AF884580

CPAexcel
CPA Review

Auditing and Attestation

Donald E. Tidrick, Ph.D., CPA, CMA, CIA
Robert A. Prentice, J.D.

EFFICIENT LEARNING SYSTEMS™

PO Box 4223 Sedona, AZ 86340-4223
888.884.5669 N.America 928.204.1066 International

Edward Foley, Chairman and Founder
Rahul Srivastava, CEO and President
Nigel Snow, VP Content Development
Gun Granath, Editor

Efficient Learning Systems, Inc.
1120 W. SR 89A, Suite D9
Sedona, AZ 86336 U.S.A.

ISBN 978-0-6156422-9-1
Edition 7.6

Printed in the United States of America

ABOUT THE CPAexcel™ CPA EXAM REVIEW COURSES

OUR AUTHORS

CPAexcel™ content is authored by a team of accounting professors and CPA exam experts from top accounting colleges such as the University of Texas at Austin (frequently ranked the #1 accounting school in the country), California State University at Sacramento, Northern Illinois University, and University of North Alabama.

Professor Allen H. Bizzell
CPAexcel Author, Mentor and Video Lecturer
Ph.D., CPA
Former Associate Dean and Accounting Faculty, University of Texas (Retired)
Associate Professor, Department of Accounting, Texas State University (Retired)

Professor Gregory Carnes
CPAexcel Author and Video Lecturer
Ph.D., CPA
Raburn Eminent Scholar of Accounting, University of North Alabama
Former Dean, College of Business, Lipscomb University
Former Chair, Department of Accountancy, Northern Illinois University

Professor B. Douglas Clinton
CPAexcel Author and Video Lecturer
Ph.D., CPA, CMA
Alta Via Consulting Professor of Management Accountancy, Department of Accountancy, Northern Illinois University

Professor Charles J. Davis
CPAexcel Author, Mentor and Video Lecturer
Ph.D., CPA
Professor of Accounting, Department of Accounting, College of Business Administration, California State University - Sacramento

Professor Donald R. Deis Jr.
CPAexcel Author and Video Lecturer
Ph.D., CPA, MBA
Ennis & Virginia Joslin Endowed Chair in Accounting, College of Business, Texas A&M University - Corpus Christi
Former Director of the School of Accountancy, University of Missouri - Columbia
Former Professor and Director of the Accounting Ph.D. Program, Louisiana State University - Baton Rouge

Professor Janet D. Gillespie
CPAexcel Author and Mentor
Ph.D.
Lecturer, Department of Accounting, McCombs School of Business, University of Texas - Austin

Professor Marianne M. Jennings
CPAexcel Author and Video Lecturer
J.D.
Professor of Legal and Ethical Studies, W.P. Carey School of Business, Arizona State University

Robert A. Prentice
CPAexcel Business Law Co-Author
Ed and Molly Smith Centennial Professor In Business Law and Distinguished Teaching Professor, J.D.
McCombs School of Business, University of Texas - Austin

Professor Pam Smith
CPAexcel Author and Video Lecturer
Ph.D., MBA, CPA
KPMG Professor of Accountancy, Department of Accountancy, Northern Illinois University

Professor Dan Stone
CPAexcel Author and Video Lecturer
Ph.D., MPA
Gatton Endowed Chair, Von Allmen School of Accountancy and the Department of Management, University of Kentucky

Professor Donald Tidrick
CPAexcel Author and Video Lecturer
Ph.D., CPA, CMA, CIA
Deloitte Professor of Accountancy, Northern Illinois University, Former Associate Chairman of the Department of Accounting, Director of the Professional Program in Accounting and Director of the CPA Review Course, University of Texas at Austin, 1991 - 2000

Table of Contents

Auditing and Attestation

Welcome

Passing the Auditing/Attestation Part of the CPA Exam
Candidates sometimes have a misperception of the auditing part of the CPA examination, believing that auditing is primarily a practice-oriented part of the exam. They may believe that having had first-hand experience doing audit work is sufficient for success on this part, or that not having had such experience is insurmountable. Sometimes candidates have a false sense of security, expressing the view that "Auditing is just common sense!" However, their view often changes when they see the specificity of the CPA exam questions that focus on the relevant concepts and the applicable professional standards. Passing the auditing part of the CPA examination is fundamentally an academic endeavor. I believe that everything you need to pass is contained in this product -- all that is required is your commitment to carefully study it.

AICPA professional standards
The CPA examination focuses heavily on candidates' familiarity with the applicable AICPA Professional Standards in auditing. Since the AICPA prepares the exam, it should not be surprising that they emphasize their professional literature. Indeed, a substantial majority of the points in auditing focuses on candidates' knowledge of the AICPA's Statements on Auditing Standards, the Statements on Standards for Attestation Engagements, the Statements on Standards for Accounting and Review Services, and, to a lesser extent, the Statements on Quality Control Standards. The entire set of AICPA Professional Standards tested in the auditing/attestation area have been outlined and are included; and outlines of the key professional standards that are heavily tested have been linked directly to the related study outlines. Of course, the PCAOB auditing standards and IFAC's International Standards on Auditing (starting in 2011) are "fair game" for testing and are also appropriately addressed in CPAexcel.

CPAexcel materials
These CPAexcel materials strive to achieve an optimal balance between **technical depth**, covering the topics on the AICPA Content Specification Outlines, and **efficiency**, focusing on the task at hand without excess verbiage and unnecessary detail. The materials emphasize the professional standards and important concepts that are the primary object of testing in this auditing/attestation area.

I encourage you to review the study text basically in sequence, since auditing has something of a chronological order -- including planning, evidence gathering, and reporting. Read the study text carefully, and read the supplemental outlines of the important professional standards that are linked to the study text. And, very importantly, take the time to work on the proficiency questions and the multiple-choice questions that are central to CPAexcel's successful approach.

Multiple-choice questions
Even though the number of professional standards has increased over the years, these standards often deal with only incremental changes to similar prior standards. In many cases, the underlying issues and concepts have not changed very significantly. This part of the exam is not quantitative by nature, so questions cannot be updated by simply changing the "numbers." If you make a diligent effort studying these past exams' multiple-choice questions, you will very likely see some "old friends" on your examination, or, at the very least, some questions that are very similar to what you have practiced.

Final review
In addition to diligently studying the study text and the supplemental outlines of the identified key professional standards and practicing proficiency questions and exam questions, candidates invariably benefit from an intensive final review. The study text is designed to facilitate an efficient review and I encourage you to spend two or three days prior to the exam reviewing the study text to refresh your memory of important concepts.

Work hard and enjoy the resulting accomplishment for the rest of your life!

~ Professor Donald Tidrick

Professional Responsibilities
In AUD, I am responsible for the 16%-20% devoted to Professional Responsibilities, including primarily the AICPA's Code of Professional Conduct, PCAOB and SEC ethics rules, GAO and Department of Labor ethics guidelines, and the IFAC Code of Ethics for Professional Accountants.

I expect few topics on the exam to receive more attention than the independence rules contained in the Code of Professional Conduct. Once you have those mastered, then you will have an easier time with the similar (but different) independence rules contained in the GAO guidelines (for auditing governmental units and recipients of government funds), the Department of Labor guidelines (for auditing ERISA benefit plans), and, importantly, the IFAC Code of Ethics. As both business and the audit profession continue to globalize, I expect the IFAC Code to receive considerable attention. It is a new topic for the exam, but an important topic. As you study it you will notice how it compares to the AICPA Code of Professional Conduct's "Conceptual Framework" and realize that the similarity is not coincidental. A conscious effort at a global convergence of reporting, auditing, and ethical standards is under way.

The tax-related provisions of the AICPA Code of Professional Conduct are now in REG, as the Code's ethical provisions have been divided. But the non-tax rules for integrity, objectivity, conflicts of interest, advertising, consulting standards, and the like are all here with the independence rules. Those are also very important, particularly because they apply to CPAs in all lines of work - audit, tax, consulting, etc.

The SEC and PCAOB material contained in this part deals primarily, though not exclusively, with additional Sarbanes-Oxley provisions aimed generally at improving the quality of financial information flowing to investors. The SOX rules regarding non-audit services that can be provided to public company audit clients and the required cooling-off period for CPAs who wish to leave an accounting firm and go to work for an audit client are particularly important.

~ Professor Robert Prentice

Auditing and Attestation Professors

Professor Donald E. Tidrick is currently Deloitte Professor of Accountancy in the Department of Accounting at Northern Illinois University. From 1991 - 2000, Dr. Tidrick was on faculty at the University of Texas at Austin, where he was Associate Chairman of the Department of Accounting, Director of the Professional Program in Accounting and Director of UT's CPA Review Course. Among other professional distinctions, Dr. Tidrick serves on the Educators' Advisory Panel for the Comptroller General of the United States and he is a member of the Ethics Committee of the Illinois CPA Society.

Professor Robert A. Prentice is the Ed and Molly Smith Centennial Professor of Business Law at the University of Texas at Austin and has taught both UT's and other CPA courses for fifteen years. He created a new course in accounting ethics and regulation that he has taught for the last decade. Professor Prentice has written several textbooks, many major law review articles on securities regulation and accountants' liability, and has won more than thirty teaching awards.

Financial Statement Audits

Accounting vs. Auditing

After studying this lesson, you should be able to:

1. *Explain the respective responsibilities of management and the auditor in financial reporting.*
2. *Outline the role of and distinction between GAAP and GAAS.*

I. **Financial Accounting --** Focuses on the preparation of the general-purpose financial statements (balance sheet, income statement, statement of cash flows, and statement of retained earnings), which are representations of management.

   A. Distributed to interested parties such as actual or potential shareholders and creditors, major customers and suppliers, employees, regulators, for their decision-making (resource allocation) needs.

   B. Users' decision making will involve different issues and they may have different information priorities and concerns, but most will want to evaluate whether management has performed well.

   C. Since management's performance will be evaluated, at least in part, by financial statements prepared by management itself, users need to know whether the financial statements are reliable when evaluating the performance of management.

II. **The Auditor's Primary Role --** Is to provide an impartial (independent) assessment of the reliability of management's financial statements.

   A. Public companies are required by the Securities and Exchange Commission to have their financial statements audited - auditors must adhere to PCAOB auditing standards when auditing the financial statements of public companies (also referred to as "issuers" as in issuers of securities to the public).

   B. Private companies - auditors must adhere to auditing standards of the AICPA's Auditing Standards Board when auditing the financial statements of private companies (also referred to as "nonissuers").

      1. Influential creditors may require or negotiate audited financial statements, perhaps through debt covenants.

      2. Management may choose to have the financial statements audited to obtain a more favorable cost of capital or to gain insights from the auditors about the adequacy of internal controls and how the company compares to others in the industry with whom the auditors may be acquainted.

   [See "AU110 (SAS 1) - Responsibilities and Functions of the Independent Auditor"]

Definitions:
Standards: Important criteria that measure quality.

Generally Accepted Accounting Principles (GAAP): The standards by which the quality of the financial statements is judged.

Generally Accepted Auditing Standards (GAAS): The standards by which the quality of the auditor's performance is judged.

GAAS

After studying this lesson, you should be able to:

1. *Identify the ten Generally Accepted Auditing Standards (GAAS).*
2. *Understand the guidance that is applicable to GAAS, including Statements on Auditing Standards, interpretive publications, and other auditing publications.*
3. *Identify the two types of professional requirements ("unconditional requirements" and "presumptively mandatory requirements") and the language associated with each.*

> **Note:** Remember the acronym **"TID-PIE-GCDO"** -- Training, Independence, Due professional care (general standards); Planning, Internal control, Evidence (field work standards); GAAP, Consistency, Disclosure, Opinion (reporting standards) -- A mnemonic for remembering the 10 standards of GAAS. The "key" words are part of the memory aid. The "standard" is the whole phrase that follows each of the key words.

I. **Generally Accepted Auditing Standards (GAAS) --** There are ten standards that comprise GAAS and that serve as the criteria to evaluate the quality of the auditor's performance.

[See "AU150 (SAS 95, as Amended) - GAAS"]

II. **General Standards --** There are three of these (**"TID"**). They are "personal" in nature as they relate to qualities that the auditor brings to the assignment:

A. **Training --** "The auditor must have adequate technical training and proficiency to perform the audit."

B. **Independence --** "The auditor must maintain independence in mental attitude in all matters relating to the audit."

C. **Due professional care --** "The auditor must exercise due professional care in the performance of the audit and the preparation of the report."

III. **Field Work Standards --** There are three of these (**"PIE"**). They are related to the evidence-gathering activities that form the foundation for the auditor's conclusions.

A. **Planning and supervision --** "The auditor must adequately plan the work and must properly supervise any assistants."

B. **Internal control --** "The auditor must obtain a sufficient understanding of the entity and its environment, including its internal control, to assess the risk of material misstatement of the financial statements whether due to fraud or error, and to design the nature, timing, and extent of further audit procedures."

C. **Evidence --** "The auditor must obtain sufficient appropriate audit evidence by performing audit procedures to afford a reasonable basis for an opinion regarding the financial statements under audit."

IV. **Reporting Standards --** There are four of these (**"GCDO"**). Each of them says something about the language that is required in the auditor's report.

A. **GAAP --** "The auditor must state in the auditor's report whether the financial statements are presented in accordance with generally accepted accounting principles (GAAP)."

B. **Consistency --** "The auditor must identify in the auditor's report those circumstances in which such principles have not been consistently observed in the current period in relation to the preceding period."

C. **Disclosure --** "When the auditor determines that informative disclosures are not reasonably adequate, the auditor must so state in the auditor's report."

D. Opinion -- "The auditor must either express an opinion regarding the financial statements, taken as a whole, or state that an opinion cannot be expressed, in the auditor's report. When the auditor cannot express an overall opinion, the auditor should state the reasons therefore in the auditor's report. In all cases where an auditor's name is associated with financial statements, the auditor should clearly indicate the character of the auditor's work, if any, and the degree of responsibility the auditor is taking, in the auditor's report."

V. Guidance Applicable to GAAS -- SAS No. 95, "Generally Accepted Auditing Standards" (as amended) specifies GAAS and describes the guidance that is applicable to GAAS.

A. Statements on Auditing Standards (SASs) -- Interpretations of GAAS must be followed by auditors when AICPA auditing standards are applicable. (Specifically, Rule 202, "Compliance With Standards," of the AICPA Code of Professional Conduct requires that auditors adhere to standards promulgated by the Auditing Standards Board.) The AICPA Professional Standards codify these SASs as AU section numbers using the 10 Generally Accepted Auditing Standards as a framework.

1. The auditor is expected to have sufficient knowledge of the SASs to identify those applicable to the audit.
2. The auditor should be prepared to justify any departures from the SASs.
3. Materiality and audit risk also underlie the application of the 10 standards (GAAS) and the SASs, particularly those related to field work and reporting.

B. "Interpretive publications" -- Consist of auditing interpretations of the SASs, auditing guidance included in AICPA Audit and Accounting Guides, and AICPA auditing Statements of Position (**and the appendices to the SASs**).

1. Interpretive publications are **not** auditing standards.
2. These are issued under the authority of the Auditing Standards Board after all ASB members have had an opportunity to comment on the interpretive publication.
3. Auditors should be aware of (and consider) interpretive publications applicable to their audits. When auditors do not apply such auditing guidance, they should be prepared to explain how they complied with the SAS provisions related to such interpretive publications.

C. "Other auditing publications" -- Include articles in the *Journal of Accountancy* and the AICPA's *CPA Letter* (and other professional publications), continuing professional education programs, textbooks, etc.

1. Other auditing publications have no authoritative status - they may help the auditor understand and apply the SASs, however.
2. To assess appropriateness of the other auditing publications - consider the degree to which the publication is recognized as helpful in applying the SASs and the degree to which the author is recognized as an authority on auditing matters. (Other auditing publications reviewed by the AICPA Audit and Attest Standards staff are presumed to be appropriate.)

VI. Categories of Professional Requirements -- The various AICPA standards (i.e., Statements on Auditing Standards, Statements on Standards for Attestation Engagements, Statements on Standards for Accounting and Review Services, and Statements on Quality Control Standards) distinguish between **two types of professional requirements:**

A. "Unconditional requirements" -- Must comply with the requirement without exception (indicated by "must" in applicable standards);

Note:
Explanatory material -- descriptive guidance within the body of the standards that does not impose a "requirement" (indicated by "may," "might," or "could" in applicable standards).

B. **"Presumptively mandatory requirements" --** In rare circumstances, the practitioner may depart from such a "requirement," but must document the justification for the departure and how the alternate procedures performed were adequate to meet the objective of the "requirement" (indicated by "should" in applicable standards).

[See "AU120 (SAS 102) and AT20 (SSAE 13) - Defining Professional Requirements"]

Quality Control Standards (SQCS)

After studying this lesson, you should be able to:

1. *Describe the relationship of GAAS to the AICPA's Statements on Quality Control Standards (SQCS).*
2. *List the six elements that comprise a firm's quality control system.*

[See "QC10 - A Firm's System of Quality Control"]

I. **Relationship of GAAS to the Statements on Quality Control Standards --** An individual audit engagement is governed by GAAS, whereas a CPA firm's collective portfolio of accounting and auditing services (the "A&A" practice, which involves clients' financial statements and, thereby, involves the "public interest") is governed by the AICPA's Statements on Quality Control Standards. SQCS are issued by the Auditing Standards Board.

II. **Focus of the System of Quality Control --** A CPA firm is required to have a "system of quality control" for **accounting and auditing services** (covering audit, attestation, compilation, and review services; not applicable to tax or consulting services) to provide reasonable assurance that engagements are performed in accordance with professional standards and regulatory and legal requirements, and that the issuance of reports are appropriate in the circumstances.

   A. **Nature and scope --** The policies and procedures will vary with the circumstances (e.g., firm size and number of offices, complexity of services offered, experience of professional staff).

   B. **Inherent limitations --** Similar to any internal control system, a quality control system provides **reasonable** (a high, but not absolute) **assurance**, reflecting implicit cost-benefit trade-offs.

III. **Six Elements of a Quality Control System --** These are interrelated (e.g., monitoring and the quality of personnel involved affect the other elements).

   A. **Leadership responsibilities for quality --** Policies and procedures should promote an internal culture that emphasizes a commitment to quality (the "tone at the top").

   B. **Relevant ethical requirements --** Policies and procedures should address the independence of personnel as necessary (should obtain written confirmation of compliance with independence requirements from all appropriate personnel at least annually).

   C. **Acceptance and continuance of clients and engagements --** Policies and procedures should carefully assess the risks associated with each engagement (including issues related to management integrity) and to only undertake engagements that can be completed with professional competence.

   D. **Human resources --** Policies and procedures should address important personnel issues (including initial hiring, assignments to engagements, professional development and continuing professional education, and promotion decisions).

   E. **Engagement performance --** Policies and procedures should focus on compliance with all applicable firm and professional standards and regulatory requirements, and encourage personnel to consult as necessary with professional (or other) literature or other human resources within or outside of the firm for appropriate guidance.

   F. **Monitoring --** Policies and procedures should provide an ongoing assessment of the adequacy of the design and the operating effectiveness of the system of quality control.

IV. Differences of Opinion -- The firm should establish policies and procedures for dealing with and resolving differences of opinion within the engagement team, with those consulted, and between the engagement partner and the engagement quality control reviewer (including that the conclusions reached are documented and implemented and that the report is not released until the matter is resolved).

V. Documentation of the Operation of Quality Control Policies and Procedures -- The firm should establish policies and procedures requiring appropriate documentation of the operation of each element of the system of quality control.

Overview of Audit Process

After studying this lesson, you should be able to:

1. *Identify the primary dimensions that comprise the audit process: a) Engagement planning; b) Internal control considerations; c) Reporting.*

I. Engagement Planning

A. Decide whether to accept (or continue) the engagement - see the quality control standards regarding client acceptance/continuation issues.

B. Perform risk assessment procedures.

C. Evaluate requirements for staffing and supervision.

D. Prepare the required written audit program that specifies the nature, timing, and extent of auditing procedures for every audit area (usually prepared after control risk has been assessed, so that detection risk can be appropriately set in each audit area).

II. Internal Control Consideration

A. Obtain an understanding for planning purposes as required, emphasizing the assessment of the risk of material misstatement in individual audit areas and document the understanding of internal control.

B. If contemplating "reliance" on certain identified internal control strengths as a basis for reducing substantive testing, the auditor must then perform **tests of controls** to determine that those specific controls are working as designed.

III. Substantive Audit Procedures (evidence gathering) -- Note that the word "substantive" is derived from "substantiate," which means "to verify."

A. Analytical procedures -- Those evidence-gathering procedures that suggest "reasonableness" (or "unreasonableness") based upon a comparison to appropriate expectations or benchmarks, such as prior year's financial statements, comparability to industry data (including ratios) or other interrelationships involving financial and/or nonfinancial data.

B. Tests of details -- Those evidence-gathering procedures consisting of either of two types:

1. **Tests of ending balances --** Where the final balance is assessed by testing the composition of the year-end balance (e.g., testing a sample of individual customers' account balances that make up the general ledger accounts receivable control account balance).

2. **Tests of transactions --** Where the final balance is assessed by examining those debits and credits that caused the balance to change from last year's audited balance to the current year's balance.

IV. Reporting -- Conclusions are expressed in writing using standardized language to avoid miscommunication.

Auditor's Report

After studying this lesson, you should be able to:

1. *Describe the structure and content of the so-called "standard unqualified" audit report.*

Note:
The standard three paragraph unqualified auditor's report should be memorized!

I. Introductory Paragraph (3 sentences)

A. Identify company's financial statements.

B. Identify management's responsibilities.

C. Identify auditor's responsibility.

II. Scope Paragraph (5 sentences)

A. Audit conducted in accordance with GAAS.

B. Reasonable assurance about material misstatement.

C. Examined evidence on a test basis.

D. Assessed principles used and estimates made.

E. Audit provides reasonable basis for opinion.

III. Opinion Paragraph (1 long sentence and mention GAAP) -- Express an opinion that the financial statements are fairly stated in conformity with GAAP (or other applicable accounting framework).

Standard Unqualified Auditor's Report

Independent Auditor's Report

We have audited the balance sheets of ABC Company at December 31, 20X2 and 20X1, and the related statements of income, retained earnings, and cash flows for the years then ended. These financial statements are the responsibility of the Company's management. Our responsibility is to express an opinion on these financial statements based on our audits.

We conducted our audits in accordance with auditing standards generally accepted in the United States of America. Those standards require that we plan and perform the audit to obtain reasonable assurance about whether the financial statements are free of material misstatement. An audit includes examining, on a test basis, evidence supporting the amounts and disclosures in the financial statements. An audit also includes assessing the accounting principles used and significant estimates made by management, as well as evaluating the overall financial statement presentation. We believe that our audits provide a reasonable basis for our opinion.

In our opinion, the financial statements referred to above present fairly, in all material respects, the financial position of ABC Company at December 31, 20X2 and 20X1, and the results of their operations and their cash flows for the years then ended, in conformity with accounting principles generally accepted in the United States of America.

/s/ CPA firm (signed by audit engagement partner)

Date (The auditor's report should not be dated earlier than the date on which the auditor has obtained sufficient appropriate audit evidence to support the opinion.)

Standard Unqualified Auditor's Report (with explicitly identified sentences)

Introductory paragraph

We have audited the balance sheets of ABC Company at December 31, 20X2 and 20X1, and the related statements of income, retained earnings, and cash flows for the years then ended.

These financial statements are the responsibility of the Company's management.

Our responsibility is to express an opinion on these financial statements based on our audits.

Scope paragraph

We conducted our audits in accordance with auditing standards generally accepted in the United States of America.

Those standards require that we plan and perform the audit to obtain reasonable assurance about whether the financial statements are free of material misstatement.

An audit includes examining, on a test basis, evidence supporting the amounts and disclosures in the financial statements.

An audit also includes assessing the accounting principles used and significant estimates made by management, as well as evaluating the overall financial statement presentation.

We believe that our audits provide a reasonable basis for our opinion.

Opinion paragraph

In our opinion, the financial statements referred to above present fairly, in all material respects, the financial position of ABC Company at December 31, 20X2 and 20X1, and the results of their operations and their cash flows for the years then ended, in conformity with accounting principles generally accepted in the United States of America.

Different Types of Engagements

After studying this lesson, you should be able to:

1. *Recognize which AICPA Professional Standards are applicable to engagements to review and/or compile financial statements of a private company and which are applicable to other attestation engagements.*
2. *Be aware that "engagement letters" are required for any engagement to audit, review, or compile an entity's financial statements under AICPA Professional Standards.*

I. **Statements on Standards for Accounting and Review Services (SSARSs) --** When associated with the financial statements of a private company, but that association is something less than a full-scope "audit" engagement.

   A. **Compilation --** When the CPA is engaged simply to assemble into financial statement format the financial records of a private company, without expressing any degree of assurance on the reliability of those financial statements.

   B. **Review --** When the CPA is engaged to provide a lower level of assurance (relative to that of an audit) on financial statements of a private company by performing limited procedures, including reading the financial statements, performing analytical procedures, and making appropriate inquiries of client personnel.

II. **Statements on Standards for Attestation Engagements (SSAEs) --** When associated with written representations or subject matter other than financial statements (e.g., management may make representations about superior product performance that may be made more reliable by independent verification).

III. **Responsibilities Vary for Different Types of Engagements**

   A. **Understanding with the client --** AICPA Professional Standards require the auditor to establish an understanding with the client as to the services to be rendered and the parties' respective responsibilities. The auditor must document that understanding in a written engagement letter between the auditor and the client entity.

   B. **Levels of assurance --** The level of assurance varies with the type of service involved and should be addressed in the engagement letter between the CPA and the client entity.

      1. **Audit --** Conveys a high level of assurance about financial statements.
      2. **Review --** Conveys a lower (i.e., "moderate") level of assurance about financial statements (for a private company only).
      3. **Compilation --** Conveys no assurance about the financial statements (for a private company only).

   C. **Other attest engagements --** Can convey either a high or moderate level of assurance about nonfinancial statement representations. (The subject matter of the engagement is other than financial statements and, hence, more flexibility exists to negotiate with the client about the level of assurance to be conveyed and/or the procedures to be used as a basis for conclusions.)

> **Note:**
> *An Engagement Letter is Now Required for Audits, Reviews, and Compilations!* In the past, an engagement letter was not technically required, but that has changed. A written engagement letter must be obtained for engagements to audit, review, or compile an entity's financial statements under AICPA Professional Standards.

Planning Activities

Pre-Engagement Issues

After studying this lesson, you should be able to:

1. *Understand the auditor's requirement under applicable Statements on Quality Control Standards to specifically consider the "acceptance and continuance of clients and engagements."*
2. *Understand the successor auditor's responsibility to communicate with the predecessor auditor about specific matters when an entity changes auditors.*

I. **Statements on Quality Control Standards --** Recall the AICPA's "Statements on Quality Control Standards (SQCS)" that are applicable to a CPA's financial statement-related services.

   A. One of the six elements of a quality control system is **"acceptance and continuance of clients and engagements."** (Auditors should avoid clients whose management lacks integrity or clients that are viewed as too risky due to industry considerations or entity-specific issues.)

   B. The auditor should also evaluate his or her compliance with applicable ethics requirements, especially regarding independence issues and competencies to properly perform the engagement, before doing other significant audit-related activities.

II. **Required Communications** – Required communications between the new ("successor") auditor and the prior ("predecessor") auditor when the client entity changes auditors.

[See "AU315 (SAS 84) - Predecessor Successor Communications"]

   A. The successor (the prospective new auditor) is **required** to initiate an inquiry of the predecessor (the former auditor) about certain specific matters before accepting the engagement. The inquiry may be written or verbal, but the successor and predecessor are both required to obtain the entity's permission in advance to discuss entity-specific matters (due to confidentiality issues). If the client entity does not facilitate that communication, the successor auditor should view that as an indication of high risk.

      1. Facts known to the predecessor related to management's integrity.
      2. Significant disagreements over accounting or auditing issues that occurred between the predecessor auditor and management - perhaps related to the "opinion shopping" issue (for example, the client may be seeking a more lenient auditor with respect to revenue or expense recognition issues).
      3. Any communications the predecessor had with those charged with governance about sensitive matters, such as fraud, illegal acts, and significant internal control issues.
      4. The predecessor's understanding of the reason(s) for the client's change in auditors. Since the successor has already heard management's explanation, this may corroborate (or call into question) management's explanation of circumstances leading to the change.

   B. The successor may also choose to inquire about any other matters that could affect the conduct of the audit (e.g., any difficult to audit areas that the predecessor encountered).

   C. The successor also normally asks the (prospective) client's permission to request access to the **predecessor's audit documentation** (usually having ongoing audit relevance) -- the predecessor should be reasonably accommodating in that regard, but valid reasons may exist for refusing to allow the successor access to those working papers (for example, ongoing litigation issues).

Question:
What if successor believes that the financial statements covered by the predecessor's report require revision?

Answer:
Try to arrange a meeting with the three parties (i.e., the successor, predecessor, and client management) -- if the client refuses to meet to discuss issues reflecting on the appropriateness of the previously issued financial statements, the successor should consider the risks of being the entity's auditor.

D. **Early appointment** of the auditor facilitates planning and may lead to more efficient field work (e.g., "interim" work); late appointment may make it impossible to issue an unqualified opinion.

Question:
What if the auditor is unable to observe beginning inventory?

Answer:
If unable to verify the beginning inventory, the auditor may be unable to reach a conclusion about cost of goods sold and, hence, net income. As a result, the auditor may not be able to express an opinion on the fairness of the income statement, statement of cash flows, or statement of retained earnings. However, the auditor could still express an opinion on the balance sheet itself.

Planning and Supervision

After studying this lesson, you should be able to:

1. *Understand the auditor's responsibility to adequately plan an audit engagement and to properly supervise members of the audit team based on applicable AICPA Professional Standards.*

I. **Recall the First Field Work Standard of GAAS --** "The auditor must adequately plan the work and must properly supervise any assistants."

II. **Planning and Supervision --** The fundamental interpretation of that Field Work Standard is provided by Statement on Auditing Standards No. 108, "Planning and Supervision."

[See "AU311 (SAS 108) - Planning and Supervision"]

A. **The relative emphasis on planning and supervision --** Varies with the particular circumstances, including the size and complexity of the entity, the auditor's experience with that entity, and the auditor's understanding of the entity and its environment, including its internal control.

B. **Audit planning --** Involves developing the overall audit strategy for the expected conduct, organization, and staffing of the audit.

C. **Basic auditor responsibility --** Must plan the audit to be responsive to the assessment of the risk of material misstatement based on the auditor's understanding of the environment, including internal control. (Note that this is an "iterative process" that begins with engagement acceptance and continues throughout the audit. The auditor may obtain disconfirming evidence that might cause a revision of the overall audit strategy.)

D. **Appointment of the auditor --** May accept an engagement after the fiscal year-end, but early appointment is preferable and enables the auditor to plan the audit prior to the balance sheet date. (The auditor should discuss with those charged with governance and management any circumstances that might interfere with the expression of an unqualified opinion.)

E. **Developing the "overall audit strategy" --** The auditor should

1. Determine the characteristics of the engagement that define its scope (including the basis of reporting, industry-specific reporting requirements, and locations of the entity).

2. Identify the reporting objectives of the engagement that may affect the timing of the audit and the nature of required communications (including reporting deadlines and dates for expected communications with those charged with governance, etc.).

3. Consider other factors that influence the focus of the audit team (including determination of materiality levels, preliminary identification of high risk audit areas, expectations about reliance on the operating effectiveness of internal control, and identification of recent developments affecting the entity or the industry).

4. Note that developing this overall audit strategy will affect resource allocation, including the number of audit team members assigned, the level of experience assigned, the timing of the work (interim versus year-end), and the extent of supervision required.

F. **Developing the "audit plan" (after the overall audit strategy has been developed) --** The audit plan is more detailed than the audit strategy; the audit plan specifies the nature, timing, and extent of planned audit procedures to be performed to obtain sufficient appropriate audit evidence through the efficient use of the auditor's resources. (Note that the audit plan is commonly referred to as the "audit program.") The audit plan should include:

1. A description of the nature, timing, and extent of planned "risk assessment procedures" sufficient to assess the risk of material misstatement.
2. A description of the nature, timing, and extent of planned "further audit procedures" (consisting of tests of controls and substantive tests) at the relevant assertion level for each material class of transactions, account balance, and disclosure.
3. A description of other audit procedures to be carried out in compliance with GAAS.

G. **Determining the extent of the involvement of professionals having specialized skills**

1. The auditor should consider whether specialized skills are needed to perform the audit (either on the auditor's staff or an outside professional, usually referred to as a "specialist"). If that professional is part of the audit team, the responsibilities for supervision are the same as for other assistants.
2. For example, the auditor may add a professional having information technology (IT) skills to the audit team to assist with an audit involving complex IT systems -- the IT professional may help with (1) inquiring of an entity's IT personnel how transactions are initiated, authorized, recorded, processed, and reported (and how IT controls are designed); (2) inspecting systems documentation; (3) observing the operation of IT controls; and (4) planning and performing tests of IT controls.

H. **Communicating in planning with those charged with governance and with management --** The auditor should discuss with those charged with governance the overall audit strategy and timing of the audit, including the parties' respective responsibilities. The auditor should discuss issues with management, as necessary, to coordinate the planned procedures with the entity's personnel.

I. **Supervision --** The extent of supervision varies with the circumstances, including the complexity of the subject matter and the qualifications (and experience) of the staff involved. Elements of supervision include directing the work of assistants, keeping informed of significant issues encountered, reviewing the work performed, and dealing with differences of opinion among firm personnel.

1. Discussion regarding fraud -- the auditor with final responsibility for the audit should communicate with members of the audit team regarding the susceptibility of the financial statements to misstatement due to error or fraud (and emphasize the need to maintain professional skepticism).
2. Informing assistants of their responsibilities and objectives of the work assigned -- the auditor with final responsibility for the audit should direct assistants to bring up any issues they believe are significant to the financial statements or to the auditor's report, including any difficulties they encountered in performing the audit.
3. Differences of opinion among audit team members -- the auditor with final responsibility for the audit should ensure that audit team members are aware of the procedures to be followed when those involved in the audit have differences of opinion about accounting and auditing issues.
4. An assistant should be permitted to document his or her disagreement with the conclusions reached if, after appropriate consultation, he or she believes it is necessary to be disassociated with the matter.
5. The basis for the final resolution of the matter should be documented.

Engagement Letters

After studying this lesson, you should be able to:

1. *Understand the auditor's responsibility to obtain a required written understanding with the client entity about the engagement (an "engagement letter") and the specific matters normally involved in accordance with applicable AICPA Professional Standards.*

I. **The Engagement Letter --** The auditor should establish an understanding with the client about the services to be performed (and each party's respective responsibilities). That understanding should be documented in a written communication with the client (usually referred to as an "engagement letter").

   A. Note that this is an important change attributable to SAS No. 108, "Planning and Supervision," issued in 2006. (Prior to the issuance of SAS No. 108, auditors were required to "obtain an understanding" but that understanding was not then required to be in writing.)

II. **Matters that are Normally Covered in an Engagement Letter**

   A. The objective of the audit is the expression of an opinion on the financial statements.

   B. Management is responsible for the entity's financial statements, for the design and implementation of internal control over financial reporting, for compliance with applicable laws and regulations, and for making all financial records and related information available to the auditor.

   C. Management will provide the auditor with a letter at the conclusion of the engagement to document certain representations made to the auditor during the engagement (called a "management representations letter").

   D. The auditor is responsible for conducting the audit in accordance with GAAS (or PCAOB auditing standards for "issuers"), which standards require the auditor to provide reasonable, rather than absolute, assurance about the fairness of the financial statements.

   E. The auditor is responsible for obtaining an understanding of internal control sufficient to properly plan the audit and to determine the nature, timing, and extent of audit procedures to be performed. The auditor is responsible for communicating any identified significant deficiencies in internal control to those charged with governance.

   F. Management is responsible for adjusting the financial statements for any material misstatements and for stating that the effects of any uncorrected misstatements are immaterial, individually and in the aggregate, to the financial statements taken as a whole.

   G. Other matters that are typically addressed include the following: arrangements regarding client assistance (such as preparation of schedules of analysis and the availability of documents and the participation of the entity's internal auditors); arrangements involving "specialists" who may participate as members of the audit team and who contribute technical expertise outside of accounting and auditing issues; arrangements involving a predecessor auditor and/or the involvement of other accountants; details regarding fees and billing arrangements; any limitations regarding the liability of the auditor or the auditee (such as indemnification when not prohibited by applicable laws or regulations); circumstances whereby access to the audit documentation may be granted to others; additional services to be provided (such as tax or consulting services or services to meet certain regulatory requirements); and the extent and timing of interim audit procedures to be performed.

III. Sample Engagement Letter

CPA Firm's Letterhead

(Date)

Ms. Nancy Pritchett*

ABC Company**

1803 King Avenue

Columbus, OH 43212

Dear Ms. Pritchett:

This letter confirms our understanding of the services we will provide to ABC Company for the fiscal year ended December 31, 20XX. Moreover, this letter constitutes the entire agreement between us regarding the services covered by this letter, and it supersedes any prior proposals, correspondence, and understandings, whether written or oral.

Services and Related Report

We will audit the balance sheet of ABC Company as of December 21, 20XX, and the related statements of income, retained earnings, and cash flows for the year then ended, for the purpose of expressing an opinion on them. Upon completion of our audit, we will provide you with our audit report on those financial statements.

Our Responsibilities and Limitations

Our responsibility is to express an opinion on the financial statements based on our audit, and is limited to the period covered by our audit. If circumstances preclude us from issuing an unqualified opinion, we will discuss the reasons with you in advance. If, for any reason, we are unable to complete the audit or are unable to form an opinion, we may decline to express an opinion or decline to issue a report for the engagement.

We are responsible for conducting the audit in accordance with generally accepted auditing standards. Those standards require that we obtain reasonable, but not absolute, assurance about whether the financial statements are free of errors or fraud that would have a material effect on the financial statements, as well as other illegal acts having a direct and material effect on the financial statements. Accordingly, a material misstatement may remain undetected. An audit is not designed to detect errors, fraud, or the effects of illegal acts that might be immaterial to the financial statements. We will inform you of all matters of fraud that come to our attention. We will also inform you of any illegal acts that come to our attention, unless they are clearly inconsequential.

We will obtain an understanding of internal control over financial reporting sufficient to properly plan the audit and to determine the nature, timing, and extent of audit procedures to be performed. The audit will not be designed to provide assurance on internal control over financial reporting or to detect significant deficiencies in internal control. However, we will report to you any significant deficiencies in internal control that we identify.

An audit includes examining, on a test basis, evidence supporting the amounts and disclosures in the financial statements. Judgment is required in determining the areas and number of transactions selected for our testing. An audit also includes assessing the accounting principles used and significant estimates made by management, as well as evaluating the overall financial statement presentation. Our procedures will include appropriate tests of documentary evidence supporting the transactions recorded in the accounts, tests of the physical existence of inventory, and direct confirmation of accounts receivable and certain other assets and liabilities by correspondence with selected customers, banks, legal counsel, and creditors. At the conclusion of our audit, we will request certain written representations from senior management about the financial statements and related matters.

Management's Responsibilities

The financial statements are the responsibility of the Company's management. That responsibility includes properly recording transactions in the accounting records and establishing and maintaining internal control sufficient to permit the preparation of financial statements in conformity with generally accepted accounting principles.

The Company's management is responsible for adjusting the financial statements to correct any material misstatements and for affirming to us in the representation letter that the effects of any uncorrected misstatements aggregated by us during the engagement and pertaining to the latest period presented are immaterial, both individually and in the aggregate, to the financial statements taken as a whole. Management is also responsible for ensuring that the Company complies with all applicable laws and regulations.

The Company's management is also responsible for making available to us, on a timely basis, all of the Company's original accounting records and related information and documentation and company personnel to whom we may direct our inquiries. That includes providing access to us to the minutes of all meetings of stockholders, the board of directors, and committees of the board of directors for which such minutes are taken.

Timing, Fees, and Other Matters

Assistance to be supplied by the Company's personnel, including the preparation of certain specific schedules and analyses of accounts, is described in a separate attachment. Timely completion of this work is necessary for us to complete our audit on a timely basis.

The results of our audit tests, the responses to our inquiries, and the written representation furnished by management, comprise the evidence that we will reply upon in forming our opinion on the financial statements. The resulting audit documentation for this engagement is the property of (*name of the CPA firm*) and access will be limited to authorized persons to protect the confidentiality of company-specific information.

As part of our engagement for the year ending December 31, 20XX, we will review the federal and state income tax returns for ABC Company. We will be available during the year to consult with you on the tax effects of any proposed transactions or anticipated changes in your business activities.

Our fees will be billed as work progresses and are based on the amount of time required plus out-of-pocket expenses incurred by our audit team. Individual hourly rates vary according to the degree of responsibility involved and the experience and skill required. We will notify you on a timely basis of any circumstances we encounter that might affect our initial estimate of total fees, which we anticipate will range from $xx,xxx to $xx,xxx, excluding the aforementioned out-of-pocket expenses. Invoices are payable upon presentation.

If this letter accurately reflects your understanding, please sign where indicated in the space provided below and return it to us. We appreciate the opportunity to serve you and look forward to a mutually enjoyable association.

Sincerely yours,

(Name of the CPA Firm)

____

Engagement Partner's Signature

Accepted and agreed to:

____

(ABC Company Representative's Signature)

(Title)

(Date)

*The engagement letter should be addressed to whoever engaged the CPA firm (which might be the entity's CEO, board of directors, or someone else). The client representative responsible for the engagement who signs the engagement letter should be given a copy of the signed engagement letter and the CPA firm should retain the original letter for engagement documentation purposes.

**Assume that ABC Company is a "nonissuer" (i.e., a private company) such that PCAOB auditing standards do not apply. Hence, there is no mention here of PCAOB auditing standards or the audit of internal control that is applicable to SEC registrants under the Sarbanes-Oxley Act of 2002.

Materiality

After studying this lesson, you should be able to:

1. *Understand the concept of materiality that is essential in evaluating the "fairness" of the financial statements within some range of acceptability viewed as materiality.*
2. *Understand the distinction between the auditor's "planning-stage" and "evaluation-stage" materiality judgments, as well as the quantitative and qualitative considerations that might influence the auditor's judgments about materiality.*

I. Professional Guidance is Provided by SAS No. 107, "Audit Risk and Materiality in Conducting an Audit"

[See "AU312 (SAS 107) - Audit Risk and Materiality"]

II. "Materiality" -- The concept of materiality can be described as "an understanding of what is important" in financial reporting based on the auditor's perception of the users' needs.

A. A couple of definitions of "Materiality:"

1. From the **auditing standards** (per SAS No. 107):

> "The concept of materiality recognizes that some matters, either individually or in the aggregate, are important for fair presentation of financial statements in conformity with GAAP, while other matters are not important."

2. From the FASB's Conceptual Framework project (Statement on Financial Accounting Concepts No. 2):

> "The **magnitude** of an omission or misstatement of accounting information that, in the light of **surrounding circumstances**, makes it probable that the judgment of a reasonable person relying on the information would have been changed or influenced by the omission or misstatement." *(Note that this definition emphasizes that materiality judgments involve both **quantitative** and **qualitative** considerations.)*

B. The auditor should consider materiality in two distinct contexts (even though materiality issues are normally addressed throughout the audit process):

1. Planning-stage materiality -- What size misstatements is the audit program (i.e., audit plan) designed to catch? In this setting, the materiality judgment is like a fisherman's net where decisions must be made in advance as to the size of the fish (in this case, the size of the misstatements) intended to be caught.

2. Evaluation-stage materiality -- At the conclusion of the field work, does the evidence suggest that the financial statements are "fairly" stated (within a reasonable range, defined by "materiality")? This is essentially a "yes" or "no" judgment.

3. Theoretically, the materiality judgment at the beginning of the engagement (planning stage) should be the same as that at the end of the engagement (evaluation stage). However, as a practical matter, these materiality judgments will usually differ due to unforeseen information discovered during fieldwork and because the auditor can factor everything known about the entity, quantitatively and qualitatively, in making the final evaluation-stage materiality judgment.

C. Considerations that may affect the auditor's materiality judgment

1. **Quantitative guidelines --** Related to the size of misstatements of interest. Examples of frequently used general guidelines:

   a. 5% - 10% of net income or earnings before taxes.

   b. 0.50% - 2% of the larger of net sales or total assets.

   c. 5% of owners' equity for private companies.

2. **Qualitative matters --** Related to the surrounding circumstances and perceived risks -- that might affect the auditor's judgment of what is material to the users; there are too many such factors to list here, but two examples follow:

   a. **Public versus private companies --** A lower materiality threshold may apply to public companies due to more exposure to litigation (and because the owners of private companies may be closer to the day-to-day operations and, therefore, have different information needs).

   b. **Unstable versus stable industry --** A lower materiality threshold may apply to a company in an unstable industry, which is by nature more susceptible to business failure.

3. **"Tolerable misstatement" --** (sometimes referred to as "tolerable error") -- Refers to the maximum error in a population that the auditor is willing to accept; this should be established in such a way that tolerable misstatement, combined for the entire audit plan, does not exceed materiality for the financial statements taken as a whole. (Note that tolerable misstatement might be viewed as the amount of planning-stage materiality to be allocated to a specific account or individual audit area.)

Audit Risk

After studying this lesson, you should be able to:

1. *Understand the concept (and definition) of "audit risk" that underlies a risk-based audit approach relevant to planning, fieldwork, and audit reporting.*
2. *Understand the components of the "audit risk model" that are applicable to individual audit areas or major classes of transactions to be audited.*

I. Professional Guidance is Provided by SAS No. 107, "Audit Risk and Materiality in Conducting an Audit."

[See "AU312 (SAS 107) - Audit Risk and Materiality"]

II. "Audit Risk"

A. Definition of Audit Risk -- "The risk that the auditor may unknowingly fail to appropriately modify his or her opinion on financial statements that are materially misstated." Note that the concept of audit risk is really a probability and that audit risk and materiality are interrelated by the definition of audit risk.

> According to SAS No. 107: "Audit risk and materiality affect the application of GAAS, especially the standards of fieldwork and reporting, and are reflected in the auditor's standard report. Audit risk and materiality, among other matters, need to be considered together in designing the nature, timing, and extent of audit procedures and in evaluating the results of those procedures."

B. The presence of audit risk is indicated in the auditor's report by reference to **"reasonable assurance,"** meaning that audit risk cannot be reduced to a zero probability (which would imply "absolute assurance"). Another Statement on Auditing Standards comments on the concept of "reasonable assurance" as follows: "...the auditor must plan and perform the audit to obtain sufficient appropriate audit evidence so that audit risk will be limited to a low level... The high, but not absolute, level of assurance that is intended to be obtained by the auditor is expressed in the auditor's report as obtaining reasonable assurance..." (Note that "reasonable assurance" means a "high level of assurance" and a "low level of audit risk.")

III. Basic Auditor Responsibility -- The auditor should properly plan and perform the audit to obtain reasonable assurance that material misstatements, whether caused by errors or fraud, are detected.

IV. Considerations at the Financial Statement Level -- The one overriding audit planning objective is to limit **audit risk** to an appropriately low level (as determined by the auditor's judgment), which involves the following:

A. Determining the extent and nature of the auditor's risk assessment procedures.

B. Identifying and assessing the risk of material misstatement.

C. Determining the nature, timing, and extent of further audit procedures.

D. Evaluating whether the financial statements taken as a whole are presented fairly in conformity with GAAP.

V. The Audit Risk Model -- The SAS No. 107 "audit risk model" is applicable at the level of an individual account balance, class of transactions, or disclosure level, but it is not applicable at the overall financial statement level. This "audit risk model" can be expressed in terms of its three component risks (inherent risk, control risk, and detection risk):

AR = IR x CR x DR

Definitions:
Inherent risk (IR): The probability that a material misstatement would occur in the particular audit area in the absence of any internal control policies and procedures.

Control risk (CR): The probability that a material misstatement that occurred in the first place would not be detected and corrected by internal controls that are applicable.

Detection risk (DR): The probability that a material misstatement that was not prevented or detected and corrected by internal control was not detected by the auditor's substantive audit procedures (that is, an undetected material misstatement exists in a relevant assertion).

VI. Variations on the Above SAS No. 107 "Audit Risk Model"

A. AR = RMM x DR, where:

1. "Risk of material misstatement" (RMM) -- the auditor's combined assessment of inherent risk and control risk (if IR and CR are not separately assessed).

Note that RMM = IR x CR

B. AR = RMM x TD x AP, where:

1. DR can be broken into two components involving the likelihood that the auditor's two basic categories of substantive procedures fail to detect a material misstatement that exists (1) **"tests of details risk"** (TD) and (2) **"substantive analytical procedures risk (AP)."**

Note that DR = TD x AP

C. AR = IR x CR x TD x AP

VII. Quantification of Risk Components

A. The component risks do not necessarily have to be quantified; for example, they could be assessed qualitatively as high, medium, or low.

B. Each component is considered from left to right in order: **audit risk** is set, **then inherent risk** is assessed, **then control risk** is assessed, and finally the implications for the appropriate level of **detection risk** are considered.

C. "Detection risk" is the only component risk that is **specifically the auditor's responsibility** -- "inherent risk" arises because of the particular audit area under investigation and "control risk" reflects management's responsibility to design and implement internal controls. Note that the auditor must "assess" inherent risk and control risk, but the auditor actually makes the decisions that, in effect, result in some level of detection risk, which should take into consideration the auditor's assessment of the risk of material misstatement.

1. If IR and CR are seen by the auditor as too high, the auditor must compensate by decreasing DR.
2. If IR and CR are perceived as low, the auditor may consider accepting a higher DR.

D. Changing DR is accomplished by adjusting the nature, timing, and/or extent of the auditor's substantive audit procedures -- these might be viewed as the auditor's three strategic variables that, in effect, "set" DR based on the auditor's professional judgment:

1. **Nature --** What specific audit procedures to perform (perhaps shifting the relative emphasis placed on the "soft evidence" analytical procedures versus the "hard evidence" tests of details)?
2. **Timing --** When will the procedures be performed, at an "interim" date (prior to year-end) or at "final" (after year-end when the books have been closed)?
3. **Extent --** Are large samples required for the auditor's test work or can somewhat smaller sample sizes be justified? How extensively should substantive procedures be performed?

Documentation/Communication - Mty and AR

After studying this lesson, you should be able to:

1. *Understand the specific matters related to audit risk and materiality that the auditor is obligated to document.*
2. *Understand the specific matters related to audit risk and materiality that the auditor is obligated to communicate to management.*

I. **Documentation Requirements --** The auditor should document the following matters:

A. The levels of materiality (and tolerable misstatement) used in the audit -- and the basis on which those levels were determined.

B. A summary of uncorrected identified "known" and "likely" misstatements (except those that are deemed to be "trivial").

Definitions:
Known misstatements: Specific misstatements identified during the audit (such as misapplications of accounting principles or misstatements of facts).

Likely misstatements: (1)Misstatements that arise from management's accounting estimates that the auditor considers unreasonable; or (2) that result from inferences obtained from an application of audit sampling.

C. The auditor's conclusion as to whether any uncorrected misstatements, individually or in the aggregate, do, or do not, cause the financial statements to be materially misstated (note that the auditor should also consider the effect of undetected misstatements in evaluating whether the financial statements are fairly stated), and the basis for that conclusion.

D. All identified (known and likely) misstatements that have been corrected by management (except those that are deemed to be "trivial").

II. **Communication of Identified Misstatements to Management**

A. The auditor must accumulate all identified known and likely misstatements (except those deemed to be "trivial") and communicate them to the appropriate level of management on a timely basis.

B. The auditor should request management to correct all known misstatements (except those that are "trivial"), including the effect of any prior period misstatements.

C. When a likely misstatement from sampling indicates a material misstatement -- the auditor should request management follow up to identify the necessary correction (the auditor should reevaluate as necessary).

D. When a likely misstatement involves differences regarding estimates -- the auditor should request management to review the assumptions and methods used to develop management's estimate (the auditor should reevaluate as necessary).

E. If management decides not to correct some (or all) of the identified misstatements communicated by the auditor -- the auditor should obtain an understanding of management's reasoning and consider the implications to the auditor's report.

Analytical Procedures

After studying this lesson, you should be able to:

1. *Know the definition of "analytical procedures."*
2. *Know the three purposes served by analytical procedures in an audit engagement (two of which are required in an audit under GAAS).*
3. *Understand the four "key" considerations that determine the efficiency and effectiveness of analytical procedures used for substantive purposes.*

[See "AU329 (SAS 56) - Analytical Procedures"]

Definition:
Analytical procedures: Evaluations of financial information made by a study of plausible relationships among both **financial and nonfinancial** data (sometimes referred to as "tests of reasonableness")

I. Analytical Procedures Serve Three Distinct Purposes

A. Required during planning -- Directs attention:

1. Helps auditor understand the client's activities.
2. Helps target risky areas where misstatements may be more likely.
3. Primarily based on financial data, but may use nonfinancial data, too (e.g., sales per square foot is a widely used benchmark in the retail industry).

B. Constitutes a form of **substantive evidence** during fieldwork (widely used, but not technically required for this purpose) - the effectiveness and efficiency of analytical procedures for substantive purposes depends on four factors:

1. **Nature of assertion --** Analytical procedures may be particularly effective in testing for omissions (regarding the "completeness" assertion) of transactions that would be hard to detect with procedures that focus on recorded amounts; in other words, tests of details may not be effective when underlying source documents do not exist for transactions that went totally unrecorded, so analytical procedures may represent the best chance of detecting such omissions.
2. **Plausibility and predictability of relationship --** Developing a meaningful "expectation" to compare to the entity's recorded amount is critically important to the skillful use of analytical procedures
   - **a.** Relationships in a stable environment are usually more predictable than those in a dynamic environment.
   - **b.** Relationships involving income statement accounts tend to be more predictable than those involving balance sheet accounts (since the income statement deals with a period of time rather than a single moment in time).
   - **c.** Relationships involving transactions subject to management discretion tend to be less predictable.
3. **Availability and Reliability of Data --** Reliability increases when the data used are reliable, which is enhanced when the data are (1) obtained from independent external sources; (2) are subject to audit testing (either currently or in the past); or (3) are developed under conditions of effective internal control.

4. **Precision of Expectation --** The likelihood of detecting a misstatement decreases as the level of aggregation of the data increases. In other words, relationships of interest to the auditor may be obscured by the noise in the data at high levels of aggregation (e.g., analyzing sales by month broken down by product line is more likely to be helpful to the auditor than simply comparing the current year's sales in total to the prior year's sales).

C. **Required as a Final Review --** This represents one last opportunity to verify the appropriateness of the auditor's conclusions reached before the auditor's report is issued.

Detecting Fraud

After studying this lesson, you should be able to:

1. *Understand (and be able to state) the auditor's fundamental responsibility to detect and communicate matters related to fraud in a financial statement audit.*
2. *Identify and distinguish between the two types of "fraud" that might be relevant to a financial statement audit, as discussed in the AICPA Professional Standards.*
3. *Identify the three categories of "risk factors" that the auditor is required to consider when assessing the risk of material misstatement due to fraud in accordance with AICPA Professional Standards.*

I. Auditor's Responsibilities -- The auditor's responsibilities to detect and communicate issues related to fraud are currently addressed by SAS No. 99, "Consideration of Fraud in a Financial Statement Audit."

[See "AU316 (SAS 99) - Consideration of Fraud"]

A. Two types of misstatements that are relevant to the auditor's consideration of fraud:

1. **Fraudulent financial reporting --** Where misstatements are intended to deceive financial statement users (for example, the intent is to inflate the entity's stock price).
2. **Misappropriation of assets --** Theft of assets causing the financial statements to be misstated due to false entries intended to conceal the theft.

II. Auditor's Basic Responsibility Relates to Planning

A. In general, the auditor is required to design (plan) the audit to provide "reasonable assurance" of detecting misstatements that are material to the financial statements.

> **Note:** AICPA Professional Standards focus on the auditor's responsibility for providing reasonable assurance of detecting material misstatements, **whether due to error or fraud**. The distinction depends upon whether the misstatement is intentional (which is the essence of fraud) or not. Intent may be difficult to determine, for example, when addressing accounting estimates.

B. Specifically, audit team members must have a discussion to consider how and where the financial statements might be susceptible to material misstatement due to fraud and to emphasize the importance of maintaining professional skepticism.

C. The auditor should also discuss the potential for management override of internal controls.

> **Question:**
> Does failure to detect a material misstatement imply a substandard audit?
>
> **Answer:**
> No! An auditor may be unable to detect a material misstatement due to forgery, collusion, or upper management involvement, etc.

III. **Inquiry and Analytical Procedures --** To obtain information needed to identify the risks of material fraud -- the auditor emphasizes "inquiry" and "analytical procedures." (Note that inquiries should be documented in the "Management Representation Letter" at the end of fieldwork!)

A. **Inquiry --** Inquire of management personnel about their knowledge of fraud, suspected fraud, or allegations of fraud; inquire about specific controls that management has implemented to mitigate fraud risks; inquire about management's communications with those charged with governance about fraud-related issues; may choose to inquire of others (e.g., audit committee, internal auditors, operating personnel, in-house legal counsel, etc.) about fraud-related issues.

B. **Analytical procedures --** Specifically perform analytical procedures involving revenue accounts; in general, consider any unexpected results associated with analytical procedures.

C. There is a presumption that improper revenue recognition is a fraud risk -- the auditor should ordinarily presume a risk of material misstatement due to fraud related to revenue recognition and perform appropriate procedures (such as analytical procedures).

IV. **Conditions of Fraud -** The auditor is required specifically to assess the risk of material misstatement due to fraud - SAS 99 requires consideration of three conditions generally associated with fraud: (1) incentive/pressure; (2) opportunity; and (3) attitude/rationalization. These three categories of risk factors are sometimes referred to as the "fraud triangle."

A. **Fraudulent financial reporting -** Example risk factors the auditor should consider:

1. **Incentive/pressure --** Reasons that management might be motivated to commit fraudulent financial reporting.

a. **Financial stability/profitability -** Threatened by economic conditions, for example: operating losses threaten bankruptcy; recurring negative cash flows from operations; vulnerability to rapid changes due to technology or other factors; increasing business failures in the industry; unusual profitability relative to the industry

b. **Excessive pressure to meet the expectations of outsiders -** For example: overly optimistic press releases; marginal ability to meet exchange listing requirements; difficulty meeting debt covenants; need to obtain additional financing to stay competitive.

2. **Opportunities -** Circumstances that might give management a way to commit fraudulent financial reporting.

a. **Nature of the industry or the entity's operations -** For example: significant related-party transactions not in the ordinary course of business; ability to dominate suppliers or customers in a certain industry sector; unnecessarily complex transactions close to year-end raise "substance over form" issues; significant bank accounts or business operations in "tax-haven" jurisdictions with no clear business justification; major financial statement elements that involve significant estimates by management that are difficult to corroborate.

b. **Ineffective monitoring of management -** For example: domination of management by a single person or small group without compensating controls; ineffective oversight by those charged with governance.

c. **Complex or unstable organizational structure -** For example: organization consists of unusual legal entities; high turnover of senior management, counsel, or board members.

d. **Internal controls are deficient -** For example: inadequate monitoring of controls; high turnover rates in accounting, internal auditing, and information technology staff; ineffective accounting and information systems (significant deficiencies are material weaknesses).

3. **Attitudes/rationalizations --** Attitudes, behaviors or justifications that might be associated with fraudulent financial reporting:

a. Lack of commitment to establishing and enforcing ethical standards.

b. Previous violations of securities laws (or other regulations).

c. Excessive focus by management on the entity's stock price.

d. Management's failure to correct reportable conditions.

e. Pattern of justifying inappropriate accounting as immaterial.

f. Management has a strained relationship with the predecessor or current auditor.

B. **Misappropriation of assets --** Example risk factors the auditor should consider:

1. **Incentive/pressure --** Reasons that an employee or member of management might be motivated to commit the misappropriation: employees who have access to cash (or other assets susceptible to theft), have personal financial problems, or have adverse relationships with the entity under audit, (including anticipated future layoffs or recent changes to their benefits or compensation levels).

2. **Opportunities --** Circumstances that might give someone a way to commit the misappropriation.

a. When assets are inherently vulnerable to theft -- e.g., large amounts of liquid assets are on hand; inventory items are small, but valuable.

b. Inadequate internal control over assets -- e.g., inadequate segregation of duties; inadequate documentation or reconciliation for assets; inadequate management understanding related to information technology.

3. **Attitudes/rationalizations --** Attitudes, behaviors or justifications that might be associated with that justify misappropriation: generally, the auditor cannot observe these attitudes, but should consider such matters when discovered.

a. Employee's behavior indicates dissatisfaction with the entity under audit.

b. Changes in employee's behavior or lifestyle are suspicious.

c. Employee exhibits disregard for internal control related to assets by overriding existing controls or failing to correct known deficiencies.

C. **Consideration of the effects of the risk factors**

1. The auditor should use judgment in considering the individual or collective effects of the risk factors -- the effects of these risk factors vary widely.

2. Specific controls may mitigate implied risks or specific control deficiencies may add to the risks.

D. Conditions may be **discovered during fieldwork** that cause the assessment of these risks in the planning stage to be modified.

1. **Discrepancies in the accounting records --** Including inaccuracies or unsupported balances.

2. **Conflicting or missing evidence --** Including missing documents or absence of original documents (e.g., only copies are available).

3. **Problematic relationship between the auditor and the client --** Including restricted access to records or personnel and undue time pressures.

E. **Responses to risk assessment --** In response to this risk assessment related to fraud, the auditor may conclude that the planned procedures should be modified or that control risk should be reconsidered.

1. May need to adjust the nature, timing, and extent of audit procedures to appropriately determine the planned level of detection risk - the auditor should incorporate a degree of "unpredictability" in audit testing (e.g., visit locations on an unannounced basis).

2. May need to assign more experienced personnel or information technology specialists to the engagement.

3. May need to focus in more detail on certain audit areas (e.g., areas that are highly subjective or apparently complex).

F. **Management override --** Auditors should plan procedures specifically to address management override of internal control. Management override means that upper management may not be affected by controls that are imposed on subordinates throughout the organization. (Therefore, management may be able to sidestep those controls without leaving an audit trail for discovery.)

1. **Examine adjusting journal entries --** The auditor should be especially attentive to nonstandard journal entries (involving unusual accounts or amounts and those involving complex issues or significant uncertainty); should also be especially attentive to journal entries near the end of the reporting period (both the fiscal year and applicable interim reporting periods, such as quarterly reports).

2. **Evaluate accounting estimates for bias --** The auditor should consider performing a **"retrospective review,"** which means evaluating prior years' estimates for reasonableness in light of facts occurring after those estimates were made. (In other words, did later events support or refute the appropriateness of management's estimates in prior periods? That may affect the auditor's perception of the reliability of management's estimates in the current period.)

3. **Evaluate the business rationale for any unusual transactions --** The auditor should look for appropriate authorization by those charged with governance.

Fraud - Evaluation/Communication

After studying this lesson, you should be able to:

1. *Understand the auditor's responsibility to evaluate fraud issues in light of the overall results of audit procedures performed.*
2. *Identify the specific fraud issues that the auditor should document.*
3. *Understand the auditor's responsibility to communicate identified fraud issues to management, those charged with governance, or others.*

I. **Evaluation of Audit Test Results --** The auditor should consider the accumulated results of audit procedures and the auditor's observations throughout the engagement. (This assessment of the accumulated results is primarily a **qualitative** matter based on the auditor's judgment.)

A. When evaluating misstatements of the financial statements in general, consider whether such misstatements could be indicative of fraud -- e.g., evaluate the organizational level involved.

B. If the misstatement is (or may be) the result of fraud and the effect could be material to the financial statements (or if the auditor has been unable to evaluate the materiality involved):

1. Discuss the issues and any further investigation required with an appropriate level of management (at least one level above those believed to be involved) and with those charged with governance (especially if senior management appears to be involved).
2. Consider the implications to other aspects of the audit (e.g., does this matter reflect on management integrity more generally?). The auditor may consider withdrawing from the engagement, although the AICPA states, "It is not possible to definitively describe when withdrawal is appropriate."
3. Attempt to obtain additional evidence to determine the facts as to the cause and whether the financial statements are misstated.

II. **Required Documentation --** The auditor must document the following matters related to the consideration of fraud in the financial statement audit:

A. The discussion among engagement personnel about fraud in planning the audit, including how and when the discussion occurred, the team members who participated, and the subject matter discussed.

B. The procedures performed to obtain information necessary to assess the risks of material fraud.

C. Specific risks of material fraud that were identified, including a description of how the auditor responded to those identified risks (including the linkage of audit procedures to the risk assessment).

D. Reasons supporting the auditor's conclusion if improper revenue recognition was not identified as a risk of material misstatement due to fraud.

E. The results of procedures performed to further address the risk of management override of controls.

F. Other conditions and analytical relationships that caused the auditor to perform additional auditing procedures.

G. The nature of the communication about fraud made to management, those charged with governance, and others.

III. Required Communications when Fraud is Detected or Suspected

A. If the fraud is not material to the financial statements and senior management is not involved in the fraud, the **appropriate level of management** (defined to be at least one level above where the fraud occurred) should be notified.

B. If the fraud is material to the financial statements or if senior management is involved in the fraud, those charged with governance should be notified.

C. The auditor should consider whether any identified fraud risk factors may constitute a **"significant deficiency" (or material weakness)** regarding internal control that should be reported to senior management and those charged with governance.

D. **"Whistle-blowing" --** Informing others (outside) the entity is ordinarily prohibited by the auditor's client confidentiality requirements, subject to four basic exceptions:

1. The auditor must respond truthfully to a valid legal subpoena.
2. The auditor must comply with applicable legal and regulatory requirements (including complying with the SEC's 8-K requirements about important matters, such as the entity's decision to change auditors).
3. The auditor must respond appropriately to a successor auditor's inquiries when the former client has given permission for the predecessor auditor to respond to the successor's questions.
4. The auditor must report fraud to the applicable funding agency under the requirements of government auditing standards.

Detecting Illegal Acts

After studying this lesson, you should be able to:

1. *State the auditor's fundamental responsibility to detect and communicate matters related to illegal acts in a financial statement audit.*

I. **Auditor's Basic Responsibilities to Detect Illegal Acts --** These responsibilities are about the same as for fraud.

[See "AU317 (SAS 54) - Illegal Acts by Clients"]

A. **Planning**

1. Must design the audit to provide "reasonable assurance" of detecting illegal acts having a **direct and material effect** on the financial statements (e.g., illegalities related to compliance with applicable securities laws).
2. The auditor is less likely to detect acts relating to the entity's operating activities, rather than financial reporting activities (for example, the auditor might not be the mostly likely party to detect illegal disposals of hazardous waste materials).

II. **Fieldwork --** Make inquiries of management about the entity's compliance with applicable laws and their knowledge of any such illegal acts having financial statement consequences (include reference in the "management representation letter" at the end of fieldwork).

III. **If Auditor Determines that an Illegal Act May Have Occurred**

A. Gather additional evidence to determine the facts -- about the nature and financial statement effect of any such illegal acts.

B. Discuss with the appropriate level of management (at least one level above those believed to be involved) and those charged with governance.

C. May have to consult with client's attorney or other specialists, since determination of illegality is usually outside of auditor's expertise.

D. Consider implications to other audit areas -- for example, does such an act reflect on management's integrity?

IV. **Reporting Effects of Detected Illegal Acts**

A. Ask management to revise the financial statements appropriately; if management will not make required adjustments, the auditor should appropriately modify the opinion (due to GAAP departure).

B. If unable to determine the magnitude of the misstatement, the auditor may have to disclaim or qualify the opinion (due to scope limitation).

C. Inform management and those charged with governance, but **not** outside authorities due to **confidentiality** (which prohibits "whistleblowing" -- same "exceptions" as for disclosing fraud).

Using the Work of a 'Specialist'

After studying this lesson, you should be able to:

1. *Understand the meaning of the term "specialist" as used by the AICPA.*
2. *Identify the considerations that would be relevant to an auditor's selection of a particular specialist.*
3. *Determine when it would be appropriate for the auditor to make reference to the involvement of the specialist in the auditor's report.*

I. **When a Specialized Measurement or Valuation is Required for the Engagement --** An appropriate expert outside of the auditor's firm (called a "specialist") may be hired to assist the auditors and participate in the engagement as a member of the audit team. This determination is usually made at the planning stage of an audit.

[See "AU336 (SAS 73) - Using the Work of Specialists"]

A. **Examples --** Actuaries, appraisers, engineers, geologists (involves some specialized expertise outside of accounting or auditing).

B. **Decision to use --** When there are audit issues related to valuation, quantity or quality, or interpreting technical requirements; the auditor is still responsible for understanding the methods, assumptions, and conclusions of the specialist with respect to the entity's financial statements.

C. **Selection of a specialist --** Consider professional credentials, reputation, and any relationship to the client (obviously prefer unrelated parties!).

D. **Reference to the specialist in the auditor's report**

1. Unqualified opinion:
   a. Usually, do not refer to the specialist (that might be misunderstood), since a "division of responsibility" is not permitted; the auditor is responsible for the opinion expressed.
   b. However, the auditor may choose to add an explanatory paragraph that references the report or findings of the specialist, if that will facilitate the readers' understanding.
2. Modified opinions (qualified, adverse, or disclaimer) -- the audit report may reference the report or findings of the specialist, if that will facilitate the readers' understanding of the reason(s) for the modified opinion.

Communications/Those Charged with Governance

After studying this lesson, you should be able to:

1. *State the specific matters that the auditor is required to communicate "with those charged with governance" (and be able to define that term).*
2. *Understand the impact that ineffective two-way communication with those charged with governance may have on the audit engagement.*

I. Primary Definitions and Audit Responsibility

[See "AU380 (SAS 114) – Communication with Those Charged with Governance"]

> **Definitions:**
> *Those charged with governance*: The person(s) with responsibility for overseeing the strategic direction of the entity and obligations related to the accountability of the entity (encompasses the term "board of directors" or "audit committee" used elsewhere in the auditing standards).
>
> *Management*: The person(s) responsible for achieving the objectives of the entity and who has or have the authority to establish policies and make decisions by which those objectives are to be pursued.

A. **Basic auditor responsibility --** The auditor must communicate those matters that are significant and relevant to the responsibilities of those charged with governance in overseeing the financial reporting process.

> **Note:**
> The auditor is not required to perform any specific procedures to identify such matters to communicate with those charged with governance.

II. Communication with Management -- The auditor may choose to discuss some matters with management before communicating them with those charged with governance, unless that is inappropriate (for example, the auditor would not normally discuss issues involving management's competence or integrity). Likewise, the auditor may choose to discuss some matters with the internal auditor(s) before communicating the matters with those charged with governance.

III. Matters Required to be Communicated with Those Charged with Governance -- (Although the auditor may choose to communicate additional matters.)

A. **The auditor's responsibilities under GAAS --** May be communicated by an engagement letter.

B. **The planned scope and timing of the audit --** Including how the auditor plans to address the significant risks of material misstatement; the general approach to internal control relevant to the audit; the factors considered in determining materiality; and the auditor's use of the internal audit function and how they can best work together.

C. **Significant findings from the audit --** Including the following matters:

1. **Qualitative aspects of the entity's significant accounting policies --** Discuss the quality (not just the acceptability) of significant accounting practices.
2. **Significant difficulties encountered during the audit --** Including significant delays caused by management, unreasonable time pressure, unavailability of expected information, etc.
3. **Disagreements with management over accounting and auditing matters --** Whether or not the disagreements were satisfactorily resolved.

4. **Uncorrected misstatements --** Including all known and likely misstatements identified during the audit (excluding any that are considered "trivial").
5. **Management consultations with other accountants --** May represent possible "opinion shopping" activities by management, so discuss the matters that were subject to consultation.
6. **Significant issues discussed (or subject to correspondence) --** With management in connection with the auditor's engagement retention.
7. **Independence issues --** The auditor may discuss circumstances or relationships potentially affecting independence, which the auditor considered, in concluding that the auditor's independence is not impaired.

IV. **The Communication Process --** Generally, the communication may be oral or in writing (effective communication may include formal presentations, written reports, or informal discussions, as determined by the auditor's judgment).

A. Should communicate the significant findings from the audit in writing when oral communication is inadequate in the auditor's judgment.

B. When a significant matter is discussed with an individual member of those charged with governance (such as the chair of the audit committee) -- the auditor should evaluate whether the matter should be summarized in a subsequent communication to all those charged with governance.

C. **Timing of communications --** The auditor should communicate on a timely basis so that those charged with governance can take appropriate action (however, that timing may vary depending upon the circumstances).

D. **Adequacy of the communication process --** The auditor should evaluate whether the two-way communication has been adequate for purposes of the audit.

1. An inadequate two-way communication may suggest an unsatisfactory control environment, which the auditor should consider.
2. If the two-way communication is inadequate -- the auditor should consider whether a scope limitation may exist and consider the possible effect on the assessment of the risks of material misstatement (this might warrant modification of the opinion, or even withdrawal).

V. **Documentation of the Communication --** The auditor should document matters communicated orally (when communicated in writing, the auditor should keep a copy of that communication).

VI. **Other Statements on Auditing Standards --** Other statements require that certain specific matters should be communicated to those charged with governance regarding:

A. **Illegal acts --** Communicate any illegal acts that come to the auditor's attention.

B. **Going concern issues --** When substantial doubt about the entity's ability to continue as a going concern remains after considering management's strategy, the auditor should communicate (1) the nature of the conditions identified; (2) the possible effect on the financial statements and disclosures; and (3) the effects on the auditor's report.

C. **Fraud --** The auditor should (1) inquire of the audit committee about the risks of fraud and the audit committee's knowledge of any fraud or suspected fraud; (2) communicate any fraud discovered involving senior management and any fraud that causes a material misstatement (whether or not management is involved); and (3) obtain an understanding with those charged with governance regarding communications about misappropriations committed by lower-level employees.

D. **Communicating internal control matters identified in an audit --** The auditor should communicate to management and those charged with governance any identified significant deficiencies in internal control (including material weaknesses).

Internal Control - Concepts and Standards

Internal Control Concepts 1

After studying this lesson, you should be able to:

1. *Understand the auditor's responsibility to obtain an understanding of an entity's internal control in connection with the second standard of field work under GAAS.*
2. *Explain three different ways that an auditor might document the understanding of internal control.*

I. **Review Phase --** The auditor should obtain an initial understanding of internal controls and document that understanding.

A. Obtain an **understanding of internal control** and the flow of documents related to transactions through:

1. Inquiry of appropriate personnel.
2. Observation of client activities.
3. Review of documentation -- including the client's accounting manuals, prior-year's audit documentation (working papers), etc.

B. The auditor's internal control analysis tends to focus on major transaction cycles.

C. **"Transaction cycle" --** Is a group of essentially homogeneous transactions.

D. **Implication --** A specific transaction cycle is the highest level of aggregation about which meaningful generalizations of control risk can be made, since control risk is constant within that transaction cycle.

E. **Examples of typical transaction cycles --** For which a given type of transaction is subject to essentially the identical configuration of internal control policies and procedures (hence, within a transaction cycle, all transactions have the same control risk):

1. Revenue/receipts.
2. Expenditures/disbursements.
3. Payroll.
4. Financing/investing activities.
5. Inventory, especially if inventory is manufactured, rather than purchased.

F. **Document understanding --** The auditor must **document that understanding** -- The extensiveness of the review and documentation varies with the circumstances (e.g., the emphasis on understanding internal controls increases if reliance on internal control is planned):

1. **Flow charts of transaction cycles --** A graphical depiction of the client's accounting systems for major categories of transactions (with emphasis on the origination, processing, and distribution of important underlying accounting documents).

a. **Advantages --** A fairly systematic approach that is unlikely to overlook important considerations; tailored to client-specific circumstances; fairly easy for others to review and understand; fairly easy to update from year to year.

b. **Disadvantages --** Can be rather tedious and time consuming to prepare initially; the auditor might fail to recognize relevant internal control deficiencies by getting too absorbed in the details of the client's system.

Common flow charting symbols:

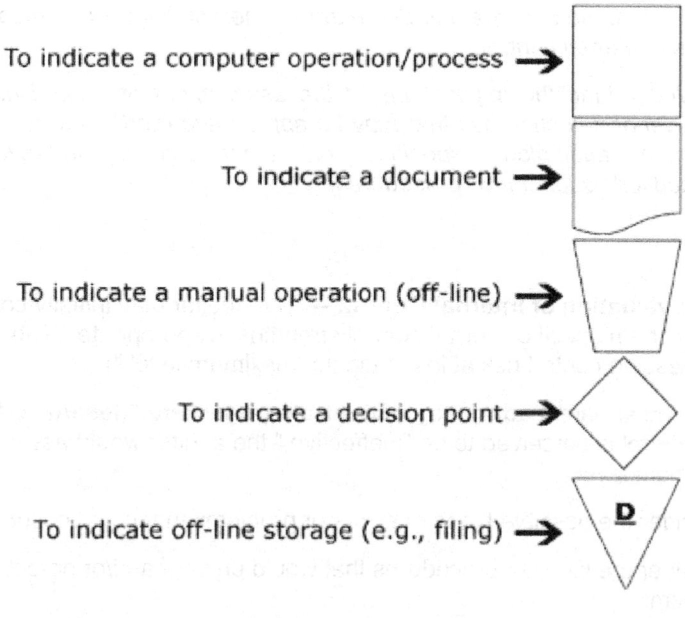

2. **Internal control questionnaires (ICQs) --** Questionnaires consisting of a listing of questions about client's control procedures and activities; a "no" answer is usually designed to indicate a control weakness.
   a. **Advantages --** Generic questionnaires can be prepared in advance for clients in various industry categories with every conceivable question, so that no important question related to controls is likely to be omitted; deficiencies are easily identified by a client's "no" response to any question.
   b. **Disadvantages --** Generic questionnaires are not tailored to client-specific circumstances and irrelevant questions are annoying to client personnel; the client personnel responding to the checklist of questions may conceal deficiencies by inaccurate answers without the auditor's knowledge.
3. **Narrative write-ups --** A written memo describing the important control-related activities in the transaction cycles under consideration.
   a. **Advantages --** Tailored to a client's unique circumstances; can be as detailed or general as desired; relatively easy to prepare the memo (and easy for reviewers to read it).
   b. **Disadvantages --** Relatively easy to overlook relevant internal control issues (strengths or weaknesses) because the analysis is fairly unstructured; can be tedious to make changes over time to a detailed, hard copy memo when the client's policies and procedures have changed. (This may require starting over with a new memo to accommodate any changes, although this is not a problem when using modern word processing software.)

G. **Perform a "walkthrough" --** The auditor may select a few transactions to trace them through the client's accounting system. The purpose is merely to get some feedback as to whether the auditor has accurately understood (and documented) the way the client entity is processing transactions. The walkthrough is not considered "evidence" or a form of documentation and should not be confused with "tests of control."

Internal Control Concepts 2

After studying this lesson, you should be able to:

1. *Understand the purpose of performing "tests of control" and the circumstances that warrant performing such tests of control.*
2. *Understand the meaning of the term "inherent limitations" in connection with internal control.*
3. *Understand the implications of the assessment of control risk to the level of detection risk that may be appropriate (and, thereby, the effect on the "audit plan" -- specifically on the nature, timing, and extent of the auditor's substantive procedures).*

I. **Preliminary Evaluation of Internal Control --** The auditor may initially consider whether "reliance" on certain specific internal control strengths is appropriate. (The auditor may consider "assessing control risk at less than the maximum level.")

   A. Consider the apparent **adequacy of controls (regarding "design" effectiveness)** -- If internal control is perceived to be "ineffective," the auditor would assess control risk at the maximum level.

      1. Consider the possible types of errors or problems that could occur.
      2. Consider the kinds of procedures that would prevent and/or detect such errors or problems.
      3. Determine whether such controls are in place.
      4. Evaluate the implications of any identified weaknesses.

   B. Consider **cost-benefit tradeoffs** -- Reliance on internal controls "buys" a reduction of substantive audit work to some degree, but it "costs" additional effort to perform tests of control (and this may or may not be cost beneficial, even if the design of internal control is perceived to be effective).

   C. The auditor should document the basis for conclusions about internal control -- either way, whether internal control is perceived to be effective or ineffective.

II. **Perform "Tests of Controls" --** If reliance is planned (regarding "operating effectiveness") -- "reliance" means the same thing as "to assess control risk at less than the maximum level" for purposes of accepting a somewhat higher level of detection risk.

   A. Perform "tests of controls" -- but only for those specific control policies and procedures (strengths) on which reliance is planned.

   B. The purpose of performing tests of control is to verify that the controls that looked good "on paper" (design effectiveness) were actually working as intended throughout the period (**operating effectiveness**).

   C. Circumstances that warrant performing tests of control (associated with a "reliance" strategy): (1) when the auditor's risk assessment includes an expectation regarding the operating effectiveness of controls; or (2) when the performance of substantive procedures alone do not limit audit risk to an acceptably low level.

   D. Select a sample of transactions and verify that the control procedures of interest were, in fact, performed on the transactions in the sample which usually requires that the control procedure be documented as it is performed. (Undocumented controls may be tested by the auditor's "observation" of the controls.)

III. Re-evaluate Planned Reliance Based on the Results of These Tests of Controls -- Determine whether the results of the tests of controls are consistent with the planned reliance on internal controls. (What looked good on paper may not be working satisfactorily in reality.)

IV. Develop a Detailed Audit Plan -- (Also referred to as an "audit program") The auditor should prepare a written audit plan that specifies the nature, timing, and extent of further audit procedures to be performed; and the auditor should document the conclusions about control risk in planning the audit:

A. A wholly substantive audit approach means "no reliance" on internal control (which means the same thing as "assessing control risk at the maximum level"). In other words, the auditor plans to meet the audit risk objectives by performing only substantive audit procedures without any expectation about the operating effectiveness of internal control.

B. Auditors may base their audit conclusions on both tests of controls and substantive audit procedures, although the auditor must always perform substantive procedures to some extent (i.e., the auditor cannot rely entirely on the operating effectiveness of internal control as a sole basis for conclusions), related to "detection risk" in the SAS No. 107 audit risk model.

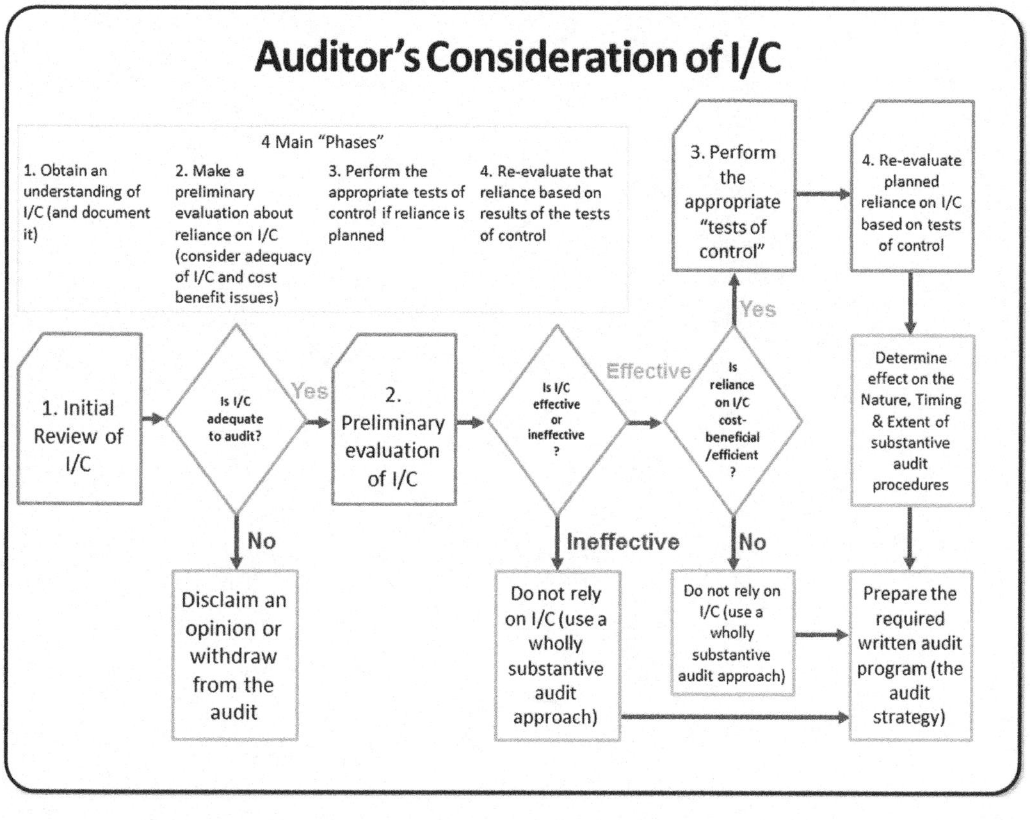

V. Inherent Limitations -- The design and implementation of internal control is a management function (not the auditor's responsibility!) and management must evaluate the applicable costs and benefits in the design and implementation of their internal control policies and procedures:

A. The costs of internal controls should not outweigh the benefits attributable to those controls -- as a result, controls provide reasonable (not absolute) assurance.

B. Mistakes may occur due to employees' misunderstandings, misjudgments, carelessness, fatigue, etc.

C. Segregation of duties may break down due to collusion (a conspiracy among employees or management to circumvent internal controls) or management's "override" of controls -- override refers to management imposing controls downward on subordinates without intending to be affected by those controls themselves.

Question:
Why must auditors consider an entity's internal control in planning the audit engagement?

Answer:
In order to plan an effective and efficient audit, auditors must assess control risk as a basis for setting the appropriate level of "detection risk" related to their substantive auditing procedures (specifically, to determine the nature, timing, and extent of those substantive procedures).

Internal Control Standards 1

After studying this lesson, you should be able to:

1. *Understand the auditor's responsibility to perform risk assessment procedures.*
2. *Understand the entity and its environment, including internal control (with emphasis on the five interrelated components of internal control), in accordance with AICPA Professional Standards.*

I. Responsibilities under AICPA Professional Standards

A. AICPA Professional Standards interpret the auditor's basic responsibilities to consider internal controls required by the second Standard of Fieldwork of GAAS: "The auditor must obtain a sufficient understanding of the entity and its environment, including its internal control, to assess the risk of material misstatement of the financial statements whether due to fraud or error, and to design the nature, timing, and extent of further audit procedures."

[See "AU314 (SAS 109) - Understanding the Entity and Its Environment"]

B. SAS No. 109 focuses on the auditor's requirements related to (1) risk assessment procedures; (2) understanding the entity and its environment, including its internal control; (3) assessing the risks of material misstatement; and (4) documentation.

II. Risk Assessment Procedures -- The auditor should perform "risk assessment procedures" to obtain an understanding of the entity and its environment, including its internal control (the nature, timing, and extent of the risk assessment procedures vary with the engagement's circumstances, such as the entity's size and complexity and the auditor's experience with it).

A. Inquiries of management and others -- The auditor obtains information from inquiries made of management and others, including internal auditors, production and marketing personnel, those charged with governance, and outsiders (such as external legal counsel or valuation experts used by the entity).

B. Observation and inspection -- Including observation of entity operations, inspection of documents (e.g., internal control manuals), reading reports prepared by management and those charged with governance (e.g., minutes of meetings), and visits to the entity's facilities.

C. Analytical procedures -- Analytical procedures performed in planning may assist the auditor in understanding the entity and its environment and identify specific risks relevant to the audit.

D. Review information -- About the entity and its environment obtained in prior periods. The auditor should consider whether changes may have affected the relevance of that information (perhaps by making inquiries or performing a walkthrough of transactions through the entity's systems).

E. Discussion among audit team members -- The audit team should discuss the susceptibility of the entity's financial statements to material misstatements.

1. **Key members should be involved in the discussion --** But that requires professional judgment to determine who should be included. (For a multi-location audit, there may be multiple discussions for key members at each major location.)
2. **Objective of this discussion --** For members of the audit team to understand the potential for material misstatements of the financial statements (due to error or fraud) in specific areas assigned to them and how their work may affect other parts of the audit.

3. **The discussion should include "critical issues" --** Areas of significant audit risk, potential for management override of controls; important controls; materiality at the financial statement level and the account level; etc.

III. Understanding the Entity and Its Environment -- Including its internal control.

A. The auditor's understanding of the entity and its environment consists of understanding the following: (1) industry, regulatory, and other external factors; (2) nature of the entity; (3) objectives and strategies and related business risks that may cause material misstatement of the financial statements; (4) measurement and review of the entity's financial performance; and (5) internal control.

1. **Industry, regulatory, and other external factors --** There may be specific risks of material misstatement due to the nature of the business, the degree of regulation or other economic, technical, and competitive issues.
2. **Nature of the entity --** Refers to the entity's operations, ownership, governance, financing, etc. (Understanding these considerations may help the auditor understand the classes of transactions, account balances, and disclosures that are relevant to the financial statements.)
3. **Objectives and strategies --** And related business risks that may cause material misstatement of the financial statements. Strategies are operational approaches by which management intends to achieve its objectives. Business risks result from circumstances that could adversely affect the entity's ability to achieve its objectives. (Note that the auditor does not have a responsibility to identify all business risks.)
4. **Measurement and review of the entity's financial performance --** Performance measures (and their review) indicate aspects of the entity's performance that management considers important, which may help the auditor to understand whether such pressures increase the risks of material misstatement.
5. **Obtain a sufficient understanding of internal control --** By performing risk assessment procedures to evaluate the design of controls relevant to the audit to identify types of potential misstatements. (Note that inquiry alone is not sufficient to evaluate the design and implementation of a control.) Consider factors that affect the risks of material misstatement; and design tests of controls, if applicable, and substantive procedures.

> **Note:**
> The auditor must perform substantive tests to some degree for all significant audit areas - cannot assess control risk so low that substantive testing is omitted entirely!

B. **The Auditor's Consideration of Internal Control --** (Internal control may also be referred to as "internal control structure.") The auditor should obtain a sufficient understanding of internal control to evaluate the design of controls relevant to the audit.

> **Definition:**
> *Internal control*: A process -- effected by those charged with governance, management, and other personnel -- designed to provide reasonable assurance about the achievement of the entity's objectives with regard to reliability of financial reporting, effectiveness and efficiency of operations, and compliance with applicable laws and regulations.

C. **The auditor's primary consideration --** Whether (and how) a specific control prevents, or detects and corrects, material misstatements in relevant assertions related to classes of transactions, account balances, or disclosures.

D. Internal control consists of five interrelated components:

1. **Control environment --** Policies and procedures that determine the overall control consciousness of the entity, sometimes called "the tone at the top."

> The auditor should evaluate the following elements that comprise the entity's control environment: (1) communication and enforcement of integrity and ethical values; (2) commitment to competence; (3) participation of those charged with governance (including their interaction with internal and external auditors); (4) management's philosophy and operating style; (5) the entity's organizational structure; (6) the entity's assignment of authority and responsibility (including internal reporting relationships); and (7) human resource policies and practices.

2. **Risk assessment --** The policies and procedures involving the identification, prioritization, and analysis of relevant risks as a basis for managing those risks.

> The auditor's responsibilities include: (1) inquiring about business risks that management has identified relevant to financial reporting and considering their implications to the financial statements; (2) considering how management identified (and decided how to manage) business risks relevant to financial reporting; and (3) considering the implications to the risk assessment process when the auditor identifies business risks that management failed to identify.

3. **Information and communication systems --** Policies and procedures related to the identification, capture, and exchange of information in a form and time frame that enable people to carry out their responsibilities.

> The auditor's responsibilities include: (1) obtaining sufficient knowledge to understand the classes of transactions that are significant to the financial statements and the procedures and relevant documents related to financial reporting; (2) obtaining an understanding of how incorrect processing of transactions is resolved; (3) obtaining an understanding of the automated (IT) and manual procedures used to prepare the financial statements and how misstatements may occur; (4) obtaining an understanding of how transactions originate with the entity's business processes; and (5) obtaining sufficient knowledge to understand how the entity communicates financial reporting roles and responsibilities.

4. **Control activities --** The policies and procedures that help ensure that management directives are carried out especially those related to (1) authorization, (2) segregation of duties, (3) safeguarding assets, and (4) asset accountability.

> The auditor's responsibilities include: (1) obtaining an understanding of how IT affects control activities relevant to planning the audit (especially with respect to "application controls" and "general controls"); and (2) considering whether the entity has established effective controls related to IT (especially with respect to maintaining the integrity of information and the security of data).

5. **Monitoring --** The policies and procedures involving the ongoing assessment of the quality of internal control effectiveness over time.

> The auditor should obtain an understanding of the sources of the information related to the entity's monitoring activities and the basis upon which management considers the information to be reliable.

E. **Inherent Limitations of Internal Control --** Internal control provides reasonable, not absolute, assurance about achieving the entity's objectives; internal control may be ineffective due to human failures (mistakes and misunderstandings) and controls may be circumvented by collusion or management override of controls. The cost of an internal control procedure should not exceed the benefit expected to be derived from it.

Internal Control Standards 2

After studying this lesson, you should be able to:

1. *Assess the risk of material misstatement.*
2. *Document various internal control matters.*
3. *Link audit responses to the risks of material misstatement at the financial statement level and at the relevant assertion level, in accordance with AICPA Professional Standards.*

I. Assessing the Risk of Material Misstatement

A. **Auditor's responsibility --** The auditor should identify and assess the risks of material misstatement at the financial statement level and at the relevant assertion level related to classes of transactions, account balances, and disclosures

B. **Internal control considerations --** A weak control environment (such as management's lack of competence) may have pervasive financial statement effects and require an overall response by the auditor; the auditor's understanding of internal control may raise questions about the auditability of the entity's financial statements (e.g., sufficient appropriate evidence may not be available).

C. **"Significant risks" --** Risks that the auditor believes require special audit consideration; the auditor should consider the nature of the risks identified (whether risk may relate to fraud, significant economic developments, the complexity of transactions, related-party transactions, subjective measurement, or nonroutine transactions that are unusual for the entity).

D. **Risks for which substantive procedures alone do not provide sufficient appropriate audit evidence --** The auditor should evaluate the design and implementation of controls over such risks, since it is not possible to reduce detection risk to an acceptably low level with substantive procedures by themselves (for example, when IT is a significant part of the entity's information system and transactions are initiated, authorized, recorded, processed, and reported electronically without an audit trail).

E. **Revision of risk assessment --** Risk assessment is an iterative process and the assessment of risks may change as additional evidence is obtained. (For example, when performing tests of controls, evidence may be obtained that controls are ineffective, or when performing substantive procedures, misstatements may be detected that suggest that controls are ineffective).

II. Documentation -- The form of the documentation requires professional judgment and varies with the circumstances, including the complexity of the entity and the extent to which IT is used (the documentation may include narrative descriptions, questionnaires, flowcharts, and checklists).

A. The auditor should document the following:

1. The discussion with members of the audit team about the potential for misstatements due to error or fraud (including how and when that discussion occurred, the subject matter discussed, the team members involved, and significant decisions reached about the planned responses to those risks).
2. Major elements of the understanding of each of the five components of internal control to assess the risk of material misstatement, the sources of information used for that understanding, and the risk assessment procedures performed.

3. The assessment of the risks of material misstatement (both at the financial statement level and at the relevant assertion level) and the basis for that assessment.

4. The risks identified and the related controls the auditor evaluated.

[See "AU318 (SAS 110) - Performing Audit Procedures in Response to Assessed Risks"]

B. SAS No. 110 "provides guidance on determining overall responses and designing and performing further audit procedures to respond to the assessed risk of material misstatement at the financial statement and relevant assertion levels in a financial statement audit, and on evaluating the sufficiency and appropriateness of the audit evidence obtained."

C. SAS No. 110 focuses on the auditor's requirements related to: (1) overall responses to the risks of material misstatement at the financial statement level; (2) responses to the risks of material misstatement at the relevant assertion level (in determining the nature, timing, and extent of further audit procedures, including tests of the operating effectiveness of controls and substantive procedures); (3) evaluating the sufficiency and appropriateness of the audit evidence obtained; and (4) documentation.

III. Overall Responses to the Risks of Material Misstatement at the Financial Statement Level

A. May assign more experienced staff to the engagement; provide closer supervision; use specialists; use more unpredictable audit procedures; and/or make appropriate changes in the nature, timing, or extent of further audit procedures.

B. May influence the auditor's strategy in using a "substantive approach" or a "combined approach" that uses both tests of controls (regarding operating effectiveness of controls) and substantive procedures.

IV. Responses to the Risks of Material Misstatement at the Relevant Assertion Level -- In determining the nature, timing, and extent of further audit procedures, including tests of the operating effectiveness of controls and substantive procedures

A. Substantive procedures must be performed to some degree for all relevant assertions related to each material class of transactions, account balance, or disclosure (the auditor cannot rely totally on internal control).

B. **Nature --** Refers to the purpose of further audit procedures (tests of controls or substantive procedures) and their type (inspection, observation, inquiry, confirmation, recalculation, reperformance, or analytical procedures).

C. **Timing --** Refers to when the further audit procedures are performed (at year-end or before year-end); performing substantive procedures at year-end is usually more effective with a higher risk of material misstatement.

D. **Extent --** Refers to the quantity of an audit procedure to be performed (such as sample size) based on the auditor's judgment; computer-assisted audit techniques (CAATs) may be used to extensively test electronic transactions/files.

E. **Tests of Controls --** To determine the operating effectiveness of controls

1. The auditor should perform tests of controls when the auditor's risk assessment includes an expectation of the operating effectiveness of controls. (Note that this is frequently referred to as "relying" on internal control as a partial basis for the auditor's conclusions, or "assessing control risk at less than the maximum level.")

2. The auditor should also perform tests of control when substantive procedures alone do not provide sufficient appropriate evidence at the relevant assertion level (for example, when the entity uses IT extensively and no audit trail exists).

3. **Nature of tests of controls --** Including inquiries of entity personnel; inspection of documents, reports, or files, indicating performance of the control; observation of the application of the control; and auditor reperformance of the control (note that inquiry alone is not sufficient to test controls). When controls are not documented, the auditor may be able to obtain evidence about operating effectiveness by observation or the use of CAATs.

4. **Timing of tests of controls --** When obtaining evidence about the effectiveness of controls for an interim period, the auditor should determine what evidence is required for the remaining period. If planning to rely on controls that have changed since last tested, the auditor should test those controls currently. If planning to rely on controls that have not changed since last tested, the auditor should test the operating effectiveness of those controls at least every third year (that is, no more than two years should pass before retesting such controls).

> **Note:**
> When the auditor identifies a significant risk of material misstatement, but plans to rely on the effectiveness of controls that mitigate that risk, the auditor should test those controls in the current period.

5. **Extent of tests of controls --** When a control is applied on a "transaction basis" (for example, matching approved purchase orders to suppliers' invoices) and if the control operates frequently, the auditor should use audit sampling techniques to test operating effectiveness; when a control is applied on a "periodic basis" (for example, monthly reconciliation of the accounts receivable subsidiary ledger to the general ledger), the auditor should perform procedures appropriate for testing smaller populations.

F. **Substantive Procedures --** Issues related to the auditor's search for material misstatements will be discussed later in connection with "audit evidence" topics.

V. Evaluating the Sufficiency and Appropriateness of the Audit Evidence Obtained

A. An audit is an iterative process, so the planned audit procedures may need to be modified; for example, identified misstatements from substantive procedures may alter the auditor's judgment about the effectiveness of controls.

B. Consider all relevant audit evidence -- the auditor should consider all relevant audit evidence, whether it appears to corroborate or contradict the relevant assertions.

VI. Documentation -- The auditor should document the following:

A. The overall responses to address the assessed risk of misstatement at the financial statement level.

B. The nature, timing, and extent of the further audit procedures.

C. The linkage of those procedures with the assessed risks at the relevant assertion level.

D. The results of the audit procedures.

E. The conclusions reached in the current audit about the operating effectiveness of controls tested in a prior audit.

Internal Control - Required Communications

After studying this lesson, you should be able to:

1. *Know the meaning of the terms "significant deficiency" and "material weakness."*
2. *Understand the auditor's responsibility to communicate identified internal control deficiencies to management and those charged with governance in accordance with AICPA Professional Standards.*

I. Required Communications Related to Internal Control Deficiencies (weaknesses)

A. Guidance is provided by SAS No. 115 -- "Communicating Internal Control Related Matters Identified in an Audit." This SAS defines the terms "deficiency," "significant deficiency," and "material weakness." (The term "reportable condition" is no longer used, which makes AICPA terminology more consistent with that of the PCAOB.)

[See "AU325 (SAS 115) - Internal Control"]

Definitions:
Control deficiency: When the design or operation of a control does not allow management or employees, in the normal course of performing their assigned functions, to prevent or detect misstatements on a timely basis.

Deficiency in design: When a control necessary to meet the control objective is missing, or when the control objective is not always met, even if the control operates as designed.

Deficiency in operation: When a properly designed control does not operate as designed, or when the person performing the control does not have the authority or competence to effectively perform the control.

Significant deficiency: A deficiency (or combination of deficiencies) in internal control that is less severe than a material weakness, yet important enough to merit attention by those charged with governance.

Material weakness: A deficiency (or combination of deficiencies) in internal control such that there is a reasonable possibility that a material misstatement of the entity's financial statements will not be prevented or detected and corrected on a timely basis.

II. Evaluating Control Deficiencies -- The auditor must determine whether identified deficiencies are "significant deficiencies" or "material weaknesses."

A. The auditor should consider both the likelihood and potential magnitude of misstatement in making that evaluation - multiple control deficiencies affecting the same financial statement item increases the likelihood of misstatement.

B. The auditor may wish to consider the possible mitigating effects of compensating controls that can reduce the severity of the effects of a deficiency.

C. Risk factors that affect whether there is a reasonable possibility that a deficiency will result in a misstatement include the following:

1. The nature of the accounts, classes of transactions, disclosures, and assertions involved.

2. The susceptibility of the related asset or liability to loss or fraud.
3. The subjectivity, complexity, or extent of judgment involved.
4. The interaction or relationship of the control with other controls.
5. The interaction among the deficiencies.
6. The possible future consequences of the deficiency.

D. Specific indicators of material weaknesses include the following:

1. Identification of any fraud involving senior management (whether or not material);
2. Restatement of previously issued financial statements to correct a material misstatement due to error or fraud;
3. Identification of a material misstatement in the financial statements by the auditor that would not have been identified by the entity's internal control; and
4. Ineffective oversight of the entity's financial reporting and internal control by those charged with governance.

III. **Communicating Identified Control Deficiencies --** The auditor must communicate the significant deficiencies and material weaknesses identified in the audit.

A. **Form of communication --** Identified significant deficiencies and material weaknesses must be communicated to management and those charged with governance in writing.

B. **Timing --** The required communication is best made by the "report release date" and should be made no later than 60 days following the report release date. (The "report release date" is the date that the auditor grants the entity permission to use the auditor's report in connection with the audited financial statements.)

C. **Early communication is permitted --** The auditor may choose to verbally communicate certain significant deficiencies and material weaknesses during the audit (e.g., to permit timely correction). However, all identified significant deficiencies and material weaknesses must still be communicated in writing no later than 60 days following the report release date, including those matters communicated orally during the audit.

D. **Other matters --** The auditor may choose to communicate other matters believed to be beneficial to the entity (including deficiencies that are not "significant deficiencies") either in writing or verbally. (If communicated verbally, the auditor must document such communication.)

E. The written communication about significant deficiencies and material weaknesses should:

1. State that the purpose of the audit was to express an opinion on the financial statements, not to express an opinion on the effectiveness of internal control.
2. State that the auditor is not expressing an opinion on the effectiveness of internal control.
3. State that the auditor's consideration of internal control was not designed to identify all significant deficiencies or material weaknesses.
4. Include the definition of the terms material weakness and significant deficiency, as applicable.
5. Identify the matters that are considered to be material weaknesses and significant deficiencies, as applicable.

> **Note:**
> The auditor may include additional statements regarding the general inherent limitations of internal control, including the possibility of management override, but such comments are not required.

6. State that the communication is intended solely for the use of management, those charged with governance, and others within the organization (should not be used by anyone other than those specified parties) - if such a communication is required to be given to a governmental authority, that specific reference may be added.

Sample Written Communication about Internal Control Deficiencies:

In planning and performing our audit of the financial statements of ABC Company (the "Company") as of and for the year ended December 31, 20XX, in accordance with auditing standards generally accepted in the United States of America, we considered the Company's internal control over financial reporting (internal control) as a basis for designing our auditing procedures for the purpose of expressing our opinion on the financial statements, but not for the purpose of expressing an opinion on the effectiveness of the Company's internal control. Accordingly, we do not express an opinion on the effectiveness of the Company's internal control.

Our consideration of internal control was for the limited purpose described in the preceding paragraph and was not designed to identify all deficiencies in internal control that might be significant deficiencies or material weaknesses and therefore, there can be no assurance that all deficiencies, significant deficiencies, or material weaknesses have been identified. However, as discussed below, we identified certain deficiencies in internal control that we consider to be material weaknesses (and other deficiencies that we consider to be significant deficiencies - *add this phrase only if applicable*).

A deficiency in internal control exists when the design or operation of a control does not allow management or employees, in the normal course of performing their assigned functions, to prevent, or detect and correct misstatements on a timely basis. A material weakness is a deficiency, or a combination of deficiencies, in internal control, such that there is a reasonable possibility that a material misstatement of the entity's financial statements will not be prevented, or detected and corrected on a timely basis. (We consider the following deficiencies in the Company's internal control to be material weaknesses:)

(*Describe the material weaknesses that were identified.*)

(A significant deficiency is a deficiency, or a combination of deficiencies, in internal control that is less severe than a material weakness, yet important enough to merit attention by those charged with governance. We consider the following deficiencies to be significant deficiencies in internal control:)

(*Describe the significant deficiencies that were identified.*)

This communication is intended solely for the information and use of management, (*identify those charged with governance*), others within the organization, and (*identify any specified governmental authorities*) and is not intended to be and should not be used by anyone other than these specified parties.

F. The auditor should not issue a written communication stating that no significant deficiencies were identified - however, the auditor is permitted to add a comment that no material weaknesses were identified, perhaps as requested to submit to a governmental authority.

G. Management may issue a written response to the auditor's communication to indicate corrective action taken or planned or stating management's belief that the costs of correction exceed the benefits - if such a written response is included with the auditor's communication, the auditor should add a paragraph to disclaim an opinion on management's written response.

Implications of an Internal Audit Function

After studying this lesson, you should be able to:

1. *Understand the independent auditor's responsibilities to evaluate the internal auditors' competence and objectivity when considering the role of an entity's internal audit function for purposes of assessing control risk and/or providing assistance with substantive procedures.*

[See "AU322 (SAS 65) - Internal Audit Function"]

I. **Determine the Relevance of the Internal Auditors' Activities to the Audit --** In connection with understanding internal control and assessing control risk.

A. **Audit procedures --** Vary with the circumstances (a matter of professional judgment) but typically include:

1. **Inquire --** About the internal auditors' organizational status (that is, to whom the internal audit function reports), their access to records and any limitations on their activities, their application of professional standards and audit plans.

2. **Review --** Documentation about the internal auditors' processes for identifying and assessing the entity's risks and the allocation of resources; review internal auditors' reports and documentation supporting their reports.

B. When the internal auditors' activities **are deemed relevant**, the independent auditor must decide whether placing **"reliance"** on the internal auditors' work is **efficient (cost beneficial)** -- If so, the independent auditor must assess the internal auditors' competence and objectivity.

1. **Competence --** Related to education, certification, experience, performance evaluations, etc.

2. **Objectivity --** Organizational status of the internal auditors (independence is enhanced by having the internal audit function report to those charged with governance, such as the entity's audit committee or board of directors); policies to maintain their independence.

3. If the independent auditors plan to rely on the internal audit function as a type of internal control strength to influence the substantive audit procedures, they must perform appropriate tests of controls.

II. **The Independent Auditor May Use the Internal Auditors --** To provide **direct assistance** to the independent auditors for substantive purposes (whether or not they are relying on the internal audit function in connection with their assessment of control risk).

A. Must assess the internal auditors' competence and objectivity.

B. Must supervise, review, evaluate, and test the internal auditors' work to an appropriate extent.

C. The independent auditor expressing the opinion on the fairness of the financial statements has the ultimate responsibility for the work completed and conclusions reached.

> **Note:**
> There is no "division of responsibility" regarding the participation of the internal auditors. **Do not** refer to the internal auditors' assistance in the audit report!

Internal Control - Transaction Cycles

Specific Transaction Cycles

After studying this lesson, you should be able to:

1. *Understand what is meant by the term "transaction cycle" and why auditors tend to focus on transaction cycles when assessing control risk.*
2. *Identify several examples of transaction cycles that an auditor might consider.*

I. **A "Transaction Cycle" --** A transaction cycle is a group of essentially homogeneous transactions. The bulk of a company's economic activities can be grouped into a relative few categories called transaction cycles.

II. **Implication --** Within a given category of transactions, control risk is essentially constant, since all transactions within that category are processed subject to the same configuration of internal control policies and procedures.

III. **Transaction Cycles Covered in This Module**

   A. Revenue/receipts.

   B. Expenditures/disbursements.

   C. Payroll.

   D. Inventory, especially manufactured inventory (since purchased inventory would be similar to expenditures/disbursements as presented here).

   E. Fixed assets.

   F. Investing/financing.

> **Note:**
> The applicable SAS actually describes "control activities" in terms of four specific considerations: (1) authorization; (2) segregation of duties; (3) safeguarding assets; and (4) asset accountability.

> **Exam Tip:** As a tool to analyze the audit considerations of internal control policies and procedures in each transaction cycle, remember that internal controls should "SCARE"!! This is intended to be a helpful memory aid simply to recall some basic points of emphasis that are useful to auditors in looking at the relative strength or weakness of controls in a particular transaction cycle. In this context, "SCARE" represents: (1) Segregation of duties, (2) Comparisons, (3) Access, (4) Records, and (5) Execution of transactions.

IV. **The Framework "SCARE" --** Is easy to remember and is helpful in identifying relevant internal considerations that are consistent with the concepts emphasized in the AICPA Professional Standards:

   A. **Segregation of duties --** Involves separating "incompatible functions" to the extent possible. The same employee should not normally authorize (execution function) transactions, have access to the related assets (custody function), and perform accounting activities (record keeping function) in the ordinary course of duties. In essence, these three activities are like points on a triangle and each point of the triangle should ideally be vested in different employees, subject to cost-benefit considerations.

   B. **Comparisons --** There are certain comparisons that ought to be made, either comparing actual assets on hand to what the accounting records indicate should be on hand (e.g., the entity's annual physical observation of inventory) or comparing related accounting documents on a timely basis for consistency (e.g., before paying a vendor's invoice, someone should verify that the goods reflected on that invoice agree with what was received per the receiving report, which agrees with the entity's purchase order). This is important in establishing proper asset accountability!

C. **Access --** Access to assets (and to important accounting documents) should be limited to authorized personnel. (Of course, this is important in safeguarding assets and in establishing accountability for assets.)

D. **Records --** It is important to have adequate records and documentation to support the record keeping function and to establish proper asset accountability!

E. **Execution --** Transactions should be recorded as management authorized. (Authorization and execution are essentially the same concept.)

Revenue/Receipts - Sales

After studying this lesson, you should be able to:

1. *Identify the primary accounting documents and internal control objectives associated with an entity's revenue-receipts cycle (with emphasis on sales recognition).*
2. *Understand the primary control activities normally associated with an entity's revenue-receipts cycle (with emphasis on sales recognition).*

I. Flow Chart of Typical Internal Controls for Sales

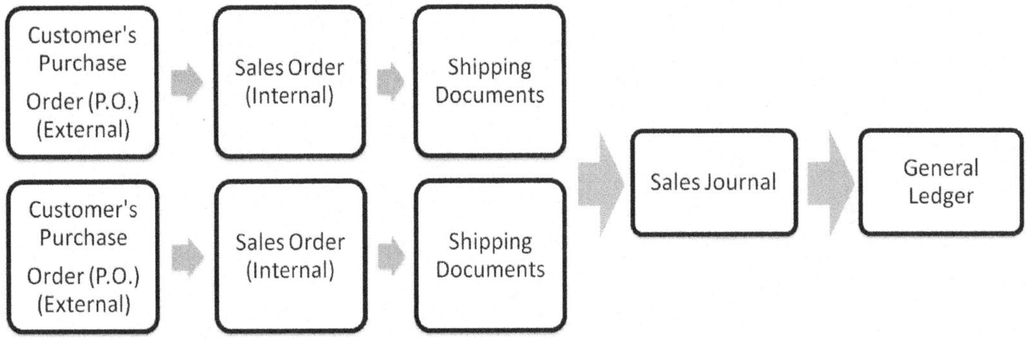

II. Internal Control Objectives -- Objectives of internal controls in this area are to provide reasonable assurance that:

A. Goods and services are provided in accordance with management's authorization (and based on approved orders).

B. Terms of sale (including prices and any discounts) are in accordance with management's authorization.

C. Credit terms and limits are properly established (as authorized).

D. Deliveries of goods and services result in accurate and timely billings.

E. Any sales-related discounts and adjustments (including returns) are in accordance with management's authorization.

III. Audit Considerations Framed by "SCARE"

A. Segregation of duties

1. An independent employee should review the statements to customers.
2. Credit to customers granted by an independent department (separate from sales staff which may be paid on commission and which may have an incentive to view everyone as "creditworthy").
3. Returns are accounted for by an independent clerk in the shipping/receiving area.

B. Comparisons

1. **Trial balance reconciled to ledger --** An aged trial balance for accounts receivable is reconciled to the general ledger (control) account -- to establish the mathematical accuracy of the general ledger; the aging provides important information about the quality of receivables and the need for follow-up.

2. **Monthly statements --** Are sent to all customers -- to provide information to customers about their account balances and payments received.

3. **Sales invoices and orders**

   a. **Sales invoices --** Are matched with a **sales order** (perhaps the **customer's purchase order** (P.O.)) and applicable **shipping documents.**

      i. An appropriate employee should verify that the merchandise ordered was, in fact, shipped and properly billed.

      ii. An appropriate employee should examine these documents for proper cutoff (to record the sale in the proper period).

C. **Access --** Including direct (physical) and indirect (by computer) access.

1. Computer passwords limit unauthorized access.

2. Cash receipts are handled by someone without access to accounts receivable record keeping.

D. **Records --** Regarding the adequacy of underlying documentation; e.g., key documents that constitute the "audit trail" should be prenumbered and the numerical sequence should be accounted for to establish control over these documents.

1. Sales invoices are prenumbered (and the numerical sequence is accounted for).

2. Shipping documents for outbound shipments are prenumbered (and the numerical sequence is accounted for).

3. "Receivers" (shipping documents used exclusively for inbound shipments) are prenumbered (and the numerical sequence is accounted for).

E. **Execution of Transactions --** Should be as authorized.

1. Management should review the terms of sales transactions and note that approval on the sales invoice (billing).

2. Management should usually establish "general" approvals of transactions within specified limits and specifically approve transactions outside of those prescribed limits.

3. Management should specifically approve all adjusting journal entries.

Revenue/Receipts - Cash

After studying this lesson, you should be able to:

1. *Identify the primary accounting documents and internal control objectives associated with an entity's revenue-receipts cycle (with emphasis on cash collection).*
2. *Understand the primary control activities normally associated with an entity's revenue-receipts cycle (with emphasis on cash collection).*

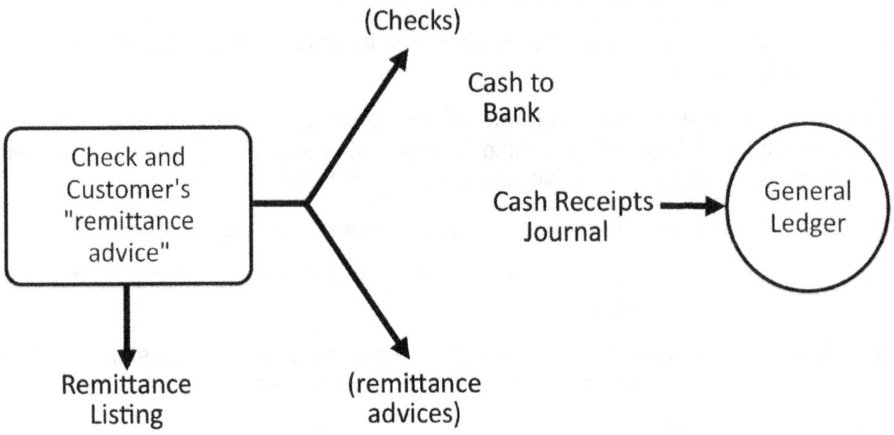

I. Internal Control Objectives -- Objectives of internal controls in this area are to provide reasonable assurance that:

A. Access to cash receipts records and accounts receivable records is limited to authorized personnel.

B. Detailed cash and account balance records are reconciled with control accounts and bank statements at least monthly.

C. All cash receipts are correctly recorded in the period received.

II. Audit Considerations Framed by "SCARE"

A. S̲egregation of duties

1. A listing of cash receipts (sometimes referred to as a **"remittance listing"** or "log of cash receipts") is prepared upon opening the mail in the mail room; checks are restrictively endorsed immediately ("for deposit only...").
2. Cash-related activities are handled by separate personnel as appropriate:
   a. Opening the mail, handling the checks received, and verifying the accuracy of the payment indicated on the enclosed "remittance advice," the stub returned with the customer's payment on account.
   b. Making the deposit -- should be daily.
   c. Applying payments received to the appropriate customers' accounts receivable.
   d. Preparing the bank reconciliation on a timely basis.

B. Comparisons

1. The initial cash receipts listing from the mail room should be compared to the total according to the cash receipts journal, and traced to that day's bank deposit.
2. Receipts should be deposited daily, **not** accumulated in someone's desk drawer for an occasional deposit.
3. The cash accounts should be reconciled with the bank statements on a timely basis by someone not involved in handling cash receipts or updating the accounting records.

C. Access -- Including direct and indirect access.

1. Employees with access to cash receipts should be "bonded" -- bonding is a type of insurance for which the employer pays an insurance premium and which involves background checks.
2. Access to cash receipts (including access to documents) should be limited to those authorized -- includes appropriate use of passwords.
3. The company might use a "lockbox" whereby payments from customers are directly received by the bank, thereby avoiding the company's mail room.

D. Records -- Should be adequate:

1. In general, there should be adequate documentation supporting transactions and account balances (important documents should be prenumbered and the numerical sequence properly accounted for).
2. For cash transactions received "on site," there should be adequate "point of sale" cash registers and use of prenumbered receipts.

E. Execution of transactions as authorized

1. Adjusting journal entries should be approved by management.
2. Bank reconciliations should be appropriately reviewed with the reviewer's approval indicated.

Expenditures/Disbursements

After studying this lesson, you should be able to:

1. *Identify the primary accounting documents and internal control objectives associated with an entity's expenditure/disbursements cycle.*
2. *Understand the primary control activities normally associated with an entity's expenditure/disbursements cycle.*

I. Flow Chart of Typical Internal Controls for Expenditures/Disbursements

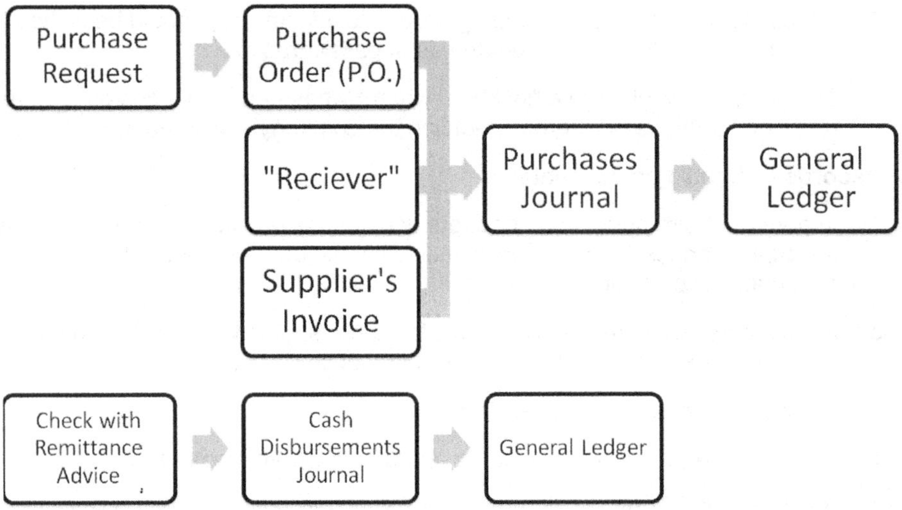

II. Objectives of Internal Controls over Purchases and Accounts Payable -- To provide reasonable assurance that:

A. Goods and services are obtained in accordance with management's authorization and based on approved orders -- considering quantity, quality, vendors, etc. (usually handled by a separate "Purchasing Department" to centralize these activities).

B. The terms of acquisitions (including prices and quantities) are in accordance with management's authorization.

C. All goods and services received are accurately accounted for on a timely basis.

D. Adjustments to vendor accounts are made according to management's authorization.

E. Only authorized goods and services are accepted and paid for (and payments are timely to take advantage of any cash discounts for prompt payment).

F. Amounts payable for goods and services received are accurately recorded and properly classified.

G. Access to purchasing, receiving, and accounts payable records is limited to authorized personnel.

III. Objectives of Internal Controls over Cash Disbursements -- To provide reasonable assurance that:

A. Disbursements are for authorized expenditures as approved by management.

B. Disbursements are recorded at the proper amounts and with the appropriate classifications.

C. Periodic comparisons are made between the supporting detailed records (including bank reconciliations) with the general ledger control accounts.

D. Any adjusting journal entries for cash accounts are in accordance with management's authorization.

E. Access to cash and disbursement records is limited to authorized personnel.

IV. Audit Considerations Framed by "SCARE" -- Related to the expenditures/ disbursement transactions cycle.

A. Segregation of duties

1. A separate purchasing department handles the purchasing activities (after a duly approved request for goods or services has been received from the department making the request).
2. The purchasing personnel are independent of those in receiving and accounting (recordkeeping).
3. The accounts payable personnel are likewise independent of those involved with purchasing, receiving, and cash disbursements.
4. Bank reconciliations are prepared by someone not having other involvement in handling cash receipts, cash disbursements, or record keeping.

B. Comparisons

1. An appropriate employee should compare the suppliers' monthly statements with recorded payables.
2. An appropriate employee should compare the purchase order, "receiver," and vendor's invoice for agreement to establish that the invoice is for goods and services received and as authorized. (The invoice should be approved before payment is made and available cash discounts should be taken.)

C. Access -- Including direct and indirect access.

1. Employees with the ability to initiate cash disbursements should be "bonded."
2. Access to cash disbursements or to related documents should be limited to authorized personnel.

D. Records -- Should be adequate.

1. Detailed records should be maintained to support the general ledger payable account.
2. Prenumbered purchase orders should be used (and the numerical sequence accounted for).
3. Prenumbered checks should be used (and the numerical sequence accounted for).
4. There should be appropriate physical control over unused checks to limit access to authorized personnel.
5. The supporting documents (including vendors' invoices) should be canceled as "paid" immediately upon payment to prevent double payments.

E. Execution of Transactions -- As authorized.

1. All adjusting journal entries should be approved by management.
2. Only authorized personnel should be able to order goods and services on the company's behalf.

3. The department requesting the purchase of goods or services should indicate their acceptance of the goods or services received and approval, before payment is made.

4. Two signatures should be required on checks. (Any signature plates should be protected.)

F. Note the difference between a **"vouchers payable"** system and an **"accounts payable"** system:

1. An **accounts payable** system keeps track of payables by the name of the vendor. (Hence, payables are identified by the total amount owed to the various individual suppliers.)

2. A **vouchers payable** system keeps track of individual transactions without summarizing amounts owed by vendor. (There can be numerous vouchers payable to an individual vendor, but the payables are identified by voucher number, not by vendor name.)

Payroll Cycle

After studying this lesson, you should be able to:

1. *Identify the primary accounting documents and internal control objectives associated with an entity's payroll cycle.*
2. *Understand the primary control activities normally associated with an entity's payroll cycle.*

I. Flow Chart of Typical Internal Controls for Payroll

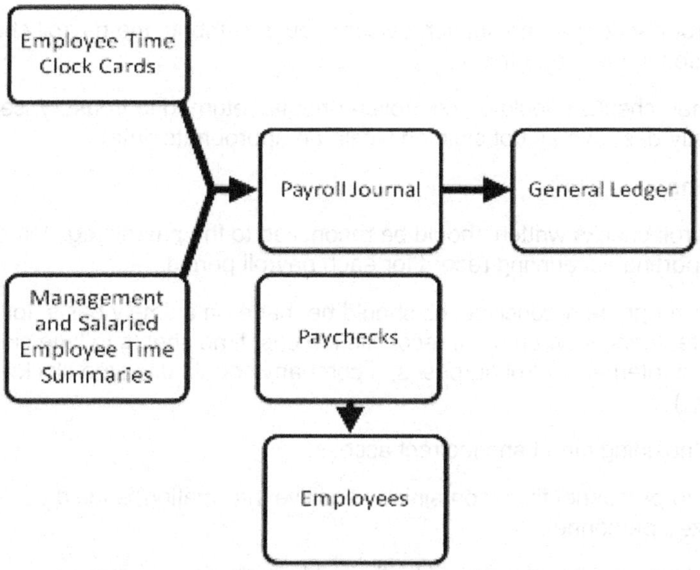

II. Objectives of Internal Controls over Payroll -- To provide reasonable assurance that:

A. Payroll withholdings and deductions are based on appropriate supporting authorizations;

B. Compensation is made only to valid employees at authorized rates and for services actually rendered.

C. Gross pay, withholdings, deductions, and net pay are correctly computed.

D. Payroll costs and liabilities are appropriately classified and summarized in the proper periods.

E. Appropriate comparisons are made of personnel, payroll, and work records at reasonable intervals.

F. Net pay and related withholdings are remitted to the appropriate employees and agencies.

G. Access to sensitive personnel files and payroll records is limited to authorized personnel.

III. Audit Considerations Framed by "SCARE"

A. Segregation of duties

1. The following activities should be performed by different personnel when circumstances permit:
    a. Establishing and maintaining employee files in the personnel department.
    b. Timekeeping.
    c. Payroll preparation.
    d. Check distribution.
    e. Reconciling the payroll bank account.
2. The treasurer should sign the payroll checks.
3. An appropriate departmental supervisor should distribute the payroll checks to employees in that department.
4. Unclaimed checks should be controlled (that is, returned to treasury, secured, and eventually destroyed if not claimed within an appropriate time).

B. Comparisons

1. The payroll checks written should be reconciled to the payroll register, serving as the supporting accounting record for each payroll period.
2. Other appropriate reconciliations should be made on a timely basis: for example, in a manufacturing environment, reconcile job cost time sheets to time clock cards. (For strict internal control purposes, a company should use time clocks where possible.)

C. Access -- Including direct and indirect access:

1. Access to personnel files (containing sensitive information) should be limited to authorized personnel.
2. Access to payroll checks should be limited to authorized personnel.
3. Personnel with access to payroll checks should be "bonded."

D. Records -- Should be adequate.

1. A company should maintain current and accurate payroll information (which should be periodically matched with the personnel files).
2. Payroll checks should be prenumbered (and the numerical sequence accounted for).
3. A company should maintain a separate checking account specifically for payroll transactions to establish more accountability and control over these important transactions.

E. Execution of Transactions -- as authorized.

1. Payroll should be authorized by a responsible official.
2. Payroll computations should be verified by an independent person.
3. Overtime payments should be approved by management.
4. Payroll for management should also be appropriately reviewed and approved.

Miscellaneous Cycles

After studying this lesson, you should be able to:

1. *Identify the internal control objectives associated with miscellaneous transaction cycles (manufactured inventory, fixed assets, and investing/financing).*
2. *Understand the primary control activities normally associated with these miscellaneous transaction cycles.*

I. Production/Manufacturing Inventory

A. The Major Objectives of Internal Controls -- In this area, are to provide reasonable assurance that:

1. The resources obtained and used in production (including raw materials, work-in-process, and finished goods) are accurately recorded on a timely basis;
2. Transfers of finished products to customers or others are accurately recorded;
3. Related expenditures are appropriately classified;
4. Access to all categories of inventory (and inventory-related documents) is limited to authorized personnel;
5. Comparisons of actual inventory on hand are made to recorded amounts at least annually.

B. Audit Considerations Framed by "SCARE"

1. **Segregation of duties**
   a. To the extent possible, the company should separate the authorization of inventory-related transactions, the custody of (or access to) inventory, and the accounting record keeping activities.
   b. Sales returns (inventory) should be immediately counted by the receiving clerk and a "receiver" prepared to verify the quantity and condition of goods returned.
2. **Comparisons**
   a. Actual inventory should be compared periodically to recorded inventory (and any unusual differences should be investigated).
   b. In a manufacturing context, appropriate reconciliations should be made of underlying accounting records (including applicable job order cost sheets or process cost worksheets) to the applicable inventory-related general ledger accounts.
3. **Access --** Including direct (physical) and indirect (by computer) access.
   a. Access should be limited to authorized personnel (physical security controls).
   b. Access to the important accounting documents, including applicable shipping documents, should be limited to authorized personnel.
4. **Records --** Should be adequate.
   a. The company should use prenumbered purchase orders for raw materials and components of production, along with prenumbered "receivers." (The numerical sequence of these documents should be properly accounted for.)
   b. The company should consider using a perpetual inventory system for items with high cost per unit.

c. The company should maintain adequate support for related general ledger control accounts.

5. **Execution of Transactions --** Should be as authorized.

a. The acquisition and distribution of inventory should be consistent with management's authorization.

b. Management should establish general approvals of transactions within specified limits, and specifically approve transactions above those limits.

c. Any adjusting journal entries (including sales returns and allowances, or adjustments to inventory, such as write-downs) should be approved by management.

II. **Fixed Assets Cycle --** The major objectives of internal controls in this area are to provide reasonable assurance that:

A. Transactions involving property, plant, and equipment are accurately recorded and classified; and in accordance with management's authorization.

B. Estimates used in the determination of depreciation, depletion, and amortization of the assets' cost basis are reasonable and consistent over time; any changes should be properly approved.

C. Fixed assets are reasonably secure from loss with appropriate property insurance in force.

D. Supporting detailed records are maintained and periodically compared to the assets on hand.

E. Any adjusting journal entries related to fixed assets are approved by management.

III. **Investing/Financing Cycle --** The major objectives of internal controls in this area are to provide reasonable assurance that:

A. Transactions involving investments and financing are accurately recorded and classified on a timely basis; and as authorized by management.

1. **"Investing" --** As used here, refers to decisions related to the composition of the company's investment assets, current and noncurrent.

2. **"Financing" --** Refers to decisions related to the structure of the company's noncurrent liabilities and stockholders' equity sections of the balance sheet.

B. Investment assets should be reasonably secure from loss with procedures established to monitor the associated risks. (Access should be limited to authorized personnel with appropriate segregation of duties.)

C. Supporting detailed records should be maintained and compared periodically to actual investment-related assets of the company.

D. Any adjusting journal entries related to investment-related assets, liabilities, or stockholders' equity are approved by management.

Audit Evidence - Concepts and Standards

Overview of Substantive Procedures

After studying this lesson, you should be able to:

1. *Know the two categories of "substantive" audit procedures (and the two categories of "'tests of details").*
2. *Know the meaning of the term "analytical procedures," the three purposes served by analytical procedures, and the four considerations that determine the efficiency and effectiveness of analytical procedures used for substantive purposes.*
3. *Be familiar with the fundamental ratios that are most often associated with the auditor's analytical procedures and which are frequently tested.*

I. **SAS No. 107 Audit Risk Model --** Recall the SAS No. 107 "audit risk model" that applies to an individual account balance, class of transactions, or disclosure level [note that this audit risk model does not apply at the overall financial statement level]: AR = IR x CR x DR; where **detection risk** is the only component within the auditor's direct influence and which is essentially **"set" by specifying the nature, timing, and extent of the auditor's substantive audit procedures.**

   A. **Nature --** What specific procedures to perform? (How much emphasis should the auditor place on "tests of details" (which tend to be labor intensive and expensive, but which provide a relatively stronger basis for conclusions for most financial statement assertions) versus "analytical procedures" (which tend to be less labor intensive and less expensive, but which provide a relatively weaker basis for conclusions for most financial statement assertions).)

   B. **Timing --** When to perform the procedures, at an "**interim**" date (before the books are closed) or at "**final**" date (after the balance sheet date and after the books are closed)?

   C. **Extent --** How large should the samples be? (Since the work is performed on a "test basis," should the sample sizes be relatively **large** or **small**?)

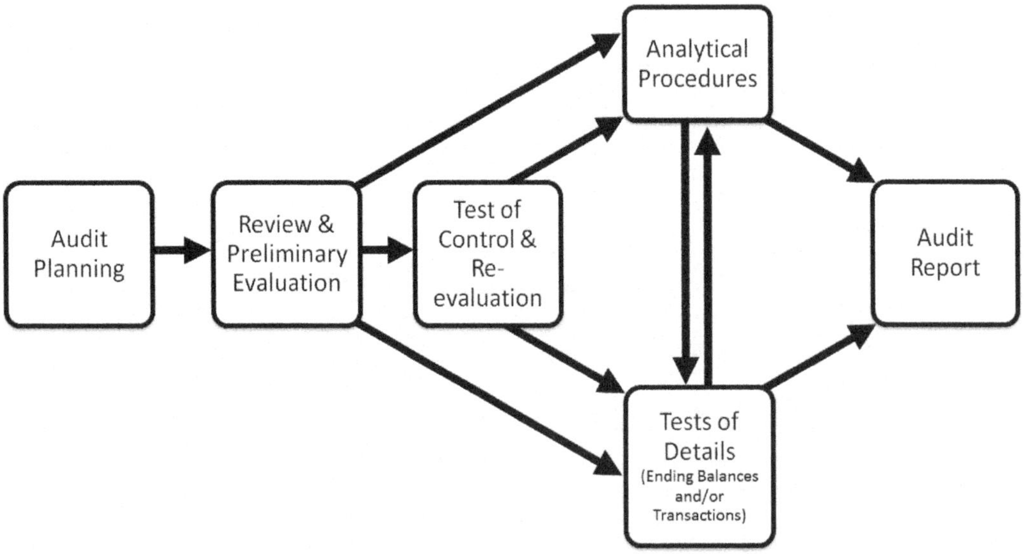

D. SAS No. 110 -- Performing Audit Procedures in Response to Assessed Risks and Evaluating the Audit Evidence Obtained, states:

> "When ... the auditor has determined that it is not possible or practicable to reduce the detection risks at the relevant assertion level to an acceptably low level with audit evidence obtained only from substantive procedures, he or she should perform tests of controls to obtain audit evidence about their operating effectiveness. For example ..., the auditor may find it impossible to design effective substantive procedures that by themselves provide sufficient appropriate audit evidence at the relevant assertion level when an entity conducts its business using information technology (IT) and no documentation of transactions is produced or maintained, other than through the IT system."

Question:
Under these circumstances, what would be the consequences if the required tests of controls indicate that internal control is ineffective and cannot be relied on?

Answer:
If the auditor's substantive procedures by themselves are insufficient and if internal control is ineffective, the auditor would not have obtained sufficient appropriate evidence to afford a reasonable basis for the opinion. In other words, these circumstances would constitute a scope limitation!

II. Substantive Audit Procedures -- Directly related to the financial statement amounts. (Recall that the word **"substantive"** is derived from "substantiate," which means **to verify** Substantive procedures are those audit procedures designed to verify the entity's financial statement elements or, in other words, to search for material misstatements if there are any.)

A. Tests of Details -- Relatively precise (but expensive, labor-intensive) procedures (where the results of the procedures suggest whether the client's recorded amounts are right or not).

Definitions:
Tests of Ending Balances: Verifying the client's recorded amounts by directly testing the composition of the ending account balance.

Tests of Transactions: Verifying the client's recorded amounts by testing those relative few debits and credits (the transactions) that caused the account balance to change from last year's audited balance to this year's recorded balance.

B. Analytical Procedures -- Recall the AICPA definition of "analytical procedures" -- "evaluations of financial information made by a study of plausible relationships among both financial and nonfinancial data."

1. **Analytical procedures serve three distinct purposes --** two of which are required in an audit.
   a. **Required** in audit planning;
   b. Useful (but **not required**) as a form of substantive evidence; and
   c. **Required** as a final review before issuing the audit report to assess the appropriateness of conclusions reached.

[See "AU329 (SAS 56) - Analytical Procedures"]

Note:
These tests of reasonableness involve analyzing trends and interrelationships -- the "key" is developing a meaningful expectation by which to judge the reasonableness of the client's recorded amount.

2. The AICPA states that the effectiveness and efficiency of analytical procedures used for substantive purposes depends on the following **4 factors** or considerations:

   a. **Nature of assertion --** Substantive analytical procedures may be particularly effective in testing for omissions of transactions that would be hard to detect with procedures that focus on recorded amounts. (In other words, the skillful use of analytical procedures may be more effective than tests of details in addressing the "completeness" assertion, since there may be no supporting documents to examine for transactions that were not recorded in the first place!)

   b. **Plausibility and predictability of relationship --** Developing a meaningful expectation to compare to the client's recorded balance is critical to the skillful use of analytical procedures, so the predictability of the relationship is very important.

      i. Relationships in a stable environment are usually more predictable than those in a dynamic environment.

      ii. Relationships involving income statement accounts tend to be more predictable than those involving balance sheet accounts (since the income statement deals with a period of time rather than a single moment in time).

      iii. Relationships involving transactions subject to management discretion tend to be less predictable.

   c. **Availability and reliability of data --** The reliability increases when the data used is (1) obtained from independent outside sources; (2) is subject to audit testing (either currently or in the past); or (3) is developed under conditions of effective internal control.

   d. **Precision of the expectation --** The likelihood of detecting a misstatement decreases as the level of aggregation of the data increases. (That is, procedures would be less effective for "high altitude" global comparisons than for more focused, specific comparisons. In other words, relationships of interest to the auditor might be obscured by the noise in the data at a high level of aggregation, whereas those relationships might be more identifiable at a lower level of aggregation. For example, the auditor could focus on sales by month broken down by product line instead of simply comparing current annual sales currently to the prior year.)

3. **Selected Ratios --** Such ratios may be tested in Auditing & Attestation as "analytical procedures" or in Financial Accounting & Reporting as "financial statement analysis."

Definition:
Liquidity ratios (also known as solvency ratios): Measures of an entity's short-term ability to meet its obligations.

   a. *Working capital* = current assets - current liabilities. (This is a definition, not a ratio.)

   b. *Current ratio* = current assets/ current liabilities.

   c. *Quick ratio* (acid-test ratio) = (cash + marketable securities + A/R)/ current liabilities.

   d. *Current cash to debt ratio* = net cash from operations/ average current liabilities.

Definition:
Activity ratios (also known as turnover or efficiency ratios): Measures of an entity's effectiveness putting its assets to use.

- **e.** *Asset turnover* = net sales/ average total assets.
- **f.** *Receivable turnover* = net (credit) sales/ average trade receivable (net).
- **g.** *Number of days sales in receivables* = 365 days/ receivable turnover.
- **h.** *Inventory turnover* = cost of goods sold/ average inventory.
- **i.** *Number of days sales in inventory* = 365 days/ inventory turnover.

Definition:
Profitability ratios: Measures of an entity's operating success (failure) for a period of time.

- **j.** *Profit margin on sales* = net income/ net sales.
- **k.** *Gross profit percentage* = (sales - cost of goods sold)/ sales.
- **l.** *Rate of return on assets* = net income/ average total assets.
- **m.** *Rate of return on common stockholders' equity* = (net income - dividends attributable to preferred stockholders)/ average common stockholders' equity.
- **n.** *Earnings per share* = (net income - preferred dividends)/average number of common shares outstanding.
- **o.** *Price earnings ratio* ("P-E ratio") = market price of stock/ earnings per share.

Definition:
Coverage ratios (also known as leverage ratios): Measures of the entity's ability to meet its obligations over time. (That is, measures of long-term risk to creditors and the extent to which the entity has borrowed up to its available capacity.)

- **p.** *Debt to total assets ratio* = total liabilities/ total assets.
- **q.** *Debt to equity ratio* = total liabilities/ total stockholders' equity.
- **r.** *Times interest earned* = income before interest expense and income taxes/ interest expense.
- **s.** *Cash to debt coverage ratio* = net cash from operations/ average total liabilities.

Nature of Evidence 1

After studying this lesson, you should be able to:

1. *Know what constitutes "audit evidence."*
2. *Understand the meaning of the terms "sufficient" and "appropriate."*
3. *Understand the meaning of the term "assertion" and know the assertions associated with each of the three categories of assertions according to AICPA Professional Standards.*

I. The Nature of Audit Evidence -- This SAS interprets the Third Standard of Field Work of GAAS: "The auditor must obtain sufficient appropriate audit evidence by performing audit procedures to afford a reasonable basis for an opinion regarding the financial statements under audit."

[See "AU326 (SAS 106) - Audit Evidence"]

II. Audit Evidence

> **Definitions:**
> *Audit Evidence*: All the information used by the auditor in arriving at the conclusions on which the audit opinion is based and includes the information contained in the accounting records underlying the financial statements and other information.
>
> *Accounting records*: Records related to initial entries, including general and special journals; and supporting records, such as general and subsidiary ledgers, support for adjustments, worksheets, supporting cost allocations, checks, invoices, purchase orders, contracts, etc.
>
> *Other information constituting audit evidence*: Includes minutes of meetings, confirmations, industry analysts' reports, internal control manuals, and any other information obtained by inquiry, observation, and inspection.

> **Note:** The auditor should obtain audit evidence by testing the accounting records, by analysis, review, and reconciling related information; however, the accounting records by themselves do not provide sufficient appropriate audit evidence.

III. Sufficient Appropriate Audit Evidence -- "Sufficient" refers to the quantity of evidence, whereas "appropriate" refers to the quality of evidence in terms of its relevance and reliability.

A. The quantity of evidence required (related to "sufficient") is directly related to the risk of misstatement (the greater the risk, the more evidence is needed) and inversely related to the quality of evidence (the higher the quality, the less evidence is needed).

B. "Reliability" is affected by the source and nature of evidence and depends upon individual circumstances -- however the SAS offers the following guidelines:

1. Evidence obtained directly by the auditor is more reliable than evidence obtained indirectly or by inference. (e.g., observation of the application of a control is more reliable than inquiry of entity personnel about the application of a control).

2. Evidence is more reliable when obtained from independent (knowledgeable) sources outside the entity;

3. Evidence generated internally is more reliable when the related controls are effective;

4. Evidence is more reliable when it exists in documentary form (whether paper or electronic); and

5. Evidence provided by original documents is more reliable than evidence based on photocopies/facsimiles (faxes).

C. The auditor should consider the reliability of information used, but the auditor is not normally responsible for authenticating the entity's documents. The auditor should obtain evidence about the accuracy and completeness of information used to perform further audit procedures (either in connection with the actual audit procedure or by testing controls related to the information).

D. More assurance is obtained from consistent audit evidence obtained from different sources or of a different nature ("corroborating" information) than from evidence considered individually -- when evidence from different sources is inconsistent, the auditor should determine what audit procedures are needed to resolve the inconsistency.

E. Professional judgment is required for "reasonable assurance" and the auditor does not examine all available evidence -- the auditor may appropriately consider the cost of information relative to its usefulness (although cost alone is not a valid basis for omitting an audit procedure); audit evidence is usually "persuasive" (or suggestive) and is rarely "conclusive" (or compelling) -- the auditor should not be satisfied with evidence that is less than persuasive.

IV. **Using "Assertions" to Obtain Audit Evidence --** In stating that the financial statements are consistent with GAAP, management makes several "assertions" (which are implicit or explicit statements of fact).

A. Historically, the auditing standards discussed five traditional financial statement assertions: (1) existence/occurrence; (2) completeness; (3) rights and obligations; (4) valuation and allocation; and (5) presentation and disclosure.

B. An important change associated with SAS No. 106 (which is intended, in part, to make U.S. auditing standards somewhat more consistent with international auditing standards) is that U.S. professional standards now classify assertions in three separate categories for the auditor's consideration, related to (1) account balances; (2) presentation and disclosure; and (3) classes of transactions and events.

C. **Four assertions about "account balances at period end"**

1. **Existence --** That assets, liabilities, and equity interests exist;

2. **Completeness --** That all assets, liabilities, and equity interests that should have been recorded have been recorded; (There are no omissions.)

3. **Rights and obligations --** That the entity holds or controls the rights to assets, and liabilities are the obligations of the entity; (Any restrictions on the rights to the assets or obligations for the liabilities must be disclosed.)

4. **Valuation and allocation --** That assets, liabilities, and equity interests are included in the financial statements at appropriate amounts (relative to the requirements of GAAP) and any resulting valuation or allocation adjustments are appropriately recorded.

D. **Four assertions about "presentation and disclosure"**

1. **Occurrence and rights and obligations --** That disclosed events and transactions have occurred and pertain to the entity;

2. **Completeness --** That all disclosures that should have been included have been included; (There are no omissions of required disclosures.)
3. **Classification and understandability --** That financial information is appropriately presented, described, and clearly expressed;
4. **Accuracy and valuation --** That financial and other information are disclosed fairly and at appropriate amounts.

E. **Five assertions about "classes of transactions and events during the period"**

1. **Accuracy --** That amounts and other data have been recorded appropriately;
2. **Occurrence --** That transactions and events that have been recorded have occurred (they are properly recorded and valid);
3. **Completeness --** That all transactions and events that should have been recorded have been recorded (there are no omissions);
4. **Cutoff --** That transactions and events have been recorded in the correct accounting period;

> **Note:** "Cutoff" is actually redundant in this context, since establishing "occurrence" (that the recorded transactions are properly recorded) and "completeness" (that there are no omissions of transactions that should have been recorded) together establish that the transactions, in fact, have been recorded in the correct accounting period ("cutoff"). However, "cutoff" is an important issue that auditors must address, so this redundancy emphasizes an important auditing concept.

5. **Classification --** That transactions and events have been recorded in the proper accounts.

Categories of Assertions			
	Account Balances at End of Period	**Presentation & Disclosure**	**Transactions & Events During the Period**
Existence/Occurrence	**Applicable**	**Applicable**	**Applicable**
Completeness	**Applicable**	**Applicable**	**Applicable**
Rights & obligations	**Applicable**	N/A separately (included with Occurrence)	N/A
Accuracy & Valuation; or Valuation & Allocation	**Applicable**	**Applicable**	**Applicable**
Classification; or Classification & Understandability	N/A	**Applicable**	**Applicable**
Cutoff	N/A -- implicit	N/A	**Applicable**

F. This SAS points out that the auditor may use the assertions as presented above or express them differently as long as the relevant issues have been addressed -- for example, the auditor may combine the assertions about transactions and events with those about account balances; and the auditor may decline to identify a separate assertion about "cutoff" if occurrence and completeness have been established.

G. The auditor should use "relevant assertions" (those that have a meaningful bearing on whether the account is fairly stated) to assess the risk of material misstatement -- the auditor should evaluate the nature of the assertion, the volume of transactions or data involved, and the complexity of the systems (including IT) by which the entity processes and controls the information related to the assertion.

Nature of Evidence 2

After studying this lesson, you should be able to:

1. *Know the three categories of audit procedures.*
2. *Understand the auditor's responsibility to plan and perform substantive procedures to be responsive to the assessed risks of material misstatement, according to AICPA Professional Standards.*

I. **Audit Procedures for Obtaining Evidence --** The auditor's basis for conclusion is comprised of three categories of procedures: (1) risk assessment procedures; (2) tests of controls; and (3) substantive procedures.

> **Definitions:**
> *Risk assessment procedures*: To obtain an understanding of the entity and its environment, including internal control, to assess the risk of material misstatement.
>
> *Tests of controls*: Performed in order to obtain information about the operating effectiveness of controls in preventing or detecting and correcting material misstatements at the relevant assertion level. (Note that the auditor must perform tests of controls when the risk assessment includes an expectation of the operating effectiveness of controls or when the substantive procedures alone do not provide sufficient appropriate audit evidence.)
>
> *Substantive procedures*: Performed in order to detect material misstatements at the relevant assertion level (consisting of tests of details and analytical procedures). (Note that the auditor should perform substantive procedures for all relevant assertions related to each material class of transactions, account balance, and disclosure.)

II. **Menu of Specific Substantive Audit Procedures --** The auditor may use computer-assisted audit techniques (CAATs) to assist when information is in electronic form:

A. **Inspection of records/documents --** Examining records or documents, whether internal or external, whether paper electronic, or other media;

B. **Inspection of tangible assets --** Physical examination of the assets;

C. **Observation --** Looking at a process or procedure being performed by others;

D. **Inquiry --** Seeking information of knowledgeable persons inside or outside the entity and evaluating their responses. (Note that inquiry alone does not provide sufficient appropriate audit evidence either for substantive purposes or for tests of controls.)

E. **Confirmation --** Obtaining a representation directly from a knowledgeable third party;

F. **Recalculation --** Checking the mathematical accuracy of documents;

G. **Reperformance --** The auditor's execution of procedures or controls originally performed as part of the entity's internal controls;

H. **Analytical procedures --** Includes "scanning" to review accounting data to identify unusual items to be tested further. (CAATs may be especially useful in identifying significant or unusual items.)

[See "AU318 (SAS 110) - Performing Audit Procedures in Response to Assessed Risks"]

> **Note:**
> Analytical procedures are defined as "evaluations of financial information made by a study of plausible relationships among both financial and nonfinancial data."

III. The Auditor Should Plan and Perform Substantive Procedures -- To be responsive to the assessed risks of material misstatements. The purpose of substantive procedures is to detect material misstatements at the relevant assertion level.

A. Perform some substantive procedures for all relevant assertions related to each material class of transactions, account balance, and disclosure (regardless of the assessed risk of material misstatement), since there are inherent limitations to internal control and the assessment of risk is judgmental.

B. Substantive procedures should include the following related to the financial reporting process -- (1) agree the financial statement information to the underlying accounting records; and (2) examine material journal entries and other adjustments made during the preparation of the financial statements.

C. **Nature of substantive procedures --** These should be responsive to the planned level of detection risk; they consist of (1) tests of details and (2) substantive analytical procedures (should consider testing the controls over the preparation of information used in connection with analytical procedures)

D. **Timing of substantive procedures --** May be performed at an interim date (before year-end) or at final (at or after year-end)

1. Performing substantive procedures at an interim date increases detection risk -- the auditor should perform additional substantive procedures (or substantive procedures combined with tests of control) to mitigate the increased risk and provide a reasonable basis for extending the audit conclusions from the interim date to year-end.
2. Need not necessarily rely on internal controls (that is, test the operating effectiveness of controls) to extend the audit conclusions from the interim date to year-end -- however, the auditor should consider whether only performing additional substantive procedures is sufficient.
3. When planning to perform substantive analytical procedures for the period following the interim date -- consider whether the period-end balances are reasonably predictable as to amount, relative significance, and composition.

E. **Extent of substantive procedures --** Determine the implications to sample sizes (considering the planned level of detection risk, materiality, tolerable misstatement, expected misstatement, and the nature of the population).

F. **Evaluating the sufficiency and appropriateness of the audit evidence obtained**

1. **Consider all relevant audit evidence --** Whether it appears to corroborate or to contradict the relevant assertions in the financial statements.
2. The sufficiency and appropriateness of audit evidence as a basis for the auditor's conclusions are matters of professional judgment -- the auditor's judgment may be influenced by factors such as the following:
    a. The significance of the potential misstatement and the likelihood that it may have a material effect;
    b. The understanding of the entity and its environment, including internal control;
    c. The effectiveness of management's responses and controls to address the risks;
    d. The results of audit procedures performed (including whether the procedures identified instances of fraud or error);
    e. The persuasiveness of audit evidence obtained;
    f. The source and reliability of available information; and

g. The experience gained in previous audits with such misstatements.

3. **Documentation --** As covered in the course materials on Internal Controls, the auditor should document the following matters:

    a. The overall responses to address the assessed risk of misstatement at the financial statement level;

    b. The nature, timing, and extent of the further audit procedures;

    c. The linkage of those procedures with the assessed risks at the relevant assertion level;

    d. The results of the audit procedures; and

    e. The conclusions reached in the current audit about the operating effectiveness of controls tested in a prior audit.

Audit Documentation

After studying this lesson, you should be able to:

1. *Understand the auditor's responsibilities to prepare and obtain documentation in accordance with AICPA Professional Standards.*
2. *Know the major differences between AICPA Professional Standards and PCAOB Auditing Standards with respect to documentation "completion" requirements and "retention" requirements.*
3. *Know the distinction between the auditor's "permanent file" and the current year's audit documentation.*

I. Purposes of Audit Documentation

[See "AU339 (SAS 103) - Audit Documentation"]

A. Provides the principal support for the auditor's report (regarding procedures performed and conclusions reached).

B. Documents the auditor's compliance with GAAS -- especially the Field Work Standards.

1. That the work was adequately planned and supervised.
2. That internal control was reviewed and evaluated as necessary.
3. That the procedures applied and the evidence obtained provide a reasonable basis for the opinion expressed.

C. Audit documentation (still often called "working papers") assists in controlling the audit work - that is, breaking the overall audit project into manageable tasks that can be delegated to the various members of the audit team (while documenting the work performed and the conclusions reached and identifying the work yet to be completed).

II. Ownership and Custody Issues

A. Ownership -- Audit documentation is the auditor's property (should safeguard it and establish a formal retention policy).

B. Confidentiality -- Subject to restrictions imposed by AICPA ethics rules on confidentiality. (Auditor should prevent unauthorized access.)

C. Auditors should apply appropriate controls over the audit documentation to protect the integrity of the information at all stages of the audit, to prevent unauthorized changes, and to limit access to authorized personnel.

III. SAS No. 103 Requirements -- Audit documentation that is required by SAS No. 103. (The Auditing Standards Board issued SAS No. 103 to make their documentation requirements more consistent with, but not identical to, those of the PCAOB and international auditing standards.):

A. Audit documentation should permit an experienced auditor without prior connection to the audit to understand (a) the nature, timing, and extent of procedures performed; (b) the results of those procedures; (c) the conclusions reached on significant matters; and (d) whether the accounting records agree or reconcile with the audited financial statements.

B. Audit documentation should include **abstracts or copies of significant contracts or agreements examined** -- if needed by an experienced auditor to understand the basis for conclusions.

C. Audit documentation should **identify the specific items tested** by the auditor (or the "identifying characteristics" of items tested in connection with the substantive procedures and any tests of control).

D. The auditor should also **document audit findings or issues that are "significant"** (including actions taken to address them and the basis for conclusions reached), and should also document discussions of significant findings or issues with management (including issues discussed, when and with who. Such findings and issues include:

1. Significant matters regarding the selection, application, and consistency of accounting principles.
2. Circumstances causing difficulty in applying necessary audit procedures.
3. Results of audit procedures indicating a possible material misstatement.
4. Findings that could result in modification of the audit report.
5. Audit adjustments (whether or not recorded by management) that could have a material effect individually or when aggregated.

E. If information is identified that contradicts or is inconsistent with the auditor's final conclusions -- should document how the auditor addressed the contradiction or inconsistency in forming the conclusions.

F. Identification of preparer and reviewer -- the auditor should document who performed the audit work and who reviewed the specific audit documentation.

G. Should document the **"report release date"** -- defined as the date the auditor grants the entity permission to use the auditor's report.

IV. **Revisions --** To audit documentation after the date of the auditor's report:

A. **"Documentation completion date" --** The auditor should complete the assembly of the final audit file no later than 60 days after the "report release date." (The PCAOB specifies a limit of 45 days for audits of public companies.)

B. **Before the documentation completion date --** The auditor may add information received after the report date or delete unnecessary documentation.

C. **After the documentation completion date --** Must not delete audit documentation before the end of the retention period; may add to the documentation but must document any materials added, by whom, when, reasons for the change, and the effect on the auditor's conclusions.

D. **Retention requirements --** SAS No. 103 requires that the audit documentation be retained for at least five years from the report release date. (The PCAOB requires retention for at least seven years for audits of public companies.)

V. **Additional Documentation --** An earlier SAS required additional documentation in three specific areas. (Appendix A of SAS No. 103 enumerates the specific documentation requirements of various other SASs.):

A. **Aggregated misstatements --** Must document:(1) the nature and effect of misstatements that the auditor aggregates; and (2) the auditor's conclusions as to whether the aggregated misstatements are material to the financial statements.

B. **Analytical procedures --** Must document:(1) the expectation and factors (sources) considered in developing it, when not otherwise apparent;(2) the results of the comparison of that expectation to the recorded amounts (or to ratios based on recorded amounts); and (3) any additional procedures performed (and the results of those procedures) to investigate unexpected differences from that comparison.

C. **Going concern issues --** Must document:(1) the conditions giving rise to the going concern issue;(2) elements of management's plan considered important to overcoming the situation;(3) evidence obtained to evaluate the significant elements of management's plans;(4) conclusion as to whether "substantial doubt" remains; and(5) conclusion as to whether an explanatory paragraph should be added to the auditor's report.

VI. **Quantity of Content --** The quantity, type, and content of the audit documentation depends on the auditor's professional judgment -- factors that should be considered include the following:

A. The risk of material misstatement in the area involved.

B. The amount of judgment involved in performing the work and interpreting the results (including the nature of the procedures involved).

C. The nature and extent of any exceptions identified.

D. The significance of the evidence to the assertion involved.

E. The need to document a conclusion not readily determinable from the documentation of the work performed.

VII. **Types of "Files" Related to Audit Working Papers**

A. **Permanent file --** Involves matters having ongoing audit significance:

1. Description of client's industry, brief history of client, and a description of the client's facilities;
2. Abstracts or copies of important legal documents and important long-term contracts -- documents such as the company's articles of incorporation and bylaws and contracts such as debt agreements, leases, and labor contracts (including pension plans and profit-sharing agreements);
3. Documentation of the auditor's understanding of internal control for the major transaction cycles;
4. **Historical financial information --** Such as ratio analysis of the client's operations or other data having ongoing usefulness.

B. **Current year's audit files --** Including documentation of important administrative matters (such as the audit team's time budget) along with the supporting working papers related to the financial statement items.

1. Audit plan (still often called the audit program).
2. Memoranda (documenting planning activities, consideration of fraud, assessment of internal control, etc.).
3. Abstracts or copies of relevant client documents (including minutes of board of directors' meetings).
4. Letters (confirmations, attorney letters, management representation letter, engagement letter, etc.).
5. Analyses and schedules (either prepared by client personnel or by the auditor).

C. **Bulk file --** Where documentation that is too voluminous can be stored (for example, magnetic tapes, extensive computer printouts).

D. **Correspondence file -- W**here letters and e-mail messages to and from clients are organized so that the audit team can conveniently review communications related to each client organization.

E. **Report file --** Where prior years' audit reports and management letters are organized (by client) so that the audit team can conveniently review formal reports previously issued for each client.

Confirmation

After studying this lesson, you should be able to:

1. *Know the distinction between a "positive" and "negative" confirmation.*
2. *Understand the auditor's responsibility to perform "alternate procedures" for when no response has been received for a positive confirmation attempt.*

[See "AU330 (SAS 67) – The Confirmation Process"]

I. **Tailor Objectives/Assertions --** The auditor should tailor confirmations to the specific audit objectives/assertions -- Confirmations are most useful in addressing the existence/occurrence assertion. There are **two basic types** of confirmation requests:

A. **Positive confirmation request --** Where a response is requested whether or not the other party agrees with the client's recorded amount (so a nonresponse is viewed as a "loose end" that must be addressed).

1. When individual accounts are large.
2. Requires second (or possibly third) requests for nonresponses.
3. If no response is obtained, the auditor must perform "**alternate procedures**."

B. **Negative confirmation request --** Where a response is only requested in the event of **disagreement** (so a nonresponse is viewed as evidence of agreement by the recipient):

1. Could easily misinterpret a nonresponse as suggesting "agreement" when, instead, the other party did not even open the envelope!
2. Therefore, usually requires a larger sample size than would positive confirmations.
3. May justify using negative confirmations when:
   a. There is a large number of small accounts;
   b. Control risk is low (that is, when controls are effective);
   c. Recipients are expected to pay attention to the request.

C. **Alternative procedures --** Are usually required when no response is received for a **positive confirmation** request:

1. **Receivables --** Usually verify that cash was received subsequent to the date of the confirmation request (or, second best, would be to examine the documents underlying the apparent validity of the recorded transaction).
2. **Payables --** Usually verify subsequent cash disbursements as a payment on the account.

II. **Control of Requests and Responses --** Must "maintain control over the confirmation requests and responses" -- if the response is by fax, consider a direct call to the respondent; if the response is verbal, encourage a written reply.

III. **Responding to Risks of Material Misstatement --** SAS No. 110, Performing Audit Procedures in Response to Assessed Risks and Evaluating the Audit Evidence Obtained, states, "When... the auditor has determined that an assessed risk of material misstatement at the relevant assertion level is a significant risk, the auditor should perform substantive procedures that are specifically responsive to that risk.

Example:
If the auditor identified that management is under pressure to meet earnings expectations, there may be a risk that management is inflating sales by improperly recognizing revenue related to sales agreements with terms that preclude revenue recognition or by invoicing sales before shipment. In these circumstances, the auditor may, for example, design external written confirmation requests not only to confirm outstanding amounts, but also to confirm the details of the sales agreements, including date, any rights of return, and delivery terms. In addition, the auditor may find it effective to supplement such external written confirmations with inquiries of nonfinancial personnel in the entity regarding any changes in sales agreements and delivery terms.

Accounting Estimates

After studying this lesson, you should be able to:

1. *Understand the auditor's responsibilities when auditing accounting estimates for reasonableness in accordance with AICPA Professional Standards.*

[See "AU342 (SAS 57) – Auditing Accounting Estimates"]

I. **Basic Auditor Responsibility --** The auditor should evaluate the "reasonableness" of any significant accounting estimates relative to the requirements of GAAP.

   A. The risk of material misstatements associated with estimates varies with: (1) the complexity and subjectivity of the **process** involved; (2) the availability and reliability of **data** involved; and (3) the number, significance, and uncertainty of **assumptions** involved.

   B. To evaluate the reasonableness of an estimate, the auditor usually concentrates on key factors and assumptions that are:

      1. Significant to the accounting estimate;
      2. Sensitive to variations;
      3. Deviations from historical patterns;
      4. Subjective and susceptible to misstatement and bias.

   C. The auditor's procedures primarily consist of **inquiry** and **review**. The auditor must obtain an understanding of how the estimate was made:

      1. Inquire of appropriate personnel to obtain an understanding of how management developed the estimate;
      2. Based on that understanding the auditor uses one (or a combination) of the following approaches to evaluate the reasonableness of the accounting estimate:

         a. **Review --** and test the process used by management - also, identify the relevant controls and the sources and reliability of data involved. (Evaluate whether the assumptions are consistent with the supporting data, including applicable historical and industry data.)

         b. **Develop --** an independent expectation for comparison to management's estimate.

         c. **Review --** subsequent events for additional evidence or outcomes that might corroborate or refute management's estimates (including reading the minutes of meetings of those charged with governance, etc.).

Note:
This involves analytical procedures covered earlier.

Fair Value Measurements and Disclosures

After studying this lesson, you should be able to:

1. *Understand the auditor's responsibilities for auditing fair value measurements and disclosures in accordance with AICPA Professional Standards.*

[See "AU328 (SAS 101) - Auditing Fair Value Measurements and Disclosures"]

I. The AICPA Issued SAS No. 101 -- To establish standards and provide **general guidance** on auditing fair value measurements and disclosures contained in financial statements.

- **A.** SAS No. 101 does not deal with specific types of assets, liabilities, transactions, or industry-specific practices - the Auditing Standards Board points out that specific guidance will be issued as needed (for example, the Auditing Standards Board previously issued a separate pronouncement to address certain specific financial statement elements: SAS No. 92, "Auditing Derivative Instruments, Hedging Activities, and Investments in Securities").
- **B.** Prior to the issuance of SAS No. 101, such fair value issues were implicitly covered by "Auditing Accounting Estimates" (SAS No. 57).

II. Summary of SAS No. 101

- **A.** The auditor must obtain sufficient appropriate evidence to provide reasonable assurance that fair value measurements and disclosures comply with GAAP. Management is responsible for the financial statements, including the fair value measurements and disclosures, which are inherently imprecise.

> **Note:**
> The auditor is not responsible for predicting the future!

- **B.** The auditor must obtain an understanding of the entity's process (and relevant controls) for determining the fair value measurements and disclosures sufficient to develop an effective audit approach.
- **C.** The auditor must evaluate whether the fair value measurements and disclosures conform to GAAP. The auditor should also determine that the methods used to determine fair value are consistently and appropriately applied.
- **D.** GAAP requires or permits a variety of fair value measurements and disclosures in financial statements; and GAAP varies in the depth of guidance provided for these matters. The SAS states that:

> "The existence of published price quotations in an active market is the best evidence of fair value."

- **E.** When there are no observable market prices, the auditor should evaluate the entity's valuation method - the auditor should consider whether:
  1. Management has appropriately applied any criteria provided by GAAP.
  2. The valuation method is appropriate in the circumstances.
  3. The valuation method is appropriate relative to the business, industry, and environment of the entity.
- **F.** **Using a "specialist" --** The auditor should consider whether to engage a specialist to assist with the examination of the fair value measurements and disclosures.

G. **Planned audit procedures may vary significantly in terms of nature, timing, and extent --** Fair value measurements may range from simple to complex with varying degrees of risk of misstatement. Substantive testing may involve (1) testing management's significant assumptions, the valuation model, and the underlying data; (2) developing independent fair value estimates as corroboration; or (3) reviewing subsequent events and transactions for evidence bearing on the appropriateness of the fair value measurements.

H. **Management representations --** The auditor normally obtains written representations from management regarding the reasonableness of significant assumptions and whether those assumptions reflect management's intent and ability to carry out specific actions relevant to the use of fair value measurements or disclosures (may choose to include additional representations from management regarding the appropriateness of the methods and assumptions used, the adequacy of disclosure, and the effects of subsequent events).

I. **Communication with those charged with governance**

> The auditor should determine that those charged with governance are informed about the process used by management in formulating particularly sensitive accounting estimates, including fair value estimates, and about the basis for the auditor's conclusions regarding the reasonableness of those estimates.

Lawyer's Letters

After studying this lesson, you should be able to:

1. *Understand procedures the auditor would perform related to legal liability issues.*
2. *Understand the agreement between the AICPA and American Bar Association regarding matters that can be communicated to the auditor in the "lawyer's letter" in response to a "letter of inquiry" (with emphasis on "asserted" and "unasserted claims").*
3. *Be familiar with the language used in a typical "letter of inquiry to legal counsel."*

[See "AU337 (SAS 12) - Inquiry of Client Lawyer"]

I. Audit Procedures Related to Legal Contingencies

A. Management is the primary source of information about these legal contingencies. The auditor should make appropriate **inquiries** of management.

B. **Review** minutes of all meetings of those charged with governance where significant issues affecting the financial statements likely would be discussed.

C. To corroborate management's responses to the auditor's inquiries about the identity of lawyers who have rendered significant legal services to the client -- the auditor should examine the charges to the related expense account and then examine (vouch to) the appropriate underlying invoices.

D. Send a **"letter of inquiry"** to those lawyers who have rendered litigation-related services -- the lawyer's response to the letter of inquiry is simply called the **"lawyer's letter"** (or attorney's letter); the primary purpose of the lawyer's letter is to corroborate management's responses to the auditor's inquiries about legal contingencies.

II. Inquiries of the Client's Lawyer(s) -- The letter of inquiry normally includes the entity's listing of pending legal matters that the lawyer is handling (classified separately as "Asserted Claims" and "Unasserted Claims") to facilitate the lawyer's response.

III. Asserted Claims -- With respect to asserted claims and active litigation -- "asserted" means that someone has already filed a claim or has at least announced the intention to make such a claim, which is synonymous with the AICPA's term **"pending or threatened litigation."** (According to the American Bar Association, the lawyer should inform the auditor directly about any omissions of asserted claims in the lawyer's letter responding to the letter of inquiry.)

IV. Unasserted Claims -- With respect to unasserted claims and potential litigation - "unasserted" means that the entity has exposure to litigation, but no one has yet announced an intention to sue.

A. The lawyer cannot (according to the American Bar Association) inform the auditor directly about omissions of unasserted claims in the letter of inquiry.

B. However, lawyers must tell their client about any such omissions and request that client management then inform the auditors.

C. Note that this issue (whether the entity's lawyer has informed management of any omission of an unasserted claim that management should discuss with their auditors) is specifically addressed in the management representation letter.

1. Must be probable that a claim will be asserted.
2. Must have at least a reasonable possibility of a material unfavorable outcome.

V. Scope Limitation -- A limitation in the lawyer's response is a scope limitation sufficient to preclude an unqualified opinion (a nonresponse would likely result in a disclaimer of opinion due to a major scope limitation).

VI. Sample Letter of Inquiry to Legal Counsel

Illustrative Letter of Inquiry to Legal Counsel

(Prepared on Client's Letterhead)

(*Date* [1])

(*Name of Lawyer*)

(*Address of Lawyer*)

Dear__________________:

In connection with an audit of our financial statements at (*balance-sheet date*) and for the (*period*) then ended, management of the Company has prepared, and furnished to our auditors (*state name and address of auditors*), a description and evaluation of certain contingencies, including those set forth below involving matters with respect to which you have been engaged and to which you have devoted substantive attention on behalf of the Company in the form of legal consultation or representation. These contingencies are regarded by management of the Company as material for this purpose.[2] Your response should include matters that existed at (*balance-sheet date*) and during the period from that date to the date of your response.

Pending or Threatened Litigation (excluding unasserted claims)

(Ordinarily, the information would include the following: (1) the nature of the litigation; (2) the progress of the case to date; (3) how management is responding or intends to respond to the litigation (for example, to contest the case vigorously or to seek an out-of-court settlement); and (4) an evaluation of the likelihood of an unfavorable outcome and an estimate, if one can be made, of the amount or range of potential loss.)

Please furnish to our auditors such explanation, if any, that you consider necessary to supplement the foregoing information, including an explanation of those matters as to which your views may differ from those stated and an identification of the omission of any pending or threatened litigation, claims, and assessments or a statement that the list of such matters is complete.

Unasserted Claims and Assessments (considered by management to be probable of assertion, and that, if asserted, would have at least a reasonable possibility of an unfavorable outcome)

(Ordinarily, the information would include the following: (1) the nature of the litigation; (2) how management intends to respond if the claim is asserted; and (3) an evaluation of the likelihood of an unfavorable outcome and an estimate, if one can be made, of the amount or range of potential loss.)

Please furnish to our auditors such explanation, if any, that you consider necessary to supplement the foregoing information, including an explanation of those matters as to which your views may differ from those stated.

We understand that whenever, in the course of performing legal services for us with respect to a matter recognized to involve an unasserted possible claim or assessment that may call for financial statement disclosure, if you have formed a professional conclusion that we should disclose or consider disclosure concerning such possible claim or assessment, as a matter of professional responsibility to us, you will so advise us and will consult with us concerning the question of such disclosure and the applicable requirements of Statement of Financial Accounting Standards No. 5. Please specifically confirm to our auditors that our understanding is correct.

Please specifically identify the nature of and reasons for any limitation on your response.

(The auditor may request the client to inquire about additional matters, for example, unpaid or unbilled charges or specified information on certain contractually assumed obligations of the company, such as guarantees of indebtedness of others.)

Very truly yours,

(*Authorized Signature for Client*)[3]

---

[1]Sending of this letter should be timed so that the lawyer's response is dated as close as practicable to the date of the auditor's report. However, the auditor and client should consider early mailing of a draft inquiry as a convenience for the lawyer in preparing a timely response to the formal letter of inquiry.

[2]Management may indicate a specific materiality limit if an understanding has been reached with the auditor.

[3]If a client has not needed to retain legal counsel, the auditors may express an unqualified opinion on the financial statements even though they have not obtained a letter from legal counsel of the Company. In these circumstances, the auditors should obtain written representation from the Company that legal counsel has not been retained for matters concerning business operations that may involve current or prospective litigation.

Management Representations Letters

After studying this lesson, you should be able to:

1. *Understand the auditor's responsibility to obtain a required management representations letter in accordance with AICPA Professional Standards.*
2. *Be familiar with the language used in a typical management representations letter.*

[See "AU333 (SAS 85) - Management Representations"]

I. Document Verbal Responses

- **A.** An auditor is required to obtain written representations from management to corroborate management's verbal responses to important inquiries by the auditor.
- **B.** This letter from management is addressed directly to the auditors.
- **C.** Should be signed by those members of management with overall responsibility for financial and operating matters - ordinarily the chief executive officer (CEO) and the chief financial officer (CFO).
    1. Their unwillingness to sign the management representations letter would be a scope limitation probably resulting in a disclaimer of opinion or withdrawal from the engagement.
    2. If any such representations are contradicted by other evidence -- investigate the circumstances and evaluate the implications to reliance on other management representations.
- **D.** The representations letter should cover all periods encompassed by the auditor's report. (If current management was not present for all periods covered, tailor the representations to the circumstances.)
- **E.** Date of the management representations letter -- the representations should be made as of the date of the auditor's report.

II. The Specific Content of the Representations Depend on the Circumstances -- Usually include the following provisions as applicable.

- **A. Regarding the financial statements**
    1. That management is responsible for the fairness of the financial statements.
    2. That management believes in the fairness of the presentation according to GAAP.
- **B. Regarding the completeness of information**
    1. That all financial records were made available to the auditor.
    2. That all minutes of meetings of those charged with governance (such as the board of directors) were complete and made available to the auditor.
    3. That there were no communications from regulatory bodies about noncompliance or deficiencies in financial reporting.
    4. That there are no known material unrecorded transactions.
    5. That the effects of uncorrected misstatements are immaterial to the financial statements, individually and in the aggregate.

C. AICPA professional standards require that a **summary of any such uncorrected misstatements must be included or attached to the management representation letter**. The summary should include sufficient information to provide management and those charged with governance with an understanding of the nature, amount, and effect of the uncorrected misstatements. Similar items may be aggregated.

D. Regarding recognition, measurement, and disclosure

1. Regarding fraud: (1) that there has been no fraud involving management or employees having significant roles related to internal control; (2) that there has been no fraud involving others that could have a material effect on the financials; (3) that management has no knowledge of any allegations of fraud or suspected fraud affecting the entity; and (4) that management acknowledges responsibility for the design and implementation of programs and controls to prevent and detect fraud.
2. That there are no plans that would affect the carrying values or classification of the assets and liabilities.
3. That there were no related party transactions other than those identified and properly accounted for.
4. That there are no contingencies (including guarantees) other than those properly presented in the financial statements.
5. Any known significant estimates and material concentrations have been properly disclosed (in accordance with AICPA Statement of Position 94-6, "Disclosure of Certain Significant Risks and Uncertainties").
6. That there were no violations of laws, regulations, or contracts requiring disclosure or accrual as a contingent loss.
7. That there are no unasserted claims or assessments which the client's lawyer has directed management to discuss with the auditors. (See SAS No. 12 regarding omissions of "unasserted claims" that the entity's lawyer advises management to discuss with the auditor.)
8. That satisfactory title is held for all assets and that there are no encumbrances on such assets, nor has any asset been pledged as collateral.

E. Subsequent events -- That no events occurred subsequent to the balance sheet date (through the date of the letter) that would require financial statement adjustment or disclosure.

F. Other circumstances -- The representation letter can be tailored to include any other industry or company-specific circumstances of interest. (For example, the auditor could choose to address what constitutes "materiality," either quantitatively or qualitatively.)

See the following Sample Management Representations Letter.

Illustrative Management Representation Letter

(Prepared on the Entity's Letterhead)

(*Date*)

To: (Independent Auditor)

We are providing this letter in connection with your audit(s) of the (*identification of financial statements*) of (*name of entity*) as of (*dates*) and for the (*periods*) for the purpose of expressing an opinion as to whether the (consolidated) financial statements present fairly, in all material respects, the financial position, results of operations, and cash flows of (*name of entity*) in conformity with accounting principles generally accepted in the United States of America. We confirm that we are responsible for the fair presentation in the (consolidated) financial statements of financial position, results of operations, and cash flows in conformity with generally accepted accounting principles.

Certain representations in this letter are described as being limited to matters that are material. Items are considered material, regardless of size, if they involve an omission or misstatement of accounting information that, in the light of surrounding circumstances, makes it probable that the judgment of a reasonable person relying on the information would be changed or influenced by the omission or misstatement.

We confirm, to the best of our knowledge and belief, (as of (*date of auditor's report*)) the following representations made to you during your audit(s):

1. The financial statements referred to above are fairly presented in conformity with accounting principles generally accepted in the United States of America.

2. We have made available to you all -

a. Financial records and related data.

b. Minutes of the meetings of stockholders, directors, and committees of directors, or summaries of actions of recent meetings for which minutes have not yet been prepared.

3. There have been no communications from regulatory agencies concerning noncompliance with or deficiencies in financial reporting practices.

4. There are no material transactions that have not been properly recorded in the accounting records underlying the financial statements.

5. We believe that the effects of the uncorrected financial misstatements summarized in the accompanying schedule are immaterial, both individually and in the aggregate, to the financial statements taken as a whole.

6. We acknowledge our responsibility for the design and implementation of programs and controls to prevent and detect fraud.

7. We have no knowledge of any fraud or suspected fraud affecting the entity involving

a. Management,

b. Employees who have significant roles in internal control, or

c. Others where the fraud could have a material effect on the financial statements.

8. We have no knowledge of any allegations of fraud or suspected fraud affecting the entity received in communications from employees, former employees, analysts, regulators, short sellers, or others.

9. The company has no plans or intentions that may materially affect the carrying value or classification of assets and liabilities.

10. The following have been properly recorded or disclosed in the financial statements -

a. Related-party transactions, including sales, purchases, loans, transfers, leasing arrangements and guarantees, and amounts receivable from or payable to related parties.

b. Guarantees, whether written or oral, under which the company is contingently liable.

c. Significant estimates and material concentrations known to management that are required to be disclosed in accordance with the AICPA's Statement of Position 94-6, "Disclosure of Certain *Significant Risks and Uncertainties*." (Significant estimates are estimates at the balance sheet date that could change materially within the next year. Concentrations refer to volumes of business, revenues, available sources of supply, or markets or geographic areas for which events could occur that would significantly disrupt normal finances within the next year.)

12. The company has satisfactory title to all owned assets, and there are no liens or encumbrances on such assets nor has any asset been pledged as collateral.

13. The company has complied with all aspects of contractual agreements that would have a material effect on the financial statements in the event of noncompliance.

To the best of our knowledge and belief, no events have occurred subsequent to the balance sheet date and through the date of this letter that would require adjustment to or disclosure in the aforementioned financial statements.

(*Signed by CEO and CFO*)

Related Party Issues

After studying this lesson, you should be able to:

1. *Know the definition of the term "related parties."*
2. *Understand the auditor's responsibility to address related-party issues in accordance with AICPA Professional Standards.*

[See "AU334 (SAS 45) - Related Parties"]

I. Definition of Related Parties (from FASB Statement No. 57, "Related Party Disclosures")

> **Definition:**
> *Related parties*: "Affiliates of the enterprise; entities for which investments are accounted for by the equity method by the enterprise; trusts for the benefit of employees, such as pension and profit-sharing trusts that are managed by or under the trusteeship of management; principal owners of the enterprise; its management; members of the immediate families of principal owners of the enterprise and its management; and other parties with which the enterprise may deal if one party controls or can significantly influence the management or operating policies of the other to an extent that one of the transacting parties might be prevented from fully pursuing its own separate interests." (The essence of this definition is that one party has the ability to influence the conduct of the other party.)

II. Procedures Used to Identify the Existence of Related Parties

A. Inquire of management as to any related entities.

B. Review prior year's working papers for continuing engagements.

C. Might inquire of the predecessor auditors for a first-year engagement (if applicable).

D. Review any applicable SEC filings (for public companies) that list related parties.

E. Review stockholder listings of closely held companies to identify major stockholders.

III. Procedures Used to Identify Transactions with the Related Parties

A. Inquire of management as to the existence of any such transactions; (Review any conflict-of-interest statements furnished to the company by management.)

B. Review minutes of board of directors' meetings for mention of significant activities with related parties;

C. Review the accounting records for any large, unusual, or nonrecurring transactions, especially near the end of the reporting period;

D. Examine underlying documents for unusual or large transactions (such as investment transactions) and transactions that have terms or conditions that are inconsistent with prevailing market conditions (such as loans with abnormal interest rates or without stated maturity dates):

   1. Guarantees of loans (either payable or receivable) might be identified on confirmations of such loans;
   2. Transactions with major customers, suppliers, borrowers, or lenders might indicate undisclosed relationships;

3. Invoices from law firms might indicate work performed for related parties or related party transactions.

E. If related party transactions are identified, the auditor should apply any procedures deemed necessary to understand the nature of the transactions and their effect on the financial statements.

1. Obtain an understanding of the business purpose of the transaction.

2. Determine whether the transaction has been authorized by the board of directors or other appropriate officials.

3. Evaluate the reasonableness of amounts to be disclosed.

IV. **The Historical Cost Principle --** In accounting is based on the notion of an exchange price negotiated in an "arms-length" transaction, which results in an accurate measure of the value exchanged. However, related parties could potentially set the transaction price at whatever value they wish, without regard to the "real" economic value. Auditors are generally not in a position to provide reliable, independent appraisals of transaction prices between related parties. As a result, auditors are primarily concerned with the adequacy of disclosure about transactions between related parties.

Subsequent Events

After studying this lesson, you should be able to:

1. *Know what is meant by the term "subsequent events" and be able to distinguish those that require financial statement adjustment from those that require disclosure without adjustment.*
2. *Understand the auditing procedures associated with identifying subsequent events issues.*
3. *Recognize the effect that subsequent events issues may have on dating the auditor's report.*

[See "AU560 (SAS 1) - Subsequent Events"]

[See "AU530 (SAS 1) - Dating the Auditor's Report"]

Definition:
Subsequent Events: Events or transactions occurring after the balance sheet date but prior to the issuance of the audit report, which require financial statement **adjustment** or **disclosure.**

I. **Requiring Adjustment --** Where such an event provides new or better information about circumstances in existence as of the balance sheet date.

Example:
A lawsuit that could only be estimated at the balance sheet date was settled for a fixed amount prior to the issuance of the audit report; with the benefit of this new information, there is no need to estimate the financial statement consequences, since the actual consequence is now known and can be used to adjust the income statement and balance sheet effects.

II. **Requiring Disclosure Only --** Where disclosure of a material event or transaction is necessary so that the financial statements will not be misleading, even though the subsequent events issue is unrelated to circumstances existing at the balance sheet date.

Example:
After the balance sheet date a tornado wiped out the company's facilities and the company had no casualty insurance; disclosure would be required to prevent financial statement readers from being misled about the entity's circumstances, but adjustment would not be required since the financial statement presentation was appropriate at year-end.

III. **Audit Procedures that should be Performed**

A. Inquire of management. (Include an appropriate reference to such subsequent events in the management representations letter.)

B. Review the minutes of meetings of those charged with governance (include all meetings up to the date of the audit report).

C. The lawyer's letter may be relevant to this issue (regarding legal contingencies).

D. Scan journals and ledgers subsequent to year-end (through fieldwork) for any "unusual" items.

IV. Dating the Auditor's Report -- (Especially for subsequent events.)

A. Dating the auditor's report (in general) -- Should not be dated earlier than the date on which the auditor has obtained "sufficient appropriate audit evidence to support the opinion."

1. Prior auditing standards (before SAS No. 103, Audit Documentation, was issued) emphasized the "completion of field work" as the relevant date for the audit report.

2. Current standards emphasize that the audit report should not be dated before the completion of field work, and may be dated later than that. For example, management must take responsibility for the financial statement presentation, including footnotes; and the auditor must review and evaluate the audit documentation before having "sufficient appropriate evidence" both of which may follow the so-called completion of field work.

B. Subsequent event -- Dating the auditor's report when a subsequent event occurs after the completion of field work but prior to the issuance of the auditor's report

1. If the financial statements are adjusted without accompanying disclosure, the report should be dated whenever the auditor has obtained sufficient appropriate audit evidence (which may be the completion of field work or later).

2. If the financial statements are (a) adjusted along with additional footnote disclosure; or (b) disclosure is added without adjustment - the audit report may be either "**dual dated**" (using one date for the overall audit report and a later date to address a specific subsequent event) or the entire audit report may be dated as of the later date (which makes the auditor responsible, in general, for all subsequent events up to that later date).

> **Example:**
> "Dual dating" the audit report: "February 16, 20X1, except for Note XY, as to which the date is March 1, 20X1"

C. Reissuance of the Auditor's Report -- After the date of the original audit report.

1. Using the original report date - this indicates that the auditor did not examine records, transactions, or events after that original date.

2. If a material subsequent event has occurred after the date of the original report - the auditor may decide not to reissue the original audit report.

   a. When adjustment is required to the financial statements previously reported on the adjustment should be made "with disclosure" since the financial statements are changed relative to those previously reported.

   b. When a subsequent event requires "adjustment with disclosure" or "disclosure only" (without adjustment) - the audit report should be either "dual dated" or the entire report should have a later date.

   c. When a subsequent event requires "disclosure only" - the subsequent event can be addressed by management adding a separate footnote to the entity's financial statements labeled something like "Event (Unaudited) Subsequent to the Date of the Independent Auditor's Report" (then the reissued report could use the original date).

Going Concern Issues

After studying this lesson, you should be able to:

1. *Know the indicators that would cause the auditor to have "substantial doubt about an entity's ability to continue as a going concern" (and the audit procedures that would likely detect such issues).*
2. *Understand the additional evidence-gathering responsibilities (and documentation requirements) the auditor has when the auditor has substantial doubt about the entity's ability to continue as a going concern.*
3. *Understand the audit reporting implications of such going concern issues.*

[See "AU341 (SAS 59) - Going Concerns"]

I. **Audit Procedures to Identify Whether There is "Substantial Doubt" --** About the entity's ability to continue as a going concern. Note that the auditor's routine procedures would ordinarily be sufficient to identify circumstances leading to a going concern issue. (Procedures to specifically search for going concern issues are usually not required.)

   A. Analytical procedures.

   B. Review for subsequent events.

   C. Review compliance with terms of loan agreements. (Non-compliance with debt covenants usually results in that debt becoming immediately due and payable!)

   D. Read minutes of meetings of those charged with governance for any discussion of significant issues.

   E. Inquire of client's attorney(s) about lawsuits.

II. **Indicators of "Substantial Doubt" --** About the entity's ability to continue as a going concern:

   A. **Negative trends --** recurring losses, negative cash flows, or working capital deficiencies.

   B. **Other indicators --** defaults on debt, violations of debt covenants, disposals of major assets, or restructuring of debt.

   C. **Internal matters --** labor problems, dependence on single projects or customers, or harmful long-term commitments.

   D. **External matters --** lawsuits, catastrophic losses, harmful legislation, a downturn in the economy causing many companies in an adversely affected industry to fail, or a loss of major customers or suppliers.

III. **Evidence-Gathering Responsibilities --** When the auditor has "substantial doubt about the entity's ability to continue as a going concern" -- the auditor's reporting responsibilities extend to 1 year after the balance sheet date.

> **Note:**
> The auditor cannot be expected to predict the future, however!

   A. Inquire about management's strategy to overcome the financial difficulties - to dispose of assets, to borrow or restructure existing debt, to delay expenditures, or to issue additional stock. (These are **"mitigating factors"** that might be expected to generate meaningful cash inflows or reduce the entity's cash outflows.)

   B. Plan and perform audit procedures to evaluate the feasibility of those elements of management's plans deemed most important.

IV. Reporting Responsibilities -- When substantial doubt remains about the entity's ability to continue as a going concern.

- **A.** Consider the adequacy of disclosure relative to the requirements of GAAP.
- **B.** The auditor may add an **explanatory paragraph** (after the opinion paragraph) to draw the reader's attention to the going concern uncertainties if the client's disclosure of these uncertainties is adequate and the auditor intends to issue an **unqualified opinion.**
- **C.** The auditor could possibly disclaim an opinion if sufficient appropriate evidence cannot be obtained to evaluate the adequacy of the client's financial statement treatment of these uncertainties in relation to GAAP (as a scope limitation).

V. Documentation Requirements -- The auditor should document the following matters related to going concern issues:

- **A.** The conditions that caused the auditor to believe that there is substantial doubt about the entity's ability to continue as a going concern.
- **B.** The work performed in connection with the auditor's evaluation of management's plans.
- **C.** The auditor's conclusion as to whether substantial doubt about the entity's ability to continue as a going concern for a reasonable period of time remains or is alleviated by management's strategy.
- **D.** The consideration and effect of that conclusion on the financial statements, disclosures, and the audit report.

VI. Required Communication with Those Charged with Governance -- When substantial doubt about the entity's ability to continue as a going concern remains, the auditor should communicate: (1) the nature of the conditions identified; (2) the possible effect on the financial statements and disclosures; and (3) the effects on the auditor's report.

Audit Evidence - Specific Audit Areas

Introduction to Auditing Individual Areas

After studying this lesson, you should be able to:

1. *Identify the four assertions for account balances at the end of the period as broad audit objectives applicable to balance sheet line items for which the auditor must gather evidence as a basis for evaluation.*
2. *Identify certain audit procedures that are generally applicable to each of these assertions and other audit procedures that are generally applicable to every individual audit area.*

I. **Audit Procedures Generally Applicable to the Four "Assertions" for Account Balances --** Note that these assertions represent broad audit objectives for which the auditor must gather evidence to determine whether the financial statement elements are fairly presented in accordance with the applicable accounting framework (e.g., GAAP).

A. **Existence --** Related to the validity of recorded items.

1. **Confirmation --** (Especially when concerned about overstatements.) For example, cash, accounts receivable, inventory held by others, and investments held by others.
2. **Observation --** Especially for inventory or investment securities held by the entity.
3. **Agree (vouch) to underlying documents --** Agree items from the accounting record to the supporting source documents to evaluate the appropriateness of recorded items. For example, as an alternate procedure for accounts receivable; to verify additions to property, plant, and equipment accounts; and for various liabilities, such as notes payable.

B. **Completeness --** Related to omissions of amounts that should have been recorded.

1. **Cutoff tests --** Trace from supporting source documents back to the accounting records looking for omissions. For example, trace from shipping documents to cost of goods sold or to the sales journal, or perform a "search for unrecorded liabilities."
2. **Analytical procedures --** These are applicable to every audit area, but be specific: calculate a particular ratio or compare something specific to another specific thing!

C. **Rights and obligations --** Related to any restrictions to the entity 's rights to their assets or to the obligations for their liabilities.

1. **Inquire of applicable client personnel --** Inquire about compensating balances with banks, the use of specific assets as collateral for debts, review debt agreements for collateral, etc.; the management representation letter should document these inquiries regarding important matters.
2. **Examine authorization of transactions --** To ascertain whether any unusual conditions apply.

D. **Valuation and allocation --** Related to the appropriateness of dollar measurements.

1. **Recalculate account balances --** (Verify the client's calculations). For example, for depreciation expense and prepaid insurance.
2. **Trace to subsequent cash receipts or disbursements --** Includes tracing to cash receipts or cash disbursements journal and to the applicable bank statement.
3. **Analytical procedures --** Review the aged trial balance for accounts receivable to evaluate the allowance for uncollectibles. (Test the accuracy of the aged categories by examining underlying invoices; review "receivers" for returns of sales.)

4. **Examine published price quotations for fair value measurements, when applicable --** Verify mathematical accuracy. (Verify that the supporting ledgers or other accounting records agree to the reported balance per the general ledger before performing other audit procedures on those supporting accounting records for purposes of reaching a conclusion about the fairness of the general ledger account balance involved.) -- "Foot" and "cross-foot" the underlying records to verify that they, in fact, add up.

II. **Audit Procedures Generally Applicable to Every Individual Audit Area**

A. **Consider the implication of internal control --** Remember the acronym "**SCARE**" ("segregation, comparison, access, records, and execution" discussed in connection with "Internal Control Concepts") to identify control activities of interest to the auditor relevant to planning the **nature, timing, and extent of substantive procedures** that underlie detection risk, based on the assessed level of control risk.

B. **Substantive procedures usually performed in every individual audit area**

1. Agree the financial statement elements (or the trial balance from which the financial statement elements are derived) to the underlying accounting records (i.e., to the general ledger).
2. Scan the entity's journals and ledgers for any "unusual" items.
3. Make appropriate inquiries of management and other personnel (and document those important inquiries and management's responses in the management representations letter).
4. Perform specific analytical procedures - consider historical trends and events within the industry.

Cash

After studying this lesson, you should be able to:

1. *Verify the appropriateness of each of the items on an entity's bank reconciliation supporting the entity's reported cash balance.*
2. *Be familiar with the content of the standard bank confirmation form.*
3. *Understand what is meant by the term "kiting" and how the auditor might address that issue.*

I. Review the Client's Bank Reconciliation for Each Cash Account

A. Request a **"cutoff" bank statement** approximately 10 days after year-end, to test the reconciling items on the year-end bank reconciliation: (This request must come from management to the entity's financial institution to provide information directly to the entity's auditors.):

1. **Deposits in-transit --** Verify that items listed as deposits in transit on the bank reconciliation have been processed as deposits on the cutoff bank statement (testing for "existence/occurrence" regarding the validity of those reconciling items); these should appear in chronological order on the cutoff bank statement.

2. **Outstanding checks --** Look for checks processed with the cutoff bank statement and having a date prior to year-end; trace those items to the client's list of outstanding checks for "completeness." (Note that checks outstanding at year-end will not necessarily clear the bank in order or within the period encompassed by the cutoff bank statement.)

B. **Confirm** directly with the bank the balance according to the bank statement (Usually confirm 2 separate bank-related matters: (1) cash balances with emphasis on the "existence" assertion; and (2) liabilities to the bank with emphasis on the "completeness" assertion) -- Note that such evidence obtained from independent sources outside the client organization is viewed as very reliable evidence.

Sample Bank Reconciliation As of 12/31/X1:

Balance per bank @ 12/31/X1	$X[1]
Add: Deposits in Transit	X[2]
Less: Outstanding checks	(X)[3]
Adjusted balance as of 12/31/X1	$X
Balance per books @ 12/31/X1	X[4]
Add: Credits directly by bank (e.g., interest)	X[5]
Less: Charges by bank (service charges, etc.)	(X)[5]
Adjusted balance as of 12/31/X1	$X

Legend:

[1] Confirmed as of 12/31/X1... (A-3).

[2] Agreed to bank cutoff statement (A-4).

[3] Reviewed canceled checks (dated December or earlier and processed in January) returned with bank cutoff statement (A-4); no omissions from the outstanding check listing were noted.

[4] Agreed to General Ledger as of 12/31/X1.

[5] Agreed to client's December bank statement.

STANDARD FORM TO CONFIRM ACCOUNT BALANCE INFORMATION WITH FINANCIAL INSTITUTIONS

____
CUSTOMER NAME

Financial Institution's Name and Address [ ] [ ]

We have provided to our accountants the following information as of the close of business on ____________, 20____, regarding our deposit and loan balances. Please confirm the accuracy of the information, noting any exceptions to the information provided. If the balances have been left blank, please complete this form by furnishing the balance in the appropriate space below.* Although we do not request nor expect you to conduct a comprehensive, detailed search of your records, if during the process of completing this confirmation additional information about other deposit and loan accounts we may have with you comes to your attention, please include such information below. Please use the enclosed envelope to return the form directly to our accountants.

1. At the close of business on the date listed above, our records indicated the following deposit balance(s):

ACCOUNT NAME	ACCOUNT NO.	INTEREST RATE	BALANCE*

2. We were directly liable to the financial institution for loans at the close of business on the date listed above as follows:

ACCOUNT NO./ DESCRIPTION	BALANCE*	DATE DUE	INTEREST RATE	DATE THROUGH WHICH INTEREST IS PAID	DESCRIPTION OF COLLATERAL

_______________________ (Customer's Authorized Signature)   _______________________ (Date)

The information presented above by the customer is in agreement with our records. Although we have not conducted a comprehensive, detailed search of our records, no other deposit or loan accounts have come to our attention except as noted below.

_______________________ (Financial Institution Authorized Signature)   _______________________ (Date)

_______________________ (Title)

EXCEPTIONS AND/OR COMMENTS

Please return this form directly to our accountants: [ ] [ ]

* Ordinarily, balances are intentionally left blank if they are not available at the time the form is prepared.

Approved 1990 by American Bankers Association, American Institute of Certified Public Accountants, and Bank Administration Institute. Additional forms available from: AICPA—Order Department, P.O. Box 1003, NY, NY 10108-1003

D 451 5951

II. Multiple Checking Accounts with Transfers Among Them

A. Prepare a schedule of interbank (or intercompany) transfers to verify that both sides of the transfer are properly accounted for (that is, verify that the cash receipts journal and the cash disbursements journal both reflect the transfer in the same proper period) and to detect any **"kiting."**

B. Kiting is an overstatement of the true cash balance at year-end caused by recording the receipt, while failing to record the disbursement, associated with a transfer between cash accounts. (Note that recording the disbursement, while failing to record the receipt part of a transfer between cash accounts would result in a misstatement -- however, it would be an understatement of the cash balance and, therefore, would be inconsistent with kiting, which results specifically in an overstatement.)

III. **If Fraud (Misappropriation) is Suspected --** The auditor may prepare a **"proof of cash"** -- This compares the beginning balance per the bank plus deposits minus checks clearing the bank versus the beginning balance per the books plus receipts minus disbursements according to the books.

IV. **Petty Cash --** May count cash on hand at the client's request. (If the auditor chooses to perform any specific audit procedures for an immaterial account, such as petty cash, analytical procedures are usually sufficient, such as simply comparing the current year's general ledger balance to the prior year's general ledger balance.)

V. **Inquire of Management --** About any **restrictions on cash balances.** If there is a minimum balance requirement for cash, then that restriction should be disclosed.

Note:
The "management representations letter" usually addresses any "compensating balances" (minimum balance requirements) that constitute a restriction on spendable cash. (The usual management representations comment that addresses all general restrictions on the entity's rights to its assets is: "The company has satisfactory title to all owned assets, and there are no liens or encumbrances on such assets nor has any asset been pledged as collateral.")

Accounts Receivable

After studying this lesson, you should be able to:

1. *Recognize that the four assertions for account balances at the end of the period represent a framework for preparing an audit plan to evaluate the fairness of accounts receivable.*
2. *Know how to identify appropriate substantive audit procedures to address each of those assertions when auditing accounts receivable.*

I. **Recall the Four "Assertions" --** That SAS No. 106, "Audit Evidence", identifies for account balances at the end of the period: (1) existence; (2) completeness; (3) rights and obligations; and (4) valuation and allocation.

   A. Related to the **"Existence/Occurrence" Assertion** -- Confirm selected individual customers' accounts.

   B. Verify that the subsidiary A/R ledger agrees or reconciles with the A/R general ledger balance:

      1. Recall that the "accounting records" constitute one category of evidence. (The second category is "other information" according to SAS 106 covered in the review module on Audit Evidence.)

      2. It is important to establish the logical connection between the detailed accounting records being used for the audit procedure (in this case, the subsidiary ledger of individual customer accounts) and that which is the object of the auditor's intended conclusions (specifically, the general ledger balance for A/R).

   C. **Confirm all accounts --** That are determined to be individually material and confirm selected other accounts on a test-basis.

      1. **Positive confirmations --** Request a response whether the individual customer agrees or disagrees with the stated balance; a nonresponse indicates a situation that should be followed up by the auditor.

      2. **Negative confirmations --** Request a response only if the individual customer disagrees with the stated balance.

         a. A non-response is taken as evidence supporting the client's representation.

         b. The risk is that the recipient of the request might have thrown it away without even verifying the balance owed.

         c. Accordingly, negative confirmations are usually used only for rather small balances under conditions of effective internal control (that is, low control risk).

   D. **Investigate all "exceptions" (disagreements) received --** Determine whether the client's records are accurate and, if not, whether the financial statements are materially misstated.

   E. If no response is received to a **positive confirmation** request, the auditor should send a second confirmation request, and perform **"alternate procedures"** if still no response is received.

      1. **Subsequent cash receipts (the preferred alternate procedure) --** Trace collections on the account subsequent to the date of the confirmation to the cash receipts journal and to the bank statement (suggests the balance was valid if it was subsequently collected).

2. **Vouch to (inspect) the underlying documents (the last resort if the account has not been collected) --** Examine the documents (customer's purchase order, client's sales invoice, and shipping documents) supporting the validity ("occurrence") of the transactions comprising the account balance.

II. **Related to the "Valuation" Assertion --** Evaluate the reasonableness of management's estimates of "allowance for uncollectibles" and the "allowance for sales returns."

A. Note that confirmations may contribute, in part, to the auditor's conclusions about the **fairness of the dollar valuation**; however, that contribution relates to establishing the reasonableness of the gross A/R and additional procedures are required to assess the net realizable value of the A/R.

B. **Review the client's aged trial balance of accounts receivable**

1. Inquire about any large, delinquent items.
2. Estimate the percentage of uncollectible accounts within each category of age (based on prior year's working papers tempered by current economic conditions).

C. Review **"receivers" (documents used by the entity's receiving department to capture deliveries) after year-end** for sales returns; consider prior years' returns in view of current economic conditions.

D. Review **adjusting journal entries** (e.g., write-offs) for appropriate authorization.

III. **Related to the "Completeness" Assertion**

A. Perform a **"cutoff" test** of sales. (Examine the shipping documents for the last few shipments before year-end and the first few shipments after year-end; compare these shipping documents with the related sales invoices to assess whether the sales were recorded in the appropriate period.)

B. Compare these shipping documents around the end of the period with the related sales invoices (related to the sales journal) to assess whether the sales were recorded in the appropriate period.

C. Proper "cutoff" involves two assertions ("existence/occurrence" and "completeness"). Usually the auditor performs certain specific audit procedures directed at testing the validity of recorded transactions (i.e., existence/occurrence) but "completeness" is primarily addressed by these cutoff procedures (along with applicable analytical procedures).

IV. **Related to the "Rights and Obligations" Assertion --** Inquire of management:

A. About receivables pledged as collateral for debts (and review loan agreements to identify such collateral).

B. About shipments on consignment that are not actual sales.

C. About any receivables due from employees or management that should be classified separately from ordinary trade receivables.

D. Document such inquiries (and management's response) in the management representations letter.

Note:
Lapping is an attempt to cover up a theft of receipts, where a clerk might try to apply a later receipt to the prior customer's account (and so on) until the scam ends by writing off someone's account as uncollectible. Lapping is a type of fraud (specifically, misappropriation of assets) that is associated with an improper segregation of duties whereby someone with access to the customer's payment also has the authority to make entries in the accounting records to cover up the theft.

Inventory

After studying this lesson, you should be able to:

1. *Recognize that the four assertions for account balances at the end of the period represent a framework for preparing an audit plan to evaluate the fairness of inventory.*
2. *Identify appropriate substantive audit procedures to address each of those assertions when auditing inventory.*

> Recall the four "assertions" that SAS No. 106, Audit Evidence, identifies for account balances at the end of the period: (1) existence; (2) completeness; (3) rights and obligations; and (4) valuation and allocation.

I. **Existence Assertion --** Related to the "existence" assertion -- The auditor participates in the client's physical count of inventory (the observation of inventory):

[See "AU331 (SAS 1) Inventories"]

A. **Note --** The **client counts** the entire inventory and the **auditor observes** the client's taking of the inventory (while taking independent "test counts") -- the auditor participates in this process for two primary reasons, referred to as "dual purpose" tests.

1. **Internal Control Objectives --** The auditor should study the client's written procedures and instructions given to the employees or others counting the inventory to assess the adequacy of the design of these procedures in achieving an accurate physical count; the auditor's focus here is assessing control risk related to inventory reporting.
2. **Substantive Audit Objectives --** The auditor should take a sample of inventory items and verify the physical existence of quantities reflected in the client's detailed records supporting the ending inventory; the auditor's focus here is assessing the fairness of the reported inventory.

B. **Related audit procedures --** Emphasizing quantities:

1. Review the client's written inventory-taking procedures to determine that the physical count will be complete and accurate (regarding dates, locations, personnel involved, and instructions about accounting for the prenumbered inventory tags, cutoff procedures, and error resolution procedures).
2. Assessing the accuracy of the client's reported inventory **quantities.** The auditor should perform test counts for a sample of the prenumbered inventory tags, trace these counts into the client's count sheets (to verify the accuracy of the client's counts on a test basis) and to the client's final inventory listing that supports the general ledger balance. Note that the entity's final inventory listing (reflecting both quantities and dollar amounts) serves as the "subsidiary ledger" for inventory and represents the dollar amount for inventory to which the general ledger account will be adjusted.
3. Focus on the client's prenumbered inventory tags. Determine that all tags have been properly accounted for (that is, all tags are used, unused and returned, or have been voided and returned to a responsible official).
4. The auditor should be alert for and inquire about obsolete or damaged items (for example, dusty or damaged cartons); the auditor should also be alert for empty containers or hollow spaces.

C. If there is a material amount of inventory stored in a **public warehouse,** the auditor can confirm such inventory with the custodian (or could consider physical observation).

II. **Valuation Assertion --** Related to the "Valuation" assertion:

A. **"Price tests" --** Regarding the **unit costs** (not selling prices!) attributed to inventory items:

1. Affected by the client's inventory methods (perpetual versus periodic inventory system) and cost flow assumptions (LIFO, FIFO, average).

2. For merchandising (non-manufacturing) inventory: examine the appropriate underlying invoices.

3. For manufactured inventory -- Review the supporting job order cost records (or the process cost worksheets) and test to underlying documents.

B. **Test extensions --** Recalculate the product of quantity times cost/unit for selected items:

1. Add up these extensions to verify that the items tested are reflected in the total of the detailed inventory listing supporting the client's general ledger balance -- this can be described as "verifying the mathematical accuracy" to establish the connection between the general ledger balance and the supporting detailed listing.

2. Scan the detailed inventory listing for any unusual items.

3. Review the client's reconciliation (or the adjusting journal entry) of the general ledger balance to the detailed inventory listing.

C. **Lower of cost or market considerations --** Inquire of management as to the existence of any damaged, obsolete, or excess inventory items that might require a write-down from historical cost to net realizable value; be attentive to these issues when participating in the observation of inventory.

III. **Completeness Assertion --** Related to the "completeness" assertion. Procedures that might identify material omissions of inventory:

A. Test **inventory cutoff** (recall "FOB-shipping point" versus "FOB-destination" as a technical issue determining when title to goods is transferred):

1. **Related to increases in inventory --** Review "receivers" (receiving documents used by the entity's receiving department to capture deliveries) for a few days before and after year-end (part of "purchases" cutoff test).

2. **Related to decreases to inventory --** Review shipping documents for a few days before and after year-end (related to "sales" and, hence, "cost of goods sold" cutoff test).

B. **Analytical procedures (perhaps by location or by product-line) --** Compare the current year to the prior year and inquire about any significant differences in:

1. Gross profit rates.

2. Inventory turnover (primarily applicable to the "valuation" assertion regarding slow-moving inventory).

3. Shrinkage rates.

4. Total inventory.

IV. **Rights and Obligations Assertion**

A. Inquire of management about any inventory that might be held on consignment or pledged as collateral for borrowings (and review loan agreements to identify such collateral).

B. Document such inquiries (and management's response) in the management representations letter.

V. Other Issues Related to Auditing Inventory

A. **Use of specialists --** An auditor may need to engage an outside expert if the determination of **quantities** and/or **quality** is too complex (for example, electronics, precious jewels).

B. If an auditor is unable to verify the **beginning** inventory for a first-year audit, but is able to verify the **ending** inventory:

1. The auditor may render an opinion on the balance sheet and disclaim an opinion on the income statement, statement of retained earnings, and the statement of cash flows (due to the inability to verify cost of goods sold and, hence, net income).
2. It may be possible to establish the reasonableness of a new client's beginning inventory from alternate procedures -- through the use of analytical procedures or by reviewing a predecessor auditor's working papers.

Investments

Derivative instruments, hedging activities, and investments in securities. In September 2000, the AICPA issued a new Statement on Auditing Standards (SAS 92) to clarify the auditor's responsibilities with respect to: (1) derivative instruments; (2) hedging activities; and (3) investments in securities (that is, all debt and equity securities, including those accounted for using the "equity method"). Note: In view of the recent issuance of this pronouncement, some degree of testing of this topic seems likely!

After studying this lesson, you should be able to:

1. *Understand the auditor's responsibilities under AICPA Professional Standards when auditing investments (including derivative instruments and hedging activities).*
2. *Recognize that the four assertions for account balances at the end of the period represent a framework for preparing an audit plan to evaluate the fairness of investments.*
3. *Identify appropriate substantive audit procedures to address each of those assertions when auditing investments.*

[See "AU332 (SAS 92) - Auditing Investments"]

I. **Introduction --** With respect to (1) derivative instruments and (2) hedging activities, GAAP is determined by the FASB's Statement of Financial Accounting Standards No. 133, "Accounting for Derivative Instruments and Hedging Activities." (Other pronouncements specify GAAP for investments in securities.)

A. **Definitions and Context**

Definitions:
Derivative: A derivative instrument is a financial instrument or other contract with the following three characteristics: (a) it has one or more **"underlyings"** and one or more **"notional amounts"** or payment provisions or both; (b) it requires no initial net investment (or an initial net investment that is smaller than would be expected to have a similar response to changes in market forces); and (c) its terms require or permit net settlement. (It can be settled by a means outside the contract or by delivery of an asset.)

Hedge: "A hedge is a defensive strategy designed to protect an entity against the risk of adverse price or interest-rate movements on certain of its assets, liabilities, or anticipated transactions. A hedge is used to avoid or reduce risks by creating a relationship by which losses on certain positions are expected to be counterbalanced in whole or in part by gains on separate positions in another market."

Note: The AICPA notes that GAAP (SFAS No. 133) does not define "hedge" and offered the above definition.

1. **The FASB identified four fundamental decisions --** Underlying its rules for accounting for derivative instruments and hedging activities:
    a. Derivative instruments represent rights and obligations that should be reported in the financial statements. (They meet the definitions of assets and liabilities.)

b. Only assets and liabilities should be reported as such.

c. "Fair value" is the most relevant measure for financial instruments, in general, and the only relevant measure for derivative instruments, in particular - generally, changes in the fair value of hedged items should be recognized in earnings as gains or losses.

d. Special accounting for a derivative designated a "hedging instrument" should be limited to certain qualifying items.

2. **Accounting for changes in the fair value of a derivative --** (That is, gains and losses) Depends on the designation and intended use of the derivative -- for a derivative not designated a "hedging instrument," the gain or loss is recognized in earnings in the period of the change.

   a. For a derivative designated a **fair value hedge** (i.e., hedging the fair value of a recognized asset or liability) -- the **gain or loss is recognized in earnings** in the period of the change. (The net effect on earnings will be limited to the ineffective result of hedging, since the change in the fair value of the related asset or liability will offset the change in the fair value hedge at least partially.)

   b. For a derivative designated a "**cash flow hedge**" (i.e., hedging the variable cash flows of a forecasted transaction) -- **the effective portion of the hedge is reported in "other comprehensive earnings"** (outside earnings until the forecasted transactions impacts earnings); the ineffective portion is reported as a gain or loss in earnings in the period of the change.

   c. For a derivative designated as hedging the foreign currency exposure of a net investment in foreign operations -- the gain or loss is reported in "other comprehensive earnings" (outside earnings) as part of the "cumulative translation adjustment."

   d. If an entity elects to apply such "hedge accounting" -- at the inception of the hedge, must establish the method to be used to assess the effectiveness of the hedge.

II. **Auditing Derivative Instruments, Hedging Activities, and Investment Securities --** The auditing standards emphasize the auditor's responsibility to consider the component risks of the "audit risk model."

> Recall that AR = IR x CR x DR

A. **Inherent Risk Assessment --** The auditor should consider the following:

1. **Entity's experience --** Inherent risk increases if the client is inexperienced in using such derivatives. (Likewise, inherent risk increases if the client must significantly rely on outside parties and is unable to question the underlying methodology or assumptions.)

2. **Complexity of the instrument --** Inherent risk increases with the complexity of the instrument (especially in determining fair value).

3. **Management's objectives --** There is an inherent risk that the instrument will be ineffective for unexpected changes in market conditions:

   a. **Credit risk --** Risk of loss caused by a counterpart's failure to meet its obligation.

   b. **Market risk --** Adverse changes due to market forces (e.g., interest rates, currency exchange rates, price changes).

   c. **Basis risk --** Risk of loss due to ineffective hedging.

d. **Legal risk --** The risk that legal action precludes performance by one or more parties to the agreement (similar to credit risk).

4. **Evolving nature of derivatives --** GAAP may lag behind the development of new financial instruments, which may require interpretation of existing guidance and assumptions about future conditions.

5. **Whether the transaction involves an exchange of cash --** it may be more difficult to detect contracts that are not associated with initial cash flows.

6. **A derivative that is an "embedded feature" --** Of a contract is more difficult to detect than a derivative that is "freestanding."

B. **Control Risk Assessment --** The auditor must obtain an understanding of internal controls affecting derivatives, hedging activities, and investments in securities; and, if assessing control risk at less than the maximum, the auditor must perform appropriate tests of control for the identified control strengths.

> **Note:**
> If the client has a lot of derivative-related transactions, it is not usually feasible to assess control risk at the maximum!

1. **Recall the five components of internal controls that the auditor is obligated to understand --** (1) control environment; (2) risk assessment; (3) information and communication system; (4) control activities; and (5) monitoring.

2. **"Control activities" --** Are the policies and procedures that provide reasonable assurance that management's specific objectives will be achieved; With "SCARE" as a framework, look for the following control activities for derivatives and hedging activities:

> **Note:**
> Recall that "control activities" can be remembered by "SCARE" -- which stands for: (1) **segregation of duties**; (2) **comparisons** that should be made; (3) **access** to assets; (4) adequacy of the **records**; and (5) **execution of transactions** (proper authorization).

a. **Segregation of duties --** Independent staff monitor derivative activities.

b. **Comparisons --** Reconciliations are appropriately made of derivative positions.

c. **Access --** Constraints are defined (and enforced) for derivative traders, risk managers, and senior management.

d. **Records --** Derivative positions are accurately conveyed to risk measurement systems; controls and financial results are regularly reviewed.

e. **Execution of transactions --** Senior management approves transactions exceeding specified limits and approves departures from stated strategies; limits are reviewed when there are changes in strategy or market conditions.

3. **The services of a service organization --** May be part of an entity's information system, having implications to the assessment of control risk (see "Service Organizations" (AU324 SAS 70)).

> **Note:**
> Merely "holding" securities by itself would not be considered part of the entity's information system requiring an assessment of control risk.

a. When initiating the purchase or sale of securities and acting as an investment adviser or manager.

b. When handling cash receipts or disbursements related to holding securities or otherwise maintaining records of transactions.

c. When providing fair values (pricing services) used by an entity for reporting purposes.

C. **Detection Risk --** Designing the substantive procedures (based on the auditor's judgment about the **nature**, **timing**, and **extent** of those procedures considered necessary.)

1. **Considerations in designing these procedures --** (Based on inherent risk and control risk assessments) The size of the entity; its experience with such derivatives and securities; the types and complexity of the derivatives and securities; and the

controls affecting the derivatives and securities (especially controls over segregation of duties, access/custody, recording, and authorization).

2. **The auditing standards emphasize the five traditional financial statement "assertions"** for which audit procedures should be performed: (1) **existence or occurrence**; (2) **completeness**; (3) **valuation**; (4) **rights and obligations**; and (5) **presentation and disclosure.**

3. **Existence or occurrence --** Procedures to consider:

    a. CONFIRM -- Confirm transactions or terms with the issuer, holder, or counterparty.

    b. INSPECT -- Physically inspect the security and read the applicable contract or supporting documents.

4. **Completeness --** Procedures to consider:

    a. **INQUIRE --** Inquire of management about operating activities that might identify risks involving derivatives; inquire of counterparties used in the past who are not presently used.

    b. **READ --** Read the financial instruments and other agreements; read minutes of meetings of those charged with governance and other supporting documents.

    c. **ANALYTICAL PROCEDURES --** Perform analytical procedures (e.g., comparisons between the current and prior account details).

5. **Valuation --** Procedures to consider

    a. **When the valuation is based on cost**

        i. Inspect documentation of the purchase price.

        ii. Inspect the security or confirm with holder.

        iii. Recalculate amortization of discount/premium.

    b. **When the valuation is based on the investee's financial results (i.e., the "equity method") --** Inquire about management's ability to exercise "significant influence" over the investee

        i. Review investee's financial statements (preferably along with the audit report).

        ii. Inquire of management about any declines in market value (and whether "other than temporary").

    c. **When the valuation is based on fair value**

        i. Determine the appropriate quoted market price (from financial publications or pricing services or from broker-dealers when they are market makers).

        ii. When no quoted market price is available, obtain estimates from broker-dealers using proprietary valuation models (such as the Black-Scholes option pricing model).

        iii. Assess the reasonableness of such estimates by management or others.

        iv. If collateral is important to the valuation, ascertain the existence, fair value, and the investor's rights to that collateral.

        v. For changes in fair value, determine that the financial statements comply with GAAP (e.g., such changes for an "available-for-sale security" are reported in other comprehensive income, whereas such changes for a "trading security" are reported in earnings).

   vi. Inquire about any impairments that are "other than temporary" and evaluate the reasonableness of management's replies.

6. **Rights and obligations --** Procedures to consider:
   a. **READ --** Read the financial instruments and other agreements. (Also, read minutes of meetings of those charged with governance and other supporting documents regarding collateral and repurchase agreements.)
   b. **CONFIRM --** Confirm significant terms with the holder or counterparty.
7. **Presentation and disclosure --** Review the form and content of the financial statements (including classifications and level of detail) and compare the presentation and disclosure with the requirements of GAAP.
8. **Management representations --** Usually obtain written representations in the "management representations letter" regarding assertions about derivatives and securities that are affected by management's stated "intent and ability."

III. Summary of Procedures Used in Auditing Traditional Investment Securities -- (That is, Stocks and Bonds):

A. **Related to the "Existence" Assertion --** The auditor mainly uses inspection and confirmation.
   1. Physically inspect any securities in the possession of the client.
   2. Confirm any stocks and bonds held by an independent custodian.

B. **Related to the "Completeness" Assertion --** The auditor primarily uses analytical procedures to detect omissions.
   1. Review investment income or loss accounts:
      a. Verify revenue through confirmation when held by an independent custodian.
      b. May trace cash receipts to a bank statement.
      c. May recalculate the interest income on debt instruments or dividends received on stock investments.
   2. Compare dividends, interest, or other investment income (loss) to prior year's working papers for reasonableness; dividends can be verified by consulting "dividend record books" produced by commercial investment advisory services.
   3. Review the minutes of the meetings of those charged with governance for approval of any large transactions.

C. **Related to the "Valuation" assertion --** The appropriate audit procedures will vary with the type of security involved.
   1. **For bonds --** Verify the interest earned by calculations (based on the face value, interest yield, and period held); review the amortization of any premium or discount; inquire about management's intention to hold the security to maturity.
   2. **For investments (in stocks or bonds) which are "marked to market" --** As required by the applicable accounting standards.
      a. Compare the carrying value at the beginning of the period to the prior year's working papers; agree to underlying documents, examine canceled checks for any current year additions to investments and trace the proceeds of any sales to a bank statement.
      b. Verify the year-end fair market value (trace to an independent outside source, such as *The Wall Street Journal* or other appropriate quotation) - disclose as required by the applicable accounting standards.

c. Inquire of management about any "impairments" that may be "other than temporary."

3. **For investments in stock accounted for by the equity method**

   a. Compare the carrying value at the beginning of the period to the prior year's audit working papers; agree transactions to underlying documents and examine canceled checks for any current year's additions to investments.

   b. Examine the investee's current year audited financial statements to verify the investor's percentage share of income (loss) and any dividend distributions.

   c. Inquire of management about any "impairments" relative to the investment's carrying value.

D. **Related to the "Rights and Obligations" assertion --** The auditor primarily uses inquiry and review.

1. Inquire about management's "intent and ability" affecting investment classifications (and document the inquiry in the management representations letter):

   a. **Trading securities**

      i. **Balance sheet --** Reported at fair value (in current assets).

      ii. **Income statement --** Unrealized holding gains/losses are reported on the **income statement** (include interest and dividends, too.)

   b. **Available-for-sale securities**

      i. **Balance sheet --** Reported at fair value (either current or noncurrent assets, as applicable); use "unrealized holding 'gains and losses'" as a separate component of stockholders' equity.

      ii. **Income statement --** Now the **unrealized holding gains/losses** are reported in "**other comprehensive income**," not "net income"!

   c. **Held-to-maturity (debt) securities**

      i. **Balance sheet --** Reported at amortized cost basis (either current or non-current assets, as applicable).

      ii. **Income statement --** No recognition of fluctuations in market value! Report interest as revenue.

2. Inquire of management about any restrictions applicable to investments (including any securities pledged as collateral for debt).

3. Review cash receipts and cash disbursements subsequent to year-end for material transactions affecting investments, perhaps requiring disclosure.

Fixed Assets

Since the composition of the fixed assets' balance is usually substantially carried over from one period to the next, the auditor usually emphasizes substantive tests of transactions (that is, the continuing auditor usually verifies the ending balance by examining the debits and credits that caused the balance to change from the prior year).

After studying this lesson, you should be able to:

1. *Recognize that the four assertions for account balances at the end of the period represent a framework for preparing an audit plan to evaluate the fairness of fixed assets.*
2. *Identify appropriate substantive audit procedures to address each of those assertions when auditing fixed assets.*

Recall the four "assertions" that SAS No. 106, Audit Evidence, identifies for account balances at the end of the period: (1) existence; (2) completeness; (3) rights and obligations; and (4) valuation and allocation.

Note:
Instead of performing "tests of ending balances," the continuing auditor will normally verify the appropriateness of the year-end balance of fixed assets by performing substantive "tests of transactions." In other words, if there are relatively few transactions that have caused the fixed asset balance to change from last year to this year, the auditor will, in effect, back into the ending balance by taking the beginning balance (audited last year), add any additions, and subtract any disposals. Since there are likely only a few additions and/or disposals, it is more efficient to examine those few transactions, rather than verify a sample of the individual items that comprise the year-end fixed asset balance.

I. **Existence Assertion --** Related to the "existence" assertion:

   A. Consider the adequacy of the accounting records -- Verify that the client's detailed fixed asset listing supports the related general ledger account balance.

   B. **For additions --** Vouch to (inspect) the underlying documents (examine the purchase order, vendor's invoice, and the entity's canceled check if payment has been made); look for approval in the minutes of meetings of those charged with governance if the addition is a "major" one.

   C. **For disposals --** Trace any proceeds received to the cash receipts journal and bank statement; review for appropriate approval.

II. **Valuation Assertion --** Related to the "valuation" assertion:

   A. Review the calculations for depreciation expense -- compare the useful lives and methods used to prior years for consistency, and recalculate on a test basis.

   B. Consider whether there have been any "impairments" of long-lived assets requiring a write-down from the historical cost-based carrying value - make appropriate inquiries of management (and document such inquiries and management's response in the management representations letter).

III. **Completeness Assertion --** Related to the "completeness" assertion.

   A. Review the client's "repairs and maintenance expense" account and examine underlying documents for material items to determine whether any of those recorded expenses should instead be capitalized.

   B. Review any lease agreements to determine if lease capitalization might be required.

IV. **Rights and Obligations Assertion --** Related to the "rights and obligations" assertion.

   A. Inquire of management about any fixed assets pledged as security for borrowings (and review loan agreements to identify such collateral).

B. Document such inquiries (and management's response) in the management representations letter.

Current Liabilities

After studying this lesson, you should be able to:

1. *Recognize that the four assertions for account balances at the end of the period represent a framework for preparing an audit plan to evaluate the fairness of current liabilities.*
2. *Know how to identify appropriate substantive audit procedures to address each of those assertions when auditing current liabilities.*

I. **Accounts Payable (or Vouchers Payable) --** Primarily use substantive tests of ending balances.

A. Recall the difference between **accounts payable and vouchers payable** systems described in the review materials related to Internal Control -- Transaction Cycles:

1. **Accounts Payable --** In an accounts payable system, the payables are tracked by the name of the vendor. (The total payable to another party, which constitutes a receivable to them, is susceptible to confirmation if desired.)
2. **Vouchers Payable --** In a vouchers payable system, the payables are tracked by individual transaction without summarizing the amounts owed by vendor name. (The total payable to another party is not susceptible to confirmation, only individual transactions could be confirmed.)

B. Recall the four "assertions" that SAS No. 106, "Audit Evidence," identifies for account balances at the end of the period: (1) existence; (2) completeness; (3) rights and obligations; and (4) valuation and allocation.

C. Related to the **"Completeness" Assertion** (for liabilities, the auditor's primary concern involves "completeness" not "existence"!). Perform a **"search for unrecorded liabilities."** (This is done toward the end of field work to provide the best chance of detecting any significant unrecorded liabilities.)

1. Review cash disbursements **subsequent to year-end** and, for all disbursements over some specified dollar amount (>$X), examine the related vendors' invoices and the entity's related receiving documents to identify transactions that should have been reported as liabilities as of year-end; compare those apparent liabilities to the details comprising the recorded payables to identify apparent liabilities that are unrecorded.
2. Examine any unpaid invoices on hand at the date of the "search" along with the entity's related receiving documents to identify any transactions that should have been reported as a liability as of year-end.
3. Inquire of management about their knowledge of any unrecorded liabilities and whether all invoices have been made available to the auditor. (Document such inquiries and management's response in the management representations letter.)

D. Related to the "existence" and "valuation" assertions:

1. Verify the mathematical accuracy of payables by comparing the general ledger balance to the supporting detailed listing of payables.
2. Vouch selected items to the underlying vendor's invoices.
3. Could "confirm" selected payables, but usually do not --Confirmation primarily establishes the validity ("existence") of the recorded items, but there is a relatively low risk that the company would overstate its true liabilities; the far bigger risk is that material liabilities may have been omitted (i.e., "completeness").

4. Usually "valuation" is not a significant audit issue, since there is a presumption that the client will pay 100% of what is owed; the auditor should look to see that the client takes advantage of any available cash discounts for prompt payment.

E. Related to the **"rights and obligations" assertion** -- Inspect the specific terms of the payables and inquire about any related party transactions. (Separately classify notes payable for borrowings from accounts payable for ordinary operating activities.)

II. **Other Current Liabilities --** The auditor uses analytical procedures extensively to evaluate other miscellaneous payables:

A. **Wages and salaries payable --** The auditor can compute the estimated accrual, in view of the number of days to be accrued relative to a whole pay period.

B. **Dividends payable --** The auditor can compute, in view of the declared dividends/share (per the minutes of meetings of those charged with governance) times the number of shares outstanding.

C. **Interest payable (and the related interest expense) --** The auditor can compute an estimate of accrued interest for the time period involved, based on the interest rate (and payment dates) specified in the underlying debt agreements.

Long-Term Liabilities

After studying this lesson, you should be able to:

1. *Recognize that the four assertions for account balances at the end of the period represent a framework for preparing an audit plan to evaluate the fairness of long-term liabilities.*
2. *Identify appropriate substantive audit procedures to address each of those assertions when auditing long-term liabilities.*

> Recall the four "assertions" that SAS No. 106, "Audit Evidence," identifies for account balances at the end of the period: (1) existence; (2) completeness; (3) rights and obligations; and (4) valuation and allocation.

I. Related to the "Completeness" Assertion -- Use substantive tests of transactions (to address decreases in debt):

- **A.** Verify due dates for payments in the loan agreements.
- **B.** Trace cash disbursements from the accounting records to the bank statement.
- **C.** Examine canceled notes if paid in full.
- **D.** Could confirm year-end balances, but confirmations are most applicable to establishing the validity of recorded items (that is, existence).

II. Related to the "Existence/Occurrence" Assertion -- Use substantive tests of transactions (to address increases in debt):

- **A.** Obtain copies of new loan agreements for the auditor's review and documentation.
- **B.** Verify authorization of new debt in minutes of meetings of those charged with governance.
- **C.** Trace receipts from the accounting records to the bank statement.

III. Related to the "Valuation" Assertion -- There are few measurement issues associated with most liabilities, but long-term liabilities should be based on present values:

- **A.** Trace related cash receipts and disbursements from the accounting records to the bank statements.
- **B.** Examine the underlying loan contracts related to the stated dollar amounts.
- **C.** Recalculate the amortization of any premium or discount using the effective interest method.
- **D.** Apply analytical procedures to the related expense accounts (e.g., interest) -- Note that the balance sheet item and the related income statement item are usually addressed on the same audit documentation (working paper).

IV. Related to the "Rights and Obligations" Assertion -- The auditor should make appropriate inquiries of management and review the loan documents:

- **A.** Debt covenants -- Important restrictions should be disclosed. (Note that violations of such covenants can cause the entire balance to become immediately payable.)
- **B.** Collateral -- Any assets pledged as security for the debt should be disclosed.

C. The current portion of long-term debt should be reclassified to current liabilities -- Read the loan documents to identify the principal to be paid within the next year; examine the cash payments for the current-year installment paid if the debt is scheduled to be paid in equal installments.

Stockholders' Equity

After studying this lesson, you should be able to:

1. *Recognize that the four assertions for account balances at the end of the period represent a framework for preparing an audit plan to evaluate the fairness of stockholders' equity.*
2. *Identify appropriate substantive audit procedures to address each of those assertions when auditing stockholders' equity.*

> Recall the four "assertions" that SAS No. 106, "Audit Evidence," identifies for account balances at the end of the period: (1) existence; (2) completeness; (3) rights and obligations; and (4) valuation and allocation.

I. Related to the "Existence" Assertion -- Confirm the outstanding shares of stock if there is an external registrar. (Verify that the stock was issued in accordance with the company's articles of incorporation and with the approval of those charged with governance.)

II. Related to the "Completeness" Assertion

- **A.** Review the minutes of meetings of those charged with governance to identify authorized transactions.
- **B.** Account for all certificate numbers to establish that no unauthorized shares were issued.

III. Related to the "Rights and Obligations" Assertion

- **A.** Review the minutes of board meetings to verify that any stock and dividend transactions were duly authorized by those charged with governance.
- **B.** Review contracts with employee stock option plans to verify compliance with such agreements.
- **C.** Inquire of management about any restrictions that might exist on the availability of retained earnings for purposes of dividend distribution -- the financial statements should disclose any restrictions on retained earnings available for dividend distribution.

IV. Related to the "Valuation" Assertion

- **A.** Review cash receipts and disbursements (and minutes of meetings of those charged with governance) for increases or decreases in stock accounts.
- **B.** Compare the subsidiary ledger to the general ledger stock accounts. (Examine stock certificates or read the applicable minutes of meetings of those charged with governance to verify the par or stated value per share.)

Payroll

When the auditor chooses to examine the payroll function handled "in-house" by the company (as opposed to an outside payroll service), recall the internal control considerations associated with the payroll transaction cycle covered in the lesson Specific Transaction Cycles.

After studying this lesson, you should be able to:

1. *Recognize that the five assertions for transactions and events during the period represent a framework for preparing an audit plan to evaluate the fairness of income statement items, such as payroll expense.*
2. *Identify appropriate substantive audit procedures to address payroll expense.*

> Recall the five "assertions" that SAS No. 106, "Audit Evidence," identifies for "classes of transactions and events for the period under audit": (1) accuracy; (2) occurrence; (3) completeness; (4) cutoff; and (5) classification.

I. Related to the "Accuracy and Existence" Assertions

A. Examine personnel records on a test basis, to determine that the levels of compensation and support for all deductions exist for all employees. (Officers' compensation should be documented in the minutes of meetings of those charged with governance.)

B. Trace selected transactions from the payroll register to the general ledger and to the payroll bank account.

C. Recalculate selected entries on the payroll register.

II. Related to the "Completeness" Assertion

A. Review time reports and time cards to verify support for production records.

B. Apply analytical procedures (and recalculation) to verify that the payroll-related accruals at year-end are reasonable.

III. Related to the "Cutoff" Assertion --

Cutoff is effectively addressed when "occurrence" and "completeness" have been addressed; in other words, when the auditor has established that recorded transactions are properly recorded and that there are no omissions of transactions that should have been recorded, the auditor has established that the transactions have been recorded in the correct accounting period.

> As stated in SAS No. 106, "... there may not be a separate assertion related to cutoff of transactions and events when the occurrence and completeness assertions include appropriate consideration of recording transactions in the correct accounting period."

IV. Related to the "Classification" Assertion

A. The comments related to accuracy and occurrence apply to recording the transactions in the proper accounts, as well.

B. Review outside reports related to pension, other post-retirement benefits (e.g. insurance), and profit-sharing plans.

C. Verify payroll deductions and taxes, trace cash disbursements for withholdings to appropriate agencies.

D. Note that ordinarily, income statement elements (including revenue and expense items) are primarily audited by analytical procedures. Typically, tests of details will be performed only when the analytical procedures suggest that a risk of material misstatement exists and that a more detailed investigation is warranted. Payroll-related expenses would normally be subject to such analytical procedures, too. The discussion above is presented to provide insights about how such transactions could be tested in detail if the auditor deemed that appropriate.

Audit Sampling

Introduction to Sampling

After studying this lesson, you should be able to:

1. *Understand the distinction between "statistical" and "non-statistical" audit sampling.*
2. *Understand the distinction between "sampling risk" and "non-sampling risk."*
3. *Understand the distinction between "false rejection" (a Type I Error) and "false acceptance" (a Type II Error) comprising "sampling risk" applicable to tests of control substantive procedures.*

[See "AU350 (SAS 39, as amended) - Audit Sampling"]

> **Definition:**
> *Sampling*: An "... application of an audit procedure to less than 100% of the items within an account balance or class of transactions for the purpose of evaluating some characteristic of the balance or class."

I. There are Two General Approaches to Sampling -- May depend on the auditor's perceptions of cost/benefit tradeoffs.

A. Non-statistical sampling -- Also called "judgmental" sampling.

B. Statistical -- The benefits relate to objectivity:

1. Relates to the **sufficiency** of the evidence -- The determination of the sample size in a statistical sampling application establishes how much evidence is required.
2. The results may seem more defensible to others (such as the courts).
3. A common misconception is that "statistical sampling" eliminates the need for judgment. Actually, numerous judgments must be made; however, these judgments are made more explicit.
4. Sampling applications occur in either of 2 contexts:

> **Definitions:**
> *Attributes Sampling*: Sampling to decide whether internal controls are working as designed (tests of controls).
>
> *Variables Sampling*: Sampling to decide whether account balances (such as inventory or receivables) are fairly stated (substantive tests of details).

II. Uncertainty and Audit Sampling -- Risk Considerations -- Recall the definition of **"Audit Risk"** -- The probability that the auditor fails to modify the opinion on financial statements containing a material misstatement. An appendix in SAS No. 111 provides the following model for auditors who want to evaluate the risk components explicitly:

> AR = RMM * AP * TD, where
>
> AR = audit risk;
>
> RMM = risk of material misstatement, consisting of the combined assessments of inherent risk and control risk;
>
> AP = risk that analytical procedures performed for substantive purposes will not detect a material misstatement that occurred;
>
> TD = risk that tests of details will fail to detect a material misstatement that was not otherwise detected.

III. Whether "Non-statistical" Sampling or "Statistical" Sampling is Used -- The auditor is fundamentally seeking a sample that is truly representative of the population, so that the auditor gets an accurate signal about the population's characteristics in a highly efficient way.

IV. "Sampling Risk" -- Is the risk that the sample may not be truly representative of the population; in other words, the chance of an erroneous conclusion that the auditor takes by examining a subset of the population, rather than the entire population.

A. "Type I Errors" (False Rejection)

1. Tests of controls => "the risk of **under-reliance** on internal controls" (also known as "risk of assessing control risk too high").
2. Substantive testing => "the risk of incorrect rejection".
3. Type I errors relate to **"efficiency"** -- the auditor will probably achieve the appropriate conclusions, although not in the most efficient manner (perhaps taking more than one sample, maybe at the urging of the client who has faith in the effectiveness of the internal control or the fairness of the financial statement element).

B. "Type II Errors" (False Acceptance)

1. Tests of controls => "the risk of **over-reliance** on internal controls" (also known as "risk of assessing control risk too low").
2. Substantive testing => "the risk of incorrect acceptance".
3. Type II errors relate to **"effectiveness"** -- now the auditor may have failed to meet the overall objective, which is to limit audit risk to an acceptably low level. (The client will have no incentive to argue about this conclusion, so the auditors will not have any reason to take a second look.)

> **Note:**
> If there were no variation within a population (that is, if all items were homogeneous), the auditor would only need a sample of one item to assess the whole population! The variability of the population causes the sample size to increase and is responsible for the sampling risk.

V. Nonsampling Risk -- Refers to any other mistakes by the auditor (that is, other than sampling risk), not a direct consequence of using a sampling approach:

A. Inappropriate auditing procedures.

B. Failure to correctly identify "errors" or amounts sampled, misinterpreting the results, etc.

Attributes Sampling

After studying this lesson, you should be able to:

1. *Understand the meaning of the term "attributes sampling."*
2. *Know the eight steps that comprise an attributes sampling application.*
3. *Know how to determine the sample size for an attributes sampling application using AICPA tables.*

I. **Attributes Sampling --** Statistical sampling for the purpose of identifying the percentage frequency of a characteristic in a population of interest to the auditor; this term is usually used to refer to audit sampling to ascertain the operating effectiveness of internal control (where, for each transaction in the sample, the control procedure of interest was either performed or not performed - there are only two outcomes, similar to 'hit or miss' or "heads or tails")

II. **Eight Steps Comprise an Attributes Sampling**

A. **Identify the Sampling Objective --** That is, the purpose of the test.

B. **Define what Constitutes an "Occurrence" --** Sometimes called a "deviation" or "error" when a control procedure of interest was not properly performed.

C. **Identify the Relevant Population**

1. Specify the relevant time period.
2. Specify the "sampling unit" -- what it is that the auditor is selecting (e.g., sales transactions).

D. **Determine the Sampling Method --** How the specific items (or transactions) are to be selected for the sample.

1. **Statistical Sampling Approaches**
   a. **Random Number --** Each transaction has the same probability of being selected (the best approach).
   b. **Systematic --** For example, selecting every 100th item.
2. **Judgmental Sampling Approaches --** not appropriate for attributes sampling!
   a. **Block --** A group of contiguous items (e.g., the sales transactions for the entire month of June).
   b. **"Haphazard" --** Arbitrary selection, with no "conscious" biases. Subconscious biases may exist without the auditor's awareness, however.

E. **Determine the Sample Size --** (Based on AICPA tables.)

Factor (holding all others constant)	Relationship
Expected error rate (related to the variation in population)	**Direct**
Tolerable (deviation) rate (related to precision)	**Inverse**
Risk of over-reliance	**Inverse**
Risk of under-reliance (implicit)	**Inverse**
Population size (implicit)	**Direct**

F. **Select the Sample --** Identify the "occurrences" associated with all the items in the sample.

G. **"Evaluate" the sample results --** This means make a decision as to whether the auditor can rely on the effectiveness of the internal control procedure under consideration.

1. Calculate the **observed deviation rate** = (# errors)/n.
2. Determine the "point estimate," the best single indicator of the percentage of times that the control procedure was performed as designed in the population (ignoring, for the moment, the uncertainty surrounding whether the sample is truly representative of the population).
3. Calculate a "confidence interval" for the **achieved upper precision limit** (in view of the actual errors observed). There are AICPA tables to determine the achieved upper precision limit. (*The topic determination of confidence intervals is not likely to be tested on the CPA exam!*)
4. Compare the achieved upper precision limit to the stated **tolerable rate**; the auditor can only rely on the internal control procedure if the error rate, based on the upper bound of the confidence interval (the "achieved upper precision limit" from the tables) is less than or equal to the stated tolerable rate.
5. Consider the **qualitative characteristics** of the internal control deviations for any implication to the rest of the audit.
6. Make the appropriate decision -- Should the auditor rely on the specific control procedure (that is, **assess control risk at less than the maximum**) or not?

H. **Document the auditor's sampling procedures**

III. **Attributes Sampling Example**

Statistical Sample Sizes for Tests of Controls

Five-Percent Risk of Overreliance

Expected Population	**Tolerable Rate**					
Deviation Rate	**2%**	**3%**	**4%**	**5%**	**6%**	**7%**
.25	236	157	117	93	78	66
.50	*	157	117	93	78	66
.75	*	208	117	93	78	66
1.00	*	*	156	**93**	78	66
1.25	*	*	156	124	78	66
1.30	*	*	192	124	103	66
1.75	*	*	227	153	103	88
2.00	*	*	*	181	127	88

* Sample size is too large to be cost-effective for most audit applications.

Note:
This table has been adapted from material copyrighted by the American Institute of Certified Public Accountants, Inc.

IV. Attributes Sampling - Numerical Example

A. Suppose that an auditor specified the following parameters for a statistical sampling application related to internal controls in the revenue/receipts transaction cycle:

Acceptable risk of over-reliance on Internal Control (a Type II error) **5%**

(The auditor is willing to rely on the control procedure if the statistical test indicates that the control is working as prescribed at least 95% of the time.)

Estimated population deviation rate 1%
Tolerable deviation rate 5%

B. Requirement -- Identify the required sample size using the AICPA tables for attributes sampling.

C. Solution -- The 5% **risk of over-reliance** (Type II Error) determines the applicable page of the AICPA tables; the 5% **tolerable rate** determines the applicable column of the AICPA table; and the 1% **estimated population deviation rate** determines the applicable row of the AICPA table.

1. The resulting sample size is **93**.

Variables Sampling

After studying this lesson, you should be able to:

1. *Understand the meaning of the term "variables sampling" and the various specific approaches (difference estimation, ratio estimation, mean-per-unit estimation, and probability-proportionate-to-size sampling).*
2. *Know the eight steps that comprise a variables sampling application.*
3. *Know the factors that affect sample size for a variables sampling application.*
4. *Understand the role of "stratification" in audit sampling.*

I. **Relies Heavily on the Classic "Normal Distribution" --** (With the bell-shaped curve.)

   A. This distribution is determined by two parameters:

      1. The **mean**, related to central tendency; and
      2. **Variance** (or its square root, standard deviation), related to dispersion or variability.

> **Note:** If 68% of the area is under the bell-shaped curve, it is within one standard deviation of the mean; if 95.5% of the area, is within two standard deviations of the mean .

II. **Basic Steps --** The eight **basic steps in a variables sampling plan** are practically the same as in the attributes sampling case:

   A. Identify the **sampling objective** -- the purpose of "variables sampling" is to determine the inferred audit value of a population of interest (e.g., for accounts receivable or inventory).

   B. Identify the relevant population:

      1. Specify what constitutes the sampling unit;
      2. Be careful to assure that conclusions are properly extended to the appropriate population (i.e., completeness of the population).

> **Note:** Auditors should examine all the items that are individually material (i.e., we are not "sampling" these).

   C. **Select the specific sampling technique --** The choices are difference estimation, ratio estimation, mean-per-unit estimation, or probability-proportionate-to-size sampling.

   D. **Calculate the sample size --** Since tables do not exist for this in variables sampling. Recall the **five factors and relationships** to sample size identified for attributes sampling applications -- These factors are still applicable to variables sampling.

   See the following illustration.

Factor (holding all others constant)	Relationship
Estimated population standard deviation (related to the variation in population)	**Direct**
Allowance for sampling risk (also called "tolerable misstatement") [related to precision]	**Inverse**
Risk of incorrect acceptance (Type II)	**Inverse**
Population size (explicitly considered for variables sampling)	**Direct**
Risk of incorrect rejection (Type I error, only implicitly considered)	**Inverse**

The **basic formula**, based on classical statistics:

n = (S * Z-coefficient * N /A)^2

where:

n represents the sample size to be determined;

S represents the estimated population standard deviation (related to the variability of the population);

Z-coefficient represents a measure of reliability for some level of specified "confidence" (typically about 2);

N represents the size of the population (number of accounts or items of inventory, etc.);

A represents the specified allowance for sampling risk, related to the statistical concept of "precision."

> **Exam Tip:** It is very unlikely that the AICPA will require calculations of sample size! However, they frequently test these **concepts**. In particular, they might ask questions related to the factors that influence the sample size and whether that influence is directly or inversely related. The formula identified above is a useful way to keep these relationships straight.

E. Determine the **method of selection** -- **random** (the preferred approach) or systematic.

F. **Conduct the sample**

G. **Evaluate the sample** and project to population:

1. Calculate a point estimate (the implied audit value) for the population based on the sample's audited values.
2. Construct a confidence interval to determine whether to accept or reject the client's recorded balance as consistent with the audit evidence.

> **Exam Tip:** The AICPA has rarely tested calculations in this area. On a few occasions, they have required calculations of a "point estimate" for a population; however, calculations of the confidence interval surrounding a point estimate are beyond the scope of the CPA examination!

H. **Document the auditor's sampling procedures** and judgments.

> **Definition:**
> *Stratification*: The auditor may reduce the overall variability within a population by classifying similar items into "sub-populations" (within each group, the variability may be much smaller); the resulting aggregate sample size may be smaller as a result of reducing the combined effects of variability.

III. **Variables Sampling - Specific Sampling Techniques --** Note that the CPA exam has rarely emphasized calculations related to statistical sampling; however, the exam has historically tested the concepts related to sampling.

A. **Difference estimation --** This approach involves identifying the dollar differences between the sample's audit values and applicable book values.

1. **Sample size --** As previously described. (Note that we usually need at least 30 differences between audit and book values in our sample when using "difference estimation.")

2. Estimate the population's implied audit value.

a. Calculate the average difference between the audit value and book value for items in the sample:

> d = (av - bv)/n

b. Extend that average difference to the population by multiplying it by the number of items in the population:

> D = d * N

c. Calculate the implied population audit value (the "point estimate") by adding the calculated difference for the population to the population's book value:

> AV = BV + D, where D can be either positive or negative

3. Construct a confidence (precision) interval around the population's audit value to compare to the client's recorded balance - beyond the scope of the CPA Examination.

B. **Ratio estimation --** This approach involves identifying the ratio of the audit values and book values for the sampled items.

1. Note that this approach is useful when the dollar-amount of the differences between the audit and the book values are expected to be proportional to the book values.

2. Sample size - as previously described.

3. Estimate the population's implied audit value:

a. Calculate the "ratio" for the sample, where the ratio has the sample's audit value in the numerator and the sample's book value in the denominator:

> R = av/bv

b. Estimate the population's audit value (a "point estimate") by multiplying the population's book value by that "ratio:"

AV = R * BV

4. Construct a confidence (precision) interval around the population's audit value to compare to the client's recorded balance - beyond the scope of the CPA Examination.

C. Mean-per-unit estimation (MPU)

1. Useful when difference or ratio estimation cannot be used - for example, for inventory when perpetual records do not exist (that is, there is no "book" value for each individual sample item).
2. Sample size - as previously described.
3. Estimate the population's implied audit value.
    a. Calculate the average audit value for items in the sample:

PU = av/n

    b. Multiply that average (MPU) times the number of items in the population:

AV = MPU * N

4. Construct a confidence (precision) interval around the population's audit value to compare to the client's recorded balance - beyond scope of CPA Exam!

D. Probability-proportional-to-size (PPS) sampling

1. The "sampling unit" is an individual dollar (when a given dollar is selected for the sample, it attaches to the related account or item which is then examined in its entirety); note that individually material items are automatically selected.
2. Useful if there are relatively few differences between audit and book values; otherwise, the sample size can become very large and the PPS application then becomes inefficient.
3. The main advantage is efficiency - it can achieve the maximum possible stratification (which then minimizes the effects of variability on sample size).
4. The main disadvantage is that PPS does not work very well in auditing negative balances (understatements) or zero (unrecorded) balances. Applies best to audit concerns involving overstatements (for example, accounts receivable or inventory when few misstatements are expected).
5. Note about determining sample size:

n = reliability factor * Book Value (from tables) / tolerable error

Example Problems

Difference Estimation Problem

I. **Calculating a "Point Estimate" --** Using statistical sampling to assist in verifying the year-end accounts payable balance, an auditor has accumulated the following data (based on a 1984 AICPA Exam question):

	No. of Accounts	Book Balance	Audit Value
Population	4100	$5,000,000	??
Sample	200	$250,000	$300,000

II. **Required --** Using **difference estimation**, calculate the implied value for the year-end accounts payable balance.

Difference Estimation Solution

I. **Calculating a "Point Estimate" --** Using statistical sampling to assist in verifying the year-end accounts payable balance, an auditor has accumulated the following data (based on a 1984 AICPA Exam question):

	No. of Accounts	Book Balance	Audit Value
Population	4100	\$5,000,000	??
Sample	200	\$250,000	\$300,000

II. **Required --** Using **difference estimation**, calculate the implied value for the year-end accounts payable balance.

A. First, calculate the average difference for items in the sample:

> d = (av - bv)/n => (\$300,000 - \$250,000)/ 200 = \$250

B. Second, extend that average difference to the population by multiplying it by the number of items in the population:

> D = d * N => \$250 * 4100 = \$1,025,000

C. Third, estimate the population's audit value by adding that difference to the population's book value:

> AV = BV + D => \$5,000,000 + \$1,025,000 = **\$6,025,000**

> **Exam Tip:** Even though ratio estimation and difference estimation calculate different "point estimates," that does not mean that the auditor would reach different conclusions about the fairness of the client's book balance. The calculation of the applicable confidence intervals would also differ accordingly. However, the calculation of confidence intervals is currently beyond the scope of the CPA exam.

Ratio Estimation Problem

I. **Calculating a "Point Estimate" --** Using statistical sampling to assist in verifying the year-end accounts payable balance, an auditor has accumulated the following data (based on a 1984 CPA Exam question):

	No. of Accounts	Book Balance	Audit Value
Population	4100	$5,000,000	??
Sample	200	$250,000	$300,000

II. **Required --** Using **ratio estimation**, calculate the implied value for the year-end accounts payable balance.

Ratio Estimation Solution

I. **Calculating a "Point Estimate" --** Using statistical sampling to assist in verifying the year-end accounts payable balance, an auditor has accumulated the following data (based on a 1984 CPA Exam question):

	No. of Accounts	Book Balance	Audit Value
Population	4100	$5,000,000	??
Sample	200	$250,000	$300,000

II. **Required --** Using **ratio estimation**, calculate the implied value for the year-end accounts payable balance.

"Ratio" = av/bv => $300,000/$250,000 = 1.2

A. Estimated population Audit Value = "ratio" * population Book Value

=> 1.2 * $5,000,000 = **$6,000,000**

MPU Estimation Problem

I. **Calculating a "Point Estimate" --** Using statistical sampling to assist in verifying the year-end accounts payable balance, an auditor has accumulated the following data (based on a 1984 CPA Exam question):

	No. of Accounts	Book Balance	Audit Value
Population	4100	$5,000,000	??
Sample	200	$250,000	$300,000

II. **Required --** Using **mean-per-unit estimation**, calculate the implied value for the year-end accounts payable balance.

MPU Estimation Solution

I. **Calculating a "Point Estimate" --** Using statistical sampling to assist in verifying the year-end accounts payable balance, an auditor has accumulated the following data (based on a 1984 CPA Exam question):

	No. of Accounts	**Book Balance**	**Audit Value**
Population	4100	$5,000,000	??
Sample	200	$250,000	$300,000

II. **Required --** Using **mean-per-unit estimation**, calculate the implied value for the year-end accounts payable balance.

A. First, calculate the "mean-per-unit" (that is, the average audit value for items in the sample):

MPU = av/n => $300,000/200 = $1500 per unit

B. Second, calculate the implied audit value for the population by multiplying that MPU times the number of items in the population:

av = MPU * N => $1500 * 4100 = **$6,150,000**

Exam Tip: Even though MPU estimation calculates a different "point estimate" than ratio estimation or difference estimation, it does not mean that the auditor would reach different conclusions about the fairness of the client's book balance. The calculation of the applicable confidence intervals would also differ accordingly. However, the calculation of confidence intervals is currently beyond the scope of the CPA exam.

PPS Sampling Problem

I. **A Numerical Problem -- Sample Size for PPS Sampling**

II. Hill has decided to use probability-proportional-to-size (PPS) sampling, sometimes called dollar-unit sampling, in the audit of a client's accounts receivable balances. Hill plans to use the following PPS sampling table:

Reliability Factors for Errors of Overstatement					
Number of Overstatements	**Risk of Incorrect Acceptance**				
	1%	**5%**	**10%**	**15%**	**20%**
0	4.61	3.00	2.31	1.90	1.61
1	6.64	4.75	3.89	3.38	3.00
2	8.41	6.30	5.33	4.72	4.28
3	10.05	7.76	6.69	6.02	5.52
4	11.61	9.16	8.00	7.27	6.73

Additional Information	
Tolerable misstatement (net of effect of expected misstatement)	$ 24,000
Risk of incorrect acceptance	20%
Number of misstatements allowed	1
Recorded amount of accounts receivable	$240,000
Number of accounts	360

III. **Required --** What sample size should Hill use?

PPS Sampling Solution

I. A Numerical Problem -- Sample Size for PPS Sampling

II. Hill has decided to use probability-proportional-to-size (PPS) sampling, sometimes called dollar-unit sampling, in the audit of a client's accounts receivable balances. Hill plans to use the following PPS sampling table:

Reliability Factors for Errors of Overstatement					
Number of Overstatements	Risk of Incorrect Acceptance				
	1%	5%	10%	15%	20%
0	4.61	3.00	2.31	1.90	1.61
1	6.64	4.75	3.89	3.38	3.00
2	8.41	6.30	5.33	4.72	4.28
3	10.05	7.76	6.69	6.02	5.52
4	11.61	9.16	8.00	7.27	6.73

Additional Information	
Tolerable misstatement (net of effect of expected misstatement)	$ 24,000
Risk of incorrect acceptance	20%
Number of misstatements allowed	1
Recorded amount of accounts receivable	$240,000
Number of accounts	360

III. Required -- What sample size should Hill use?

A. n = reliability factor from tables* Book Value / tolerable error

B. => (3.0 * $240,000) / $24,000 = **30**

IT (Computer) Auditing

IT Controls - General Controls

After studying this lesson, you should be able to:

1. *Understand the meaning of the term "general controls" relevant to an IT (computerized) environment.*
2. *Know the five categories of such general controls.*

I. **The Study and Evaluation of Internal Control --** This is somewhat different in a computerized environment:

   A. **The basic control objectives are the same, however!**

   B. Particular considerations in an Electronic Data Processing (EDP) (often referred to as an Information Technology (IT)) environment:

      1. A **disadvantage** is that the **segregation of duties** may be undermined -- If someone gets unauthorized access to the computer system, it may be difficult to separate incompatible activities.

      2. Another **disadvantage** is that the usual **audit trail may be lacking.** (There may be no "paper trail" auditors are accustomed to following.)

      3. An **advantage** is that **computer processing is uniform** -- Computers don't have "good" days and "bad" days; if a particular transaction is processed correctly one time, an identical transaction will be processed correctly, too.

   C. The **specific evidence gathering procedures** may differ.

II. **General Controls --** Controls that have pervasive effects on all the specific applications; there are five categories of "general controls:"

   A. **Organization and Operation**

      1. **Segregation of duties --** Especially within the EDP department; also between the EDP and various user departments.

      2. Focus on the **primary areas of responsibility** -- As much as possible, try to separate the following activities within the EDP department:

         a. **Systems analyst --** Responsible for designing the system.

         b. **Programmer --** Responsible for writing the code that makes up the programs.

         c. **Operator --** Responsible for running the system.

         d. **Librarian --** Responsible for keeping track of the programs and files and verifying that access is limited to authorized personnel.

         e. **Security --** Responsible for protecting the programs and data files and implementing procedures to safeguard the system.

   B. **Systems development and documentation --** Regarding the appropriate authorization and documentation of new systems; any changes should be appropriately documented.

   C. **Hardware and systems software**

      1. **"Built In" Controls**

         a. **Parity check --** Especially related to transmissions of information between system hardware components. (A "bit" added to each character so that the loss of any portion of the data might be detected.)

b. **Echo check --** Especially related to transmissions of information over the phone lines. (A signal that what was "sent" was, in fact, "received.")

c. **Diagnostic routines --** That check internal operations of hardware components (usually when booting up the system).

d. **Boundary protection --** For running multiple jobs concurrently.

2. **Operating system --** Controls and instructions built into the software that runs the hardware.

D. **Access --** The access to data, software, and the hardware should be limited to authorized personnel.

E. **Data and procedures --** Including physical safeguards that can protect the data files:

1. **File labels --** Internal and external labels that might prevent using a file for an unintended or inappropriate use.

2. **File protection rings --** A processing control related to magnetic tapes that prevents critical data from being over written (similar to a "read only" switch on a floppy disk).

3. **File protection plans --** Duplicates or prior generations. ("Grandfather" and "father" versions that can be used to recreate a current file by updating earlier files with current transaction data.)

IT Controls - Application Controls

After studying this lesson, you should be able to:

1. *Understand the meaning of the term "application controls" relevant to an IT (computerized) environment.*
2. *Know the three categories of application controls (input, processing, and output) and specific examples of controls associated with each such category.*

I. **Application Controls --** Related to the specific computer processing applications; now the emphasis is placed on the specific input, processing, and output activities.

A. **Input**

1. **Objectives --** That the input of data is accurate and as authorized.
2. **Examples**

a. **Preprinted forms --** So that employees will know exactly where to look for particular items of information.

b. **Keypunch --** Verification/duplication.

c. **Control totals --** Where useful comparisons are made to verify that all of the data were input properly.

i. **"Batch totals" --** Totals that actually mean something (for example, the day's cash withdrawals at an ATM location).

ii. **"Hash totals" --** Totals that have no meaningful interpretation per se, even though a total can be arithmetically determined (for example, adding up employees' social security numbers to verify that no employees were dropped from a payroll application).

iii. **Record count --** Keeping track of the number of records processed to determine that the appropriate number was accounted for.

d. **Logic checks --** Refers to certain computer edit routines that might signal when erroneous data have been input:

i. **Limit tests --** Are the data all within some predetermined range? (For example, a payroll program may specify an upper limit for how many hours can be legitimately worked.)

ii. **Validity checks --** Are the data recognized as legitimate possibilities (for example, gender codes could only be "M" or "F")?

iii. **Missing data checks --** Are there any omissions from any fields in which data should have been present?

iv. **Check digits --** A check digit is an arithmetic manipulation of a numerical field that captures the information content of that field and then gets "tacked" onto the end of that numeric field.

e. **Error resolution procedures --** Whenever the control procedures flag a data input problem, there should be procedures to pull out the item, fix the problem, and then put the item back in line for data entry.

B. **Processing**

1. **Objectives --** That the processing of data is accurate and as authorized.

2. **Examples**

    a. **Control totals --** Same as for the corresponding section under "Input" above.

    b. **Checkpoint/restart --** For particularly long processing runs, there should be built in "checkpoint/restart" procedures so that, if the program crashes, it does not have to be restarted from the very beginning.

    c. **Limit on processing time --** A predetermined limit for computer processing time might be specified; if that time is exceeded, the program can assume an error has occurred and shut down the processing run.

    d. **Internal (e.g., "headers") and external labels --** Should be used on all files to reduce the likelihood of mistakes caused by using the wrong files.

    e. **Error resolution procedures (the same idea as for "input") --** Whenever the control procedures flag a data processing problem, there should be procedures to pull out the item, fix the problem, and then put the item back in line for the necessary data processing.

C. **Output**

1. **Objectives --** That the output of data (and the distribution of any related reports) is accurate and as authorized.

2. **Examples**

    a. **Control totals (same idea as for "Input" and "Processing")**

    b. **Output limits --** A predetermined page (or time) limit might be specified; if those limits are exceeded, the program can assume an error has occurred and stop the output activity.

    c. **Error resolution procedures --** (the same idea as for "Input" and "Processing"). Whenever the control procedures flag a data output problem, there should be procedures to pull out the item, fix the problem, and then put the item back in line for proper output.

IT Evidence-Gathering Procedures

The auditor's evidence gathering procedures may be affected by a computerized environment -- "auditing through the computer" (as opposed to "auditing around the computer").

After studying this lesson, you should be able to:

1. *Understand the costs and benefits associated with developing generalized audit software versus customizing software to a specific entity's circumstances.*
2. *Understand specific procedures that the auditor may perform in an IT environment to test relevant controls.*

I. **Audit Software (focus is on substantive test work) --** Especially to access the client's files, but may also be used to help achieve the audit objectives:

A. **Generalized software --** Canned audit programs to access and test client's files; initially expensive to develop, but can be efficient if used on numerous engagements.

B. **Customized software --** Programs specifically written to access the files of a particular client; may be cheaper in the short-run, but more expensive in the long-run if such costs are incurred for many clients.

C. **Data mining software --** Commercially available software (such as ACL or Idea) can be easily used to access client's electronic data and perform a broad range of substantive audit tasks (such as performing analytical procedures and sampling for confirmation work).

II. **Procedures Related to Tests of Controls --** When those IT-related controls are internal and unobservable:

A. **Test data --** Introducing "dummy" transactions under the auditor's control:

1. Include some known errors to test the client's internal controls by checking whether the client's system catches those known errors.
2. The auditor need not include every possible type of error; include only those kinds of errors that are of interest to the auditor.
3. But be careful not to contaminate the client's database.

B. **Integrated test facility (ITF) --** Create a fictitious division or department within the client and process the "dummy" data along with the client's "live" data; again, be careful not to contaminate the client's actual files.

C. **Parallel simulation --** Processing the client's actual data on the auditor's software and then comparing auditor's output to client's output for agreement.

D. **Tagging specific client transactions and tracing them through the client's system --** Such "tagging" is analogous to an electronic tag attached to an animal in the wilderness so that researchers can follow the animal's movement.

E. **Embedded Audit Modules --** and audit hooks) - Systems that don't have a permanent audit trail require that any "auditing" occurs while processing take place.

Note:
Test data, ITF, and parallel simulation test how well the client's systems work (after the fact), especially in detecting errors.

Note:
Tagging, embedding audit modules, and audit hooks test the working of the system while processing takes place.

1. **Embedded audit modules --** Routines that are built into the application program to perform an on-going audit function.

2. **Audit hooks --** An exit point that is built into the application program where an audit module can be added subsequently.

> **Note:**
> Inquiry, observation, and inspection can be used to gather evidence about external, observable EDP-related controls that are not otherwise documented.

Other IT Considerations

After studying this lesson, you should be able to:

1. *Understand a variety of other terms and concepts associated with processing and networking in an IT environment.*

I. **Hardware versus Software**

  A. **Hardware --** The central processing unit (CPU) and all the other related equipment.

  B. **Software --** The systems programs and all the applications programs:

    1. **Operating system --** The set of instructions that runs the CPU and the related peripheral equipment.

    2. **Compiler --** Translates the source program into object program:

      a. **Source program --** Written in a specific programming language (for example, FORTRAN, COBOL).

      b. **Object program --** The instructions in machine readable form.

II. **Modes of Operation --** Related to when the transactions are processed:

  A. **Batch processing --** When transactions are collected for periodic processing (for example, daily updates for an ATM machine).

  B. **On-line, real-time processing**

    1. **"On-line" --** Means that the user is in direct communication with the computer's central processing unit (CPU).

    2. **"Real-time" --** Means that the data files are immediately updated.

III. **Service Organizations --** Independent computer centers may be engaged to process a client's transactional data; using such a service organization is a form of "out-sourcing" and represents an alternative to having a company's own IT department.

IV. **Distributed Systems --** Involves a single database, which is literally distributed across multiple computers connected by a communication link - in other words, a network of remote computers connected to the main system (i.e. a "host" server) whereby each location can then have input/output, processing, and printing capabilities.

V. **Database Systems --** A set of interconnected files that eliminates the redundancy associated with maintaining separate files for different subsets of the organization; a key concern is limiting the users' access to the appropriate parts of the database as authorized.

VI. **"Hierarchical" vs. "Relational" Database Structures**

  A. **Hierarchical --** Data elements at one level encompass the data elements immediately below (constructed like a company's "organizational chart") - these structures are largely outdated.

  B. **Relational --** An integrated database having the structure of a spreadsheet (where each row consists of fields related to a particular customer or item and each column consists of a specific information field that is applicable to each customer or item).

VII. **Networks --** Basic definitions

  A. **Local area network (LAN) --** A network of hardware and software interconnected throughout a building or campus (usually limited to a few miles in scope).

  B. **Wide area network (WAN) --** A larger version of a LAN that might span a whole city or country.

C. **Value added network (VAN) --** A network that facilitates "EDI" transactions (see the section on e-commerce below) between the buying and selling companies in such transactions, but the VAN is maintained by an independent company.

D. **Internet --** A worldwide network of privately controlled computers.

E. **Intranet --** A local area network that uses Internet technology to facilitate communications throughout a particular organization (perhaps using a "firewall" to insulate the organization's system from unauthorized, outside entry).

F. **Extranet --** Same as "Intranet," except that important external constituents (e.g. major customers or suppliers) are also connected.

VIII. Electronic Commerce

A. **Electronic funds transfer (EFT) --** Involves the transfer of monies between financial accounts (usually associated with financial institutions).

B. **Electronic data interchange (EDI) --** Involves an electronic transaction between companies (one is selling, the other is buying).

1. The usual hard copy documents (e.g., purchase orders, sales invoices) don't exist!
2. The goal is greater efficiency and less paperwork - should result in lower receivable/payable balances.
3. **Point-to-point (point of sale) transactions --** Involve direct computer-to-computer communication between the parties.
4. **Value Added Network --** As indicated above, an independent company may develop the electronic infrastructure to facilitate these electronic business activities (along with support services).

IX. Using the Internet -- Security and information reliability remain major concerns, although no direct investment is specifically required to engage in e-commerce transactions. (Note that the AICPA developed "*WebTrust*" as an assurance service to address such concerns for a consumer/buyer.)

Audit Reports

Introduction to Audit Reports

After studying this lesson, you should be able to:

1. *Know how to accurately state the four Standards of Reporting of GAAS.*
2. *Know the structure and content of the "standard unqualified" audit report.*
3. *Know the various audit report types that are alternatives to the "standard unqualified" audit report.*

I. **The Four Standards of Reporting of GAAS --** Recall the memory aid "GCDO" representing the "key" words to remember the standards: GAAP, Consistency, Disclosure, and Opinion.

A. **First Standard of Reporting --** The auditor must state in the auditor's report whether the financial statements are presented in accordance with generally accepted accounting principles (GAAP).

1. Note that this is an "explicit" requirement - the auditor should specifically mention GAAP (or other applicable accounting framework) in expressing an opinion on the fairness of the financial statements.

B. **Second Standard of Reporting --** The auditor must identify in the auditor's report those circumstances in which such principles (GAAP) have not been consistently observed in the current period in relation to the preceding period.

1. Note that this is an "implicit" requirement - if there has been no change in the accounting measurement principles used, then the auditor would not mention consistency in the auditor's report.

C. **Third Standard of Reporting --** When the auditor determines that informative disclosures are not reasonably adequate, the auditor must so state in the auditor's report.

1. Note that this is an "implicit" requirement - if disclosure is adequate then the auditor would not mention disclosure in the auditor's report.

D. **Fourth Standard of Reporting --** The auditor must either express an opinion regarding the financial statements, taken as a whole, or state that an opinion cannot be expressed, in the auditor's report. When the auditor cannot express an overall opinion, the auditor should state the reasons therefore in the auditor's report. In all cases where an auditor's name is associated with financial statements, the auditor should clearly indicate the character of the auditor's work, if any, and the degree of responsibility the auditor is taking, in the auditor's report.

1. Note that the third word of the introductory paragraph of the auditor's report clearly indicates the nature of the association with the entity's financial statements: "We have audited ...."

II. **Standard Unqualified Report --** Consists of three paragraphs.

A. **Introductory paragraph (three sentences) --** (1) Identify the nature of the engagement and the subject matter involved; (2) identify management's responsibility; and (3) identify the auditor's responsibility.

B. **Scope paragraph (five sentences) --** Identify the standards applicable to the audit and describe what an audit consists of: (1) that the audit was conducted according to GAAS; (2) that the audit provides reasonable assurance about material misstatement;

(3) that evidence is gathered on a test basis; (4) an audit includes assessing the accounting principles used and significant estimates made by management; and (5) express a belief that the audit provides a reasonable basis for the opinion.

C. **Opinion paragraph (one sentence) --** Express an opinion that the financial statements are fairly stated in conformity with GAAP (or other applicable accounting framework).

Standard Unqualified Auditor's Report

Independent Auditor's Report

We have audited the balance sheets of ABC Company at December 31, 20X2 and 20X1, and the related statements of income, retained earnings, and cash flows for the years then ended. These financial statements are the responsibility of the Company's management. Our responsibility is to express an opinion on these financial statements based on our audits.

We conducted our audits in accordance with auditing standards generally accepted in the United States of America. Those standards require that we plan and perform the audit to obtain reasonable assurance about whether the financial statements are free of material misstatement. An audit includes examining, on a test basis, evidence supporting the amounts and disclosures in the financial statements. An audit also includes assessing the accounting principles used and significant estimates made by management, as well as evaluating the overall financial statement presentation. We believe that our audits provide a reasonable basis for our opinion.

In our opinion, the financial statements referred to above present fairly, in all material respects, the financial position of ABC Company at December 31, 20X2 and 20X1, and the results of their operations and their cash flows for the years then ended, in conformity with accounting principles generally accepted in the United States of America.

/s/ CPA firm (signed by audit engagement partner)

Date (The auditor's report should not be dated earlier than the date on which the auditor has obtained sufficient appropriate audit evidence to support the opinion.)

III. **Alternatives to the Standard Unqualified Audit Report --** These are discussed in detail in subsequent lessons.

A. **Unqualified but modified audit report --** An unqualified audit report that contains differences in reporting language relative to the standard unqualified audit reporting language.

B. **Qualified audit report --** An audit report in which the auditor expresses one or more reservations about (1) the financial statement presentation (i.e., a qualification for a GAAP departure) or (2) the audit engagement (i.e., a scope limitation that prevents the auditor from gathering certain desired audit evidence); the auditor nonetheless expresses an overall opinion that the financial statements are fairly stated despite identifying the particular reservation(s).

C. **Adverse audit report --** An audit report in which the auditor states that the financial statements are not fairly stated (can only be due to an accounting measurement issue that causes the financial statement presentation to be misleading).

D. **Disclaimer of opinion --** An audit report in which the auditor does not express any opinion on the fairness of the financial statements (either because of an impairment in the auditor's independence or because of a serious scope limitation that prevented the auditor from obtaining sufficient appropriate evidence as a reasonable basis for an expression of opinion).

Unqualified but Modified - Three Paragraphs

After studying this lesson, you should be able to:

1. *Identify the two circumstances that might result in modification of the "standard" unqualified audit report while still presenting the audit report in three paragraphs (introduction, scope, and opinion) and the language to be used in the auditor's report to address each of those circumstances.*

I. **"Modifications" Relative to the So-Called "Standard" Unqualified Audit Report --** While still expressing an unqualified opinion in an audit report consisting of three paragraphs.

A. **Limited reporting engagement --** When the auditor is reporting on just one of the basic financial statements (e.g., just the balance sheet); the only impact on the auditor's report is to replace the usual reference to "financial statements" (plural) with the appropriate reference to the "balance sheet" (singular).

Sample Audit Report for a Limited Reporting Engagement

Independent Auditor's Report

We have audited the accompanying balance sheet of ABC Company as of December 31, 20X1. This financial statement is the responsibility of the Company's management. Our responsibility is to express an opinion on this financial statement based on our audit.

We conducted our audit in accordance with auditing standards generally accepted in the United States of America. Those standards require that we plan and perform the audit to obtain reasonable assurance about whether the balance sheet is free of material misstatement. An audit includes examining, on a test basis, evidence supporting the amounts and disclosures in the balance sheet. An audit also includes assessing the accounting principles used and significant estimates made by management, as well as evaluating the overall balance sheet presentation. We believe that our audit of the balance sheet provides a reasonable basis for our opinion.

In our opinion, the balance sheet referred to above presents fairly, in all material respects, the financial position of ABC Company as of December 31, 20X1, in conformity with accounting principles generally accepted in the United States of America.

II. **The Auditor's Report Based in Part on the Report of Other Auditors** -- The principal auditor may convey a **division of responsibility** when other auditors participate in part of the overall audit engagement; the principal auditor still has the ultimate responsibility for the audit conclusions expressed:

A. The principal auditor is not required to make reference to the participation of other auditors -- Usually make that reference when other auditors have been involved to a material degree (unless the other auditors are with an affiliated firm, in which case, no mention would be made).

1. **Procedures --** Inquire about the other auditors' professional reputation and obtain their representation as to independence (may request to review their audit programs and working papers, too).
2. **Reporting --** If the principal auditor decides to mention the involvement of other auditors, usually identify the proportion of the financial statements audited by them (Note: usually mention them as "other auditors" but not specifically by name).

B. Reference to the other auditors affects each paragraph of the audit report to some extent.

Sample Audit Report Indicating a Division of Responsibility

Independent Auditor's Report

We have audited the consolidated balance sheets of ABC Company and subsidiaries as of December 31, 20X2 and 20X1, and the related consolidated statements of income, retained earnings, and cash flows for the years then ended. These financial statements are the responsibility of the Company's management. Our responsibility is to express an opinion on these financial statements based on our audits. **We did not audit the financial statements of B Company, a wholly-owned subsidiary, which statements reflect total assets of $______ and $______ as of December 31, 20X2 and 20X1, respectively, and total revenues of $______ and $______ for the years then ended. Those statements were audited by other auditors whose report has been furnished to us, and our opinion, insofar as it relates to the amounts included for B Company, is based solely on the report of the other auditors.**

We conducted our audits in accordance with auditing standards generally accepted in the United States of America. Those standards require that we plan and perform the audit to obtain reasonable assurance about whether the financial statements are free of material misstatement. An audit includes examining, on a test basis, evidence supporting the amounts and disclosures in the financial statements. An audit also includes assessing the accounting principles used and significant estimates made by management, as well as evaluating the overall financial statement presentation. **We believe that our audits and the report of other auditors provide a reasonable basis for our opinion.**

In our opinion, **based on our audits and the report of other auditors**, the consolidated financial statements referred to above present fairly, in all material respects, the financial position of ABC Company and subsidiaries as of December 31, 20X2 and 20X1, and the results of their operations and their cash flows for the years then ended in conformity with accounting principles generally accepted in the United States of America.

The "division of responsibility" affects each paragraph of the auditor's report (as indicated here in **bold**), although the introductory paragraph is most affected. The introductory paragraph is the only place where the other auditor's relative involvement is specified in terms of the balance sheet and income statement amounts audited by other auditors.

Unqualified but Modified - Four Paragraphs

After studying this lesson, you should be able to:

1. *Identify the circumstances that might result in an unqualified audit report containing an explanatory paragraph.*
2. *State the auditor's responsibilities with respect to "supplementary information" (including supplementary information that is required by recognized accounting standard-setting bodies, reporting on supplementary information in relation to the financial statements, and supplementary information which is otherwise included in a document containing the audited financial statements).*
3. *Identify the one specific circumstance requiring the explanatory paragraph to precede the opinion paragraph of an unqualified audit report.*

> **Note:**
> Instances where the "explanatory paragraph" **must follow** the opinion paragraph.

I. **"Modification" --** "Modifications" (relative to the "standard" unqualified audit report) involving the presence of an "**explanatory paragraph**," while still expressing an unqualified opinion -- the resulting unqualified audit report consists of four paragraphs.

II. **Uncertainties (Including "Going Concern" Issues)**

A. When the outcome of financial statement-related uncertainties is not susceptible to reasonable estimation and the auditor cannot determine whether the entity's financial statements should be modified (e.g., when the auditor has substantial doubt about the entity's ability to continue as a going concern);

B. If the financial statement treatment is inconsistent with the requirements of GAAP or other applicable accounting framework (e.g., disclosure is inadequate) -- then the auditor should treat the matter as a GAAP departure and modify the audit report accordingly;

C. If the financial statement treatment (including disclosure) is consistent with the requirements of GAAP or other applicable accounting framework -- the auditor may add an explanatory paragraph following the opinion paragraph to clarify the surrounding issues.

III. **Inconsistency in the Application of Accounting Measurement Principles --** When the entity has a material change in its accounting measurement principles from one acceptable alternative to another acceptable alternative under GAAP (or other applicable accounting framework).

A. If the financial statement treatment is inconsistent with the requirements of GAAP or other applicable accounting framework -- then the auditor should treat the matter as a GAAP departure and modify the audit report accordingly;

B. If the financial statement treatment is consistent with the requirements of GAAP or other applicable accounting framework -- the auditor should draw attention to the accounting change by adding the explanatory paragraph following the opinion paragraph ;

C. Adding such an explanatory paragraph is how the auditor complies with the requirements of the Second Reporting Standard (regarding "consistency") of GAAS -- if no reference to consistency is made in the auditor's report, financial statement readers may presume that there were no material changes in accounting principles relative to any prior year financial statements that are presented.

IV. Required Supplementary Information -- the auditor's responsibility with respect to information that a designated accounting standard setter (e.g., the FASB, GASB, or FASAB) requires to accompany an entity's basic financial statements for the purpose of placing the basic financial statements in an appropriate operational, economic, or historical context is the focus of SAS No. 120, "Required Supplementary Information."

[See "AU558 (SAS 120) - Required Supplementary Information"]

A. Procedures To Be Performed with Respect to Required Supplementary Information

1. Inquire of management about the methods of preparing the information (including whether it is presented according to prescribed guidelines; whether the methods of measurement/presentation have changed relative to the prior period; and whether any significant assumptions are applicable);
2. Compare the information for consistency (with the basic financial statements, with management responses to audit inquiries, and other knowledge obtained during the audit of the entity's financial statements);
3. Inform those charged with governance of any significant difficulties encountered with management over required supplementary information.

B. Reporting -- The auditor should add an explanatory paragraph (after the opinion paragraph) to refer to the required supplementary information as appropriate.

1. When the required supplementary information is included and the auditor has performed the necessary procedures (and there are no material departures from applicable accounting guidelines);
2. When the required supplementary information is omitted (or when some of the required supplementary information is missing and some is presented);
3. When material departures from prescribed guidelines have been identified;
4. When the auditor has doubts as to whether the required supplementary information is presented in accordance with prescribed guidelines;
5. When the auditor is unable to perform the required procedures.

C. Note that the required supplementary information is outside of the basic financial statements, so the auditor's opinion cannot be affected by the presentation or omission of that information

V. Reporting on Supplementary Information in Relationship to the Financial Statements -- (Excluding "required supplementary information") -- The auditor's responsibility when engaged to report on the fairness of supplementary information in relation to an entity's financial statements is the focus of SAS No. 119, "Supplementary Information in Relation to the Financial Statements as a Whole."

[See "AU551 (SAS 119) - Information Accompanying Documents"]

> **Note:**
> Instances where the "explanatory paragraph" **may either precede or follow** the opinion - note that it is always acceptable to place the explanatory paragraph after the opinion paragraph.

A. Procedures to be performed with respect to the supplementary information -- The auditor should use the same materiality level as for the financial statements.

1. Inquire of management about the purpose of the supplementary information and the criteria used to prepare it;
2. Inquire of management about any significant assumptions used;
3. Obtain an understanding about the methods (and consistency of methods) used;
4. Compare/reconcile the supplementary information to the financial statements or to the underlying records used for the financial statements;

5. Determine whether the supplementary information complies with applicable criteria;
6. Evaluate the appropriateness and completeness of the supplementary information based on the audit of the entity's financial statements;
7. Obtain required written representations from management.

B. **Reporting --** When reporting on supplementary information in relation to the financial statements, the auditor should either (1) add an explanatory paragraph after the opinion paragraph; or (2) issue a separate report on the supplementary information.

1. If the auditor expresses an adverse opinion or disclaimer of opinion on the financial statements -- the auditor cannot express an opinion on the supplementary information;
2. If the auditor believes the supplementary information is misstated -- discuss proposed revision with management; and if management does not revise the information, the auditor should modify the opinion on the supplementary information (or withhold the auditor's separate report on it).

C. These provisions also apply when the audited financial statements are "readily available" to intended users of the supplementary information -- "readily available" means the user can obtain the audited financial statements without further action by the entity (e.g., being available upon request is not considered readily available).

VI. **Emphasis of a Matter --** Since the audit report is the responsibility of the auditor, the auditor may emphasize any matters considered important (e.g., to describe the significance of related party transactions or the status of major litigation).

VII. **Other Information in a Document Containing the Audited Financial Statements**

[See "AU550 (SAS 118) - Other Information in Documents"]

A. The auditor's responsibilities with respect to the other information.

1. The auditor should read the other information to identify material inconsistencies with the audited financial statements.
2. The auditor should communicate the auditor's responsibility regarding the other information to those charged with governance.
3. For material "inconsistencies" identified in other information obtained <u>prior</u> to the audit report release date -- if management refuses to make appropriate revisions, the auditor should communicate the matter with those charged with governance and either (a) include an explanatory paragraph in the auditor's report to describe the inconsistency; (b) withhold the auditor's report; or (c) withdraw from the engagement (if that is permitted under applicable law or regulation).
4. For material "inconsistencies" identified in other information obtained <u>subsequent</u> to the audit report release date -- the auditor may review the steps taken by management to ensure that those receiving the previously issued financial statements are informed of the need for revision to the other information; if management refuses to make appropriate revision, the auditor should notify those charged with governance (and take further action, such as seeking advice from the auditor's legal counsel)
5. For material "misstatements of fact" (that is, incorrect presentation of other information that is unrelated to matters in the audited financial statements) -- the auditor should discuss the matter with management and encourage management to consult with a qualified third party (such as legal counsel); if management refuses to make appropriate revisions, the auditor should communicate the matter with those charged with governance (the auditor may also decide to withhold the auditor's report or withdraw from the engagement, subject to advice from the auditor's legal counsel).

B. Including an explanatory paragraph -- The auditor is not required to reference the other information in the auditor's report, but may choose to include an explanatory paragraph so that readers will not infer an unintended level of assurance regarding the other information.

C. Examples of "other information" -- (1) A report by management (or those charged with governance) on operations; (2) financial summaries or highlights; (3) employment data; (4) planned capital expenditures; (5) financial ratios; (6) names of officers and directors; and (7) selected quarterly data (note that information contained in analyst briefings or contained on the entity's Web site is specifically excluded as "other information").

> **Note:**
> Current auditing standards do not differentiate between other information in document prepared by the client entity versus other information in an "auditor-submitted document," which was a distinction in earlier auditing standards that have now been superseded.

VIII. Omitted Quarterly Data for SEC Registrants ("Issuers")

A. If quarterly data required under Regulation S-K has been omitted - the auditor of the entity's financial statements should add an explanatory paragraph to the auditor's report pointing out that fact.

B. If the quarterly data has been presented, but not reviewed according to applicable standards - the auditor of the entity's financial statements should add an explanatory paragraph to the auditor's report disclaiming an opinion on that data.

IX. Unusual Circumstances Requiring Departure from Promulgated GAAP

A. This gives auditors a somewhat hypothetical "trap door" in the event of some peculiar and unforeseen circumstance whereby adherence to an official accounting standard would itself cause an entity's financial statements to become misleading. "Fairly stated" financial statements is the most important consideration, so departure from such an accounting standards would be justified along with a required explanatory paragraph.

> **Note:**
> In one instance, the "explanatory paragraph" **must precede** the opinion paragraph.

B. Note that there is a very strong presumption that complying with accounting pronouncements issued by recognized standard-setting bodies (such as the FASB) will not cause misleading financial statements, so the auditor would have the substantial burden of justifying such a departure from promulgated GAAP.

X. When the Opinion on the Prior Period's Financial Statements Differs from the Opinion Previously Expressed

A. Suppose, for example, that a qualified opinion was expressed on last year's financial statements due to a GAAP departure that management refused to adjust; further suppose that management has now corrected the previously identified deficiency, so that an unqualified opinion can now be given on when those (corrected) financial statements are presented for comparative purposes.

B. The explanatory paragraph must come before the opinion paragraph to prepare readers for a different conclusion than what was expressed in the prior period .

Qualified for Scope Limitation

After studying this lesson, you should be able to:

1. *Understand when and how to express a qualified audit opinion for a scope limitation affecting the auditor's basis for conclusions.*

I. **Meaning of a "Qualified" Opinion --** The auditor is expressing one or more reservations either about the financial statement presentation (that is, a "GAAP departure") or about the basis for the auditor's conclusions (that is, a "scope limitation" where the auditor was unable to perform a desired audit procedure) while still concluding that the financial statements, taken as a whole, are fairly stated and that the auditor has obtained sufficient, appropriate audit evidence as a reasonable basis for the auditor's conclusions.

II. **Scope Limitation --** When the auditor has been unable to perform a desired audit procedure.

A. If the auditor is able to perform other procedures to adequately compensate for the inability to perform a specific audit procedure, then there is no need to mention the inability to perform a specific procedure.

B. If the auditor is not able to perform other procedures to adequately compensate for the inability to perform a specific audit procedure, but nonetheless believes that sufficient, appropriate audit evidence has been obtained as a reasonable basis for conclusions about the financial statements taken as a whole -- the auditor can express a qualified opinion for a scope limitation.

> **Example:**
> The auditor has been unable to obtain audited financial statements for an investee entity when the investment is accounted for using the "equity method" and the period's investment income is based on the investor's share of the investee's net income (or perhaps a client's record retention policy may have eliminated some documentary evidence), but alternative audit procedures are viewed as adequate.

1. Resulting auditor's report.

   a. Same introductory paragraph.

   b. **Scope paragraph --** The first sentence is modified to: "Except as discussed in the following paragraph, we conducted our audits in accordance with auditing standards generally accepted in the United States of America."

   c. **Explanatory paragraph --** (Preceding the opinion) to explain the specific scope limitation and prepare the reader to understand why the resulting opinion is qualified;

   d. **Opinion paragraph --** The beginning of the sentence is modified to: "In our opinion, except for the effects of such adjustments, if any, as might have been determined to be necessary had we been able to gather evidence regarding ..."

Sample Audit Report Qualified for Scope Limitation

Independent Auditor's Report

Same first paragraph as the standard report.

Except as discussed in the following paragraph, we conducted our audits in accordance with auditing standards generally accepted in the United States of America. Those standards require that we plan and perform the audit to obtain reasonable assurance about whether the financial statements are free of material misstatement. An audit includes examining, on a test basis, evidence supporting the amounts and disclosures in the financial statements. An audit also includes assessing the accounting principles used and significant estimates made by management, as well as evaluating the overall financial statement presentation. We believe that our audits provide a reasonable basis for our opinion.

We were unable to obtain audited financial statements supporting the Company's investment in a foreign affiliate stated at $______ and $______ at December 31, 20X2 and 20X1, respectively, or its equity in earnings of that affiliate of $______ and $______, which is included in net income for the years then ended as described in Note X to the financial statements; nor were we able to satisfy ourselves as to the carrying value of the investment in the foreign affiliate or the equity in its earnings by other auditing procedures.

In our opinion, **except for the effects of such adjustments, if any, as might have been determined to be necessary had we been able to examine evidence regarding the foreign affiliate investment and earnings**, the financial statements referred to in the first paragraph above present fairly in all material respects, the financial position of ABC Company as of December 31, 20X2 and 20X1, and the results of its operations and its cash flows for the years then ended in conformity with accounting principles generally accepted in the United States of America.

C. If a scope limitation is so severe as to prevent the auditor from obtaining sufficient appropriate audit evidence to afford a reasonable basis for an opinion -- the auditor would express a "disclaimer of opinion" (which is discussed in a separate lesson).

Qualified for GAAP Departure

After studying this lesson, you should be able to:

1. *Understand when and how to express a qualified audit opinion for a GAAP departure affecting the fair presentation of an entity's financial statements.*

I. **Meaning of a "Qualified" Opinion --** The auditor is expressing one or more reservations either about the financial statement presentation (that is, a "GAAP departure") or about the basis for the auditor's conclusions (that is, a "scope limitation" where the auditor was unable to perform a desired audit procedure) while still concluding that the financial statements, taken as a whole, are fairly stated and that the auditor has obtained sufficient, appropriate audit evidence as a reasonable basis for the auditor's conclusions.

II. **GAAP Departure (or Departure from Other Applicable Accounting Framework) --** A qualified opinion would be expressed when the GAAP departure is material, but the financial statements taken as a whole are still viewed as fairly stated (for inadequate disclosures or deficiencies in the application of accounting measurement principles).

A. For inadequate disclosure (including omissions of required information):

1. If practicable, include the omitted (or correcting) information in the auditor's report;

2. The auditor would not be expected to prepare an omitted statement of cash flows or present omitted segment information in the auditor's report. The AICPA has withdrawn an earlier SAS on "segment information" citing the applicability of AU431 ("Adequacy of Disclosure"). The auditor should determine whether the entity's financial statements comply with the requirements of GAAP, including that dealing with segment information specifically. If required information is omitted, the auditor should express a qualified or an adverse opinion, as applicable, and provide the information in the auditor's report "if practicable."

Sample Audit Report Qualified for Inadequate Disclosure

Independent Auditor's Report

Same first and second paragraphs as the standard report.

The Company's financial statements do not disclose (**describe the nature of the omitted disclosures**). In our opinion, disclosure of this information is required by accounting principles generally accepted in the United States of America.

In our opinion, **except for the omission of the information discussed in the preceding paragraph**, ...

See the following sample report.

Sample Audit Report Qualified for Inadequate Disclosure (Omission of Cash Flows)

Independent Auditor's Report

We have audited the accompanying balance sheets of ABC Company as of December 31, 20X2 and 20X1, and the related statements of income and retained earnings for the years then ended. These financial statements are the responsibility of the Company's management. Our responsibility is to express an opinion on these financial statements based on our audit.

Same second paragraph as the standard report.

The Company declined to present a statement of cash flows for the years ended December 31, 20X2 and 20X1. Presentation of such statement summarizing the Company's operating, investing, and financing activities is required by accounting principles generally accepted in the United States of America.

In our opinion, **except that the omission of a statement of cash flows results in an incomplete presentation as explained in the preceding paragraph**, the financial statements referred to above present fairly, in all material respects, the financial position of ABC Company as of December 31, 20X2 and 20X1, and the results of its operations for the years then ended in conformity with accounting principles generally accepted in the United States of America.

[See "AU431 (SAS 32) - Adequacy of Disclosure"]

B. For deficiencies in the application of accounting measurement principles (e.g., not capitalizing lease obligations as required by GAAP) -- if practicable, the auditor's report should identify the financial statement effects of the misapplication of GAAP (or departures from other applicable accounting framework).

Sample Audit Report Qualified for Accounting Principles

Independent Auditor's Report

Same first and second paragraphs as the standard report.

The Company has excluded, from property and debt in the accompanying balance sheets, certain lease obligations that, in our opinion, should be capitalized in order to conform with accounting principles generally accepted in the United States of America. If these lease obligations were capitalized, property would be increased by $______ and $______, long-term debt by $______ and $______, and retained earnings by $______ and $______ as of December 31, 20X2 and 20X1, respectively. Additionally, net income would be increased (decreased) by $______ and $______ and earnings per share would be increased (decreased) by $______ and $______, respectively, for the years then ended.

In our opinion, **except for the effects of not capitalizing certain lease obligations as discussed in the preceding paragraph**, the financial statements referred to above present fairly, in all material respects, the financial position of ABC Company as of December 31, 20X2 and 20X1, and the results of its operations and its cash flows for the years then ended in conformity with accounting principles generally accepted in the United States of America.

C. Resulting auditor's report:

1. Same introductory paragraph;
2. Same scope paragraph;

3. Explanatory paragraph (preceding the opinion) to explain the specific GAAP departure and prepare the reader to understand why the resulting opinion is qualified;
4. **Opinion paragraph --** For a deficiency in disclosure, the beginning of the sentence is modified to: "In our opinion, **except for the omission of the information discussed in the preceding paragraph,** ..."; for a deficiency in the application of accounting principles, the beginning of the sentence is modified to: "In our opinion, **except for the effects of not capitalizing certain lease obligations as discussed in the preceding paragraph,** ..."

D. If a GAAP departure (or departure from another applicable accounting framework) is so severe as to cause the financial statements to be misleading taken as a whole (that is, not fairly stated) -- the auditor would express an "adverse opinion" (which is discussed in a separate lesson).

Adverse Opinion

After studying this lesson, you should be able to:

1. *Understand how to express an adverse audit opinion due to a GAAP departure causing an entity's financial statements to be misleading.*

I. **Meaning of an "Adverse" Opinion --** The auditor expresses a conclusion that the financial statements taken as a whole are not fairly stated (which can only be caused by a major GAAP departure -- or departure from another applicable accounting framework --that renders the financial statement presentation misleading).

II. **Resulting Auditor's Report**

A. Same introductory paragraph;

B. Same scope paragraph;

C. One or more explanatory paragraph(s) to explain the specific GAAP departure and prepare the reader to understand why the adverse opinion is expressed;

D. **Opinion paragraph --** For an adverse opinion, the opinion paragraph is modified to: "In our opinion, because of the effects of the matters discussed in the preceding paragraph(s), the financial statements referred to above do not present fairly, in conformity with accounting principles generally accepted in the United States of America, the financial position of ABC Company as of December 31, 20X2 and 20X1, or the results of its operations or its cash flows for the years then ended."

Sample Audit Report for an Adverse Opinion

<u>Independent Auditor's Report</u>

Same first and second paragraphs as the standard report.

As discussed in Note X to the financial statements, the Company carries its property, plant and equipment accounts at appraisal values, and provides depreciation on the basis of such values. Further, the Company does not provide for income taxes with respect to differences between financial income and taxable income arising because of the use, for income tax purposes, of the installment method of reporting gross profit from certain types of sales. Generally accepted accounting principles require that property, plant and equipment be stated at an amount not in excess of cost, reduced by depreciation based on such amount, and that deferred income taxes be provided.

Because of the departures from generally accepted accounting principles identified above, as of December 31, 20X2 and 20X1, inventories have been increased $_____ and $_____ by inclusion in manufacturing overhead of depreciation in excess of that based on cost; property, plant and equipment, less accumulated depreciation, is carried at $_____ and $_____ in excess of an amount based on the cost to the Company; and deferred income taxes of $_____ and $_____ have not been recorded; resulting in an increase of $_____ and $_____ in retained earnings and in appraisal surplus of $_____ and $_____, respectively. For the years ended December 31, 20X2 and 20X1, cost of goods sold has been increased $_____ and $_____, respectively, because of the effects of the depreciation accounting referred to above and deferred income taxes of $_____ and $_____ have not been provided, resulting in an increase in net income of $_____ and $_____, respectively.

In our opinion, **because of the effects of the matters discussed in the preceding paragraphs, the financial statements referred to above do not present fairly, in conformity with accounting principles generally accepted in the United States of America, the financial position of ABC Company as of December 31, 20X2 and 20X1, or the results of its operations or its cash flows for the years then ended.**

III. **GAAP Departure --** If a GAAP departure (or departure from an other applicable accounting framework) is material, but less severe such that the financial statements taken as a whole are viewed as "fairly stated" -- the auditor would express a "qualified opinion" (which is discussed in a separate lesson).

Disclaimer of Opinion

After studying this lesson, you should be able to:

1. Understand when and how to express a disclaimer of opinion.

I. When the "Auditor" is Associated with Unaudited Financial Statements or When Lacking Independence

A. Guidance is provided by SAS 26, "Association with Financial Statements"

[See "AU504 (SAS 26) - Association with Financial Statements"]

B. Report consists of one sentence

1. **When associated with unaudited financial statements --** "... the financial statements were not audited by us and, accordingly, we do not express an opinion on them."
2. **When lacking independence --** "We are not independent with respect to ... the financial statements and, accordingly, we do not express an opinion on them." (Note: Do **NOT** try to describe the details as to why independence is lacking -- that might be misunderstood.)

C. Clearly **mark each page** of the financial statements as **"UNAUDITED"** -- to prevent readers from misunderstanding.

D. Do not describe any procedures that may have been performed -- Again, that might be misunderstood.

E. Must modify the disclaimer to point out the effects of any known GAAP departures -- That is, known deficiencies related to the financial statements cannot be ignored just because a disclaimer is given.

II. Major Scope Limitation -- Where the auditor is unable to gather sufficient appropriate evidence required as a basis for the opinion. (Omit the usual scope paragraph!)

A. Due to client imposed limitations -- for example, senior management refuses to sign the management representations letter.

B. Or due to other circumstances -- for example, due to weak internal controls, the auditor cannot be reasonably sure that all cash sales have been captured by the client's accounting system.

See the following example.

Sample Audit Report for a Disclaimer of Opinion Due to Scope

Independent Auditor's Report

We were engaged to audit the accompanying balance sheets of ABC Company as of December 31, 20X2 and 20X1, and the related statements of income, retained earnings, and cash flows for the years then ended. These financial statements are the responsibility of the Company's management.

Second paragraph of standard report (about scope) should be omitted.

The Company did not make a count of its physical inventory in 20X2 or 20X1, stated in the accompanying financial statements at $_____ as of December 31, 20X2, and at $_____ as of December 31, 20X1. Further, evidence supporting the cost of property and equipment acquired prior to December 31, 20X1, is no longer available. The Company's records do not permit the application of other auditing procedures to inventories or property and equipment.

Since the Company did not take physical inventories and we were not able to apply other auditing procedures to satisfy ourselves as to inventory quantities and the cost of property and equipment, the scope of our work was not sufficient to enable us to express, and we do not express, an opinion on these financial statements.

Reports on Comparative Financial Statements

After studying this lesson, you should be able to:

1. *Modify the continuing auditor's report when different types of opinions are expressed for the current year's financial statements and the prior year's financial statements that are presented on a comparative basis.*
2. *Identify the appropriate reporting treatment when the prior year's financial statements have been audited by other auditors ("predecessor"), depending upon whether the predecessor's previous audit report is presented or is not presented along with the current ("successor") auditor's report on the current period's financial statements.*

Reference in the fourth reporting standard to the financial statements taken as a whole applies not only to the financial statements of the current period, but also to those of one or more prior periods that are "presented on a comparative basis ...." (SAS 26).

Note: Financial statements are usually presented on a "comparative basis," meaning that the current year financial statements are presented along with one or more prior year's financial statements serving as a reference point to the reader. The auditor is not required to express the same type of opinion on the current year as in the prior year. The opinion should be appropriate to the financial statements of a given period, but need not be the same for each period presented on a comparative basis. When the auditor has audited each period's financial statements that are presented, the auditor's report should encompass the periods presented.

I. **Prior Year Qualified, Current Year Unqualified --** For example, the auditor may express an unqualified opinion on the prior year's financial statements and a qualified opinion on the current year's financial statements.

   [See Sample Report "Prior Year Qualified, Current Year Unqualified"]

II. **Prior Year Disclaimer, Current Year Unqualified --** For example, the auditor may express a disclaimer of opinion on the prior year's income statement, statement of retained earnings, and cash flows; and express an unqualified opinion on the current year's financial statements.

   [See Sample Report "Prior Year Disclaimer, Current Year Unqualified"]

III. **Different Opinion than Previously Expressed --** When the opinion now expressed on the prior year's financial statements is different from the opinion previously expressed on those financial statements (e.g., management has now corrected a GAAP departure that previously resulted in a qualified opinion), an explanatory paragraph must be added <u>prior</u> to the opinion paragraph to prepare the reader for this change in the opinion expressed.

   [See Sample Report "Different Opinion than Previously Expressed"]

Note:
When an entity has changed auditors and the new auditor (successor) has audited the current period's financial statements and the former auditor (predecessor) has audited the prior period's financial statements, financial statements should still be presented on a comparative basis.

IV. **Predecessor's Report Reissued for Comparison --** When the predecessor auditor's report will be reissued for comparison with the current year's financial statements, the predecessor auditor should consider whether the previous report is still appropriate:

A. Read the current year's financial statements (and the successor auditor's audit report) and compare with the prior year's financial statements for consistency.

B. The predecessor auditor should obtain an updated representation letter from management documenting the fact that nothing affects the financial statements as previously reported.

V. **Predecessor's Report Not Presented --** When the predecessor auditor's report is **not** presented along with the current year's audit report, the successor auditor should modify the introductory paragraph to indicate the following:

A. State that the prior year's financial statements were audited by other auditors.

B. Identify the date and type of the report that was issued on the prior years' financial statements - whether unqualified, qualified, adverse, or disclaimer was issued.

C. Identify the reasons for any modification of the report, if other than a standard report.

[See Sample Report "Predecessor's Prior Year Report Not Presented"]

Omitted Procedures/Facts Discovered After Report

After studying this lesson, you should be able to:

1. *Understand the auditor's responsibility to perform omitted procedures that should have been performed prior to issuing the auditor's report.*
2. *Understand the auditor's responsibility upon discovering facts existing at the date of the auditor's report that suggest that the previously issued audit report is incorrect.*

I. **Consideration of Omitted Procedures After the Report Date --** What are the auditor's responsibilities upon realization that, subsequent to the issuance of the audit report, auditing procedures considered necessary were, in fact, omitted?

[See "AU390 (SAS 46) – Consideration of Omitted Procedures"]

A. Do nothing further if other redundant **auditing procedures that were performed compensate** for the omitted procedure.

B. More likely, the auditor will have to (belatedly) perform the omitted procedure(s):

1. If the results support the opinion already issued, document that fact in the working papers.
2. If the results conflict with the opinion already issued, the auditor should consult with legal counsel. (See the following section on Subsequent Discovery)

II. **Subsequent Discovery of Facts Existing at the Date of the Auditor's Report --** What should the auditor do if facts are discovered after the audit report has been issued that, if known earlier, would have changed the type of report issued? (Note that auditor ordinarily has no responsibility to continue the investigation of financial statements previously reported on ...):

[See "AU561 (SAS 1) - Subsequent Discovery"]

A. Request management's assistance to:

1. Inform all known users not to rely on the financial statements and the previous audit report.
2. Issue revised financial statements with an appropriate audit report as soon as possible.

B. If management does not provide the requested assistance:

1. Notify those charged with governance (such as each member of the board of directors) about management's lack of cooperation.
2. Notify management and those charged with governance, applicable regulators, and any known users that they should not rely on the previous financial statements and the auditor's report thereon.
3. Consult with an attorney about the auditor's legal liability exposure.

Other Reporting Topics

After studying this lesson, you should be able to:

1. *Understand the implications to the auditor when an entity's financial statements have been prepared for use exclusively outside of the United States.*
2. *Understand the reporting requirements to the auditor when associated with "condensed" financial statements or "selected" financial data.*
3. *Understand the auditor's responsibilities under the Securities Act of 1933 as stated in AICPA Professional Standards.*
4. *Recognize the circumstances that result in restricted distribution of the auditor's report and the language that should be used to restrict the use of the auditor's report.*
5. *Know how to "dual date" the auditor's report for a subsequent event issue, and understand the various meanings of the phrase "taken as a whole" and prohibition against "piecemeal" opinions.*

I. Reporting on Financial Statements Prepared for Use in Other Countries

[See "AU534 (SAS 51) - Reports for Other Countries"]

A. **Applicability --** When a U.S. auditor is engaged to report on a U.S. entity's financial statements prepared for use **exclusively** outside the U.S.

B. **Procedures**

1. Must follow U.S. **GAAS -- general and fieldwork standards.**
2. Must understand the foreign country's accounting principles -- Consult with others having appropriate expertise; may follow "international financial reporting standards." (IFRS)
3. Obtain management's written representation as to the intended use of these financial statements solely outside the U.S.

C. **Reporting**

1. If the financial statements are prepared for use solely outside U.S. -- the auditor has a choice as to the format of the audit report (may use either a modified version of the U.S. report or the format preferred in the foreign country).
2. If the financial statements are intended for distribution within U.S. -- must use the U.S. format for report (modified, if necessary, for departures from U.S. GAAP).

II. Reporting on Condensed Financial Statements and Selected Financial Data

[See "AU552 (SAS 42) - Selected Financial Data"]

A. **Applicability --** When reporting on condensed financial statements for an entity having complete audited financial statements filed with regulators; or when reporting on selected financial data presented in a document that includes the audited financial statements.

B. **Reporting considerations**

1. State that the auditor has reported on the complete financial statements -- Indicate the date and type of report issued.
2. Indicate whether the condensed financial statement information is fairly stated relative to the complete set of audited financial statements.

Note:
This information should be clearly marked "condensed" -- This is **NOT GAAP**, since many important disclosures are omitted.

III. **Filings Under Federal Securities Statutes**

[See "AU711 (SAS 37) – Filings Under Federal Security Statutes"]

A. **Responsibilities under Federal securities statutes - the Securities Act of 1933 --** promotes fair disclosure and prohibits fraud in initial public offerings of securities.

1. **Management's** responsibilities are the same as with the financial statements used for other purposes - that is, the financial statements are the representations of management.
2. The **independent accountant's** responsibilities are similar to other types of reporting - Section 11 of the 1933 Act prohibits false or misleading statements (or material omissions) in registration statements.
   a. Section 11 defense - after a reasonable investigation, the independent accountant had reasonable grounds to believe that the financial statements were fairly stated (but the CPA has the burden of proof).
   b. Statutory responsibility is determined in light of the circumstances on the effective date of the registration statement.
   c. The CPA should read the relevant parts of any prospectus filed under the 1933 Act to verify that the independent accountant's name is not being used inappropriately. (Note that a "prospectus" is an informational document required to be filed with the SEC in connection with a registration statement to offer securities for sale; the prospectus cannot be used to finalize sales of such securities until the registration statement is declared effective by the SEC.)
   d. When the registration statement references the interim financial information reviewed by the accountant - the prospectus should clearly indicate that the review report is not part of the registration statement within the meaning of the 1933 Act.

B. **Subsequent events procedures in connection with filings under the Securities Act of 1933**

1. Extend the procedures regarding subsequent events from the audit report date up to (or as near as practicable) to the effective date of the registration statement.
2. Following field work, the auditor may usually rely on inquiries of appropriate client personnel - obtain written representations from management regarding those financial and accounting matters.
3. An auditor who has reported on the financial statements from prior periods, but not the most recent audited financial statements included in the registration statement, is responsible for events subsequent to the date of the prior-period's audited financial statements.
   a. Should read the applicable portions of the prospectus and registration statement.
   b. Should obtain a letter of representations from the successor auditor as to whether the successor's audit identified any matters that might have a material effect on the prior period's financial statements.

Note:
For guidance related to subsequent events and subsequently discovered facts -- see AU560 and AU561.

IV. Restricting the Use of an Auditor's Report

A. Guidance is provided by SAS 87, "Restricting the Use of an Auditor's Report."

[See "AU532 (SAS 87) - Restricting the Use of an Auditor's Report"]

B. "Restricted use" reports are restricted to specified parties, whereas "general use" reports are unrestricted.

C. Reports *must be restricted* for any of three reasons

1. **The report is based on criteria (from contracts or regulations) that are not GAAP or "other comprehensive basis of accounting" --** restrict the report to the parties to the contract or to the applicable regulatory agency.
2. **The report is based on specific procedures requested by specified parties who take responsibility for the sufficiency of those procedures --** restrict the report to those specified parties.
3. **The report is issued as a "by product" of the financial statement audit --** a "by product" report is incidental to the audit, not the primary focus of the engagement.
   - **a.** Examples: reports on internal control matters noted in an audit, matters communicated to those charged with governance, or reports on compliance with contractual or regulatory requirements.
   - **b.** Distribution should be restricted to the following: those charged with governance (e.g., audit committee or board of directors); management; or others within the organization; parties to the contract; or a specified regulatory agency.

D. Language used for a restricted-use report

1. Add a separate paragraph at the end of the report - "This report is intended solely for the information and use of (the specified parties) and is not intended to be and should not be used by anyone other than the specified parties."
2. Restriction should be clearly identified, but the auditor is not responsible for preventing the client's unauthorized distribution of the restricted-use report.

V. Miscellaneous

A. "Dual dating" the report -- The audit report should be dated when sufficient appropriate audit evidence has been obtained (which cannot precede the last day of fieldwork):

1. The audit report may specify a later date applicable to a particular footnote added to the financial statements (for example, when addressing a "subsequent event").
2. An example of dual dating would be dating the audit report as follows: "February 16, 20xx, except for Note Y, as to which the date is March 1, 20xx."
3. Dating the entire report as of that single, later date (when the subsequent event issue was addressed) would imply that the auditor was responsible for gathering evidence broadly applicable to the financial statements up to that later date.

B. "Piecemeal" opinions -- Describing different conclusions about selected elements of the financial statements than expressed about the financial statements "taken as a whole:"

1. **"Taken as a whole" --** Includes the individual financial statements (such as the balance sheet by itself); the current year's set of financial statements; and the set of current year's financial statements along with any prior years' financial statements included for comparative purposes.

2. "Piecemeal" opinions on audited financial statements are prohibited - The auditor cannot comment that certain elements within the financial statements are fairly stated, while disclaiming or expressing an adverse opinion on the financial statements taken as a whole.

3. A CPA can be engaged to issue a "special report" (different than an "audit report"), which might involve attesting to the fairness of one or more individual elements of the financial statements; but, again, that is a distinctly different type of engagement than auditing the financial statements taken as a whole. (Special reports are addressed in a separate lesson of CPAexcel.)

Review Report on Interim Financial Statements

After studying this lesson, you should be able to:

1. *Understand the objective of a review of interim financial information of a nonissuer and the conditions that are required to conduct such a review.*
2. *Distinguish between the auditing standards that are applicable to a review of interim financial information for an issuer and for a nonissuer.*
3. *Describe the procedures that are applicable to a review of interim financial information (whether for an issuer or a nonissuer).*
4. *Understand how to express a review report on interim financial information subject to AICPA standards (whether for an issuer or a nonissuer).*

> **Note:** In 2003, the PCAOB adopted the AICPA's then-existing Professional Standards on a transitional basis. Those standards included SAS No. 100 ("Interim Financial Information"), which continues to apply to reviews of interim financial information of "issuers." In 2009, the AICPA issued SAS No. 116 ("Interim Financial Information"), which supersedes SAS No. 100 and applies to reviews of interim financial information of "nonissuers," since responsibility for guidance applicable to issuers resides with the PCAOB. As a practical matter, the requirements of SAS Nos. 100 and 116 are very similar, although not identical.

Reviewing the Interim Financial Information of a "Issuer"

[See Previous "AU722 (SAS 100) - Interim Financial Information"]

I. Applicability

A. SAS No. 100 continues to govern a review of an issuer's "interim financial information," defined as information or statements covering a period less than a full year (or for a 12-month period ending on a date different than the entity's fiscal year-end)

II. Objective

A. To provide the accountant with a basis for communicating whether material modifications are known that should be made for the interim financial information to comply with GAAP

III. Procedures Associated with such a Review

A. Read the information -- including minutes of board meetings and "other information" accompanying the interim information in reports to regulatory agencies or holders of securities

B. Analytical procedures -- perform appropriate analytical procedures to evaluate the reasonableness of the financial items involved

C. Inquiry -- inquire of management and other appropriate personnel about a variety of specific issues relevant to the financial information; obtain a required management representations letter to document these important inquiries

D. Documentation -- the principal record of the procedures performed and conclusions reached; should include any findings or issues considered to be "significant"

IV. Example Report (as presented in the PCAOB's Auditing Standard No. 1)

Report of Independent Registered Public Accounting Firm

We have reviewed the accompanying (describe the interim financial information or statements reviewed) of ABC Company as of September 30, 20X3 and 20X2, and for the three-month and nine-month periods then ended. This interim financial information (statements) is (are) the responsibility of the company's management.

We conducted our review in accordance with the standards of the Public Company Accounting Oversight Board (United States). A review of interim financial information consists principally of applying analytical procedures and making inquiries of persons responsible for financial and accounting matters. It is substantially less in scope than an audit conducted in accordance with the standards of the Public Company Accounting Oversight Board, the objective of which is the expression of an opinion regarding the financial statements taken as a whole. Accordingly, we do not express such an opinion.

Based on our review, we are not aware of any material modifications that should be made to the accompanying interim financial information (statements) for it (them) to be in conformity with U.S. generally accepted accounting principles.

/Signature/

/City and State or Country/

/Date/

Reviewing the Interim Financial Information of a "Nonissuer"

[See "AU722 (SAS 116) - Interim Financial Information"]

I. Applicability

A. SAS No. 116 applies when performing reviews of "interim financial information" of nonissuers (e.g., non-public companies participating in private equity exchanges or otherwise preparing interim financial information that conforms with SEC requirements); this SAS removes the earlier guidance for reviews involving "issuers," since such guidance is now under the authority of the PCAOB.

B. Interim financial information - financial information or statements covering a period less than a full year or for a 12-month period ending on a date other than the entity's fiscal year end (may be condensed or in the form of a complete set of financial statements).

C. Conditions for conducting a review of interim financial information - (1) the entity's most recent annual financial statements have been audited (either by the accountant or a predecessor); (2) the accountant has been engaged to audit the entity's current-year financial statements (or has audited the latest annual financial statements and expects to be engaged to audit the current year); (3) the client prepares its interim financial information in accordance with the same reporting framework used for annual purposes; and (4) if the information is "condensed," several additional conditions exist.

II. Objective of the Review of the Interim Information -- To provide the accountant with a basis for communicating an awareness of any material modifications that should be made to conform with the applicable financial reporting framework (such as GAAP or other comprehensive basis of accounting).

III. Procedures Applicable to the Interim Financial Information -- Mostly inquiries and analytical procedures:

A. Read the information -- Read the interim financial information for consistency with the applicable financial reporting framework; read the minutes of the meetings of those charged with governance (and any committees thereof) and of shareholders; and obtain evidence that the interim information agrees/reconciles with the accounting records.

B. **Analytical procedures --** Expectations developed for a review of interim information tend to be less precise than those developed for an audit.

1. Compare the current and preceding interim financial information for reasonableness; and compare the interim and year-to-date information with the corresponding period(s) of the prior year.
2. Consider the apparent reasonableness of interrelationships (involving both financial and non-financial information, as applicable) - may wish to consider information in a director's information package or in a senior committee's briefing materials.
3. Compare the client's recorded amounts with the auditor's expectations in view of current economic conditions and industry events.
4. Compare disaggregated revenue data - e.g., compare revenue reported by month and by product line or by business segment for the current interim period with comparable prior periods.

C. **Inquire --** Of persons responsible for financial and accounting matters; and must obtain written representations from management for all interim information presented and for all periods covered by the review regarding:

1. The financial information: management's responsibility, etc.
2. Internal control issues (including any changes since the prior year's audit) about management's responsibilities for programs and controls to prevent and detect fraud, and management's knowledge of any fraud or suspected fraud, including any allegations from employees, former employees, or others.
3. The completeness and availability of information.
4. A variety of recognition, measurement, and disclosure issues.
5. Any subsequent events and litigation issues. Usually do not send a "letter of inquiry" to the entity's lawyer(s) when reviewing interim information.
6. Other matters as deemed appropriate, for example, may inquire about management's plans when a going concern issue has been identified (however, need not obtain evidence to corroborate any "mitigating factors").

IV. **Review Report on a Nonissuer's Interim Financial Information --** Usually consists of three paragraphs:

A. Identify the interim financial statements and indicate management's responsibility;

B. Indicate adherence to AICPA standards; describe the procedures for a review; indicate that the scope is "substantially less" than an audit and disclaim opinion;

C. Express conclusions in the form of "**negative assurance**" that "we are not aware of any material modifications that should be made ..." (modify as necessary for any known deficiencies).

See the following example.

Independent Accountant's Report

We have reviewed the accompanying (describe the interim financial information or statements reviewed) of ABC Company and consolidated subsidiaries as of September 30, 20X1, and for the three-month and nine-month periods then ended. This interim financial information is the responsibility of the company's management.

We conducted our review in accordance with standards established by the American Institute of Certified Public Accountants. A review of interim financial information consists principally of applying analytical procedures and making inquiries of persons responsible for financial and accounting matters. It is substantially less in scope than an audit conducted in accordance with auditing standards generally accepted in the United States, the objective of which is the expression of an opinion regarding the financial statements taken as a whole. Accordingly, we do not express such an opinion.

Based on our review, we are not aware of any material modifications that should be made to the accompanying interim financial information for it to be in conformity with (identify the applicable financial reporting framework; for example, accounting principles generally accepted in the United States of America).

/Signature/

/Date/

D. Note that each page of the interim information should be clearly marked "unaudited."

E. Modification of the accountant's review report:

1. Departure from the applicable financial reporting framework - add appropriate modification in an explanatory paragraph before the concluding paragraph.
2. Inadequate disclosure (note that disclosure requirements for interim information are less extensive than for annual financial statement purposes) - modify the report and provide the necessary disclosure, if practicable, in an explanatory paragraph before the concluding paragraph.
3. Going concern issues - if disclosure is adequate, the accountant is not required to modify the review report. However, the accountant may add an explanatory paragraph for emphasis after the concluding paragraph.

F. **Incomplete review --** When the accountant is unable to perform the procedures considered necessary to achieve the objectives of the review (e.g., management fails to provide the necessary written representations).

1. An incomplete review is not an adequate basis for issuing a review report.
2. The accountant should appropriately communicate any known material modifications that are necessary even if no review report is issued.

V. Additional Provisions of SAS No. 116

A. **Issuance of a written report --** An accountant is ordinarily **not required** to issue a written report on a review of interim financial information, unless the entity states in a written communication containing the interim financial information that it has been reviewed or otherwise references the accountant's association with it.

B. **Required knowledge of the entity's business and its internal control --** The accountant should obtain sufficient knowledge of the entity's business and its internal control related to the preparation of financial information to (1) identify the types and likelihood of potential material misstatements; and (2) tailor the specific inquiries and analytical procedures to the engagement.

C. **Provides guidance --** When performing an "initial review" - defined as when the accountant has not audited the financial statements of the previous year end.

1. Make appropriate inquiries of the predecessor accountant and review the predecessor's documentation to obtain knowledge of the entity's business and its internal control to plan the review engagement.
2. If unable to obtain that knowledge from the predecessor, the successor should perform alternative procedures to obtain the necessary knowledge of required matters.

D. **Establish an understanding in writing --** Requires the accountant to establish an understanding in writing with the client regarding the engagement to review interim financial information (including the objectives of the engagement; the limitations of the engagement; management's responsibilities; the accountant's responsibilities; and the expected form of the communication, whether written or oral).

E. **Provides guidance related to communications --** With management and those charged with governance regarding the review of interim financial information (such as the need for material modifications, possible fraud or illegal acts, significant deficiencies or material weaknesses in internal control, or other matters).

F. **Provides guidance regarding documentation requirements --** Should include any findings/issues considered to be "significant" (e.g., any indications that the interim information could be materially misstated, actions taken to address such findings, and the basis for the final conclusions reached).

Sample Reports

Standard Unqualified Report

Independent Auditor's Report

We have audited the balance sheets of ABC Company at December 31, 20X2 and 20X1, and the related statements of income, retained earnings, and cash flows for the years then ended. These financial statements are the responsibility of the Company's management. Our responsibility is to express an opinion on these financial statements based on our audits.

We conducted our audits in accordance with auditing standards generally accepted in the United States of America. Those standards require that we plan and perform the audit to obtain reasonable assurance about whether the financial statements are free of material misstatement. An audit includes examining, on a test basis, evidence supporting the amounts and disclosures in the financial statements. An audit also includes assessing the accounting principles used and significant estimates made by management, as well as evaluating the overall financial statement presentation. We believe that our audits provide a reasonable basis for our opinion.

In our opinion, the financial statements referred to above present fairly, in all material respects, the financial position of ABC Company at December 31, 20X2 and 20X1, and the results of their operations and their cash flows for the years then ended, in conformity with accounting principles generally accepted in the United States of America.

/s/ CPA firm (signed by audit engagement partner)

Date (The auditor's report should not be dated earlier than the date on which the auditor has obtained sufficient appropriate audit evidence to support the opinion.)

Standard Unqualified Report (Sentences)

Introductory Paragraph

We have audited the balance sheets of ABC Company at December 31, 20X2 and 20X1, and the related statements of income, retained earnings, and cash flows for the years then ended.

These financial statements are the responsibility of the Company's management.

Our responsibility is to express an opinion on these financial statements based on our audits.

Scope Paragraph

We conducted our audits in accordance with auditing standards generally accepted in the United States of America.

Those standards require that we plan and perform the audit to obtain reasonable assurance about whether the financial statements are free of material misstatement.

An audit includes examining, on a test basis, evidence supporting the amounts and disclosures in the financial statements.

An audit also includes assessing the accounting principles used and significant estimates made by management, as well as evaluating the overall financial statement presentation.

We believe that our audits provide a reasonable basis for our opinion.

Opinion Paragraph

In our opinion, the financial statements referred to above present fairly, in all material respects, the financial position of ABC Company at December 31, 20X2 and 20X1, and the results of their operations and their cash flows for the years then ended, in conformity with accounting principles generally accepted in the United States of America.

Limited Reporting Engagement

Independent Auditor's Report

We have audited the accompanying balance sheet of ABC Company as of December 31, 20X1. This financial statement is the responsibility of the Company's management. Our responsibility is to express an opinion on this financial statement based on our audit.

We conducted our audit in accordance with auditing standards generally accepted in the United States of America. Those standards require that we plan and perform the audit to obtain reasonable assurance about whether the balance sheet is free of material misstatement. An audit includes examining, on a test basis, evidence supporting the amounts and disclosures in the balance sheet. An audit also includes assessing the accounting principles used and significant estimates made by management, as well as evaluating the overall balance sheet presentation. We believe that our audit of the balance sheet provides a reasonable basis for our opinion.

In our opinion, the balance sheet referred to above presents fairly, in all material respects, the financial position of ABC Company as of December 31, 20X1, in conformity with accounting principles generally accepted in the United States of America.

Division of Responsibility

Independent Auditor's Report

We have audited the consolidated balance sheets of ABC Company and subsidiaries as of December 31, 20X2 and 20X1, and the related consolidated statements of income, retained earnings, and cash flows for the years then ended. These financial statements are the responsibility of the Company's management. Our responsibility is to express an opinion on these financial statements based on our audits. **We did not audit the financial statements of B Company, a wholly-owned subsidiary, which statements reflect total assets of $______ and $______ as of December 31, 20X2 and 20X1, respectively, and total revenues of $______ and $______ for the years then ended. Those statements were audited by other auditors whose report has been furnished to us, and our opinion, insofar as it relates to the amounts included for B Company, is based solely on the report of the other auditors.**

We conducted our audits in accordance with auditing standards generally accepted in the United States of America. Those standards require that we plan and perform the audit to obtain reasonable assurance about whether the financial statements are free of material misstatement. An audit includes examining, on a test basis, evidence supporting the amounts and disclosures in the financial statements. An audit also includes assessing the accounting principles used and significant estimates made by management, as well as evaluating the overall financial statement presentation. **We believe that our audits and the report of other auditors provide a reasonable basis for our opinion.**

In our opinion, **based on our audits and the report of other auditors**, the consolidated financial statements referred to above present fairly, in all material respects, the financial position of ABC Company and subsidiaries as of December 31, 20X2 and 20X1, and the results of their operations and their cash flows for the years then ended in conformity with accounting principles generally accepted in the United States of America.

Note:
The "division of responsibility" affects each paragraph of the auditor's report (as indicated here in **bold**), although the introductory paragraph is most affected. The introductory paragraph is the only place where the other auditor's relative involvement is specified in terms of the balance sheet and income statement amounts audited by other auditors.

Qualified for Inadequate Disclosure

Independent Auditor's Report

(Same first and second paragraphs as the standard report)

The Company's financial statements do not disclose **(describe the nature of the omitted disclosures)**. In our opinion, disclosure of this information is required by accounting principles generally accepted in the United States of America.

In our opinion, **except for the omission of the information discussed in the preceding paragraph**, ...

Qualified for Omission of Cash Flows

Independent Auditor's Report

We have audited the accompanying balance sheets of ABC Company as of December 31, 20X2 and 20X1, and the related statements of income and retained earnings for the years then ended. These financial statements are the responsibility of the Company's management. Our responsibility is to express an opinion on these financial statements based on our audit.

(Same second paragraph as the standard report.)

The Company declined to present a statement of cash flows for the years ended December 31, 20X2 and 20X1. Presentation of such statement summarizing the Company's operating, investing, and financing activities is required by accounting principles generally accepted in the United States of America.

In our opinion, **except that the omission of a statement of cash flows results in an incomplete presentation as explained in the preceding paragraph,** the financial statements referred to above present fairly, in all material respects, the financial position of ABC Company as of December 31, 20X2 and 20X1, and the results of its operations for the years then ended in conformity with accounting principles generally accepted in the United States of America.

Qualified for Accounting Principles

Independent Auditor's Report

(Same first and second paragraphs as the standard report.)

The Company has excluded, from property and debt in the accompanying balance sheets, certain lease obligations that, in our opinion, should be capitalized in order to conform with accounting principles generally accepted in the United States of America. If these lease obligations were capitalized, property would be increased by $______ and $______, long-term debt by $______ and $______, and retained earnings by $______ and $______ as of December 31, 20X2 and 20X1, respectively. Additionally, net income would be increased (decreased) by $______ and $______ and earnings per share would be increased (decreased) by $______ and $______, respectively, for the years then ended.

In our opinion, **except for the effects of not capitalizing certain lease obligations as discussed in the preceding paragraph**, the financial statements referred to above present fairly, in all material respects, the financial position of ABC Company as of December 31, 20X2 and 20X1, and the results of its operations and its cash flows for the years then ended in conformity with accounting principles generally accepted in the United States of America.

Qualified for Scope Limitation

Independent Auditor's Report

(Same first paragraph as the standard report.)

Except as discussed in the following paragraph, we conducted our audits in accordance with auditing standards generally accepted in the United States of America. Those standards require that we plan and perform the audit to obtain reasonable assurance about whether the financial statements are free of material misstatement. An audit includes examining, on a test basis, evidence supporting the amounts and disclosures in the financial statements. An audit also includes assessing the accounting principles used and significant estimates made by management, as well as evaluating the overall financial statement presentation. We believe that our audits provide a reasonable basis for our opinion.

We were unable to obtain audited financial statements supporting the Company's investment in a foreign affiliate stated at $______ and $______ at December 31, 20X2 and 20X1, respectively, or its equity in earnings of that affiliate of $______ and $______, which is included in net income for the years then ended as described in Note X to the financial statements; nor were we able to satisfy ourselves as to the carrying value of the investment in the foreign affiliate or the equity in its earnings by other auditing procedures.

In our opinion, **except for the effects of such adjustments, if any, as might have been determined to be necessary had we been able to examine evidence regarding the foreign affiliate investment and earnings**, the financial statements referred to in the first paragraph above present fairly in all material respects, the financial position of ABC Company as of December 31, 20X2 and 20X1, and the results of its operations and its cash flows for the years then ended in conformity with accounting principles generally accepted in the United States of America.

Adverse Opinion

Independent Auditor's Report

(Same first and second paragraphs as the standard report.)

As discussed in Note X to the financial statements, the Company carries its property, plant and equipment accounts at appraisal values, and provides depreciation on the basis of such values. Further, the Company does not provide for income taxes with respect to differences between financial income and taxable income arising because of the use, for income tax purposes, of the installment method of reporting gross profit from certain types of sales. Generally accepted accounting principles require that property, plant and equipment be stated at an amount not in excess of cost, reduced by depreciation based on such amount, and that deferred income taxes be provided.

Because of the departures from generally accepted accounting principles identified above, as of December 31, 20X2 and 20X1, inventories have been increased $_____ and $_____ by inclusion in manufacturing overhead of depreciation in excess of that based on cost; property, plant and equipment, less accumulated depreciation, is carried at $_____ and $_____ in excess of an amount based on the cost to the Company; and deferred income taxes of $_____ and $_____ have not been recorded; resulting in an increase of $_____ and $_____ in retained earnings and in appraisal surplus of $_____ and $_____, respectively. For the years ended December 31, 20X2 and 20X1, cost of good sold has been increased $_____ and $_____, respectively, because of the effects of the depreciation accounting referred to above and deferred income taxes of $_____ and $_____ have not been provided, resulting in an increase in net income of $_____ and $_____, respectively.

In our opinion, **because of the effects of the matters discussed in the preceding paragraphs, the financial statements referred to above do not present fairly, in conformity with accounting principles generally accepted in the United States of America, the financial position of ABC Company as of December 31, 20X2 and 20X1, or the results of its operations or its cash flows for the years then ended.**

Disclaimer of Opinion

Independent Auditor's Report

We were engaged to audit the accompanying balance sheets of ABC Company as of December 31, 20X2 and 20X1, and the related statements of income, retained earnings, and cash flows for the years then ended. These financial statements are the responsibility of the Company's management.

(Second paragraph of standard report (about scope) should be omitted.)

The Company did not make a count of its physical inventory in 20X2 or 20X1, stated in the accompanying financial statements at $_____ as of December 31, 20X2, and at $_____ as of December 31, 20X1. Further, evidence supporting the cost of property and equipment acquired prior to December 31, 20X1, is no longer available. The Company's records do not permit the application of other auditing procedures to inventories or property and equipment.

Since the Company did not take physical inventories and we were not able to apply other auditing procedures to satisfy ourselves as to inventory quantities and the cost of property and equipment, the scope of our work was not sufficient to enable us to express, and we do not express, an opinion on these financial statements.

Prior Year Unqualified, Current Year Qualified

<u>Independent Auditor's Report</u>

(Same first and second paragraphs as the standard report.)

The Company has excluded, from property and debt in the accompanying 20X2 balance sheet, certain lease obligations that were entered into in 20X2 which, in our opinion, should be capitalized in order to conform with accounting principles generally accepted in the United States of America. If these lease obligations were capitalized, property would be increased by $_____, long-term debt by $_____, and retained earnings by $_____ as of December 31, 20X2, and net income and earnings per share would be increased (decreased) by $_____ and $_____, respectively, for the year then ended.

In our opinion, **except for the effects on the 20X2 financial statements of not capitalizing certain lease obligations as described in the preceding paragraph,** the financial statements referred to above present fairly, in all material respects, the financial position of ABC Company as of December 31, 20X2 and 20X1, and the results of its operations and its cash flows for the years then ended in conformity with accounting principles generally accepted in the United States of America.

Prior Year Disclaimer, Current Year Unqualified

Independent Auditor's Report

(Same first paragraph as the standard report.)

Except as explained in the following paragraph, we conducted our audits in accordance with auditing standards generally accepted in the United States of America. Those standards require that we plan and perform our audit to obtain reasonable assurance about whether the financial statements are free of material misstatement. An audit includes examining, on a test basis, evidence supporting the amounts and disclosures in the financial statements. An audit also includes assessing the accounting principles used and significant estimates made by management, as well as evaluating the overall financial statement presentation. We believe that our audits provide a reasonable basis for our opinion.

We did not observe the taking of the physical inventory as of December 31, 20X0, since that date was prior to our appointment as auditors for the Company, and we were unable to satisfy ourselves regarding inventory quantities by means of other auditing procedures. Inventory amounts as of December 31, 20X0, enter into the determination of net income and cash flows for the year ended December 31, 20X1.

Because of the matter discussed in the preceding paragraph, the scope of our work was not sufficient to enable us to express, and we do not express, an opinion on the results of operations and cash flows for the year ended December 31, 20X1.

In our opinion, the balance sheets of ABC Company as of December 31, 20X2 and 20X1, and the related statements of income, retained earnings, and cash flows for the year ended December 31, 20X2, present fairly, in all material respects, the financial position of ABC Company as of December 31, 20X2 and 20X1, and the results of its operations and its cash flows for the year ended December 31, 20X2, in conformity with accounting principles generally accepted in the United States of America.

Different Opinion than Previously Expressed

Independent Auditor's Report

(Same first and second paragraphs as the standard report.)

In our report dated March 1, 20X2, we expressed an opinion that the 20X1 financial statements did not fairly present financial position, results of operations, and cash flows in conformity with generally accepted accounting principles because of two departures from such principles: (1) the Company carried its property, plant, and equipment at appraisal values, and provided for depreciation on the basis of such values, and (2) the Company did not provide for deferred income taxes with respect to differences between income for financial reporting purposes and taxable income. As described in Note X, the Company has changed its method of accounting for these items and restated its 20X1 financial statements to conform with generally accepted accounting principles. Accordingly, our present opinion on the 20X1 financial statements, as presented herein, is different from that expressed in our previous report.

In our opinion, the financial statements referred to above present fairly, in all material respects, the financial position of ABC Company as of December 31, 20X2 and 20X1, and the results of its operations and its cash flows for the years then ended in conformity with accounting principles generally accepted in the United States of America.

Predecessor's Prior Year Report Not Presented

<u>Independent Auditor's Report</u>

We have audited the balance sheet of ABC Company as of December 31, 20X2, and the related statements of income, retained earnings, and cash flows for the year then ended. These financial statements are the responsibility of the Company's management. Our responsibility is to express an opinion on these financial statements based on our audit. **The financial statements of ABC Company as of December 31, 20X1, were audited by other auditors whose report dated March 31, 20X2, expressed an unqualified opinion on those statements.**

(Same second paragraph as the standard report.)

In our opinion, the 20X2 financial statements referred to above present fairly, in all material respects, the financial position of ABC Company as of December 31, 20X2, and the results of its operations and its cash flows for the year then ended in conformity with accounting principles generally accepted in the United States of America.

Note:
The successor auditor now confines the opinion to the current year's financial statements audited, while noting the nature (and date) of the predecessor auditor's report on the prior year's financial statements presented for comparative purposes.

Other Types of Reports

Reports on Application of Accounting Principles

After studying this lesson, you should be able to:

1. *Understand an accountant's responsibilities under AICPA Professional Standards when engaged to express a written report or verbal advice about the application of an entity's accounting principles to specific transactions or the type of opinion that might be expressed on an entity's specific financial statements.*

[See "AU625, modified by SAS 97 (SAS 50) – Reports on the Application of Accounting Principles"]

I. **Applicability --** When giving a written report or verbal advice:

   A. On the application of accounting principles to "specific transactions" - SAS No. 97 prohibits issuing a written report on the application of accounting principles to a **hypothetical** transaction!

   B. On the type of opinion that might be issued on specific financial statements.

II. **Procedures --** Note that the "General Standards" apply.

   A. Obtain an understanding of the form and substance of the transaction(s) -- consult with the **"continuing accountant"** to verify the facts (must request permission from the client to initiate that contact).

   B. Review applicable GAAP - consider the appropriate analogies or precedents (consult with others if necessary).

III. **Reporting --** Any written report should be addressed to the principal(s) to the transaction or to their representatives.

   A. Briefly describe the nature of engagement and refer to the applicable AICPA standards.

   B. Describe the relevant facts, circumstances, and assumptions (identify the principals to any specific transactions).

   C. Conclusions -- describe the appropriate accounting principles to be applied or the resulting type of opinion to be issued (along with the underlying reasons).

   D. Point out that the preparers of the financial statements have the responsibility for the proper accounting treatment **and that they should consult with their continuing accountant.**

Special Reports

After studying this lesson, you should be able to:

1. *Understand the five specific topics associated with the AICPA's reference to "special reports" and the auditor's responsibilities under applicable AICPA Professional Standards.*

[See "AU623 (SAS 62) - Special Reports"]

The AICPA term "special reports" encompasses five specific topics: (1) financial statements prepared using a "comprehensive basis other than GAAP" (sometimes referred to as an "other comprehensive basis" of accounting); (2) auditing specified elements, accounts, or financial statement items (something less than a financial statement taken as a whole); (3) reporting on contractual or regulatory compliance issues in connection with audited financial statements; (4) reporting on special-purpose financial presentations to comply with contractual or regulatory requirements; and (5) reporting on financial information presented in prescribed forms or schedules.

I. **Financial Statements (Other Comprehensive Basis of Accounting -- OCBOA) --** Prepared under a comprehensive basis other than GAAP. Note the First Standard of Reporting of GAAS (regarding GAAP) does not apply.

   A. **Examples**

      1. Financial statements prepared following regulatory accounting principles, not GAAP (sometimes called "RAP accounting").
      2. Financial statements prepared using the cash-basis of accounting.
      3. Financial statements prepared using income tax principles.
      4. Financial statements prepared using any other definite criteria having "substantial support" (e.g., price-level basis of accounting).

   B. **Reporting --** Usually consists of four paragraphs (see the example of such a report):

      1. **Introduction --** Same as the standard audit report.
      2. **Scope --** Same as the standard audit report.
      3. **Explanatory --** Describe the basis used (refer to the appropriate financial statement note) and point out that the "other comprehensive basis" is not GAAP.
      4. **Opinion --** About the same as the standard audit report, but refer (again) to the financial statement note describing the basis used.

   See the following example.

Sample Audit Report for Financial Statements Prepared on the Cash Basis

Independent Auditor's Report

We have audited the accompanying statements of assets and liabilities arising from cash transactions of XYZ Company as of December 31, 20x2 and 20x1, and the related statements of revenue collected and expenses paid for the years then ended. These financial statements are the responsibility of the Company's management. Our responsibility is to express an opinion on these financial statements based on our audits.

We conducted our audits in accordance with auditing standards generally accepted in the United States of America. Those standards require that we plan and perform the audit to obtain reasonable assurance about whether the financial statements are free of material misstatement. An audit includes examining, on a test basis, evidence supporting the amounts and disclosures in the financial statements. An audit also includes assessing the accounting principles used and significant estimates made by management, as well as evaluating the overall financial statement presentation. We believe that our audits provide a reasonable basis for our opinion.

As described in Note X, these financial statements were prepared on the basis of cash receipts and disbursements, which is a comprehensive basis of accounting other than generally accepted accounting principles.

In our opinion, the financial statements referred to above present fairly, in all material respects, the assets and liabilities arising from cash transactions of XYZ Company as of December 31, 20x2 and 20x1, and its revenue collected and expenses paid during the years then ended, **on the basis of accounting described in Note X**.

Notice that the financial statements are named in a way to avoid confusing them with financial statements prepared under GAAP.

C. **Additional Reporting Considerations**

1. If using regulatory accounting principles -- restrict the distribution of the report to the company and applicable regulators.
2. Any reservations should be described in an additional explanatory paragraph (preceding the opinion paragraph).
3. Must evaluate the adequacy of disclosure -- but the auditor does **not** have to quantify the difference between GAAP and the other basis used.
4. Should be careful to label the financial statements in a way that would not be confused with financial statements prepared under GAAP.

II. **Reporting on Specified Elements, Accounts, or Financial Statement Items When Such Elements Have Been Audited --** Note that the Fourth Standard of Reporting of GAAS (regarding an opinion on the financial statements "taken as a whole") does not apply.

A. **Examples --** Rentals, royalties, profit participation, or provision for income taxes.

B. Note that **SAS No. 62 applies** when **auditing** these items.

C. SSAEs apply when "reviewing" individual elements of the financial statements.

D. **Reporting --** Usually consists of four paragraphs:

1. **Introduction --** Identify element(s) audited.
2. **Scope --** Indicate the audit work performed.
3. **Explanatory --** Describe the basis used (and refer to any relevant agreement or contract).

4. **Opinion --** About the same as standard audit report, but refer to the contract or financial statement note describing the basis used.

E. **Additional reporting considerations --** (See the example of such a report)

1. If presented to comply with a contract or other agreement (not GAAP) -- restrict the distribution of the report to the contracting parties.
2. If the specified item is based upon **net income** (e.g., profit participation) -- must have audited the complete financial statements to express an opinion on that "bottom-line" item (and the CPA must refer to that audit report on the financial statements taken as a whole).
3. Any reservations should be described in an additional explanatory paragraph (preceding the opinion).

Sample Audit Report on a Profit Participation

Independent Auditor's Report

We have audited, in accordance with generally accepted auditing standards, the financial statements of XYZ Company for the year ended December 31, 20x1, and have issued our report thereon, dated March 10, 20x2. We have also audited XYZ Company's schedule of Reed Smith's profit participation for the year ended December 31, 20x1. This schedule is the responsibility of the Company's management. Our responsibility is to express an opinion on this schedule based on our audit.

We conducted our audit of the schedule in accordance with auditing standards generally accepted in the United States of America. Those standards require that we plan and perform the audit to obtain reasonable assurance about whether the schedule of profit participation is free of material misstatement. An audit includes examining, on a test basis, evidence supporting the amounts and disclosures in the schedule. An audit also includes assessing the accounting principles used and significant estimates made by management, as well as evaluating the overall schedule presentation. We believe that our audit provides a reasonable basis for our opinion.

We have been informed that the documents that govern the determination of Reed Smith's profit participation are (a) the employment agreement between Reed Smith and XYZ Company dated February 1, 20x0, (b) the production and distribution agreement between XYZ Company and Television Network Incorporated dated March 1, 20x0, and (c) the studio facilities agreement between XYZ Company for the year ended December 31, 20x1, in accordance with the provisions of the agreements referred to above.

In our opinion, the schedule of profit participation referred to above presents fairly, in all material respects, Reed Smith's participation in the profits of XYZ Company for the year ended December 31, 20x1, in accordance with the provisions of the agreements referred to above.

This report is intended solely for the information and use of the board of directors and management of XYZ Company and Reed Smith and should not be used for any other purpose.

Notice that, since the object of this report is "profit participation" (a bottom-line concept), the auditor also must have audited the entire income statement and make reference to the related audit report.

III. **Compliance with Contractual Agreements --** (or regulatory requirements) related to audited financial statements.

A. **Examples --** Payments into sinking funds, maintenance of stipulated ratios, or compliance with other such debt covenants.

B. **Reporting --** Can issue a separate report for this purpose or combine this report with the report on the financial statements.

1. State that the financial statements were audited -- cannot report on compliance with these agreements if the audit of the financial statements resulted in an adverse or disclaimer of opinion.
2. Identify the specific covenants and provide **negative assurance** ("... nothing came to our attention that caused us to believe that the Company failed to comply ...").
3. Restrict the distribution of the report to the parties to the agreement (or to the applicable regulatory agency).

IV. **Special-purpose Financial Presentations --** To comply with contractual agreements or regulatory provisions.

A. Financial statements presented on a prescribed basis resulting in an **incomplete presentation** (but otherwise consistent with GAAP) -- for example, a statement of assets sold and liabilities transferred to comply with a contract.

B. Financial statements prepared on a basis of accounting prescribed in an agreement (**not in conformity with GAAP** or other comprehensive basis; no "substantial support") -- for example, financial statements prepared for the purpose of obtaining a bank loan.

C. **Reporting --** Usually consists of five paragraphs:

1. **Introduction**
2. **Scope**
3. **Explanatory --** Indicate the intent of the presentation and refer to the financial statement note describing the basis of presentation (or noting that it is not intended to be a complete presentation).
4. **Opinion**
5. Restrict the **distribution** of the report (unless filed with a government agency, such as the SEC, and intended for the public).

V. **Financial Information Presented in Prescribed Forms or Schedules --** When a preprinted form uses reporting language that the auditor views as inappropriate, the auditor should edit the form appropriately or refer to (and attach) a separate report.

Service Organizations

Reports on the Processing of Transactions by Service Organizations -- When the auditor's client has "out-sourced" the processing of transactions to another company that provides such processing services.

After studying this lesson, you should be able to:

1. *Understand the service auditor's requirements under AICPA Professional Standards when engaged to report on internal control over financial reporting at a service organization.*
2. *Understand the user auditor's responsibilities under AICPA Professional Standards when relevant internal controls over financial reporting applicable to an entity's financial statements reside at a service organization to whom certain transactional processing has been outsourced.*

[See "AU324 (SAS 70) - Service Organizations"]

[See "AT801 (SSAE 16) - Reporting on Control at a Service Organization"]

I. Distinction Between the "Service Auditor" and the "User Auditor"

Definitions:

Service Auditor: Practitioner who reports on controls at a service organization.

User Auditor: An auditor who audits and reports on the financial statements of a user entity. (In other words, the auditor whose client has out-sourced the processing of its transactions to the service organization for whom such processing may be more efficient; the user auditor must consider relevant internal controls of the service organization in auditing the financial statements of such a client.)

II. Applicability

A. **The attestation standards apply to internal control reporting by the service auditor --** Engagements leading to either of two types of reports on internal control applicable to a service organization.
   1. **On the adequacy of the design of internal control --** (called a "type 1 engagement" by AICPA Professional Standards) Whether the control policies and procedures are suitably designed and placed in operation.
   2. **On the operating effectiveness of internal control (based on tests of controls) --** (called a "type 2 engagement" by AICPA Professional Standards) Whether the policies and procedures are suitably designed and working effectively to provide reasonable assurance of achieving the stated control objectives.

B. **The auditing standards apply to the user auditor's responsibility to obtain an understanding of internal control over financial reporting relevant to the audit of an entity's financial statements --** Must consider the implications of the service organization's internal controls in planning the audit of the financial statements of a client receiving such transaction processing services.

C. **Examples of such services --** Bank trust departments, mortgage banks that service mortgages for others, IT centers (for example, processing checks for financial institutions or handling the details of subscriptions for magazine publishers).

III. Responsibilities of Service Auditors (governed by SSAEs) -- Must be independent of **service** organization, but **not** necessarily independent of all **user** entities.

A. Procedures

1. **Inquiry --** Of service organization management and other personnel.
2. **Inspection --** Of documentation (flowcharts, narrative memoranda, or questionnaires).
3. **Observation --** Of internal control activities.
4. Obtain management's written representations as deemed appropriate.
5. If reporting on the operating effectiveness of internal control - the service auditor must perform appropriate **tests of controls.**

B. Reporting on the adequacy of the design of internal control -- (That is, reporting on the internal control policies and procedures placed in operation - also known as a "type 1" engagement) - the service auditor's report ordinarily consists of the following sections:

1. **Scope --** identify the nature of the engagement and the **specific date** involved.
2. Service organization's responsibilities.
3. Service auditor's responsibilities - reference the attestation standards established by the AICPA and describe an examination; also, **disclaim an opinion on operating effectiveness.**
4. Inherent limitations of internal control.
5. Opinion - (1) that the description fairly presents the system that was designed and implemented as of the specific date; and (2) that the controls related to the stated control objectives were suitably designed to provide reasonable assurance that the control objectives would be achieved if the controls operated effectively as of the specific date.
6. Restricted use - distribution should be restricted to the service organization, user entities, and the user entities' independent auditors.

C. Reporting on the operating effectiveness of internal control -- (That is, reporting on the policies and procedures placed in operation **and** on their operating effectiveness - also known as a "type 2" engagement) - the service auditor's report ordinarily consists of the following sections:

1. Scope - identify the nature of the engagement and the period involved.
2. Service organization's responsibilities.
3. Service auditor's responsibilities - reference the attestation standards established by the AICPA and describe an examination.
4. Inherent limitations of internal control.
5. Opinion - (1) that the description fairly presents the system that was designed and implemented throughout the period; (2) that the controls related to the stated control objectives were suitably designed to provide reasonable assurance that the control objectives would be achieved if the controls operated effectively throughout the period; and (3) that the controls tested operated effectively throughout the period.
6. Description of tests of controls - reference the pages of the service auditor's report identifying the specific controls tested and the nature, timing, and results of those tests.
7. Restricted use - distribution should be restricted to the service organization, user entities, and the user entities' independent auditors.

> **Note:**
> Management specifies the control objectives to be tested - Should cover a reporting period of **at least 6 months.**

D. Responsibilities of user auditors (governed by SASs) -- Related to assessing control risk at the user entity.

1. The service auditor's report may be useful in obtaining an understanding of internal control issues relevant to a users' entity's financial statements.
2. User auditor may "rely" on the operating effectiveness of internal controls of the service organization:
    a. When the service auditor has performed appropriate tests of effectiveness for specified objectives.
    b. When the user auditor has performed tests of controls at the user entity (or at the service organization).
3. If **substantive procedures** are performed by the service auditors:
    a. User auditor should inquire about the service auditor's professional reputation.
    b. May initiate communication with service auditor about procedures or conclusions.
    c. Report - do **NOT** refer to the service auditor's report; cannot indicate any division of responsibility here!

Background Commentary Regarding SAS No. 70 & SSAE No. 16:

When SAS No. 70, "Service Organizations," was issued in 1992, its provisions applied both to user auditors and to service auditors. In 2010, as part of the Auditing Standards Board's efforts to achieve greater convergence of U.S. standards with international standards, the ASB issued SSAE No. 16, "Reporting on Controls at a Service Organization," which addresses the service auditor's responsibilities when engaged to report on a service organization's internal controls.

The ASB has already issued a "clarified" Statement on Auditing Standards to address the user auditor's responsibilities with respect to internal control issues involving service organizations. That clarified SAS will supersede the guidance in SAS No. 70, but SAS No. 70 continues in effect until the ASB issues its completed set of clarified standards, perhaps some time in 2011.

In May, 2010, the AICPA published a Q&A on this evolving professional guidance applicable to service organizations. The AICPA stated, "The guidance for user auditors, currently in AU section 324 of the SASs, will be unchanged until the new SAS for user auditors, which has been approved by the ASB, becomes effective. The new SAS does not contain any significant changes for user auditors. However, the ASB believes that because the new SAS is written in clarity format, it will be easier for user auditors to use and, thereby, meet their responsibilities."

This same Q&A identifies the two major changes affecting service auditors by SSAE No. 16 (relative to the original guidance contained in SAS No. 70):

1. Management of the service organization will now be required to provide the service auditor with a written assertion about the fairness of the presentation of the description of the system and about the suitability of the design and, in a type 2 engagement, the operating effectiveness of the controls; that assertion will either accompany the service auditor's report or be included in the service organization's description.

2. In a type 2 engagement, the description of the service organization's system and the service auditor's opinion on the description will cover a period (the same period as the period covered by the service auditor's tests of the operating effectiveness of controls). In SAS No. 70, the description of the service organization's system in a type 2 report was as of a specified date, rather than for a period.

Comfort Letters

After studying this lesson, you should be able to:

1. *Understand the purpose associated with "comfort letters" provided by accountants to underwriters and other financial intermediaries in connection with an entity's stock issuance.*
2. *Understand the basic structure of such comfort letters and the nature of the assurance specifically provided by the entity's accountants/auditors.*

[See "AU634 (SAS 86) - Letters for Underwriters"]

Guidance now provided by SAS No. 86, "Amendment to SAS No. 72, Letters for Underwriters and Certain Other Requesting Parties."

I. **Purpose --** Section 11 of the Securities Act of 1933 provides for liability to underwriters and certain others (such as a broker-dealer or a financial intermediary) when there is a material omission or misstatement to a registration statement.

   A. A **"comfort letter"** from the independent accountants may help underwriters or others having a statutory due diligence defense under Section 11 of the Act establish a "reasonable investigation" (that is, **"due diligence"**).

   B. Comfort letters are not required and are not filed with the SEC.

   C. The scope is specified in the underwriting agreement (between the client and the underwriters or others); a copy of the agreement should be given to the accountants.

   D. The accountants should meet with the underwriters (or certain other requesting parties) to establish their specific needs and give them a "draft" of the comfort letter in advance to avoid misunderstandings.

   E. The accountants should avoid implying that the procedures performed were adequate for the underwriter's (or other parties') purposes.

II. **A Typical Comfort Letter --** Usually consists of the following

   A. An introductory paragraph that identifies the particular registration statement and the audited financial statements and schedules with which the accountant is associated;

   B. A statement as to the independence of the accountants;

   C. **Positive expression of opinion --** Whether the **audited** financial statements and schedules **comply as to form** with the requirements of the Act and the SEC;

   D. **Negative assurance --** Whether the **unaudited** condensed interim financial information complies as to form with the requirements of the Act and the SEC;

   E. **Negative assurance --** Whether any material modifications should be made to the unaudited condensed consolidated financial statements;

   F. **Negative assurance --** Whether there has been any change during a specified period in capital stock, increase in long-term debt, or any decrease in other specified financial statement items;

   G. A concluding paragraph that limits the distribution of the comfort letter to specified parties for the purposes stated;

III. Other Reporting Considerations

A. Dating of the letter -- usually dated on or shortly before the effective date of the registration.

B. Addressee -- should only be addressed to the client, named underwriters, broker-dealer, or the financial intermediary related to the securities.

C. Comment on the previously audited financial statements referred to in the registration statement.

   1. Give **positive assurance** (opinion) as to whether the audited financial statements comply with the **form** and content required by the SEC.

   2. Use the following language: "In our opinion (include the phrase 'except as disclosed in the registration statement,' if applicable) the consolidated financial statements and financial statement schedules audited by us and included in the registration statement comply as to form in all material respects with the applicable accounting requirements of the Act and the related published rules and regulations."

D. Commenting on the **unaudited financial statements, condensed interim financial information, or capsule financial information** -- must first have knowledge of internal control over financial reporting.

   1. **Unaudited financial statements and schedules and unaudited condensed interim financial information --** Can give negative assurance that such information complies as to form with SEC requirements.

   2. **Capsule financial information --** (Unaudited summarized interim information in narrative or tabular form) -- At most, can give negative assurance; in some cases, may be required to structure comments as procedures and findings.

E. Commenting on financial **forecasts; subsequent changes**; or **tables, statistics, and other financial information.**

   1. **Forecasts --** Must have knowledge of the entity's accounting and financial reporting; can attach the forecast's compilation report, if applicable.

   2. **Subsequent changes --** Comments usually relate to any changes in capital stock, increase in long-term debt, or decreases in other specified financial statement items (subsequent to latest financial statements included in registration).

   3. Can give negative assurance if within 135 days of the most recent period for which an audit or review was performed -- procedures are usually limited to reading the minutes and making inquiries of management.

   4. **Tables, statistics, and other financial information --** Limited to matters related to accounting records and subject to controls over financial reporting; should not comment on non-accounting matters such as square footage of facilities, number of employees, or sales backlog information.

F. Letter should state that the accountants make no representation involving legal interpretations.

Government Auditing Standards

After studying this lesson, you should be able to:

1. *Understand the distinction between "GAAS" and "GAGAS" (issued by the U.S. Government Accountability Office) and the additional responsibilities resulting from those Government Auditing Standards.*
2. *Understand the circumstances causing the Single Audit Act to be applicable.*

I. **Government Auditing Standards --** (also known as Generally Accepted Government Auditing Standards or GAGAS) are issued by the U.S. Government Accountability Office (GAO's "Yellow Book") under the authority of the Comptroller General - GAGAS go beyond the fieldwork and reporting standards of GAAS and must be followed when required by law, regulation, or agreement.

   A. **Additional reporting requirements regarding internal control --** Government Auditing Standards require a written report on internal control in all audits under GAGAS; when the auditor communicates "significant deficiencies," the auditor should obtain a response from officials of the entity as to their views about those findings (and include a copy of any written response in the auditor's report).

   B. **Additional reporting requirements regarding compliance with applicable laws and regulations --** Government Auditing Standards require a written report on compliance with applicable laws and regulations and distinguish between (1) "general requirements" that apply to all federal financial programs and (2) "specific requirements" that apply to a particular program by statutory (legislative) requirement.

   C. **Additional reporting requirements regarding illegal acts --** Government Auditing Standards require the auditor to report any known instances of illegal acts that could result in "criminal prosecution."

II. **Single Audit Act of 1984, as Updated --** Requires state and local governmental entities having expenditures of federal assistance aggregating at least $500,000 in a given fiscal year to be audited under the Single Audit Act.

   A. Requires a "single" coordinated audit of the aggregate federal financial assistance that has been provided to a state or local governmental entity (with emphasis on defined "major" assistance programs) - this is intended to result in greater efficiency than having multiple programs subject to separate program-specific audits.

   B. Requires an audit of the entity's financial statements, additional tests for the entity's compliance with applicable governmental requirements, and reviews of the entity's internal control systems.

Compliance Audits

After studying this lesson, you should be able to:

1. *Understand the circumstances causing AU 801 (SAS No. 117), "Compliance Audits," to be applicable, along with understanding the auditor's responsibilities under SAS No. 117.*

SAS No. 117 establishes standards and provides guidance regarding applicable engagements.

[See "AU801 – Compliance Audits"]

I. **Applicability --** When an auditor is engaged to perform a "compliance audit" in accordance with (1) generally accepted auditing standards (GAAS), (2) Government Auditing Standards (also called "Generally Accepted Government Auditing Standards" (GAGAS) from GAO's "Yellow Book" issued under the authority of the Comptroller General of the United States), and (3) a governmental audit requirement requiring an expression of opinion on compliance with applicable compliance requirements.

   A. SAS No. 117 applies to the compliance audit, but not to the financial statement audit part of such an engagement - example engagements for which SAS No. 117 applies includes an audit under OMB Circular A-133, "Audits of States, Local Governments, and Non-Profit Organizations;" also includes a department-specific requirement such as "U.S. Department of Housing and Urban Development Audit Requirements Related to Entities Such as Public Housing Agencies, Nonprofit and For-Profit Housing Projects, and Certain Lenders."

   B. **Objectives of the audit --** (1) to express an opinion on whether the entity complied with applicable compliance requirements (at the level specified in the governmental audit requirements); and (2) to identify audit/reporting requirements in the governmental audit requirement that are supplementary to GAAS and GAGAS and to evaluate those requirements

   C. **Definition of "governmental audit requirement" --** A governmental requirement established by law, regulation, rule, or provision of contracts or grant agreements requiring that an entity undergo an audit of its compliance with applicable compliance requirements related to one or more government programs.

II. **Compliance Auditing - Requirements and Guidance**

   A. **SAS No. 117 incorporates the AICPA's "risk assessment" standards**

      1. The auditor should perform risk assessment procedures to obtain an understanding of the applicable compliance requirements and internal controls over compliance - the nature and extent of the risk assessment procedures may vary with the circumstances (such as the complexity of the compliance requirements and the depth of the auditor's knowledge of internal control over compliance).

      2. The auditor should assess the risks of material noncompliance (whether due to fraud or error) for each applicable compliance requirement and consider whether any of those are "pervasive" to compliance.

      3. The auditor should perform further audit procedures in response to the assessed risks - develop an overall response to any risks that are "pervasive" to the entity's compliance; perform appropriate tests of details; and perform tests of controls when there is an expectation of operating effectiveness or when required to do so. (Note that an example of a "pervasive" risk of noncompliance would be financial difficulty that increases the risk that grant funds will be used for unauthorized purposes.)

B. Supplementary audit requirements -- The auditor should identify "supplementary audit requirements" (beyond GAAS and GAGAS) specified in the governmental audit requirement.

1. Some governmental audit requirements specifically identify the applicable compliance requirements, whereas others provide a framework for the auditor to determine the applicable compliance requirements.
2. OMB Circular A-133, "Audits of States, Local Governments and Non-Profit Organizations," provides a framework ("Compliance Supplement") to determine the compliance requirements.

C. Written representations -- The auditor should obtain written representations from management tailored to the entity and the governmental audit requirement.

D. Subsequent events -- The auditor should perform procedures up to the date of the auditor's report to identify subsequent events related to the entity's compliance (e.g., reports from grantors regarding noncompliance or information about noncompliance obtained through other professional engagements for the entity); an example of a subsequent event warranting disclosure is the discovery of noncompliance causing the grantor to stop the funding .

E. Evaluating the evidence and forming an opinion -- Most governmental audit requirements specify that the auditor's opinion on compliance is at the "program" level (and materiality is usually determined based on the program taken as a whole).

1. The auditor should consider "likely questioned costs" (not just "known questioned costs") and other noncompliance that may not result in questioned costs.
2. The auditor may include a variety of factors in assessing the risk of noncompliance, including: (a) the complexity of the compliance requirements; (b) how long the entity has been subject to those compliance requirements; (c) the degree of judgment involved in compliance; and (d) the entity's compliance in prior years.

F. Reporting -- The auditor may issue (1) a separate report on compliance only; (2) a combined report on compliance and on internal control over compliance; or (3) a separate report on internal control over compliance.

See the following example.

Combined Report on Compliance With Applicable Requirements and Internal Control Over Compliance

Independent Auditor's Report

(Addressee)

Compliance

We have audited (entity's name) compliance with the (identify the applicable compliance requirements or reference the document that describes the applicable compliance requirements) applicable to (entity's) (identify the government program(s) audited or refer to a separate schedule that identifies the program(s)) for the year ended June 30, 20X1. Compliance with the requirements referred to above is the responsibility of (entity's) management. Our responsibility is to express an opinion on (entity's) compliance based on our audit.

We conducted our audit of compliance in accordance with auditing standards generally accepted in the United States of America; the standards applicable to financial audits contained in Government Auditing Standards issued by the Comptroller General of the United States; and (name of the governmental audit requirement or program-specific audit guide). Those standards and (name of the governmental audit requirement or program-specific audit guide) require that we plan and perform the audit to obtain reasonable assurance about whether noncompliance with the compliance requirements referred to above that could have a material effect on (identify the government program(s) audited or refer to a separate schedule that identifies the program(s)). An audit includes examining, on a test basis, evidence about (entity's) compliance with those requirements and performing such other procedures as we considered necessary in the circumstances. We believe that our audit provides a reasonable basis for our opinion. Our audit does not provide a legal determination of (entity's) compliance with those requirements.

In our opinion, (entity's name) complied, in all material respects, with the compliance requirements referred to above that are applicable to (identify the government program(s) audited) for the year ended June 30, 20X1.

Internal Control Over Compliance

Management of (entity's name) is responsible for establishing and maintaining effective internal control over compliance with the compliance requirements referred to above. In planning and performing our audit, we considered (entity's) internal control over compliance to determine the auditing procedures for the purpose of expressing our opinion on compliance, but not for the purpose of expressing an opinion on the effectiveness of internal control over compliance. Accordingly, we do not express an opinion on the effectiveness of (entity's) internal control over compliance.

A deficiency in internal control over compliance exists when the design or operation of a control does not allow management or employees, in the normal course of performing their assigned functions, to prevent, or detect and correct, noncompliance on a timely basis. A material weakness in internal control over compliance is a deficiency, or combination of deficiencies in internal control over compliance, such that there is a reasonable possibility that material noncompliance with a compliance requirement will not be prevented, or detected and corrected, on a timely basis.

This report is intended solely for the information and use of management, (identify the body or individuals charged with governance), others within the entity, (identify the legislative or regulatory body), and (identify the grantor agency(ies)) and is not intended to be and should not be used by anyone other than these specified parties.

(Signature)

(Date)

G. **Documentation --** The auditor should document the risk assessment procedures performed, responses to the assessed risks of material noncompliance, the basis for materiality levels, and compliance with applicable "supplementary audit requirements."

H. **Communication --** The auditor should communicate the following matters with those charged with governance: the auditor's responsibilities under GAAS, GAGAS, and the governmental audit requirements; an overview of the planned scope and timing of the compliance audit; and any significant findings.

I. **Reissuance of the compliance report --** When reissuing a compliance report, the auditor should add an explanatory paragraph describing why the report is being reissued and noting any changes from the previously issued report; if additional audit procedures are performed, the auditor's report date should be updated.

SSARSs - Framework

After studying this lesson, you should be able to:

1. *Know the "framework" applicable to SSARSs, consisting of requirements ("unconditional" and "presumptively mandatory") and explanatory material.*
2. *Know the "hierarchy" applicable to compilation and review engagements, consisting of SSARSs, interpretive publications, and other publications.*

I. **Statements on Standards for Accounting and Review Services (SSARSs) --** Are issued by the AICPA's "Accounting and Review Services Committee" (ARSC). These standards apply to **reviews** and **compilations** of financial statements for nonpublic entities (referred to as "**nonissuers**").

A. **Compilation --** Assists management in presenting financial information in the form of financial statements without providing any assurance; "Although a compilation is **not an assurance engagement**, it is an attest engagement." (AR 60.05)

B. **Review --** The objective is to obtain "limited assurance" that there are no material modifications that should be made to the financial statements; "A review engagement is **an assurance engagement** as well as an attest engagement." (AR 60.07)

II. **Framework for Compilation and Review Engagements --** SSARS contain both "requirements" and "explanatory material."

[See "AR60 - Reporting on Compilation and Review Engagements"]

A. **Requirements --** There are two categories: "unconditional" and "presumptively mandatory."

1. **"Unconditional requirements" --** The accountant is required to comply with an unconditional requirement without exception (indicated by the words "**must**" or "**is required**")

2. **"Presumptively mandatory requirements" --** Indicated by the word "**should.**"

a. The accountant is also required to comply with a "presumptively mandatory requirement" -- but it allows for the possibility of exception.

b. In rare circumstances, the accountant may depart from a presumptively mandatory requirement. he accountant must document the justification for the departure and how the alternative procedures performed in the circumstances were sufficient to achieve the objectives of the presumptively mandatory requirement.

III. **Explanatory Material --** Defined as the text within a SSARS (excluding any related appendices or interpretations) that may provide further explanation on the professional requirements or describe other procedures or actions possibly applicable to the auditor (practitioner).

A. Such explanatory material is intended to be descriptive and does not impose a professional requirement.

B. Explanatory material is identified by the terms **"may," "might," or "could."**

IV. Hierarchy of Compilation and Review Standards and Guidance

A. **SSARSs --** They provide a measure of quality and the objectives to be achieved in both a compilation and review engagement. (Compliance is enforceable by Rule 202 of the AICPA Code of Professional Conduct, *"Compliance With Standards,"* which requires accountants to adhere to standards promulgated by the ARSC.)

B. **"Interpretive publications"**

1. Consist of compilation and review interpretations (and appendices) of the SSARSs, AICPA Audit and Accounting Guides, and AICPA auditing Statements of Position, to the extent applicable to compilation and review engagements.
2. Accountants should be aware of (and consider) interpretive publications applicable to compilations and reviews. When accountants do not apply such guidance, they should be prepared to explain how they complied with the SSARS provisions related to such interpretive publications

C. **"Other compilation and review publications" --** Other publications have no authoritative status, but they may help the accountant understand and apply the SSARS (for example, articles in the *Journal of Accountancy* and the AICPA's *CPA Letter*, continuing professional education programs, textbooks).

SSARSs - Compilations

After studying this lesson, you should be able to:

1. *Know what is meant by the term "compilation."*
2. *Understand the accountant's responsibilities for a compilation engagement.*
3. *Know the structure of the accountant's report for a compilation engagement.*

> **Definition:**
> *Compilation*: A compilation is a service, the objective of which is to assist management in presenting financial information in the form of financial statements without undertaking to obtain or provide any assurance that there are no material modifications that should be made. (The accountant functions primarily as an "assembler" of the financial statements using financial data provided by management.)

I. Establishing an Understanding -- The accountant should establish an understanding (regarding the engagement's objectives, management's responsibilities, the accountant's responsibilities, and the limitations of the engagement, among other matters) with management and document that in writing with an engagement letter.

[See "AR80 - Compilation of Financial Statements"]

II. Compilation Performance Requirements

A. Should have or obtain an understanding of the industry and the entity itself, including the accounting principles and practices used;

B. **Read the financial statements --** The accountant should read the entity's financial statements to see if they are appropriate in form and free of obvious material errors;

C. **Other compilation procedures --** The accountant is not required to verify the information supplied by the entity, but should obtain additional or revised information when the accountant believes the financial statements are materially misstated;

D. **Documentation --** The accountant should document the work performed in accordance with SSARSs; the extent of the documentation varies with the circumstances, but should include: (1) the engagement letter; (2) any findings or issues that are considered "significant;" and (3) any communications (whether oral or written) to the appropriate level of management about fraud or illegal acts.

III. Reporting

A. **Elements of the compilation report**

1. **Title --** "Accountant's Compilation Report" or "Independent Accountant's Compilation Report"
2. Addressee
3. **Introductory paragraph --** Identify the financial statements and the nature of the engagement; include a disclaimer of any level of assurance;
4. **Management's responsibility --** For the financial statements and related internal control;

5. **Accountant's responsibility --** To conduct the compilation in accordance with SSARSs issued by the AICPA;
6. Signature of the accountant (either manual or printed);
7. Date of the report (the date of completion of the compilation).

> **Compilation Report on Financial Statements**
>
> Accountant's Compilation Report
>
> (Appropriate Salutation)
>
> I (we) have compiled the accompanying balance sheet of XYZ Company as of December 31, 20XX, and the related statements of income, retained earnings, and cash flows for the year then ended. I (we) have not audited or reviewed the accompanying financial statements and, accordingly, do not express an opinion or provide any assurance about whether the financial statements are in accordance with accounting principles generally accepted in the United States of America.
>
> Management (owners) is (are) responsible for the preparation and fair presentation of the financial statements in accordance with accounting principles generally accepted in the United States of America and for designing, implementing, and maintaining internal control relevant to the preparation and fair presentation of the financial statements.
>
> My (our) responsibility is to conduct the compilation in accordance with Statements on Standards for Accounting and Review Services issued by the American Institute of Certified Public Accountants. The objective of a compilation is to assist management in presenting financial information in the form of financial statements without undertaking to obtain or provide any assurance that there are no material modifications that should be made to the financial statements.
>
> (Signature of accounting firm or the accountant, as appropriate)
>
> (Date)

B. Additional comments about the compilation report

1. Each page of the financial statements should reference the compilation report (see "Accountant's Compilation Report").
2. The report should not describe any other procedures that were performed;
3. Financial statements that omit substantially all disclosures may be compiled, as long as the omission of disclosures is not intended to mislead readers (must add a paragraph to the compilation report that comments on the omission of substantially all disclosures);
4. If the accountant is not independent -- The accountant is permitted to compile the entity's financial statements since no assurance is provided;
5. Emphasis of a matter -- the accountant may choose to add a paragraph to the compilation report to emphasize a matter (for example, going concern issues, related party transactions, subsequent events, etc.); such a paragraph is not a substitute for proper disclosure, so an emphasis paragraph can only be used for a matter that has been disclosed in the financial statements.

> **Note:**
> If lacking independence, the accountant must add a final paragraph to the report to state that fact. May choose to add a single sentence without any explanation, or may instead choose to disclose the reason(s) for the impairment of independence. If commenting on the reason(s), the accountant must include all of the reasons involved, not just selected reasons.

C. Departures from the applicable accounting framework (for example, GAAP) -- Add a separate paragraph to the compilation report; however, if such modification of the report is not an adequate way to disclose the departure, the accountant should instead withdraw from the engagement.

IV. Change in an Engagement from an Audit (or Review) to a Compilation -- Before agreeing to such a change, the accountant should consider: (1) the reason for the client's request (e.g., whether a scope limitation is imposed by the client or by circumstances); (2) the additional effort required to complete the audit or review; and (3) the estimated additional cost to complete the audit or review. (If there is a reasonable basis for making such a change, the compilation report should not mention the original engagement or the reason(s) for the change.)

SSARSs - Reviews

After studying this lesson, you should be able to:

1. *Know what is meant by the term "review" for a nonissuer.*
2. *Understand the accountant's responsibilities for a review engagement under SSARSs.*
3. *Know the structure of the accountant's report for a review engagement under SSARSs.*

Definition:
Review: A review is a service, the objective of which is to obtain limited assurance that there are no material modifications that should be made to the financial statements in order for the statements to be in conformity with the applicable financial reporting framework. (Note that "A review is an assurance engagement as well as an attest engagement." The level of assurance for a review is described as "negative assurance.")

[See "AR90 - Review of Financial Statements"]

I. **Establishing an Understanding --** The accountant should establish an understanding (regarding the engagement's objectives, management's responsibilities, the accountant's responsibilities, and the limitations of the engagement, among other matters) with management and document that in writing with an engagement letter.

II. **Review Performance Requirements**

   A. Should have or obtain an understanding of the industry and the entity itself, including the accounting principles and practices used;

   B. **Designing and performing review procedures --** A review consists primarily of performing analytical procedures and making inquiries of management and other client personnel; (Those procedures constitute "review evidence")

   C. **Analytical procedures --** Comparing expectations developed by the accountant to recorded amounts or ratios based on recorded amounts; such procedures may be performed at the financial statement level or at the detailed account level;

   D. **Inquiries and other review procedures --** The accountant should direct inquiries to management about a variety of matters; should also read the minutes of board meetings, etc.; should read the financial statements for apparent compliance with the applicable financial reporting framework; and obtain reports from other accountants who have audited or reviewed financial statements of any significant components of the entity;

   E. **Incorrect, incomplete, or otherwise unsatisfactory information --** If the accountant believes that the financial statements may be materially misstated, the accountant should perform additional procedures to obtain limited assurance that there are no material modifications that should be made to the financial statements;

   F. **Management representations --** Written representations are required from management for all financial statements and periods covered by the accountant's review report. (If current management was not present for all such periods, the accountant should still obtain written representations from current management for all such periods.)

III. Documentation -- The accountant should document the work performed in accordance with SSARSs; the extent of the documentation varies with the circumstances, but should include: (1) the engagement letter; (2) the analytical procedures performed; (3) additional procedures performed as a follow-up to the analytical procedures; (4) significant matters addressed by inquiries; (5) any findings that are "significant;" (6) any significant "unusual matters" considered and their disposition; (7) communications (whether oral or written) to the appropriate level of management regarding fraud or illegal acts; and (8) the management representation letter.

IV. Reporting

A. Elements of the review report

1. **Title --** "Independent Accountant's Review Report"
2. Addressee
3. **Introductory paragraph --** Identify the financial statements and the nature of the engagement; state that a review is substantially less in scope than an audit and include a disclaimer of opinion ;
4. **Management's responsibility --** For the financial statements and related internal control;
5. **Accountant's responsibility --** To conduct the review in accordance with SSARSs issued by the AICPA;
6. Results of the engagement (expressed as "negative assurance");
7. Signature of the accountant (either manual or printed);
8. Date of the report (not before the date of completion of the review).

Review Report on Financial Statements

<u>Independent Accountant's Review Report</u>

(Appropriate Salutation)

I (we) have reviewed the accompanying balance sheet of XYZ Company as of December 31, 20XX, and the related statements of income, retained earnings, and cash flows for the year then ended. A review includes primarily applying analytical procedures to management's (owners') financial data and making inquiries of company management (owners). A review is substantially less in scope than an audit, the objective of which is the expression of an opinion regarding the financial statements as a whole. Accordingly, I (we) do not express such an opinion.

Management (owners) is (are) responsible for the preparation and fair presentation of the financial statements in accordance with accounting principles generally accepted in the United States of America and for designing, implementing, and maintaining internal control relevant to the preparation and fair presentation of the financial statements.

My (our) responsibility is to conduct the review in accordance with Statements on Standards for Accounting and Review Services issued by the American Institute of Certified Public Accountants. Those standards require me (us) to perform procedures to obtain limited assurance that there are no material modifications that should be made to the financial statements. I (We) believe that the results of my (our) procedures provide a reasonable basis for our report.

Based on my (our) review, I am (we are) not aware of any material modifications that should be made to the accompanying financial statements in order for them to be in conformity with accounting principles generally accepted in the United States of America.

(Signature of accounting firm or the accountant, as appropriate)

(Date)

B. **Additional comments about the review report**

1. Each page of the financial statements should reference the review report (see "Independent Accountant's Review Report").
2. **An "incomplete review" (scope limitation) --** When the accountant is unable to perform the inquiry and analytical procedures considered necessary; cannot issue a review report under these circumstances;
3. **Emphasis of a matter --** The accountant may choose to add a paragraph to the review report to emphasize a matter (for example, going concern issues, related party transactions, subsequent events, etc.); such a paragraph is not a substitute for proper disclosure, so an emphasis paragraph can only be used for a matter that has been disclosed in the financial statements.

C. **Departures from the applicable accounting framework (for example, GAAP) --** Add a separate paragraph to the review report; however, if such modification of the report is not an adequate way to disclose the departure, the accountant should instead withdraw from the engagement .

V. **Change in an Engagement from an Audit to a Review --** Before agreeing to such a change, the accountant should consider: (1) the reason for the client's request (e.g., whether a scope limitation is imposed by the client or by circumstances); (2) the additional effort required to complete the audit; and (3) the estimated additional cost to complete the audit. (If there is a reasonable basis for making such a change, the review report should not mention the original engagement or the reason(s) for the change.)

SSARSs - Other Topics

After studying this lesson, you should be able to:

1. *Understand the accountant's reporting responsibilities under SSARSs for comparative financial statements (both for a continuing accountant and for a successor accountant).*
2. *Understand the accountant's responsibilities under SSARSs when engaged to compile specified "elements" of a financial statement.*
3. *Understand the accountant's responsibilities under SSARSs when engaged to compile "pro forma" financial information.*
4. *Understand the accountant's responsibilities for other miscellaneous topics under SSARSs, including for communicating with the predecessor, for compilation reports on financial statements in certain prescribed forms, and for the accountant's association with personal financial statements solely for purposes of financial planning.*

I. Review and Compilation Reports on Comparative Financial Statements

[See "AR200 - Reporting on Comparative Financial Statements"]

A. For a recurring engagement

1. Can review (or compile) both years' financial statements;
2. Can review one year's financial statements and compile the financials of another year - add an additional paragraph at the end of the current year's report (describing the nature and date of the prior year's report);
3. Can remove a prior reference to a GAAP departure for the prior year's financial statements (when that GAAP problem was later resolved) - add an appropriate explanatory paragraph;
4. Can review or compile the current year's financial statements and audit the prior year's financial statements. Note that the Statements on Auditing Standards (SASs) govern the reporting requirements when auditing any given year's financial statements.

B. If not a recurring engagement (i.e., there are new accountants for the current year) and if the prior year's financial statements are presented for comparative purposes:

1. If a predecessor accountant reviewed or compiled the prior year's financial statements - indicate that fact in an explanatory paragraph (specifying the nature and date of the predecessor's report) ;
2. Indicate that the (current) accountant takes no responsibility for the prior year's financial statements.

II. Compilation of Specified Elements – The accountant may be engaged to compile "specified elements, accounts, or items of a financial statement."

[See "AR110 - Compilation of Specified Elements"]

A. Establish an understanding -- (Preferably in writing) as to the services to be performed - describe the nature and limitations of those services and the nature of the report to be issued.

1. The understanding should specifically include that the engagement cannot be relied upon to disclose errors, fraud or illegal acts.

2. The understanding should also include that the accountant will inform the appropriate level of management of any material errors and of any information coming to the accountant's attention that fraud or an illegal act may have occurred (need not report matters regarding illegal acts that are "clearly inconsequential").

B. **Performance requirements --** Read the compiled elements, accounts or items and consider whether that information appears to be free of obvious material errors.

C. **Reporting requirements --** Each page of the compiled elements, accounts, or items should include a reference such as "See Accountant's Compilation Report."

1. **Not required to be independent --** But if not independent, disclose that lack of independence;

2. The accountant may "assist" with the compilation of specified elements, accounts, or items of a financial statement without issuing a compilation report (if not actually engaged to compile such information) - should consider issuing a compilation report anyway when associated with such information so that users will not attribute unwarranted assurance.

III. **Compilation of Pro Forma Financial Information --** The accountant may be engaged to compile "pro forma financial information." Note that presentations of "pro forma financial information" are not within the definition of "financial statements."

[See "AR120 - Compilation of Pro Forma Financial Information"]

A. **General comments --** Label the pro forma information in a way that distinguishes it from historical financial information.

1. Objective of pro forma information -- to show the significant effects on historical financial information associated with a transaction (actual or proposed) had the transaction occurred at an earlier date.

2. To compile the pro forma financial information -- the accountant must have compiled, reviewed, or audited the historical financial statements on which the pro forma information is based.

B. **Establish an understanding --** (Preferably in writing) as to the services to be performed -- describe the nature and limitations of those services and the nature of the report to be issued.

1. The understanding should specifically include that the engagement cannot be relied upon to disclose errors, fraud or illegal acts.

2. The understanding should also include that the accountant will inform the appropriate level of management of any material errors and of any information coming to the accountant's attention that fraud or an illegal act may have occurred (need not report matters regarding illegal acts that are "clearly inconsequential").

C. **Performance requirements --** Read the compiled pro forma financial information (including the summary of significant assumptions) and consider whether that information appears to be free of obvious material errors.

D. **Reporting requirements --** Each page of the compiled pro forma financial information should include a reference such as "See Accountant's Compilation Report."

1. Not required to be independent -- but if not independent, disclose that lack of independence without describing the specific reason for it.

2. The accountant may "assist" with the compilation of pro forma financial information without issuing a compilation report (if not actually engaged to compile such information) -- should consider issuing a compilation report anyway when associated with such information so that users will not attribute unwarranted assurance.

3. The report should not describe any other procedures performed by the accountant before or during the compilation engagement.

IV. When an accountant submits unaudited financial statements to the client that are *not expected to be used by a third party* -- The accountant must either (1) issue a compilation report or, alternatively, (2) document an understanding with the client by an engagement letter and a management representation letter in which, among other things to be addressed, management states that the financial statements are for internal use only and are not to be used by third parties.

> **Note:** In this case, the engagement letter allows the accountant to submit the unaudited financial statements without having to issue a compilation report. Include a reference on each page of the financial statements restricting their use to management only! If unauthorized distribution of these financial statements is discovered, discuss the matter with management and if they are uncooperative, the accountant should notify known third parties not to use the financial statements (and probably should consult with his or her attorney, too).

V. Miscellaneous Issues Related to Reviews and Compilations

A. If there is a change of the public(issuer)/nonpublic(nonissuer) status of a client -- the current status of the entity governs what standards apply to the engagement.

B. Communication between the successor and the predecessor accountants -- not required to communicate with the predecessor, but the successor may certainly choose to:

[See "AR400 - Predecessor Successor Communications"]

1. Requires the client's permission (due to confidentiality considerations).
2. The successor may also ask to review the predecessor's documentation. (The predecessor is not necessarily obligated to permit such a review, however.)

C. Compilation reports on financial statements in certain prescribed forms:

[See "AR300 - Compilation Reports in Prescribed Forms"]

1. When unaudited financial statements of a nonissuer are presented in a prescribed form (not GAAP) -- for banks, trade associations, or credit agencies.
2. Add an explanatory paragraph at the end of the compilation report indicating that the prescribed form differs from GAAP -- the second paragraph should refer to "... in the form prescribed by ..."
3. Any other known deficiencies should be identified in the report.

D. Personal financial statements included with personal financial plans:

[See "AR600 - Personal Financial Statements"]

1. When the accountant helps prepare personal financial statements related to developing an individual's personal financial plans or goals -- a compilation report is not required. (The financial statements must not be used for any other purpose, however.)
2. The report should state the purpose of these financial statements is intended solely to help develop the financial plan, and note that the financial statements have not been audited, reviewed, or compiled; and indicate that the financial statements may be incomplete.

Sample Reports

Financial Statements Prepared on the Cash Basis

Independent Auditor's Report

We have audited the accompanying statements of assets and liabilities arising from cash transactions of XYZ Company as of December 31, 20x2 and 20x1, and the related statements of revenue collected and expenses paid for the years then ended. These financial statements are the responsibility of the Company's management. Our responsibility is to express an opinion on these financial statements based on our audits.

We conducted our audits in accordance with auditing standards generally accepted in the United States of America. Those standards require that we plan and perform the audit to obtain reasonable assurance about whether the financial statements are free of material misstatement. An audit includes examining, on a test basis, evidence supporting the amounts and disclosures in the financial statements. An audit also includes assessing the accounting principles used and significant estimates made by management, as well as evaluating the overall financial statement presentation. We believe that our audits provide a reasonable basis for our opinion.

As described in Note X, these financial statements were prepared on the basis of cash receipts and disbursements, which is a comprehensive basis of accounting other than generally accepted accounting principles.

In our opinion, the financial statements referred to above present fairly, in all material respects, the assets and liabilities arising from cash transactions of XYZ Company as of December 31, 20x2 and 20x1, and its revenue collected and expenses paid during the years then ended, **on the basis of accounting described in Note X**.

Note:
Notice that the financial statements are named in a way to avoid confusing them with financial statements prepared under GAAP.

Profit Participation

Independent Auditor's Report

We have audited, in accordance with generally accepted auditing standards, the financial statements of XYZ Company for the year ended December 31, 20x1, and have issued our report thereon, dated March 10, 20x2. We have also audited XYZ Company's schedule of Reed Smith's profit participation for the year ended December 31, 20x1. This schedule is the responsibility of the Company's management. Our responsibility is to express an opinion on this schedule based on our audit.

We conducted our audit of the schedule in accordance with auditing standards generally accepted in the United States of America. Those standards require that we plan and perform the audit to obtain reasonable assurance about whether the schedule of profit participation is free of material misstatement. An audit includes examining, on a test basis, evidence supporting the amounts and disclosures in the schedule. An audit also includes assessing the accounting principles used and significant estimates made by management, as well as evaluating the overall schedule presentation. We believe that our audit provides a reasonable basis for our opinion.

We have been informed that the documents that govern the determination of Reed Smith's profit participation are (a) the employment agreement between Reed Smith and XYZ Company dated February 1, 20x0, (b) the production and distribution agreement between XYZ Company and Television Network Incorporated dated March 1, 20x0, and (c) the studio facilities agreement between XYZ Company for the year ended December 31, 20x1, in accordance with the provisions of the agreements referred to above.

In our opinion, the schedule of profit participation referred to above presents fairly, in all material respects, Reed Smith's participation in the profits of XYZ Company for the year ended December 31, 20x1, in accordance with the provisions of the agreements referred to above.

This report is intended solely for the information and use of the board of directors and management of XYZ Company and Reed Smith and should not be used for any other purpose.

Note:
Notice that, since the object of this report is "profit participation" (a bottom-line concept), the auditor also must have audited the entire income statement and make reference to the related audit report.

Compliance for Governmental Entities

Sample Audit Report on Compliance for Governmental Entities (Assuming No Material Instances of Noncompliance)

Combined Report on Compliance with Applicable Requirements and Internal Control Over Compliance

Independent Auditor's Report

(Addressee)

Compliance

We have audited (entity's name) compliance with the (identify the applicable compliance requirements or reference the document that describes the applicable compliance requirements) applicable to (entity's) (identify the government program(s) audited or refer to a separate schedule that identifies the program(s)) for the year ended June 30, 20X1. Compliance with the requirements referred to above is the responsibility of (entity's) management. Our responsibility is to express an opinion on (entity's) compliance based on our audit.

We conducted our audit of compliance in accordance with auditing standards generally accepted in the United States of America; the standards applicable to financial audits contained in Government Auditing Standards issued by the Comptroller General of the United States; and (name of the governmental audit requirement or program-specific audit guide). Those standards and (name of the governmental audit requirement or program-specific audit guide) require that we plan and perform the audit to obtain reasonable assurance about whether noncompliance with the compliance requirements referred to above that could have a material effect on (identify the government program(s) audited or refer to a separate schedule that identifies the program(s)). An audit includes examining, on a test basis, evidence about (entity's) compliance with those requirements and performing such other procedures as we considered necessary in the circumstances. We believe that our audit provides a reasonable basis for our opinion. Our audit does not provide a legal determination of (entity's) compliance with those requirements.

In our opinion, (entity's name) complied, in all material respects, with the compliance requirements referred to above that are applicable to (identify the government program(s) audited) for the year ended June 30, 20X1.

Internal Control Over Compliance

Management of (entity's name) is responsible for establishing and maintaining effective internal control over compliance with the compliance requirements referred to above. In planning and performing our audit, we considered (entity's) internal control over compliance to determine the auditing procedures for the purpose of expressing our opinion on compliance, but not for the purpose of expressing an opinion on the effectiveness of internal control over compliance. Accordingly, we do not express an opinion on the effectiveness of (entity's) internal control over compliance.

A deficiency in internal control over compliance exists when the design or operation of a control does not allow management or employees, in the normal course of performing their assigned functions, to prevent, or detect and correct, noncompliance on a timely basis. A material weakness in internal control over compliance is a deficiency, or combination of deficiencies in internal control over compliance, such that there is a reasonable possibility that material noncompliance with a compliance requirement will not be prevented, or detected and corrected, on a timely basis.

This report is intended solely for the information and use of management, (identify the body or individuals charged with governance), others within the entity, (identify the legislative or regulatory body), and (identify the grantor agency(ies)) and is not intended to be and should not be used by anyone other than these specified parties.

(Signature)

(Date)

> **Note:** Notice that this report contains a **disclaimer** of opinion with respect to **overall** compliance; **positive assurance** with respect to compliance with **"items tested;"** and **negative assurance** with respect to compliance with **"items not tested."**

Sample Review Report on Financial Statements

Independent Accountant's Review Report

I (we) have reviewed the accompanying balance sheet of XYZ Company as of December 31, 20XX, and the related statements of income, retained earnings, and cash flows for the year then ended. A review includes, primarily, applying analytical procedures to management's (owners') financial data and making inquiries of company management (owners). A review is substantially less in scope than an audit, the objective of which is the expression of an opinion regarding the financial statements as a whole. Accordingly, I (we) do not express such an opinion.

Management (owners) is (are) responsible for the preparation and fair presentation of the financial statements in accordance with accounting principles generally accepted in the United States of America and for designing, implementing, and maintaining internal control relevant to the preparation and fair presentation of the financial statements.

My (our) responsibility is to conduct the review in accordance with Statements on Standards for Accounting and Review Services issued by the American Institute of Certified Public Accountants. Those standards require me (us) to perform procedures to obtain limited assurance that there are no material modifications that should be made to the financial statements. I (We) believe that the results of my (our) procedures provide a reasonable basis for our report.

Based on my (our) review, I am (we are) not aware of any material modifications that should be made to the accompanying financial statements in order for them to be in conformity with accounting principles generally accepted in the United States of America.

(Signature of accounting firm or the accountant, as appropriate)

(Date)

Sample Compilation Report on Financial Statements

Sample Compilation Report on Financial Statements of a Nonissuer (Assuming No Known Material GAAP Departures)

Compilation Report on Financial Statements

Accountant's Compilation Report

(Appropriate Salutation)

I (we) have compiled the accompanying balance sheet of XYZ Company as of December 31, 20XX, and the related statements of income, retained earnings, and cash flows for the year then ended. I (we) have not audited or reviewed the accompanying financial statements and, accordingly, do not express an opinion or provide any assurance about whether the financial statements are in accordance with accounting principles generally accepted in the United States of America.

Management (owners) is (are) responsible for the preparation and fair presentation of the financial statements in accordance with accounting principles generally accepted in the United States of America and for designing, implementing, and maintaining internal control relevant to the preparation and fair presentation of the financial statements.

My (our) responsibility is to conduct the compilation in accordance with Statements on Standards for Accounting and Review Services issued by the American Institute of Certified Public Accountants. The objective of a compilation is to assist management in presenting financial information in the form of financial statements without undertaking to obtain or provide any assurance that there are no material modifications that should be made to the financial statements.

(Signature of accounting firm or the accountant, as appropriate)

(Date)

Other Professional Services

Attestation Standards

After studying this lesson, you should be able to:

1. *Know the definition of "attest engagement" and the three different kinds of attest engagements identified in the definition of "attest engagement" - examination, review, and agreed-upon procedures.*
2. *Know the 11 Attestation Standards.*
3. *Understand the guidance that is applicable to attest engagements, including Statements on Standards for Attestation Engagements (SSAEs), interpretive publications, and other attestation publications.*
4. *Know the two types of professional requirements ("unconditional requirements" and "presumptively mandatory requirements") and the language associated with each.*

[See "AT101 (SSAE 10 as amended) - Attestation Standards"]

Definitions:
Attest Engagement: (Revised by SSAE 10) - When a CPA practitioner is engaged to issue (or does issue) an examination, a review, or an agreed-upon procedures report on subject matter, or an assertion about the subject matter that is the responsibility of another party. (Now the CPA can report directly on the subject matter or on the responsible party's assertion - previously required a written assertion!)

Assertion: Any declaration about whether the subject matter is in conformity with the criteria selected (previously had to be in writing!).

Responsible Party: The person(s) responsible for the subject matter (or a party who has a reasonable basis for making a written assertion about the subject matter) - being able to identify a responsible party is a prerequisite for an attest engagement.

I. There are 11 Attestation Standards (similar, but not identical, to GAAS)

A. General Standards (remember: T-K-C-I-D)

1. **T**echnical training in the <u>attest function</u>.

"The practitioner must have adequate technical training and proficiency to perform the attestation engagement."

2. **K**nowledge in the <u>subject matter of assertion</u> (since the subject matter is now something other than traditional GAAP-based financial statements...).

"The practitioner must have adequate knowledge of the subject matter."

3. **C**riteria - measurement criteria are "<u>suitable and available</u>." (The criteria should be chosen by the client or the responsible party.)

"The practitioner must have reason to believe that the subject matter is capable of evaluation against criteria that are suitable and available to users."

a. **Suitable --** Objective; measurable; complete; and relevant. (Criteria established by "due process" procedures are usually suitable.)

b. **Available --** Can be publicly available; in the presentation of the subject matter or assertion; in the practitioner's report; understood by users; or available to the specified parties.

4. **I**ndependence

> "The practitioner must maintain independence in mental attitude in all matters relating to the engagement."

5. **D**ue professional care

> "The practitioner must exercise due professional care in the planning and performance of the engagement and the preparation of the report."

B. Standards of field work (remember: P-E)

1. **P**lanning and supervision.

> "The practitioner must adequately plan the work and must properly supervise any assistants."

2. **E**vidence.

> "The practitioner must obtain sufficient evidence to provide a reasonable basis for the conclusion that is expressed in the report."

> **Note:** The CPA should usually consider obtaining a written representation letter from the responsible party - the responsible party's refusal to furnish written representations, when deemed necessary, is a scope limitation (modify report for examination; withdraw from a review).

C. Standards of reporting (remember: N-C-R-L)

1. **N**ature of engagement. (In general, whether it is an "examination," a "review," or "agreed-upon procedures" engagement - subject to some technical exceptions where the choices may differ!)

> "The practitioner must identify the subject matter or the assertion being reported on and state the character of the engagement in the report."

2. **C**onclusions (whether the assertion is reliable).

> "The practitioner must state the practitioner's conclusion about the subject matter or the assertion in relation to the criteria against which the subject matter was evaluated in the report."

3. **R**eservations.

> "The practitioner must state all of the practitioner's significant reservations about the engagement, the subject matter, and, if applicable, the assertion related thereto in the report."

a. **About the engagement --** As to the criteria used or the scope of work.

b. **About the presentation --** As to the reliability of the assertion.

4. **L**imited use reports. (The distribution of reports for **"agreed-upon procedures"** engagements must be **restricted to specific users.)**

> "The practitioner must state in the report that the report is intended solely for the information and use of the specified parties under the following circumstances:
>
> 1. When the criteria used to evaluate the subject matter are determined by the practitioner to be appropriate only for a limited number of parties who either participated in their establishment or can be presumed to have an adequate understanding of the criteria.
>
> 2. When the criteria used to evaluate the subject matter are available only to specified parties.
>
> 3. When reporting on subject matter and a written assertion has not been provided by the responsible party.
>
> 4. When the report is on an attestation engagement to apply agreed-upon procedures to the subject matter."

> **Note:** Add a paragraph at the end of the report to restrict its distribution. The practitioner can negotiate to restrict the distribution of any report, but some reports must be restricted. The practitioner is not responsible for controlling the client's distribution of reports!

II. **Usual Menu of Attestation Engagements under these Standards --** Note that the SSAEs apply to attest engagements that are not otherwise covered by other standards (that is, by SASs or SSARSs); must establish "an understanding" with the client (including the nature of services involved and the parties' respective responsibilities).

III. **Examination --** Expressing a high level of assurance (that is, a positive expression of opinion and, therefore, a low level of "attestation risk").

A. The report should identify any material deficiencies noted:

1. **For a scope limitation --** Issue a qualified or disclaimer of opinion.

2. **Problems with presentation --** Issue a qualified or adverse opinion.

B. Can also add an explanatory paragraph to emphasize other matters as desired.

C. Can be issued for general distribution:

1. Describe the nature of the engagement and the scope of work performed.

2. Refer to the applicable professional standards governing the work.

IV. **Review --** Expressing a lower (sometimes called "moderate") level of assurance (that is, negative assurance and, therefore, a moderate level of "attestation risk"):

A. The report should identify any material deficiencies noted.

B. Can also add an explanatory paragraph to emphasize other matters.

C. Indicate that the scope of the work was less than an examination and disclaim an opinion.

V. **Agreed-Upon Procedures --** Where the practitioner and the "specified parties" agree upon the specific procedures to be performed (and the specified parties take responsibility for the sufficiency of the procedures for their purposes!).

[See "AT201 (SSAE 10) - Agreed-Upon Procedures"]

VI. **Limit the Distribution of the Report --** To the "specified users" who participated in identifying the procedures to be used (and who take responsibility for the sufficiency of the procedures!).

A. Usually communicate directly with specified users in advance to obtain their acknowledgment of the sufficiency of procedures.

B. If unable to communicate directly - may meet this requirement by (a) comparing the procedures to the specified users' written requirements; (b) discussing the procedures with representatives of the specified users; or (c) reviewing contracts or correspondence involving the specified users.

C. Adding "non-participant parties" - obtain the party's statement as to the sufficiency of the procedures (usually in writing); can even add parties after the report has been issued. (Practitioner can provide written acknowledgment that the party has been added.)

D. Procedures may evolve or be modified over time - there is flexibility as long as the specified parties take responsibility for the sufficiency of the procedures for their purposes.

E. Avoid vague terminology - don't use terms like "general review; limited review; check; or test" unless clearly defined by the parties.

F. Involvement of internal auditors and other client personnel - basically the same as for their involvement with an audit. (The practitioners cannot take the internal auditors' work as their own or report in a way that implies 'shared responsibility' for that work.)

G. Obtain "an understanding" with the client as to services to be performed and respective responsibilities (should agree upon materiality limits, the involvement of "specialists," etc.).

VII. **Basic Agreed-Upon Procedures Reports**

A. Identify the subject matter (or assertion); refer specifically to "attestation standards established by the (AICPA)." Note that specified parties are responsible for the sufficiency of procedures.

B. Conclusions presented in the form of **"PROCEDURES and FINDINGS"** (either enumerate in the body of the report or refer to the applicable appendix or exhibit where the procedures and findings are identified). Note that no other assurance is given.

C. Indicate that this is not an examination and disclaim an opinion.

D. Restrict the distribution of the report to the specified parties.

VIII. **Additional Reporting Considerations**

A. "Materiality" does not apply unless defined in advance.

B. Explanatory language can be added as deemed appropriate (to describe the condition of records or control; to explain that the practitioner has no responsibility to update the report, etc.).

C. Scope limitations - try to obtain agreement from the specified parties to modify the agreed-upon procedures; if such agreement cannot be obtained, describe any restrictions in the report (or else withdraw from the engagement).

IX. SSAE Hierarchy

[See "AT50 (SSAE 14) - SSAE Hierarchy"]

A. Attestation standards -- Practitioners must comply with SSAEs. (These are enforceable under Rule 202 "Compliance With Standards" of the AICPA Code of Professional Conduct.)

B. Attestation interpretations -- (Consisting of Interpretations of the SSAEs, appendices to the SSAE, etc.) Practitioners should be prepared to explain how they complied with the SSAE provisions involved when such guidance is not applied.

C. Other attestation publications -- (Consisting of articles in professional journals and newsletters, continuing professional education programs, textbooks, etc.) These have no authoritative status, so practitioners may choose to apply such guidance when they deem it relevant and appropriate, perhaps considering the author's reputation, etc.

X. Categories of Professional Requirements

[See "AT20 (SSAE 13) - Defining Professional Requirements"]

A. "Unconditional requirements" -- Must comply without exception (indicated by "must" in SSAEs);

B. "Presumptively mandatory requirements" -- In rare circumstances, the practitioner may depart from such a "requirement", but must document the justification for the departure and how the alternate procedures performed were adequate to meet the objective of the "requirement" (indicated by "should" in SSAEs);

Note:
Descriptive guidance that does not impose a "requirement" (indicated by "may," "might," or "could" in SSAEs).

Financial Forecasts and Projections

After studying this lesson, you should be able to:

1. *Know the two different types of prospective financial statements: forecasts and projections.*
2. *Know the three kinds of engagements (and the structure of the reports) associated with prospective financial statements: examination, compilation, and agreed-upon procedures.*
3. *Know what is meant by the term "partial presentation" of a forecast based on the AICPA's minimum presentation guidelines.*

[See "AT301 (SSAE 10) - Financial Forecasts/Projections"]

I. **There are Two Types of "Prospective Financial Statements" --** Note that "prospective" involves a forward-looking, rather than historical, perspective:

   A. **Forecasts --** Represents the predicted financial statement outcome (that is, the "best guess").

   B. **Projections --** Represents the expected financial statement outcome based on certain specified hypothetical assumptions (more of a "what if ...?" scenario).

II. **Examination of Such Prospective Financial Statements**

   A. **Responsibilities --** Evaluate the presentation of the prospective financial statement information and evaluate the underlying assumptions for reasonableness.

   B. **Basic examination report issues --** Usually three paragraphs (four if limiting the distribution of the report to specified users):

      1. **First paragraph (describe the engagement) --** Identify the prospective financial statements presented; identify management's responsibility and the practitioner's responsibility.
      2. **Second paragraph (AICPA standards) --** State that examination complied with AICPA standards and express belief about reasonable basis for opinion.
      3. **Third paragraph (express opinion) --** State that presentation conforms with AICPA guidelines and that underlying assumptions provide a reasonable basis for the prospective financial statement information (caution that the results may not be achieved).

See the following example.

Examination Report on Forecasted Financial Statements

Independent Accountant's Report

To the Board of Directors and Stockholders

ABC Company

We have examined the accompanying forecasted balance sheet, statements of income, retained earnings, and cash flows of ABC Company as of December 31, 20X1, and for the year then ending. ABC Company's management is responsible for the forecast. Our responsibility is to express an opinion on the forecast based on our examination.

Our examination was conducted in accordance with attestation standards established by the American Institute of Certified Public Accountants and, accordingly, included such procedures as we considered necessary to evaluate both the assumptions used by management and the preparation and presentation of the forecast. We believe that our examination provides a reasonable basis for our opinion.

In our opinion, the accompanying forecast is presented in conformity with guidelines for presentation of a forecast established by the American Institute of Certified Public Accountants, and the underlying assumptions provide a reasonable basis for management's forecast. However, there will usually be differences between the forecasted and actual results, because events and circumstances frequently do not occur as expected, and those differences may be material. We have no responsibility to update this report for events and circumstances occurring after the date of this report.

/s/ CPA firm (signed by engagement partner)

Date (usually the last day of field work)

C. **Additional examination report issues**

   1. **Only a "forecast" can be issued for general distribution; the CPA must restrict the distribution of the report for a "projection."** (Add an additional paragraph to limit the distribution of the report.)
   2. If the prospective information is presented as a **range**, add an additional paragraph to the report pointing out that fact.
   3. May add an explanatory paragraph to emphasize a matter as desired.
   4. **Modification of the opinion**
      a. Issue a **qualified** or **adverse opinion** - when the presentation departs from AICPA guidelines.
      b. Issue an **adverse opinion** if the presentation is not in conformity with AICPA guidelines or if the underlying assumptions are not reasonable.
      c. **Disclaim** an opinion if the scope of the examination is insufficient.

III. **Compilation of Prospective Financial Statement Information --** No assurance is given, the CPA is merely assembling the information in prospective form.

A. **Responsibilities --** Disclose all significant assumptions; read the information and consider whether it is consistent with AICPA guidelines; even though no assurance is given for a compilation, consider whether the compiled information is obviously inappropriate.

B. **Reporting --** Usually consists of two paragraphs. (three if limiting the distribution of the report to specified users.)

1. **First paragraph --** Identify the prospective financial statement information compiled and state that the compilation was made in accordance with AICPA standards.
2. **Second paragraph --** Point out that a compilation is limited in scope (and disclaim an opinion); caution that the results may not be achieved; and state that the accountant takes no responsibility for any events after the report date.

C. The CPA must **restrict the distribution of the report on a "projection."** (Add an additional paragraph to limit the distribution of the report.)

D. If the prospective information is presented as a **range**, add an additional paragraph to the report pointing out that fact.

E. May add an explanatory paragraph to emphasize a matter as desired.

F. Any identified **deficiencies and omissions** must be noted.

G. Do not have to be independent to compile prospective financial statements (since not conveying any assurance) - if **lacking independence**, add a sentence at the end of the compilation report pointing out that fact.

IV. Applying Agreed-Upon Procedures to Prospective Financial Statement Information

A. Specified users participate in **determining the particular procedures** to be performed -- usually meet with the users to discuss their needs (or to provide them with a draft of the anticipated report in advance to reduce misunderstandings).

B. **Reporting --** Usually consists of four paragraphs:

1. Identify the prospective financial statement information, the specified users, the type of engagement, and refer to AICPA standards.
2. Enumerate the procedures performed and the resulting findings.
3. State that the scope was less than an examination under AICPA guidelines and caution that the results may not be achieved; state that the accountant takes no responsibility for events occurring after the report date and **disclaim an opinion.**
4. **Restrict the distribution of the report to the specified users for all "agreed-upon procedures" engagements!**

V. Restricted Reports -- The following reports on prospective financial statement information must be restricted:

A. Any type of report on a **projection** (since projections are too easily misunderstood to be appropriate for general distribution!).

B. An **agreed-upon procedures** report on a forecast.

C. Any type of report on a **"partial presentation"** of a forecast (where any omission of the AICPA **minimum presentation guidelines** causes a presentation to be inappropriate for general distribution).

D. **Minimum presentation guidelines**

1. Sales or gross revenues;
2. Gross profit or cost of sales;
3. Unusual or infrequently occurring items;
4. Provision for income taxes;
5. Discontinued operations or extraordinary items;
6. Income from continuing operations;
7. Net income;

8. Basic and diluted earnings per share;
9. Significant changes in financial position;
10. Description of what the responsible party intends the prospective financial statements to represent;
11. Summary of significant assumptions;
12. Summary of significant accounting policies.

VI. Prospective Financial Statements Included in a Document with Other Information

A. Practitioner-submitted document -- Includes prospective financial information along with historical financial statements (on which the practitioner reports - as an audit, review, or compilation).

1. Must also report on the prospective information (as an examination, compilation, or agreed-upon procedures).
2. The only exception is prospective information that is labeled a "budget" (not extending beyond the end of the fiscal year) - indicate that the budget was not compiled or examined and disclaim an opinion.

B. Client-prepared document -- Includes prospective financial information and historical financial statements (and the practitioner has reported on one or the other, but not both) - do not consent to the use of the practitioner's name unless the other subject matter is covered by an appropriate report (or there is an indication that the practitioner takes no responsibility for the other subject matter).

Pro Forma Financial Information

After studying this lesson, you should be able to:

1. *Know what is meant by the term "pro forma" financial information.*
2. *Understand the accountant's responsibilities under SSAEs when engaged to examine or review such pro forma financial information.*

[See "AT401 (SSAE 10) - Pro Forma Financial Information"]

I. **"Pro Forma" Financial Information --** Shows the significant effects on historical financial information that might have been had a transaction (actual or proposed) occurred at an earlier date.

II. **Examples --** The effects of a business combination, disposal of a significant segment of the business, change in capitalization, or issuance of securities and application of the proceeds.

III. **Required Conditions for Reporting on Pro Forma Financial Information**

A. The document containing the pro forma information includes or references the complete historical financial statements.

B. The accountant has **audited** or **reviewed** the related historical financial statements. (Note that the level of assurance on the pro forma information cannot exceed the level of assurance on the historical financial statements!)

C. The practitioner should have an appropriate level of knowledge of the accounting and financial reporting practices of the entity involved (having audited or reviewed the entity's financial statements would provide that).

IV. **There are Two Basic Types of Engagements Related to Pro Forma Financial Statements**

A. **Examination of pro forma financial information --** Results in "positive assurance."

B. **Review of pro forma financial information --** Results in "negative assurance."

See the following example.

Examination Report on Pro Forma Financial Information

Independent Accountant's Report

We have examined the pro forma adjustments reflecting the transactions (or event) described in Note 1 and the application of those adjustments to the historical amounts in the accompanying pro forma financial condensed balance sheet of ABC Company as of December 31, 20X1, and the pro forma condensed statement of income for the year then ended. The historical condensed financial statements are derived from the historical financial statements of ABC Company, which were audited by us, and of XYZ Company, which were audited by other accountants, appearing elsewhere herein. Such pro forma adjustments are based upon management's assumptions described in Note 2. ABC Company's management is responsible for the pro forma financial information. Our responsibility is to express an opinion on the pro forma financial information based on our examination.

Our examination was conducted in accordance with attestation standards established by the American Institute of Certified Public Accountants and, accordingly, included such procedures as we considered necessary in the circumstances. We believe that our examination provides a reasonable basis for our opinion.

The objective of this pro forma financial information is to show what the significant effects on the historical financial information might have been had the transaction (or event) occurred at an earlier date. However, the pro forma condensed financial statements are not necessarily indicative of the results of operations or related effects on financial position that would have been attained had the above-mentioned transaction (or event) actually occurred earlier.

In our opinion, management's assumptions provide a reasonable basis for presenting the significant effects directly attributable to the above-mentioned transaction (or event) described in Note 1, the related pro forma adjustments give appropriate effect to those assumptions, and the pro forma column reflects the proper application of those adjustments to the historical financial statement amounts in the pro forma condensed balance sheet as of December 31, 20X1, and the pro forma condensed statement of income for the year then ended.

Note: Additional paragraph(s) may be added to emphasize certain matters relating to the attest engagement or the subject matter.

Review Report on Pro Forma Financial Information

Independent Accountant's Report

We have reviewed the pro forma adjustments reflecting the transactions (or event) described in Note 1 and the application of those adjustments to the historical amounts in the accompanying pro forma financial condensed balance sheet of XYZ Company as of March 31, 20X2, and the pro forma condensed statement of income for the three months then ended. The historical condensed financial statements are derived from the historical unaudited financial statements of XYZ Company, which were reviewed by us, and of ABC Company, which were reviewed by other accountants, appearing elsewhere herein. Such pro forma adjustments are based upon management's assumptions described in Note 2. XYZ Company's management is responsible for the pro forma financial information.

Our review was conducted in accordance with attestation standards established by the American Institute of Certified Public Accountants. A review is substantially less in scope than an examination, the objective of which is the expression of an opinion on management's assumptions, the pro forma adjustments and the application of those adjustments to historical financial information. Accordingly, we do not express such an opinion.

The objective of this pro forma financial information is to show what the significant effects on the historical financial information might have been had the transaction (or event) occurred at an earlier date. However, the pro forma condensed financial statements are not necessarily indicative of the results of operations or related effects on financial position that would have been attained had the above-mentioned transaction (or event) actually occurred earlier.

Based on our review, nothing came to our attention that caused us to believe that management's assumptions do not provide a reasonable basis for presenting the significant effects directly attributable to the above-mentioned transaction (or event) described in Note 1, that the related pro forma adjustments do not give appropriate effect to those assumptions, or that the pro forma column does not reflect the proper application of those adjustments to the historical financial statement amounts in the pro forma condensed balance sheet as of March 31, 20X2, and the pro forma condensed statement of income for the three months then ended.

Note: Additional paragraph(s) may be added to emphasize certain matters relating to the attest engagement or the subject matter.

C. The **objective of such an engagement** is to provide some degree of assurance as to (1) whether management's assumptions provide a reasonable basis for presenting the effects of the transactions (events), (2) whether the pro forma adjustments reflect those assumptions, and (3) whether the historical financial statements are appropriately adjusted.

V. **Procedures --** Obtain an understanding of the transaction, read any contracts involved and minutes of board meetings, make inquiries, discuss the assumptions with management, evaluate the computations involved, obtain "sufficient evidence" underlying the adjustments. (Note that an examination requires more evidence than a review.)

VI. **Examination Report Usually Consists of Four Paragraphs**

A. **First paragraph --** Identify the nature of the engagement, describe the pro forma information involved, and identify respective responsibilities.

B. **Second paragraph --** State that the examination was performed according to **attestation standards established by the AICPA** and express belief that the examination provides a reasonable basis for the opinion.

C. **Third paragraph --** Identify the objective of the pro forma information -- "The objective of this pro forma financial information is to show what the significant effects on the historical financial information might have been had the transaction (or event) occurred at an earlier date."

D. **Fourth paragraph --** Express positive assurance (an opinion) on three matters:

1. Whether management's assumptions provide a reasonable basis for presenting the significant effects.
2. Whether the adjustments appropriately reflect those assumptions.
3. Whether the pro forma column reflects the proper adjustments of the historical financial statements.

VII. **Basic Review Report Structure --** Usually consists of four paragraphs (essentially the same structure as the examination report, except "negative assurance" is expressed, instead of an opinion).

VIII. **Other Examination or Review Report Considerations**

A. Modify the report for any scope limitations or other known deficiencies (must convey any known deficiencies noted even if the engagement is a review).

B. The practitioner may negotiate to restrict the distribution of any pro forma report.

C. The report on pro forma information can be added to the practitioner's report on the historical financial statements, or presented separately. (If combined, and the two reports have different dates, the combined report should be "dual-dated.")

Compliance Attestation

After studying this lesson, you should be able to:

1. *Know the two types of engagements applicable to an entity's compliance issues: examination and agreed-upon procedures.*
2. *Understand the accountant's responsibilities under SSAEs when engaged to examine or perform agreed-upon procedures regarding an entity's compliance issues.*

[See "AT601 (SSAE 10) - Compliance Attestation"]

I. **Applicability --** When reporting on an entity's written assertion about compliance with requirements of laws, regulations, or contracts; or an assertion about the effectiveness of its internal controls related to such compliance.

   A. There are two types of engagements related to "compliance attestation:" - (1) examination; and (2) agreed-upon procedures (a "review" is not permitted!).

   B. For either an examination or agreed-upon procedures engagement - obtain management's written representations letter as evidence supporting the engagement

II. **Examination --** Involves a positive expression of opinion relative to the established criteria. See the example of an examination report.

Sample Examination Report on Compliance with Specified Requirements

Independent Accountant's Report

We have examined management's assertion about (*name of entity*)'s compliance with (*list specified compliance requirements*) during the (*period*) ended (*date*) included in the accompanying (*title of management report*). Management is responsible for (*name of entity*)'s compliance with those requirements. Our responsibility is to express an opinion on management's assertion about the Company's compliance based on our examination.

Our examination was made in accordance with standards established by the American Institute of Certified Public Accountants and, accordingly, included examining, on a test basis, evidence about (*name of entity*)'s compliance with those requirements and performing such other procedures as we considered necessary in the circumstances. We believe that our examination provides a reasonable basis for our opinion. Our examination does not provide a legal determination on (*name of entity*)'s compliance with specified requirements.

In our opinion, management's assertion (*identify management's assertion - for example that XYZ Company complied with the aforementioned requirements for the year ended December 31, 19x1*) is fairly stated, in all material respects.

   A. Consider **"attestation risk"** (including the component risks: inherent, control, and detection risks).

   B. **Obtain an understanding of the specific compliance requirements --** Laws, regulations, contracts, etc. (Consider recent regulatory reports and inquiries with appropriate persons inside and outside of the client organization.)

C. **This is very similar to audit requirements --** For example, the CPA must plan the engagement appropriately; obtain sufficient evidence (including appropriate tests of controls); must perform tests of controls when assessing control risk at less than the maximum; must communicate any significant deficiencies noted; and modify the report as needed.

D. **If material noncompliance is found --** Issue a qualified or adverse opinion. (In this case, report directly on the subject matter, not the written assertion.)

III. **Agreed-Upon Procedures**

A. **Objective --** To present specific findings to assist users in evaluating the entity's compliance with specified requirements (or the effectiveness of internal control over compliance) based on agreed-upon procedures.

Sample Agreed-Upon Procedures Report on Compliance with Specified Requirements

Independent Accountant's Report

To the Audit Committees and Managements of ABC Inc. and XYZ Fund

We have performed the procedures enumerated below, which were agreed to by the audit committees and managements of ABC Inc. and XYZ Fund, solely to assist you in evaluating the accompanying Statement of Investment Performance Statistics of XYZ Fund (prepared in accordance with the criteria specified therein) for the year ended December 31, 20X1. XYZ Fund's management is responsible for the statement of investment performance statistics. This agreed-upon procedures engagement was conducted in accordance with attestation standards established by the American Institute of Certified Public Accountants. The sufficiency of these procedures is solely the responsibility of those parties specified in this report. Consequently, we make no representation regarding the sufficiency of the procedures described below either for the purpose for which this report has been requested or for any other purpose.

We were not engaged to and did not conduct an examination, the objective of which would be the expression of an opinion on the accompanying Statement of Investment Performance Statistics of XYZ Fund. Accordingly, we do not express such an opinion. Had we performed additional procedures, other matters might have come to our attention that would have been reported to you.

This report is intended solely for the information and use of the audit committees and managements of ABC Inc. and XYZ Fund, and is not intended to be and should not be used by anyone other than these specified parties.

/signature/

(Date)

Note: Include paragraphs to enumerate **procedures and findings** - or reference appendix (appendices) where these procedures and findings are identified.

B. **Extents of procedures --** These procedures may be as limited or as extensive as the specified users desire, subject to the following conditions:

1. That the users participate in establishing the procedures -- need not necessarily discuss these matters directly with the users; (could base the procedures on the users' requirements or based on correspondence with them; but the CPA should then distribute a draft of the anticipated report or a proposed engagement letter with a request for the users' comments).

2. The users must take responsibility for the adequacy of these agreed-upon procedures for their purposes.

C. **Restrictions on scope --** If there are restrictions on scope due to circumstances - try to get an agreement from the users for modifying the agreed-upon procedures (otherwise must describe the restrictions in the report or else withdraw from the engagement).

D. **Other report modifications involving an explanatory paragraph**

1. If noncompliance is detected:
2. If a material uncertainty exists. (For example, litigation or a regulatory investigation may establish uncertainty about compliance.)
3. When compliance hinges upon interpretations of laws, etc. - consider whether "reasonable criteria" exist; may add an explanatory paragraph that describes the source of interpretations made by management.

E. Do not include "negative assurance" - **CANNOT** offer a "review" related to compliance!

Reporting on Internal Control in an Integrated Audit

After studying this lesson, you should be able to:

1. *Understand the auditor's responsibilities when reporting on internal control over financial reporting in an integrated audit of a non-issuer's financial statements in accordance with AICPA Professional Standards.*
2. *Be familiar with the structure of the report on internal control over financial reporting for such an engagement, whether the report is issued separately or combined with the audit report on the entity's financial statements.*

Note:
These AICPA standards are not applicable to reports on internal control for public companies ("issuers") which are subject to PCAOB standards!

I. Internal Control -- This section presents the AICPA's attestation standards related to reporting on internal control over financial reporting in an "integrated audit" of a non-issuer's financial statements. The AICPA issued SSAE No. 15 to supersede an earlier SSAE and, thereby, more closely align its standards with PCAOB Auditing Standard No. 5.

[See "AT501 (SSAE 15) - Entity Internal Control"]

II. Applicability -- When engaged to perform an examination of the design and operating effectiveness of an entity's internal control over financial reporting ("examination of internal control") that is integrated with an audit of the entity's financial statements ("integrated audit").

A. Timing of an examination of internal control - usually engaged to examine internal control over financial reporting as of the end of the entity's fiscal year. (If engaged to examine internal control for a period of time, the examination should be integrated with an audit of the financial statements covering the same period.)

B. SSAE No. 15 does not apply to other engagements related to internal control that are addressed by other standards, such as (1) engagements to examine the suitability of design of internal control; (2) engagements to examine controls over the effectiveness and efficiency of operations; (3) engagements to examine controls over compliance with laws and regulations; (4) engagements to report on controls at a service organization; and (5) engagements to apply agreed-upon procedures on controls. (Note that an auditor should not accept an engagement to review an entity's internal control over financial reporting.)

III. Underlying Concepts of SSAE No. 15

A. If one or more "material weaknesses" exist then the entity's internal control cannot be considered effective - accordingly, the auditor should plan and perform the examination to obtain sufficient appropriate evidence to obtain reasonable assurance about whether material weaknesses exist as of the date specified.

B. The auditor is not required to search for deficiencies that are less severe than a material weakness (that is, not required to look for significant deficiencies).

C. The auditor should use the same suitable and available control criteria to perform the examination of internal control as management uses for its evaluation of the effectiveness of the entity's internal control.

D. Four conditions must be met for the auditor to examine internal control:

1. Management must accept responsibility for the effectiveness of the entity's internal control;

2. Management must evaluate the effectiveness of the entity's internal control using suitable and available criteria (for example, COSO's Internal Control-Integrated Framework);

3. Management must support its assertion about the effectiveness of the entity's internal control with sufficient appropriate evidence;

4. Management must provide its written assertion about the effectiveness of the entity's internal control in a report that accompanies the auditor's report. (If management refuses to furnish a written assertion, the auditor should withdraw from the engagement.)

E. The auditor's basic responsibilities - the auditor should plan and perform the integrated audit to achieve the objectives of both engagements simultaneously; that is, design the tests of control to (1) obtain sufficient appropriate evidence to support the auditor's opinion on internal control as of the period end and (2) obtain sufficient appropriate evidence to support the auditor's control risk assessments for purposes of the audit of the financial statements.

IV. **Planning the Engagement --** The auditor uses the same risk assessment process to focus attention on the areas of highest risk in both engagements.

A. **Scaling the examination --** The size and complexity of the entity, its business processes, and the business units may affect the way in which the entity achieves its control objectives. (Less control testing may be needed for smaller, less complex entities.)

B. **Entities with multiple locations --** The auditor should assess the risk of material misstatement associated with the various locations/business units and correlate the amount of work with the degree of risk.

C. **Fraud risk assessment --** The auditor should incorporate the results of the fraud risk assessment performed in the financial statement audit.

D. **Using the work of others --** The auditor should assess the competence and objectivity of persons whose work the auditor plans to use. (The auditor's need to perform the work increases with the risk associated with a control.)

E. **Materiality --** The auditor should use the same materiality for both engagements.

F. **Use a "top-down approach" --** The auditor should (1) begin at the financial statement level; (2) use the auditor's understanding of the overall risks to internal control; (3) focus on "entity-level controls" (e.g., the control environment, the entity's risk assessment process, monitoring controls, etc.); (4) focus on accounts, disclosures, and assertions that have a reasonable possibility of material misstatement to the financial statements; (5) verify the auditor's understanding of the risks in the entity's processes (including "walkthroughs"); and (6) select controls for testing based on the assessed risk of material misstatement to each relevant assertion.

V. **Testing Controls and Evaluating Identified Deficiencies --** The evidence that should be obtained increases with the risk of the control being tested. (The objective is to express an opinion on the entity's overall internal control, not on the effectiveness of individual controls.)

A. **Evaluating "design effectiveness" --** Procedures include a mix of inquiry, observation of the entity's operations, and inspection of relevant documentation. (A walkthrough is usually sufficient to evaluate design effectiveness.)

B. **Evaluating "operating effectiveness" --** Procedures include a mix of inquiry, observation of the entity's operations, inspection of relevant documentation, recalculation, and reperformance of the control. (Note that these procedures are presented in order of increasing persuasiveness of the resulting evidence.)

C. **The severity of a deficiency --** Depends on the magnitude of the potential misstatement and the degree of likelihood (whether there is a "reasonable possibility") of a failure; it does not require that an actual misstatement occur.

D. **Risk factors affecting whether a misstatement may occur --** (1) the nature of the accounts, classes of transactions, disclosures, and assertions involved; (2) the susceptibility of the related asset or liability to loss or fraud; (3) the subjectivity, complexity, or judgment involved; (4) the interaction of the control with other controls; (5) the interaction among the deficiencies; and (6) the possible future consequences of the deficiency.

E. **Multiple deficiencies --** May cause a material weakness even though the deficiencies individually may be less severe.

F. **Compensating controls --** May mitigate the severity of a deficiency, although they do not eliminate the deficiency entirely.

G. **Indicators of material weaknesses --** (1) discovery of any fraud involving senior management; (2) restatement of previously issued financial statements to correct a material misstatement; (3) identification of any material misstatement during the audit that was not detected by internal control; and (4) ineffective oversight of reporting and controls by those charged with governance.

VI. Concluding Procedures

A. Review reports of other parties - the auditor should review the reports of others (such as internal auditors) during the year that address internal control issues.

B. Obtain written representations from management specific to internal control matters - management's failure to provide these representations is a scope restriction.

C. Communicate certain internal control matters identified during the integrated audit.

   1. Any identified material weaknesses and significant deficiencies - should be communicated in writing by the report release date. (For governmental entities only, the written communication must occur within 60 days of the report release date.)

   2. Any lesser deficiencies - should be communicated in writing to management within 60 days of the report release date (and should inform those charged with governance of that communication).

   3. Communicating an absence of deficiencies - the auditor should **not** issue any report stating that "no material weaknesses" (or that "no significant deficiencies") were identified in an integrated audit.

VII. Reporting on Internal Control

A. **Separate or combined reports --** The auditor may choose separate reports on the financial statements and on internal control or a combined report on both. (If issuing separate reports, the auditor should add a paragraph to each report referencing the other report.)

   See the following example.

Sample Combined Report on Internal Control and Financial Statements

Independent Auditor's Report

(Introductory paragraph)

We have audited the accompanying balance sheet of ABC Company as of December 31, 20XX, and the related statements of income, retained earnings, and cash flows for the year then ended. We also have audited[1] ABC Company's internal control over financial reporting as of December 31, 20XX based on (*identify criteria*). ABC Company's management is responsible for these financial statements, for maintaining effective internal control over financial reporting, and for its assertion of the effectiveness of internal control over financial reporting, included in the accompanying (*title of management's report*). Our responsibility is to express an opinion on these financial statements and an opinion on ABC Company's internal control over financial reporting based on our examination audits.

(Scope paragraph)

We conducted our audit of the financial statements in accordance with auditing standards generally accepted in the United States of America and our audit of internal control over financial reporting in accordance with attestation standards established by the American Institute of Certified Public Accountants. Those standards require that we plan and perform the audits to obtain reasonable assurance about whether the financial statements are free of material misstatement and whether effective internal control over financial reporting was maintained in all material respects. Our audit of the financial statements included examining, on a test basis, evidence supporting the amounts and disclosures in the financial statements, assessing the accounting principles used and significant estimates made by management, as well as evaluating the overall financial statement presentation. Our audit of internal control over financial reporting included obtaining an understanding of internal control over financial reporting, assessing the risk that a material weakness exists, and testing and evaluating the design and operating effectiveness of internal control based on the assessed risk. Our audits also included performing such other procedures as we considered necessary in the circumstances. We believe that our audits provide a reasonable basis for our opinions.

(Definition paragraph)

An entity's internal control over financial reporting is a process effected by those charged with governance, management, and other personnel, designed to provide reasonable assurance regarding the preparation of reliable financial statements in accordance with (*applicable financial reporting framework, such as accounting principles generally accepted in the United States of America*). An entity's internal control over financial reporting includes those policies and procedures that (1) pertain to the maintenance of records that, in reasonable detail, accurately and fairly reflect the transactions and dispositions of the assets of the entity; (2) provide reasonable assurance that transactions are recorded as necessary to permit preparation of financial statements in accordance with (*applicable financial reporting framework, such as accounting principles generally accepted in the United States of America*), and that receipts and expenditures of the entity are being made only in accordance with authorizations of management and those charged with governance; and (3) provide reasonable assurance regarding prevention, or timely detection and correction of unauthorized acquisition, use, or disposition of the entity's assets that could have a material effect on the financial statements.

(Inherent limitations paragraph)

Because of its inherent limitations, internal control over financial reporting may not prevent, or detect and correct misstatements. Also, projections of any evaluation of effectiveness to future periods are subject to the risk that controls may become inadequate because of changes in conditions, or that the degree of compliance with the policies or procedures may deteriorate.

(Opinion paragraph)

In our opinion, the financial statements referred to above present fairly, in all material respects, the financial position of ABC Company as of December 31, 20XX, and the results of its operations and its cash flows for the year then ended in conformity with accounting principles generally accepted in the United States of America. Also in our opinion, ABC Company maintained, in all material respects, effective internal control over financial reporting as of December 31, 20XX, based on (*identified criteria*).

(Signature)

(Date)

[1] SSAE No. 15 includes the following statement: "Because the examination of internal control is integrated with the audit of the financial statements and an examination provides the same level of assurance as an audit, the auditor may refer to the examination of internal control as an audit in his or her report or other communications."

B. **Report date --** Should be dated when the auditor has obtained sufficient appropriate evidence to support the auditor's opinion. (If issuing separate reports, the reports should have the same date for an integrated audit.)

C. **Unqualified opinion on management's assertion about internal control or on the operating effectiveness of internal control (directly) --** The structure of the auditor's report consists of six paragraphs: (1) Introductory paragraph; (2) Scope paragraph; (3) Definition paragraph; (4) Inherent limitations paragraph; (5) Opinion paragraph; and (6) Audit of financial statements paragraph.

Sample Examination Report on Management's Assertion

Independent Auditor's Report

(Introductory paragraph)

We have examined management's assertion, included in the accompanying (*title of management report*), that ABC Company maintained effective internal control over financial reporting as of December 31, 20XX based on (*identify criteria*). ABC Company's management is responsible for maintaining effective internal control over financial reporting, and for its assertion of the effectiveness of internal control over financial reporting, included in the accompanying (*title of management's report*). Our responsibility is to express an opinion on ABC Company's internal control over financial reporting based on our examination.

(Scope paragraph)

We conducted our examination in accordance with attestation standards established by the American Institute of Certified Public Accountants. Those standards require that we plan and perform the examination to obtain reasonable assurance about whether effective internal control over financial reporting was maintained in all material respects. Our examination included obtaining an understanding of internal control over financial reporting, assessing the risk that a material weakness exists, and testing and evaluating the design and operating effectiveness of internal control based on the assessed risk. Our examination also included performing such other procedures as we considered necessary in the circumstances. We believe that our examination provides a reasonable basis for our opinion.

(Definition paragraph)

An entity's internal control over financial reporting is a process effected by those charged with governance, management, and other personnel, designed to provide reasonable assurance regarding the preparation of reliable financial statements in accordance with [applicable financial reporting framework, such as accounting principles generally accepted in the United States of America]. An entity's internal control over financial reporting includes those policies and procedures that (1) pertain to the maintenance of records that, in reasonable detail, accurately and fairly reflect the transactions and dispositions of the assets of the entity; (2) provide reasonable assurance that transactions are recorded as necessary to permit preparation of financial statements in accordance with (*applicable financial reporting framework, such as accounting principles generally accepted in the United States of America*), and that receipts and expenditures of the entity are being made only in accordance with authorizations of management and those charged with governance; and (3) provide reasonable assurance regarding prevention, or timely detection and correction of unauthorized acquisition, use, or disposition of the entity's assets that could have a material effect on the financial statements.

(Inherent limitations paragraph)

Because of its inherent limitations, internal control over financial reporting may not prevent, or detect and correct misstatements. Also, projections of any evaluation of effectiveness to future periods are subject to the risk that controls may become inadequate because of changes in conditions, or that the degree of compliance with the policies or procedures may deteriorate.

(Opinion paragraph)

In our opinion, management's assertion that ABC Company maintained effective internal control over financial reporting as of December 31, 20XX is fairly stated, in all material respects, based on (*identified criteria*).

(Audit of financial statements paragraph)

We also have audited, in accordance with auditing standards generally accepted in the United States of America, the (*identify financial statements*) of ABC Company and our report dated (*date of report, which should be the same as the date of the report on the examination of internal control] expressed [include nature of opinion*).

(Signature)

(Date)

See the following example.

Sample Examination Report on the Effectiveness of Internal Control

Independent Auditor's Report

(Introductory paragraph)
We have examined ABC Company's internal control over financial reporting as of December 31, 20XX based on (*identify criteria*). ABC Company's management is responsible for maintaining effective internal control over financial reporting, and for its assertion of the effectiveness of internal control over financial reporting, included in the accompanying (*title of management's report*). Our responsibility is to express an opinion on ABC Company's internal control over financial reporting based on our examination.

(Scope paragraph)
We conducted our examination in accordance with attestation standards established by the American Institute of Certified Public Accountants. Those standards require that we plan and perform the examination to obtain reasonable assurance about whether effective internal control over financial reporting was maintained in all material respects. Our examination included obtaining an understanding of internal control over financial reporting, assessing the risk that a material weakness exists, and testing and evaluating the design and operating effectiveness of internal control based on the assessed risk. Our examination also included performing such other procedures as we considered necessary in the circumstances. We believe that our examination provides a reasonable basis for our opinion.

(Definition paragraph)
An entity's internal control over financial reporting is a process effected by those charged with governance, management, and other personnel, designed to provide reasonable assurance regarding the preparation of reliable financial statements in accordance with (*applicable financial reporting framework, such as accounting principles generally accepted in the United States of America*). An entity's internal control over financial reporting includes those policies and procedures that (1) pertain to the maintenance of records that, in reasonable detail, accurately and fairly reflect the transactions and dispositions of the assets of the entity; (2) provide reasonable assurance that transactions are recorded as necessary to permit preparation of financial statements in accordance with (*applicable financial reporting framework, such as accounting principles generally accepted in the United States of America*), and that receipts and expenditures of the entity are being made only in accordance with authorizations of management and those charged with governance; and (3) provide reasonable assurance regarding prevention, or timely detection and correction of unauthorized acquisition, use, or disposition of the entity's assets that could have a material effect on the financial statements.

(Inherent limitations paragraph)
Because of its inherent limitations, internal control over financial reporting may not prevent, or detect and correct misstatements. Also, projections of any evaluation of effectiveness to future periods are subject to the risk that controls may become inadequate because of changes in conditions, or that the degree of compliance with the policies or procedures may deteriorate.

(Opinion paragraph)
In our opinion, ABC Company maintained, in all material respects, effective internal control over financial reporting as of December 31, 20XX, based on (*identified criteria*).

(Audit of financial statements paragraph)

We also have audited, in accordance with auditing standards generally accepted in the United States of America, the (*identify financial statements*) of ABC Company and our report dated (*date of report, which should be the same as the date of the report on the examination of internal control*) expressed (*include nature of opinion*).

(Signature)

(Date)

D. Adverse opinions -- The auditor should express an adverse opinion if there is one or more material weaknesses in internal control (in this case, report directly on the effectiveness of internal control, not on management's assertion); should also consider the implications to the audit of the entity's financial statements.

Sample Report with Adverse Opinion on the Effectiveness of Internal Control

<u>Independent Auditor's Report</u>

(Introductory paragraph)

We have examined ABC Company's internal control over financial reporting as of December 31, 20XX based on (*identify criteria*). ABC Company's management is responsible for maintaining effective internal control over financial reporting, and for its assertion of the effectiveness of internal control over financial reporting, included in the accompanying (*title of management's report*). Our responsibility is to express an opinion on ABC Company's internal control over financial reporting based on our examination.

(Scope paragraph)

We conducted our examination in accordance with attestation standards established by the American Institute of Certified Public Accountants. Those standards require that we plan and perform the examination to obtain reasonable assurance about whether effective internal control over financial reporting was maintained in all material respects. Our examination included obtaining an understanding of internal control over financial reporting, assessing the risk that a material weakness exists, and testing and evaluating the design and operating effectiveness of internal control based on the assessed risk. Our examination also included performing such other procedures as we considered necessary in the circumstances. We believe that our examination provides a reasonable basis for our opinion.

(Definition paragraph)

An entity's internal control over financial reporting is a process effected by those charged with governance, management, and other personnel, designed to provide reasonable assurance regarding the preparation of reliable financial statements in accordance with (*applicable financial reporting framework, such as accounting principles generally accepted in the United States of America*). An entity's internal control over financial reporting includes those policies and procedures that (1) pertain to the maintenance of records that, in reasonable detail, accurately and fairly reflect the transactions and dispositions of the assets of the entity; (2) provide reasonable assurance that transactions are recorded as necessary to permit preparation of financial statements in accordance with (*applicable financial reporting framework, such as accounting principles generally accepted in the United States of America*), and that receipts and expenditures of the entity are being made only in accordance with authorizations of management and those charged with governance; and (3) provide reasonable assurance regarding prevention, or timely detection and correction of unauthorized acquisition, use, or disposition of the entity's assets that could have a material effect on the financial statements.

(Inherent limitations paragraph)

Because of its inherent limitations, internal control over financial reporting may not prevent, or detect and correct misstatements. Also, projections of any evaluation of effectiveness to future periods are subject to the risk that controls may become inadequate because of changes in conditions, or that the degree of compliance with the policies or procedures may deteriorate.

(Explanatory paragraph)

A material weakness is a deficiency, or a combination of deficiencies, in internal control over financial reporting, such that there is a reasonable possibility that a material misstatement of the entity's financial statements will not be prevented, or detected and corrected on a timely basis. The following material weakness has been identified and included in the accompanying (*title of management's report*).

(*Identify the material weakness described in management's report.*)

(Opinion paragraph)

In our opinion, because of the effect of the material weakness described above on the achievement of the objectives of the control criteria, ABC Company has not maintained effective internal control over financial reporting as of December 31, 20XX, based on (*identified criteria*).

(*Audit of financial statements paragraph*)

We also have audited, in accordance with auditing standards generally accepted in the United States of America, the (*identify financial statements*) of ABC Company. We considered the material weakness identified above in determining the nature, timing, and extent of audit tests applied in our audit of the 20XX financial statements, and this report does not affect our report dated (*date of report, which should be the same as the date of the report on the examination of internal control*), which expressed (*include nature of opinion*).

(Signature)

(Date)

E. **Other report modifications --** (1) if elements of management's report are incomplete or improperly presented (add an explanatory paragraph); (2) if there is a scope limitation (either withdraw or disclaim an opinion); (3) if the opinion is based partially on the report of another auditor; or (4) management's report contains other additional information, such as commentary about corrective action taken (disclaim an opinion on the other information).

Management's Discussion and Analysis (MD&A)

After studying this lesson, you should be able to:

1. *Understand the accountant's responsibilities (and the structure of the report) when* ***examining*** *an entity's MD&A presentation in accordance with AICPA Professional Standards.*
2. *Understand the accountant's responsibilities (and the structure of the report) when* ***reviewing*** *an entity's MD&A presentation in accordance with AICPA Professional Standards.*

[See "AT701 (SSAE 10) - MD&A"]

I. **Applicability**

A. When attesting to MD&A that has been prepared according to the requirements of the SEC and that MD&A is presented in annual reports or in other documents.

B. Can even apply to a nonpublic entity that provides a written assertion that the SEC requirements were used as criteria for the presentation of the MD&A.

1. **Precondition to accept an MD&A engagement --** Must have audited the annual financials for the latest period applicable to the MD&A presentation; any other financials involved must have been audited (or at least reviewed if interim/quarterly financials) by the practitioner or a predecessor auditor.

II. **Examination of MD&A - Results in Positive Assurance**

A. **Purpose --** To express an opinion on whether:

1. **Required elements --** The presentation includes the elements required by the SEC:
   a. Discussion of **financial condition** (liquidity and capital resources);
   b. Discussion of **changes in financial condition**;
   c. Discussion of **results of operations.**
2. **Historical amounts --** The historical financial amounts are accurately derived from the financials.
3. **Basis for conclusions --** The underlying information, assumptions, etc., provide a reasonable basis for the disclosures within the MD&A.

B. There are **four assertions** implicitly embodied in the MD&A presentation:

1. **Occurrence --** Whether reported events actually occurred during the period.
2. **Consistency with the financials --** Whether historical amounts have been accurately derived from the financials.
3. **Completeness of the explanation --** Whether the description of matters comprising the MD&A presentation is complete.
4. **Presentation and disclosure --** Whether information in the MD&A is properly classified, described, and disclosed.

C. **Primary dimensions of an examination of MD&A**

1. **Planning the examination (similar to an audit engagement) --** Develop an overall strategy that limits **"attestation risk"** to an acceptably low level.

a. Inherent risk - varies with the assertion involved.

b. Control risk (same as previously discussed).

c. Detection risk (same as previously discussed).

2. **Consideration of internal control applicable to MD&A (similar to an audit) --** Pertains to assessment of control risk, documenting the understanding, and communication of significant deficiencies.

3. **Obtain sufficient evidence --** Varies with the circumstances but includes reading the MD&A for consistency with the financials, examining related documents, reading minutes, reading communications from the SEC, and obtaining written representations from management, among other things.

4. **Consideration of subsequent events --** (SEC expects MD&A to reflect events at or near the filing date) -- Read minutes and available interim financials; make inquiries of management and obtain appropriate representations in writing.

D. **Reporting on MD&A --** Financial statements with the auditor's report should accompany the document containing the MD&A (or be incorporated by reference to documents filed with the SEC).

1. **Title --** "Independent Accountant's Report."

2. **Standard examination report consists of four paragraphs**

a. **Introductory paragraph (four sentences)**

i. Identify MD&A presentation.

ii. Identify management's responsibility.

iii. Identify accountant's responsibility.

iv. Refer to related audit report.

b. **Scope paragraph (three sentences)**

i. Refer to attestation standards established by AICPA.

ii. Describe scope of examination.

iii. Say that examination provides reasonable basis for opinion.

c. **Explanatory paragraph (three sentences)**

i. Comment on the need for estimates and assumptions.

ii. Comment on the role of future expectations.

iii. State that actual results may differ.

d. **Opinion paragraph (one long sentence) --** Whether (1) the presentation includes elements required by SEC; (2) the historical amounts are accurately derived; and (3) the underlying information and assumptions provide a reasonable basis for the MD&A.

3. **Dating report --** As of completion of the examination procedures.

4. **Modifications of the standard report.**

a. **Reservations as to presentation --** Results in a **qualified** or **adverse** opinion.

b. **Reservations as to scope --** Results in a **qualified** opinion or a **disclaimer** of opinion.

c. **Division of responsibility --** May refer to another practitioner's report on MD&A for a specific component as a partial basis for one's own report.

d. **Emphasis of a matter --** Presented as a separate paragraph (e.g. information included beyond the SEC's requirements).

Sample Examination Report on (Annual) MD&A When Reporting Directly on the Subject Matter, Not on Management's Assertion

Independent Accountant's Report

(Introductory paragraph)

We have examined ABC Company's Management's Discussion and Analysis taken as a whole, included (incorporated by reference) in the Company's (insert description of registration statement or document). Management is responsible for the preparation of the Company's Management's Discussion and Analysis pursuant to the rules and regulations adopted by the Securities and Exchange Commission. Our responsibility is to express an opinion on the presentation based on our examination. We have audited, in accordance with auditing standards generally accepted in the United States of America, the financial statements of ABC Company as of December 31, 20X3 and 20X2, and for each of the years in the three-year period ended December 31, 20X3, and in our report dated [Month and day], 20X4, we expressed an unqualified opinion on those financial statements.

(Scope paragraph)

Our examination of Management's Discussion and Analysis was conducted in accordance with attestation standards established by the American Institute of Certified Public Accountants, and, accordingly, included examining, on a test basis, evidence supporting the historical amounts and disclosures in the presentation. An examination also includes assessing the significant determinations made by management as to the relevancy of information to be included and the estimates and assumptions that affect reported information. We believe that our examination provides a reasonable basis for our opinion.

(Explanatory paragraph)

The preparation of Management's Discussion and Analysis requires management to interpret the criteria, make determinations as to the relevancy of information to be included, and make estimates and assumptions that affect reported information. Management's Discussion and Analysis includes information regarding the estimated future impact of transactions and events that have occurred or are expected to occur, expected sources of liquidity and capital resources, operating trends, commitments, and uncertainties. Actual results in the future may differ materially from management's present assessment of this information because events and circumstances frequently do not occur as expected.

(Opinion paragraph)

In our opinion, the Company's presentation of Management's Discussion and Analysis includes, in all material respects, the required elements of the rules and regulations adopted by the Securities and Exchange Commission; the historical financial amounts included therein have been accurately derived, in all material respects, from the Company's financial statements; and the underlying information, determinations, estimates, and assumptions of the Company provide a reasonable basis for the disclosures contained therein.

(Signature)

(Date)

III. Review of MD&A - Results in Negative Assurance

A. **Purpose --** To report whether the practitioner has any reason to believe that:

1. The presentation does **not** include the elements required by the SEC;
2. The historical financial amounts are **not** accurately derived from the financials;

3. The underlying information, assumptions, etc., do **not** provide a reasonable basis for the disclosures within the MD&A.

B. **Primary dimensions of a review of MD&A**

1. Obtain an understanding of the SEC requirements regarding MD&A.
2. Plan the engagement - develop an overall strategy.
3. Consider relevant portions of internal control affecting MD&A presentation.
4. Apply **analytical procedures** and make **inquiries** of management (usually do not have to obtain corroboration).
5. Consideration of subsequent events.
6. Obtain written representations from management.

C. **Standard review report --** Usually consists of five paragraphs (if including a "restricted use" paragraph at the end of the report); the accountant may review the entity's annual MD&A presentation or an interim MD&A presentation.

1. **Title --** "Independent Accountant's Report"
2. **Introductory paragraph (three sentences) - delete the sentence on accountant's responsibility**
   a. Identify MD&A presentation.
   b. Identify management's responsibility.
   c. Refer to related audit report.
3. **Scope paragraph (four sentences) - add a disclaimer**
   a. Refer to attestation standards established by the AICPA.
   b. Describe a review engagement.
   c. Say that scope is less than that of an examination.
   d. Disclaim an opinion.
4. **Explanatory paragraph (three sentences) - same as for an examination report**
   a. Comment on the need for estimates and assumptions.
   b. Comment on the role of future expectations.
   c. State that actual results may differ.
5. **Conclusions paragraph (one long sentence) --** Negative assurance as to whether presentation does not include elements required by SEC, historical amounts are not accurately derived, and underlying information and assumptions do not provide a reasonable basis for the MD&A.
6. **Restricted use paragraph (one sentence) --** Restrict the distribution when the MD&A presentation and the practitioner's report are not intended to be filed with the SEC under the 1933 and 1934 Securities Acts.
7. **Dating report --** As of completion of the review procedures.
8. **Modifications of the standard report --** Reservations as to presentation; reservations as to scope (not rendering review incomplete); division of responsibility; or emphasis of a matter.

Assurance Services

After studying this lesson, you should be able to:

1. *Know the definition of "assurance services" and understand the distinction between "auditing," "attestation," and "assurance."*
2. *Be familiar with the AICPA's established assurance services, including WebTrust, SysTrust, and PrimePlus/ElderCare.*
3. *Recognize the "Assurance Services Executive Committee" as the AICPA senior committee with responsibility for identifying evolving assurance opportunities and for developing criteria and guidance to support these AICPA initiatives.*

Definition:

Assurance Services: Independent professional services that improve the quality or context of information for decision makers. (Quality includes the "reliability" and "relevance" of information and "context" refers to how the decision maker uses the information.)

I. **Relationship of "Assurance" to "Auditing" and "Attestation" --** Auditing and attestation both involve enhancing the *reliability* of information (auditing specifically focuses on historical financial statement subject matter, whereas attestation is not limited to financial statements subject matter); assurance is broader than attestation, since assurance may address the relevance of information in addition to the *reliability* of information.

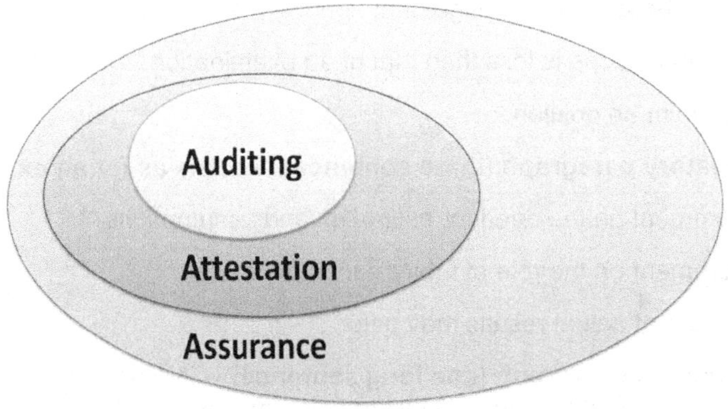

II. **AICPA Assurance Services**

A. **"Trust Services" --** The AICPA and Canadian Institute of Chartered Accountants developed "SysTrust" (to provide assurance on "systems" generating information and representations generally) and "WebTrust" (to provide assurance specifically related to e-commerce activities).

1. Five principles and criteria associated with Trust Services (these are organized in 4 broad areas: policies, communications, procedures, and monitoring):

    a. **Security --** The system is protected from unauthorized access.

    b. **Availability --** The system is available for operation and use as committed or agreed.

   c. **Processing integrity --** System processing is complete, accurate, timely, and authorized.

   d. **Confidentiality --** Information designated as confidential is protected as committed or agreed.

   e. **Privacy --** Personal information is collected, used, retained, and disclosed in conformity with the commitments in the entity's privacy notice and with criteria set forth in generally accepted privacy principles issued by the AICPA/CICA.

2. **Web Trust --** To earn the WebTrust seal (which provides assurance to participants about transaction integrity and information security in e-commerce transactions with an entity's Web site), the entity must comply with all five of the principles above and engage a CPA licensed to provide WebTrust-related services; the seal displays a digital certificate and can be displayed until the designated expiration date (the WebTrust seal is managed by a third-party "seal manager").

3. **SysTrust --** To earn the CPA's unqualified opinion for a SysTrust engagement, an entity's system would also have to meet the above Trust Services principles; the SysTrust engagement would evaluate management's written assertions about the effectiveness of controls over the entity's system relative to applicable attestation standards.

B. **PrimePlus** (formerly known as "ElderCare") **Services --** PrimePlus has a connotation primarily involving financial/lifestyle planning issues, whereas ElderCare has a connotation primarily involving healthcare (the AICPA says it will continue to support both brands).

> **Definition:**
>
> *PrimePlus/ElderCare services*: "A unique and customizable package of professional services - both financial and nonfinancial - intended to help older adults maintain, for as long as possible, their desired lifestyle and financial independence."

1. **Financial services** include the following: receiving, disposing, and accounting for client receipts; making bill payments and handling banking services; submitting claims to insurance companies; estate planning; providing tax planning and tax return preparation; evaluating investments and trust activity; managing portfolios; protecting elderly from predators; etc.

2. **Nonfinancial services** include the following: coordinating support and healthcare services; communicating family expectations to care providers; managing real estate and other assets; establishing performance monitoring systems; managing real estate and other assets; coordinating services involving healthcare, legal, and other professionals; etc.

3. Markets for PrimePlus/ElderCare services - there are three primary markets: (a) older clients themselves; (b) children of older adults; and (c) other professionals who deal with those older adults (such as lawyers and healthcare professionals).

C. The AICPA has established a senior committee known as the "**Assurance Services Executive Committee**" (ASEC) to oversee the ongoing development of assurance services.

1. ASEC's role - to identify trends and assurance opportunities; to develop assurance guidance (including applicable criteria); to communicate those opportunities and guidance to AICPA members; and to create alliance with industry, government, or others to facilitate those assurance opportunities.

2. ASEC has appointed several task forces to focus on developing assurance opportunities: (a) XBRL Assurance Task Force (regarding the development of guidance on the assurance of XBRL-related documents); (b) Trust/Data Integrity Task Force (regarding the development of principles/criteria for assurance on the security, availability, process integrity of systems and the confidentiality and privacy of information); and (c) Risk Assurance Task Force (regarding enterprise risk management issues).

Sample Reports

Examination of Forecast

Independent Accountant's Report

To the Board of Directors and Stockholders

ABC Company

We have examined the accompanying forecasted balance sheet, statements of income, retained earnings, and cash flows of ABC Company as of December 31, 20X1, and for the year then ending. ABC Company's management is responsible for the forecast. Our responsibility is to express an opinion on the forecast based on our examination.

Our examination was conducted in accordance with attestation standards established by the American Institute of Certified Public Accountants and, accordingly, included such procedures as we considered necessary to evaluate both the assumptions used by management and the preparation and presentation of the forecast. We believe that our examination provides a reasonable basis for our opinion.

In our opinion, the accompanying forecast is presented in conformity with guidelines for presentation of a forecast established by the American Institute of Certified Public Accountants, and the underlying assumptions provide a reasonable basis for management's forecast. However, there will usually be differences between the forecasted and actual results, because events and circumstances frequently do not occur as expected, and those differences may be material. We have no responsibility to update this report for events and circumstances occurring after the date of this report.

/s/ CPA firm (signed by engagement partner)

Date (usually the last day of field work)

AUP of Forecast

Sample Agreed-Upon Procedures Report on Forecast Financial Information

Independent Accountant's Report on Applying Agreed-Upon Procedures

Board of Directors - XYZ Corporation

Board of Directors - ABC Company

At your request, we have performed certain agreed-upon procedures, as enumerated below, with respect to the forecasted balance sheet and the related forecasted statements of income, retained earnings, and cash flows of DEF Company, a subsidiary of ABC Company, as of December 31, 20XX, and for the year then ending. These procedures, which were agreed to by the Boards of Directors of XYZ Corporation and ABC Company, were performed solely to assist you in evaluating the forecast in connection with the proposed sale of DEF Company to XYZ Corporation. DEF Company's management is responsible for the forecast.

This agreed-upon procedures engagement was conducted in accordance with attestation standards established by the American Institute of Certified Public Accountants. The sufficiency of these procedures is solely the responsibility of the specified parties. Consequently, we make no representation regarding the sufficiency of the procedures described below either for the purpose for which this report has been requested or for any other purpose.

[Include paragraphs to enumerate (or reference) procedures and findings]

We were not engaged to and did not conduct an examination, the objective of which would be the expression of an opinion on the accompanying prospective financial statements. Accordingly, we do not express an opinion on whether the prospective financial statements are presented in conformity with AICPA presentation guidelines or on whether the underlying assumptions provide a reasonable basis for the presentation. Had we performed additional procedures, other matters might have come to our attention that would have been reported to you. Furthermore, there will usually be differences between the forecasted and actual results, because events and circumstances frequently do not occur as expected, and those differences may be material. We have no responsibility to update this report for events and circumstances occurring after the date of this report.

This report is intended solely for the information and use of the Boards of Directors of ABC Company and XYZ Corporation and is not intended to be and should not be used by anyone other than these specified parties.

Compilation of Forecast

Accountant's Compilation Report

We have compiled the accompanying forecasted balance sheet, statements of income, retained earnings, and cash flows of ABC Company as of December 31, 20X1, and for the year then ending, in accordance with attestation standards established by the American Institute of Certified Public Accountants.

A compilation is limited to presenting in the form of a forecast information that is the representation of management and does not include evaluation of the support for the assumptions underlying the forecast. We have not examined the forecast and, accordingly, do not express an opinion or any other form of assurance on the accompanying statements or assumptions. Furthermore, there will usually be differences between the forecasted and actual results, because events and circumstances frequently do not occur as expected, and those differences may be material. We have no responsibility to update this report for events and circumstances occurring after the date of this report.

Examination of Pro Forma

Independent Accountant's Report

We have examined the pro forma adjustments reflecting the transactions [or event] described in Note 1 and the application of those adjustments to the historical amounts in the accompanying pro forma financial condensed balance sheet of ABC Company as of December 31, 20X1, and the pro forma condensed statement of income for the year then ended. The historical condensed financial statements are derived from the historical financial statements of ABC Company, which were audited by us, and of XYZ Company, which were audited by other accountants, appearing elsewhere herein. Such pro forma adjustments are based upon management's assumptions described in Note 2. ABC Company's management is responsible for the pro forma financial information. Our responsibility is to express an opinion on the pro forma financial information based on our examination.

Our examination was conducted in accordance with attestation standards established by the American Institute of Certified Public Accountants and, accordingly, included such procedures as we considered necessary in the circumstances. We believe that our examination provides a reasonable basis for our opinion.

The objective of this pro forma financial information is to show what the significant effects on the historical financial information might have been had the transaction [or event] occurred at an earlier date. However, the pro forma condensed financial statements are not necessarily indicative of the results of operations or related effects on financial position that would have been attained had the above-mentioned transaction [or event] actually occurred earlier.

Note:
Additional paragraph(s) may be added to emphasize certain matters relating to the attest engagement or the subject matter.

In our opinion, management's assumptions provide a reasonable basis for presenting the significant effects directly attributable to the above-mentioned transaction [or event] described in Note 1, the related pro forma adjustments give appropriate effect to those assumptions, and the pro forma column reflects the proper application of those adjustments to the historical financial statement amounts in the pro forma condensed balance sheet as of December 31, 20X1, and the pro forma condensed statement of income for the year then ended.

Review of Pro Forma

Independent Accountant's Report

We have reviewed the pro forma adjustments reflecting the transactions [or event] described in Note 1 and the application of those adjustments to the historical amounts in the accompanying pro forma financial condensed balance sheet of XYZ Company as of March 31, 20X2, and the pro forma condensed statement of income for the three months then ended. The historical condensed financial statements are derived from the historical unaudited financial statements of XYZ Company, which were reviewed by us, and of ABC Company, which were reviewed by other accountants, appearing elsewhere herein. Such pro forma adjustments are based upon management's assumptions described in Note 2. XYZ Company's management is responsible for the pro forma financial information.

Our review was conducted in accordance with attestation standards established by the American Institute of Certified Public Accountants. A review is substantially less in scope than an examination, the objective of which is the expression of an opinion on management's assumptions, the pro forma adjustments and the application of those adjustments to historical financial information. Accordingly, we do not express such an opinion.

The objective of this pro forma financial information is to show what the significant effects on the historical financial information might have been had the transaction [or event] occurred at an earlier date. However, the pro forma condensed financial statements are not necessarily indicative of the results of operations or related effects on financial position that would have been attained had the above-mentioned transaction [or event] actually occurred earlier.

Note: Additional paragraph(s) may be added to emphasize certain matters relating to the attest engagement or the subject matter.

Based on our review, nothing came to our attention that caused us to believe that management's assumptions do not provide a reasonable basis for presenting the significant effects directly attributable to the above-mentioned transaction [or event] described in Note 1, that the related pro forma adjustments do not give appropriate effect to those assumptions, or that the pro forma column does not reflect the proper application of those adjustments to the historical financial statement amounts in the pro forma condensed balance sheet as of March 31, 20X2, and the pro forma condensed statement of income for the three months then ended.

Examination for Compliance

Independent Accountant's Report

We have examined management's assertion about (*name of entity*)'s compliance with (*list specified compliance requirements*) during the (*period*) ended (*date*) included in the accompanying (*title of management report*). Management is responsible for (*name of entity*)'s compliance with those requirements. Our responsibility is to express an opinion on management's assertion about the Company's compliance based on our examination.

Our examination was made in accordance with standards established by the American Institute of Certified Public Accountants and, accordingly, included examining, on a test basis, evidence about (*name of entity*)'s compliance with those requirements and performing such other procedures as we considered necessary in the circumstances. We believe that our examination provides a reasonable basis for our opinion. Our examination does not provide a legal determination on (*name of entity*)'s compliance with specified requirements.

In our opinion, management's assertion (*identify management's assertion - for example that XYZ Company complied with the aforementioned requirements for the year ended December 31, 19x1*) is fairly stated, in all material respects.

AUP for Compliance

Independent Accountant's Report

To the Audit Committees and Managements of ABC Inc. and XYZ Fund

We have performed the procedures enumerated below, which were agreed to by the audit committees and managements of ABC Inc. and XYZ Fund, solely to assist you in evaluating the accompanying Statement of Investment Performance Statistics of XYZ Fund (prepared in accordance with the criteria specified therein) for the year ended December 31, 20X1. XYZ Fund's management is responsible for the statement of investment performance statistics. This agreed-upon procedures engagement was conducted in accordance with attestation standards established by the American Institute of Certified Public Accountants. The sufficiency of these procedures is solely the responsibility of those parties specified in this report. Consequently, we make no representation regarding the sufficiency of the procedures described below either for the purpose for which this report has been requested or for any other purpose.

> **Note:**
> Include paragraphs to enumerate **procedures and findings** - or reference appendix (appendices) where these procedures and findings are identified.

We were not engaged to and did not conduct an examination, the objective of which would be the expression of an opinion on the accompanying Statement of Investment Performance Statistics of XYZ Fund. Accordingly, we do not express such an opinion. Had we performed additional procedures, other matters might have come to our attention that would have been reported to you.

This report is intended solely for the information and use of the audit committees and managements of ABC Inc. and XYZ Fund, and is not intended to be and should not be used by anyone other than these specified parties.

/signature/

[Date]

Examination of MD&A

Sample Examination Report on (Annual) MD&A When Reporting Directly on the Subject Matter, Not an Assertion

Independent Accountant's Report

Introductory paragraph

We have examined ABC Company's Management's Discussion and Analysis taken as a whole, included (incorporated by reference) in the Company's (insert description of registration statement or document). Management is responsible for the preparation of the Company's Management's Discussion and Analysis pursuant to the rules and regulations adopted by the Securities and Exchange Commission. Our responsibility is to express an opinion on the presentation based on our examination. We have audited, in accordance with auditing standards generally accepted in the United States of America, the financial statements of ABC Company as of December 31, 20X3 and 20X2, and for each of the years in the three-year period ended December 31, 20X3, and in our report dated (Month and day), 20X4, we expressed an unqualified opinion on those financial statements.

Scope paragraph

Our examination of Management's Discussion and Analysis was conducted in accordance with attestation standards established by the American Institute of Certified Public Accountants, and, accordingly, included examining, on a test basis, evidence supporting the historical amounts and disclosures in the presentation. An examination also includes assessing the significant determinations made by management as to the relevancy of information to be included and the estimates and assumptions that affect reported information. We believe that our examination provides a reasonable basis for our opinion.

Explanatory paragraph

The preparation of Management's Discussion and Analysis requires management to interpret the criteria, make determinations as to the relevancy of information to be included, and make estimates and assumptions that affect reported information. Management's Discussion and Analysis includes information regarding the estimated future impact of transactions and events that have occurred or are expected to occur, expected sources of liquidity and capital resources, operating trends, commitments, and uncertainties. Actual results in the future may differ materially from management's present assessment of this information because events and circumstances frequently do not occur as expected.

Opinion paragraph

In our opinion, the Company's presentation of Management's Discussion and Analysis includes, in all material respects, the required elements of the rules and regulations adopted by the Securities and Exchange Commission; the historical financial amounts included therein have been accurately derived, in all material respects, from the Company's financial statements; and the underlying information, determinations, estimates, and assumptions of the Company provide a reasonable basis for the disclosures contained therein.

Review of MD&A

Sample Review Report on (Interim) MD&A When Reporting Directly on the Subject Matter, Not an Assertion

Independent Accountant's Report

Introductory paragraph

We have reviewed ABC Company's Management's Discussion and Analysis taken as a whole, included in the Company's [insert description of registration statement or document]. Management is responsible for the preparation of the Company's Management's Discussion and Analysis pursuant to the rules and regulations adopted by the Securities and Exchange Commission. We have reviewed, in accordance with standards established by the American Institute of Certified Public Accountants, the interim financial information of ABC Company as of June 30, 20X2 and 20X1, and for the three-month and six-month periods then ended, and have issued our report thereon dated July XX, 20X6

Scope paragraph

We conducted our review of Management's Discussion and Analysis in accordance with attestation standards established by the American Institute of Certified Public Accountants. A review of Management's Discussion and Analysis consists principally of applying analytical procedures and making inquiries of persons responsible for financial, accounting, and operational matters. It is substantially less in scope than an examination, the objective of which is the expression of an opinion on the presentation. Accordingly, we do not express such an opinion.

Explanatory paragraph

The preparation of Management's Discussion and Analysis requires management to interpret the criteria, make determinations as to the relevancy of information to be included, and make estimates and assumptions that affect reported information. Management's Discussion and Analysis includes information regarding the estimated future impact of transactions and events that have occurred or are expected to occur, expected sources of liquidity and capital resources, operating trends, commitments, and uncertainties. Actual results in the future may differ materially from management's present assessment of this information because events and circumstances frequently do not occur as expected.

Concluding paragraph

Based on our review, nothing came to our attention that caused us to believe that the Company's presentation of Management's Discussion and Analysis does not include, in all material respects, the required elements of the rules and regulations adopted by the Securities and Exchange Commission, that the historical financial amounts included therein have not been accurately derived, in all material respects, from the Company's financial statements, or that the underlying information, determinations, estimates, and assumptions of the Company do not provide a reasonable basis for the disclosures contained therein.

Restricted use paragraph - omit if intended to be filed with the SEC under Securities Acts

This report is intended solely for the information and use of (list or refer to specified parties) and is not intended to be and should not be used by anyone other than the specified parties.

Sarbanes-Oxley Act of 2002 and the PCAOB

PCAOB Responsibilities

The Sarbanes-Oxley Act of 2002 (SOA) was enacted by Congress in response to a series of highly visible financial reporting frauds and audit failures that undermined investor confidence in the U.S. capital markets. Said to be the most significant revision of securities laws since the 1930s, SOA ended self-regulation of the accounting profession and created the Public Company Accounting Oversight Board (PCAOB), a private-sector not-for-profit corporation, to provide a new regulatory mechanism over auditors of public companies, among other things.

After studying this lesson, you should be able to:

1. *Know the five primary responsibilities of the Public Company Accounting Oversight Board established by the Sarbanes-Oxley Act of 2002.*
2. *Understand the primary sections ("Titles") of the Sarbanes-Oxley Act of 2002 that directly affect auditors of public companies ("issuers").*

I. The Sarbanes-Oxley Act of 2002 and the PCAOB

A. Public Company Accounting Oversight Board (PCAOB) - five primary responsibilities

1. **Registration of public accounting firms --** U.S. and non-U.S. accounting firms that prepare audit reports of any U.S. public company ("issuer" of securities) must register with the PCAOB. (This includes non-U.S. accounting firms that play a substantial role in the preparation of such audit reports.)
2. **Inspections of registered public accounting firms --** PCAOB is directed to conduct a continuous program of inspections that assess compliance with SOA, PCAOB rules, SEC rules, and applicable professional standards. (A written report is required for each such inspection.)
   - **a.** Firms that provide audit reports for at least 100 issuers - PCAOB must inspect annually.
   - **b.** Firms that provide audit reports for fewer than 100 issuers - PCAOB must inspect every three years ("triennially").
3. **Standard setting --** PCAOB is directed to establish auditing and related attestation, quality control, ethics and independence standards and rules to be used by registered public accounting firms in the preparation of audit reports for issuers. (The Office of the Chief Auditor and the Standing Advisory Group (SAG) assist PCAOB in establishing such auditing and professional practice standards.)
4. **Enforcement --** PCAOB has broad authority to investigate registered public accounting firms and persons associated with such firms.
   - **a.** PCAOB rules require cooperation by registered public accounting firms and associated persons - must produce documents and provide testimony as directed. (PCAOB may also seek information from others, including clients of registered firms.)
   - **b.** PCAOB sanctions may range from revocation of a firm's registration or barring a person from participating in audits of public companies to lesser sanctions such as monetary penalties or imposition of remedial measures, including additional training or new quality control procedures.

5. **Funding --** PCAOB's budget is funded by (1) registration and annual fees from public accounting firms and (2) an annual "accounting support fee" assessed on issuers (based on their relative monthly market capitalization).

II. Overview of the Sarbanes-Oxley Act of 2002

A. **Purpose of the legislation --** To address a series of perceived corporate misconduct and alleged audit failures (including Enron, Tyco, and WorldCom, among others) and to strengthen investor confidence in the integrity of the U.S. capital markets.

B. The Sarbanes-Oxley Act of 2002 consists of 11 "Titles" (the first four of which are directly applicable to auditors).

C. **Title I --** Established the PCAOB, gave standard-setting authority to the PCAOB (regarding auditing, quality control, and independence standards), and created its role in overseeing the accounting firms required to register with the PCAOB.

D. **Title II --** Established independence requirements for external auditors, which addressed perceived conflicts of interest (limiting non-audit services, establishing a five-year rotation for the audit partner and review partner, and restricting members of the audit firm from taking key management positions (including CEO, CFO, controller, or chief accounting officer) during the one-year period preceding the audit engagement).

   1. Services that the auditor is prohibited from providing: (1) bookkeeping or other services related to the accounting records; (2) financial information systems design and implementation; (3) appraisal or valuation services; (4) actuarial services; (5) internal audit outsourcing services; (6) management functions or human resources; (7) broker or dealer, investment advisor, or investment banking services; (8) legal services and expert services unrelated to the audit; and (9) any other service that the PCAOB determines is impermissible.

   2. The issuer's audit committee is required to approve any non-audit services (including tax services) that are not specifically prohibited.

E. **Title III --** Established requirements related to "corporate responsibility" to make executives take responsibility for the accuracy of financial reporting (including a requirement for certification by the entity's "principal officers") and to make it illegal for management to improperly influence the conduct of an audit.

F. **Title IV --** Addressed a variety of "enhanced financial disclosures," the most well known of which deals with required internal control reporting (Section 404), among other matters.

Auditing Standard No. 1

After studying this lesson, you should be able to:

1. *Know the audit report (and review report) requirements applicable to issuers under PCAOB Auditing Standard No. 1.*

I. **"References in Auditors' Reports to the Standards of the (PCAOB)" --** Approved by the SEC on May 14, 2004.

II. **Standards Adopted --** PCAOB adopted the AICPA's auditing standards in existence on April 16, 2003, as "interim standards, on an initial, transitional basis."

III. **Required Changes --** Made the following required changes to the auditor's report, relative to AICPA guidelines.

   A. **Title of the report --** Replaced "Independent Auditor's Report" with "**Report of Independent Registered Public Accounting Firm**."

   B. **Scope paragraph --** Replaced reference to "auditing standards generally accepted in the United States of America" with "**the standards of the Public Company Accounting Oversight Board (United States)**."

   C. **Opinion paragraph --** Replaced reference to "accounting principles generally accepted in the United States of America" with "**U.S. generally accepted accounting principles**."

   D. **Signature --** Required firms to **add their city and state** (or country, as applicable) along with their signature and date of their audit report.

IV. **Examples of Reporting Language Specified by PCAOB**

Sample Audit Report Using the PCAOB's Template: Report No. 1

Report of Independent Registered Public Accounting Firm

We have audited the accompanying balance sheets of ABC Company at December 31, 20X3 and 20X2, and the related statements of operations, stockholders' equity, and cash flows for each of the three years in the period ended December 31, 20X3. These financial statements are the responsibility of the Company's management. Our responsibility is to express an opinion on these financial statements based on our audits.

We conducted our audits in accordance with the standards of the Public Company Accounting Oversight Board (United States). Those standards require that we plan and perform the audit to obtain reasonable assurance about whether the financial statements are free of material misstatement. An audit includes examining, on a test basis, evidence supporting the amounts and disclosures in the financial statements. An audit also includes assessing the accounting principles used and significant estimates made by management, as well as evaluating the overall financial statement presentation. We believe that our audits provide a reasonable basis for our opinion.

In our opinion, the financial statements referred to above present fairly, in all material respects, the financial position of ABC Company at December 31, 20X3 and 20X2, and the results of its operations and its cash flows for each of the three years in the period ended December 31, 20X3, in conformity with U.S. generally accepted accounting principles.

(Signature)

(City and State or Country)
(Date)

Sample Review Report Using the PCAOB's Template: Report No. 2

Report of Independent Registered Public Accounting Firm

We have reviewed the accompanying (*describe the interim financial information or statements reviewed*) of ABC Company as of September 30, 20X3 and 20X2, and for the three-month and nine-month periods then ended. This interim financial information (statements) is (are) the responsibility of the company's management.

We conducted our review in accordance with the standards of the Public Company Accounting Oversight Board (United States). A review of interim financial information consists principally of applying analytical procedures and making inquiries of persons responsible for financial and accounting matters. It is substantially less in scope than an audit conducted in accordance with the standards of the Public Company Accounting Oversight Board, the objective of which is the expression of an opinion regarding the financial statements taken as a whole. Accordingly, we do not express such an opinion.

Based on our review, we are not aware of any material modifications that should be made to the accompanying interim financial information (statements) for it (them) to be in conformity with U.S. generally accepted accounting principles.

(Signature)

(City and State or Country)

(Date)

Auditing Standard No. 3

After studying this lesson, you should be able to:

1. *Know the PCAOB documentation requirements under Auditing Standard No. 3.*
2. *Know the primary differences between PCAOB documentation requirements for issuers relative to AICPA documentation requirements for nonissuers (regarding documentation retention and the documentation completion date).*

I. **"Audit Documentation" --** Approved by the SEC on August 25, 2004.

> **Definition:**
>
> *Audit Documentation*: The written record of the basis for the auditor's conclusions that provides the support for the auditor's representations. Also serves as a **basis for the review** of the quality of the audit work - the documentation should be prepared in sufficient detail to permit an experienced auditor without prior connection to the engagement to understand the procedures performed and the conclusions reached (and to determine who performed the work and on what date).

II. **Basic Documentation Requirement --** (1) Demonstrate that the engagement complied with PCAOB standards; (2) support the basis for the auditor's conclusions regarding every relevant financial statement assertion; and (3) demonstrate that the underlying accounting records agree to or reconcile with the financial statement elements.

III. **Documentation of Specific Matters**

A. Document audit procedures involving inspection of documents (including walkthroughs, tests of controls, and substantive tests of details) - identify the specific items tested (or the source and specific selection criteria); include abstracts or copies of significant contracts or agreements examined.

B. For matters documented in a "**central repository**" or in a particular office of the public accounting firm (including issues such as auditor independence, staff training, client acceptance/retention, etc.) - the audit documentation should appropriately reference the central repository.

C. Must document all "**significant findings or issues**" (also document the actions taken to address them and the basis for the conclusions reached) - including the application of accounting principles, circumstances causing modification of planned audit procedures, matters that could result in modification of the auditor's report, material misstatements, significant deficiencies or material weaknesses in internal control over financial reporting, difficulties in applying audit procedures, and disagreements among members of the engagement team about final conclusions on significant matters, among other things.

D. All significant findings or issues must be identified in an "**engagement completion document**" in sufficient detail so that a reviewer can obtain a thorough understanding of the matters.

IV. **Retention of and Subsequent Changes to Audit Documentation**

A. Must retain audit documentation for **seven years** from the "**report release date**" - the report release date is when the auditor grants permission to use the auditor's report in connection with the issuance of the company's financial statements. (Recall that the AICPA requires a retention period of five years for audits of "nonissuers.")

B. A complete and final set of audit documentation should be assembled no later than **45 days** after the report release date - that is called the "**documentation completion date**." (Recall that the AICPA allows auditors of "nonissuers" to have a maximum of 60 days for this purpose.)

C. After the documentation completion date - no documentation can be deleted, but documentation can be added (must indicate the date the information was added, the name of the person preparing the additional documentation, and the reason for adding it).

D. The office of the firm issuing the auditor's report is responsible for ensuring that all documentation complies with PCAOB requirements - documentation of other auditors associated with the engagement (in other offices of the firm or in different firms) must be retained or accessible to the office issuing the report.

Auditing Standard No. 4

After studying this lesson, you should be able to:

1. *Know the PCAOB requirements, in general, when engaged to report on whether a previously reported material weakness in internal control over financial reporting continues to exist under Auditing Standard No. 4.*
2. *Know management's specific responsibilities before an auditor can report on whether a previously reported material weakness in internal control over financial reporting continues to exist.*
3. *Understand the auditor's specific responsibilities when reporting on whether a previously reported material weakness in internal control over financial reporting continues to exist.*

I. **"Reporting on Whether a Previously Reported Material Weakness Continues to Exist"** -- Approved by the SEC on February 6, 2006.

II. **Applicability --** When engaged to report on whether a previously reported material weakness in internal control over financial reporting continues to exist as of a date specified by management. (The date specified by management must be a date after that of management's most recent annual assessment.) PCAOB standards do not require reporting on whether a previously reported material weakness continues to exist, so such an engagement is voluntary.

III. **The Auditor's Objective --** In an engagement to report on whether a previously reported material weakness continues to exist to express an opinion about the existence of a specifically identified material weakness as of a specified date (does not relate to the overall effectiveness of internal control over financial reporting); may report on more than one material weakness as part of the same engagement.

IV. **Conditions for Engagement Performance --** Cannot report on whether a previously reported material weakness continues to exist unless all of the following are met:

   A. Management accepts responsibility for the effectiveness of internal control over financial reporting;

   B. Management evaluates the effectiveness of the specific control(s) that it believes addresses the material weakness using the same control criteria that management used for its most recent annual assessment of internal control over financial reporting and management's stated control objective(s);

   C. Management asserts that the specific control(s) identified is (are) effective in achieving the stated control objective;

   D. Management supports its assertion with sufficient evidence, including documentation;

   E. Management presents a written report that will accompany the auditor's report that contains all the elements required by the PCAOB.

      1. Statement of management's responsibility for establishing and maintaining effective internal control over financial reporting;
      2. Statement identifying the control criteria used by management to conduct the required annual assessment of internal control;
      3. Identification of the material weakness that was identified as part of management's annual assessment (or by the auditor's report on it);

4. Identification of the control objective(s) addressed by the specified controls and a statement that the specified controls achieve the stated control objective(s) as of a specified date;
5. Statement that the identified material weakness no longer exists as of the specified date because the specified controls address the material weakness.

V. **Performing the Engagement**

A. An individual material weakness may be associated with a single stated control objective (or more than one) - a "stated control objective" is the specific control objective identified by management that, if achieved, would result in the material weakness no longer existing.

B. Auditor uses materiality at the financial-statement level, rather than at the individual account-balance level, in evaluating whether a material weakness exists.

C. Obtaining an understanding of internal control over financial reporting:

1. The extensiveness of the required understanding of internal control increases with the pervasiveness of the effects of the material weakness.
2. Must perform a walkthrough for all major classes of transactions that are directly affected by controls specifically identified by management as addressing the material weakness - an auditor who has reported on internal control in accordance with Auditing Standard No. 5 for the most recent annual assessment is not required to perform a walkthrough for this engagement.
3. Successor auditors may determine that they are unable to obtain a sufficient basis for reporting on whether a previously reported material weakness continues to exist without performing a complete audit of internal control over financial reporting in accordance with Auditing Standard No. 5 .

D. Testing and evaluating whether a material weakness continues to exist:

1. If management has not supported its assertion with sufficient evidence (a required condition) - the auditor cannot complete this engagement.
2. Auditor should evaluate the appropriateness of management's chosen date - for example, controls that operate daily and continuously can be as of almost any date of management's choosing; controls that operate over the company's period-end reporting process can usually only be tested in connection with a period-end.
3. Auditor should obtain evidence about the effectiveness of all controls specifically identified in management's assertion (all controls that are necessary to achieve the stated control objective should be specifically identified and evaluated) - determine whether the specified control operated as designed and whether the person performing the control possesses the authority and qualifications to perform the control effectively.

E. Using the work of others - the auditor may consider the work of others in deciding the nature, timing, or extent of the work that should be performed. (The auditor should perform any walkthroughs, however, because of the judgment involved.)

F. Obtain written representations from management about various matters (ranging from management's responsibility for establishing and maintaining internal control, management's evaluation of the effectiveness of the specified controls, describing any fraud issues, and stating whether there were material subsequent events, among other matters).

VI. **Auditor's Report --** On whether a previously reported material weakness continues to exist may only issue an **unqualified opinion** or a **disclaimer of opinion** (cannot issue a qualified opinion - any limitation on the scope precludes an expression of opinion).

A. See the sample below for a "continuing auditor" who has previously reported on the company's internal control over financial reporting in accordance with Auditing Standard No. 5 as of the company's most recent year-end.

B. Report modifications - for any of the following conditions:

1. Other material weaknesses that were reported previously by the company as part of the company's annual assessment of internal control are not addressed by the auditor's opinion.
2. A significant subsequent event has occurred since the date reported on.
3. Management's report contains additional information - express a disclaimer of opinion on the additional information.

Sample Auditor's Report for a Continuing Auditor Expressing an Opinion That a Previously Reported Material Weakness No Longer Exists

<u>Report of Independent Registered Public Accounting Firm</u>

We have previously audited and reported on management's annual assessment of XYZ Company's internal control over financial reporting as of December 31, 200X based on (*identify control criteria, for example, "criteria established in Internal Control - Integrated Framework issued by the Committee of Sponsoring Organizations of the Treadway Commission (COSO)."*) Our report, dated (*date of report*), identified the following material weakness in the Company's internal control over financial reporting:

(*Describe material weakness*)

We have audited management's assertion, included in the accompanying (*title of management's report*), that the material weakness in internal control over financial reporting identified above no longer exists as of (*date of management's assertion*) because the following control(s) addresses the material weakness:

(*Describe control(s)*)

Management has asserted that the control(s) identified above achieves the following stated control objective, which is consistent with the criteria established in (*identify control criteria used for management's annual assessment of internal control over financial reporting*): (*state control objective addressed*). Management also has asserted that it has tested the control(s) identified above and concluded that the control(s) was designed and operated effectively as of (*date of management's assertion*). XYZ Company's management is responsible for its assertion. Our responsibility is to express an opinion on whether the identified material weakness continues to exist as of (*date of management's assertion*) based on our auditing procedures.

Our engagement was conducted in accordance with the standards of the Public Company Accounting Oversight Board (United States). Those standards require that we plan and perform the engagement to obtain reasonable assurance about whether a previously reported material weakness continues to exist at the company. Our engagement included examining evidence supporting management's assertion and performing such other procedures as we considered necessary in the circumstances. We obtained an understanding of the company's internal control over financial reporting as part of our previous audit of management's annual assessment of XYZ Company's internal control over financial reporting as of December 31, 200X and updated that understanding as it specifically relates to changes in internal control over financial reporting associated with the material weakness described above. We believe that our auditing procedures provide a reasonable basis for our opinion.

In our opinion, the material weakness described above no longer exists as of (*date of management's assertion*).

We were not engaged to and did not conduct an audit of internal control over financial reporting as of (*date of management's assertion*), the objective of which would be the expression of an opinion on the effectiveness of internal control over financial reporting. Accordingly, we do not express such an opinion. This means that we have not applied auditing procedures sufficient to reach conclusions about the effectiveness of any controls of the company as of any date after December 31, 200X, other than the control(s) specifically identified in this report. Accordingly, we do not express an opinion that any other controls operated effectively after December 31, 200X.

Because of its inherent limitations, internal control over financial reporting may not prevent or detect misstatements. Also, projections of any evaluation of the effectiveness of specific controls or internal control over financial reporting overall to future periods are subject to the risk that controls may become inadequate because of changes in conditions or that the degree of compliance with the policies or procedures may deteriorate.

(Signature)

(City and State/or Country)

(Date)

Auditing Standard No. 5

After studying this lesson, you should be able to:

1. *Understand the auditor's responsibilities when reporting on internal control over financial reporting in an integrated audit of an issuer's financial statements in accordance with PCAOB Auditing Standard No. 5.*
2. *Be familiar with the structure of the report on internal control over financial reporting for such an engagement, whether the report is issued separately or combined with the audit report on the entity's financial statements.*

I. **"An Audit of Internal Control Over Financial Reporting That Is Integrated with An Audit of Financial Statements" --** Approved by the SEC on July 25, 2007.

II. **Applicability of Standard --** When engaged to "perform an audit of management's assessment of the effectiveness of internal control over financial reporting" (ICFR); the objective of such an engagement is to express an opinion on the effectiveness of ICFR.

III. **Some Important Definitions**

  A. **"Control deficiency" --** When the design or operation of a control does not allow management or employees, in the normal course of performing their assigned functions, to prevent or detect misstatements on a timely basis.

    1. **Deficiency in design --** When a control necessary to meet the control objective is missing or when an existing control is not properly designed so that, even if the control operates as designed, the control objective is not always met.

    2. **Deficiency in operation --** When a properly designed control does not operate as designed or when the person performing the control does not possess the necessary authority or qualifications to perform the control effectively.

  B. **"Material weakness" --** A deficiency, or a combination of deficiencies, in ICFR such that there is a reasonable possibility that a material misstatement of the company's annual or interim financial statements will not be prevented or detected on a timely basis. (If one or more material weaknesses exist, the company's ICFR is not considered to be effective.)

  C. **"Significant deficiency" --** A deficiency, or a combination of deficiencies, in ICFR that is less severe than a material weakness, yet important enough to merit attention by those responsible for oversight of the company's financial reporting.

IV. **Planning the Audit --** The audit of ICFR should be integrated with the audit of the financial statements (that is, the tests of controls should be designed to address both the objectives of the audit of ICFR and the audit of the financial statements).

  A. **Role of risk assessment --** "Risk assessment underlies the entire audit process described by this standard, including the determination of significant accounts and disclosures and relevant assertions, the selection of controls to test, and the determination of the evidence necessary for a given control."

    1. There is a direct relationship between the risk of material weakness and the amount of audit attention that is needed.

    2. Materiality - should use the same materiality considerations in planning the audit of ICFR as for the audit of the company's annual financial statements.

B. **Using the work of others --** The auditor may use the work of others to reduce the work the auditor might otherwise have to perform.

1. Includes internal auditors, other company personnel, service auditors (when a service organization is involved), and third parties working under the direction of management or the audit committee; the auditor should assess the competence and objectivity of those whose work the auditor plans to use.
2. As the risk associated with a control increases, the auditor should take increasing responsibility for performing the work instead of using the work of others.

V. **Using a "Top-down" Approach --** Begins at the financial statement level and with the auditor's understanding of the overall risks to ICFR; the auditor then focuses on "entity-level" controls and works down to significant accounts and disclosures and their relevant assertions.

A. Identifying entity-level controls - the auditor must test those entity-level controls that are important to the conclusion about the effectiveness of ICFR.

1. **Entity-level controls --** Include controls related to the control environment, controls over management override, the company's risk assessment process, controls to monitor results of operations or other controls, controls over the period-end financial reporting process; and policies that address significant business control and risk management practices.
2. **Control environment --** Because of its importance to ICFR, the auditor must evaluate the control environment at the company.
3. **Period-end financial reporting process --** Because of its importance to ICFR, the auditor must evaluate the period-end financial reporting process.

B. Identifying significant accounts and disclosures and their relevant assertions.

1. **Relevant assertions --** Those financial statement assertions that have a reasonable possibility of containing a material misstatement. (Auditing Standard No. 5 specifically refers to (1) existence or occurrence; (2) completeness; (3) valuation or allocation; (4) rights and obligations; and (5) presentation and disclosure.)
2. **Risk factors --** The auditor should consider risk factors relevant to the identification of significant accounts and disclosures and their relevant assertions, including the nature of the account or disclosure; size and composition of the account; susceptibility to misstatement, volume of activity and complexity of transactions; and changes from the prior period, among others.

C. Understanding likely sources of misstatement:

1. **The auditor should achieve these control objectives --** (a) Understand the flow of transactions related to the relevant assertions; (b) verify that the auditor has identified the points within the company's processes at which a material misstatement could arise; (c) identify the controls that management has implemented to address these potential misstatements; and (d) identify the controls that management has implemented over the company's assets that could materially misstate the financial statements.
2. **Performing walkthroughs --** Following a transaction from origination through the company's processes until reflected in the financial records is frequently the most effective way to achieve the objectives above. (Procedures usually include inquiry, observation, inspection of relevant documentation, and reperformance of controls.)

D. Selecting controls to test - the auditor should test those controls that are important to the conclusion about whether the company's controls sufficiently address the assessed risk of misstatement to each relevant assertion.

VI. Testing Controls

A. **Nature of tests of controls --** (From least to most evidence) Inquiry, observation, inspection of relevant documentation, and re-performance of a control:

   1. **Testing design effectiveness --** Procedures include inquiry of appropriate personnel, observation of the company's operations, and inspection of relevant documentation (may be addressed by appropriate walkthroughs).

   2. **Testing operating effectiveness --** Procedures include inquiry of appropriate personnel, observation of the company's operations, inspection of relevant documentation, and re-performance of the control.

B. **Timing of tests of controls --** Testing controls over a greater period of time provides more evidence than testing over a shorter period of time; testing closer to the date of management's assessment provides more evidence than testing performed earlier in the year.

C. **Extent of tests of controls --** The more extensively a control is tested, the greater the evidence to evaluate the effectiveness of the control.

D. **Roll-forward procedures --** When operating effectiveness has been tested at an interim date, the auditor should consider what additional testing for the remaining period may be necessary.

VII. Evaluating Identified Deficiencies

A. **Basic responsibility --** The auditor must evaluate identified control deficiencies to determine whether, individually or in combination, they constitute material weaknesses as of the date of management's assessment (based on whether there is a "reasonable possibility" that the controls will fail to prevent or detect a material misstatement, not whether a misstatement has actually occurred).

B. **Indicators of material weaknesses --** Examples include (1) identification of fraud involving senior management (whether or not material); (2) restatement of previously issued financial statements; (3) identification by the auditor of a material misstatement of the financial statements in the current period; and (4) ineffective oversight of the company's external financial reporting and internal control by the company's audit committee.

C. **Communicating identified deficiencies**

   1. The auditor must communicate (in writing) all **material weaknesses** identified to **management and the audit committee**.

   2. The auditor must also communicate (in writing) other **significant deficiencies** identified to the **audit committee**.

   3. The auditor should communicate (in writing) all other deficiencies in ICFR to **management** and inform the audit committee that such a communication has been made.

   4. If the auditor concludes that the audit committee's oversight of financial reporting and ICFR is ineffective - must communicate that conclusion in writing to the board of directors.

VIII. Reporting on Internal Control over Financial Reporting

A. Separate or combined reports - the auditor may choose to issue a combined report on the financial statements and on ICFR or separate reports.

B. Title of report should include the word "independent" (e.g., "Report of Independent Registered Public Accounting Firm").

C. Combined report - an unqualified report on the financial statements and on ICFR consists of five paragraphs: (1) introduction; (2) scope; (3) definition; (4) inherent limitations; and (5) opinion.

D. Separate reports - the auditor should add an additional paragraph to the audit report on the financial statements that references the report on ICFR; and the auditor should add an additional paragraph to the report on ICFR that references the audit report on the financial statements.

E. Report date - if separate reports are issued, they should be dated the same (the date as of which the auditor has obtained sufficient competent evidence).

F. If one or more material weakness exists - the auditor must express an adverse opinion (unless there is a scope limitation).

1. When expressing an adverse opinion - the auditor's report must include the definition of a material weakness and refer to management's assessment of the material weakness. (If not included in management's assessment, the auditor's report should state that fact.)
2. Should determine the effect the adverse opinion on ICFR has on the opinion on the entity's financial statements.

G. If there is a scope limitation - the auditor should disclaim an opinion or withdraw from the engagement.

Sample Report on the Effectiveness of Internal Control Over Financial Reporting

(Separate From Audit Report on Financial Statements)

Report of Independent Registered Public Accounting Firm

Separate Audit Report on ICFR

(*Introductory paragraph*)

We have audited ABC Company's internal control over financial reporting as of December 31, 20X2, based on (*Identify control criteria, for example, "criteria established in Internal Control - Integrated Framework issued by the Committee of Sponsoring Organizations of the Treadway Commission (COSO)"*). ABC Company's management is responsible for maintaining effective internal control over financial reporting and for its assessment of the effectiveness of internal control over financial reporting, included in the accompanying (*title of management's report*). Our responsibility is to express an opinion on the company's internal control over financial reporting based on our audit.

(*Scope paragraph*)

We conducted our audit in accordance with the standards of the Public Company Accounting Oversight Board (United States). Those standards require that we plan and perform the audit to obtain reasonable assurance about whether effective internal control over financial reporting was maintained in all material respects. Our audit of internal control over financial reporting included obtaining an understanding of internal control over financial reporting, assessing the risk that a material weakness exists, and testing and evaluating the design and operating effectiveness of internal control based on the assessed risk. Our audit also included performing such other procedures as we considered necessary in the circumstances. We believe that our audit provides a reasonable basis for our opinion.

(*Definition paragraph*)

A company's internal control over financial reporting is a process designed to provide reasonable assurance regarding the reliability of financial reporting and the preparation of financial statements for external purposes in accordance with generally accepted accounting principles. A company's internal control over financial reporting includes those policies and procedures that (1) pertain to the maintenance of records that, in reasonable detail, accurately and fairly reflect the transactions and dispositions of the assets of the company; (2) provide reasonable assurance that transactions are recorded as necessary to permit preparation of financial statements in accordance with generally accepted accounting principles, and that receipts and expenditures of the company are being made only in accordance with authorizations of management and directors of the company; and (3) provide reasonable assurance regarding prevention or timely detection of unauthorized acquisition, use, or disposition of the company's assets that could have a material effect on the financial statements.

(*Inherent limitations paragraph*)

Because of its inherent limitations, internal control over financial reporting may not prevent or detect misstatements. Also, projections of any evaluation of effectiveness to future periods are subject to the risk that controls may become inadequate because of changes in conditions, or that the degree of compliance with the policies or procedures may deteriorate.

(*Opinion paragraph*)

In our opinion, ABC Company maintained, in all material respects, effective internal control over financial reporting as of December 31, 20X2, based on (*identify control criteria, for example, "criteria established in Internal Control - Integrated Framework issued by the Committee of Sponsoring Organizations of the Treadway Commission (COSO)"*).

(*Explanatory paragraph*)

We have also audited, in accordance with the standards of the Public Company Accounting Oversight Board (United States), the (*identify financial statements*) of ABC Company and our report dated (*date of report, which should be the same as the date of the report on the effectiveness of internal control over financial reporting*) expressed (*include nature of opinion*).

(Signature)

(City and State or Country)

(Date)

See the following example.

Sample Combined Audit Report on Financial Statements and on the Effectiveness of Internal Control Over Financial Reporting

Report of Independent Registered Public Accounting Firm

Combined Audit Reports on Financial Statements and ICFR

(*Introductory paragraph*)

We have audited the accompanying balance sheets of ABC Company as of December 31, 20X2 and 20X1, and the related statements of income, stockholders' equity and comprehensive income, and cash flows for each of the years in the three-year period ended December 31, 20X2. We have also audited ABC Company's internal control over financial reporting as of December 31, 20X2, based on (*Identify control criteria, for example, "criteria established in Internal Control - Integrated Framework issued by the Committee of Sponsoring Organizations of the Treadway Commission (COSO)"*). ABC Company's management is responsible for these financial statements, for maintaining effective internal control over financial reporting, and for its assessment of the effectiveness of internal control over financial reporting, included in the accompanying (*title of management's report*). Our responsibility is to express an opinion on these financial statements and an opinion on the company's internal control over financial reporting based on our audits.

(*Scope paragraph*)

We conducted our audits in accordance with the standards of the Public Company Accounting Oversight Board (United States). Those standards require that we plan and perform the audits to obtain reasonable assurance about whether the financial statements are free of material misstatement and whether effective internal control over financial reporting was maintained in all material respects. Our audits of the financial statements included examining, on a test basis, evidence supporting the amounts and disclosures in the financial statements, assessing the accounting principles used and significant estimates made by management, and evaluating the overall financial statement presentation. Our audit of internal control over financial reporting included obtaining an understanding of internal control over financial reporting, assessing the risk that a material weakness exists, and testing and evaluating the design and operating effectiveness of internal control based on the assessed risk. Our audits also included performing such other procedures as we considered necessary in the circumstances. We believe that our audits provide a reasonable basis for our opinions.

(*Definition paragraph*)

A company's internal control over financial reporting is a process designed to provide reasonable assurance regarding the reliability of financial reporting and the preparation of financial statements for external purposes in accordance with generally accepted accounting principles. A company's internal control over financial reporting includes those policies and procedures that (1) pertain to the maintenance of records that, in reasonable detail, accurately and fairly reflect the transactions and dispositions of the assets of the company; (2) provide reasonable assurance that transactions are recorded as necessary to permit preparation of financial statements in accordance with generally accepted accounting principles, and that receipts and expenditures of the company are being made only in accordance with authorizations of management and directors of the company; and (3) provide reasonable assurance regarding prevention or timely detection of unauthorized acquisition, use, or disposition of the company's assets that could have a material effect on the financial statements.

(*Inherent limitations paragraph*)

Because of its inherent limitations, internal control over financial reporting may not prevent or detect misstatements. Also, projections of any evaluation of effectiveness to future periods are subject to the risk that controls may become inadequate because of changes in conditions, or that the degree of compliance with the policies or procedures may deteriorate.

(*Opinion paragraph*)

In our opinion, the financial statements referred to above present fairly, in all material respects, the financial position of ABC Company as of December 31, 20X2 and 20X1, and the results of its operations and its cash flows for each of the years in the three-year period ended December 31, 20X2 in conformity with accounting principles generally accepted in the United States of America. Also in our opinion, ABC Company maintained, in all material respects, effective internal control over financial reporting as of December 31, 20X2, based on (*identify control criteria, for example, "criteria established in Internal Control - Integrated Framework issued by the Committee of Sponsoring Organizations of the Treadway Commission (COSO)"*).

(Signature)

(City and State or Country)

(Date)

Auditing Standard No. 6

After studying this lesson, you should be able to:

1. *Understand the auditor's responsibilities under PCAOB Auditing Standard No. 6 to identify issues related to "consistency" involving either a change in accounting principle or a restatement to correct previously issued financial statements.*

I. **"Evaluating Consistency of Financial Statements" --** Approved by the SEC on September 16, 2008.

II. **PCAOB Auditing Standard No. 6 --** Establishes requirements and provides direction for the auditor's evaluation of the consistency of financial statements and the effect of that evaluation on the auditor's report (regarding the second reporting standard of Generally Accepted Auditing Standards).

   A. Identifies two types of issues related to consistency that might affect the auditor's report: (1) a change in accounting principle; and (2) an adjustment to correct a misstatement in previously issued financial statements (i.e., "restatements").

   B. When reporting on two or more periods - evaluate the consistency between those periods and with the prior period, if that prior period is presented along with the financial statements reported on.

III. **Changes in Accounting Principle --** Involving a change from one generally accepted accounting principle to another, including the situation where the accounting principle formerly used is no longer generally accepted.

   A. GAAP is specified by FASB Statement No. 154, "Accounting Changes and Error Corrections." Auditing Standard No. 6 points out that, when a company uses retrospective application to account for a change in accounting principle, the financial statements generally will be viewed as consistent. (However, the previous years' financial statements will appear different from those that the auditor previously reported on.)

   B. When there is a change in accounting principle - the auditor should evaluate whether **(1) the newly adopted principle is GAAP; (2) the method of accounting for the effect of the change conforms to GAAP; (3) the disclosures related to the change are adequate; and (4) the company has justified that the alternative accounting principle is preferable.**

      1. When the four criteria have been met - the auditor should add an explanatory paragraph to the auditor's report to identify the inconsistency.

      2. When the four criteria have not been met - the auditor should treat the matter as a GAAP departure and modify the audit report appropriately.

      3. When an investor uses the "equity method" and the investee has a change in accounting principle that is material to the investor's financial statements - the auditor should add an explanatory paragraph to emphasize the matter.

   C. When there is a change in accounting estimate effected by a change in accounting principle - the auditor should evaluate and report on the matter like other changes in accounting principle.

   D. When there is a change in the reporting entity resulting from a transaction or event, such as the purchase or disposition of a subsidiary - it does not require recognition in the auditor's report. (However, if there is a change in the reporting entity that does not result from such a transaction or event, then an explanatory paragraph would be required.)

IV. Correction of a Material Misstatement in Previously Issued Financial Statements

A. The correction of a material misstatement in previously issued financial statements should be recognized in the auditor's report by the addition of an explanatory paragraph.

B. Restatements of previously issued financial statements require related disclosures to be made - the auditor should evaluate the adequacy of the company's disclosures.

V. Change in Classification

A. Changes in classification in previously issued financial statements normally do not require recognition in the auditor's report (unless the change represents a change in accounting principle or the correction of a material misstatement).

B. Accordingly, the auditor should evaluate a material change in financial statement classification (and the related disclosure) to determine whether such a change is also a change in accounting principle or a correction of a material misstatement.

PCAOB Auditing Standard No. 6 is substantially similar to the AICPA's AU Section 420, "Consistency of Application of (GAAP)" (primarily from SAS No. 1, as amended). Auditing Standard No. 6 is more up-to-date and cites FASB Statement No. 154 as defining GAAP, whereas AU Section 420 cites the old APB Opinion No. 20 and includes a discussion involving "pooling of interests" that once was relevant to consolidations.

Perhaps the major difference is that Auditing Standard No. 6 requires the auditor to add an explanatory paragraph to address consistency issues associated with restatements (corrections of errors). AU Section 420 specifically states that "error correction not involving principle" (e.g., mathematical mistakes, oversight, or misuse of facts) need not be identified in the auditor's report.

Auditing Standard No. 7

After studying this lesson, you should be able to:

1. *Understand the auditor's responsibilities for an "engagement quality review" (and for concurring approval of issuance) under PCAOB Auditing Standard No. 7.*
2. *Know the primary differences between the requirements of PCAOB Auditing Standard No. 7 and the AICPA's Statements on Quality Control Standards (SQCS).*

I. "Engagement Quality Review" Approved by the SEC, January 2010

II. Introduction and Overview

A. Applicability of standard - requires an engagement quality review (and concurring approval of issuance) for engagements conducted under PCAOB standards (1) for an audit and (2) for a review of interim financial information.

B. Objective of the engagement quality reviewer - to perform an evaluation of the significant judgments made by the engagement team and the related conclusions reached and in preparing any engagement report(s).

C. Qualifications of an engagement quality reviewer - (1) must be an "associated person" of a registered public accounting firm; and (2) must have competence, independence, integrity, and objectivity:

1. **"Associated person" of a registered public accounting firm --** should be able to withstand any pressure from the engagement partner or others and may be someone from outside the firm; if the reviewer is from within the firm, he/she should be a partner or have an equivalent position. (There is no such requirement for a reviewer from outside the firm.)
2. **Competence --** must be qualified to serve as the engagement partner on the engagement under review.
3. **Objectivity --** the engagement quality reviewer (and any assisting personnel) should not make engagement team decisions or assume any responsibilities of the engagement team.
4. **"Cooling off" restriction --** the person serving as engagement partner during either of the two audits preceding the audit subject to engagement quality review is not permitted to serve as engagement quality reviewer (unless the registered firm qualifies for a specific exemption to this requirement).

> **Note:**
> "An outside reviewer who is not already associated with a registered public accounting firm would become associated with the firm issuing the report if he or she ... (1) receives compensation from the firm issuing the report for performing the review or (2) performs the review as agent for the firm issuing the report."

III. Engagement Quality Review for an Audit or a Review under PCAOB Standards

A. Engagement quality review process -- to evaluate the significant judgments and conclusions of the engagement team, the engagement quality reviewer should (1) hold discussions with the engagement partner and other members of the engagement team; and (2) review documentation.

B. Evaluation of engagement documentation -- the engagement quality reviewer should evaluate whether the documentation that was reviewed (1) indicates that the engagement team responded appropriately to significant risks; and (2) supports the conclusions reached by the engagement team.

C. **Concurring approval of issuance**

1. The engagement quality reviewer cannot express such approval if there is any "significant engagement deficiency" (when (a) the engagement team failed to obtain sufficient appropriate evidence; (b) the engagement team reached an inappropriate overall conclusion; (c) the engagement report is not appropriate; or (d) the firm is not independent of its client).
2. The firm cannot give permission to the client to use the engagement report until the engagement quality reviewer provides concurring approval of issuance.

IV. **Documentation of an Engagement Quality Review**

A. Documentation should contain sufficient information to permit an experienced auditor, having no prior association with the engagement, to understand the procedures performed and conclusions reached by the engagement quality reviewer.

B. Documentation of an engagement quality review should be included in the engagement documentation (and be subject to other PCAOB requirements regarding retention of and changes to audit documentation).

V. **Auditing Standard No. 7 Identified Several Differences Relative to AICPA's Statements on Quality Control Standards (SQCS)**

A. **Engagement quality review --** SQCS do not require an engagement quality review for any type of engagement, whereas Auditing Standard No. 7 establishes such a requirement.

B. SQCS do not impose a "cooling off" restriction or a requirement that the reviewer must be an associated person of a registered public accounting firm.

C. **Concurring approval of issuance --** SQCS require any engagement quality review performed be completed before the engagement report is released without requiring a concurring approval of issuance.

D. **Documentation retention and changes --** SQCS do not specifically require that engagement quality review documentation must be retained with other engagement documentation and be subject to specific policies regarding retention and changes.

PCAOB Risk Assessment Standards

After studying this lesson you should be able to:

1. *Recognize the set of pronouncements that comprise the PCAOB's "risk assessment" project.*
2. *Understand the auditor's fundamental responsibilities associated with the various risk assessment Auditing Standards issued by the PCAOB.*
3. *Know the primary differences between the risk-assessment-related standards of the PCAOB and those of the AICPA.*

I. **PCAOB "Risk Assessment Standards" --** The PCAOB issued a suite of eight Auditing Standards comprising their "risk assessment" project in 2010 (approved by the Securities and Exchange Commission in December, 2010). In general, these PCAOB risk assessment standards are remarkably similar to the risk assessment standards previously issued by the AICPA (Statements on Auditing Standards) and by the International Federation of Accountants (International Standards on Auditing), although a few (mostly minor) differences are identified below.

   A. PCAOB Auditing Standard No. 8, "Audit Risk"

   B. PCAOB Auditing Standard No. 9, "Audit Planning"

   C. PCAOB Auditing Standard No. 10, "Supervision of the Audit Engagement"

   D. PCAOB Auditing Standard, No. 11, "Consideration of Materiality in Planning and Performing an Audit"

   E. PCAOB Auditing Standard, No. 12, "Identifying and Assessing Risks of Material Misstatement"

   F. PCAOB Auditing Standard, No. 13, "The Auditor's Responses to the Risks of Material Misstatement"

   G. PCAOB Auditing Standard, No. 14, "Evaluating Audit Results"

   H. PCAOB Auditing Standard, No. 15, "Audit Evidence"

II. **PCAOB vs. AICPA --** Compare those eight PCAOB risk assessment standards with the five Statements on Auditing Standards issued by the AICPA's Auditing Standards Board in 2006 comprising the Auditing Standards Board's "risk assessment" project.

   A. Statement on Auditing Standards No. 106, "Audit Evidence"

   B. Statement on Auditing Standards No. 107, "Audit Risk and Materiality in Conducting an Audit"

   C. Statement on Auditing Standards No. 108, "Planning and Supervision"

   D. Statement on Auditing Standards No. 109, "Understanding the Entity and Its Environment and Assessing the Risks of Material Misstatement"

   E. Statement on Auditing Standards No. 110, "Performing Audit Procedures in Response to Assessed Risks and Evaluating the Audit Evidence Obtained"

III. **Structural Differences --** There are some obvious structural differences between these PCAOB risk assessment standards relative to those of the Auditing Standards Board.

   A. In three instances, the PCAOB essentially split a single Statement on Auditing Standards (SAS) into 2 related PCAOB Auditing Standards (AS).

1. SAS No. 107 encompassed both "audit risk and materiality" - the PCAOB issued a separate AS on "audit risk" and another AS on "materiality" issues.
2. SAS No. 108 encompassed both "planning and supervision" - the PCAOB issued a separate AS on "planning" and another on "supervision" issues.
3. SAS No. 110 encompassed both "performing audit procedures to assessed risks and evaluating the audit evidence obtained" - the PCAOB issued a separate AS on "performing audit procedures in response to assessed risks" and another on "evaluating the audit evidence obtained."

B. These PCAOB Auditing Standards are applicable to integrated audits of an issuer's financial statements and the internal controls over financial reporting - in contrast these AICPA's Statements on Auditing Standards focus solely on audits of non-issuers' financial statements.

IV. **Summaries --** Summaries of the essence of these PCAOB risk assessment standards.

A. **PCAOB Auditing Standard No. 8, "Audit Risk"**

1. Auditor's objective - to conduct the audit of financial statements in a manner that reduces audit risk to an appropriately low level.
2. "Reasonable assurance" means reducing audit risk to an appropriately low level - the auditor must plan and perform the audit to obtain reasonable assurance about whether the financial statements are free of material misstatements due to error or fraud.
3. The auditor should assess the risks of material misstatement at two levels: (1) at the financial statement level (where the risk of material misstatement is pervasive and potentially involves many assertions); and (2) at the assertion level (where the risk of material misstatement involves inherent risk and control risk).

B. **PCAOB Auditing Standard No. 9, "Audit Planning"**

1. Auditor's objective - to plan the audit so that the audit is conducted effectively.
2. "Planning the audit includes establishing the overall audit strategy for the engagement and developing an audit plan, which includes, in particular, planned risk assessment procedures and planned responses to the risks of material misstatement. Planning is not a discrete phase of an audit but, rather, a continual and iterative process that might begin shortly after (or in connection with) the completion of the previous audit and continues until the completion of the current audit."
   a. Overall strategy - involves rather high level audit resource allocation issues involving the scope, timing, and direction of the audit (guides the development of the more specific audit plan).
   b. Audit plan - deals with the planned nature, timing, and extent of the risk assessment procedures, the tests of controls, the substantive procedures, and any other procedures required to comply with PCAOB standards.
3. Engagement partner responsibilities - "The engagement partner is responsible for the engagement and its performance. Accordingly, the engagement partner is responsible for planning the audit and may seek assistance from appropriate engagement team members in fulfilling this responsibility."(AS No. 9 seems a bit more direct in discussing the engagement partner's responsibilities, whereas SAS No. 108 is more indirect in saying, "The auditor with final responsibility for the audit may delegate portions of the planning and supervision of the audit to other firm personnel.")

C. PCAOB Auditing Standard No. 10, "Supervision of the Audit Engagement"

1. Auditor's objective - to supervise the audit engagement so that the work is performed as directed and supports the conclusions reached.
2. The extent of supervision required varies with the engagement's circumstances, including the size and complexity of the company, the nature of the work assigned to engagement personnel, the capabilities of each engagement team member, and the risks of material misstatement. (The extent of supervision should be commensurate with those risks.)
3. Engagement partner responsibilities - "The engagement partner is responsible for the engagement and its performance. Accordingly, the engagement partner is responsible for proper supervision of the work of engagement team members and for compliance with PCAOB standards, including standards regarding using the work of specialists, other auditors, internal auditors, and others who are involved in testing controls." (Once again, AS No. 10 is a bit more direct than the corresponding SAS No. 108 in discussing the engagement partner's responsibilities.)

D. PCAOB Auditing Standard, No. 11, "Consideration of Materiality in Planning and Performing an Audit"

1. Auditor's objective - to apply the concept of materiality appropriately in planning and performing audit procedures.
2. The auditor should plan and perform the audit to detect misstatement that, individually or in the aggregate, would result in material misstatement of the financial statements.
3. The auditor should use the same materiality considerations for planning the audit of internal control over financial reporting as for the audit of the financial statements.
4. The materiality level for the financial statements should be expressed as a specified amount to determine the nature, timing, and extent of audit procedures.
5. The auditor should determine tolerable misstatement for purposes of assessing risks of material misstatement at the account or disclosure levels.

E. PCAOB Auditing Standard, No. 12, "Identifying and Assessing Risks of Material Misstatement"

1. Auditor's objective - to identify and appropriately assess the risks of material misstatement, thereby providing a basis for designing and implementing responses to the risks of material misstatement.
2. The auditor should perform risk assessment procedures sufficient to provide a reasonable basis for identifying and assessing the risks of material misstatement and designing further audit procedures.
3. These risk assessment procedures should include (a) obtaining an understanding of the company and its environment; (b) obtaining an understanding of internal control over financial reporting; (c) considering information from the client acceptance/retention evaluation, planning activities, prior audits, and other engagements for the company; (d) performing analytical procedures; and (e) inquiring of the audit committee, management, and others within the company about the risks of material misstatement.
4. The auditor should begin by identifying and assessing the risks of material misstatement at the financial statement level and then work down to the significant accounts and disclosures and their relevant assertions.

F. **PCAOB Auditing Standard, No. 13, "The Auditor's Responses to the Risks of Material Misstatement"**

1. Auditor's objective - to address the risks of material misstatement through appropriate overall audit responses and audit procedures.
2. Overall responses - the auditor should consider (a) making appropriate assignments of responsibilities based on capabilities of team members; (b) providing appropriate supervision; (c) incorporating a degree of unpredictability in planned procedures; (d) evaluating the company's selection and application of significant accounting principles (especially in subjective areas); and (e) determining whether it is necessary to make pervasive changes to the nature, timing, and extent of audit procedures.
3. Responses involving the nature, timing, and extent of audit procedures - the auditor should address the assessed risks of material misstatement for each relevant assertion of each significant account and disclosure.
    a. There are two categories of audit procedures performed in response to the assessed risks of material misstatement: (1) tests of controls; and (2) substantive procedures.
    b. The auditor should perform substantive procedures that are responsive to any identified "significant risks" (including fraud risks).
    c. In responding to fraud risks, the auditor should address the risk of management override of controls by examining journal entries, reviewing accounting estimates for biases, and evaluating the business rationale for significant unusual transactions.

G. **PCAOB Auditing Standard, No. 14, "Evaluating Audit Results"**

1. Auditor's objective - to evaluate the results of the audit to determine whether the audit evidence obtained is sufficient and appropriate to support the opinion.
2. The auditor must reach a conclusion as to whether sufficient appropriate audit evidence has been obtained to support the opinion.
3. The auditor should consider all relevant audit evidence (whether it corroborates or contradicts the financial statements) and evaluate the following:
    a. The results of analytical procedures performed as the overall review.
    b. Misstatements (other than "trivial" ones) accumulated during the audit (with emphasis on uncorrected misstatements).
    c. The qualitative aspects of the company's accounting practices, including potential for management bias.
    d. Conditions identified related to fraud risk.
    e. The presentation of the financial statements (including disclosures) relative to the applicable financial reporting framework.
    f. The sufficiency and appropriateness of the evidence obtained.

H. **PCAOB Auditing Standard, No. 15, "Audit Evidence"**

1. Auditor's objective - to plan and perform the audit to obtain appropriate audit evidence that is sufficient to support the opinion.
2. Sufficient appropriate audit evidence.
    a. Sufficiency relates to the QUANTITY of evidence required - the amount of evidence needed increases as the risk of material misstatement increases; the amount of evidence needed decreases as the quality of the underlying evidence increases.

b. Appropriateness relates to the QUALITY of evidence, which involves (1) relevance and (2) reliability.

3. Financial statement assertions are factual representations that are implicitly or explicitly made by management - the PCAOB identified the five traditional financial statement assertions previously presented in a now-superseded Statement on Auditing Standards.

    a. Existence - that the assets or liabilities exist at a given date or that the recorded transactions have occurred during a given period.

    b. Completeness - that there are no omissions of transaction or accounts that should have been recorded.

    c. Rights and obligations - that the company has the rights to the assets and the obligations for the liabilities at a given date.

    d. Valuation or allocation - that the financial statement elements are presented at appropriate amounts relative to the applicable accounting framework.

    e. Presentation and disclosure - that the elements of the financial statements are properly classified, described, and disclosed relative to the applicable accounting framework.

> **Note:**
> The PCAOB's discussion about these five traditional financial statement assertions is a relatively major difference compared to the AICPA's Statement on Auditing Standards dealing with audit evidence. The current SAS presents the discussion of assertions in three categories: (1) account balances at the period end (four assertions); (2) transactions and events during the period (five assertions); and presentation and disclosure (four assertions).
> The Auditing Standards Board replaced an earlier SAS that had focused on the five traditional financial statement assertions in order to make U.S. auditing standards more consistent with International Standards on Auditing.
> The PCAOB AS addressed the alternative treatments of assertions: "The auditor may base his or her work on financial statement assertions that differ from those in this standard if the assertions are sufficient for the auditor to identify the potential misstatements... "

V. **Summary of Differences --** Summary of fundamental differences between the PCAOB risk assessment standards and the AICPA Auditing Standards Board risk assessment standards.

A. The PCAOB risk assessment standards apply to integrated audits of issuers (encompassing both the company's financial statements and internal control over financial reporting), whereas the AICPA risk assessment standard apply solely to audits of non-issuers' financial statements.

B. The PCAOB issued eight risk assessment standards, whereas the AICPA issued five risk assessment standards - in three instances, the AICPA combined topics into a single standard that the PCAOB addressed in separate standards.

C. The PCAOB standards tended to provide a bit more specific guidance in certain areas (such as the engagement partner's responsibilities) that were addressed in somewhat more general terms in the AICPA standards.

D. A more significant difference involves the treatment of "assertions" in their respective standards dealing with the topic of audit evidence - the PCAOB focuses on the five traditional financial statement assertions (as presented in an earlier SAS that has since been superseded in an attempt to align U.S. auditing standards more closely with international standards); the resulting current AICPA standard classifies 13 assertions into three categories: (1) account balances at the period end (for which there are four assertions); (2) transactions and events for the period (for which there are five assertions); and (3) presentation and disclosure (for which there are four assertions).

International Auditing Issues

IFAC and International Standards on Auditing

After studying this lesson, you should be able to:

1. *Understand the nature of the International Federation of Accountants (IFAC) and its role as a global standard-setting body in auditing, ethics, public sector accounting, and education.*
2. *Understand the role of IFAC's "International Auditing and Assurance Standards Board" (IAASB) as a global auditing standard-setting body, in general, and the structure of the IAASB's International Standards on Auditing (ISAs), in particular.*
3. *Understand the role of IFAC's "International Ethics Standards Board for Accountants" (IESBA) as a global ethics standard-setting body, which is responsible for IFAC's Code of Ethics for Professional Accountants.*
4. *Understand the primary differences between clarified ISAs and existing PCAOB Auditing (and Interim) Standards and, thereby, the primary differences between ISAs and AICPA Professional Standards.*

I. The International Federation of Accountants (IFAC)

A. Membership

1. IFAC is comprised of more than 150 member and associate organizations, which collectively represent more than 2.5 million accounting professionals globally.
2. U.S. CPAs are represented through the AICPA's membership in IFAC -- individual CPAs cannot be members of IFAC.

B. Brief history

1. IFAC was established in 1977 with the following purposes: (a) to develop and support high quality international standards; (b) to facilitate cooperation among member bodies; (c) to collaborate with other international organizations; and (d) to serve as the primary international spokesperson for the accountancy profession.
2. Over time, IFAC has expanded its focus to become increasingly involved in regulation of the international profession and coordinating interactions among the largest public accounting firms (through the "Forum of Firms" representing more than twenty large firms/affiliations of firms that perform transnational audits), among other activities.

II. **IFAC's Role as a Standard-Setting Body --** IFAC has four specific standard-setting boards.

A. The International Auditing and Assurance Standards Board (IAASB)

1. **Purposes --** To set high quality standards related to auditing, review, other assurance services, and quality control; and to facilitate convergence of national and international standards.
2. **Composition of IAASB --** The Board is comprised of eighteen members: ten are nominated by member bodies; three are so-called "public" members; and five are nominated by the "Transnational Auditors Committee" (TAC is the acting executive committee of the "Forum of Firms"); there are also four "observers" (non-voting), including one from the U.S. PCAOB.

> **Note:**
> **IFRSs** are issued by the **International Accounting Standards Board** (IASB), which is an independent accounting-standard setter and is not part of IFAC! IFAC is not the global "accounting" standard-setting body.

3. **Standards issued by the IAASB**

    a. **International Standards on Auditing (ISAs) -- Applicable to the audit of historical financial information**; ISAs distinguish professional requirements from explanatory material in each standard (similar to recently issued AICPA Statements on Auditing Standards that are modeled on the structure of ISAs).

    b. **Other standards issued by the IAASB --** International Standards on Review Engagements (ISREs) applicable to the review of historical financial information; International Standards on Assurance Engagements (ISAEs) applicable to assurance engagements not involving historical financial information; International Standards on Related Services (ISRSs) applicable to agreed-upon procedures and compilation engagements; and International Standards on Quality Control (ISQCs) applicable to a firm's services under those ISAs, ISAEs, and ISRSs.

4. **Due process --** The IAASB adheres to due process in the issuance of ISAs, which includes issuance of exposure drafts and a period for public comments; a separate "basis for conclusions" is issued for every final pronouncement that addresses comments received.

5. "International Auditing Practice Statements" provide guidance and assistance to practitioners in implementing ISAs (similar Practice Statements are issued with respect to ISAEs and ISRSs).

6. **IAASB's "Clarity Project" --** In line with its commitment to facilitate convergence between national and international standards (and similar to a comparable initiative of the AICPA's Auditing Standards Board), the IAASB initiated a "Clarity Project."

    a. **Purpose of the Clarity Project --** To enhance the quality of practice by making standards as clear/understandable and capable of consistent application as possible.

    b. **Impact on ISAs --** Each ISA specifies an objective and establishes the auditor's responsibilities in relationship to that objective.

7. **Public Interest Oversight Board (PIOB) --** Provides oversight of the IAASB to ensure that IFAC's auditing standards are responsive to the public interest and to enhance investor confidence in these standards.

B. **The International Ethics Standards Board for Accountants (IESBA)**

1. **Purposes --** To set ethical standards and provide related guidance to accounting professionals and to promote good ethical practices globally.

2. Ethical standards issued by the IESBA comprise the Code of Ethics for Professional Accountants; the IESBA also issues Interpretations of the Code of Ethics.

3. **Due process --** The IESBA follows the same due process as the IAASB.

4. **Public Interest Oversight Board (PIOB) --** Provides oversight of the IESBA to ensure that IFAC's ethics standards are responsive to the public interest.

C. The International Public Sector Accounting Standards Board (IPSASB) issues international standards dealing with accounting issues affecting local, regional, and national governmental entities and their constituents. (The Board's pronouncements are called "International Public Sector Accounting Standards.")

D. The International Accounting Education Standards Board (IAESB) issues international standards dealing with accounting education around the world with particular emphasis on (1) the elements of accreditation (including tests of professional competence) and (2) continuing professional education. (The Board's pronouncements are called "International Education Standards.")

III. Comparison of International Standards on Auditing (ISAs) and the PCAOB's Auditing Standards -- Based on a 2009 study (conducted by the Maastricht Accounting, Auditing and Information Management Research Center on behalf of the European Union).

A. **Objective of the Study --** Identify the primary differences between IFAC's clarified ISAs and the PCAOB Auditing (and Interim) Standards and the effect of those differences on audit practice and the perceptions of financial statement users.

B. The 2009 Maastricht study identified five primary areas where ISAs and PCAOB standards differ in ways that might be significant to auditing:

1. **Evaluating and reporting on internal control over financial reporting --** PCAOB auditing standards require the auditor to report on internal control over financial reporting in an "integrated audit" (as mandated by the Sarbanes-Oxley Act, specifically Sections 302 and 404); whereas, there is no similar requirement under ISAs for an integrated audit or an expression of opinion on internal control over financial reporting.

2. **Documentation requirements --** The PCAOB is viewed as somewhat more specific ("prescriptive") in their documentation requirements (for example, an engagement completion memorandum is necessary); whereas, ISA documentation requirements are viewed more generally as a matter of professional judgment.

3. **Reference to "other auditors" --** PCAOB auditing standards permit the primary auditor to signal a division of responsibility by referring to other auditors; whereas, no such reference is permitted under ISAs.

4. **Going concern issues --** PCAOB standards focus on the foreseeable future defined as a period not to exceed twelve months; whereas, ISAs are not limited to twelve months in addressing such going concern issues.

C. The 2009 Maastricht study identified minor differences regarding **auditing related party transactions** (ISA requirements are more extensive than PCAOB standards) and **inquiry of a client's attorney** about litigation, etc. (PCAOB requirements are more extensive than ISAs).

D. Other than the differences identified above - the 2009 Maastricht study indicated that there were practically no differences between PCAOB standards and ISAs for other audit-related topics (including materiality, quality control, analytical procedures, confirmations, written representations, sampling, responsibilities for fraud and illegal acts, fair values, subsequent events, the role of an entity's internal audit function, using specialists, audit communications, etc.).

E. The PCAOB "risk assessment" standards issued in 2010 result in additional differences relative to International Standards on Auditing - the most significant difference is that the PCAOB Auditing Standards focus on five traditional financial statement assertions, whereas the ISAs focus on 13 assertions across three categories of assertions (which is consistent with the treatment of the Auditing Standards Board's corresponding Statement on Auditing Standards).

> An article entitled "Auditing Standards Don't Have Far to Converge" (dated August 21, 2009) on WebCPA commented about the 2009 Maastricht study as follows:
>
> "A new study indicates that differences between the international and U.S. auditing standards are fairly negligible and won't present the challenge now facing the convergence of U.S. GAAP with International Financial Reporting Standards.... However, there will remain significant differences because of Sarbanes-Oxley requirements for separate reporting by auditors on internal control over financial reporting."

Professional Responsibility

Code of Professional Conduct

The AICPA Code of Professional Conduct consists of (1) Principles (which provide a broad framework) and (2) Rules of Conduct (which govern the specifics of members' performance of professional services). Bylaws require adherence to the Rules and to technical standards promulgated under them. By the time one studies the Principles, the Rules, Interpretations of the Rules of Conduct, and specific Ethics Rulings, one is immersed in a considerable amount of detail. There is probably more information in this course than you need to pass the test. Your attention should center upon the areas emphasized in the outline (especially the tables that summarize key rulings) and upon the past test questions.

After studying this lesson, you should be able to:

1. *Understand the basic organizational structure of the AICPA's Code of Professional Conduct.*

I. Code of Professional Conduct

A. Introduction

1. The Code applies to all AICPA members.
    a. By accepting membership, CPAs assume an obligation of self-discipline above the simple requirements of the law.
2. Even nonmembers are expected to follow the Code.
3. Reason for adoption of a distinguishing mark of a profession is an acceptance of responsibility to the public.

B. Code Provisions -- Where applicable (i.e., some do not apply to CPAs not in public practice), Code provisions establish *minimum* levels of acceptable professional conduct.

C. Principles are Organized into Six Articles

1. Responsibilities;
2. The Public Interest;
3. Integrity;
4. Objectivity and Independence;
5. Due Care; and
6. Scope and Nature of Services.

D. Supplementation -- The Principles are supplemented by Rules of Conduct, Interpretations, and Rulings.

E. Article I - Responsibilities -- "In carrying out their responsibilities as professionals, members should exercise sensitive professional and moral judgments in all their activities."

F. Article II - The Public Interest -- "Members should accept the obligation to act in a way that will serve the public interest, honor the public trust, and demonstrate commitment to professionalism."

1. Accountants are expected to act with integrity, objectivity, due professional care, and a desire to serve the public.

G. Article III - Integrity -- "To maintain and broaden public confidence, members should perform all professional responsibilities with the highest sense of integrity."

1. Integrity requires the observance of the principles of:
    a. Objectivity;
    b. Independence; and
    c. Due Care.
2. Integrity provides that service and the public trust should not be subordinated to personal gain and advantage.

H. Article IV - Objectivity and Independence -- "A member should maintain objectivity and be free of conflicts of interest in discharging professional responsibilities. A member in public practice should be independent in fact and appearance when providing auditing and other attestation services."

1. Objectivity is a state of mind, featuring:
    a. Impartiality;
    b. Intellectual honesty; and
    c. Freedom from conflicts of interest.
2. Independence precludes relationships that even appear to impair objectivity in performing attest functions.

Requirements

	Audit	Compilation	Tax	Consulting
Integrity	Yes	Yes	Yes	Yes
Objectivity	Yes	Yes	Yes	Yes
Independence in Fact	Yes	No	No	No
Independence in Appearance	Yes	No	No	No

I. Article V - Due Care -- "A member should observe the profession's technical and ethical standards, strive continually to improve competence and the quality of services, and discharge professional responsibility to the best of the member's ability."

1. Competence and diligence are key components of due care.
2. Competence is a synthesis of education and experience.
3. Competence may require consultation or referral when a professional engagement exceeds the member's personal competence.
4. Due care requires adequate planning and supervision for any professional activity undertaken.

J. Article VI - Scope and Nature of Services -- "A member *in public practice* should observe the Principles of the Code of Professional Conduct in determining the scope and nature of services to be provided."

1. In addition to serving the public interest and evidencing integrity, objectivity, and due care, professionals should consider whether their attest activities may render inappropriate the offering of other services to an attest client.
2. Additionally, members should:
    a. Have in place appropriate internal quality control procedures;

b. avoid conflicts of interest, as potentially between the role as auditor and a role providing other services, and
   i. Sarbanes-Oxley (SOX) (2002) dramatically limits the forms of consulting services that audit firms may offer to audit clients that are public companies;
   ii. For private company audit clients, AICPA guidelines still apply. They allow quite a bit of consulting by auditors.
c. assess whether an activity is consistent with their role as professionals.

Independence

Introduction and Independence

For those involved in the attest function, nothing can be more important than being conversant with the rules regarding independence.

After studying this lesson you should be able to :

1. *Understand the basic situations where independence is required.*
2. *Know how to identify basic conflicts that produce the need for independence rules.*
3. *Comprehend the basics of the AICPA's "Conceptual Framework" for analyzing independence issues.*

I. Introduction

A. Especially with the SEC and PCAOB looking over auditors' shoulders, independence problems can lead to all sorts of liability. Two simple but critical points to take away from this section are:

1. Those involved in tax and consulting need not be independent; and

2. For those involved in the attest function, independence in appearance is as important as independence in fact.

> "A member **in public practice** shall be independent in the performance of professional services as required by standards promulgated by bodies designated by the Council."

3. **Areas of Concern --** Those who perform the attest function must act independently. Whereas consultants and tax professionals may be advocates for their clients, auditors owe their highest duty of loyalty not to the attest client but to the consumers of the financial statements.

4. There are four major areas of concern regarding independence:

a. **Financial ties to clients --** An auditor should not own stock in a client;

b. **Employment ties to a client --** An auditor should not be on a client's board of directors;

c. **Nonaudit services provided to clients --** An auditor should not audit financial statements that he himself has produced on the client's behalf; and

d. **Auditors' family ties to clients --** An auditor's spouse should not be CEO or a large stockholder of an audit client.

B. **Rule 101 --** The AICPA Code of Ethics addresses independence in Rule 101 but, to the extent that the Code conflicts with federal guidelines promulgated by the Securities Exchange Commission (SEC) and the Public Company Accounting Oversight Board (PCAOB), its provisions must give way.

II. The Conceptual Framework

A. Before we examine the four major areas of independence problems (financial relationships, employment relationships, consulting services, and family relationships), it is worth noting that although there are many, many rules to learn, even this multitude cannot cover every possible situation. To give guidance for situations that are not specifically provided for in the rules, the AICPA in 2006 promulgated a "conceptual framework" for handling such situations.

B. The idea is that by adopting a "risk-based" approach, CPAs may be able to determine how to handle unique, problematic situations. This risk-based approach involves three steps:

1. Identifying and evaluating threats to independence.
2. Determining whether safeguards already eliminate or sufficiently mitigate identified threats and whether threats that have not yet been mitigated can be eliminated or sufficiently mitigated by safeguards.
3. If no safeguards are available to eliminate an unacceptable threat or reduce it to an acceptable level, independence would be considered impaired.

C. There are three types of safeguards that might prevent impairment of independence:

1. Safeguards created by the profession, legislation, or regulation, such as: education and training requirements, external reviews of a firm's quality control system, and professional monitoring and disciplinary procedures.
2. Safeguards created by the client, such as: hiring skilled and experienced personnel, a tone at the top emphasizing fair financial reporting, and effective corporate governance structures.
3. Safeguards implemented by the accounting firm, such as policies and procedures designed to implement and monitor quality control, documented independence policies, and policies and procedures designed to monitor the firm or partner's reliance on revenue from a single client.

Who Must Be Independent?

After studying this lesson you should be able to :

1. *Describe all the categories of "covered members" who must comply with the AICPA's independence rules.*

I. Who Must Be Independent?

A. Those who participate on the attest engagement team, including those who perform concurring and second partner reviews, all employees and contractors retained by the firm who participate in the attest engagement, irrespective of their functional classification (tax, consulting, etc), but not individuals who perform only routine clerical functions, such as word processing and photocopying;

B. Those who are in a position to influence the attest engagement:

1. Those who evaluate the performance or recommend compensation of the attest engagement partner.
2. Those who directly supervise the attest engagement partner and all successively senior levels through the firm's chief executive.
3. Those who consult with the attest engagement team during the engagement regarding technical or industry-specific issues, transactions, or events.
4. Those who provide quality control or other oversight of the attest engagement, including internal monitoring.

C. Other partners or professionals of the firm:

1. Partners and managers who provide 10 or more hours of non-attest services to the client.
2. Other partners in the office in which the lead attest engagement partner primarily practices in connection with the attest engagement.

D. The firm.

E. Entities controlled by any of the above.

II. Who is a "Covered Member"?

See the following table.

	Covered	Not Covered
The Firm	X	
Partners who work on the engagement	X	
Managers who work on the engagement	X	
Staff members who work on the engagement	X	
Receptionists and copy staff who work on the engagement		X
Partners in the office of the lead attest partner who don't work on the engagement	X	
Managers in the office of the lead attest partner who don't work on the engagement (unless they perform 10 hours of non-attest service)		X*
Partners in other offices		X*
Those who do concurring and second partner reviews	X	
Those in a position (by reason of review, setting compensation, etc.) to influence members of the engagement team	X	

* Although these persons are generally not "covered members," even they and all other professional employees in the firm, may not own more than 5% of an audit client's stock nor serve as director, officer, other manager, promoter, underwriter, voting trustee, or trustee of a pension or profit-sharing plan of an audit client.

Financial Interests

After studying this lesson you should be able to :

1. *Understand the basic rules that must be followed to maintain financial independence from an audit client.*

I. Financial Relationships --

Financial Relationships -- The first major way an auditor may impair his or her independence is to develop inappropriate financial relationships with a client. Interpretation 101-1 spells out the key rules that seek to prevent an auditor or audit firm from having any important financial interest in a client, whether that interest is held directly or indirectly.

A. Interpretation 101-1 -- Independence is impaired if, during the period of professional engagement or at time of expression of opinion:

	Impaired	Not Impaired
Member (or firm) had material direct financial interest in client	X	
Member had immaterial direct financial interest in client	X	
Member had material indirect financial interest in client	X	
Member had immaterial indirect financial interest in client		X
Member committed to obtain material indirect financial interest in client	X	
Member had any material joint investment with client	X	
Member had any loan to or from client, officer, or stockholder (except as permitted by 101-5)	X	
CM accepts gift that is not clearly insignificant to the recipient	X	
Member leases to or from client via a capital lease	X	
Member leases to or from client via an operating lease		X
Member has not been paid for more than a year	X	
Member has put investment in client in a blind trust	X	
Member participates in or receives benefits from, an employee benefit plan that is a client or sponsored by a client	X	
Partner or professional employee and/or his or her immediate family owned 5% or more of client's equity stock*	X	

*Under new AICPA revision, being a trustee or executor creates a problem only if (i) the covered member had authority to make investment decisions for the estate or trust, or (ii) the trust or estate owned or was committed to acquiring more than 10% of the client ownership interests, or (iii) the value of the trust or estate's holdings in the client exceeded 10% of the total assets of the trust or estate.

B. Direct vs. indirect financial interests -- To help clarify the distinction between direct and indirect financial interests (because interests that are both indirect and immaterial do not impair independence), the AICPA issued new guidelines in 2006 that look like this:

1. A **financial interest** is an ownership interest in an equity or a debt security issued by an entity, including rights and obligations to acquire such an interest and derivatives directly related to such an interest.
2. A **direct financial interest** is a financial interest:
   a. owned directly by an individual or entity (including those managed on a discretionary basis by others); or
   b. under the control of an individual or entity (including those managed on a discretionary basis by others); or

c. beneficially owned through an investment vehicle, estate, trust, or other intermediary when the beneficiary:

   i. controls the intermediary; or

   ii. has the authority to supervise or participate in the intermediary's investment decisions.

3. An **indirect financial interest** is a financial interest beneficially owned through an investment vehicle, estate, trust, or other intermediary when the beneficiary neither controls the intermediary nor has the authority to supervise or participate in the intermediary's investment decisions.

4. A financial interest is **beneficially owned** when an individual or entity is not the recorded owner of the interest but has a right to some or all of the underlying benefits of ownership. These benefits include the authority to direct the voting or the disposition of the interest or to receive the economic benefits of the ownership of the interest.

C. **Interpretation 101-5 --** Loans from financial institution clients. Generally, covered members shouldn't loan to or borrow from a financial institution client or its subsidiary. However, if obtained pursuant to normal lending procedures, terms, and requirements, two types of loans are permitted:

	Permitted	Not Permitted
Grandfathered Loans		
1) Loans from Financial Institution (FI) before it became a client	X	
2) Loan from FI which then sold loan to attest client	X	
3) Loan to CPA before s/he joined firm which had FI as client	X	
4) Falling behind on repayment of #1-3		X
5) Renegotiating #1-3		X
6) Collateral on loans #1-3 (if secured) worth less than loan balance		X
Other Permitted Loans		
7) Auto loan from current client if collateralized by the auto	X*	
8) Loan of surrender value of insurance policy	X	
9) Passbook loans collateralized by cash deposits ("passbook loans")	X	
10) Credit cards and cash advanced on checking accounts < $10,000	X	

*The AICPA recently established similar rules for the leasing of an automobile.

D. **Interpretation 101-6 --** Effect of threatened litigation upon independence.

	Impaired	Not Impaired
Suit by present management alleging deficient audit	X	
Suit by member against present management for fraud or deceit	X	
Strong possibility present management will sue for deficient audit	X	
Suit over billing dispute or other matter not related to audit (such as consulting or tax matters) if it is for nonmaterial amount		X
Suit against auditor by client's shareholders (assuming no cross claim by member against management claiming fraud)		X
Suit against auditor by client's creditors (assuming no cross claim by member against management claiming fraud)		X

E. Interpretation 101-8 -- CPA's financial interests in nonclients may impair independence when those nonclients have financial interests in the CPA's clients.

> **Example:**
> CPA Firm owns 60% of XYZ Co. stock.
>
> XYZ Co. owns 51% of ABC Co.
>
> CPA Firm audits ABC Co.

F. Additional financial threats to independence -- In this section, we note some new rules that address some intractable problems with independence that arise from financial ties.

1. **Unsolicited financial interests --** For example, what if an audit engagement team member's aunt just out of the blue gives her a block of stock as a gift, and the stock happens to have been issued by an audit client? The rule on unsolicited financial interests provides for the following:

   a. If a "covered member" receives a gift or inheritance of stock in an audit client, no independence problem exists so long as the covered member disposes of the stock as soon as practicable, but definitely within 30 days.

   b. If a "covered member" becomes aware that he or she will receive a gift or inheritance of stock in a client but does not yet have the right to dispose of it, independence would be considered to be impaired unless (a) the covered member does not participate on the attest engagement team, and (b) the covered member disposes of the stock as soon as practicable after acquiring the power to do so but definitely within 30 days.

G. Mutual funds -- Obviously, if Sam audits XYZ Mutual Fund, he cannot own a direct interest in the mutual fund. But can he own an interest in ABC Corp. if XYZ holds ABC shares in its portfolio? The rule looks like this:

1. An interest in a mutual fund is a direct financial interest, but the mutual fund investor's interest in the underlying securities held by the fund would be indirect.
2. If the mutual fund is diversified, a covered member's ownership of 5% or less of the shares of the fund would not be considered a material indirect interest in the underlying investments.
3. If a covered member (CM) owns more than 5% of the shares of a diversified fund, or if the fund is not diversified, then the member should evaluate the underlying investments to determine if their indirect interest is material.

H. Direct and indirect interests - retirement, savings, compensation or similar plans

1. Investments held by a retirement, savings, compensation, or similar plan sponsored by a CM's firm would be considered *direct financial interests* of the firm.
2. If a CM or his or her immediate family member (IMF) self-directs the investments in a retirement, savings, compensation, or similar plan, or has the ability to supervise or participate in the plan's investment decisions, the investments held by the plan would be considered *direct financial interests* of the CM. Otherwise, the underlying plan investments would be considered *indirect financial interests* of the CM.
3. Investments held in a defined benefit plan would not be considered financial interests of the CM unless the CM or his or her IFM is a trustee of the plan or otherwise has the ability to supervise or participate in the plan's investment decisions.

4. Allocated shares held in an employee stock ownership plan (ESOP) would be considered *indirect financial interests* that are beneficially owned until such time as the CM or his or her IFM has the right to dispose of the financial interest. Once the participant has the right to dispose of the financial interest, the financial interest is considered a *direct financial interest*.

5. Rights to acquire equity interests, restricted stock awards, or other SBCA (Share-Based Compensation Arrangements) are considered *direct financial interests*, regardless of whether such financial interests are vested or exercisable.

I. **Gifts and entertainment --** What happens if a covered member accepts gifts or entertainment from an attest client? Or from one of its key employees or an owner of 10% of its stock? The answer for gifts is slightly different than the answer for entertainment.

   1. Answer for gifts: Independence would be considered impaired if the firm, a member of the attest engagement team, or one in a position to influence the engagement accepted a gift from an attest client, unless the value is *clearly insignificant to the recipient*.

   2. Answer for entertainment: Independence is not considered impaired if a covered member accepts entertainment, provided the entertainment is "*reasonable in the circumstances.*"

Employment Relationships

After studying this lesson you should be able to :

1. *Understand the basic rules that must be followed in order to avoid employment relationships that could compromise audit independence in fact or appearance.*

I. Employment Relationships -- The second way that an auditor can impair independence is to develop an employment relationship with an audit client. Clearly, a member of the audit team should not work for the client while on the audit team.

	Impaired	Not Impaired
Member was trustee of any trust or executor of any estate with direct or material indirect interest in client*	X	
Member was trustee of any pension or profit sharing plan of client	X	
Member is on client's board of directors	X	
Member is promoter of client's stock	X	
Member is officer of client	X	
Member is a voting trustee of a client	X	
Also, partner or professional employee (who are not otherwise "covered members") and/or his or her immediate family cannot be employed by client or serve as director, promoter, underwriter, voting trustee, or trustee of any pension or profit-sharing trust of the client	X	

*Under new AICPA revision, being a trustee or executor creates a problem only if (i) the covered member had authority to make investment decisions for the estate or trust, or (ii) the trust or estate owned or was committed to acquiring more than 10% of the client ownership interests, or (iii) the value of the trust or estate's holdings in the client exceeded 10% of the total assets of the trust or estate.

A. Interpretation 101-4 -- A CPA who is a director of a nonprofit organization where the board is large and representative of community leadership is not lacking in independence if:

1. the position is purely honorary;
2. the CPA is identified as honorary on external materials;
3. the CPA does no more than contribute the use of his/her name; and
4. the CPA does not vote or participate in management affairs.

B. Former client employees now working for the audit firm -- What if an audit client's employee wishes to go to work for the audit firm? What safeguards would preserve independence? In May 2010, a new interpretation of Rule 101 addressed this area.

1. **Covered client employees --** The interpretation covers people who were:
   a. employed by a client; or
   b. associated with a client as an officer, director, promoter, underwriter, voting trustee, or trustee for a pension or profit sharing trust of the client.
2. **The rule --** A firm's independence is impaired if one of these people participated on the attest engagement team or became a person in a position to influence the team when the attest engagement covers any period of time when the person was employed by, or associated with, the audit client.

3. While such a former client employee simply cannot become a team member or person in a position to influence, he or she could become another sort of covered member (such as an OPIO - other partner in the office) without impairing the audit firm's independence so long as he or she dissociates himself or herself from the client prior to becoming a covered member. Dissociation includes all of the following five steps:
    a. Ceasing to participate in all client employee health and welfare benefit plans, unless the client is legally required to allow the covered member to participate in the plan (e.g., COBRA), and the covered member pays 100% of his or her portion of the cost;
    b. Ceasing to participate in all other employee benefit plans by liquidating or transferring all vested benefits in the client's defined benefit plans, defined contribution plans, and similar arrangements at the earliest date permitted under the plan;
        i. If the person does not join the audit team or become a person in a position to influence it, he or she need not liquidate or transfer vested benefits if to do so would incur a significant penalty under the terms of the plan.
    c. Disposing of any direct or material indirect financial interest in the client;
    d. Collecting or repaying any loans to or from the client other than those specifically permitted or grandfathered by Interpretation 101-5; and
    e. Assessing other relationships to the client to determine if they create threats to independence that would require the application of safeguards to reduce threats to an acceptable level.

C. **Cooling-off period**

1. Sarbanes-Oxley imposes a one-year *"cooling-off period"* that requires the lead partner, the concurring partner, or any other member of the audit engagement team who provides more than 10 hours of audit, review, or attest services to observe a one-year cooling-off period before going to work for a client: (a) as CEO, CFO, controller, CAO, or any equivalent officers, (b) in any financial oversight role, and (c) preparing financial statements. Because the focus is the year preceding commencement of the audit of the current year's financial statements, the time period could effectively last as long as 23 months.
2. When a member of the attest engagement team (or a person in a position to influence that team) intends to seek or discuss potential employment or association with an attest client or is in receipt of a specific offer of employment from an attest client, independence will be impaired with respect to that client unless:
    a. the person promptly reports such consideration or offer to an appropriate person in the firm;
    b. the person removes himself or herself from the engagement until the offer is rejected or the position is no longer sought. When a "covered member" learns that another person on the attest engagement team (or a person in a position to influence) is considering employment with a client, that member should alert the firm. The firm must then consider what additional procedures may be necessary to provide "reasonable assurance" that the person performed his/her work for the client with objectivity and integrity.
3. What about covered members formerly employed by, or associated with, a client? For example, what if a member of the engagement team used to work for the audit client?
    a. An individual who was formerly (i) employed by a client or (ii) associated with a client as an officer, director, promoter, underwriter, voting trustee, or trustee for a pension or profit-sharing trust of the client would impair independence if the individual:

i. participated on the attest engagement team or was an individual in a position to influence the attest engagement for the client when the attest engagement covers any period that includes his or her former employment or association with that client; or

ii. was otherwise a covered member with respect to the client unless the individual first disassociates from the client by (a) terminating any relationships with the client, (b) disposing of any direct or material indirect financial interest in the client, (c) ceases to participate in all employee benefit plans sponsored by the client, and (d) liquidates and transfers all vested benefits in the client's benefit plans (but need not liquidate or transfer if there is a significant penalty attached).

Nonaudit Services

After studying this lesson you should be able to :

1. *Realize that where public company audit clients are concerned, Sarbanes-Oxley mandates that most of these services not be provided at all.*
2. *Understand what an audit client can and cannot do in terms of nonaudit services (consulting) for a private company audit client without impairing independence.*

I. Nonaudit Services to Audit Clients

A. A third concern in the independence realm is the provision of nonaudit services to audit clients. The worry is that auditors will subordinate their objective judgment in order to keep the client happy and purchasing consulting services.

B. The following are now the rules only for audits of private companies. Sarbanes-Oxley overrides for audits of public companies and does not allow most of these activities.

1. **Interpretation 101-3 --** When a CPA performs nonattest services for an attest client, that member must be careful not to perform management functions, not to make management decisions, and not to appear to do these things. Also, the member must not take custody of client assets.
2. The client must agree to:
    - **a.** make all management decisions and perform all management functions;
    - **b.** designate an individual who possesses suitable skill, knowledge, and/or experience, preferably within senior management, to oversee the services;
    - **c.** evaluate the adequacy and results of the services performed;
    - **d.** accept responsibility for the results of the services; and
    - **e.** establish and maintain internal controls, including monitoring ongoing activities.
3. The member should be satisfied that the client will be able to meet these criteria and make informed judgments on the results of the member's nonattest services.
4. Before performing nonattest services, the member should establish and document in writing his or her understanding with the BOD or audit committee regarding:
    - **a.** the objectives of the engagement;
    - **b.** the services to be performed;
    - **c.** the client's acceptance of responsibility;
    - **d.** the member's responsibilities; and
    - **e.** any limitations to the engagement.
5. The following are activities that would impair a member's independence:
    - **a.** Authorizing, executing, or consummating a transaction, or otherwise exercising authority on behalf of a client or having the authority to do so;
    - **b.** Preparing source documents, in electronic or other form, evidencing the occurrence of a transaction;
    - **c.** Having custody of client assets;

d. Supervising client employees in the performance of their normal recurring activities;

e. Reporting to the board of directors on behalf of management;

f. Serving as a client's stock transfer or escrow agent, registrar, general counsel, or its equivalent; or

g. Establishing or maintaining internal controls, including performing ongoing monitoring activities for a client.

6. The following guidelines give specifics regarding various areas of practice:

Bookkeeping	Impaired	Not Impaired
Record transactions in client's general ledger		X
Prepare F/S based on trial balance information		X
Propose standard, adjusting, or correcting journal entries, provided that client reviews and member is satisfied that client understands nature and impact		X
Make changes in records w/o client approval	X	
Approve or authorize client transactions	X	
Prepare source documents or originate data	X	
Make changes to source documents w/o client approval	X	

Nontax Disbursement	Impaired	Not Impaired
Use payroll time record provided by client to generate unsigned checks or process client's payroll		X
Transmit client approved payroll or other disbursement information to a financial institution chosen by client		X
Accept responsibility to authorize payment of client funds	X	
Accept responsibility to sign or cosign checks	X	
Maintain client's bank account, take custody of client funds, or make credit or banking decisions for client	X	
Approve vendor invoices for payments	X	

Benefit Plan Administration	Impaired	Not Impaired
Communicate summary plan data to plan trustee		x
Advise client management regarding impact of plan provisions		x
Process transactions initiated by plan participants		x
Prepare account valuations		x
Prepare and transmit participant statement to plan participants		x
Make policy decisions on client's behalf	x	
Interpret plan for participants w/o management's concurrence	x	
Make disbursements on plan's behalf	x	
Take custody of plan assets	x	
Serve as a plan fiduciary	x	

Investment - Advisory or Management	Impaired	Not Impaired
Recommend allocation of funds that a client should invest in various asset classes		x
Perform bookkeeping and reporting of client's portfolio balance		x
Review management of client's portfolio by others to determine if managers are meeting client's investment objectives		x
Transmit client's investment selection to broker		x
Make investment decisions on client's behalf	x	
Execute transactions to buy or sell for client	x	
Take custody of client assets, such as a security purchased	x	

Corporate Finance - Consulting/Advisory	Impaired	Not Impaired
Assist in developing corporate strategies		x
Assist in identifying or introducing client to sources of capital		x
Assist in analyzing effects of proposed transactions		x
Assist in drafting offering documents		x
Advise client in transaction negotiations		x
Commit the client to a transaction or consummate on client's behalf	x	
Act as a promoter, underwriter, broker-dealer, or guarantor of client's securities	x	
Act as a distributor of client's private placement memoranda	x	
Maintain custody of client securities	x	

Executive or Employee Search	Impaired	Not Impaired
Recommend position description or candidate specifications		x
Solicit, screen, and recommend candidates on client-approved criteria		x
Advise employer on employee hiring or benefits		x
Hire or terminate client employees	x	
Commit client to employee compensation or benefits	x	

Business Risk Consulting	Impaired	Not Impaired
Provide assistance in assessing client's business risks and control processes		x
Recommend a plan for improving control processes and assisting in implementation		x
Make or approve business risk decisions	x	
Present business risk consideration to board on management's behalf	x	

Information Systems	Impaired	Not Impaired
Install or integrate a client's financial information system (FIS), that was not designed or developed by member		x
Assist in setting up the client's chart of accounts and financial statement format with respect to the client's FIS		x
Provide training and instruction to client's employees		x
Design or develop a client's FIS	x	
Design, develop, install, or integrate a client's FIS that is unrelated to the client's F/S or accounting records		x
Make other than insignificant modifications to source code underlying a client's existing FIS.	x	
Supervise client personnel in the daily operation of its FIS	x	
Operate client's local area network (LAN)	x	

Appraisal, Valuation, or Actuarial	Impaired	Not Impaired
Results would be material to the F/S and services involve a high degree of subjectivity*	x	
Services not requiring a high degree of subjectivity**		x
Services performed for nonfinancial statement purposes***		x

*Ex: valuing ESOP, business combination, or appraisals of assets and liabilities.

**Ex: valuing a client's pension or postemployment benefit liabilities.

***Ex: appraising or actuarial services for tax planning, estate and gift taxation, and divorce proceedings.

7. **Internal audit outsourcing**

   a. Regarding internal audit outsourcing, an auditor should not perform internal auditing for an audit client unless he/she ensures that the client understands its responsibility for establishing, maintaining, and directing the internal audit function (IAF).

b. The member should ensure that client management: (i) designates a competent manager to be responsible for the IAF; (ii) determines the scope, risk, and frequency of internal audit activities; (iii) evaluates the findings and results arising from those activities; and (iv) evaluates the adequacy of the audit procedures performed and the resultant findings.

c. Additionally, the member should be satisfied that the client's board of directors or audit committee is informed about the member's and the client's respective roles. That said, certain internal audit activities would, in any event, impair independence. These include, as examples:

Internal Audit Consulting	Impaired	Not Impaired
Performing ongoing monitoring activities or control activities (e.g., reviewing customer credit info as part of sales process) that affects execution of transactions	x	
Determining which, if any, recommendations for improving internal control system should be implemented	x	
Reporting to the board or audit committee on behalf of management regarding internal audit affairs	x	
Approving or being responsible for the overall internal audit work, including determining internal audit risk and scope, project priorities, and frequency of performance of audit procedures	x	
Being connected with the client as an employee or in any management position	x	

Forensic Accounting Services	Impaired	Not Impaired
Expert witness for a client	x	
Expert witness for a large group where attest clients are (a) <20% of members, voting interest, and claims of the group, (b) aren't "lead" plaintiffs, and (c) don't have sole decision-making power to select expert witness		x
Litigation consulting: providing advice to attest client (w/o serving as expert witness)		x
Litigation consulting: serving as trier of fact, special master, court-appointed expert, or arbitrator	x	
Litigation consulting: mediator		x

Tax Compliance Services	Impaired	Not Impaired
Assuming that the CPA does not have custody or control over the client's funds and a client employee reviews and approves the tax return prior to transmission to taxing authority, and, if required for filing, signs the tax return, then:		
- Preparing tax return		x
- Transmitting tax return to taxing authority		x
- Transmitting payment		x
Signing and filing a tax return *on behalf of client management*	x*	
Representing client in administrative proceedings before a taxing authority		x
Representing client in court or a public hearing to resolve a tax dispute	x	
*Signing and filing a tax return on behalf of client management impairs independence, unless several restrictive conditions are met: (a) the member has legal authority to do so; (b) the taxing authority has prescribed procedures in place for a client to permit a member to file a tax return on behalf of the client (e.g., Forms 8879 or 8453), and such procedures meet, at a minimum, standards for electronic return originators outlined in Form 8879; and (c) an individual in client management provides the member with a signed statement that clearly identifies the return being filed and represents that (i) such individual is authorized to sign and file the return; (ii) such individual has reviewed the tax return, including its accompanying schedules and statements, and it is true, correct, and complete to the best of his or her knowledge and belief; and (iii) such individual authorized the member to sign and file on behalf of the client.		

8. Although the SEC and PCAOB considered banning the provision of tax services, they ultimately decided not to. The PCAOB rules now provide, however, that a public company's auditor's independence is impaired regarding a tax client if:

a. the firm enters into a contingent fee arrangement with an audit client;

b. the firm provides marketing, planning, or opinion services in favor of the tax treatment of a "confidential transaction," or if the transaction is based on an "aggressive" interpretation of tax law; and/or

c. the firm provides tax services to members of management who serve in a financial-reporting oversight role for a client (or for his or her immediate family).

i. Also, when a firm seeks the permission of an audit client's audit committee to provide tax services, it must describe the proposed services in writing to the committee, discuss with the committee the potential effects on independence, and document that discussion.

Family Relationships

After studying this lesson you should be able to :

1. *Know how to describe the rules that govern family relationships and the independence problems that those relationships can produce.*
2. *Explain the different rules that apply to immediate family members on the one hand and close relatives on the other.*

I. Family Members

A. A fourth independence concern relates to family members. Obviously, an auditor would have difficulty being objective and independent if a close relative were CEO of the audit company. The rules establish two sets of relatives - an inner circle known as "immediate family members" and a broader circle known as "close relatives."

B. Interpretation 101-1 -- The meaning of certain independence terminology and the effect of family relationships on independence.

C. Immediate family members

1. **Defined --** Spouse, spousal equivalent, and dependents (whether or not related).
2. **Financial interest --** In determining *materiality* of a financial interest, a covered member's interest must be combined with that of their IFMs.
3. **Employment --** An IFM may be employed by an attest client in a position other than a *key position*.
    a. A "key position" is one in which an individual (i) has primary responsibility for significant accounting functions that support material components of the financial statements; (ii) has primary responsibility for the preparation of the financial statement; or (iii) has the ability to exercise responsibility for the preparation of the financial statements, including when the individual is a member of the board of directors or similar governing body, president,CEO, CFO,COO, CAO, general counsel, controller, director of internal audit, director of financial reporting, or any equivalent position.
4. **Benefit Plans --** Immediate family members may work for audit clients and may obviously work for other firms. Both types of employers (particularly the former) may provide benefit plans with interests in audit clients. Immediate family members' participation in these benefit plans can create independence issues and in 2010, the AICPA issued very detailed rules covering such plans, breaking the rules into three broad categories:
    a. Share-Based Compensation Arrangements (SBCA)
    b. Nonqualified Deferred Compensation Plans (NDCP)
    c. Employee Benefit Plans other than SBCA and NDCP
5. **Share-Based Compensation Arrangements (SBCA) --** These are broken into the following three categories:
    a. SBCA resulting in *beneficial financial interest* in attest clients are permitted, provided that:
        i. the covered member is neither on the attest engagement team nor in a position to influence;
        ii. the IFM does not serve as a trustee for the SBCA and does not have the ability to supervise or participate in selection of investment options;

iii. when the beneficial interests are distributed or the IFM has the right to dispose of the shares, the IFM disposes of the shares as soon as practicable but within 30 days, or exercises his or her put option to require the employer to repurchase the beneficial interest as soon as permitted; and

iv. benefits payable from the SBCA to the IFM upon any termination of employment are funded by investment operations other than the employer's financial interests, and any unfunded benefits payable are immaterial to the covered member at all times during the payout period.

b. Share-based compensation arrangements resulting in *rights* to acquire shares in an attest client, such as an employee stock option plan or restricted stock rights plan are permitted, provided that:

i. the covered member is neither on the attest engagement team nor in a position to influence; and

ii. the IFM exercises or forfeits these rights once he or she is vested and the closing market price of the underlying stock equals or exceeds the exercise price for ten consecutive days (market period). The exercise or forfeiture should occur as soon as practicable, but no later than 30 days after the end of the market period. In addition, if the IFM exercises his or her right to acquire the shares, he or she should dispose of the shares as soon as practicable but no later than 30 days after the exercise date.

c. Share-based compensation arrangements based upon *stock appreciation* of an attest client's underlying shares are permitted, provided that:

i. the SBCA (e.g., a stock appreciation plan) does not provide for the issuance of rights to acquire the employer's financial interests;

ii. the covered member neither participates on the attest engagement team nor is in a position to influence the attest engagement;

iii. the IFM exercises or forfeits his or her vested compensation rights if the underlying price of the employer's shares equals or exceeds the exercise price for ten consecutive days (market period). Exercise or forfeiture should occur as soon as practicable but no later than 30 days after the end of the market period; and

iv. any resulting compensation payable to the IFM that is outstanding for more than 30 days is immaterial to the covered member during the payout period.

6. **Nonqualified Deferred Compensation Plans --** Individual family members may participate in an NDCM as a result of permitted employment at an attest client, provided that:

a. the covered member neither participates on the attest engagement team nor is in a position to influence it;

b. the amount of the deferred compensation payable to the IFM is funded through life insurance, an annuity, a trust, or similar vehicle and any unfunded portion is immaterial to the covered member; and

c. any funding of the deferred compensation does not include financial interests in the attest client.

7. **Employee Benefit Plans Other than SBCAs and NDCMs**

a. Individual family members may *participate* in such plans as a result of permitted employment in an attest client, provided that:

i. the plan is offered to all employees in comparable employment positions;

ii. the IFM does not serve in a position of governance for the plan; and

iii. the IFM does not have the ability to supervise or participate in the plan's investment decisions or in the selection of investment options that will be made available to plan participants.

b. An IMF may *hold a direct or material indirect financial interest* in an attest client through participation in a plan, provided that:

i. the covered member neither participates on the attest engagement team nor is in a position to influence it;

ii. such investment is an unavoidable consequence of such participation; and

iii. in the event that a plan option to invest in a nonattest client becomes available, the IMF selects such option and disposes of any direct or material indirect financial interest in the attest client as soon as practicable but no later than 30 days after such option becomes available.

D. **Close relatives --** Parent, sibling, or nondependent child. Independence is considered impaired if:

1. an individual participating on the attest engagement team has a close relative who had:

a. a key position with the client, or

b. a financial interest in the client that:

i. the individual knows or has reason to believe was material to the close relative; **or**

ii. enabled the close relative to exercise significant influence over the client.

2. an individual in a position to influence the attest engagement or any partner in the office in which the lead attest engagement partner primarily practices in connection with the attest engagement, has a close relative who had:

a. a key position with the client; or

b. a financial interest in the client that:

i. the individual or partner knows or has reason to believe was material to the close relative; **and**

ii. enabled the close relative to exercise significant influence over the client (5% threshold).

E. **Immediate family members**

See the following table.

	IFM of Audit Team	IFM of PTI*	IFM 10 hours Non-Audit	IFM of OPIO**
Key Position With Client	No	No	No	No
Non-Key Position	Yes	Yes	Yes	Yes
Participate in Client Benefit Plan	No	No	Yes	Yes

*PTI is shorthand for a "person in a Position To Influence." Example: supervisors, those who decide compensation, etc. of the audit team.

*OPIO means "Other Partners in the Office" of the auditor in charge of an account. Example: The Austin office of PwC audits Dell. All partners in that office, including tax partners, would be OPIOs.

NOTE: "No" indicates impairment.

F. Close relatives

	CR of Audit Team	CR of PTI	CR Partner of OPIO
Key position with client	No	No	No
Financial interest in client that is not material or enables significant influence	No	Yes	Yes
Financial interest in client that is material and enables significant influence	No	No	No

Rule 102 - Integrity and Objectivity

Every CPA, whether involved in auditing, tax work, or consulting must comply with standards of integrity and objectivity. Unlike independence principles, these are not confined mainly to the audit function. In a close case, common sense should prevail, as the AICPA Code of Conduct specifies that, ultimately, integrity is judged in terms of what is "right and just."

After studying this lesson you should be able to :

1. *Comprehend the rules regarding such threats to professionalism as conflicts of interest, client advocacy, and subordination of professional judgment.*
2. *Understand the meaning of basic concepts of integrity and objectivity.*

> "In the performance of any professional service, a member:
>
> A. Shall maintain objectivity and integrity;
>
> B. Shall be free of conflict of interest; and
>
> C. Shall not knowingly misrepresent facts or subordinate his or her judgment to others."

I. **Interpretation 102-1** -- Not only may a member not knowingly make a **false representation**, but that member may not permit or direct another to make a false entry in an entity's financial statement, according to Interpretation 102-1.

II. **Interpretation 102-2** -- A **conflict of interest** may occur if a CPA performing a professional service has a significant relationship with another person, entity, product, or service that could be viewed as impairing the CPA's objectivity, according to Interpretation 102-2.

A. **Exception - This is not a problem if:**

1. full disclosure is made to the client; and
2. the client consents.

B. **Examples of potential conflicts of interest:**

1. A member is asked to perform litigation services for a plaintiff in a lawsuit against one of the firm's audit clients.
2. A member has provided tax planning advice to a married couple that is now divorcing and is asked by both parties to provide services during the divorce proceedings.
3. In giving financial advice, a member suggests that the client invest in a business in which the member has a financial interest;
4. A member provides tax or financial planning services for several members of a family who may have opposing interests.
5. A member has a significant financial interest in a company that is a major competitor of a client for which the member performs management consulting services.
6. A member serves on a city's board of tax appeals, which considers matters involving several of the member's tax clients.

7. A member has been approached to provide services to the potential buyer of real estate owned by a client of the member's firm.
8. A member refers a tax or financial planning client to an insurance broker which refers clients to the member under an exclusive arrangement to do so.
9. A member recommends or refers a client to a service bureau in which the member or partners in the member's firm hold material financial interests.

III. **Interpretation 102-3 --** Provides that a member must respond accurately to his or her employer's external accountant's inquiries. SOX, of course, makes it a crime to lie to outside auditors.

IV. **Interpretation 102-4 --** Consider the situation where an auditor disagrees with his or her supervisor regarding the proper recording of transactions or preparation of financial statements. In order to ensure that a member's **professional judgment** is never improperly subordinated, Interpretation 102-4 provides that a member who has such a disagreement with his or her supervisor should take the following steps:

A. The member should consider whether

1. the entry or the failure to record a transaction in the records; or
2. the financial statement presentation or the nature or omission of disclosure in the financial statements as proposed by the supervisor; or
3. represents an acceptable alternative and does not materially misrepresent the facts.

B. If appropriate research and consultation indicate that the supervisor's position has authoritative support and does not result in a material misrepresentation, the member may accept the supervisor's position and need do nothing further.

C. If the member concludes that the supervisor's position would lead to material misstatement of records or financial statements, the member should make his/her concerns known to the appropriate levels of management, such as the supervisor's immediate superior, the audit committee, the board of directors, etc. The concerns should be documented.

D. If, after discussing the matter with the appropriate persons in the organization, the member concludes that appropriate action will not be taken, the member should consider whether or not s/he should continue the employment relationship and whether s/he has a responsibility to contact a regulatory authority or the organization's external accountant. An attorney should be consulted.

V. **Interpretation 102-5 --** Reminds members who teach or engage in **research and scholarship** that their activities are professional services and should be rendered with objectivity and integrity, that they shall be free of conflicts of interest, and that they shall not knowingly misrepresent facts or subordinate their judgment.

VI. **Interpretation 102-6 -- Client advocacy** can raise interesting dilemmas. Interpretation 102-6 recognizes that a member may be requested by a client to perform tax or consulting services that involve acting as an advocate for the client, and that auditors may be asked to be advocates in support of their clients' positions on accounting or financial reporting issues. Again, these are professional services and should be rendered with objectivity and integrity, free of conflicts of interest, and without subordination of judgment.

A. **Inappropriate Services --** Additionally, if the requested services involving client advocacy appear to stretch the bounds of performance standards or to compromise credibility, the member should consider whether it is appropriate to perform such services.

VII. Examples of Integrity and Objectivity Issues Embodied in Past Ethics Rulings

Question: A member in public practice uses an entity that the member, individually or collectively with his or her firm or with members of his or her firm, does not control (as defined by accounting principles generally accepted in the United States) or an individual not employed by the member (a third-party service provider) to assist the member in providing professional services (for example, bookkeeping, tax return preparation, consulting, or attest services, including related clerical and data entry functions) to clients. Must the member disclose the use of the third-party service provider to the client?

Answer:
Yes. Integrity requires a member to be honest and candid. Clients might not have an expectation that a member would use a third-party service provider to assist the member in providing the professional services. Accordingly, before disclosing confidential client information to a third-party service provider, a member should inform the client, preferably in writing, that the member may use a third-party service provider. This disclosure does not relieve the member from his or her confidentiality obligations. If the client objects to the member's use of a third-party service provider, the member should provide the professional services without using the third-party service provider or the member should decline the engagement. A member is not required to inform the client when he or she uses a third-party service provider to provide administrative support services (for example, record storage, software application hosting, or authorized e-file tax transmittal services) to the member.

Question: A member has been approached by a private company, for which s/he may or may not perform other professional services, to provide personal financial planning or tax services for its executives. The executives are aware of the company's relationship with the member, if any, and have also consented to the arrangement. The performance of the services could result in the member recommending to the executives actions that may be adverse to the company. What rules of conduct should the member consider before accepting and during the performance of the engagement?

Answer:
Before accepting and during the performance, the member should consider the applicability of Rule 102. If a member believes that he or she can perform the personal financial planning or tax services with objectivity, the member would not be prohibited from accepting the engagement. The member should also consider informing the company and the executives of possible results of the engagement. During the performance of the services, the member should consider his or her professional responsibility to the clients under Rule 301. However, if the client is a public company, SOX would prohibit its auditor from providing tax planning services to the client's top executives.

General Standards and Accounting Principles

No matter what type of professional service a CPA is providing - audit, tax, consulting, etc. - that CPA must act with professional competence.

After studying this lesson you should be able to :

1. *Understand the basic requirements for every professional engagement (tax, audit, or consulting).*
2. *Understand what it means to act with professional competence.*

I. **Rule 201 --** Remember (because these are often possible selections on multiple choice questions) that professional competence entails, among other things, undertaking only tasks that you are competent to perform, exercising due professional care in the completion of those tasks, adequately planning those tasks and supervising those who perform them for you, and obtaining sufficient relevant data to serve as a basis for any conclusions you reach or recommendations you make.

II. **General Standards --** A member must comply with the following standards for all professional engagements:

   A. **Professional competence --** Undertake only those professional services that the member or member's firm can reasonably expect to be completed with professional competence;

   B. **Due professional care --** Exercise due professional care in the performance of professional services;

   C. **Planning and supervision --** Adequately plan and supervise the performance of professional services;

   D. **Sufficient relevant data --** Obtain sufficient relevant data to afford a reasonable basis for conclusions or recommendations in relation to any professional services performed.

III. **Interpretations**

   A. An agreement to perform professional services implies that the member has the necessary competence to perform those services according to professional standards, applying his or her knowledge and skill with reasonable care and diligence, but the member does not assume a responsibility for infallibility of knowledge or judgment.

   B. Competence to complete an engagement includes:

      1. the technical qualifications of CPA and staff;
      2. the ability to supervise and evaluate work;
      3. the knowledge of the technical subject matter;
      4. the capability to exercise judgment in its application; and
      5. the ability to research the subject matter and consult with others where necessary.

Rule 203 - Accounting Principles and Interpretations

As a practical matter, if financial statements do not comply with GAAP, a jury will likely find at least negligence by the accountant.

After studying this lesson you should be able to :

1. *Know the circumstances under which GAAP need not be followed.*
2. *Understand the procedures for properly departing from GAAP.*

I. **Rule 203 --** As a practical matter, if financial statements do not comply with GAAP, a jury will likely find at least negligence by the accountant. However, if the financial statements do comply it is still possible (although, fortunately, somewhat unlikely) that a jury might find the accountant negligent on grounds that, in this particular case, more than compliance with GAAP and GAAS was necessary for a careful job.

II. **Principles --** Members cannot provide positive or negative assurance that financial statements are in conformity with GAAP if the statements contain departures from GAAP that have a material effect on statements taken as a whole, except when unusual circumstances would render financial statements following GAAP misleading. When such unusual circumstances exist, the CPA must disclose:

   A. the departure;

   B. the approximate effects of the departure; and

   C. the reasons why compliance with GAAP would mislead.

III. **Interpretations**

   A. **Interpretation 203-1 --** CPAs are allowed departure from SFAS (Statements of Financial Accounting Standards issued by FASB to establish GAAP) only when results of SFAS will be misleading, as where, for example:

      1. new legislation has been passed; or

      2. new forms of business transaction have evolved.

   B. **Interpretation 203-2 --** FASB and GASB Interpretations are covered by Rule 203.

   C. **Interpretation 203-3 --** A member shall not state affirmatively that financial statements or other financial data of an entity are presented in conformity with GAAP if such statements or data contain any departure from an accounting principle promulgated by a body designed by the AICPA to establish such principles that has a material effect on the statements or data taken as a whole.

Responsibilities to Clients

CPAs owe a number of responsibilities to their clients, many arising out of simple agency law. Two that often receive attention on the CPA exam relate to matters of confidentiality and contingency fees. Always remember that if a client consents to disclosure of confidential information, the CPA cannot be held liable for disclosure.

After studying this lesson you should be able to :

1. *Understand when it is proper for CPAs to charge contingent fees.*
2. *Understand a CPA's responsibility to maintain client confidences.*
3. *Comprehend the rules regarding the availability of an accountant-client testimonial privilege.*

I. Rule 301 -- "A member in public practice shall not disclose any confidential client information without the specific consent of the client."

A. Exceptions -- This prohibition does not:

1. relieve a member of his or her professional obligations;
2. affect the member's obligation to comply with validly issued subpoenas and summonses, and with applicable laws and government regulations;
3. prohibit review of a member's professional practice under AICPA or state CPA society rules; or
4. preclude a member from initiating or responding to a complaint filed by the professional ethics division or trial board of the AICPA or a duly constituted state disciplinary body.

II. Interpretation 301-3 -- A review of a member's professional practice (which is a confidentiality exception) is authorized to include a review in conjunction with a prospective purchase, sale, or merger of all or part of a member's practice so long as the member takes appropriate precautions (such as through written confidentiality agreements) so that the prospective purchaser does not disclose any information obtained in the course of the review, since such information is deemed to be confidential client information.

A. Confidential information -- Members reviewing a practice in connection with a prospective purchase or merger shall not use to their advantage nor disclose any member's confidential client information that comes to their attention.

B. Examples of confidentiality issues embodied in past ethics rulings

Question: May a member in public practice disclose the name of a client for whom the member or the member's firm performed professional services?

Answer:
Rule 301 allows a member to disclose the name of a client, whether publicly or privately owned, without the client's specific consent unless the disclosure of the client's name constitutes the release of confidential information. For example, if the member's practice is solely in the bankruptcy area, release of a client's name might also disclose that the client is having financial difficulties, which could be confidential information.

C. Chart illustrating some of the key rules -- When may client confidences be disclosed?

	May Disclose	May Not Disclose
Unless recognized exceptions apply		X
In order to comply with Rule 202 obligations to comply with professional standards	X	
In order to comply with Rule 203 obligations to follow GAAP	X	
In order to comply with an enforceable subpoena or summons	X	
Pursuant to AICPA review of professional practice	X	
Initiating complaint or responding to inquiry made by a recognized investigative or disciplinary body	X	
To potential purchaser of practice who has signed a confidentiality agreement	X	
Of working papers to CPA after that CPA has purchased practice		X
Any time client consents	X	

D. Accountant-client privilege

1. Traditionally, there has been no federal accountant-client privilege comparable to the attorney-client privilege.
2. Some states have adopted such a privilege statutorily, however, and it applies only in the courts of those states.
3. In the Internal Revenue Service Restructuring and Reform Act of 1998, Congress created a confidentiality privilege between clients and the CPAs who represent them before the IRS. The privilege essentially covers all tax advisers, including accountants. However, it applies only to noncriminal matters before federal courts in which a federal tax authority is involved. It does not apply:
    a. in criminal cases;
    b. in matters not before the IRS or federal courts in cases brought by or against the United States;
    c. to tax advice on state or local matters; or
    d. to written tax shelter advice.

III. Contingent Fees - Rule 302

A. General rule -- A member in public practice shall not:

1. Perform for a contingent fee any professional services for, or receive such a fee from, a client for whom the member or the member's firm performs:
    a. an audit or review of a financial statement; or
    b. a compilation of a financial statement when the member expects, or might reasonably expect, that a third party will use the financial statement and the report does not disclose a lack of independence; or
    c. an examination of prospective financial information.

2. Prepare an original or amended tax return or claim for a tax refund for a contingent fee for any client.

B. **Public authority exception --** A fee is not regarded as contingent if fixed by the courts or other public authorities.

C. **Variable fees --** A member's fees may vary depending on various factors, including the complexity of services rendered.

D. **Permissible situations --** Interpretation 302-1 provides the following examples of situations in the tax area where a contingent fee would be permitted:

1. Representing a client in an examination by a revenue agent of the client's federal or state income tax return.
2. Filing an amended federal or state income tax return claiming a tax refund based on a tax issue that is either the subject of a test case (involving a different taxpayer) or with respect to which the taxing authority is developing a position.
3. Filing an amended federal or state income tax return (or refund claim) claiming a tax refund in an amount greater than the threshold for review by the Joint Committee on Internal Revenue Taxation ($1 million) or state taxing authority.
4. Requesting a refund of either overpayments of interest or penalties charged to a client's account or deposits of taxes improperly accounted for by the federal or state taxing authority in circumstances where the taxing authority has established procedures for the substantive review of such refund requests.
5. Requesting, by means of "protest" or similar document, consideration by the state or local taxing authority of a reduction in the "assessed value" of property under an established taxing authority review process for hearing all taxpayer arguments relating to assessed value.
6. Representing a client in connection with obtaining a private letter ruling or influencing the drafting of a regulation or statute.

E. **Non-permissible situation --** Interpretation 302-1 gives the following example of a circumstance where a contingent fee would not be permitted:

1. Preparing an amended federal or state income tax return for a client claiming a refund of taxes because a deduction was inadvertently omitted from the return originally filed. There is no question of the propriety of the deduction; rather the claim is filed to correct an omission.

F. **Examples of contingent fee issues embodied in past ethics rulings**

Question:
Rules 302 and 503 prohibit, among other acts, the receipt of contingent fees for the performance of certain services and the receipt of a commission for the referral of products or services under certain circumstances. When is a contingent fee or commission deemed to be received?

Answer:
A contingent fee or a commission is deemed to be received when the performance of the related services is complete and the fee or the commission is determined. For example, if in one year a member sells a life insurance policy to a client and the member's commission payments are determined to be a fixed percentage of the future years' renewal premiums, the commission is deemed to be received in the year the policy is sold.

G. Summary chart -- Summarizing some of the basic rules regarding contingency fees:

	Permitted	Not Permitted
1. Performing audit or review		X
2. Perform compilation knowing third party may use it		X
3. Examine prospective financial information		X
4. Perform any service for client while also performing #1-3.		X
5. Prepare original or amended tax return or claim for refund		X
6. Represent client in an examination by revenue agent	X	
7. File amended tax return based on tax issue that is subject of a test case involving a different taxpayer	X	
8. Prepare an amended tax return for a client claiming a refund that is clearly due the client due to an inadvertent omission		X

IV. Ethics Rulings for Rules 301 and 302

A. A member may utilize outside computer services to process tax returns as long as there is no release of confidential information.

B. Members may reveal the names of clients without client consent unless such disclosure releases confidential information.

C. In divorce proceedings, a member who has prepared joint tax returns for the couple should consider both individuals to be clients for purposes of requests for confidential information relating to prior tax returns. Under such circumstances, the CPA should consider reviewing the legal implications of disclosure with an attorney.

D. A member's spouse may provide services to a member's attest client for a contingent fee and may refer products or services for a commission.

V. Contingent Fees -- The PCAOB has provided that a public company auditor cannot perform any tax services for the client on a contingent fee basis. It has also ruled that independence is impaired if:

A. The firm provides marketing, planning, or opinion services in favor of the tax treatment of a "confidential transaction," or if the transaction is based on an "aggressive" interpretation of tax law; and/or

B. The firm provides tax services to members of management who serve in financial-reporting oversight roles for a client (or to their immediate family).

Rule 501- Acts Discreditable

"A member shall not commit an act discreditable to the profession."

After studying this lesson you should be able to :

1. *Know the particular responsibilities of a CPA regarding retention of client documents.*
2. *Understand the general types of acts that discredit a CPA and may justify expulsion from the AICPA.*

I. **Interpretation 501-1 --** The AICPA has recently delineated new categories of records and provided new rules regarding when they may be retained in the face of a client request for their return.

   A. *Client-provided records* (such as accounting or other records given by the client to the member) should be returned to the client.

   B. *Client records prepared by the member* (such as tax returns or general ledgers) should usually be returned to the client, but may be withheld if the client has not paid the fee for preparation of the documents.

   C. *Supporting records* (information not reflected in the client's books and records that are otherwise unavailable to the client, such as adjusting, closing, or consolidating journal entries produced by the member) should also be returned, unless fees for preparing them are due.

   D. Members' *working papers* (such as audit programs, analytical review schedules, and statistical sampling results) belong to the member and need not be provided to the client, unless state law, federal law, or contractual obligations so require.

   E. **Additional rules --** Client requests should normally be honored within 45 days. Reasonable fees may be charged for the work. Members may keep copies of all records. If applicable state or federal laws require more than AICPA provisions, they, naturally, must be followed.

II. **Interpretation 501-2 -- Discrimination and harassment in employment practices**: Discrimination (on basis of race, color, religion, sex, age, or national origin) and harassment (sexual and other forms) are discreditable acts.

III. **Interpretation 501-3 -- Failure to follow standards and/or procedures or other requirements in governmental audits**: It is a discreditable act to fail to follow appropriate procedures for governmental audits, unless the member discloses in the report that required procedures were not followed and the reasons therefore.

IV. **Interpretation 501-4 -- Negligence in the preparation of financial statements or records**: Negligently making (or permitting, or directing another to make) false or misleading journal entries is a discreditable act.

V. **Interpretation 501-5 -- Failure to follow requirements of governmental bodies, commissions, or other regulatory agencies in performing attest or similar functions**: Failing to extend procedures beyond GAAS when governmental bodies, commissions, or other regulatory agencies such as the SEC, the FCC, and state insurance commissions so require is a discreditable act.

VI. **Interpretation 501-6 -- Solicitation or disclosure of CPA examination questions**: Soliciting or knowingly disclosing the May 1996 or later Uniform CPA Examination questions and/or answers without the written authorization of the AICPA is a discreditable act.

VII. **Interpretation 501-7 -- Failure to file tax return or pay tax liability**: CPAs who fail to pay their own or their firm's tax liabilities act discreditably.

VIII. Interpretation 501-8 -- Failure to follow requirements of governmental bodies, commissions, or other regulatory agencies on indemnification and limitation of liability provisions in connection with audit and other attest services: Government agencies, such as the SEC, often oppose indemnification provisions and other limitations of liability provisions in auditors' contracts. They wish auditors to be held liable for their errors. Therefore, if an engagement letter for an audit of a public company contained an indemnification provision wherein the audit client agreed to completely reimburse the auditor for any liability it might incur arising out of the audit, the SEC would not be pleased and the auditor would have committed a discreditable act. On the other hand, the SEC does not oppose contribution (where the client would partially reimburse the auditor if the auditor paid not only its share of damages to third-parties, but the client's share as well), so a contribution provision would be allowed.

Rule 502 - Advertising

"A member in public practice shall not seek to obtain clients by advertising or other forms of solicitation in a manner that is false, misleading, or deceptive. Solicitation by the use of coercion, over-reaching, or harassing conduct is prohibited."

After studying this lesson you should be able to :

1. *Understand the limitations upon a CPA's right to advertise.*

I. **Interpretation 502-2 --** CPAs may normally engage in accurate advertising ("commercial speech"). Examples of prohibited false, misleading, or deceptive advertisements include:

   A. creating false or unjustified expectations of favorable results;

   B. implying the ability to influence any court, tribunal, regulatory agency, or similar body or official;

   C. representing that specific professional services in current or future periods will be performed for a stated fee, estimated fee, or fee range when it was likely at the time of the representation that such fees would be substantially increased and the prospective client was not advised of that likelihood; and

   D. making any other representation that would be likely to cause a reasonable person to misunderstand or be deceived.

II. **Interpretation 502-5 --** Members who obtain engagements through the efforts of third parties have the responsibility to ascertain that all promotional efforts used by the third parties comply with the rules of conduct; otherwise, the member would be doing through others what the member is prohibited from doing personally.

Example:
In a 1993 case, the Supreme Court held that an accountant could not be prohibited from making "in-person" solicitations. Lawyers may be so prohibited by their bar associations, but accountants' clients are viewed as more sophisticated and less vulnerable to high-pressure tactics.

Rule 503 - Commissions and Referral Fees

Requirements regarding commissions and referral fees.

After studying this lesson you should be able to :

1. *Understand the Code of Professional Conduct's rules regarding the propriety of collecting commissions and referral fees.*

I. A member in public practice may not accept a commission for recommending a product or service to a client when that member or his firm also perform:

A. audits or reviews of financial statements;

B. compilations to be used by third parties; and/or

C. examinations of prospective financial information.

II. When a member does accept a permitted commission or referral fee, such must be disclosed to the client.

III. Making a profit by purchasing a product from a third party and reselling it to a client does not constitute receipt of a commission and is permissible, even if the profit is not disclosed.

Rule 505 - Name

Requirements for the form of and naming of an organization.

After studying this lesson you should be able to :

1. *Be able to name an accounting firm without running afoul of the AICPA Code of Professional Conduct.*

I. Requirements for the Form of and Naming of an Organization

A. **Member restrictions --** A member may practice public accounting only in a form of organization (proprietorship, partnership, professional corporation, limited liability company, limited liability partnership, etc.) permitted by state law whose characteristics conform to AICPA resolutions.

B. **Misleading firm name**

1. A member may practice public accounting only in a form of organization permitted by law or regulation whose characteristics conform to resolutions of Council.
2. A member shall not practice public accounting under a firm name that is misleading.
3. Names of one or more past owners may be included in the firm name of a successor organization.
4. A firm may not designate itself as "Members of the American Institute of Certified Public Accountants" unless all of its CPA owners are members of the Institute.

II. Interpretation 505-2

A. A member in public practice may own an interest in a separate business that performs nonaudit services for clients.

B. If the member, individually or collectively with his firm or members of the firm, controls the separate business, then that entity and all its owners and employees must comply with the Code of Professional Conduct.

1. Example: would have to follow rules on commissions and referral fees.

C. If the member and colleagues do not control the separate business, the Code would apply to the member and colleagues, but not to the separate business or its other owners and employees.

1. In this case, the entity could enter into a contingent fee arrangement with an attest client.

III. Interpretation 505-3

A. A majority of the financial interests in an attest firm must be owned by CPAs.

B. When alternative practice structures (APS) are involved, the bottom line is that the public interest will be considered protected if CPAs who own the attest firm remain financially responsible under applicable law or regulation.

Responsibilities in Consulting Services

At least up until the exam was closed, questions regarding consulting services tended to be fairly rudimentary. The AICPA essentially wanted CPAs to know (a) that there are separate standards (SSCS) that govern the consulting function, (b) what types of activities are considered "consulting" and therefore subject to the standards, and (c) that consulting, like other areas of service, requires professional competence, which in turn, requires that CPAs not attempt tasks for which they are not competent, that they adequately plan and supervise, and that they gather sufficient relevant data.

After studying this lesson you should be able to :

1. *Be able to list the types of consulting activities covered by the Statements on Standards in Consulting Services (SSCSs).*
2. *Understand the basic principles underlying the SSCSs.*

I. **SSCS --** Consulting services that CPAs provide to their clients are governed by Statements on Standards for Consulting Services (SSCS).

II. **Consulting Services under SSCS --** Consulting services governed by these standards can include one or more of the following types of consulting services:

A. **Consultations**

> **Definition:**
> *Consultations*: To provide counsel in a short time frame based mostly, if not entirely, on existing personal knowledge about a client.

1. **Examples --** Reviewing and commenting on a client's business plan, suggesting software for further client investigation.

B. **Advisory services**

> **Definition:**
> *Advisory services*: To develop findings, conclusions, and recommendations for client consideration and decision-making.

1. **Examples --** Operational review and improvement study, analysis of accounting system, strategic planning assistance, information system advice.

C. **Implementation services**

> **Definition:**
> *Implementation services*: To place an action plan into effect.

1. **Examples --** Installing and supporting a computer system, executing steps to improve productivity, assisting with mergers.

D. **Transaction services**

> **Definition:**
> *Transaction services*: To provide services related to a specific client transaction, generally with a third party.

1. **Examples --** Insolvency services, valuation services, information related to financing, analysis of a possible merger or acquisition, litigation services.

E. Staff and other support services

> **Definition:**
> *Staff and other support services*: To provide appropriate staff and possibly other support to perform tasks specified by the client.

1. **Examples --** Data processing, facilities management, computer programming, bankruptcy trusteeship, and controllership activities.

F. Product services

> **Definition:**
> *Product services*: To provide the client with a product and associated professional services in support of the installation, use, or maintenance of the product.

1. **Examples --** Sale, delivery, installation, and implementation of training programs, computer software, and systems development methodologies.

III. Standards for Consulting Services

A. The general standards of Rule 201 of the Code of Professional Conduct that apply to consulting:

1. Professional Competence;
2. Due Professional Care;
3. Planning and Supervision; and
4. Sufficient Relevant Data.

B. Duties to client

1. A member performing consulting services:

   a. must serve client interest while maintaining:

      i. integrity, and

      ii. objectivity,

      iii. **but not**: independence.

   b. must establish understanding with the client (orally or in writing) about the nature, scope, and limitations of the services to be performed.

   c. must communicate with client regarding:

      i. conflicts of interest,

      ii. significant reservations about engagement, and

      iii. significant engagement findings, etc.

   d. must use professional judgment in applying SSCS.

IV. Independence

A. Performing consulting services for an attest client does not necessarily create a conflict of interest, but all members performing both types of services should comply with all applicable rules regarding independence.

B. Consulting spin off

1. After the Enron scandal and passage of Sarbanes-Oxley, three of the Big Four firms spun off their consulting units.

Securities and Exchange Commission (SEC)

After studying this lesson you should be able to :

1. *Understand that the SEC's basic independence rules are quite similar to the AICPAs.*
2. *Know how to describe in detail those extra SOX requirements.*
3. *Realize that Sarbanes-Oxley (SOX) created many additional independence rules regarding the audit of public companies that go beyond or conflict with the AICPA Code's Rule 101.*

I. Basic Independence Rules

A. The SEC has its own set of independence rules for auditors, but they were developed with an eye toward the AICPA rules at a time around the turn of the century when both sets of standards migrated simultaneously from a firm-oriented approach to an audit team-oriented approach.

B. Although there are some differences in terminology, the ultimate results in independence situations are almost always the same under the SEC rules and the AICPA's Rule 101.

C. Therefore, this section will not address the basic SEC rules, but will instead address important changes that the Sarbanes-Oxley Act of 2002 (SOX) mandated for the audit of public companies. Where these rules clash with the AICPA Code, they overrule the AICPA for any audit of public companies.

II. Sarbanes-Oxley Audit Provisions

A. The AICPA Code allows audit firms to provide nonaudit services (NAS) to audit clients, with certain restrictions (e.g., don't make management decisions, don't audit your own work, don't take custody of client assets). However, after the debacles of the Enron era, Congress enacted SOX to simply prohibit the performance of many NAS where the purchaser of those services is a public company audit client of the provider. So if PriceCoopersHouse (PCH) is auditing ABC Co. (a public company), PCH may not provide it with these NAS:

1. Bookkeeping or other services related to the accounting records of financial statements;
2. Financial information systems design and implementation;
3. Appraisal or valuation services, fairness opinions, or contributions-in-kind reports;
4. Actuarial services;
5. Internal audit outsourcing services;
6. Management functions or human resources;
7. Broker or dealer, investment adviser, or investment banking services;
8. Legal services and expert services unrelated to the audit;
9. Any other service that the PCAOB determines is impermissible.

B. Keep in mind that:

1. Audit firms may provide these services to nonaudit clients and to private companies (even if they are audit clients) so long as AICPA restrictions are followed.
2. Other NAS may be performed for public company audit clients, such as tax services, but only if:

a. pre-approved by the client's audit committee; and

b. disclosed in the client's periodic reports filed with the SEC.

3. Although the SEC and PCAOB decided not to bar provision of tax services to public company audit clients, the PCAOB did issue rules that bar provision of two types of tax services:

a. those involving confidential or aggressive tax transactions (tax shelters); and

b. personal tax services provided to a person in a Financial Reporting Oversight Role (FROR) at the audit client, such as the CFO.

C. Audit partner rotation. Sarbanes-Oxley did not require that public companies rotate audit *firms*.

1. However, audit firms of public companies must rotate both the lead audit partner and the reviewing audit partner at least every five years. They must then serve at least a five-year "time out" before returning to the client. So, it's five-on, five-off, five-on, etc. for the lead audit partner and the reviewing partner.

2. Other partners playing a significant role in the audit are subject to a seven-year rotation requirement with a two-year time out period. For them it is seven-on, two-off, seven-on, etc.

D. Auditor compensation

1. Under SOX, a public company audit firm is not independent if any partner earns or receives compensation based on that partner selling NAS to an audit client.

E. Audit report to audit committee

1. All audit firms for public companies are now selected and compensated by the audit committee rather than by management;

2. Each audit firm must timely report to the client's audit committee.

a. all critical accounting policies and practices to be used;

b. all alternative treatments of financial information within GAAP that have been discussed with management officials, ramifications of the use of such alternative disclosures, and the treatment preferred by the accounting firm; and

c. other material written communications between the accounting firm and the issuer's management, such as any management letter or schedule of unadjusted differences.

F. Cooling-off periods

1. Sarbanes-Oxley provides that an audit firm may not perform an audit for a client if its CEO, controller, CFO, CAO, or any person serving in an equivalent FROR was employed by the audit firm and participated in the audit during a one-year period preceding the date of the initiation of the audit.

2. If the individual worked for the audit firm but did not participate in the client's audit, it is not considered a problem.

3. Because a complete audit cycle must pass between the time that an auditor leaves the accounting firm until he or she starts to work for the client in one of these FRORs, the total cooling-off period could end up being nearly two years.

Example:
ABC Co.'s audit cycle runs May 15 to May 15. Sandy is on PriceCooperHouse (PCH)'s audit team. She resigns on June 15, just one month into an audit cycle. She must wait until the end of that cycle, and then allow a complete cycle to pass before she can go to work for ABC in an FROR capacity. Had she quit on May 14, 2011, she could have started at ABC on May 15, 2012. But if she resigned on June 15, 2011, she would have had to wait until May 15, 2013.

III. Public Company Accounting Oversight Board (PCAOB)

A. **Creation --** Sarbanes-Oxley created the PCAOB to oversee auditors of public companies.

B. The SEC role in overseeing the PCAOB and PCAOB's powers are discussed in the next section.

Sarbanes-Oxley and the PCAOB

The audit profession has traditionally been self-regulating through self-promulgated professional standards, peer reviews, etc. The 2002 Sarbanes-Oxley Act (SOX) changed this situation and directly affects the accounting profession in several ways. In this section, we focus upon the PCAOB. Impact on audit independence rules were mentioned in the preceding section on the SEC.

After studying this lesson you should be able to :

1. *Be conversant with some key Sarbanes-Oxley criminal provisions.*

I. Public Company Accounting Oversight Board (PCAOB)

A. Sarbanes-Oxley created the PCAOB to have power over auditors similar to that exercised by FINRA over broker-dealers.

1. The SEC oversees the PCAOB.
2. The PCAOB's members (five, three of whom may not be accountants) are selected by the SEC.

B. The PCAOB does not regulate firms that service only private companies.

C. Principal functions of the PCAOB

1. Register public accounting firms.
2. Establish auditing, quality control, ethics, independence, and other standards relating to the preparation of audit reports, or adopt such standards as proposed by existing professional groups or new advisory committees.
3. Conduct inspections of registered public accounting firms.
4. Conduct investigations and disciplinary proceedings concerning registered public accounting firms and associated persons.
5. Enforce compliance with SOX, the PCAOB's rules, professional standards, and the securities laws relating to the preparation of audit reports by registered public accounting firms and associated persons.
6. Perform such other services as the PCAOB or the SEC determines are necessary or appropriate to promote high professional standards, protect investors or further the public interest.

D. Registration with the PCAOB

1. In order to prepare, issue, or participate in the preparation or issuance of any audit report with respect to any public company, a public accounting firm must register with the PCAOB.
2. Information to be disclosed will include:
    - **a.** the names of all audit clients in the past year;
    - **b.** annual fees for audit and nonaudit services received from each client;
    - **c.** a statement of firm quality control policies;
    - **d.** a list of all accountants associated with the firm who participated in the audits;
    - **e.** information relating to criminal, civil, or administrative proceedings pending against the firm or any associated person in connection with any audit report;

f. copies of any disclosure filed by a client with the SEC in the last calendar year disclosing a disagreement between the auditor and the firm; and

g. any other information that the PCAOB or the SEC believe should be disclosed.

3. Each firm must also submit an annual report and pay a registration fee each year.

E. New standards

1. The PCAOB has broad power to consult experts to establish auditing, quality control, ethics, and independence standards.

2. The auditing standards must include at least these three rules:

   a. For at least seven years, auditors must retain audit work papers and other information in sufficient detail to support the conclusions reached in the audit report.

   b. An accounting firm must provide a concurring or second partner to review and approve each audit report.

   c. In each audit report, the firm must describe the scope of the auditor's testing of the internal control structure and procedures of the issuer and present the findings of such testing, an evaluation of the internal control structure, a description of material weaknesses in such internal controls, and any material noncompliance found.

3. The PCAOB has initially adopted the AICPA's independence rules, as limited and affected by SOX requirements, but is slowly issuing its own rules, such as:

   a. Rule 3526, which requires public company auditors to communicate in writing to the client's audit committee *prior to accepting an initial engagement*, relationships that might reasonably be thought to bear on the auditor's independence and to affirm annually their compliance with PCAOB independence rules; and

   b. Rule 3523, which prohibits a registered audit firm from providing tax services to executives in financial reporting oversight roles for public company audit clients.

F. Inspections of registered public accounting firms

1. The PCAOB must conduct a "program of inspections" to assess registrant's compliance with the 1934 Securities Exchange Act, SEC and PCAOB rules, and professional standards.

   a. Annual inspections are conducted for firms doing more than 100 audits per year.

   b. Inspections are conducted every three years for firms doing fewer than 100 audits.

2. Firms can seek SEC review of PCAOB inspection reports if they disagree.

3. Inspection reports are posted on the PCAOB website.

G. Investigations and disciplinary proceedings

1. The PCAOB is authorized to investigate any act, practice, or omission by a registrant to any associated person that may violate any provision of the Act, the PCAOB's rules, securities rules, or professional standards.

2. The PCAOB can require testimony and production of audit work papers or other documents.

3. The PCAOB must notify the SEC and coordinate with its enforcement division.

4. The PCAOB may refer any investigation to the SEC, other federal regulators, or, at the SEC's direction, federal prosecutors.

5. In any disciplinary proceeding, the PCAOB must bring specific charges, give notification, allow for an opportunity to defend, and keep a record of the proceedings (which will generally be nonpublic).

6. **Board sanctions may include**

    a. temporary suspension or permanent revocation of registration of a firm (only for intentional or knowing conduct, or repeated negligent conduct);

    b. temporary or permanent suspension or bar of a person from working with a registered public accounting firm (only for intentional or knowing conduct, or repeated negligent conduct);

    c. temporary or permanent limitation on the activities, functions or operations of a firm or person (only for intentional or knowing conduct, or repeated negligent conduct);

    d. a civil penalty for each violation, up to $100,000 for an individual and $2 million for an entity, or, in the case of intentional or knowing conduct repeated negligent conduct, up to $750,000 for an individual and $15 million for an entity;

    e. censure;

    f. required professional education or training; and/or

    g. any other appropriate action.

7. The PCAOB may sanction a firm or its supervisors if they failed to reasonably supervise an "associated person" who violated rules or standards.

H. Foreign accounting firms are presumptively subject to the Act, but the SEC may create exemptions.

I. **SEC oversight**

1. The SEC must approve all PCAOB rules.

2. The SEC has broad power to oversee the board, limit its activities, and remove its members.

3. Creation of the PCAOB does not limit in any way the SEC's authority to enforce the securities laws, set standards for auditors, or take legal action.

4. A violation of the Act, any SEC rule based on the Act, or any PCAOB rule is deemed equivalent to a violation of the 1934 Securities Exchange Act.

J. **Standard setting body**

1. The SEC is authorized to adopt generally accepted accounting principles (GAAP) promulgated by any body that meets certain criteria.

2. Those criteria just happen to describe FASB.

II. Auditor Independence

A. An independent auditor cannot perform the following services for an audit client:

1. Bookkeeping or other services related to the accounting records of financial statements.

2. Financial information systems design and implementations.

3. Appraisal or valuation services, fairness opinions, or contributions-in-kind reports.

4. Actuarial services.

5. Internal audit outsourcing services.

6. Management functions or human resources.

7. Broker or dealer, investment adviser, or investment banking services.
8. Legal services and expert services unrelated to the audit.
9. Any other service that the PCAOB determines is impermissible.

B. Firms may provide these services to nonaudit clients and to private companies.

C. Other nonaudit services may be performed by public audit clients *if* pre-approved by the audit committee and disclosed in the client's periodic reports.

D. **Audit partner rotation**

1. There are no requirements for issuers to rotate audit *firms*.
2. Audit firms must rotate both the lead audit partner and the reviewing audit partner at least every 5 years.

E. **Auditor report to audit committee**

1. Audit firms are now selected and compensated by the audit committee rather than management.
2. Each firm must timely report to the client's audit committee:
   a. all critical accounting policies and practices to be used;
   b. all alternative treatments of financial information within GAAP that have been discussed with management officials, ramifications of the use of such alternative disclosures, and the treatment preferred by the accounting firm; and
   c. other material written communications between the accounting firm and the issuer's management, such as any management letter or schedule of unadjusted differences.

F. **Cooling-off periods**

1. An audit firm may not perform an audit for a client if its CEO, controller, CFO, CAO, or any person serving in an equivalent capacity was employed by the firm and participated in the audit during a one-year period preceding the date of the initiation of the audit.
2. If the individual worked for the audit firm but did not participate in the client's audit, there is no problem.

III. **Other Provisions**

A. **Financial statement requirements**

1. Financial statements for public companies must reflect "all material correcting adjustments."
2. Financial statements must contain all material off-balance sheet transactions.
3. Pro forma figures must be reconciled to GAAP.

B. It is now unlawful for officers, directors, or others to coerce, manipulate, or mislead company auditors.

C. The SEC received additional authority to discipline professionals, including auditors, under Rule 102(e).

D. **Ethical standards**

1. **Interim ethical standards --** As interim ethics standards, the PCAOB adopted Rule 3500T, which applies AICPA Rule of Professional Conduct 102, along with its interpretations and rulings.

2. **Definitions --** Rule 3501 adopts several clarifying definitions (e.g., "audit client," "confidential transaction," "contingent fee"), but the terms are generally consistent with AICPA practice and do not deserve separate treatment.

3. **Reckless contribution to violations --** Most recently, the PCAOB adopted Rule 3502, which imposes a responsibility to not knowingly *or recklessly* contribute to violations of SOX, PCAOB rules, or federal securities laws. The contribution could occur by an action or by an omission. So if someone associated with a registered accounting firm takes or omits to take an action knowing, or recklessly not knowing, that the act would directly and substantially contribute to such a violation, the person has violated Rule 3502.

Government Accountability Office (GAO)

After studying this lesson you should be able to :

1. *Understand the General Accountability Office's independence rules for firms that audit government agencies and entities that receive government funds.*

I. General Accountability Office's Government Auditing Standards - Ethical Principles

A. The GAO's guidelines apply to those who conduct audits of government entities (e.g., federal, state, and local) and entities that receive government awards (e.g., colleges, trade schools, charities, local governments) in compliance with generally accepted government auditing standards (GAGAS).

B. Independence and Ethical Principles. Those who audit pursuant to GAGAS are expected to audit:

1. Independently; and

2. In accordance with these key Ethical Principles:

a. The public interest;

b. Integrity;

c. Objectivity;

d. Proper use of government information, resources, and position; and

i. Government information, resources, or positions are to be used for official purposes and not for an auditor's personal gain.

e. Professional behavior.

i. Professional behavior includes compliance with laws and regulations, avoidance of conflicts of interest, sensitivity to appearances of impropriety and putting forth an honest effort to meet technical and professional standards.

C. Independence standards

1. Audit organizations (AOs) and individual auditors, whether government or public, must be free from three types of independence impairments (and must avoid the appearance of such impairments):

a. Personal impairments;

b. External impairments; and

c. Organizational impairments.

2. ***Personal impairments* include, for example**

a. Family relationships (e.g., a close family member is an officer of the audited entity);

b. Financial interests (e.g., the auditor has an indirect material interest in the audited entity or program);

c. Employment relationships (e.g., the auditor serves in a decision making function for the audited entity);

d. Prospective employment (e.g., the auditor seeks employment with the audited organization during the audit);

   e. Self-review (e.g., auditing source documents that the same auditor prepared);
   f. Bias (e.g., preconceived ideas toward individuals, groups or organizations that could bias the audit and political, ideological, or social convictions that could bias the audit).

3. To identify personal impairments and ensure compliance with independence requirements, AOs should:
   a. establish policies and procedures to identify, report, and resolve personal impairments;
   b. communicate the AO's policies and procedures to all auditors;
   c. establish internal policies and procedures to monitor compliance;
   d. establish a disciplinary mechanism;
   e. stress the importance of independence and the expectation that auditors will always act in the public interest; and
   f. maintain documentation of steps taken to identify potential personal independence impairments.
4. If a personal impairment is identified, the AO should promptly eliminate the problem by, for example, removing the auditor from the audit or requiring the auditor to eliminate the cause of the impairment.
5. ***External impairments*** include, among others:
   a. External interference or influence that could improperly limit or modify the scope of the audit (e.g., the audited entity exerting pressure to inappropriately reduce the extent of the work performed in order to reduce costs or fees).
   b. External interference with the selection or application of audit procedures or in the selection of transactions to be examined;
   c. Unreasonable restrictions on the time allowed to complete the audit;
   d. Externally-imposed restrictions on access to records, government officials, or other individuals needed to conduct the audit.
   e. External interference over the assignment, appointment, compensation, and promotion of audit personnel;
   f. Threat of replacing auditors over a disagreement with the contents of an audit report.
6. ***Organizational impairments*** result when:
   a. the audit function is organizationally located within the reporting line of the areas under the audit; or
   b. the auditor is assigned or takes on responsibilities that affect operations of the area under audit.
7. Audit organizations are presumed to be free from organizational impairments if the AO is:
   a. at a level of government other than the one to which the audited entity is assigned (e.g., federal auditors auditing a state government program); or
   b. in a different branch of government (e.g., an executive branch program is audited by legislative auditors).
8. Audit organizations are also resumed to be free from organizational impairment if their head is elected by voters, selected by a legislative body, or appointed by a statutorily-created governing body.

9. In addition, AOs may avoid organizational impairment of independence by a number of other means, including statutory protections that do such things as prevent the audited entity from abolishing the AO, prevent the audited entity from interfering with the audit report, and grant the AO sole authority over selection, retention, and dismissal of its staff.

10. **Internal audit**

    a. The GAO guidelines urge internal auditors to use the Institute of Internal Auditors (IIA) International Standards for the Professional Practice of Internal Auditing in conjunction with GAGAS.

    b. Under GAGAS, a government internal audit function is presumed free from organizational impairments to independence for reporting internally if the AO's head:

        i. is accountable to the head or deputy head of the government entity or to those charged with governance;

        ii. reports the audit results both to the head or deputy head of the government entity and to those charged with governance;

        iii. is located organizationally outside the staff or line-management function of the unit under audit;

        iv. has access to those charged with governance; and

        v. is sufficiently removed from political pressures to conduct audits and report findings, opinions, and conclusions objectively without fear of political reprisal.

D. **Nonaudit services**

1. Nonaudit services (NAS) receive substantial attention in the GAO guidelines.

2. Auditing organizations must use professional judgment in determining whether provision of certain types of NAS to audited government entities will impair or appear to impair independence.

3. Overarching Independence Principles for NAS. When assessing the impact of NAS performance on independence, AOs must keep in mind two overarching principles (that are consistent with AICPA principles in the area of NAS):

    a. AOs must not provide NAS that involve performing management functions or making management decisions; and

    b. AOs must not audit their own work or provide NAS in situations in which the NAS are significant or material to the subject matter of the audits.

4. NAS fall into three categories:

    a. Those that do not impair independence and therefore do not require compliance with *supplemental safeguards*.

    b. Those that do not impair independence so long as the AO complies with *supplemental safeguards*.

    c. Those that impair independence in such a way that compliance with *supplemental safeguards* will not overcome the impairment.

5. **NAS that do not impair independence --** These are often performed in response to a statutory requirement, at the discretion of the authority of the AO, or for a legislative oversight body. They usually involve auditors providing technical advice based on their technical knowledge, such as:

    a. Participating in activities such as commissions and task forces to advise entity management on issues based on the auditor's knowledge;

   b. Providing tools and methodologies, such as guidance and good business practices, that can be used by management; and

   c. Providing targeted and limited technical advice to assist management in such activities as answering technical questions and providing training.

6. *NAS that do not impair independence so long as the AO complies with supplemental safeguards.* Examples in this category include:

   a. Providing basic accounting assistance;

   b. Providing payroll services when payroll is not material to the audit objectives;

   c. Providing appraisal or valuation services that are limited to services, such as reviewing the work of the entity or valuing an entity's pension, provided management has taken responsibility for all significant assumptions and data;

   d. Providing advisory services on information technology;

   e. Providing basic human resources services, such as reviewing the applications of at least three individuals in order to provide input to management for its decision regarding whom to hire;

   f. Preparing routine tax filings based on information prepared by the audited entity.

7. The *supplemental safeguards* that can prevent independence from being impaired when the AO provides the NAS mentioned in the previous section require the AO to do all of the following:

   a. Document its consideration of the NAS, including its conclusions about the impact on independence;

   b. Establish in writing an understanding with the audited entity regarding the objectives, scope of work, deliverables, and management's responsibility for the substantive outcome of the work;

   c. Exclude personnel who provided NAS from planning, conducting, or reviewing the audit work; and

   d. Do not reduce the scope or extent of the audit work below the level that would be appropriate if the NAS were being provided by a third party.

8. **NAS that impair independence so that *supplemental safeguards* cannot eliminate the impairment**. These activities are generally consistent with AICPA prohibitions on performing management functions, auditing your own work, and taking control of client assets. The GAO theory is that, by their nature, certain types of NAS directly support the audited entities' operations and would impair the AO's ability to comply with the two overarching independence principles. Examples include:

   a. Maintaining or preparing the audited entity's basic accounting or financial records that the AO will audit;

   b. Posting transactions to the audited entity's financial records;

   c. Determining account balances or capitalization criteria;

   d. Designing, developing, installing, or operating the audited entity's accounting system or other information systems that are significant to the audit;

   e. Providing payroll services that are material to the subject matter of the audit or involve making management decisions;

   f. Providing appraisal or valuation services that go beyond the limited appraisal and evaluation services described above that do not generally impair independence;

g. (In the HR realm) Recommending a single individual for a specific position that is key to the entity or program being audited;

h. Developing an entity's performance measurement system when it is significant to the subject matter of the audit;

i. Developing an entity's policies, procedures, and internal controls;

j. Performing management's assessment of internal controls when they are significant to the audit;

k. Providing services that are intended to be used as management's primary basis for making decisions that are significant to the subject matter under audit;

l. Carrying out internal audit functions; and

m. Serving as voting members of an entity's management committee or board of directors, making policy decisions that affect future direction and operation of an entity's program, supervising entity employees, developing programmatic policy, authorizing an entity's transactions, or maintaining custody of an entity's assets.

E. Professional judgment

1. The GAO standards repeatedly emphasize the importance of auditors using professional judgment in planning and performing audits.
2. Professional judgment includes:
   a. exercising reasonable care;
   b. exercising professional skepticism;
   c. applying professional knowledge in good faith and with integrity;
   d. complying with independence standards;
   e. achieving technical competence;
   f. considering the risk level of each assignment; and
   g. documenting significant decisions.

F. Competence

1. The staff assigned to perform an audit must collectively possess adequate professional competence for the task required.
2. An AO's management is responsible for hiring, training, and supervising a competent workforce.
3. Competence is derived from a blending of education and expertise.

G. Continuing professional education (CPE).

1. Auditors performing under GAGAS should complete, every two years, at least 24 hours of CPE that directly relates to government auditing and an additional 56 hours (for a total of 80 hours) of CPE that enhances the auditor's professional proficiency to perform audit or attest engagements.

Department of Labor (DOL)

After studying this lesson you should be able to :

1. *Understand the Department of Labor's independence rules for the auditing of employee benefit plans regulated by ERISA.*

I. **Department of Labor --** Interpretive Bulletin Relating to Guidelines on Independence of Accountant Retained by Employee Benefit Plan.

  A. Employee Benefit Plans (plans) are broadly regulated by the Department of Labor's (DOL's) Employee Benefits Security Administration (EBSA) pursuant to the Employee Income Retirement Security Act (ERISA).

  B. Statutory law provides that an accountant retained by a plan to examine plan financial information and render an opinion on the financial statements and schedules required to be contained in a plan's annual report must be "independent."

  C. Unfortunately, despite having been strongly urged to simply adopt AICPA guidelines for independence, DOL's guidelines, contained in 29 C.F.R. 2509-75-9, date to the 1970s and are inconsistent with modern independence rules.

  D. The rules provide that an accountant will **not** be considered independent with respect to a plan, due to the following:

    1. **Financial ties --** Independence will be considered to be impaired if during the period of the engagement, at the date of the opinion, or during the period covered by the Financial Statements, "the accountant or his or her firm or a member thereof had, or was committed to acquire, any direct financial interest or any material indirect financial interest in such plan, or the plan sponsor ..."

      a. Because this provision covers any member of an accountant's firm, its coverage is much broader than that of current AICPA guidelines.

      b. The term "member" means all partners or shareholder employees in the firm and all professional employees participating in the audit or located in an office of the firm participating in a significant portion of the audit.

    2. **Employment ties --** During the same period, the same entities may not be connected to a plan or plan sponsor as a:

      a. Promoter;

      b. Underwriter;

      c. Investment advisor;

      d. Voting trustee;

      e. Director;

      f. Officer; or

      g. Employee of the plan or plan sponsor.

    3. However, employees of a plan or plan sponsor who have left to join the accounting firm may nonetheless be deemed independent if:

      a. They have completely disassociated themselves from the plan or plan sponsor; and

      b. Do not participate in auditing Financial Statements of the plan covering any period of his or her employment by the plan or plan sponsor.

4. However, independence may be considered impaired if an accountant or a member of an accounting firm maintains financial records for the plan. An accounting firm should not audit its own work.

E. According to the rule, an engagement to provide professional services, including actuarial services, to the plan sponsor does not ruin an accountant's independence so long as the accountant does not violate the rules on financial ties and employment mentioned above.

F. However, the firm should take care not to engage in a prohibited transaction pursuant to 29 U.S.C. 1106(a)(1)(C), which prohibits certain transactions between a plan and a "party in interest" to minimize conflicts of interest and thereby prevent fiduciaries from lining their own pockets with the plan's funds.

International Federation of Accountants (IFAC)

After studying this lesson you should be able to :

1. *Understand the basic operation of the International Federation of Accountants (IFAC).*
2. *Understand the background of the IFAC Ethics Code.*
3. *Comprehend the difference between a rules-based approach and IFAC's principles-based approach to constructing a code of ethics.*
4. *Comprehend the basic provisions of the IFAC Ethics Code.*
5. *Identify similarities and differences between the IFAC Code and the AICPA's Code of Professional Conduct.*

I. Introduction

A. **The International Ethics Standards Board for Accountants --** The International Ethics Standards Board for Accountants (IESBA), one of the International Federation of Accountants (IFAC)'s standard-setting agencies, promulgated the Code of Ethics for Professional Accountants (the IFAC Code).

B. **The IFAC Code --** This code has been adopted in more than 100 countries and accountants and accounting firms operating abroad or with clients operating abroad will increasingly need to be familiar with the IFAC Code's provisions. As cross-border tax and audit work increase, the importance of the IFAC Code will grow.

C. **Standards application --** As a member of IFAC, the AICPA has pledged that it will use its best efforts to apply standards that are not lower than those of the IFAC Code. Just as there is conscious convergence in international auditing standards (e.g., the IFRS and U.S. GAAP), IFAC and the AICPA have begun to merge ethical frameworks. Therefore, the IFAC Code is broadly consistent with the AICPA Code and would generally produce similar results in similar cases. Importantly, the AICPA's Professional Ethics Executive Committee (PEEC) participates in IESBA's activities to ensure that the AICPA's views are adequately considered. If a particular country has a statute or regulation that prevents an accountant there from complying with a portion of the IFAC Code, he or she should nonetheless comply with the other applicable portions.

D. **The IFAC Code vs. the AICPA's Code of Professional Conduct --** Two major differences between the IFAC Code and the AICPA's Code of Professional Conduct stand out.

1. First, whereas the AICPA Code has many specific rules that are supplemented by a *conceptual framework* that encourages accountants to resolve gray areas by identifying *threats to compliance* with professional duties, evaluating those threats, and applying *safeguards* in order to reduce the threats so that compliance with fundamental principles is not compromised, the IFAC Code begins with that framework in its Part A. It then gives specific guidance for applying the conceptual framework in Parts B and C. The AICPA Code might be termed a rules-based approach while the IFAC Code is a principles-based approach. This is somewhat a mere difference in emphasis, especially after a recent revision to the IFAC Code changed a large number of "shoulds" to "shalls."
2. Second, IFAC's Code covers not only accountants in public practice (termed *Professional Accountants in Public Practice* [PAPPs]) but also accountants who work for businesses, governments, and other employing agencies (termed *Professional Accountants in Business* [PABs]). Thus, Part B of the IFAC Code applies Part A's guidelines to PAPPs in ways that strongly resemble much of the AICPA Code. Part C of the IFAC Code applies Part A's principles to PABs, whereas

the AICPA has generally left it to the Institute of Internal Auditors (IAA) and Institute of Management Accountants (IMA) to issue codes of conduct for that type of activity.

E. Two less significant differences are also worth mentioning at the beginning.

1. First, consistent with the international nature of its application, the IFAC Code specifically mentions *network firms* to indicate that accounting firms under common control or management that cross borders will presumptively have to be broadly considered in applying these rules. This concept was adopted in 2010 by PEEC (ET section 101.19).
2. Second, IFAC has two sections on what it terms "assurance" engagements. One section focuses on independence and other rules for financial statement audit clients. The second focuses on other sorts of assurance engagements. For example, consider a situation where an accounting firm is asked to provide assurance services regarding a consulting firm's report on the sustainability practices of a company. This is an assurance engagement even though a financial statement would not be involved (although such a company could, of course, also be a financial statement assurance engagement client). Independence standards are generally more demanding if audits of financial statements are involved.

F. The IFAC Code is also more demanding when the financial statement audit client is a *listed firm* (a public company) than when it is not.

II. Part A

A. Fundamental principles -- The IFAC Code is based on certain *fundamental principles* that accountants should not compromise. These are:

1. Integrity;
2. Objectivity;
3. Professional competence and due care;
4. Confidentiality; and
5. Professional behavior.

B. The first four of these should be familiar, as they are heavily emphasized in the AICPA's Code of Professional Conduct. *Professional behavior* means following laws and regulations and avoiding acts that would discredit the profession.

C. Types of threats -- The IFAC Code's conceptual framework involves identifying threats to these five fundamental principles. If a threat is not *clearly insignificant* (meaning both trivial and inconsequential), then various *safeguards* must be considered. There are five primary types of threats:

1. **Self-interest threats --** The threat that a financial or other interest will inappropriately influence the professional accountant's judgment or behavior. An auditor should obviously not own stock in an audit client.
2. **Self-review threats --** The threat that a professional accountant will not appropriately evaluate the results of a previous judgment made or service performed by the professional accountant, or by another individual within the professional accountant's firm or employing organization, on which the accountant will rely when forming a judgment as part of providing a current service. An auditor should not audit its own work.
3. **Advocacy threats --** The threat that a professional accountant will promote a client's or employer's position to the point that the professional accountant's objectivity is compromised.

4. **Familiarity threats --** The threat that due to a long or close relationship with a client or employer, a professional accountant will be too sympathetic to their interests or too accepting of their work.
5. **Intimidation threats --** The threat that a professional accountant will be deterred from acting objectively because of actual or perceived pressures, including attempts to exercise undue influence over the professional accountant.

D. If such threats are identified and evaluated as sufficiently significant that they might threaten compliance with fundamental principles, the professional accountant shall consider whether they may be reduced to an acceptable level by application of two types of safeguards:

1. Safeguards created by the profession, legislation or regulation; and
2. Safeguards in the work environment.

E. *Safeguards created by the profession, legislation or regulation* include, but are not restricted to:

1. education, training, and experience requirements for entry into the profession;
2. continuing professional development requirements;
3. corporate governance regulations;
4. professional standards;
5. professional or regulatory monitoring and disciplinary procedures;
6. external review by a legally empowered third part of the reports, returns, communications, or information produced by a professional accountant.

F. **Types of safeguards --** There are two general types of *safeguards in the work environment*: firm-wide safeguards and engagement-specific safeguards.

1. Examples of **firm-wide work environment safeguards** include:
   a. Leadership of the firm that stresses the importance of compliance with the fundamental principles.
   b. Leadership of the firm that establishes the expectation that members of an assurance team will act in the public interest.
   c. Policies and procedures to implement and monitor quality control of engagements.
   d. Using different partners and engagement teams with separate reporting lines for the provision of non-assurance services to an assurance client.
   e. A disciplinary mechanism to promote compliance with policies and procedures.
2. Examples of **engagement-specific work environment safeguards** include:
   a. Having a professional accountant who was not involved with the non-assurance service review the non-assurance work performed or otherwise advise as necessary.
   b. Having a professional who was not a member of the assurance team review the assurance work performed or advise as otherwise necessary.
   c. Consulting an independent third party, such as a committee of independent directors, a professional regulatory body, or another professional accountant.
   d. Discussing ethical issues with those charged with governance of the client.
   e. Involving another firm to perform or re-perform part of the engagement.

III. Part B

A. Part B applies the basic IFAC Code concepts to Professional Accountants in Public Practice (PAPPs), that is, accountants working for accounting firms. It begins by addressing basic concepts such as conflicts of interest, contingency fees, advertising, gifts, custody of client assets, and the like. Then it addresses independence rules, addressing largely the same financial, employment, family, and consulting issues as the AICPA Code.

B. In all these settings, the results tend to be pretty similar to results from the AICPA Code, in part because both have the "threat and safeguard" conceptual framework as background. As with the AICPA Code, for example, assurance team members should not own a material financial interest in an audit client, should not borrow money from an assurance client under unusually favorable terms, should not provide assurance services to a firm whose CEO is an immediate family member of a team member, etc.

C. **The IFCA Code vs. the AICPA Code - Similarities --** To illustrate the similarities, consider several examples.

1. Under the AICPA Code, five primary categories of actors must be independent (a) audit team members; (b) those in a position to influence audit team members, (c) other partners in the office of the attest engagement team partner and other partners and managers providing at least 10 hours of non-audit services, and (e) the firm itself. Additionally, any entity composed of or controlled by the first five actors must be independent.

2. The IFAC Code is similar, but different. It presumptively covers all the firms in a *network*, which is defined as a larger structure that is (a) aimed at co-operation and (b) aimed at profit or cost sharing or shares common ownership, control or management, common quality control policies and procedures, common business strategy, the use of a common brand name, *or* a significant part of professional resources. In other words, if PwC's Chicago office has an assurance engagement with ABC Co., its Rome and Hong Kong offices may have to meet independence standards.

    a. The "audit team" is broadly defined to include all members of the engagement team (including experts contracted with) and "(a)ll others within the firm who can directly influence the outcome of the assurance engagement." This includes those who recommend compensation for or supervise the assurance engagement partner (including all successive senior levels to the top of the firm), those who provide consultation regarding technical or industry specific issues, and those who provide quality control for the assurance engagement. The assurance team also includes all those within a network firm who can directly influence the outcome of the engagement.

    b. Although the IFAC Code does not include other partners or managers who provide 10 hours of non-assurance services (NAS) to an audit client in the definition of the "audit team," it does elsewhere prohibit partners and managerial employees who provide NAS to the audit client, except those whose involvement is "minimal," and their immediate family members (IFMs), from holding a direct or material indirect financial interest in the audit client.

3. The IFAC Code independence provisions are concerned with the same general areas as the AICPA Code and SOX - financial ties, employment relationships, family connections, and consulting (NAS). Many of the IFAC rules are quite similar to the AICPA Code. The IFAC Code focuses on direct and material indirect financial relationships, as does the AICPA Code. It is concerned both with employees from the accounting firm who go to the client and those who go the other direction. It has guidelines for complications caused by immediate family members (IFMs) and close family members (CFMs - comparable to the AICPA's "close relatives"). It provides guidance regarding provision of NAS such as tax services (no problem), internal audit, IT systems services, litigation support, human resources, etc. that are provided to assurance clients.

D. Although the IFAC Code is largely principles-based, it is not without definitive rules. For example, the self-interest threat to objectivity would be so great that no safeguards could be taken that would allow a member of an assurance team to own a material financial interest in an assurance client or to accept a significant gift from such a client.

1. To illustrate similarities and differences, note that the AICPA Code provides that an IFM of an audit team member cannot hold a direct or material indirect interest in an audit client. The IFAC Code agrees. The AICPA further provides that a CR of an audit team member cannot hold a financial interest in an audit client that the team member knows or has reason to know is material to the CR. The IFAC Code has a slightly different approach. It defines a CFM the same as a CR, but does not have a black-and-white rule. It calls for application of the contextual framework. First, the self-interest threat must be evaluated. Its significance will depend upon such factors as (a) the nature of the relationship between the team member and the CFM and (b) the materiality of the financial interest to the CFM. Then, safeguards shall be applied to reduce the threat to an acceptable level, such as (a) the CFM disposing as soon as practicable of all or most of the interest, (b) having a professional accountant review the work of the team member, or (c) removing the individual from the team.
2. The provisions regarding NAS services are neither as stringent as SOX provisions where public company audit clients are concerned, nor as objective as AICPA provisions. Nonetheless, they have many of the same key features as the AICPA Code - largely forbidding the PAPP from making management decisions, ensuring that the client takes ownership of the process, discouraging the PAPP from taking custody of client assets, ensuring that NAS services are provided by employees who are not on the assurance team, encouraging full disclosure, etc.
3. As an illustration of the IFAC approach to NAS, consider provision of IT systems services to a financial statement audit client. The Code notes that design and implementation of financial information technology systems that will be used to generate information forming part of the financial statements that the assurance firm will audit creates a self-review threat, which is likely to be too significant to allow unless appropriate safeguards ensure that:
    a. The audit client acknowledges its responsibility for establishing and monitoring a system of internal controls;
    b. The audit client designates a competent employee, preferably within senior management, with the responsibility to make all management decisions with respect to the design and implementation of the hardware and software system;
    c. The audit client makes all management decisions with respect to the design and implementation process;
    d. The audit client evaluates the adequacy and results of the design and implementation of the system; and
    e. The audit client is responsible for the operation of the system (hardware or software) and the data used or generated by the system.
4. The Code also suggests that the firm *consider* as a safeguard ensuring that the IT work be performed only by employees not involved in the audit engagement. If the IT engagement is design *or* implementation of financial information technology systems, the self-review threat is not as great as with a design *and* implementation engagement. Still, the firm must evaluate the threat and consider safeguards that might be appropriate.
5. Finally, the IFAC Code indicates that provisions of services in connection with the assessment, design, and implementation of *internal accounting controls* and *risk management controls* are not considered threats to independence so long as the firm or network firm personnel do not perform management functions.

IV. Part C

A. Part C's provisions for Professional Accountants in Business (PABs) are common sense provisions. They recognize that PABs have a responsibility to further the legitimate aims of their employing organizations (EOs), but emphasize a counterbalancing responsibility to comply with the fundamental principles (integrity, objectivity, etc.). These provisions address topics such as potential conflicts of interest, the duty to accurately prepare and report information, acting with sufficient expertise, coping with conflicts created by financial interests, and pressures to accept or offer improper inducements.

B. Without going through all these provisions, consider an example that will illustrate the IFAC Code's suggested approach. Assume that a PAB is being pressured to manage earnings by a CFO interested in hitting the EO's projected numbers no matter what.

1. The IFAC Code instructs the PAB to evaluate the significance of the threats arising from pressure to violate the law. Clearly, the PAB may face an intimidation threat as the CFO may expressly or impliedly threaten to demote or even to fire the PAB should he or she not comply with the improper request. Yet the PAB has an obligation to maintain information in a manner that clearly describes the true nature of the business transaction, assets or liabilities; classifies and records information in a timely and proper manner; and represents the facts accurately and completely in all material respects.
2. The IFAC Code requires the PAB to consider safeguards to reduce the threat such as:
    - **a.** Obtaining advice where appropriate from within the EO, an independent professional advisor, or a relevant professional body;
    - **b.** Utilizing a formal dispute resolution process within the EO; and
    - **c.** Seeking legal advice.
3. If these and other steps do not sufficiently reduce the threat of noncompliance to fundamental principles, the PAB may consider resigning from the EO.

Supplemental Outlines of Professional Standards

SAS

AU110 (SAS 1) - Responsibilities of Independent Auditor

SAS 1 - as amended - Issued November, 1972.

I. Distinction between responsibilities of auditor and management

A. The financial statements are the representations of management.

1. "Management is responsible for adopting sound accounting policies and for establishing and maintaining internal control that will, among other things, initiate, record, process, and report transactions (as well as events and conditions) consistent with management's assertions embodied in the financial statements."

2. The transactions reflected in the financial statements are within the direct knowledge and control of management.

B. The auditor's responsibility is to "plan and perform the audit to obtain reasonable assurance about whether the financial statements are free of material misstatement, whether caused by error or fraud."

1. Knowledge of transactions and financial statements is limited to information obtained in the audit - the auditor's responsibility for the financial statements is confined to the opinion on them.

2. May make suggestions as to the form of financial statements or even draft them based on management's records and accounts.

II. Professional qualifications required -- "... those of a person with the education and experience to practice as such." (Judgment must be the informed judgment of a qualified professional person.) (Related to the due care standard.)

III. Responsibility to the profession -- "The independent auditor also has a responsibility to his (or her) profession, the responsibility to comply with the standards accepted by his (or her) fellow practitioners." (The Rules of Conduct, part of the AICPA's Code of Professional Conduct, provide a basis for the enforcement of the profession's standards.)

AU120 (SAS 102) - Defining Professional Requirements

Statement on Auditing Standards No. 102; and Statement on Standards for ***Attestation Engagements No.13.***

I. **Defining Professional Requirements --** "Defining Professional Requirements in Statements on Auditing Standards" and "Defining Professional Requirements in Statements on Standards for Attestation Engagements" - Issued: December 2005 (Effective at Issuance)

II. **The degree of responsibility --** associated with the terms (1) "must," (2) "is required," and (3) "should" was not previously defined in the SASs and SSAEs -- these 2 standards now define those levels of responsibilities for existing and future SASs and SSAEs.

  A. Auditing Standards Board pronouncements apply to "nonissuers" -- a nonissuer refers to any entity not subject to the Sarbanes-Oxley Act or rules of the SEC.

  B. The terms discussed in SAS 102 and SSAE 13 are consistent with how the PCAOB uses these terms.

III. **SAS 102 and SSAE 13 define 2 categories of professional requirements**

  A. "Unconditional requirements" -- the auditor (practitioner) is required to comply with an unconditional requirement when the circumstances exist to which the unconditional requirement applies. (An unconditional requirement is indicated by the words "must" or "is required.") -- No exceptions!

  B. "Presumptively mandatory requirements"

    1. The auditor (practitioner) is also required to comply with a "presumptively mandatory requirement" when circumstances exist to which the presumptively mandatory requirement applies. This allows for the possibility of exception, however!

    2. In rare circumstances, may depart from a presumptively mandatory requirement -- the auditor (practitioner) must document the justification for the departure and how alternative procedures performed in the circumstances were sufficient to achieve the objectives of the presumptively mandatory requirement. (A presumptively mandatory requirement is indicated by the word "should.")

IV. **SAS 102 and SSAE 13 also discuss "explanatory material" --** defined as the text within a SAS or SSAE (excluding any related appendices or interpretations) that may provide further explanation on the professional requirements or describe other procedures or actions possibly applicable to the auditor (practitioner).

  A. Such explanatory material is intended to be descriptive and does not impose a professional requirement.

  B. Explanatory material is identified by the terms "may," "might," or "could."

AU150 (SAS 95, as Amended) - GAAS

Issued December, 2001.

I. **Distinction between auditing standards and auditing procedures**

   A. **Standards** -- deal with measures of audit quality and the objectives to be achieved.

   B. **Procedures** -- the acts that the auditor performs to comply with auditing standards.

II. **GAAS is comprised of 10 standards**

   A. There are 3 "General Standards"

      1. The auditor must have adequate technical training and proficiency to perform the audit.

      2. The auditor must maintain independence in mental attitude in all matters relating to the audit.

      3. The auditor must exercise due professional care in the performance of the audit and the preparation of the report.

   B. There are 3 "Standards of Field Work"

      1. The auditor must adequately plan the work and must properly supervise any assistants.

      2. The auditor must obtain a sufficient understanding of the entity and its environment, including its internal control, to assess the risk of material misstatement of the financial statements whether due to fraud or error, and to design the nature, timing, and extent of further audit procedures.

      3. The auditor must obtain sufficient appropriate audit evidence by performing audit procedures to afford a reasonable basis for an opinion regarding the financial statements under audit.

   C. There are 4 "Standards of Reporting"

      1. The auditor must state in the auditor's report whether the financial statements are presented in accordance with generally accepted accounting principles (GAAP).

      2. The auditor must identify in the auditor's report those circumstances in which such principles have not been consistently observed in the current period in relation to the preceding period.

      3. When the auditor determines that informative disclosures are not reasonably adequate, the auditor must so state in the auditor's report.

      4. The auditor must either express an opinion regarding the financial statements, taken as a whole, or state that an opinion cannot be expressed, in the auditor's report. When the auditor cannot express an overall opinion, the auditor should state the reasons therefore in the auditor's report. In all cases where an auditor's name is associated with financial statements, the auditor should clearly indicate the character of the auditor's work, if any, and the degree of responsibility the auditor is taking, in the auditor's report.

III. **Guidance applicable to GAAS**

   A. **Statements on Auditing Standards (SASs)** -- these serve as interpretations of GAAS and must be followed by auditors. (Rule 202 of the AICPA Code of Professional Conduct, Compliance with Standards, requires that auditors adhere to standards promulgated by the Auditing Standards Board.)

      1. The auditor is expected to have sufficient knowledge of the SASs to identify those applicable to the audit.

      2. The auditor should be prepared to justify any departures from the SASs.

      3. "Materiality and audit risk also underlie the application of the 10 standards [GAAS] and the SASs, particularly those related to field work and reporting."

   B. **"Interpretive publications"** -- consist of auditing Interpretations of the SASs, auditing guidance included in AICPA Audit & Accounting Guides, and AICPA auditing Statements of Position

1. Interpretive publications are not auditing standards
2. These are issued under the authority of the ASB after all ASB members have had an opportunity to comment of the interpretive publication.
3. Auditors should be aware of (and consider) interpretive publications applicable to their audits -- when auditors do not apply such auditing guidance, they should be prepared to explain how they complied with the SAS provisions related to such interpretive publications.

C. **"Other auditing publications" --** include articles in the Journal of Accountancy and the AICPA's CPA Letter (and other professional publications), continuing professional education programs, textbooks, etc.

1. Other auditing publications have no authoritative status -- they may help the auditor understand and apply the SASs, however.
2. To assess the appropriateness of the other auditing publications -- consider the degree to which the publication is recognized as helpful in applying the SASs and the degree to which the auditor is recognized as an authority on auditing matters. (Other auditing publications reviewed by the AICPA Audit and Attest Standards staff are presumed to be appropriate.)

AU161 (SAS 25) - GAAS and Quality Control

I. **Compliance with GAAS --** required by Rule 202, "Compliance with Standards," of the Rules of Conduct of the Code of Professional Conduct.

II. **Different focus of GAAS and quality control standards --** GAAS and quality control standards are related. (Quality controls that are adopted by a firm may affect the conduct of individual audit engagements and the conduct of a firm's whole audit practice.)

   A. **GAAS --** relate to the conduct of individual audit engagements.

   B. **Quality control standards --** relate to the conduct of a firm's **practice as a whole.**

      1. System of quality control - "a process to provide the firm with reasonable assurance that its personnel comply with applicable professional standards and the firm's standards of quality."

      2. Firm's responsibility - the firm must adopt a system of quality control in conducting an audit practice to provide it with reasonable assurance that its personnel comply with GAAS.

      3. Statements on Quality Control Standards are issued by the AICPA's Auditing Standards Board. (Note: SQCS do not address the quality control issues associated with the Sarbanes-Oxley Act of 2002 or the specific quality control requirements of the PCAOB.)

AU201 (SAS 1) - Nature of General Standards

I. **General Standards are <u>personal in nature</u>**

  A. Concerned with the auditor's qualifications.

  B. Concerned with the quality of the auditor's work.

II. **General Standards Also Apply to the Areas of Field Work and Reporting.**

AU210 (SAS 1) - Training and Proficiency

SAS #1, as amended - November, 1972.

I. Deals with the First General Standard of GAAS: -- "The auditor must have adequate technical training and proficiency to perform the audit."

II. Technical Training (education)

- **A.** Training requires proficiency in the technical subject matters of accounting and auditing beginning with formal education and extending into subsequent experience - the auditor's formal education and professional experience complement one another.
- **B.** Training must be adequate in technical scope and should include a commensurate measure of general education.
- **C.** The training of a professional includes a continual awareness of developments taking place in business and in the profession.

III. Experience

- **A.** Reflects the assignments given.
- **B.** Supervision and review (the degree varies with the circumstances) - "The auditor charged with final responsibility for the engagement must exercise a seasoned judgment in the varying degrees of his (or her) supervision and review of the work done and judgment exercised by his (or her) subordinates, who in turn must meet the responsibility attaching to the varying gradations and functions of their work."

AU220 (SAS 1) - Independence

SAS 1, as amended - Issued November, 1972.

I. Relates to the second General Standard of GAAS regarding independence in mental attitude (also known as "independence in fact") -- "The auditor must maintain independence in mental attitude in all matters relating to the assignment."

- **A.** Requires "judicial impartiality" (not the attitude of a prosecutor) - this recognizes an obligation for fairness to all who may rely upon the auditor's report.
- **B.** Emphasizes independence in fact and in appearance - both are essential to public confidence.
    - **1.** To be independent - the auditor must be intellectually honest.
    - **2.** To be recognized as independent - the auditor must be free from any obligation to (or conflict of interest in) the entity, its management, or the owners.

II. Independence is an important component of AICPA's Code of Professional Conduct

- **A.** The Code establishes precepts to guard against the "presumption" of loss of independence - since "the possession of intrinsic independence is a matter of personal quality rather than of rules that formulate certain objective tests."
- **B.** These precepts "have the force of professional law for the independent auditor."
- **C.** The SEC has adopted independence rules that differ in some respects from those of the AICPA - the independent auditor should administer the audit practice in compliance with these precepts and rules.

AU230 (SAS 1) - Due Care

Issued November, 1972 and as Amended by SAS No. 104 (Issued February, 2006).

I. **Relates to the third General Standard regarding due professional care: --** "The auditor must exercise due professional care in the performance of the audit and the preparation of the report."

  A. The auditor with final responsibility is responsible for the assignment of tasks to (and supervision of) assistants - assignments and supervision should be commensurate with their level of knowledge, skill, and ability.

  B. Due professional care imposes a responsibility upon each professional within the auditor's organization to observe the standards of fieldwork and reporting.

II. **Refers to *Cooley On Torts* that comments on due care in legal practice**

  A. Requires the "degree of skill commonly possessed by others in the same employment."

  B. Requires that the skills be applied with "reasonable care and diligence."

  C. Note that the auditor "... no man, whether skilled or unskilled, undertakes that the task he assumes shall be performed successfully, and without fault or error; he undertakes for good faith and integrity, but not for infallibility..."

  D. Implications to auditors - an auditor should possess the "degree of skill commonly possessed" by other auditors and should exercise it with "reasonable care and diligence."

III. **Professional skepticism - should be exercised throughout the audit process**

  A. Definition - "an attitude that includes a questioning mind and a critical assessment of audit evidence."

  B. "The auditor neither assumes that management is dishonest nor assumes unquestioned honesty. In exercising professional skepticism, the auditor should not be satisfied with less than persuasive evidence because of a belief that management is honest."

IV. **Reasonable assurance is obtained --** - absolute assurance is not attainable because of the nature of audit evidence and the characteristics of fraud. (Accordingly, an audit in compliance with GAAS may not detect a material misstatement.)

  A. Audit evidence is usually "persuasive" rather than "compelling" (or convincing) - since evidence is normally obtained on a test basis; since judgment is required in evaluating the audit evidence; and since accounting presentations involve significant accounting estimates for which the measurement is inherently uncertain.

  B. Fraud may prevent a properly planned/properly performed audit from detecting a material misstatement - the characteristics of fraud include:

    1. Concealment through collusion among management, employees, or third parties.

    2. Withheld or falsified documentation - an audit under GAAS rarely involves "authentication of documentation." (Nor are auditors expected to be trained or expert in such authentication.)

    3. The ability of management to override (or to instruct others to override) internal controls that otherwise appear to be effective.

  C. Implication of "reasonable assurance" to the auditor's report - "the auditor is not an insurer and his or her report does not constitute a guarantee."

  D. SAS No. 104 contributed additional language to one paragraph of this section to expand the definition of the term "reasonable assurance."

> "While exercising due professional care, the auditor must plan and perform the audit to obtain sufficient appropriate audit evidence so that audit risk will be limited to a low level that is, in his or her professional judgment, appropriate for expressing an opinion on the financial statements. The high, but not absolute, level of assurance that is intended to be

obtained by the auditor is expressed in the auditor's report as obtaining reasonable assurance about whether the financial statements are free of material misstatement (whether caused by error or fraud)."

AU311 (SAS 108) - Planning and Supervision

I. Introductory comments

A. Audit planning involves developing the overall audit strategy for the expected conduct, organization, and staffing of the audit -- the planning activities may vary with the size and complexity of the entity, with the auditor's experience with the entity, and with the understanding of the entity and its environment, including internal control.

B. Basic responsibility -- must plan the audit so that it is responsive to the assessment of the risk of material misstatement based on the auditor's understanding of the entity and its environment, including internal control.

1. Planning and supervision continue throughout the audit -- it is an "iterative process" that begins with engagement acceptance and continues throughout the audit.
2. The auditor may obtain disconfirming evidence that might cause a revision of the overall audit strategy.

II. Planning

A. Appointment of the independent auditor.

1. Early appointment is preferable and enables the auditor to plan the audit prior to the balance-sheet date.
2. May still accept an engagement after the fiscal-year end -- should discuss any circumstances with the client that might interfere with an adequate audit and the expression of an unqualified opinion.

B. Establishing an understanding with the client:

1. The auditor should establish an understanding with the client regarding the services to be performed for each engagement -- should document the understanding through a written communication with the client.
2. The understanding should include the objectives of the engagement, management's responsibilities, and the auditor's responsibilities, and the limitations of the engagement -- these matters should be communicated in the form of an "engagement letter."
3. The following matters generally should be addressed:
    a. The objective of the audit is the expression of an opinion on the financial statements;
    b. Management is responsible for the entity's financial statements and the selection/application of accounting principles;
    c. Management is responsible for establishing and maintaining effective internal control over financial reporting;
    d. Management is responsible for designing and implementing programs and controls to prevent and detect fraud;
    e. Management is responsible for compliance with applicable laws and regulations affecting the entity;
    f. Management is responsible for making all financial record available to the auditor;
    g. At the conclusion of the engagement, management is responsible for providing the auditor with a letter that confirms certain representations made during the audit;
    h. Management is responsible for adjusting the financial statements to correct material misstatements;
    i. The auditor is responsible for conducting the audit in accordance with generally accepted auditing standards -- an audit includes obtaining an understanding of the entity and its environment, including internal control, sufficient to assess the risks of material misstatement of the financial statements (and the auditor should communicate any identified significant deficiencies to those charged with governance); and

j. Limitations -- an audit is not designed to provide assurance on internal control or to identify significant deficiencies; the auditor obtains reasonable, not absolute, assurance about the risk of material misstatement, so it is possible that a material misstatement may remain undetected; an audit is not designed to detect error or fraud that is immaterial to the financial statements; and the auditor may decline to express an opinion or issue a report as a result of circumstances encountered during the engagement.

4. Other matters may also be addressed in the understanding with the client:
   a. Overall audit strategy (as discussed below);
   b. The involvement of specialists or internal auditors;
   c. Involvement of a predecessor auditor;
   d. Fees and billing arrangements;
   e. Any limitations regarding legal liability issues, such as indemnification to the auditor for liability arising from knowing misrepresentations by management;
   f. Conditions under which access to audit documentation may be granted to others;
   g. Additional services to be provided related to regulatory requirements; and
   h. Nonattest services to be provided in connection with the engagement subject to the limitations of Ethics Interpretation No. 101-3, "Performance of Nonattest Services."

C. Preliminary engagement activities:

1. Perform procedures regarding the "continuance" of the client relationship and evaluate the auditor's compliance with ethics requirements (including independence) -- this should be done prior to performing other significant activities for the current year audit. (However, these issues continue throughout the engagement as circumstances change.)
2. These preliminary engagement activities help ensure that (a) the auditor maintains the necessary independence and ability to perform the engagement; (b) there are no issues involving management integrity affecting the engagement; and (c) there is no misunderstanding with the client as to the terms of the engagement.

D. Overall audit strategy -- the effort devoted to this activity will vary according to the size of the entity and the complexity of the audit.

1. In establishing the overall audit strategy, the auditor should:
   a. Determine the characteristics of the engagement that define its scope -- including the basis of reporting, industry-specific reporting requirements, and locations of the entity;
   b. Identify the reporting objectives of the engagement to plan the timing of the audit and the nature of required communications -- e.g., interim and final reporting deadlines, dates for expected communications with management and others, etc.;
   c. Consider other important factors that will affect the focus of the audit team -- including the determination of materiality levels, preliminary identification of high risk audit areas, expectations about reliance on the operating effectiveness of internal control, and identification of relevant recent developments that involve the specific entity, the industry, financial reporting, or other matters.
2. Developing the audit strategy will influence resource allocation, including:
   a. Resources assigned to specific audit areas (e.g., level of experience);
   b. Amount of resources assigned (e.g., number of team members);
   c. Timing of those resources (e.g., interim or final);
   d. How such resources are to be managed and supervised.
3. The auditor should update and document any significant revisions to the overall audit strategy to deal with changes in circumstances.
4. After the overall audit strategy is established -- the auditor is then able to start developing a more detailed audit plan to achieve the audit objectives through the efficient use of the auditor's resources:

a. The audit plan documents the audit procedures to be used;

b. The audit plan is more detailed than the audit strategy -- it includes the nature, timing, and extent of audit procedures to be performed by audit team members in order to obtain sufficient appropriate audit evidence to reduce audit risk to an acceptably low level;

c. The audit plan should include (1) a description of the nature, timing, and extent of planned risk assessment procedures sufficient to assess the risk of material misstatement; (2) a description of the nature, timing, and extent of planned further audit procedures at the relevant assertion level for each material class of transactions, account balance, and disclosure (including whether to test the operating effectiveness of controls and planned substantive procedures); and (3) a description of other audit procedures to be carried out in compliance with generally accepted auditing standards;

d. The auditor should document any changes to the original audit plan.

E. Determining the extent of involvement of professionals possessing specialized skills.

1. The auditor should consider whether specialized skills are needed in performing the audit (either on the auditor's staff or an outside professional):

a. Should determine whether that professional will function as a member of the audit team;

b. If part of the audit team -- responsibilities for supervision are equivalent to those of other assistants;

c. If part of the audit team -- the auditor should have sufficient knowledge to communicate the objectives of the other professional's work; to evaluate whether the specified audit procedures will meet the auditor's objectives; and to evaluate the results of the audit procedures applied as they relate to the nature, timing, and extent of further planned audit procedures.

2. In determining whether a professional having information technology (IT) skills on the audit team (to determine the effect of IT on the audit, to understand the IT controls, or to design/perform tests of IT controls), the auditor should consider the following factors:

a. The complexity of the entity's systems and IT controls;

b. The significance of changes made to existing systems or the implementation of new systems;

c. The extent to which data is shared among systems;

d. The extent of the entity's participation in electronic commerce;

e. The entity's use of emerging technologies;

f. The significance of audit evidence only available electronically.

3. Audit procedures that the auditor may assign to an IT professional include (a) inquiring of an entity's IT personnel how data/transactions are initiated, authorized, recorded, processed, and reported and how IT controls are designed; (b) inspecting systems documentation; (c) observing the operation of IT controls; and (d) planning and performing tests of IT controls.

F. Communications with those charged with governance and management -- the auditor should be careful to avoid compromising the effectiveness of the audit by making the audit procedures too predictable.

1. Discussions with those charged with governance -- usually involve the overall audit strategy and timing of the audit, including any limitations, or any additional requirements.

2. Discussions with management -- usually to facilitate the conduct of the engagement (e.g., to coordinate some of the planned procedures with the work of the entity's personnel).

G. Additional considerations in initial audit engagements:

1. Before starting an initial audit engagement -- the auditor should (a) perform appropriate procedures regarding the acceptance of the client relationship (related to the CPA firm's system of quality control); and (b) communicate with the previous auditor when a change of auditors has occurred.

2. The purpose of planning the audit is the same for an initial audit or a recurring engagement -- however, for an initial audit, the auditor should generally consider some additional matters in developing the overall audit strategy and the audit plan:

    a. Arrangements to be made with the previous auditor to review the previous auditor's audit documentation;

    b. Any major issues discussed with management in connection with the initial selection as auditors, the communication of these matters to those charged with governance, and how these matters affect the overall audit strategy and audit plan;

    c. The planned audit procedures to obtain sufficient appropriate audit evidence regarding opening balances;

    d. The assignment of firm personnel with appropriate levels of capabilities and competence to address anticipated significant risks;

    e. Other procedures required by the firm's system of quality control for initial audit engagements (e.g., another partner's review of the overall audit strategy before starting significant audit procedures or to review reports prior to issuance).

III. **Supervision --** the extent of supervision that is appropriate varies with the circumstances, including the complexity of the subject matter and the qualifications of persons doing the work and their knowledge of the client's business/industry.

A. **Elements of supervision --** instructing/directing assistants, keeping informed of significant issues encountered, reviewing the work performed, and dealing with differences of opinion among firm personnel.

B. **Discussion regarding fraud --** the auditor with final responsibility for the audit should communicate with members of the audit team regarding the susceptibility of the financial statement's due to error or fraud. (Emphasize the need to maintain a questioning mind and to exercise professional skepticism.)

C. **Assistants should be informed of their responsibilities and the objectives of the audit procedures they are to perform --** the auditor with final responsibility for the audit should direct assistants to bring up any issues the assistant believes are significant to the financial statements or the auditor's report. (Assistants should also be directed to bring to the attention of the appropriate members of the firm any difficulties encountered in performing the audit, including missing documents or resistance from client personnel in providing access to information or in responding to inquiries.)

D. **Review the audit documentation --** the work performed by each assistant should be reviewed to determine whether it was adequately performed and documented and to evaluate the results. (The person with final responsibility for the audit may delegate parts of the review responsibility to others in accordance with the firm's system of quality control.)

E. **Differences of opinion among audit team members --** the auditor with final responsibility for the audit and assistants should be aware of the procedures to be followed when differences of opinion about accounting and auditing issues exist among firm personnel involved in the audit.

    1. Such procedures should permit an assistant to document his/her disagreement with the conclusions reached if, after appropriate consultation, he/she believes it necessary to be disassociated with the resolution of the issue.

    2. In such a situation, the basis for the final resolution should be documented.

IV. **Effective date --** SAS 108 is effective for audits of financial statements for periods beginning on or after December 15, 2006 (earlier application is permitted).

V. **Appendix --** matters that the auditor may consider in establishing the overall audit strategy. (These considerations are not comprehensive, nor relevant to every engagement.)

A. When establishing the scope of the audit engagement:

1. Basis of reporting used, including any necessary reconciliation to another basis of accounting;
2. Industry-specific reporting requirements -- e.g., mandatory reports;
3. Expected audit coverage -- e.g., number and locations to be included;
4. Control relationships affecting how the group is to be consolidated;
5. Extent to which locations are audited by other auditors;
6. Nature of entities to be audited, such as need for specialized knowledge;
7. Reporting currency to be used and the need for currency translation;
8. Need for statutory or regulatory audit requirements -- e.g., OMB's Circular A-133, Audits of States, Local Governments, and Non-Profit Organizations;
9. Availability of internal auditors' work and the potential reliance on that;
10. Entity's use of service organizations and available evidence about controls;
11. Expected use of audit evidence obtained in prior audits -- e.g., audit evidence related to risk assessment procedures and tests of control;
12. Effect of information technology on audit procedures -- e.g., availability of data and expected use of computer-assisted audit techniques;
13. Coordination of the audit work with any reviews of interim financial information;
14. Discussion of matters that may affect the audit with firm personnel responsible for performing other services for the entity; and
15. Availability of client personnel and data.

B. When ascertaining the reporting objectives of the engagement, the timing of the audit, and the nature of required communications:

1. Entity's timetable for reporting, including interim periods;
2. Meetings to discuss the nature, timing, and extent of the audit work with management and those charged with governance;
3. Discussions about the expected type and timing of reports to be issued and other communications (including auditor's report, management letters, and other communications to those charged with governance);
4. Discussion with management about expected communications on the status of audit work throughout the engagement and the expected deliverables;
5. Communication with auditors of other locations;
6. Expected nature and timing of communications among audit team members, including nature and timing of team meetings and review of the audit work; and
7. Any other expected communications with third parties, including any statutory or contractual reporting responsibilities.

C. When setting the scope of the audit:

1. Materiality considerations -- planning-stage materiality; identifying material locations and account balances; communicating materiality for auditors of other locations; and reconsidering materiality as procedures are performed;
2. Audit areas where there is a higher risk of material misstatement;
3. Effect of the assessed risk of material misstatement at the overall financial statement level on scope, supervision, and review;
4. Selection of the audit team and the assignment of audit work;
5. Engagement budgeting;
6. Emphasis on professional skepticism and keeping a questioning mind;

7. Results of previous audits involving operating effectiveness of internal control and nature of identified weaknesses and actions taken;
8. Management's commitment to the design and operation of internal control;
9. Volume of transactions involved;
10. Importance attached to internal control throughout the entity;
11. Significant business developments, including changes in IT and business processes, changes in key management, and acquisitions/divestments;
12. Significant industry developments -- e.g., changes in industry regulations and reporting requirements;
13. Significant accounting changes, such as GAAP; and
14. Other significant relevant developments -- e.g., changes in the legal environment.

AU312 (SAS 107) - Audit Risk and Materiality

I. Introductory Comments

A. Audit risk and materiality affect the application of GAAS, especially the standards of fieldwork and reporting and need to be considered together in designing the nature, timing, and extent of audit procedures and in evaluating the results of those procedures.

B. Audit risk -- "the risk that the auditor may unknowingly fail to appropriately modify his or her opinion on financial statements that are materially misstated."

C. Materiality -- "The concept of materiality recognizes that some matters, either individually or in the aggregate, are important for fair presentation of financial statements in conformity with GAAP, while other matters are not important."

D. Reasonable assurance -- "The auditor's responsibility is to plan and perform the audit to obtain reasonable assurance that material misstatements, whether caused by errors or fraud, are detected."

II. Materiality in the Context of an Audit

A. Consideration of materiality is a matter of professional judgment -- it is influenced by the auditor's perception of the needs of users of financial statements.

B. Statement of Financial Accounting Concepts No. 2 defines materiality -- "the magnitude of an omission or misstatement of accounting information that, in light of surrounding circumstances, makes it probable that the judgment of a reasonable person relying on the information would have been changed or influenced by the omission or misstatement." (Such judgments involve both quantitative and qualitative considerations.)

C. Users:

1. The auditor does not consider the effect of misstatements on specific individual users, since their needs may vary widely.
2. The auditor should consider the characteristics of users in order to evaluate whether misstatements could influence economic decisions of those users. Users are assumed to:
    - **a.** Have an appropriate knowledge of business and accounting and a willingness to study the information with appropriate diligence;
    - **b.** Understand that financial reporting is affected by materiality;
    - **c.** Recognize the uncertainties inherent in financial reporting; and
    - **d.** Make appropriate decisions on the basis of the financial statements.

III. Nature and Causes of Misstatements

A. Misstatements can result from errors (unintentional) or fraud (intentional) and may consist of the following:

1. An inaccuracy in gathering/processing data affecting financial statements;
2. A difference in the amount, classification, or presentation of a financial statement element relative to the requirements of GAAP;
3. The omission of a financial statement element, account, or item;
4. The omission of information that is required to be disclosed by GAAP or disclosure that is not presented in conformity with GAAP;
5. An incorrect accounting estimate arising from an oversight or misinterpretation of facts;
6. Management's judgments concerning an accounting estimate or selection of accounting policies that the auditor considers unreasonable.

B. Misstatements may be classified into 2 types -- "known" and "likely:"

1. Known misstatements -- specific misstatements identified during the audit (that is, misapplication of accounting principles or misstatements of facts);
2. Likely misstatements -- (a) arise from differences between management's and the auditor's judgments concerning accounting estimates that the auditor considers unreasonable; or (b) that result from extrapolation of audit evidence obtained from an application of sampling;

C. The auditor has no responsibility to plan and perform the audit to detect immaterial misstatements -- however, when there is evidence of potential fraud, regardless of materiality, the auditor should consider the implications to the audit (e.g., may reflect on the integrity of management or other employees).

IV. Considerations at the Financial Statement Level

A. Consider audit risk and materiality at the financial statement level in order to:

1. Determine the extent and nature of risk assessment procedures;
2. Identify and assess the risk of material misstatement;
3. Determine the nature, timing, and extent of further audit procedures;
4. Evaluate whether the financial statements taken as a whole are presented fairly in conformity with GAAP.

B. Audit risk is a function of (1) the risk that the financial statements are materially misstated and (2) the risk that the auditor will not detect such material misstatement -- consider audit risk in relation to the relevant assertions related to individual account balances, classes of transactions, and disclosures and at the overall financial statement level. (Perform risk assessment procedures to assess the risk of material misstatement both at the financial statement and relevant assertion levels.)

C. The auditor should reduce audit risk to "a low level" that is appropriate, in the auditor's judgment, for expressing an opinion on the financial statements -- audit risk may be assessed in quantitative or non-quantitative terms.

1. Considerations of audit risk and materiality are affected by the size and complexity of the entity and the auditor's experience with and knowledge of the entity and its environment, including internal control.
2. At the financial statement level -- consider risks of material misstatement that relate pervasively to the financial statements taken as a whole and which potentially affect many relevant assertions.
    a. Such risks may be especially relevant to consideration of the risk of material fraud (e.g., through management override of control).
    b. In developing responses to risks of material misstatement at the financial statement level -- consider the knowledge, skill, and ability of personnel assigned significant engagement responsibilities; whether there is a need for a specialist; and the appropriate level of supervision of assistants.
3. In an audit of an entity with operations in multiple locations or multiple components -- consider the extent to which audit procedures should be performed at selected locations or components:
    a. Nature and amount of assets and transactions associated with the location or component;
    b. Degree of centralization of records or information processing;
    c. Effectiveness of the control environment (especially management's direct control over authority delegated to others);
    d. Frequency, timing, and scope of monitoring activities at the location or component;
    e. Judgments about materiality of the location or component; and
    f. Risks associated with the location (e.g., political or economic instability).

V. Considerations at the Individual Account Balance, Class of Transactions, or Disclosure Level

A. There is an inverse relationship between audit risk and materiality considerations -- there might be a low risk that the account is misstated by an extremely large amount, but a very high risk that the account is misstated by an extremely small amount.

B. To decrease the level of audit risk, the auditor would:

1. Perform more effective audit procedures;
2. Perform audit procedures closer to year end; or
3. Increase the extent of particular audit procedures.

C. At the account balance, class of transactions, relevant assertion, or disclosure levels, audit risk (AR) consists of (1) the risk that the relevant assertions contain material misstatements (consisting of inherent risk and control risk) and (2) the risk that the auditor will not detect such misstatements (detection risk) -- these component risks may be assessed in quantitative terms (such as percentages) or in qualitative terms (such as high, medium, or low).

1. Risk of material misstatement (RMM) -- the auditor's combined assessment of inherent risk and control risk: (However, the auditor may choose to assess those components separately.)
   - **a.** Inherent risk (IR) -- the susceptibility of a relevant assertion to a misstatement that could be material, either individually or in the aggregate, assuming that there are no related controls. (External circumstances associated with business risks can also influence inherent risk -- e.g., technological developments might cause inventory obsolescence.)
   - **b.** Control risk (CR) -- the risk that a material misstatement that could occur in a relevant assertion would not be prevented or detected on a timely basis by the entity's internal control. (Some control risk will always exist due to the inherent limitations of internal control.)
2. Detection risk (DR) -- the risk that the auditor will not detect a material misstatement that exists in a relevant assertion:
   - **a.** DR relates to the substantive audit procedures -- it can be disaggregated into 2 additional components: (1) tests of details risk (TD) and (2) substantive analytical procedures risk (AP);
   - **b.** DR should be inversely related to the risk of material misstatement at the relevant assertion level;
   - **c.** Audit risk model: AR = RMM x DR; or AR = IR x CR x TD x AP. (Expresses the general relationship of associated risks -- not intended to be a mathematical formula including all factors that may influence the assessment of audit risk; may be useful when planning appropriate risk levels.)

VI. Determining Materiality for the Financial Statements Taken as a Whole When Planning

A. The auditor should determine a materiality level for the financial statements taken as a whole when establishing the overall audit strategy for the audit.

B. Determining what factors are material requires professional judgment based on the auditor's understanding of the users' needs -- the auditor may apply a percentage to a chosen benchmark as a step in this determination. (Profit before tax from continuing operations may be a suitable benchmark for profit-oriented entities, but not when the entity's earnings are volatile or when the entity is a not-for-profit entity.)

VII. Materiality for Particular Items of Lesser Amounts than the Materiality Level is Determined for the Financial Statements Taken as a Whole

A. In establishing the overall strategy for the audit, the auditor should consider whether misstatements of particular items of lesser amounts than the materiality level determined for the financial statements taken as a whole could influence the economic decisions of users -- if so, such amounts represent lower materiality levels to be considered.

B. Consider such factors as the following:

1. Whether accounting standards, laws, or regulations affect users' expectations regarding the measurement or disclosure of items (e.g., related party transactions and the compensation of management);

2. The key disclosures for the industry and the environment in which the entity operates (e.g., research and development for pharmaceuticals);
3. Whether attention is focused on the financial performance of a particular subsidiary or division (e.g., for a newly acquired business unit).

VIII. Tolerable Misstatement -- The maximum error in a population that the auditor is willing to accept (also referred to as "tolerable error" in other standards).

A. The auditor should allow for the possibility that some misstatements of lesser amounts than the overall materiality levels could, in the aggregate, result in a material misstatement of the financial statements (should determine one or more levels of tolerable misstatement).

B. The auditor should design the audit to provide reasonable assurance of detecting material misstatements large enough, individually or in the aggregate, to be quantitatively material to the financial statements -- it is not normally practical to design audit procedures to detect misstatements that could be qualitatively material.

IX. Considerations as the Audit Progresses

A. The auditor may consider materiality for planning purposes before the financial statements have been prepared (e.g., might base materiality on annualized interim information).

B. The auditor's judgment about materiality for planning purposes may differ from that used to evaluate the audit findings (since additional information may become available during fieldwork) -- if the auditor concludes that a lower materiality level than that initially determined is appropriate, the auditor should consider the implications to tolerable misstatement and to the nature, timing, and extent of audit procedures.

C. If identified misstatements (and their circumstances) indicate that other misstatements may exist that could be material -- the auditor should consider whether the overall audit strategy and audit plan should be revised (should not assume that a misstatement is an "isolated" occurrence).

D. If the aggregate of identified (known and likely) misstatements approaches the materiality level -- the auditor should consider the likelihood that other undetected misstatements could exceed the materiality level; the auditor should then reconsider the nature and extent of further audit procedures.

X. Communication of Misstatements to Management

A. The auditor must accumulate all identified known and likely misstatements (except those believed to be "trivial") and communicate them to the appropriate level of management on a timely basis -- the determination of which level of management is appropriate is based on factors such as nature, size, and frequency of misstatement and which level of management can take the necessary action.

B. The auditor should request management to correct all known misstatements (except for those believed to be "trivial"), including the effect of prior period misstatements.

C. When a likely misstatement from a sample indicates a material misstatement -- the auditor should request management to examine the class of transactions, account balance, or disclosure to identify the necessary correction. (The auditor should then reevaluate the amount of likely misstatement and perform additional audit procedures if necessary.)

D. When a likely misstatement involves differences in estimates (e.g., a difference in fair value estimate) -- the auditor should request management to review the assumptions and methods used to develop management's estimate. (The auditor should then reevaluate the amount of likely misstatement and perform additional audit procedures if necessary.)

E. If management decides not to correct some (or all) of the known and likely misstatements communicated by the auditor -- the auditor should obtain an understanding of management's reasoning and should take that into account in considering the qualitative aspects of the entity's accounting practices and the implications to the auditor's report.

XI. Evaluating Audit Findings -- the auditor must consider the effects of misstatements (known and likely), both individually and in the aggregate, that are not corrected by the entity.

A. Before considering the aggregate effect of identified uncorrected misstatements -- the auditor should consider each misstatement separately.

1. To determine its relationship to the relevant individual classes of transactions, account balances, or disclosures.
2. To determine whether it is appropriate to offset related misstatements.
3. To determine the effect of misstatements related to prior periods.

B. In aggregating misstatements, the auditor should include the effect of any known prior period misstatements.

C. When substantive analytical procedures indicate a misstatement might exist, but not its approximate amount -- the auditor should request management to investigate. (If necessary, the auditor should expand the audit procedures to determine whether a misstatement exists.)

D. If the auditor believes the estimated amount in the financial statements is unreasonable -- the auditor should treat the difference between that estimate and the closest reasonable estimate as a likely misstatement.

1. The "closest reasonable estimate" may be a range of acceptable amounts instead of a point estimate.
2. The auditor should consider whether the difference between management's estimates and that suggested by the audit evidence suggests a possible bias on the part of the entity's management (may need to consider whether other recorded estimates might also be biased).

E. Qualitative considerations affect the auditor's perception of materiality -- the following qualitative facts might be relevant to that determination:

1. The potential effect on trends (especially in profitability)
2. A misstatement that changes a loss into income, or vice versa;
3. The potential effect on compliance with loan covenants or other contracts
4. The existence of statutory or regulatory reporting requirements affecting materiality;
5. The misstatement masks a change in earnings or other trends;
6. A misstatement that increases management's compensation;
7. Misstatements involving fraud and possible illegal acts, violations of contractual provisions, and conflicts of interest;
8. A misstatement that affects recurring earnings will normally be considered more significant than one involving a nonrecurring or extraordinary item;
9. The effect of misclassifications (e.g., operating versus non-operating);
10. The significance of the misstatement to expected user needs (e.g., earnings to investors and equity amount to creditors or the effects on purchase price in buy-sell agreements);
11. Whether the object of the misstatement is essentially subjective or objective in nature;
12. Management's apparent motivation -- whether the item involves bias or is intentional; whether management is unwilling to correct the item;
13. The existence of offsetting effects of other individually significant misstatements;
14. The likelihood that a currently immaterial misstatement may become material in the future;
15. The cost of making the correction;
16. The risk that additional undetected misstatements would affect the auditor's evaluation of the fairness of the financial statements.

F. Evaluate whether the financial statements taken as a whole are free of material misstatement.

1. If the auditor believes that the financial statements are materially misstated -- the auditor should request management to make necessary corrections and, if management refuses, the auditor must determine the implications for the auditor's report.

2. The auditor should also consider the effect of undetected misstatements in concluding whether the financial statements are fairly stated.

XII. Documentation -- The auditor should document the following matters:

A. The levels of materiality (and tolerable misstatement) used in the audit and the basis on which those levels were determined;

B. A summary of uncorrected known and likely misstatements (except those that are "trivial") -- uncorrected misstatements should be documented in a manner that allows the auditor to:

1. Separately consider the effects of known and likely misstatement, including uncorrected misstatements identified in prior periods;

2. Consider the aggregate effect of misstatements on the financial statements;

3. Consider the qualitative factors that are relevant to the auditor's consideration whether misstatements are material.

C. The auditor's conclusion as to whether uncorrected misstatements, individually or in the aggregate, do or do not cause the financial statement to be materially misstated, and the basis for that conclusion;

D. All known and likely misstatements identified by the auditor that have been corrected by management (except those that are "trivial").

XIII. Effective Date -- SAS 107 is effective for audits of financial statements for periods beginning on or after December 15, 2006 (earlier application is permitted).

AU314 (SAS 109) - Understanding the Entity and Assessing Risks

I. **Overview of This Standard --** Professional judgment is needed to determine the extent of the required understanding of the entity and its environment, including its internal control.

> **Note:**
> The auditor's primary consideration is whether that understanding is sufficient to assess risks of material misstatement of the financial statements and to design and perform further audit procedures.

A. Risk assessment procedures and sources of information about the entity and its environment, including its internal control.

B. Understanding the entity and its environment, including its internal control -- provides guidance in understanding the specified aspects of the entity and its environment, and components of its internal control, in order to identify and assess risks of material misstatement, and in designing and performing further audit procedures.

C. Assessing the risks of material misstatement -- provides guidance in assessing the risks of material misstatement at the financial statement and relevant assertion levels; also provides guidance in determining whether any of the assessed risks are significant risks that require special audit consideration or risks for which substantive procedures alone do not provide sufficient appropriate evidence.

D. Documentation -- provides guidance as to required documentation

II. **Risk Assessment Procedures and Sources of Information About the Entity and Its Environment, Including Its Internal Control --** The auditor should perform "risk assessment procedures" to obtain an understanding of the entity and its environment, including its internal control. (The nature, timing, and extent of the risk assessment procedures vary with the engagement's circumstances, including the entity's size and complexity and the auditor's experience with it.)

A. Inquiries of management and others:

1. Much of the information obtained from inquiries is obtained from management -- may also make inquiries of others within the entity (including internal auditors, production personnel, marketing/sales personnel, those charged with governance, and in-house legal counsel).

2. May also make inquiries of others outside the entity (e.g., external legal counsel or valuation experts used by the entity) -- may also review information obtained from external sources (e.g., reports by analysts, banks, or rating agencies; regulatory reports, etc.).

B. Analytical procedures -- the auditor should apply analytical procedures in planning the audit to assist in understanding the entity and its environment and to identify areas that may represent specific risks relevant to the audit.

C. Observation and inspection -- including observation of entity operations; inspection of documents (business plans, records, and internal control manuals); reading reports prepared by management and those charged with governance (including interim financial reports and minutes of board meetings); and visits to the entity's facilities.

D. Review information about the entity and its environment obtained in prior periods -- determine whether changes may have affected the relevance of that information to the current audit (make inquiries and perform walk-through of systems to determine whether such changes have occurred).

E. Discussion among the audit team -- the audit team should discuss the susceptibility of the entity's financial statements to material misstatement.

1. Professional judgment is required to determine which members of the audit team should be included and how and when it occurs and the extent of the discussion. ("Key" members should be involved, including "the auditor with final responsibility.")

2. Multi-location audit -- multiple discussions may occur that involve key members of the audit team in each significant location.

3. Objective of this discussion -- for members of the audit team to understand the potential for material misstatements of the financial statements resulting from fraud or error in the specific areas assigned to them and to understand how the results of the audit procedures that they perform may affect other aspects of the audit.

4. The discussion should include "critical issues" (areas of significant audit risk), areas susceptible to management override of controls; unusual accounting procedures used by the client; important control systems; materiality at the financial statement level and at the account level; and how materiality will be used to determine the extent of testing.

5. The auditor should plan and perform the audit with an attitude of professional skepticism.

III. Understanding the Entity and Its Environment, Including Its Internal Control

A. The auditor's understanding of the entity and its environment consists of understanding the following aspects

   1. Industry, regulatory, and other external factors;

   2. Nature of the entity;

   3. Objectives and strategies and related business risks that may cause material misstatement of the financial statements;

   4. Measurement and review of the entity's financial performance; and

   5. Internal control.

B. Industry, regulatory, and other external factors -- the entity's industry may be subject to specific risks of material misstatement due to the nature of the business, the degree of regulation, or other external forces (including political, economic, social, technical, and competitive issues).

C. Nature of the entity -- refers to the entity's operations, its ownership, governance, the types of investments that it makes, the way the entity is structured, and how it is financed. (An understanding of this helps the auditor understand the classes of transactions, account balances, and disclosures that are relevant to the financial statements.)

D. Objectives and strategies and related business risks

   1. Objectives versus strategies -- objectives are the overall plans for the entity; strategies are the operational approaches by which management intends to achieve its objectives.

   2. Business risks result from circumstances that could adversely affect the entity's ability to achieve its objectives and execute its strategies:

      a. Business risk is broader than the risk of material misstatement of the financial statements -- the auditor does not have a responsibility to identify/assess all business risks;

      b. The auditor focuses on whether a business risk may result in a material misstatement of the financial statements (which is based on the entity's circumstances).

E. Measurement and review of the entity's financial performance -- performance measures and their review indicate aspects of the entity's performance that management considers important.

   1. This understanding helps the auditor consider whether such pressures may have increased the risks of material misstatement.

   2. Internally generated measures may include key performance indicators (financial and non-financial); budgets; variance analysis; subsidiary information and divisional, departmental, or other level performance reports; and comparisons to competitors.

   3. External information may include analysts' reports and credit rating agency reports -- these may be obtained from the entity being audited or from Web sites.

   4. When using performance measures for audit purposes (such as analytical procedures) -- consider whether such measures are reliable and precise enough to detect material misstatements.

F. Obtain a sufficient understanding of internal control -- by performing risk assessment procedures to evaluate the design of controls relevant to the audit to (1) identify types of potential misstatements; (2) consider factors that affect the risks of material misstatement; and (3) design tests of controls, when applicable, and substantive procedures.

   1. The design and implementation of internal control varies with an entity's size and complexity.

   2. The auditor should obtain an understanding of an entity's accounting policies . Consider if they are appropriate for its business and consistent with GAAP used in the relevant industry.

3. Controls relevant to reliable financial reporting and to the audit -- it is not necessary to assess all controls in connection with assessing the risks of material misstatement:
   a. To determine which controls should be assessed -- professional judgment is usually required involving the following considerations:
      i. Materiality;
      ii. Size of the entity;
      iii. Nature of the entity's business (including ownership characteristics);
      iv. Diversity and complexity of the entity's operations;
      v. Applicable legal and regulatory requirements;
      vi. Nature and complexity of the systems that are part of the entity's internal control, including service organizations.
   b. Controls relevant to operations and compliance – these may be relevant to an audit if they pertain to information that the auditor may evaluate or use in applying audit procedures (e.g., related to non-financial data used in analytical procedures);
   c. Controls relevant to safeguarding assets -- the auditor's consideration is generally limited to those relevant to the reliability of financial reporting.
4. Depth of understanding of internal control -- evaluating the design of a control involves considering whether the control, individually or in combination with other controls, is capable of effectively preventing or detecting and correcting material misstatements:
   a. Procedures to obtain evidence about the design and implementation of relevant controls -- (1) inquiring of entity personnel, (2) observing the application of specific controls, (3) inspecting documents and reports, and (4) tracing transactions through the information system relevant to financial reporting; (Inquiry alone is not sufficient to evaluate the design and implementation of a control.)
   b. Obtaining an understanding of control normally is not sufficient to serve as testing the operating effectiveness of controls -- however, performing audit procedures to determine whether an automated control has been implemented may serve as a test of operating effectiveness for that control, since IT processing is inherently consistent.
5. Characteristics of manual and automated elements of internal control relevant to the auditor's risk assessment:
   a. Effect of IT on controls – these may affect any of the 5 components of internal control; and may also affect the manner in which transactions are initiated, authorized, recorded, processed, and reported;
   b. Systems using IT usually consist of a combination of automated and manual controls; (The mix varies with the nature and complexity of the entity's use of IT.)
   c. IT provides potential benefits of effectiveness and efficiency for an entity's internal control -- e.g., consistent application, additional analysis, enhanced timeliness, enhanced monitoring, etc.;
   d. IT may result in certain risks to internal control -- e.g., unauthorized access to data (or potential loss of data), unauthorized changes to data or system, etc.;
   e. Manual controls may be especially suitable where judgment and discretion are required -- e.g., for large, unusual, or nonrecurring transactions; circumstances where misstatements are difficult to define or anticipate; or in monitoring the effectiveness of automated controls;
   f. Manual controls are performed by people and pose specific risks to the entity's internal control -- as a result, consistency of application cannot be assumed.
6. Limitations of internal control -- internal control provides reasonable, not absolute, assurance about achieving the entity's objectives:
   a. Human judgment -- breakdowns can occur due to human failures, including mistakes due to misunderstanding or fatigue;
   b. Controls may also be circumvented by collusion or management override of controls;

c. Smaller entities may have difficulty achieving segregation of duties due to relatively fewer employees -- for key areas, it is still possible to implement appropriate segregation of duties or other form of effective controls.

G. Components of internal control -- (1) control environment; (2) risk assessment; (3) information and communication systems; (4) control activities; and (5) monitoring

1. Control environment -- sets the tone of an organization, including the control consciousness of its people.

a. The auditor should evaluate the following elements comprising the entity's control environment:

i. Communication and enforcement of integrity and ethical values;

ii. Commitment to competence;

iii. Participation of those charged with governance (including interaction with internal and external auditors);

iv. Management's philosophy and operating style;

v. Organizational structure -- the framework for achieving its objectives;

vi. Assignment of authority and responsibility (including reporting relationships);

vii. Human resource policies and practices.

b. Auditor's responsibilities:

i. The auditor should obtain sufficient knowledge of the control environment to understand the attitudes, awareness, and actions of those charged with governance concerning the entity's internal control and its importance in achieving reliable financial reporting;

ii. Obtain sufficient appropriate audit evidence through a combination of inquiries and other risk assessment procedures (e.g., corroborating inquiries through observation or inspection of documents).

c. Pervasive effects of the control environment on assessing the risk of material misstatement -- the auditor's preliminary judgment about its effectiveness influences the nature, timing, and extent of further audit procedures to be performed. (However, the control environment is not specific enough to prevent or detect material misstatements in account balances, classes of transactions, or disclosures and related assertions.)

2. Risk assessment process -- the entity's identification, analysis, and management of risks relevant to the preparation of financial statements in conformity with GAAP.

a. Risks may arise or change due to a variety of circumstances -- e.g., changes in the operating environment; new personnel; rapid growth; new technology; expanded foreign operations; corporate restructurings; new accounting pronouncements, etc.

b. Auditor's responsibilities:

i. Consider how management identified business risks relevant to financial reporting, estimates the significance of the risks, assesses the likelihood of their occurrence, and decides upon actions for their management;

ii. Inquire about business risks that management has identified and consider whether they may result in material misstatement of the financial statements;

iii. During the audit the auditor may identify business risks (or risks of material misstatement) that management failed to identify -- consider why the entity's risk assessment process failed to identify those risks and whether the process is appropriate to its circumstances.

c. In a smaller entity -- no formal risk assessment process may be in effect, so the auditor should discuss with management how risks to the business are identified and managed.

3. Information and communication systems relevant to financial reporting -- the procedures and records to initiate, authorize, record, process, and report entity transactions and events and to maintain accountability for the related assets, liabilities, and equity.

a. The quality of system-generated information affects management's ability to prepare reliable financial reports.

b. Auditor's responsibilities:

   i. Obtain sufficient knowledge of the information system to understand:

      1. The classes of transactions that are significant to the financial statements;

      2. The procedures by which transactions are initiated, authorized, recorded, processed, and reported in the financial statements;

      3. The related accounting records supporting information and specific accounts in the financial statements;

      4. How the information system captures events and conditions (other than classes of transactions) that are significant to the financial statements;

      5. The financial reporting process used to prepare the entity's financial statements.

   ii. Obtain an understanding of how the incorrect processing of transactions is resolved;

   iii. Obtain an understanding of the automated and manual procedures an entity uses to prepare financial statements and related disclosures, and how misstatements may occur -- including procedures that:

      1. Enter transaction totals into the general ledger; (There may be little or no visible evidence when IT is used to transfer information automatically.)

      2. Initiate, authorize, record, and process journal entries in the general ledger;

      3. Initiate and record recurring and nonrecurring adjustments to the financial statements;

      4. Combine and consolidate general ledger data;

      5. Prepare financial statements and disclosures.

   iv. Obtain an understanding of how transactions originate within the entity's business processes, which are the activities designed to develop, purchase, produce, sell and distribute an entity's products and services; ensure compliance with laws and regulations; and record information properly;

   v. Obtain sufficient knowledge of the communication component to understand how the entity communicates financial reporting roles and responsibilities -- includes policy manuals and financial reporting manuals.

4. Control activities -- the policies and procedures that help ensure that management directives are carried out, including the following specific control activities:

   a. Need not obtain an understanding of all the control activities related to each class of transactions, account balance, and disclosure in the financial statements -- ordinarily, control activities relevant to an audit include those related to: (1) authorization; (2) segregation of duties; (3) safeguarding assets; and (4) asset accountability.

   b. Auditor's responsibilities -- the auditor's primary consideration is whether (and how) a specific control activity prevents or detects and corrects material misstatements in classes of transactions, account balances, or disclosures:

      i. Obtain an understanding of how IT affects control activities relevant to planning the audit (may view the IT control activities in terms of "application controls" and "general controls"):

         1. Application controls -- related to the use of IT to initiate, authorize, record, process, and report transactions (e.g., edit checks of input data, numerical sequence checks, and manual follow-up of exception reports);

         2. General controls -- policies and procedures that related to many applications and help to ensure the continued proper operation of information systems (e.g.,

controls over data center and network operations; system software acquisition, change, and maintenance; access security; and application system acquisition, development, and maintenance);

ii. Consider whether the entity has responded adequately to the risks arising from IT by establishing effective controls -- controls over IT are effective when they maintain the integrity of information and the security of the data that such systems process.

5. Monitoring of controls -- a process to assess the quality of internal control performance over time, which involves assessing the design and operation of controls on a timely basis and taking necessary correction actions

   a. Internal auditors contribute to an entity's monitoring activities.

   b. Auditor's responsibilities – to obtain an understanding of the sources of the information related to the entity's monitoring activities and the basis upon which management considers the information to be reliable.

IV. Assessing the Risk of Material Misstatement

A. Basic responsibilities of the auditor – to identify and assess the risks of material misstatement at the financial statement level and at the relevant assertion level related to classes of transactions, account balances, and disclosures.

1. Specifically the auditor should:

   a. Identify risks throughout the process of obtaining an understanding of the entity and its environment, including relevant controls;

   b. Relate the identified risks to what can go wrong at the relevant assertion level;

   c. Consider whether the risks are of a magnitude that could result in a material misstatement of the financial statements;

   d. Consider the likelihood that the risks could result in a material misstatement of the financial statements;

2. Internal control issues:

   a. Implications of a weak control environment -- weaknesses such as management's lack of competence may have a pervasive effect and require an overall response by the auditor;

   b. Controls may be directly or indirectly related to an assertion -- the more indirect the relationship, the less effective that control may be in preventing or detecting and correcting misstatements in that assertion;

   c. The auditor's understanding of internal control may raise doubts about the auditability of the entity's financial statements -- e.g., due to concerns about the integrity of management or concerns about the condition and reliability of an entity's records that suggest that sufficient appropriate evidence is unavailable.

B. Significant risks that require special audit consideration:

1. "Significant risks" -- those risks that, in the auditor's judgment, require special audit consideration. (Note that such risks arise in most audits.)

2. The auditor should consider the following matters in considering the nature of the risks:

   a. Whether the risk may relate to fraud;

   b. Whether the risk relates to recent significant economic, accounting, or other developments requiring specific attention;

   c. Whether the risk relates to the complexity of the transactions;

   d. Whether the risk involves related-party transactions;

   e. Whether the risk involves subjective measurement;

   f. Whether the risk involves significant nonroutine transactions that appear to be unusual for the entity.

3. Nonroutine transactions - risks of material misstatement may be greater for risks relating to

significant nonroutine transactions (e.g., greater management intervention for accounting treatment; greater manual intervention for data handling; complex calculations; and related-party transactions).

4. Significant judgment matters -- risks of material misstatement may be greater for risks relating to significant judgment matters (e.g., when accounting principles for accounting estimates or revenue recognition are subject to different interpretations; or when judgment may be subjective or complex, such as judgments about fair value).

5. Internal control considerations -- an understanding of the controls related to significant risks should provide the auditor with adequate information to develop an effective audit approach. (The auditor should consider the implications for the auditor's risk assessment if management has not appropriately implemented controls over significant risks -- the auditor should also communicate any significant deficiencies or material weaknesses appropriately.)

C. Risks for which substantive procedures alone do not provide sufficient appropriate audit evidence.

1. The auditor should evaluate the design and implementation of controls over those risks for which it is not possible to reduce detection risk at the relevant assertion level to an acceptably low level with substantive procedures alone.

2. When there is highly automated processing of routine business transactions with little or no manual intervention -- audit evidence may only be available in electronic form (e.g., when a significant amount of the entity's data is initiated, authorized, recorded, processed or reported electronically, such as in an integrated IT system).

D. Revision or risk assessment -- the auditor's assessment of the risks of material misstatement at the relevant assertion level is based on available evidence and may change as additional evidence is obtained (may need to modify planned audit procedures accordingly).

1. In performing tests of controls -- evidence may be obtained that controls are not operating effectively during the audit.

2. In performing substantive procedures -- misstatements may be detected that are inconsistent with the auditor's risk assessment.

V. Documentation

A. The auditor should document the following:

1. Discussion with the audit team about potential for misstatements due to error or fraud (including how and when particular discussions occurred, subject matter discussed, team members participating, and significant decisions reached as to planned responses);

2. Key elements of the understanding of each of the components of internal control to assess the risk of material misstatement, the sources of information for that understanding, and the risk assessment procedures performed;

3. The assessment of the risks of material misstatement (both at the financial statement level and at the relevant assertion level) and the basis for that assessment;

4. The risks identified and related controls evaluated.

B. Form of documentation -- a matter of professional judgment (may include narrative descriptions, questionnaires, checklists, and flowcharts):

1. Factors affecting the form and extent of documentation -- nature, size, and complexity of the entity and its environment, including its internal control; also affected by the specific audit methodology and technology used in the audit work;

2. More extensive documentation is normally required when dealing with a complex entity and when performing extensive audit procedures (e.g., documentation in the form of a memorandum may be sufficient when the information system makes limited use of IT or for which few transactions are processed).

VI. Effective Date -- for audits of financial statements for periods beginning on or after 12/15/06 (earlier application is permitted).

AU315 (SAS 84) - Predecessor Successor Communications

I. Applicability -- when an auditor is considering an engagement to audit (or re-audit) financial statements according to GAAS.

> **Definitions:**
> *Predecessor*: An auditor who has reported on the most recently issued audited financial statements (Not applicable if the most recent audited financial statements are more than 2 years prior to the period to be audited by the successor.); or an auditor who has resigned or declined to stand for reappointment or whose services have been terminated.
>
> *Successor*: An auditor who is considering accepting an engagement (or who has already accepted, subject to communicating with the predecessor as required).

II. Change of Auditors -- the successor auditor should not accept an engagement without evaluating the (required) communications with the predecessor.

- **A.** The successor has the responsibility to initiate the communication - requires permission by the client (both for the successor to initiate the communication and for the predecessor to respond fully).
  - **1.** The communication can be written or verbal.
  - **2.** Refusal by the client to give required permission should be evaluated in deciding whether to accept the engagement.
- **B.** When more than one auditor is considering the engagement, the predecessor is not expected to respond until a successor auditor has been selected.
- **C.** Predecessor's response may be limited - due to unusual circumstances (e.g., legal liability or disciplinary hearings); successor should consider the implications of a limited response before accepting the engagement.
- **D.** The following (required) topics should be addressed:
  - **1.** Matters bearing on the integrity of management;
  - **2.** Disagreements with management over accounting or auditing matters;
  - **3.** Any communications with those charged with governance (e.g., the audit committee) about fraud, illegal acts, and internal control matters;
  - **4.** The predecessor's understanding of the reasons for the change in auditors.
- **E.** Other communications may assist in planning - not required, but advisable. (The timing is more flexible and can even occur after accepting the audit.)
  - **1.** Successor should usually request that the client authorize access to the predecessor's working papers.
  - **2.** Predecessor should usually permit review of working papers, especially related to planning, internal control, audit results, and analysis of balance sheet accounts having on-going audit significance.
  - **3.** The extent of this access is a matter for the predecessor's judgment.

III. Successor Fully Responsible -- Successor should not refer to the predecessor as a (partial) basis for the successor's conclusions - the successor is fully responsible for the nature, timing, and extent of the audit procedures and the related conclusions.

- **A. Re-audits --** of previously audited financial statements.

1. **Auditor Roles --** The auditor considering such an engagement is a "successor" and the auditor reporting on those financial statements is a "predecessor."

2. **Access to Previous Papers --** Successor should request access to the predecessor's working papers -- the extent of such access by the predecessor is a matter of judgment.

IV. Predecessor Misstatements -- Discovery of possible misstatements in connection with a predecessor auditor's report.

A. Successor should ask the client to inform the predecessor of the situation and try to arrange a meeting with the three parties involved for resolution.

B. If client refuses or if successor is unsatisfied with the resolution -- successor should evaluate implications for the engagement and whether to resign.

V. Appendices -- The SAS includes two appendices with "illustrative" acknowledgment letters - these are presented for illustrative purposes only and neither letter is required by professional standards.

A. Illustrative client consent and acknowledgment letter - the predecessor auditor may wish to request such a consent letter **from the (former) client** to reduce misunderstandings about the scope of the communications being authorized.

B. Illustrative successor auditor acknowledgment letter - the predecessor auditor may wish to request such a letter **from the successor auditor** regarding the use of the working papers.

AU316 (SAS 99) - Consideration of Fraud

I. **Introduction and Overview --** SAS 99 supersedes SAS 82, issued in 1997. (The effective date is for audits of financial statements for periods beginning on or after December 15, 2002.)

A. The SAS describes the characteristics of fraud including (1) fraudulent financial reporting and (2) misappropriation of assets.

B. Emphasizes the importance of exercising professional skepticism.

C. Requires **discussion** of the risks of material misstatement due to fraud among engagement personnel as part of planning the audit.

D. **Requirements --** Requires the auditor to gather information to identify the risks of material misstatement due to fraud:

1. Responding to the results of the assessment - requires the auditor to evaluate the entity's programs and controls that address the risks of material misstatement due to fraud;

2. Evaluating the audit evidence - requires the auditor to assess the risks of material misstatement due to fraud throughout the audit and to evaluate whether the accumulated evidence at the end of the audit affects that assessment;

3. Provides guidance about communicating fraud-related matters to management, the audit committee, and others;

4. Provides guidance about documenting the auditor's consideration of fraud.

II. **Description and Characteristics of Fraud --** General comments:

A. Definition - fraud is an intentional act that results in a material misstatement in financial statements being audited (intent may be difficult to determine).

B. Legal determination - auditors do not make a legal determination of whether fraud has occurred. (Auditors are specifically concerned with material misstatements to the financial statements.)

C. Basic responsibility: "The auditor has a responsibility to plan and perform the audit to obtain reasonable assurance about whether the financial statements are free of material misstatement."

D. **Two types of fraud are relevant**

1. **Fraudulent financial reporting** - misstatements or omissions of amounts or disclosures designed to deceive financial statement users (includes intentional misapplication of GAAP, falsification of supporting records, and misrepresentations or omissions affecting the financial statements);

2. **Misappropriation of assets** - also called theft, embezzlement, or defalcation.

E. **Associated Conditions --** Conditions generally associated with the occurrence of fraud:

1. **Incentive** - management has an inceptive or pressure to commit fraud;

2. **Opportunity** - fraud may occur due to ineffective controls or management override;

3. **Rationalization** - individuals may have personal characteristics (an attitude or values) that permit them to commit a fraudulent act.

F. **Difficulty in detecting fraud --** auditors are not trained in authenticating documents or verifying signatures, etc.

1. Fraud may be concealed through collusion (among management, employees, or others).

2. Reports alleging fraud may not be reliable (depends on motives).

3. Procedures that are effective for detecting an "error" may not be effective for detecting "fraud" - evidence that appears to be valid may be fraudulent.

III. Importance of exercising skepticism

- **A.** "Professional skepticism" is an attitude that includes a questioning mind and a critical assessment of audit evidence.
- **B.** Exercise professional skepticism in gathering and evaluating evidence - "An auditor should not be satisfied with less-than-persuasive evidence because of a belief that management is honest."

IV. Discussing Potential for Material Fraud -- Discussion among engagement personnel regarding the risks of fraud - key members of the audit team should discuss the potential for material fraud (and this communication should continue throughout the audit):

- **A.** "Brainstorm" about how and where financial statements could be affected;
- **B.** Emphasize the importance of maintaining professional skepticism;
- **C.** Discuss the internal and external factors that provide an incentive/pressure to commit fraud, provide the opportunity, and a culture/attitude that might rationalize fraud;
- **D.** Discuss the risk of management override of internal controls;
- **E.** Discuss how the auditor might respond to the risks of material misstatement due to fraud.

V. Obtaining the Information Needed to Identify the Risks of Material Fraud

- **A. Make inquiries of management** and others within the entity about risks of fraud - and modify the management representation letter appropriately to address these issues:
  1. Whether management has knowledge of fraud or suspected fraud;
  2. Whether management is aware of allegations of fraud or suspected fraud;
  3. Management's understanding about the risks of fraud within the entity;
  4. Programs and controls that the entity has established to mitigate specific fraud risks;
  5. Whether any particular operating locations/segments have higher risk of fraud (nature and extent of monitoring of those multiple locations);
  6. Whether (and how) management communicates to employees about ethical issues;
  7. Whether management has reported to the audit committee on how internal controls prevent, deter, or detect material fraud;
  8. Inquire directly of the audit committee about its views about the risk of fraud and whether it has any knowledge (or suspicions) about fraud and how the audit committee exercises oversight regarding such matters.
  9. Inquire of appropriate internal audit personnel about their views of the risks of material fraud, relevant procedures performed, whether management has responded satisfactorily to any concerns, and whether the internal auditors have knowledge or suspicions of fraud.
- **B. Making inquiries of others (outside of management) --** This may give the auditor a different perspective that is helpful since management is often in the best position to perpetrate fraud. Personnel considered should include:
  1. Operating personnel not directly involved with financial reporting.
  2. Employees involved with complex or unusual transactions.
  3. In-house legal counsel.
- **C. Inconsistent Responses --** When responses are inconsistent – the auditor should obtain additional evidence to resolve the inconsistencies.
- **D. Consider the results** of analytical procedures performed in audit planning:
  1. Consider any unexpected or unusual results for analytical procedures to identify the risks of material misstatement due to fraud;
  2. Perform analytical procedures to identify unexpected or unusual relationships involving revenue accounts (e.g., compare sales volume with production capacity; perform a trend analysis of revenues by month and sales returns by month during the year and shortly after year-end).

E. **Consider "fraud risk factors" --** conditions that indicate incentives/pressures to commit fraud, opportunities to perpetrate fraud, and/or attitudes/rationalizations to justify fraud:

1. The presence of fraud risk factors does not necessarily indicate fraud;
2. Examples given are not exhaustive, so auditor may consider others;
3. Use professional judgment in assessing the risks of material fraud.

F. **Consider other helpful information in identifying risks of material fraud --** such as the acceptance/continuance of clients and reviews of interim financial statements.

VI. **Identifying Risks that May Result in Material Fraud --** involves professional judgment in considering the type of risk (fraudulent reporting v. misappropriation of assets), the significance of the risk (materiality), the likelihood of the risk, and the pervasiveness of the risk (whether it applies to the financial statements as a whole or to specific elements).

A. **Using the information gathered to identify risks of material fraud**

1. Identification of fraud risks may be influenced by size, complexity and ownership characteristics of the entity;
2. Auditor should evaluate whether the risk are applicable to the financial statements as a whole or to specific financial statement elements - relating risks to specific elements will help in designing audit procedures;
3. Certain elements will be inherently riskier due to the high degree of management judgment and subjectivity.

B. **Presume risk of material misstatement --** Improper revenue recognition is presumed to represent a fraud risk — the auditor should ordinarily presume a risk of material misstatement due to fraud related to revenue recognition (either overstatement or understatement of revenues).

C. **Consider the risk of management override of controls --** auditor should address this risk apart from any conclusions about other identified risks.

VII. **Assess the Identified Risks After Evaluating the Applicable Programs and Controls**

A. **Evaluate Programs and Controls --** Auditor should evaluate whether entity programs and controls related to identified risks of material fraud have been suitably designed and placed in operation.

B. **Context --** Consider whether such programs and controls mitigate (or exacerbate) the identified risks of material fraud - in other words, assess the risks of material fraud in light of the evaluation of applicable programs and controls.

VIII. **Responding to the Results of the Risk Assessment**

A. **Overall responses to the** risk of **material fraud** - general considerations:

1. Assignment of personnel and supervision - Staffing should be commensurate with the assessed risks (may need to assign people having more experience or specialized skills, such as forensic and IT specialists);
2. Accounting principles - consider management's selection of measurement principles, especially in subjective or complex areas;
3. Predictability of auditing procedures - auditor should incorporate a degree of unpredictability in selecting audit procedures (e.g., adjust the timing of testing, use different sampling methods, perform procedures at different locations or on an unannounced basis, test balances not typically tested, etc.).

B. **Nature, Timing, and Extent --** Responses involving the nature, timing, and extent of audit procedures:

1. Substantive procedures and tests of operating effectiveness may be affected by the risks of material fraud (i.e., audit risk generally cannot be reduced to an appropriately low level through tests of control, due to the possibility of management override of controls);

2. The auditor's responses to identified risks may affect the nature, timing, and/or extent of audit procedures and may include more evidence from independent sources outside the entity, physical inspection of certain assets, more use of computer-assisted audit techniques to extend testing of electronic transactions and files, etc.;
3. The auditor may want to make oral inquiries of major customers and suppliers in addition to sending confirmation requests or may send confirmation requests to a specific party within an organization.

C. Additional examples of responses to identified risks of fraudulent reporting

1. Revenue recognition:
   a. Use disaggregated data to perform substantive analytical procedures related to revenue;
   b. Confirm relevant terms of contracts and the absence of side agreements;
   c. Inquire of the sales and marketing personnel or in-house counsel regarding unusual terms of sales/shipments near year-end;
   d. Perform appropriate sales and inventory cut-off procedures.
2. Inventory quantities - may need to verify contents in boxes or determine that hollow spots are not present; may need to verify the purity, grade or concentration of certain inventories.
3. Management estimates - may need to supplement other audit evidence obtained in subjective areas (e.g., may engage a specialist or may evaluate the reasonableness of prior periods' estimates on point).

D. Additional examples of responses to identified risks of **misappropriation of assets** - usually test the operating effectiveness of relevant controls and may choose to inspect related assets at or near year-end.

E. Further Responses -- Responses that further address the risk of management override of controls:

1. Examine journal entries and other adjustments for evidence of misstatement:
   a. Design appropriate procedures - obtain an understanding of the entity's reporting process and controls over adjusting entries, identify the journal entries for testing, and inquire of relevant personnel about unusual activities related to journal entries;
   b. Obtain an understanding of controls over adjustments - determine whether they are suitably designed and placed in operation;
   c. Nonstandard journal entries (e.g., for nonrecurring transactions) might not be subject to the same control - consider testing these;
   d. Usually audit testing should focus on adjustments near year-end, but the auditor might need to extend testing throughout the year.
2. Review accounting estimates for biases that could cause misstatement - perform a retrospective review of the prior year's estimates for indication of bias.
3. Evaluate the business rationale for significant unusual transactions - whether the form is overly complex, whether management has discussed the transaction with the audit committee, whether management is more focused on the accounting treatment than the economics of the transaction, whether the transaction is with related parties that do not have separate substance.

IX. Evaluating Audit Evidence

A. Assess risks of material fraud throughout the audit - conditions may be identified during fieldwork that affect the auditor's risk assessment:

1. Discrepancies in the accounting records - including improperly recorded transactions, unsupported transactions/balances, tips or complaints, etc.;
2. Conflicting or missing evidential matter - including missing documents, unavailable original document (copies only), altered documents, etc.;
3. Problematic or unusual relationships between auditor and management - including lack of cooperation, denial of access, undue time pressures, etc.

B. **Evaluate Analytical Procedures --** Evaluate whether analytical procedures (performed as substantive tests or in the overall review stage) indicate a previously unrecognized risk of material fraud – this requires professional judgment:

1. Unusual relationships involving year-end revenue and income may be relevant – e.g., unusually large amounts recorded near the end of the reporting period or income that is inconsistent with trends in cash from operations;
2. Changes in inventory, accounts payable, sales, or cost of sales - a perpetrator of fraud may not be able to manipulate all of the related accounts, causing unusual relationships;
3. Comparison of the entity's profitability to industry trends;
4. Unexpected relationship between sales volume (from the accounting records) and production statistics (from operations personnel).

C. **Evaluate risks of material fraud near the end of fieldwork --** evaluate whether the accumulated evidence affects the earlier assessment of the risks of material fraud (primarily a qualitative judgment).

D. **Responding to misstatements that may be the result of fraud --** evaluate whether senior management is involved and consider the implications to the assessment of the effectiveness of controls and to the nature, timing, and extent of substantive procedures.

1. If the auditor believes the misstatement may be the result of fraud and that the effect is material, or if the auditor has been unable to determine if it is material:
   - **a.** Attempt to gather additional evidence to determine materiality;
   - **b.** Consider the implications to other aspects of the audit;
   - **c.** Discuss the matter with the appropriate level of management (at least one level above those believed to be involved) and the audit committee (especially if senior management is involved);
   - **d.** May suggest that the client should consult with legal counsel.
2. Consider withdrawing from the engagement - depends upon the implications regarding management's integrity and the cooperation of management and the board of directors in taking appropriate action; auditor may wish to consult with legal counsel.

> **Note:**
> The AICPA states that "... it is not possible to definitively describe when withdrawal is appropriate."

X. Communicating About Possible Fraud to Management, the Audit Committee, and Others

A. **Inform Management --** Whenever there is evidence that fraud may exist - the auditor should inform the appropriate level of management.

B. **Inform Audit Committee --** When fraud causes a material misstatement or whenever senior management is involved in the fraud (even if not material) - the auditor should inform the audit committee. (Also consider whether any related internal control issues constitute a "reportable condition" that should be communicated to senior management and the audit committee.)

C. **Other Parties --** Disclosure of possible fraud to parties other than senior management and the audit committee is ordinarily inappropriate (usually precluded by legal and ethical responsibilities related to confidentiality) - a duty to disclose may exist, however:

1. To comply with certain legal and regulatory requirements;
2. To a successor auditor when communication has been authorized;
3. In response to a valid subpoena;
4. To a funding agency in accordance with Government Audit Standards.

XI. Documenting the Auditor's Consideration of Fraud -- The auditor should document the following matters

A. The discussion among engagement personnel about fraud in planning the audit - including how and when the discussion occurred, the team members who participated, and the subject matter discussed;

B. The procedures performed to obtain information necessary to assess the risks of material fraud;

C. Specific risks of material fraud that were identified, including a description of the auditor's response to those identified risks;

D. Reasons supporting the auditor's conclusion if improper revenue recognition was not identified as a risk of material misstatement due to fraud;

E. The results of procedures performed to further address the risk of management override of controls;

F. Other conditions and analytical relationships that caused the auditor to perform additional auditing procedures;

G. The nature of the communication about fraud made to management, the audit committee, and others.

AU317 (SAS 54) - Illegal Acts

I. **Basic Audit Responsibilities Related to Illegal Acts**

A. Definition of **"illegal acts"** - violations of laws or government regulations by management or employees acting on behalf of the entity.

B. Dependence on legal judgment - the determination of illegality is usually outside the auditor's expertise; however, the auditor's expertise may provide a basis for recognition that some client acts "may" be illegal.

C. Relation to financial statements - "the further removed an illegal act is from the events and transactions ordinarily reflected in the financial statements, the less likely the auditor is to become aware of the act or to recognize its possible illegality."

1. Auditor's responsibility - to consider laws and regulations that have a **direct and material effect** on the financial statements (essentially the same as for errors and fraud).

2. Other illegal acts may have material, but indirect effects on the financial statements (e.g., related to the entity's operating aspects) - the auditor ordinarily does not have a sufficient basis for recognizing such violations.

II. **Auditor's Consideration of the Possibility of Illegal Acts --** -B. Nature, timing, and extent regarding the auditor's responsibility to detect, consider the effects of, and report illegal acts that have material but **indirect** effects on an entity's financial statements.

A. Audit procedures in the absence of evidence concerning possible illegal acts:

1. Usually do not include detailed procedures specifically to detect illegal acts;

2. Usually make inquiries of management about the entity's compliance with laws and regulations (and include appropriate written representations in the "management representations letter"); read minutes of meetings of those charged with governance; obtain attorney's letter regarding legal matters.

B. Audit procedures when evidence of possible illegal acts exists - if specific information comes to the auditor's attention about such possible illegal acts, apply appropriate audit procedures to ascertain whether an illegal act has occurred:

1. Circumstances that may raise questions about possible illegal acts:

a. Unauthorized transactions, improperly recorded transactions, or transactions that do not maintain accountability for assets;

b. Investigation by a governmental agency or payment of fines, etc.;

c. Reports of regulatory agencies that identify violations;

d. Large payments for unspecified services to consultants, affiliates, or employees;

e. Sales commissions or agents' fees that appear to be excessive;

f. Unusually large payments in cash (or transfers);

g. Unexplained payments made to government officials or employees;

h. Failure to file tax returns or pay common government duties or fees.

2. Audit procedures in response to evidence of such possible illegal acts:

a. When becoming aware of a possible illegal act - the auditor should obtain an understanding of the nature of the act, the circumstances in which it occurred, and other information to evaluate the financial statement effects;

b. Inquire of management (at a level above those involved, if possible);

c. If management does not provide satisfactory information that there has been no illegal act - the auditor should consult with the entity's lawyer or other specialist about the matter and apply any additional procedures necessary (such as examining supporting documents; confirming significant information with other parties to the transaction; examining authorization of the transaction; and considering whether there may be other similar transactions/events).

III. Auditor's Responsibilities Regarding Detected Illegal Acts

A. Consider the effects on the financial statements (including the adequacy of disclosure and any fines, penalties, and damages) - consider quantitative and qualitative aspects of materiality.

B. Consider the implications to other aspects of the audit engagement - such as the reliability of management representations. (The implications of the illegal act depend on the relationship of the "perpetration and concealment," if any, of the illegal act to specific control procedures and the level of management or employees involved.)

C. Communication with those charged with governance:

1. Auditor should determine that they are informed of detected illegal acts (The auditor need not communicate matters that are "clearly inconsequential.") - the communication should describe the act, the circumstances of its occurrence, and the effect on the financial statements; if senior management is involved in an illegal act, the auditor should communicate directly with those charged with governance;
2. Communication may be written or verbal (but oral communication should be documented).

D. Effects on the audit report:

1. If the effect of an illegal act is not properly reported - issue a qualified or adverse opinion (due to a GAAP departure);
2. If unable to obtain sufficient appropriate evidence to evaluate the effects - usually disclaim (due to a scope limitation);
3. If the entity refuses to accept the auditor's modified report (either for a GAAP departure or for a scope limitation) - the auditor should withdraw from the engagement (and communicate the reasons in writing to those charged with governance);
4. The auditor may also decide to withdraw from the engagement if the entity does not take the remedial action considered necessary in the circumstances.

E. Responsibility to inform outside parties (that is, other than senior management and those charged with governance):

1. General rule - such disclosure is not permitted (due to confidentiality);
2. Exceptions - when a change in auditors requires reporting on SEC Form 8 K; when a successor auditor inquires of predecessor; in response to subpoena; and to a funding agency in accordance with requirements for the audits of entities receiving financial assistance from a government agency;

F. Responsibilities in other circumstances - an auditor may accept an engagement that has greater responsibility for detecting illegal acts than specified by AU317 (e.g., may be engaged to perform an audit in accordance with the Single Audit Act of 1984, whereby the auditor is responsible for testing and reporting on the governmental unit's compliance with applicable laws and regulations for federal financial assistance programs);

AU318 (SAS 110) - Performing Audit Procedures in Response to Assessed Risks

I. **Introduction --** This SAS "establishes standards and provides guidance on determining overall responses and designing and performing further audit procedures to respond to the assessed risk of material misstatement at the financial statement and relevant assertion levels in a financial statement audit, and on evaluating the sufficiency and appropriateness of the audit evidence obtained."

A. Overview of this SAS:

1. Overall responses -- provides guidance in responding to risks of material misstatement at the financial statement level;

2. Audit procedures responsive to risks of material misstatement at the relevant assertion level -- provides guidance in determining the nature, timing, and extent of further audit procedures, including tests of the operating effectiveness of controls and substantive procedures; (The nature, timing, and extent of these audit procedures involve the auditor's professional judgment.)

3. Evaluating the sufficiency and appropriateness of the audit evidence obtained -- provides guidance in evaluating whether the risk assessments are appropriate and to conclude whether sufficient appropriate evidence has been obtained;

4. Documentation -- provides guidance as to required documentation.

B. To reduce audit risk to an acceptably low level -- the auditor should determine overall responses to the assessed risks of material misstatement at the financial statement level and should design/perform further audit procedures that are responsive to the assessed risks of material misstatement at the relevant assertion level.

II. **Overall responses to address the risks of material misstatement at the financial statement level**

A. May include emphasizing to the audit team the need for professional skepticism; assigning more experienced staff to the engagement; using specialists; providing more supervision; using more unpredictable audit procedures; making general changes to the nature, timing, or extent of further audit procedures (such as performing substantive procedures at year end, rather than at an interim date).

B. Understanding the control environment -- affects the assessment of the risks of material misstatement at the financial statement level.

C. Effect on the auditor's general approach -- these considerations influence the auditor's decision to use a "substantive approach" or to use a "combined approach" that uses tests of controls and substantive procedures.

III. **Audit procedures responsive to risks of material misstatement at the relevant assertion level**

A. General comments -- as the risk of material misstatement increases, the audit evidence should be more reliable and relevant.

1. Considerations in designing further audit procedures to address the assessed risks at the relevant assertion level -- significance of the risk; likelihood of a material misstatement; characteristics of the class of transactions, account balance, or disclosure involved; nature of the entity's specific controls (whether automated or manual); whether the auditor plans to perform tests of controls.

2. Basis for the auditor's approach -- the assessment of risks at the relevant assertion level provides a basis for considering the appropriate audit approach (i.e., whether to use a "substantive approach" or a "combined approach" involving tests of the operating effectiveness of controls and substantive procedures).

3. Regardless of approach used -- substantive procedures must be performed for all relevant assertions related to each material class of transactions, account balance, or disclosure. (Effective controls reduce, but do not eliminate, the need for substantive procedures.)

B. Considering the nature, timing, and extent of further audit procedures.

1. **Nature**
    - a. Refers to the purpose of further audit procedures (i.e., tests of control or substantive procedures) and their type (i.e., inspection, observation, inquiry, confirmation, recalculation, reperformance, or analytical procedures).
    - b. Should obtain evidence about the accuracy and completeness of information produced by the entity's information system when that information is used in performing audit procedures (such as analytical procedures or tests of controls).
2. **Timing**
    - a. Performing the substantive procedures at (or nearer to) year end is usually more effective with an increased risk of material misstatement.
    - b. However, performing the audit procedures before the end of the period may assist in identifying issues sooner (and resolving them) or developing an effective audit approach.
    - c. Certain audit procedures can only be performed at (or after) the end of the period -- e.g., examining adjustments made during financial statement preparation or agreeing the financial statement elements to the accounting records.
3. **Extent --** refers to the quantity of an audit procedure to be performed (e.g., sample size).
    - a. Extent is determined by the auditor's judgment based on the tolerable misstatement, the assessed risk of material misstatement, and the planned degree of assurance.
    - b. CAATs -- the auditor may use computer-assisted audit techniques (CAATs) to provide extensive testing of electronic transactions and account files (may use such techniques to sample, to identify transactions with specific characteristics, or to test an entire population).

C. Tests of controls -- to determine the operating effectiveness of controls.

1. General comments:
    - a. The auditor should perform tests of controls when the auditor's risk assessment includes an expectation of the operating effectiveness of controls -- these tests should be performed only on those controls determined to be suitably designed to prevent or detect a material misstatement in a relevant assertion;
    - b. The auditor should also perform tests of controls when substantive procedures alone do not provide sufficient appropriate evidence at the relevant assertion level -- e.g., when the entity uses information technology (IT) and no documentation of transactions exists other than the IT system;
    - c. Testing the operating effectiveness of controls is different than determining that controls have been implemented -- the auditor should obtain evidence about how controls were applied at relevant times, the consistency with which they were applied, and by whom or by what means they were applied;
2. Nature of tests of controls -- ordinarily include procedures such as inquiries of entity personnel; inspection of documents, reports, or electronic files, indicating performance of the control; observation of the application of the control; and auditor reperformance of the control.
    - a. Inquiry alone is not sufficient -- perform other procedures in combination with inquiry to test controls.
    - b. When operating effectiveness is not documented (e.g., for assignment of authority/responsibility or control activities performed by a computer) -- evidence about operating effectiveness can be obtained from inquiry and other audit procedures such as observation or the use of CAATs.
    - c. "Dual purpose test" -- concurrent performance of a test of controls and a test of details on the same transaction (should consider how the outcome of the tests of controls may impact the substantive procedures to be performed).

d. Misstatements detected by performing substantive procedures should be considered when assessing the operating effectiveness of related controls -- a material misstatement not detected by an entity's controls should be viewed at least as a significant deficiency and a strong indicator of a material weakness. (The absence of misstatement does not necessarily indicate that controls were operating effectively.)

3. Timing of tests of controls -- when testing controls at a particular time, the auditor obtains evidence that the controls operated effectively only at that time.

   a. When obtaining evidence about the effectiveness of controls for an interim period -- determine what audit evidence is required for the remaining period (e.g., obtain evidence about the nature and extent of significant changes in internal control, including changes in the information systems, processes and personnel subsequent to the interim period).

   b. If planning to rely on controls that have changed since last tested -- test the operating effectiveness of those controls currently.

   c. If planning to rely on controls that have **not changed** since last tested -- test the operating effectiveness of such controls at least once in every third year in the annual audits (should not allow more than 2 years to elapse before retesting such controls).

   d. In considering whether to use audit evidence obtained in prior audits about the effectiveness of controls (and how much time can elapse before retesting) -- the auditor should consider:

      i. The effectiveness of other elements of control;

      ii. Risks arising from the nature of the control (e.g., whether automated or manual);

      iii. The effectiveness of IT controls;

      iv. The nature and extent of deviations from the control in prior audits;

      v. Whether changed circumstances might affect the effectiveness of a control that has not changed;

      vi. The risk of material misstatement and the extent of reliance on the control.

   e. Factors that ordinarily result in not relying on audit evidence obtained in prior audits (or shortening the period for retesting):

      i. A weak control environment;

      ii. Weak IT general controls;

      iii. Weak monitoring controls;

      iv. A significant manual element to the relevant controls;

      v. Personnel changes that significantly affect the application of the control;

      vi. Changing circumstances that indicate a need for change in the control.

   f. When there are multiple controls for which the auditor plans to use audit evidence obtained in prior audits -- the auditor should test the effectiveness of some of the controls each year.

   g. When the auditor identifies a significant risk of material misstatement at the relevant assertion level and plans to rely on the effectiveness of controls that mitigate that risk -- the auditor should obtain audit evidence about the operating effectiveness of those controls in the current period.

4. Extent of tests of controls:

   a. Factors the auditor may consider in determining this extent:

      i. The frequency of the performance of the control during the period;

      ii. The length of time during the audit that the auditor is relying on the control;

      iii. The relevance and reliability of audit evidence obtained regarding the effectiveness of the control at the relevant assertion level;

iv. The extent to which audit evidence is obtained from tests of other controls at the relevant assertion level;

v. The extent to which the auditor plans to rely on the effectiveness of the control to reduce substantive procedures;

vi. The expected deviation from the control -- if the expected deviation is too high, the auditor may determine that tests of controls may be inappropriate;

b. When a control is applied on a "transaction basis" (e.g., matching approved purchase orders to suppliers' invoices) and if the control operates frequently -- use an audit sampling technique to test the operating effectiveness of the control; when a control is applied on a "periodic basis" (e.g., monthly reconciliation of accounts receivable ledger to the general ledger) -- perform procedures appropriate for testing smaller populations.

c. IT processing is inherently consistent -- when an automated control is functioning as intended, perform tests to determine that the control continues to function effectively (e.g., test that relevant general controls are effective, that unauthorized changes to the program have not been made, etc.).

D. Substantive procedures -- to detect material misstatements at the relevant assertion level.

1. General comments -- should plan and perform substantive procedures to be responsive to the assessed risk of material misstatement.

   a. Types of substantive procedures -- (1) tests of details of classes of transactions, account balances, and disclosures; and (2) substantive analytical procedures.

   b. Perform substantive procedures for all relevant assertions related to each material class of transactions, account balance, and disclosure (regardless of the assessed risk of material misstatement) -- there are inherent limitations to internal control and the assessment of risk is judgmental.

   c. Substantive procedures should include the following related to the financial reporting process -- (1) agree the financial statement information to the underlying accounting records; and (2) examine material journal entries and other adjustments made during the preparation of the financial statements.

2. Nature of substantive procedures – these should be responsive to the planned level of detection risk.

   a. Substantive procedures -- consist of (1) tests of details and (2) substantive analytical procedures.

   b. Should consider testing the controls over the preparation of information used in connection with analytical procedures.

3. Timing of substantive procedures -- may be performed at an interim date or at final (after year end).

   a. Performing substantive procedures at an interim date increases the risk that misstatements at year end are undetected -- should perform additional substantive procedures (or substantive procedures combined with tests of control) to provide a reasonable basis for extending the audit conclusions from interim.

   b. Considerations that might affect the decision to perform substantive procedures at an interim date include: (1) the control environment and other relevant controls; (2) availability of information at a later date for the additional procedures; (3) the objective of the substantive procedure; (4) the assessed risk of material misstatement; (5) the nature of the class of transactions or account balance and relevant assertions; and (6) the ability of the auditor to reduce the risk of undetected misstatements.

   c. Need not necessarily test the operating effectiveness of internal controls in order to extend the conclusions from the interim date -- however, the auditor should consider whether only performing additional substantive procedures is sufficient.

   d. When planning to perform substantive analytical procedures for the period following the interim date -- consider whether the period-end balances are reasonably predictable as to amount, relative significance, and composition.

   e. Substantive procedures performed in a prior audit provide little or no evidence for the current period -- may be relevant in the current period if the prior audit evidence and related subject matter has not changed (e.g., prior evidence about the purchase cost of a building).

4. Extent of the performance of substantive procedures is usually thought of in terms of sample size, which is affected by the planned level of detection risk, tolerable misstatement, expected misstatement, and nature of the population.

E. Adequacy of presentation and disclosure -- the auditor should consider whether the financial statements are presented with appropriate classification and description of financial information (including adequate disclosure of material matters in conformity with GAAP).

IV. **Evaluating the Sufficiency and Appropriateness of the Audit Evidence Obtained --** an audit of financial statements is a cumulative and iterative process (the nature, timing, and extent of planned audit procedures may need to be modified).

A. Internal control implications -- identified misstatements from substantive procedures may alter the auditor's judgment about the effectiveness of controls.

B. Instances of fraud or error -- the auditor should not assume that an instance of fraud or error is an isolated occurrence (should consider the implications to the assessed risks of material misstatement and whether changes are warranted in the nature, timing, and extent of audit procedures to be performed).

C. Consider all relevant audit evidence -- regardless of whether it appears to corroborate or to contradict the relevant assertions in the financial statements.

D. The sufficiency and appropriateness of audit evidence as a basis for the auditor's conclusions are matters of professional judgment -- the auditor's judgment is influenced by such factors as the following:

1. The significance of the potential misstatement and its likelihood of having a material effect (individually or collectively);
2. The effectiveness of management's responses and controls to address the risks;
3. The experience gained in previous audits with such misstatements;
4. The results of audit procedures performed (including whether the procedures identified instances of fraud or error);
5. The source and reliability of available information;
6. The persuasiveness of the audit evidence obtained;
7. The understanding of the entity and its environment, including internal control;

E. Documentation -- the auditor should document the following:

1. The overall responses to address the assessed risk of misstatement at the financial statement level;
2. The nature, timing, and extent of the further audit procedures;
3. The linkage of those procedures with the assessed risks at the relevant assertion level;
4. The results of the audit procedures;
5. The conclusions reached in the current audit about the operating effectiveness of controls tested in a prior audit.

AU322 (SAS 65) - Internal Audit Function

I. **Obtaining an Understanding of the Internal Audit Function --** an important responsibility of the internal audit function is to monitor the performance of an entity's controls.

   A. When obtaining an understanding of internal control - the auditor should obtain an understanding of the internal audit function sufficient to identify the internal audit activities that are relevant to planning the audit.

   B. Necessary procedures will vary with circumstances - the auditor should ordinarily make inquiries of appropriate management and internal audit personnel and should review relevant documentation.

      1. Typical inquiries of management and internal auditors about the internal audit function:

         a. Organizational status within the entity;

         b. Application of professional standards;

         c. Audit plans (including nature, timing, and extent of work);

         d. Access to records and any limitations on the scope of their work.

      2. Review documentation:

         a. Internal audit's risk assessment and resource allocation processes;

         b. Internal audit's reports (related to the scope of internal audit work);

         c. Prior years' working papers of the external auditor.

   C. Determine the relevance of internal audit's activities to the financial statement audit.

      1. If the internal auditing activities are not relevant, the auditor need not consider the internal audit function further - unless the auditor requests the internal auditor's direct assistance.

      2. If internal audit's activities are relevant, the auditor should decide whether "reliance" on the entity's internal audit activities is efficient.

         a. If not efficient - the auditor need not consider the internal audit function further, unless requesting the internal auditor's direct assistance.

         b. If deemed efficient - the auditor must consider the effect upon the nature, timing, extent of audit work; requires procedures to test the quality and effectiveness of the internal auditor's work.

II. **Assessing the Competence and Objectivity of the Internal Auditors --** when the auditor decides that it would be efficient to consider how the internal auditors' work might affect the nature, timing, and extent of audit procedures.

   A. Competence - involves evaluating the internal auditor's education; certification(s); experience; supervision; evaluation of performance; quality of documentation, reports, and recommendations; etc.

   B. Objectivity - involves evaluating the organizational status of the internal audit function and its access to those charged with governance; and the entity's policies to maintain the individual internal auditor's objectivity in areas audited.

   C. In assessing competence and objectivity - the auditor usually considers (1) information obtained from previous experience with the internal audit function; (2) discussions with management; and (3) recent external quality reviews of the internal audit function's activities (may use professional internal auditing standards as criteria in making that assessment).

III. **Determine the Effect of the Internal Auditors' Work on the Financial Statement Audit**

   A. Related to understanding of internal control and risk assessment - at both the financial statement level and the account-balance or class-of-transaction level.

1. Financial statement level - some control issues have a pervasive effect and affect the auditor's overall audit strategy (the control environment and accounting system often have a pervasive effect); the entity's internal audit function may influence this overall assessment of risk and the auditor's decisions regarding the nature, timing, and extent of auditing procedures.

2. Account-balance or class-of-transaction level - the auditor should assess control risk for each of the significant assertions and performs tests of controls to support assessments below the maximum; when planning and performing tests of controls, the auditor may consider work performed by the internal auditors in specific audit areas.

B. Related to **substantive audit procedures** - the auditor may consider procedures performed by internal auditors to provide direct evidence about material misstatements in assertions about specific account balances or classes of transactions. (The results of such procedures may provide evidence for the auditor to consider in restricting detection risk for the related assertions.)

C. Extent of the effect of the internal auditor's work - the auditor's reliance on the internal auditor's work should be inversely related to:

1. The materiality of financial statement amounts involved;

2. The risk of material misstatement (consisting of inherent risk and control risk) involved;

3. The degree of subjectivity involved in the audit area in question.

D. Evaluating and testing the effectiveness of the internal auditor's work - the auditor should perform procedures to evaluate the quality and effectiveness of the internal auditors' work that significantly affects the nature, timing, and extent of the auditor's procedures.

E. Responsibility to report on the financial statements - still rests with the auditor. (This responsibility cannot be shared with the internal auditors, unlike using the work of other independent auditors.)

F. Coordinate audit work with the internal auditors - hold periodic meetings, provide access to internal auditors' working papers, review audit reports, etc.

IV. **Using the Internal Auditors to Provide Direct Assistance to the Auditor --** the internal auditors may assist the auditor in obtaining an understanding of internal control or in performing tests of controls or substantive tests.

A. When direct assistance is provided - the auditor should assess the internal auditors' competence and objectivity.

B. In such matters, the auditor should supervise, review, evaluate, and test the work of the internal auditors to the extent deemed appropriate.

AU324 (SAS 70) - Transactions by Service Organizations

Issued April, 1992 (Modified by SSAE No. 16 in 2010).

I. **Applicability** -- Applies specifically to a "user auditor" when auditing the financial statements of an entity that has outsourced the processing of its transactions to a service organization.

   A. Executing transactions and maintaining accountability; and/or recording transactions and processing related data

   B. Examples - bank trust departments, mortgage bankers (that service mortgages for others), IT service centers, etc.

II. **Responsibilities of User Auditors** -- Especially, in obtaining an understanding of the effect of the service organization on the internal control over financial reporting of the user entity; and in evaluating the availability of evidence.

   A. Effect of the service organization on the user entity's internal control over financial reporting - the degree of internal control interaction between the service organization and the user entity, plus the nature and materiality of the transactions involved influence the significance of the service organization's policies and procedures on the user entity's internal control.

   B. **Planning the audit** - the user auditor should consider the following:

      1. The financial statement assertions affected by the service organization;
      2. Nature of services - whether standardized and the number of user entities involved;
      3. Degree of interaction between the organizations involved;
      4. User organization's controls applied to the activities of the service organization;
      5. Terms of the contract between the organizations;
      6. Service organization's capabilities (performance, etc.);
      7. User auditor's experience with the service organization;
      8. Extent of auditable data in the user entity's possession;
      9. Existence of specific regulatory requirements beyond GAAS.

   C. **Assessing control risk** at the user entity.

      1. If information is not available to obtain a sufficient understanding of internal control - request additional specific information from the service organization (through the user entity).
      2. User auditor may assess control risk at less than the maximum level because of the policies and procedures either at the user entity or at the service organization (e.g., perhaps the user entity's controls over input and output).
      3. The service auditor's report may be useful in understanding the relevant internal control policies and procedures:
         a. By testing the user entity's controls;
         b. Service auditor's tests of operating effectiveness;
         c. User auditor's tests of the service organization's controls.
      4. User auditor is responsible for evaluating all evidence presented and assessing the effects on the user entity's internal control over financial reporting.

   D. **Substantive procedures** performed by the service auditors - procedures performed by service auditors related to balances and transactions may be used by the user auditor as audit evidence.

      1. Inquire about the service auditor's professional reputation;

2. User auditor may supplement an understanding of service auditor's procedures and conclusions by discussions with the service auditor (may request that service auditor perform "agreed-upon" procedures at the service organization, or else the user auditor can perform those procedures);
3. User auditor should ***not*** make reference to the service auditor's report - cannot make that division of responsibility!

AU325 (SAS 115) - Internal Control

"Communicating Internal Control Related Matters Identified in an Audit" - Issued: October, 2008.

I. **Supersedes SAS No. 112 Having the Same Name (issued May 2006) --** the purpose was to align the auditing standards with the attestation standards, specifically SSAE No. 15, "An Audit of Internal Control That is Integrated with an Audit of Financial Statements." (SSAE No. 15 aligns the AICPA terminology and guidance with that of the PCAOB.)

II. **Introduction --** AU325 applies whenever an auditor expresses an opinion (or disclaimer) on financial statements and provides guidance on communicating matters related to an entity's internal control over financial reporting.

   A. Controls related to the reliability of financial reporting are normally the controls that are relevant to the financial statement audit.

   B. Defines the terms "deficiency," "significant deficiency," and "material weakness."

   C. Provides guidance on evaluating the severity of control deficiencies.

   D. Requires the auditor to communicate (in writing) to management and those charged with governance, the significant deficiencies and material weaknesses identified in an audit.

      1. Auditors are not required to perform procedures to identify such deficiencies, nor do they express an opinion on the effectiveness of the entity's internal control.

      2. The auditor's awareness of such deficiencies varies with each audit (and is influenced by the nature, timing, and extent of procedures performed); and the design and formality of an entity's internal control varies with the entity's size, its industry, its culture, and management's philosophy.

III. **Definitions**

   A. **"Control deficiency" --** when the design or operation of a control does not allow management or employees, in the normal course of performing their assigned functions, to prevent or detect misstatements on a timely basis.

      1. "Deficiency in **design**" - when a control necessary to meet the control objective is missing; or when the control objective would not be met, even if the control operates as designed.

      2. "Deficiency in **operation**" - when a properly designed control does not operate as designed; or when the person performing the control does not have the authority or competence for effective performance of the control.

   B. **"Significant deficiency" --** a deficiency (or combination of deficiencies) in internal control that is less severe than a material weakness, yet important enough to merit attention by those charged with governance.

   C. **"Material weakness" --** a deficiency (or combination of deficiencies) in internal control such that there is a reasonable possibility that a material misstatement of the entity's financial statements will not be prevented, or will not be detected and corrected on a timely basis.

IV. **Evaluating control deficiencies identified as part of the audit --** the auditor must determine whether identified deficiencies (individually or in combination) are significant deficiencies or material weaknesses.

   A. The severity of a deficiency depends on (1) the magnitude of the potential misstatement and (2) whether there is a "reasonable possibility" that the controls will fail to prevent, or fail to detect and correct a misstatement. (Note: the severity of a deficiency does not depend on whether a misstatement actually occurred.)

   B. Risk factors that affect whether there is a reasonable possibility that a deficiency (or combination of deficiencies) will result in a misstatement include the following:

      1. The nature of the accounts, classes of transactions, disclosures, and assertions involved;

      2. The susceptibility of the related asset or liability to loss or fraud;

3. The subjectivity, complexity, or extent of judgment involved;
4. The interaction or relationship of the control with other controls;
5. The interaction among the deficiencies;
6. The possible future consequences of the deficiency.

C. Multiple control deficiencies affecting the same financial statement element or disclosure increase the likelihood of misstatement - the auditor should consider whether such multiple deficiencies collectively result in a significant deficiency or material weakness.

D. Compensating controls - the auditor may consider the possible mitigating effects of effective compensating controls that have been tested and evaluated in the audit. (Compensating controls limit the severity of the effects of a deficiency, but they do not eliminate the control deficiency.)

E. Indicators of material weaknesses include the following:

1. Identification of fraud involving senior management (whether material or not);
2. Restatement of previously issued financial statements to correct a material misstatement due to error or fraud;
3. Identification of a material misstatement in the financial statements by the auditor that would not have been identified by the entity's internal control;
4. Ineffective oversight of the entity's financial reporting and internal control by those charged with governance.

F. If the auditor determines that the deficiency is not a material weakness - consider whether "prudent officials" knowing the same facts/circumstances would agree.

V. Communication - Form, Content, and Timing

A. Significant deficiencies and material weaknesses identified in the audit must be communicated in writing to management and those charged with governance.

B. Timing - the required written communication is best made by the report release date and should be made no later than 60 days following the report release date. (The "report release date" is the date the auditor grants the entity permission to use the auditor's report in connection with the audited financial statements.)

C. Early communication - the auditor may communicate certain significant deficiencies and material weaknesses during the audit and early communication is not required to be in writing; however, the auditor must still communicate all significant deficiencies and material weaknesses in writing as describe above.

D. Other matters - the auditor may choose to communicate other matters that the auditor believes to be beneficial to the entity and these can be communicated in writing or verbally, but the auditor must document any such oral communication.

E. The written communication about significant deficiencies and material weaknesses should:

1. State that the purpose of the audit was to express an opinion on the financial statements, not to express an opinion on the effectiveness of internal control;
2. State that the auditor is not expressing an opinion on the effectiveness of internal control;
3. State that the auditor's consideration of internal control was not designed to identify all significant deficiencies or material weaknesses;
4. Include the definition of the terms material weakness and, where relevant, significant deficiency;
5. Identify the matters that are considered to be significant deficiencies and those that are considered to be material weaknesses;
6. State that the communication is intended solely for the use of management, those charged with governance, and others within the organization (i.e., it should not be used by anyone other than those specified parties) - if such a communication is required to be given to a governmental authority, the specific reference to that governmental authority may be added.

Note:
The auditor may include additional statements regarding the general inherent limitations of internal control, including the possibility of management override, but such comments are not required.

F. The auditor is permitted to add a comment to the written communication stating that no material weaknesses were identified (perhaps requested by the entity to submit to a governmental authority) - however, the auditor should not issue a written communication stating that no significant deficiencies were identified during the audit, due to the limited assurance provided by such a communication.

G. Management may issue a written response to the auditor's communication (perhaps due to a regulatory requirement) to indicate corrective action taken or planned or stating management's belief that the costs of correction exceed the benefits - if such a written response is included with the auditor's communication, the auditor should add a paragraph to disclaim an opinion on management's response.

Sample Written Communication About Internal Control Deficiencies:

In planning and performing our audit of the financial statements of ABC Company (the "Company") as of and for the year ended December 31, 20XX, in accordance with auditing standards generally accepted in the United States of America, we considered the Company's internal control over financial reporting (internal control) as a basis for designing our auditing procedures for the purpose of expressing our opinion on the financial statements, but not for the purpose of expressing an opinion on the effectiveness of the Company's internal control. Accordingly, we do not express an opinion on the effectiveness of the Company's internal control.

Our consideration of internal control was for the limited purpose described in the preceding paragraph and was not designed to identify all deficiencies in internal control that might be significant deficiencies or material weaknesses. For this reason no assurance can be given that all deficiencies, significant deficiencies, or material weaknesses have been identified. However, as discussed below, we identified certain deficiencies in internal control that we consider to be material weaknesses (and other deficiencies that we consider to be significant deficiencies - *add this phrase only if applicable*).

A deficiency in internal control exists when the design or operation of a control does not allow management or employees, in the normal course of performing their assigned functions, to prevent, or to detect and correct misstatements on a timely basis. A material weakness is a deficiency, or a combination of deficiencies, in internal control, such that there is a reasonable possibility that a material misstatement of the entity's financial statements will not be prevented, or be detected and corrected on a timely basis. (We consider the following deficiencies in the Company's internal control to be material weaknesses:)

(*Describe the material weaknesses that were identified.*)

(A significant deficiency is a deficiency, or a combination of deficiencies, in internal control that is less severe than a material weakness, yet important enough to merit attention by those charged with governance. We consider the following deficiencies to be significant deficiencies in internal control:)

(*Describe the significant deficiencies that were identified.*)

This communication is intended solely for the information and use of management, (*identify the body or individuals charged with governance*), others within the organization, and (*identify any specified governmental authorities*) and is not intended to be, nor should it be used by anyone other than these specified parties.

AU326 (SAS 106) - Audit Evidence

I. **Provides Guidance Regarding the Third Standard of Fieldwork --** "The auditor must obtain sufficient appropriate audit evidence by performing audit procedures to afford a reasonable basis for an opinion regarding the financial statements under audit."

II. **Concepts Underlying Audit Evidence**

A. Audit evidence -- all of the information used by the auditor in arriving at the conclusions on which the audit opinion is based, including the information contained in the accounting records underlying the financial statements and other information.

1. "Accounting records" include records related to initial entries and supporting records (such as checks, invoices, contracts, general and subsidiary ledgers, support for adjusting journal entries, worksheets supporting cost allocations, etc.).

2. The auditor should obtain audit evidence by testing the accounting records (by analysis and review, reperforming procedures followed in the financial reporting process, and reconciling related information) -- note that accounting records alone do not provide sufficient appropriate audit evidence, so the auditor should also obtain other evidence.

3. Other evidence that may be used includes minutes of meetings, confirmations, industry analysts' reports, benchmarking data for competitors, controls manuals, and other information obtained by inquiry, observation, and inspection.

B. Sufficient appropriate audit evidence -- "sufficiency" refers to the quantity of audit evidence and "appropriateness" refers to the quality of audit evidence (that is, the relevance and reliability of the evidence).

1. The amount of audit evidence normally required is directly related to the risk of misstatement (the greater the risk, the more evidence needed) and inversely related to the quality of evidence (the higher the quality, the less evidence needed).

2. "Reliability" is affected by its source and nature and depends upon individual circumstances, which may vary. Nonetheless, the following generalizations (section 3) are usually applicable.

3. Audit evidence obtained directly by the auditor is more reliable than audit evidence obtained indirectly or by inference (e.g., observation of the application of a control is more reliable than inquiry about the application of a control):

   a. Audit evidence is more reliable when obtained from independent (knowledgeable) sources outside the entity.

   b. Audit evidence generated internally is more reliable when the related controls are effective.

   c. Audit evidence is more reliable when it exists in documentary form (whether paper or electronic).

   d. Audit evidence provided by original documents is more reliable than audit evidence based on photocopies of facsimiles.

4. The auditor should consider the reliability of information used -- however an audit rarely involves authentication of documentation.

5. The auditor should obtain evidence about the accuracy and completeness of information used to perform further audit procedures -- may be performed concurrently with the actual audit procedure or by testing controls applicable to the information. (Additional procedures may be performed, such as computer-assisted audit techniques, to recalculate the information.)

6. The auditor usually obtains more assurance from consistent audit evidence obtained from different sources or of a different nature (i.e., corroborating information) than from evidence considered individually -- when evidence obtained from different sources is inconsistent, the auditor should determine what audit procedures are needed to resolve the inconsistency.

7. The auditor may appropriately consider the cost of obtaining information in relationship to its usefulness -- however, the cost alone is not a valid basis for omitting an audit procedure if there is no appropriate alternative.
8. The auditor does not examine all available information -- professional judgment is required to support the audit opinion. ("Reasonable assurance" usually involves evidence that is "persuasive" rather than "conclusive" -- however, the auditor must not be satisfied with audit evidence that is less than persuasive.)

III. Using Assertions to Obtain Audit Evidence -- in representing that the financial statements are consistent with GAAP, management makes assertions (implicitly or explicitly) about the recognition, measurement, presentation, and disclosure of information.

A. Assertions about classes of transactions and events for the period under audit.

1. 5 assertions about classes of transactions and events for the period:
   a. **Accuracy** -- amounts and other data have been recorded appropriately;
   b. **Occurrence** -- transactions and events that have been recorded have occurred;
   c. **Completeness** -- all transactions and events that should have been recorded have been recorded;
   d. **Cutoff** -- transactions and events have been recorded in the correct accounting period;
   e. **Classification** -- transactions and events have been recorded in the proper accounts.
2. 4 assertions about account balances at the period end:
   a. **Existence** -- assets, liabilities and equity interests exist;
   b. **Completeness** -- all assets, liabilities, and equity interests that should have been recorded have been recorded;
   c. **Rights and obligations** -- the entity holds or controls the rights to assets, and liabilities are the obligations of the entity;
   d. **Valuation and allocation** -- assets, liabilities, and equity interests are included in the financial statements at appropriate amounts and any resulting valuation or allocation adjustments are appropriately recorded.
3. 4 assertions about presentation and disclosure:
   a. **Occurrence; and rights and obligations** -- disclosed events and transactions have occurred and pertain to the entity;
   b. **Completeness** -- all disclosures that should have been included have been included;
   c. **Classification and understandability** -- financial information is appropriately presented, described, and clearly expressed;
   d. **Accuracy and valuation** -- financial and other information are disclosed fairly and at appropriate amounts.

B. The auditor may use the assertions as described above or may express them differently if the relevant issues have been addressed. For example, the auditor may combine the assertions about transactions and events with those about account balances; and the auditor may not identify a separate assertion about cutoff if occurrence and completeness have been established.

C. Relevant assertions are assertions that have a meaningful bearing on whether the account is fairly stated -- the auditor should use relevant assertions to assess the risk of material misstatement (this includes considering the types of potential misstatements that may occur and designing audit procedures to address the risks).

D. To determine whether a particular assertion is relevant, the auditor should evaluate:

1. The nature of the assertion;
2. The volume of transactions or data related to the assertion; and

3. The nature and complexity of the systems (including the use of IT) by which the entity processes and controls information related to the assertion.

IV. Audit Procedures for Obtaining Audit Evidence

A. The auditor should perform audit procedures as a basis for conclusions.

   1. **Risk assessment procedures** -- obtain an understanding of the entity and its environment (including internal control) to assess the risk of material misstatement;

   2. **Tests of controls** -- when necessary or desired, test the operating effectiveness of controls in preventing or detecting (and correcting) material misstatements at the relevant assertion level; and

   3. **Substantive procedures** -- detect material misstatements at the relevant assertion level (includes tests of details and analytical procedures).

B. Risk assessment procedures -- must be performed to provide a satisfactory basis for the assessment of risks at the financial statement and relevant assertion levels (must be supplemented by tests of controls, when relevant or necessary, and by substantive procedures.

C. Tests of controls are necessary when (1) the auditor's risk assessment includes an expectation of the operating effectiveness of controls or (2) the substantive procedures alone do not provide sufficient appropriate audit evidence.

D. Substantive procedures -- the auditor should plan and perform substantive procedures to be responsive to the related planned level of detection risk, including the results of any tests of controls. (Regardless of the assessed risk of material misstatement, the auditor should perform substantive procedures for all relevant assertions related to each material class of transactions, account balance, and disclosure.)

E. Some of the accounting data and other information may be available only in electronic form or only at certain points of time -- this may affect the nature and time of procedures to be used. (Source documents may be replaced with electronic messages or may be converted into electronic images and source documents may not be retained.)

F. The auditor may use computer-assisted-audit-techniques (CAATs) to assist with audit procedures described below when information is in electronic form:

   1. Inspection of records/documents -- consists of examining records or documents, whether internal or external, whether paper, electronic, or other media;

   2. Inspection of tangible assets -- consists of physical examination of the assets (provides evidence regarding existence, but not about rights/obligations or valuation);

   3. Observation -- consists of looking at a process or procedure being performed by others (limited to the point in time at which the observation occurs and observation may affect how the process/procedure is performed);

   4. Inquiry -- consists of seeking information of knowledgeable persons inside or outside the entity: (Evaluating responses to inquiries is part of the process).

      a. Consider the knowledge, objectivity, experience, responsibility, and qualifications of the individual to be questioned;

      b. Ask clear, concise, and relevant questions (either open or closed questions, as appropriate);

      c. Consider the responses/reactions and ask follow-up questions;

      d. Listen actively and effectively and evaluate the response;

      e. Consider obtaining written representations from management;

      f. Resolve any significant inconsistencies in the information obtained (consider performing additional audit procedures as needed);

      g. Inquiry alone does not provide sufficient appropriate audit evidence for substantive purposes (or to test the operating effectiveness of controls);

      h. Information to support management's intent may be limited -- their past history of carrying out stated intentions may be relevant.

5. Confirmation -- the process of obtaining a representation of information or of an existing condition (or absence of certain conditions, such as the absence of an undisclosed agreement affecting revenue recognition) directly from a third party.
6. Recalculation -- consists of checking the mathematical accuracy of documents or records.
7. Reperformance -- the auditor's independent execution of procedures or controls that were originally performed as part of the entity's internal control (e.g., reperforming the aging of accounts receivable.)
8. Analytical procedures -- consist of evaluations of financial information made by a study of plausible relationships among both financial and nonfinancial data:
   a. Analytical procedures include "scanning" -- the auditor's use of professional judgment to review accounting data to identify significant or unusual items to then test those items;
   b. Scanning includes searching for large or unusual items in the accounting records (e.g., nonstandard journal entries) as well as in transaction data (e.g., suspense accounts or adjusting journal entries) for indications of misstatements;
   c. CAATs may assist an auditor in identifying unusual items.

V. **Effective date --** SAS 106 is effective for audits of financial statements for periods beginning on or after December 15, 2006 (earlier application is permitted).

AU328 (SAS 101) - Auditing Fair Value Measurements and Disclosures

I. **Introduction** -- SAS No. 101 addresses audit considerations regarding measurement and disclosure of assets, liabilities, and specific elements of equity presented or disclosed at fair value in financial statements.

A. **Basic responsibility** -- obtain sufficient appropriate evidence to provide reasonable assurance that the fair value measurements and disclosures (FVM&D) conform to GAAP.

1. Definition of "fair value" -- "the amount at which the asset (or liability) could be bought (or incurred) or sold (or settled) in a current transaction between willing parties, that is, other than in a forced or liquidation sale."

2. GAAP prefers the use of observable market prices when available – otherwise, the auditor must use the best information available.

a. Fair value measurements for which observable market prices are unavailable are inherently imprecise -- the auditor is not responsible for predicting future conditions or outcomes that might affect the FVM&D.

b. GAAP requires or permits a variety of FVM&D in financial statements and GAAP varies in the level of guidance provided.

c. The best evidence of fair value is the existence of published price quotations in an active market.

d. When an observable market price is unavailable -- management can estimate the fair value using the assumptions that marketplace participants would use. (Management can use its own assumptions when there is no evidence that marketplace participants would use different assumptions.)

B. Management is responsible for the FVM&D (even when a specialist is used).

1. Management should establish a process for determining FVM&D.

2. Management should select appropriate valuation methods.

3. Management should identify and adequately support any significant assumptions used.

4. Management should prepare the valuation and ensure that the presentation of FVM&D is consistent with GAAP.

II. **Understanding the Entity's Process for Determining FVM&D** -- The auditor should obtain an understanding of the entity's process for determining FVM&D (including understanding relevant controls) sufficient to properly plan the audit approach.

A. The auditor should obtain a sufficient understanding of each of the 5 components of internal control -- the auditor should consider the following:

1. Controls over the process used to determine fair value measurements (including controls over data and segregation of duties);

2. The expertise/experience of persons making these measurements;

3. The role of information technology in the process;

4. Whether the accounts involved result from routine and recurring transactions versus non-routine and nonrecurring transactions;

5. The role of a service organization or any specialists in developing the FVM&D;

6. Significant management assumptions regarding the FVM&D -- including documentation supporting management's assumptions, the process used to develop these assumptions, and the process used to monitor changes in management's assumptions;

7. The integrity of change controls and security procedures over the valuation models, including approval processes;
8. Controls over the consistency, timeliness, and reliability of the data used in valuation models.

B. Based on the understanding of the entity's process (and assessment of the risk of material misstatement) the auditor determines the nature, timing, and extent of the audit procedures -- the risk of material misstatement increases with the complexity of the FVM&D.

III. Evaluating FVM&D for Conformity to GAAP

A. The auditor's evaluation of FVM&D is based on the understanding of GAAP requirements, knowledge of the business and industry, and the results of other audit procedures.

1. The auditor's knowledge of the business is especially important when the valuation method is highly complex.
2. The auditor's knowledge of the business (along with the results of other audit procedures) may help identify assets for which an impairment loss should be recognized under GAAP.

B. Audit procedures usually include inquiries of management, along with appropriate corroboration by:

1. Considering management's past record of carrying out stated intentions;
2. Reviewing written plans and documentation (e.g., budgets, minutes, etc.);
3. Considering management's stated reasons for its actions;
4. Considering management's ability to carry out its planned actions.

C. The auditor should evaluate whether the method for determining fair value measurements is consistent with prior periods.

1. Consider whether that consistency is appropriate in light of any changes in the environment or other circumstances.
2. Consider whether a change in the method for determining fair value measurements is appropriate (based on a change in GAAP requirements or a change in circumstances) -- management may be able to demonstrate that the new method is a more appropriate basis of measurement.

IV. Engaging a Specialist -- The auditor should consider whether to engage a specialist in performing substantive tests to evaluate the FVM&D. (The auditor may not have the requisite skills to plan and perform the appropriate audit procedures related to FVM&D.)

A. When planning to use the work of the specialist -- consider whether the specialist's understanding of "fair value" and the method that the specialist will use to determine fair value are consistent with those of management and GAAP.

B. The specialist is responsible for the reasonableness of assumptions and the appropriateness of the methods used -- however, the auditor should obtain an understanding of those assumptions and methods used. (If the auditor believes that the specialist's findings are unreasonable, SAS No. 73 requires the auditor to perform additional procedures.)

V. Testing the Entity's FVM&D

A. The auditor's planned audit procedures can vary significantly in nature, timing, and extent (due to the wide range of possible fair value measurements and varying levels of risk of material misstatement) -- substantive procedures may involve:

1. Testing management's significant assumptions, the valuation model, and the underlying data;
2. Developing independent fair value estimates for corroboration;
3. Reviewing subsequent events and transactions.

B. The complexity of the fair value measurements increases the risk of misstatement due to the:

1. Length of the forecast period;
2. Number and complexity of significant assumptions involved;

3. Degree of subjectivity associated with the assumptions;
4. Uncertainty associated with future outcomes tied to assumptions;
5. Lack of objective data when subjective factors are used.

C. Considerations in the development of audit procedures:

1. When the date of the fair value measurement is different than the reporting date -- the auditor should determine that management has taken into consideration the effect of events and changes in circumstances;
2. When collateral is an important factor -- the auditor should obtain evidence about the assertions involved, including the appropriateness of disclosures;
3. Inspection of an asset may be necessary to evaluate its current condition.

D. Testing management's significant assumptions, the valuation model, and the underlying data.

1. When testing the entity's FVM&D the auditor evaluates whether:
    - **a.** Management's assumptions are reasonable and consistent with market information;
    - **b.** The fair value measurement was determined appropriately (using an appropriate valuation model, if applicable);
    - **c.** Management used relevant information that was available.
2. Evaluating significant assumptions used by management (when the auditor develops an independent estimate using management's assumptions) -- the auditor should determine whether these assumptions provide a reasonable basis for FVM&D.
    - **a.** The auditor should evaluate the source and reliability of evidence supporting management's assumptions (including historical and market information as applicable).
    - **b.** The auditor focuses on significant assumptions identified by management -- especially those that are sensitive to variation or uncertainty and those that are susceptible to bias.
    - **c.** The auditor considers the sensitivity of the valuation to changes in assumptions affecting the fair value measurement.
    - **d.** The auditor considers whether management has identified the significant assumptions affecting FVM&D (if not, the auditor considers whether to employ procedures to identify those assumptions).
    - **e.** The assumptions are frequently interdependent and should be consistent with:
        - **i.** The economic environment in general, for the industry, and specific to the entity;
        - **ii.** Existing market information;
        - **iii.** Plans of the entity;
        - **iv.** Assumptions made in prior periods, if applicable; (Historical information may not be indicative of future prospects.)
        - **v.** Past experience of the entity with current circumstances;
        - **vi.** Risk associated with amounts and timing of cash flows.
3. Developing independent fair value estimates for corroboration -- the auditor may make an independent estimate of fair value (using the auditor's own assumptions) to compare with management's FVM&D.
4. Reviewing subsequent events and transactions -- the auditor may consider using events subsequent to the balance sheet date to evaluate FVM&D for those events that reflect circumstances existing at the balance sheet date.

VI. Disclosures About Fair Values -- The auditor evaluates disclosures for conformity to GAAP.

A. Obtain sufficient appropriate evidence that the valuation principles are appropriate under GAAP (and are consistently applied) and that the method of estimation and significant assumptions are adequately disclosed in conformity with GAAP.

- **B.** If an item contains a high degree of measurement uncertainty -- evaluate whether the disclosures are sufficient to convey that uncertainty.
- **C.** When disclosure of fair value information under GAAP is omitted because it cannot be determined with sufficient reliability -- the auditor should evaluate the adequacy of disclosure in the circumstances.

VII. Evaluating the Results of Audit Procedures -- The auditor should evaluate the sufficiency and appropriateness of evidence obtained from auditing FVM&D and the consistency of that evidence with other audit evidence obtained during the audit.

VIII. Management Representations -- The auditor should usually obtain written representations from management regarding the reasonableness of significant assumptions and whether those assumptions reflect management's intent and ability to carry out specific actions relevant to FVM&D.

- **A.** Obtain representations about the appropriateness of the measurement methods and assumptions used by management in determining FVM&D.
- **B.** Obtain representations about the completeness and adequacy of disclosures.
- **C.** Obtain representations as to whether subsequent events require adjustment or disclosure regarding FVM&D.

IX. Communication with Those Charged with Governance -- The auditor should determine that those charged with governance are informed about the process used by management in developing sensitive accounting estimates (including FVM&D), including the subjectivity involved and the relative materiality of the matters involved.

X. Effective Date -- SAS No. 101 is effective for audits of financial statements for periods beginning on or after June 15, 2003 (earlier application is permitted).

AU329 (SAS 56) - Analytical Procedures

I. **General Comments**

   A. Definition of **analytical procedures** -- "evaluations of financial information made by a study of plausible relationships among both **financial and non-financial** data."

      1. Involves a comparison of recorded amounts (or ratios using recorded amounts) with expectations.

      2. Sources of information for developing expectations:

         a. Financial information for prior periods;

         b. Anticipated results -- budgets, forecasts, or extensions from interim or annual data;

         c. Relationships among the elements of the current financial statements;

         d. Information (e.g., ratios) for the client's industry;

         e. The relationship of financial and non-financial information.

   B. The **underlying premise** is that relationships among data may be expected unless there are known reasons to the contrary.

   C. This SAS requires analytical procedures in **planning and review.**

   D. Analytical procedures serve 3 distinct purposes:

      1. **Assists planning --** directs attention to areas where there may be greater risks of misstatement;

      2. **As a substantive test --** constitutes a form of evidence during field work;

      3. **As an overall review --** a final opportunity to assess the appropriateness of conclusions reached.

II. **Analytical Procedures in Planning**

   A. **Purposes**

      1. To add to the auditor's understanding of the client's activities since the prior audit;

      2. To identify audit areas having greater risk (e.g. unusual transactions and activities).

   B. **Nature of data**

      1. Usually aggregated at a high level;

      2. Analytics primarily use financial data, but may also use non-financial data (e.g. sales/square foot, the number of employees, etc.).

   C. **Attention directing --** serves as a basis for inquiries.

III. **The Expected Effectiveness and Efficiency --** of analytical procedures used as substantive tests depend on 4 factors.

   A. **The nature of the assertion --** analytics may be particularly effective in testing for **omissions** that would be hard to detect with procedures dealing with recorded amounts.

   B. **The plausibility and predictability of the relationship**

      1. Relationships in a stable environment are usually more predictable than those in a dynamic environment;

      2. Relationships involving income statement accounts tend to be more predictable than those involving balance sheet accounts, since the income statement deals with a period of time rather than a moment in time;

3. Relationships involving transactions subject to management discretion tend to be less predictable.

C. **Availability and reliability of data --** data may or may not be readily available to develop the expectation for some assertions.

D. **Precision of the expectation**

1. Likelihood that unexpected differences are due to misstatements increases with the precision of the expectation;

2. Likelihood of detecting a misstatement decreases as the level of aggregation of the data increases.

IV. **Investigation and Evaluation of Significant Differences --** Unexpected differences in excess of a specified amount should be investigated (may be a consequence of the financial statement data or the expectation).

A. Inquiries of management (should corroborate management's responses as deemed appropriate).

B. Other audit procedures should be performed when a difference cannot be reasonably explained.

V. **Documentation Requirements --** when analytical procedures are used as the principal substantive test of a significant financial statement assertion.

A. The expectation and factors considered in developing it.

B. Results of the comparison of the expectation to the recorded amounts (or to ratios based on the recorded amounts).

C. Results of any additional auditing procedures performed to investigate unexpected differences.

VI. **Analytical Procedures Used in the Overall Review --** to assess the conclusions reached and to evaluate the overall financial statement presentation (including reading the financial statements and the notes and considering whether the evidence was adequate).

AU330 (SAS 67) - Confirmation Process

I. **Confirmation Procedures Related to Auditor's Assessment of Audit Risk --** - SAS 106, "Audit Evidence" expresses a presumption that "audit evidence is more reliable when it is obtained from knowledgeable independent sources outside the entity."

   A. The auditor's need for assurance from substantive procedures increases with increases in the risk of material misstatement - consider confirming terms of unusual or complex transactions.

   B. As the risk of material misstatement decreases - "the auditor may modify substantive tests by changing their nature from more effective (but costly) tests to less effective (and less costly) tests."

   C. Assertions associated with account balances - if properly designed, confirmation requests may address any one or more of these assertions; however, confirmations do not address all assertions equally well (so consider performing other procedures).

      1. Existence.

      2. Completeness.

      3. Rights and obligations.

      4. Valuation and allocation.

II. **The Confirmation Process --** - obtaining and evaluating a direct communication from a knowledgeable third party in response to a request for information about a particular item affecting financial statement assertions.

   A. The design of the confirmation request - should be tailored to specific objectives. (The auditor should consider the types of information respondents will be readily able to confirm.)

      1. Form of confirmation request - there are two types of confirmation requests: (The auditor should also consider prior experience, nature of information involved, and knowledge of respondent.)

         a. **Positive** - requests a response whether the recipient agrees or not: (Blank confirmation requests provide more assurance, but may result in a lower response rate.)

            i. Positive confirmations only provide audit evidence when a response is received from the recipient;

            ii. When a response has not been received - should send a second request (possibly a third request); perform alternate procedures if no response to follow-up attempts.

         b. **Negative** - requests a response only if the recipient does not agree (usually requires a larger sample size than for positive); may be appropriate when:

            i. There is a large number of small accounts;

            ii. The risk of material misstatement is low; and

            iii. The recipients are expected to be responsive to the request.

      2. Nature of the information being confirmed - may affect the competence of the evidence obtained and the response rate.

         a. Some accounting systems can confirm individual transactions, but not entire account balances (regarding "vouchers payable").

         b. The auditor should obtain an understanding of the substance of the client's transactions to determine the information to include on the confirmation (e.g., consider requesting confirmation of unusual agreements or transactions, such as "bill-and-hold sales").

         c. When there is a moderate (or high) risk that there may be significant oral modifications to some transactions (such as unusual payment terms or liberal rights of return) - the auditor should inquire about any such modifications to written agreements; may also confirm the terms of the agreements and whether any oral modifications exist.

B. Performing confirmation procedures - "the auditor should maintain control over the confirmation requests and responses" (that is, establish direct communication between the intended recipient and the auditor to minimize the possibility of bias due to interception and alteration of the confirmation requests or responses).

1. Facsimile (faxed) responses involve risks due to difficulty in determining the source of the responses - consider verifying the source and contents of such a response by calling the sender; request a written reply using the original confirmation request.
2. Oral confirmation - document the oral confirmation and encourage such a respondent to provide a written reply using the original confirmation request.

III. Alternative Procedures

A. Usually required when no response has been received to a positive confirmation request.

1. Receivables - usually try to verify subsequent cash receipts.
2. Payables - usually try to verify subsequent cash disbursements.

B. The auditor may omit alternative procedures if both of the following hold:

1. No unusual characteristics are associated with the non-responses;
2. Aggregate non-responses are not material - if the non-responses are viewed as 100 percent misstatements and added to the other unadjusted differences identified and the auditor's report would not be affected.

C. Evaluate whether sufficient evidence has been obtained - consider the reliability of the confirmations and alternative procedures; the nature of any exceptions; and any evidence provided by other procedures.

IV. "Confirmation of Accounts Receivable is a Generally Accepted Auditing Procedure" (including a financial institution's loans) -- The auditor should document how this presumption was overcome when the auditor has not confirmed accounts receivables (e.g., may decide not to confirm receivables if they are immaterial to the financial statements or if the risk of material misstatement is low and other substantive audit procedures are sufficient to limit audit risk to an acceptably low level).

AU331 (SAS 1) Inventories

I. **"Observation of Inventories is a Generally Accepted Auditing Procedure" --** - an auditor must justify not performing this procedure.

II. **Inventories Controlled by the Client:**

- **A.** When quantities are determined by physical count at the balance-sheet date (or within a reasonable time before or after the balance-sheet date) - the auditor should be present during the client's physical inventory and perform test counts (and make appropriate inquiries) to evaluate the effectiveness of the inventory count procedures and the degree of reliance that may be placed on the client's representations about the quantities and condition of the inventory.
- **B.** When well-kept perpetual inventory records are checked periodically by physical counts by the client - the auditor's observation procedures can usually be performed during or after the end of the period under audit.
- **C.** If statistical sampling methods are used by the client in taking physical inventory - the auditor must be satisfied that the sampling plan is reasonable and statistically valid.
- **D.** The auditor might be able to become satisfied as to prior (unobserved) inventories through tests of prior transactions and analytical procedures (e.g., gross profit rates, etc.) if the auditor is satisfied as to the current inventory.

III. **Inventories Held in Public Warehouses:**

- **A.** Usually confirm with the custodian, when material;
- **B.** If such inventories represent a significant proportion of current or total assets, other procedures may be appropriate, as follows:
  1. Observe the physical counts of the inventory;
  2. Review warehouse controls over the inventory (examine any related reports on controls by other independent accountants) - may test the owner's procedures for evaluating the performance of the warehouse custodian;
  3. If that inventory has been pledged as collateral, confirm those details with the lenders.

AU332 (SAS 92) - Auditing Investments

> **Note:**
> SAS No. 92 supersedes SAS No.81, "Auditing Investments."

I. **Applicability --** provides guidance in planning and performing auditing procedures "for assertions about derivative instruments, hedging activities, and investments in securities that are made in an entity's financial statements."

   A. **Derivative instruments and hedging activities** within scope of SAS #92:

      1. SFAS #133, "Accounting for Derivative Instruments and Hedging Activities," specifies GAAP;

      2. "Derivative" -- a financial instrument or contract with the following 3 characteristics:

         a. Has 1 or more "underlyings" and 1 or more "notional amounts" or payment provisions or both;

         b. Requires no initial net investment (or initial net investment is less than would be expected for other contracts);

         c. Terms require (or permit) net settlement; it can be readily settled by a means outside the contract; or it provides for delivery of an asset that is substantially equivalent to settlement.

   B. **Securities** within scope of SAS #92 -- applies to all securities (debt and equity securities), including those accounted for by the equity method.

II. **Need for Special Skill or Knowledge to Plan and Perform Auditing Procedures --** may require special skill or knowledge for certain assertions about derivatives (either involving persons within the auditor's firm or outside the firm).

   A. List of Skills:

      1. Obtaining an understanding of information systems (including service organizations) affecting derivatives and securities;

      2. Identifying controls placed in operation by a service organization;

      3. Understanding GAAP related to derivatives - especially with respect to measurements and disclosure;

      4. Understanding the determination of fair values of derivatives and securities - especially involving knowledge of valuation concepts;

      5. Understanding general risk management concepts and asset/liability management strategies - to assess inherent risk and control risk.

III. **Audit Risk and Materiality**

   A. **Inherent risk assessment** - considerations that may affect assessment:

      1. Management's objectives - subject to the risk that the hedge will not be affective for unexpected changes in market conditions;

      2. Complexity of the instrument's features - may affect the fair value;

      3. Whether the transaction involves the exchange of cash - may be harder to detect contracts not having initial cash flows;

      4. Entity's experience - inexperience increases inherent risk;

      5. Whether derivative is "freestanding" or an "embedded feature" of an agreement - inherent risk increases for those derivatives that are embedded in another agreement;

      6. Effect of external factors:

         a. Credit risk - related to counterparty's failure to meet its obligation;

         b. Market risk - related to adverse changes due to market factors (e.g., interest rates, currency exchange rates, etc.);

   - **c.** Basis risk - risk of loss due to ineffective hedging;
   - **d.** Legal risk - when a legal action precludes performance by one or both parties to the agreement.
7. Evolving nature of derivatives and applicable GAAP - new forms of derivatives may be developed (and GAAP may lag behind somewhat and be subject to interpretation by a variety of standard-setting bodies);
8. GAAP may require assumptions about future conditions - inherent risk increases with the number and subjectivity of those assumptions;
9. Significant reliance on outside parties - inherent risk may increase when an entity relies on external expertise (and can't challenge the specialist's methodology or assumptions, for example, affecting valuation).

B. Control risk assessment

1. Auditor must obtain an understanding of internal control to:
   - **a.** Identify types of potential misstatements;
   - **b.** Consider factors that would affect risk of material misstatement;
   - **c.** Controls should be related to managements objectives for financial reporting, operations and compliance - the following controls might be applicable to derivatives:
     - **i.** Monitoring by staff independent of derivative activities;
     - **ii.** Senior management approves derivative transactions exceeding specified limits;
     - **iii.** Senior management approves departures from approved derivative strategies;
     - **iv.** Derivative positions are accurately conveyed to risk measurement systems;
     - **v.** Reconciliations are appropriately made of derivative positions;
     - **vi.** Constraints are defined for derivative traders, risk managers, and senior management (excesses are identified and justified);
     - **vii.** Controls and financial results are regularly reviewed;
     - **viii.** Limits are reviewed when there are changes in strategy, risk tolerance, and market conditions.
2. Examples of service organization's services that are part of entity's information system:
   - **a.** Initiating purchase/sale of equity securities - when acting as an investment advisor or manager;
   - **b.** Services that are ancillary to holding securities - e.g., collecting dividends or interest; receiving notification of transactions; receiving payment from purchasers or disbursing proceeds to sellers; maintaining records of securities transactions;
   - **c.** Pricing services providing fair values used by an entity for reporting.
3. Examples of service organization's services that are not part of an entity's information system:
   - **a.** Execution of trades that are initiated by the entity or investment advisor;
   - **b.** Holding an entity's securities.
4. Assessing control risk:
   - **a.** If assessing control risk at less than the maximum -- identify specific controls relevant to the assertions and perform appropriate tests of control;
   - **b.** Considerations in designing auditing procedures -- size of the entity; entity's organizational structure; nature of entity's operations; the types, frequency, and complexity of its derivatives and securities transactions; and the controls over those transactions;

> **Note:**
> Regarding confirmations of balances and transactions -- do not provide evidential matter about the effectiveness of controls.

c. If the entity has a large number of derivatives or securities transactions (probably not practicable to assess control risk at the maximum) -- identify controls (and perform appropriate tests of controls) over authorization, recording, custody, and segregation of duties for those transactions.

IV. Designing Substantive Procedures Based on Risk Assessments -- Nature, timing, and extent.

A. **When a service organization is involved in the entity's information system, the auditor:**

1. May need to inspect documentation at the facility;
2. May need to identify controls put in place by the service organization or entity and perform appropriate tests of those controls;
3. May need to consider whether duties are appropriately segregated.

B. **Emphasize the 5 financial statements "assertions"**

1. **Existence or occurrence** - examples of procedures that might be performed a. Confirmation with the issuer of the security b. Confirmation with the holder of the security c. Confirmation of settled (or unsettled) transactions with the counterparty or broker-dealer d. Physical inspection of the security or derivative contract e. Inspect or read the applicable agreements or supporting documents f. Perform analytical procedures.
2. **Completeness** - examples of procedures that might be performed: (Note that audit risk may be an issue when derivatives may not involve an initial exchange of consideration and assessing control risk at the maximum.)
    a. Inquire of counterparties frequently used when presently not identified as a counterparty to any derivative agreements;
    b. Inspect financial instruments and other agreements;
    c. Inspect or read supporting documents subsequent to year-end;
    d. Perform analytical procedures, including comparison of current and previous account details (and investigated differences;)
    e. Read other information (e.g., minutes of board meetings);
    f. Inquire about operating activities that might present risks which could involve derivatives (e.g., foreign currency, interest rates, etc.);
    g. Inquire as to whether debt has been converted from fixed to variable (or vice versa).
3. **Rights and Obligations** - examples of procedures that might be performed:
    a. Confirm significant terms with counterparty or holder of security;
    b. Inspect financial instruments and other agreements;
    c. Consider results of reviewing minutes and reading agreements (especially regarding collateral and repurchase commitments).
4. **Valuation** - GAAP may require valuation based on cost, the investee's financial results, or fair value; impairments may or may not require recognition prior to realization:
    a. Valuation based on cost - inspect documentation of the purchase price; confirmation with the issuer or holder; test amortization of any discount or premium (by recalculation or by analytical procedures);
    b. Valuation based on investee's financial results - for investments accounted for using the equity method:
        i. Read investee's financial statements, including audit report, if available;
        ii. Perform additional procedures (e.g., review information in investor's files) if there are significant differences in year-ends or in accounting principles, etc.;
        iii. Evaluate management's conclusion about the need to recognize an impairment loss for a decline that is other than temporary - primarily consisting of review (including interim financial statements) and inquiry.
    c. Valuation based on fair value:

i. Determine whether GAAP specifies the method to be used as to fair value (and whether the stated fair value is consistent with that specified method);

ii. Quoted market prices for derivatives and securities may be available from financial publications, exchanges, NASDAQ or pricing services that use those sources - these are usually considered sufficient evidence of fair value;

iii. Quoted market prices for other derivatives and securities may be obtained from broker-dealers who are market makers for them - may require special knowledge to understand the circumstances surrounding such quotes;

iv. If quoted market prices are not available - estimates may be obtained from broker-dealers based on proprietary valuation models (e.g., Black-Scholes option pricing model);

v. May be necessary to obtain estimates from more than one source - if the pricing source is not independent of the entity or if the valuation's assumptions are highly subjective or sensitive to changes in the underlying assumptions;

vi. The auditor "does not function as an appraiser and is not expected to substitute his or her judgment for that of the entity's management." Should he or she obtain evidence about the valuation model used (e.g., present value of expected cash flows; option-pricing models; matrix pricing; option-adjusted spread models; and fundamental analysis):

1. Assess reasonableness of the model and support - may need a specialist to assess the model;

2. Calculate an independent expectation for comparison;

3. Judgment is required (for valuation, assessing effectiveness of hedge, and allocation of changes to earnings and other comprehensive income) - since these determinations may be highly subjective or sensitive to changes in underlying assumptions.

vii. If collateral is important to valuation - obtain evidence as to the existence, fair value, transferability, and investor's rights to the collateral;

viii. Accounting for changes in fair value under GAAP - auditor should gather evidence regarding the amounts reported in earnings or comprehensive income or otherwise disclosed:

1. Derivative designated as a "fair value hedge in earnings" - disclose the ineffective portion of the hedge;

2. Derivative designated as a "cash flow hedge" in 2 components – the ineffective portion is reported in earnings and the effective portion is reported in other comprehensive income;

3. Derivative not designated as a hedge (or previously designated as a hedge that is no longer effective) - reported in earnings;

4. Available-for-sale security - reported in other comprehensive income.

ix. GAAP might require recognizing in earnings any impairment loss for a decline in value that is "other than temporary" - auditor should evaluate management's conclusions (and whether management considered relevant factors).

5. **Presentation and Disclosure** - whether the classification, description, and disclosure of derivatives and securities conform to the requirements of GAAP.

a. Consider the form and content of the F/S and their notes, including terminology used, level of detail, classifications, and bases of items reported.

b. Compare the presentation and disclosure with requirements of GAAP.

C. **Additional Considerations** about hedging activities:

1. To account for a derivative as a "hedge" - management must designate the derivative as a hedge at its inception and (1) formally document the hedging relationship, (2) the entity's risk management objective and strategy, and (3) method for assessing its effectiveness;

2. Auditor should gather evidence regarding management's expectation that the hedging relationship will be highly effective at the inception and its periodic assessment of the ongoing effectiveness (as required by GAAP);

3. When a derivative is designated a "fair value hedge" -- auditor should gather evidence regarding the recorded change in the hedged item's fair value attributable to the hedged risk (gather additional evidence to determine whether GAAP has been applied);

4. When a derivative is designated a "cash flow hedge" of a forecasted transaction -- GAAP requires that the forecasted transaction is probable of occurring (not merely management's intent), supported by observable facts - the auditor should evaluate management's determination that the forecasted transaction is probable.

D. **Assertions** about securities based on management's intent and ability.

1. GAAP requires that intent and ability be considered in some cases -(1) for debt securities classified as held-to-maturity; (2) for equity securities using the equity method (as to "influence"); or (3) equity securities classified as trading or available-for-sale.

2. The auditor's responsibilities include the following:

   a. Obtain an understanding of the process used by management to classify the entity's securities;

   b. For equity method - inquire of management as to its ability to exercise significant influence;

   c. Consider whether management's activities conflict or corroborate with its stated intent;

   d. Determine whether GAAP requires management to document its intent (inspect that documentation and assess timeliness);

   e. Determine whether management's activities, contractual agreements, or entity's financial condition are consistent with having the ability to carry out its intent.

E. **Management representations** - auditors should usually obtain written representations from management regarding management's intent and ability affecting the assertions about derivatives and securities.

V. **Effective Date --** for audits of financial statements for years ending on or after June 30, 2001.

AU333 (SAS 85) - Management Representations

I. Reliance on Management Representations

> ... management makes many representations to the auditor, both oral and written, in response to specific inquiries...

> **Note:**
> SAS No. 85 supersedes SAS No. 19, "Client Representations" (issued in 1977) requires the auditor to obtain written representations from management in an audit under GAAS.

A. Written representations complement other auditing procedures to corroborate management's responses to the auditor's inquiries (also to reduce the likelihood of misunderstandings).

B. If management's representation is contradicted by other audit evidence -- investigate the circumstances and evaluate whether reliance on other management representations is appropriate.

II. Obtaining Written Representations

A. Should be obtained for all periods covered by the auditor's report (including comparative financials):

1. Addressed to the auditors;
2. Dated no later than the date of the auditor's report -- may obtain additional representations for subsequent events when "dual dating" report;
3. Signed by the CEO and CFO (or the equivalents);
4. If the current management was not present for all periods covered -- obtain representations for current management on all such periods; (Tailor the representations to the specific circumstances.)

B. The specific written representations will vary with the circumstances:

1. Regarding the financial statements:
   - **a.** Management's responsibility for the financial statements;
   - **b.** Management's belief that presentation is consistent with GAAP.
2. Regarding the completeness of information:
   - **a.** All financial records available;
   - **b.** Minutes of all meetings available;
   - **c.** Communications from regulatory bodies regarding noncompliance or deficiencies;
   - **d.** Absence of unrecorded transactions.
3. Recognition, measurement and disclosure:
   - **a.** Information regarding fraud -- involving management, employees affecting internal control, or others;
   - **b.** Plans or intentions affecting carrying values;
   - **c.** Information involving related parties;
   - **d.** Guarantees leading to contingent liabilities;
   - **e.** Significant estimates related to disclosure of risks and uncertainties;
   - **f.** Compliance issues related to laws, regulations, or contracts involving loss contingencies;
   - **g.** Unasserted claims or assessments that attorney has advised should be disclosed;
   - **h.** Assets pledged as collateral or having liens.
4. Subsequent events.

C. Representations should be tailored to include any specific industry and business circumstances -- may cover materiality (quantitatively or qualitatively).

D. If a predecessor auditor is asked to reissue or consent to reuse of an earlier audit report -- the predecessor should obtain an updated representation letter from management.

E. Scope limitations -- management's refusal to furnish written representations will preclude an unqualified opinion (and usually would result in a disclaimer of opinion or withdrawal from the engagement).

AU334 (SAS 45) - Related Parties

I. **Accounting Considerations**

A. GAAP is provided by SFAS 57, "Related Party Disclosures."

B. Emphasizes the adequacy of disclosure regarding related party relationships and transactions, especially "substance over form."

II. **Audit Procedures**

A. **Determining the existence of related parties**

1. Emphasize material transactions with parties known to be related -- review prior year's working papers to identify them.

2. Determining the existence of other related parties involves special effort.

a. Management inquiry:

b. Review SEC filings, if applicable;

c. Identify the names of officers and trustees of all pension and other trusts for the benefit of employees;

d. Review stockholder listings of closely held companies to identify major stockholders;

e. Inquire of predecessor auditors;

f. Review all material investment transactions.

B. **Detecting transactions** with identified related parties.

C. **Examples:**

1. Review the minutes of board of directors' meetings;

2. Review confirmations for guarantees (and investigate whether any such relationship constitutes a related party);

3. Review accounting records for unusual, large transactions or balances, especially near year-end.

D. **Examining documents:** Examining related party transactions that are identified (to ascertain the purpose, nature, and extent of such transactions and their effect on the financial statements):

1. Examine applicable underlying documents;

2. Determine the organization level at which approval was given (e.g. the board of directors);

3. Arrange to audit related inter-company account balances;

4. Confirm important items (e.g., guarantees).

AU336 (SAS 73) - Using the Work of Specialists

Supersedes SAS 11, "Using the Work of a Specialist," (issued December, 1975).

I. Specialist

> **Definition:**
> *Specialist*: "a person (or firm) possessing special skill or knowledge in a particular field other than accounting or auditing." (not a member of the audit staff)

A. **Examples** -- actuaries, appraisers, engineers, environmental consultants, geologists, and attorneys.

II. Decision to use a specialist -- when special knowledge is required

A. Valuation;

B. Determining the quantity and/or quality;

C. Interpreting technical requirements, etc.

III. Selecting a Specialist -- Considerations

A. Professional qualifications (licenses, certifications, etc.);

B. Reputation and standing among peers;

C. Experience in the type of work under consideration;

D. Relationship to client, if any:

1. Specialist unrelated to client is preferable;
2. May use related specialist under some circumstances (have to perform additional audit procedures if related).

IV. Effect of the Specialist's Work on the Auditor's Report

A. The auditor's responsibilities toward the specialist's work:

1. Obtain an understanding of the methods and assumptions used by the specialist;
2. Make appropriate tests of data provided to the specialist;
3. Evaluate whether the specialist's findings support the financial statement assertions.

B. If the findings support the client's representations -- conclude that there is sufficient appropriate evidence.

C. If findings do not support client's representations:

1. Perform additional procedures;
2. If still unresolved, may bring in another specialist.

D. Opinion choice --

1. If material conflicts unresolved -- qualify or disclaim due to scope limitation.
2. If client's representations are not in conformity with GAAP -- qualify or give adverse opinion.

E. Reference to specialist in audit report --

1. Unqualified -- usually do not refer to the specialist(might be misunderstood);
2. Qualified/adverse/disclaimer -- may reference the specialist if that will facilitate the reader's understanding of the reason(s) for the modification.

AU337 (SAS 12) - Inquiry of Client Lawyer

I. **Accounting Considerations**

   A. Management should have policies and procedures to identify litigation, claims, and assessments.

   B. GAAP is provided by SFAS 5, "Accounting for Contingencies."

II. **Auditing Considerations**

   A. The auditor should obtain evidence with respect to 4 factors:

      1. The existence of any such uncertainties regarding litigation, claims, or assessments;

      2. The period in which the underlying event occurred;

      3. The likelihood of an unfavorable outcome (in terms of "probable," "reasonably possible," or "remote");

      4. The amount or range of loss.

   B. **Audit procedures**

      1. **Inquiries of management:** Management is the primary source of information regarding litigation, etc. -- the auditor should make inquiries of management:

         a. About management's policies and procedures for identifying, evaluating and accounting for litigation, claims, etc., and listing all such matters known (along with a description);

         b. To obtain assurance that management has disclosed all **asserted claims** and assessments required to be disclosed according to SFAS 5;

         c. To obtain assurance that management has disclosed all **unasserted claims** that the lawyers have advised must be disclosed according to SFAS 5.

      2. **Examine documents** in client's possession regarding litigation, claims, and assessments (including invoices, correspondence, etc..)

      3. Send a letter of inquiry to the client's lawyer (discussed below).

      4. Other Procedures:

         a. Review the minutes of the board of directors' meetings;

         b. Review contracts, loan agreements, and correspondence -- regarding guarantees and commitments.

III. **Inquiry of the Client's Lawyer(s)**

   A. The "lawyer letter" is the primary source of evidence to corroborate management's representations regarding litigation, claims, and assessments.

   B. **Matters covered:** Matters to be covered should include the following:

      1. Either include management's list of actual or threatened litigation, claims, and assessments or request that the lawyer furnish such a listing of matters to which substantive attention has been given;

      2. Management's list of unasserted claims to which the lawyer has given substantive attention -- consider 2 criteria:

         a. Must be probable of assertion;

         b. Must have at least a reasonable possibility of an unfavorable outcome.

   C. **Direct comments:** The attorney should be asked to comment directly to the auditors on matters to which the attorney devoted substantive attention.

      1. **Regarding asserted claims and active litigation** (for any differences relative to management's listing):

         a. A description of the claim;

   b. The current status of the case;
   c. The client's intentions (e.g. settle or litigate vigorously?;)
   d. The likelihood of an unfavorable outcome;
   e. The amount or range of exposure to loss;

2. Regarding Unasserted Claims:
   a. The client should ask the attorney to comment on any differences relative to such matters included in client's listing of unasserted claims;
   b. For unasserted claims requiring disclosure, but, which are omitted the from the client's list:
      i. The client should request that the attorney inform **management** about the matter;
      ii. The management representation letter will then contain a provision that all such unasserted claims for which the attorney advises disclosure have, in fact, been disclosed;
      iii. The lawyer's letter should explicitly confirm an understanding that the lawyer has advised the client regarding the disclosure of any unasserted claims (omitted from the client's list), for which the attorney believes disclosure is necessary.

D. **Limitations on the scope** of the lawyer's response:

1. May appropriately limit the response to matters to which substantive attention has been given;
2. May limit the response to matters considered to be material, individually or in the aggregate -- if the lawyer and the auditor have agreed on the materiality threshold;
3. If the attorney is unable to form a conclusion about the likelihood of an unfavorable outcome and/or the amount of exposure to loss, the auditor should consider the effect of the uncertainty on the audit opinion -- add an explanatory paragraph?
4. If the attorney refuses to respond to the inquiry (in writing or verbally through a conference), the auditor should consider the refusal to be a scope limitation sufficient to preclude an unqualified opinion.

AU339 (SAS 103) - Audit Documentation

I. **Basic Requirement** -- auditors must prepare audit documentation in sufficient detail to provide a clear understanding of the work performed, the evidence obtained (and its source), and the conclusions reached.

A. Audit documentation provides the principal support the auditor's opinion and the auditor's representation that the audit complied with generally accepted auditing standards.

B. Audit documentation serves additional purposes, including assisting the audit team in planning and performing the audit; assisting with directing the audit work and supervising and reviewing that audit work; and assisting quality control reviewers and others conducting inspections or peer reviews.

C. Audit documentation is the record of procedures performed, evidence obtained, and conclusions reached - also known as "working papers" or "workpapers" whether recorded on paper or electronically:

1. Includes audit programs, analyses, memoranda, letters (such as confirmations and representations letters), checklists, correspondence regarding significant issues, abstracts or copies of important documents, and schedules of work performed, among other things.

2. Abstracts or copies of client records should be included if needed by an experienced auditor to understand the work performed and conclusions reached.

II. **Form, Content, and Extent of Audit Documentation** -- Determining the quantity, type, and content of audit documentation requires professional judgment.

A. Audit documentation should enable an experienced auditor (having no prior connection with the audit) to understand the nature, timing, and extent of procedures performed; the results of those procedures and the evidence obtained; the conclusions reached on significant matters; and whether the accounting records agree with (or reconcile to) the audited financial statements.

B. Oral explanations on their own do not represent sufficient support for the work performed or conclusions reached - may be used to clarify or explain information contained in the audit documentation, however.

C. Some matters may be documented either centrally within a firm or separately in the audit documentation for an audit engagement - for example, independence issues and staff training.

D. Consider the following factors in determining the form, content, and extent of audit documentation - nature of procedures performed; identified risk of material misstatement involved; extent of judgment involved; significance of the evidence obtained to the assertion involved; nature and extent of exceptions identified; and the need to document a conclusion (or the basis for conclusion not readily determinable from the documentation of work performed).

E. Significant findings or issues - the auditor should document significant findings or issues, actions taken to address them, and the basis for the conclusions reached.

1. Significant findings or issues include the following, for example:

a. Significant matters involving the selection, application, and consistency of accounting principles (including disclosures) - including accounting for complex/unusual transactions or accounting estimates and uncertainties;

b. Results of audit procedures indicating a possible material misstatement or need to revise the auditor's assessment of the risks of material misstatement;

c. Circumstances that caused the auditor significant difficulty in applying necessary auditing procedures;

d. Findings that could result in modification of the auditor's report;

e. Audit adjustments (whether or not recorded by management) that, individually or when aggregated with other misstatements, could have a material effect.

2. Should document discussions of significant findings or issues with management (and others) on a timely basis, including responses - document the issues discussed, when, and with whom.

F. If the auditor has identified information that contradicts or is inconsistent with the auditor's final conclusions regarding a significant finding or issue, the auditor should document how the contradiction or inconsistency was addressed in forming the conclusion. (However, the auditor need not retain documentation that is incorrect or that has been superseded.)

G. Identification of preparer and reviewer - the auditor should identify who performed the audit work (and the date such work was completed) and who reviewed the specific audit documentation (and the date the work was reviewed).

H. Documentation of specific items tested - the documentation of tests of controls and substantive tests of details should include "the identifying characteristics" of the specific items tested.

III. **Documentation of Departures from SASs --** If the auditor departs from a "presumptively mandatory requirement", the auditor must document the justification for the departure and how the procedures performed were sufficient to meet the objectives of the presumptively mandatory requirement.

IV. **Revisions to Audit Documentation After the Date of the Auditor's Report**

A. "Report release date" - the date the auditor grants the entity permission to use the auditor's report in connection with the financial statements; the report release date should be recorded in the audit documentation.

B. Changes resulting from the process of assembling and completing the audit file:

1. "Documentation completion date" - the auditor should complete the assembly of the final audit file on a timely basis, but within 60 days following the report release date (a shorter time may be specified by statutes, regulations, or firm policy);

2. Prior to the documentation completion date, the auditor may make changes to the audit documentation (for example, to delete superseded documentation, to add information received after the date of the auditor's report, etc.).

C. Changes after the documentation completion date:

1. Deletions - must not delete or discard audit documentation before the end of the specified retention period;

2. Additions - may add to audit documentation after the documentation completion date, but should document when (and by whom) such changes were made, the reasons for the changes, and the effect, if any, on the auditor's conclusions.

V. **Ownership and Confidentiality of Audit Documentation**

A. Audit documentation is the property of the auditor, who may make copies available to the entity being audited if that does not undermine independence or the validity of the audit process.

B. Retention - should retain audit documentation for a period of time sufficient to meet the auditor's needs and to satisfy any legal or regulatory requirements (should retain audit documentation for at least 5 years from the report release date).

C. Confidentiality - should adopt reasonable procedures to maintain the confidentiality of client information.

D. Auditor should apply appropriate and reasonable controls for audit documentation to:

1. Clearly determine when and by whom audit documentation was created, changed or reviewed;

2. Protect the integrity of the information at all stages of the audit;

3. Prevent unauthorized changes to the documentation; and

4. Allow access as authorized to permit proper discharge of responsibilities.

VI. **Effective Date --** Effective for audits of financial statements for periods ending on or after 12/15/06 (earlier application is permitted).

VII. **Appendix A --** Enumerates specific documentation requirements of other SASs.

VIII. Appendix B -- modifies guidance in SAS No. 1 regarding "Dating of the Independent Auditor's Report."

A. Changes the date of the auditor's report from the "date of completion of fieldwork" to require that the auditor's report "be dated no earlier than the date on which the auditor has obtained sufficient appropriate audit evidence to support the opinion on the financial statements."

B. Sufficient appropriate evidence includes evidence that the audit documentation has been reviewed and that the entity's financial statements (including disclosures) have been prepared and that management has asserted that they have taken responsibility for them.

C. Subsequent events - when a subsequent occurs after the original date of the auditor's report and before issuance of the related financial statements, the auditor may use "dual dating" or may date the report as of the later date. (When using dual dating, the responsibility for events occurring subsequent to the original report date is limited to the specific event involved.)

AU341 (SAS 59) - Going Concerns

I. **Applicability**

A. When there is substantial doubt about the entity's ability to continue as a going concern (usually related to an inability to meet obligations as they come due).

B. Does not apply when financial statements have been based on the assumption of liquidation.

C. Continuation is assumed unless there is evidence to the contrary.

II. **Audit Procedures --** Need not design audit procedures specifically to identify whether there is "substantial doubt" about the going concern assumption. (Routine procedures related to other audit objectives will be applicable to this matter as well.)

A. Analytical procedures.

B. Review of subsequent events.

C. Review of compliance with terms of loan agreements.

D. Reading of minutes of meetings of those charged with governance.

E. Inquiry of client's attorney(s) about contingencies.

F. Confirmation of details of arrangements related to financial support.

III. **Auditor's Specific Responsibilities --** - when there is substantial doubt about the entity continuing as a going concern for 1 year after the date of the financial statements being audited -- referred to as "a reasonable period of time"

A. Obtain information about management's plans intended to mitigate effects of the client's financial difficulties.

1. Nature of the underlying conditions and events:

a. Negative trends -- recurring operating losses, negative cash flows, adverse financial ratios, working capital deficiencies, etc.;

b. Other indications of financial difficulties -- defaults on debt, dividend arrearages, restructuring of debt, disposal of major assets, etc.;

c. Internal matters -- labor problems, dependence on single endeavors, harmful long-term commitments, etc.;

d. External matters -- e.g., lawsuits, legislation, catastrophic losses, loss of major customers, etc.

2. Consideration of management's plans and whether the adverse effects will be mitigated so that those plans can be implemented:

a. Plans to dispose of assets;

b. Plans to borrow or restructure debt;

c. Plans to reduce or delay expenditures;

d. Plans to increase owners' equity.

3. Plan and perform audit procedures to obtain evidence about those elements of management's plans that are most important in overcoming the adverse effects.

B. Reporting considerations when substantial doubt remains.

1. Consider the possible financial statement effects and adequacy of disclosure (may need additional disclosure when substantial doubt is alleviated by management's plans).

2. If disclosure is adequate and an unqualified opinion is issued, the auditor "should include an explanatory paragraph" (after the opinion paragraph).

3. A GAAP departure results if disclosures are inadequate.
4. "Nothing in this section, however, is intended to preclude an auditor from declining to express an opinion in cases involving uncertainties." -- the auditor should give reasons for the disclaimer in the report.
5. Regarding comparative financial statements:
   a. These need not apply to a prior period's financial statements if the underlying conditions arose in the current period;
   b. If the substantial doubt pertaining to prior financial statements has been resolved in the current period, the explanatory paragraph can be dropped.

Note:
The auditor is not responsible for predicting the future -- the failure of an entity to continue as a going concern for the next year without a modification of the audit report does not necessarily indicate a sub-standard audit. (The auditor's evaluation is based on circumstances that exist as of the date of the auditor's report.)

AU342 (SAS 57) - Accounting Estimates

I. Developing the Accounting Estimates - Management's Responsibility

A. The process consists of the following basic steps:

1. Identify situations for which estimates are needed;
2. Identify the relevant factors to be considered;
3. Accumulate necessary data;
4. Develop underlying assumptions;
5. Determine the estimate;
6. Determine compliance with GAAP (including disclosures).

B. Internal control related to accounting estimates - may reduce the likelihood of material misstatements of estimates related to the following:

1. Accumulation of needed data (including reliability);
2. Preparation of estimate by qualified personnel;
3. Adequate review and approval of the estimates and process;
4. Comparison of prior estimates with subsequent results.

II. Evaluating the Reasonableness of the Accounting Estimates - Auditor's Responsibility

A. Basic objective – to obtain sufficient appropriate evidence to provide reasonable assurance that:

1. All estimates that could be material to the financial statements are made;
2. Estimates are reasonable in the circumstances; and
3. Presentation conforms with GAAP.

B. Identifying circumstances that require accounting estimates:

1. Consider industry circumstances and new accounting pronouncements;
2. Consider information obtained by other audit procedures - e.g., inquiries of attorney, reading minutes and regulatory reports, etc.

C. Evaluate reasonableness

1. Focus on key factors and assumptions - those that are significant to the estimate, sensitive to variation, different from past results, or subject to misstatement and bias.
2. Understand how management developed the estimate.
3. Review and test management's process:
   - **a.** Identify relevant controls useful in evaluation;
   - **b.** Identify sources of data and important factors;
   - **c.** Evaluate assumptions for consistency (with each other, the supporting data, past results, etc.).

AU350 (SAS 39) - Audit Sampling

I. SAS No. 39 Issued June, 1981. SAS No. 111 Issued March, 2006.

II. General

A. Definition of "sampling" -- "... application of an audit procedure to less than 100% of the items within an account balance or class of transactions for the purpose of evaluating some characteristic of the balance or class..."

B. Two general approaches -- SAS #39 applies equally to both and either can provide sufficient evidential matter depending upon the circumstances. (The choice is based on cost-benefit considerations.)

1. Nonstatistical -- may be less costly in terms of training auditors and in designing/selecting samples to meet the statistical requirements.
2. Statistical -- benefits relate to "objectivity:"
   a. Design of sample may be more efficient;
   b. Can measure (quantify) the sufficiency of the evidence (i.e., can quantify "sampling risk"--see the following);
   c. Can evaluate the sample results in a defensible way.

C. Recall the third standard of fieldwork (regarding evidential matter). Both nonstatistical and statistical sampling can provide sufficient evidential matter; sufficiency relates to the size (and design) of the sample.

D. Ordinarily, the sample sizes should be relatively comparable whether statistical or non-statistical sampling is used.

III. Uncertainty

A. Recall the notion of "audit risk" -- that material errors will occur, will not be prevented/detected by the system of internal control, and will not be detected by the auditor's substantive procedures.

1. Audit risk -- the uncertainty inherent in applying audit procedures.

> "... the auditor should determine an acceptable audit risk and subjectively quantify his or her judgment of the risk of material misstatement (consisting of inherent risk and control risk), and the risk that substantive analytical procedures and other relevant substantive procedures would fail to detect misstatements that could occur in an assertion equal to tolerable misstatement, given that such misstatements occur and are not detected by the entity's controls."

2. A table in the appendix includes the following model for auditors who prefer to evaluate these judgment risks explicitly: TD = AR/(RMM*AP); (alternatively, AR = RMM*AP*TD):
   a. TD = Allowable risk of incorrect acceptance, that is, test of details risk..
   b. AR = Audit risk
   c. RMM = Risk of material misstatement, consisting of the combined assessments of inherent and control risks.
   d. AP = Risk that substantive analytical procedures will not detect a material misstatement.
3. Audit risk includes both "sampling risk" and "non-sampling risk."

B. Sampling risk:

1. Definition -- the risk that "... the auditor's conclusions may be different from the conclusions he would reach if the test were applied in the same way to all items in the account balance or class of transactions." (Sampling risk varies inversely with the sample size.)
2. Sampling risk has two dimensions (where the risk is that incorrect conclusions may be caused by basing one's conclusions on a sample, instead of the entire population):

a. Type I errors -- related to efficiency (a secondary concern):

i. Attributes sampling -- "risk of under-reliance" (also known as "risk of assessing control risk too high").

ii. Variables sampling -- "risk of incorrect rejection."

b. Type II errors -- related to effectiveness (the primary concern!):

i. Attributes sampling -- "risk of over-reliance" (also known as "risk of assessing control risk too low");

ii. Variables sampling -- "risk of incorrect acceptance."

C. "Nonsampling risk" -- all the aspects of audit risk that are not specifically due to sampling. (Nonsampling risk can be dealt with by adequate planning and supervision.)

IV. **Variables Sampling --** Sampling in substantive tests of details.

A. Planning samples -- the auditor should consider (1) tolerable misstatement and the expected misstatement; (2) audit risk; (3) the characteristics of the population; (4) the assessed risk of material misstatement (inherent risk and control risk); and (5) the assessed risk for other substantive procedures related to the same assertion.

1. "Tolerable misstatement" -- "the maximum monetary misstatement that the auditor is willing to accept for the balance or class"; this notion relates to the auditor's planning-state materiality judgment and should be set in such a way that tolerable misstatement, combined for the entire audit plan, does not exceed materiality for the financial statements. (Sample size is inversely related to tolerable misstatement.)

2. The allowable risk of incorrect acceptance (i.e., Type II error) increases (and, hence, the sample size decreases) with greater reliance on I/C or other related substantive tests.

3. Characteristics of the population affect the sample size:

a. Population size -- may influence sample size (that is, as the population size increases, a larger sample size is required);

b. Variation -- sample size is directly related. (The more variable the population is, the larger the sample size must be. The auditor may reduce the effect of variability by stratification of populations into more homogeneous subsets, reducing variability within subsets.)

B. Sample selection -- should be representative of the population (e.g., random, stratified random, "probability proportionate to size," and systematic sampling).

C. Performance and evaluation – are based on professional judgment.

1. Materiality:

a. Examine all individually material items;

b. If unable to apply planned audit procedures to selected sample items (e.g., the entity might not be able to locate supporting documentation) -- the auditor need not examine those items which could not alter the auditor's evaluation even if those items were viewed as errors; however, the auditor should perform appropriate alternative audit procedures if treating those items as misstatements would cause the auditor to conclude that there is, in fact, a material misstatement.

2. If the projected error is close to the tolerable error, there may be an unacceptable risk that the actual errors in the population exceed the tolerable error.

3. Qualitative aspects should be considered. Nature and cause of the misstatement, such as whether the misstatement is due to errors or to fraud. Relationship with other parts of the audit.

V. **Attributes Sampling --** Sampling to determine whether internal control procedures of interest were working effectively.

A. Planning of samples:

1. Requires an audit trail -- "Sampling generally is not applicable to tests of compliance with internal accounting control procedures that depend primarily on appropriate segregation of

duties or that otherwise provide no documentary evidence of performance." (The overall evaluation of I/C involves judgment in combining results of tests of control and the auditor's observations and inquiries about undocumented controls.)

2. "Tolerable rate" -- "...the maximum rate of deviations from a prescribed control procedure that (the auditor) would be willing to accept without altering (the) planned reliance..."

   a. Considerations:

      i. Accounting records being tested;

      ii. Related internal accounting control procedures;

      iii. Purpose of the evaluation.

   b. Suggests 5% or 10% (often higher as a practical matter)--select low level if the compliance test is the primary source of evidence regarding the control procedure.

   c. Factors that influence sample size:

      i. Tolerable error rate -- inverse relationship;

      ii. Expected error rate -- direct relationship (related to the notion of the variability of the population);

      iii. Allowable risk of over-reliance -- inverse relationship.

B. Sample selection -- the key issue is the "representativeness" of the sample. (Note that a "random" sample is assumed to be representative of the population, but may not be truly representative due to the existence of "sampling risk.")

C. Performance and evaluation:

   1. If unable to apply planned procedures to certain items, view those items as "errors;"

   2. If the observed error rate (per the sample) differs from the expected error rate (which was used to calculate sample size), recalculate the adequacy of the sample size using the error rate from the sample (usually only if the observed sample error rate is higher than the expected rate used in planning).

   3. Consider the qualitative aspects of observed errors:

      a. Nature and cause of the deviation from prescribed controls, such as whether the deviations are due to errors or fraud;

      b. Relationship with other parts of the audit.

D. Sampling concepts do not apply to risk assessment procedures performed to obtain an understanding of internal control and do not apply for certain tests of controls:

   1. Tests of automated application controls are usually tested once (or a few times) when effective (IT) general controls are present -- so, in that context, the auditor does not rely on the concepts of risk and tolerable deviation;

   2. Sampling is usually not applicable to analyses of controls for determining the appropriate segregation of duties or other analyses that do not examine documentary evidence of performance; sampling may not apply to tests of certain documented controls or to analyses of the effectiveness of security and access controls; sampling may not apply to some tests of the operation of the control environment (for example, when examining the actions of those charged with governance for assessing their effectiveness).

VI. **"Dual Purpose Samples" --** When the same sample is used to test the operating effectiveness of an identified control (control purpose) and to test the recorded monetary amount (substantive purpose).

   A. The sample size for a dual purpose test should be the larger of the samples that would otherwise have been designed for the two separate purposes.

   B. Misstatements discovered by performing substantive procedures should be considered as possible indications of a control failure when assessing the operating effectiveness of related controls. (The converse is not true -- i.e., the absence of misstatements does not imply that related controls are effective.)

AU380 (SAS 114) - The Auditor's Communication

I. **SAS No. 114 Supersedes SAS No. 61, "Communication with Audit Committees" --** the new SAS expands the auditor's responsibility beyond audit committees (or equivalent groups) specifically to "those charged with governance;" it also increases the specific matters to be communicated and provides guidance on the communication process.

A. Definitions

> **Definitions:**
>
> *Those charged with governance*: the person(s) with responsibility for overseeing the strategic direction of the entity and obligations related to the accountability of the entity (encompasses the term "board of directors" or "audit committee" used elsewhere in auditing standards).
>
> *Management*: the person(s) responsible for achieving the objectives of the entity and who have the authority to establish policies and make decisions by which those objectives are to be pursued.

B. SAS No. 114 emphasizes the importance of effective two-way communication to the audit - the SAS provides a framework for the auditor's communication with those charged with governance and identifies specific matters to be communicated (other SASs identify additional matters to be communicated)

C. Basic auditor responsibility - the auditor must communicate those matters that are significant and relevant to the responsibilities of those charged with governance in overseeing the financial reporting process. (The auditor is not required to perform specific procedures to identify other significant matters to communicate with those charged with governance.)

II. **The role of Communication**

A. The principal purposes of communication with those charged with governance are to:

1. Communicate clearly the responsibilities of the auditor, and an overview of the scope and timing of the audit;
2. Obtain information relevant to the audit from those charged with governance;
3. Provide those charged with governance with information relevant to their responsibilities in overseeing the financial reporting process.

B. This SAS focuses primarily on communications from the auditor to those charged with governance - but effective "two-way" communication is important to both parties in meeting their respective responsibilities.

III. **Communication with Those Charged with Governance**

A. Identifying with whom to communicate - the appropriate person(s) may vary depending upon the circumstances and the matter to be communicated (e.g., governance structures may vary by the entity's size and ownership characteristics).

1. Governance is usually the collective responsibility of a governing body (such as a board of directors, etc.) and a subgroup (such as the audit committee) may be assigned specific tasks - in smaller entities, one person (such as the owner-manager) may be charged with governance.
2. An understanding of the entity's governance structure and policies obtained in accordance with SAS No. 109, "Understanding the Entity and Its Environment and Assessing the Risks of Material Misstatement" is relevant in deciding with whom to communicate matters.
3. When the appropriate persons with whom to communicate are not clearly identifiable - the auditor and the engaging party should agree on the relevant person(s) with whom the auditor will communicate.

B. Communication with the audit committee (or other subgroup) - when an audit committee exists, communication with it is a key element of the auditor's communication with those charged with governance.

1. Good governance principles suggest that: (a) the auditor has access to the audit committee as needed; (b) the chair of the audit committee (and other members when relevant) meets with the auditor periodically; and (c) the audit committee meets with the auditor without management present at least annually.
2. The auditor should evaluate whether communication with a subgroup (such as the audit committee) adequately fulfills the responsibility to communication with those charged with governance - auditors may wish to make explicit in the engagement letter that they retain the right to communicate with the governing body.

IV. Communication with Management

A. The auditor may discuss matters with management before communicating them with those charged with governance - unless that is inappropriate (e.g., issues involving management's competence or integrity).

B. When the entity has an internal audit function - the auditor may discuss matters with the internal auditor(s) before communicating with those charged with governance.

C. When all those charged with governance are involved in managing the entity -matters communicated with the person(s) in a management role need not be communicated again to the same person(s) in a governance role.

V. Matters to be Communicated with Those Charged with Governance -- May choose to communicate additional matters. (Management's communication of these matters to those charged with governance does not relieve the auditor of the responsibility to also communicate them.)

A. The auditor's responsibilities under GAAS - may be communicated by the engagement letter (or other contract) if given to those charged with governance.

B. Planned scope and timing of the audit - should communicate an overview of the planned scope and timing of the audit. (Be careful to avoid reducing the effectiveness of the audit by divulging the detailed audit procedures which could cause those procedures to be too predictable.)

1. How the auditor plans to address the significant risks of material misstatement.
2. Approach to internal control relevant to the audit.
3. Materiality - focusing on the factors considered, not thresholds.
4. Internal audit function - including the auditor's use of the internal audit function and how they can best work together.

C. Significant findings from the audit - the following matters should be discussed with those charged with governance:

1. Qualitative aspects of the entity's significant accounting policies - comment on the acceptability of significant accounting practices (this may address accounting policies, accounting estimates, financial statement disclosures, the selective correction of misstatements, etc.);
2. Significant difficulties encountered during the audit - including significant delays by management in providing information; unreasonable time pressure to complete the audit; unavailability of expected information; restrictions imposed on the auditors by management; or extensive unexpected effort required to obtain sufficient appropriate audit evidence;
3. Disagreements with management over accounting or auditing matters - whether or not these are satisfactorily resolved;
4. Uncorrected misstatements - discuss any uncorrected misstatements identified and the effect on the auditor's report (These should be communicated individually, unless there are a large number of small uncorrected misstatements.); should also communicate the effect of any uncorrected misstatements related to prior periods;
5. Management's consultations with other accountants - when aware that such consultation has occurred, the auditor should discuss with those charged with governance the matters that were subject to consultation;

6. Significant issues discussed (or subject to correspondence) with management in connection with the auditor's retention - communicate any significant issues that were discussed (or subject to correspondence) with management, including business conditions affecting the entity and the application of GAAP;

7. Independence issues - the auditor may discuss circumstances or relationships that might influence independence which the auditor considered in concluding that independence is not impaired.

VI. The Communication Process

A. Establishing a mutual understanding - the auditor should communicate the form, timing, and expected general content of communications. (Effective two-way communication should include the process for taking action/reporting back on matters communicated by the auditor and matters communicated by those charged with governance.)

B. Forms of communication - generally communication may be oral or in writing: (Effective communication may include formal presentations, written reports, or informal discussions, as appropriate.)

1. The auditor should communicate in writing the significant findings from the audit when, in the auditor's judgment, oral communication is not adequate;

2. The decision to communicate orally or in writing may be influenced by: (a) whether the matter has been satisfactorily resolved; (b) whether management has already communicated the matter; (c) the size and operating structure of the entity; (d) legal or regulatory requirements; (e) the expectations of those charged with governance; and (f) whether there have been significant changes in the membership of a governing body;

3. When a significant matter is discussed with an individual member of those charged with governance (e.g., the chair of the audit committee) - the auditor may decide that it is appropriate to summarize the matter in a subsequent communication to all those charged with governance;

4. When matters are communicated in writing - the auditor should restrict the distribution of that communication to those charged with governance (and, if appropriate to management).

C. Adequacy of the communication process - the auditor should evaluate whether the two-way communication has been adequate for purposes of the audit: (If not, the auditor should take appropriate action to address the effectiveness of the communication process.)

1. Inadequate two-way communication may indicate an unsatisfactory control environment; (The auditor need not design specific procedures to support the evaluation.)

2. If the two-way communication is not adequate, this may constitute a scope limitation, so the auditor should consider the possible effect on the assessment of the risks of material misstatement, which could warrant modification of the opinion or even withdrawing from the engagement.

D. Timing of communications - should communicate on a timely basis so that those charged with governance can take appropriate action. (This timing will vary with the circumstances.)

VII. Documentation -- When the auditor has communicated orally those matters required to be communicated by this SAS, the auditor should document them. (When communicated in writing, the auditor should retain a copy of the communication.)

VIII. Effective Date -- Effective for audits of financial statements for periods beginning on or after December 15, 2006.

IX. Appendix -- Requirements in other SASs to communicate specific matters with those charged with governance:

A. SAS No. 54, "Illegal Acts" - should communicate illegal acts that come to the auditor's attention;

B. SAS No. 59, "The Auditor's Consideration of an Entity's Ability to Continue as a Going Concern" - when substantial doubt about the entity's ability to continue as a going concern remains, the auditor should communicate (1) the nature of the conditions identified; (2) the possible effect on the financial statements and disclosures; and (3) the effects on the auditor's report;

C. SAS No. 74, "Compliance Auditing Considerations in Audits of Governmental Entities and Recipients of Governmental Financial Assistance" - should communicate when the entity is subject to an audit requirement that may not be encompassed by the terms of the engagement (that is, when an audit in accordance with GAAS may not satisfy applicable legal or other requirements);

D. SAS No. 99, "Consideration of Fraud in a Financial Statement Audit" - (1) should inquire of the audit committee about the risks of fraud and the audit committee's knowledge of any fraud or suspected fraud; (2) should communicate any fraud discovered involving senior management and any fraud (whether or not senior management is involved) that causes a material misstatement to the financial statements; and (3) should obtain an understanding with those charged with governance regarding communications about misappropriations committed by lower-level employees;

E. SAS No. 112, "Communicating Internal Control Related Matters Identified in an Audit" - should communicate in writing to management and those charged with governance any identified significant deficiencies (or material weaknesses) .

AU390 (SAS 46) - Omitted Procedures

I. **Applicability --** When the auditor realizes, subsequent to the report date, that auditing procedures which were considered necessary at the report date were, in fact, omitted.

  A. AU390 applies when there is no reason to believe that the financial statements were materially misstated.

  B. AU561 applies when the auditors become aware subsequent to the report date that facts may have existed at the report date that might have affected the report had they been aware of those facts at that time.

  C. An auditor might discover such omissions as a result of a post-issuance review related to the firm's quality assurance program or related to a peer review.

II. **Requirements --** Assess whether the omitted procedure affects the auditor's ability to support the audit opinion:

  A. The omission may not have any impact -- if other procedures already performed compensate for the omitted one;

  B. If the omitted procedure apparently impairs the auditor's ability to support the opinion -- the auditor should promptly perform the omitted procedure (or perform appropriate alternative procedures);

    1. If the results of the procedure support the report issue -- document the (belated) performance of the procedure in the working papers;

    2. If the results of the procedure do not support the opinion:

      a. Consult AU561 regarding facts existing at the report date that would have affected the report had the auditor known these facts at that time;

      b. Probably consult with an attorney regarding the auditor's responsibilities to the client, regulatory bodies, and users of the financial statements.

AU410 (SAS 1) - Adherence to GAAP

I. First Standard of Reporting --

AU410 (SAS 1) Relates to the **First Standard of Reporting** - "The report shall state whether the financial statements are presented in accordance with (GAAP)."

A. Includes the accounting principles and practices.

B. Includes the methods of applying the principles and practices.

Note:
The first standard of reporting involves a statement of **opinion**, not a statement of **fact.**

AU420 (SAS 1) - Consistent Application of GAAP

I. **Relates to the Second Standard of Reporting --** "The report shall identify those circumstances in which such principles (GAAP) have not been consistently observed in the current period in relation to the preceding period."

II. **Affecting Factors --** Factors that may affect the comparability of the financial statements between years:

   A. Accounting changes **affecting consistency** (recognize in audit report);

   B. **Change** in accounting principle -- changing from one **accepted** principle to another one (requires mention in report);

   C. **Change** in reporting entity:

      1. Requiring recognition in the auditor's report:

         a. Presenting consolidated or combined financial statements in place of individual companies' financial statements;

         b. Changing which subsidiaries are reflected in the consolidated financial statements (or which companies are included in the combined financial statements);

         c. Changing among the cost, equity, and consolidation methods of accounting for subsidiaries.

      2. Changes that do not involve consistency (are not recognized in the auditor's report) include acquiring or selling a subsidiary or other business unit.

   D. **Correction of an error** in principle -- changing from an **unaccepted** principle to an accepted one:

      1. Requires recognition in the audit report as to consistency;

      2. Accounted for as a correction of an error.

   E. **Inseparable Principle -** A change in principle that is inseparable from a change in estimate requires recognition as to consistency in audit report -- treated as a change in principle;

   F. Changes that **do not affect consistency** are not recognized in the auditor's report;

   G. Change in Accounting Estimate:

      1. The auditor must verify that such a change does not involve a principle (i.e., is not "inseparable" with a principle);

      2. Disclosure in the financial statements may be required if the change in estimate is material.

   H. **Correction of an error** (not involving principle);

   I. **Changes in classification** or reclassification -- usually not so material as to require disclosure, but may require disclosure if material;

   J. **Transactions/Events -** Substantially different transactions or events – these may require disclosure when the substance of transactions or event are clearly different that those previously occurring;

   K. **Future Material Effects -** Accounting change currently not having a material effect, but expected to have a material future effect -- it may require financial statement disclosure (but does not require recognition in audit report).

III. **Other Matters**

   A. **Disclosure of changes** not affecting consistency -- although these items do not require recognition as to consistency in the audit report, disclosure of such items may be required if material; if the appropriate disclosure is not made, the auditor may have to issue a qualification as to GAAP departure.

B. Periods encompassed by this consistency standard:

1. Reporting only on the current year -- consistency involves the current year in relation to the prior year (whether or not the prior year's financial statements are presented);
2. Reporting on 2 or more years -- consistency only involves the financial statements being reported on and the prior year's financial statements if also presented;
3. **First year audits** -- the auditor should perform procedures to ascertain that the principles used in the current year are consistent with the prior year; if unable to determine that the principles were consistent, the auditor may be precluded from issuing an opinion on the results of operations and cash flows (due to a scope limitation).

AU431 (SAS 32) - Adequacy of Disclosure

I. **Relates to the Third Standard of Reporting --** "Informative disclosures in the financial statements are to be regarded as reasonably adequate unless otherwise stated in the report."

   A. If management omits required information from the financial statements or notes, the auditor should express a qualified or adverse opinion (due to a GAAP departure):

      1. If practicable, include the omitted information in the auditor's report;

      2. If the omission from the audit report is permitted by specific SASs, it is not necessary for the auditor to provide the missing information -- for example, the auditor would not have to include an omitted statement of cash flows, or omitted segment information.

   B. The auditor should obtain the client's permission to disclose any additional information that is not required to be disclosed by GAAP -- due to confidentiality considerations.

II. **When Information Required by GAAP is Omitted from the Financial Statements --** "If management omits from the financial statements, including the accompanying notes, information that is required by generally accepted accounting principles, the auditor should express a qualified or an adverse opinion and should provide the information in his report, if practicable, unless its omission from the auditor's report is recognized as appropriate by a specific Statement on Auditing Standards. In this context, practicable means that the information is reasonably obtainable from management's accounts and records and that providing the information in the report does not require the auditor to assume the position of a preparer of financial information. For example, the auditor would not be expected to prepare a basic financial statement or segment information and include it in his report when management omits such information." (AU 431.03)

AU504 (SAS 26) - Association with Financial Statements

I. **General Comments --** AU508 governs the report on audited financial statements.

  A. Intended to clarify the reference to **"associated with financial statements"** in the **Fourth Standard of Reporting.**

  B. Applies to both public and private companies when the independent accountant is engaged to examine the financial statements in accordance with GAAS.

  C. The **CPA is "associated with financial statements"** when:

    1. Consenting to the use of the CPA's name in a report or other written communication containing the financial statements;

    2. Submitting to the client (or others) the financial statements prepared by the accountant (or for which assistance in the preparation is given) -- whether or not the accountant's name is attached to the financial statements.

II. **Disclaimers of Opinion When Associated with Financial Statements**

  A. Associated with unaudited financial statements:

    1. The report consists of one sentence -- "The (financial statements) were not audited by us and, accordingly, we do not express an opinion on them."

    2. Do not describe any procedures that may have been performed -- except where the circumstances specifically permit negative assurance with regard to a review, letters to underwriters, etc.

    3. If the financial statements are prepared on a comprehensive basis other than GAAP -- the disclaimer is essentially as above, except that the financial statements should be labeled appropriately in view of the basis used.

  B. When Lacking Independence:

    1. The report consists of one sentence -- "We are not independent with respect to ... the (financial statements) and, accordingly, we do not express an opinion on them."

    2. For a nonpublic entity -- guidance for review and compilation engagements is provided by the Statements on Standards for Accounting and Review Services.

  C. Circumstances requiring a modified disclaimer:

    1. GAAP departure identified (including inadequate disclosure) -- failing revision by the client, the auditor should describe the departure in the disclaimer if practicable;

    2. When the effects of the departure are not reasonably estimable, the auditor should indicate that fact;

    3. If management chooses to omit all disclosures, including them in the accountant's report becomes impracticable.

III. **Statements in Comparative Form --** When unaudited financial statements are presented in comparative form with the audited financial statements:

  A. **Unaudited statements:** Any financial statements that have not been audited should be **clearly marked "unaudited"** to indicate their status;

  B. **Prior period implications:** Either the report on the prior period should be reissued or the report on the current period should include a separate paragraph describing the responsibility assumed, if any, for the prior period's financial statements;

  C. **Included paragraph:** When the report on the current period includes a separate paragraph, it should include:

    1. A statement of the service performed in the current period;

2. The date of the report regarding that service;
3. A description of any material modifications of that report;
4. A statement that the service was less in scope than an audit and that the service does not provide a basis for an opinion:
    a. For a public client -- disclaim an opinion;
    b. For a private client -- if the service was a compilation or a review, appropriately describe such service.

AU508 (SAS 58) - Reports on Financial Statements

I. **Applicability**

A. Does not apply to unaudited financial statements (see AU504).

B. "Taken as a whole" applies to individual financial statements as well as to a set of financial statements.

II. **Unqualified Audit Report** -- The standard audit report:

A. **Title** includes the word "independent;"

B. **Addressee** -- the company, board of directors, or stockholders;

C. **Introductory paragraph** -- consists of 3 sentences:

1. Identifies the financial statements audited;
2. States that the financial statements are management's responsibility;
3. States that the auditor's responsibility is to express an audit opinion on the financial statements.

D. **Scope paragraph** -- consists of 5 sentences:

1. States that the audit was conducted in accordance with GAAS;
2. States that GAAS requires the auditor to plan and perform the audit to obtain "reasonable assurance" as to whether the financial statements are materially misstated;
3. States that an audit includes examining evidence on a test basis related to the amounts and disclosures of the financial statements;
4. States that an audit includes assessing the accounting principles used and significant estimates made (as well as evaluating the overall financial statement presentation);
5. States the belief that the audit provides a reasonable basis for the opinion.

E. **Opinion paragraph** -- (one sentence) State the opinion as to whether the financial statements are presented fairly, in all material respects, in conformity with GAAP;

F. **Signature** of the auditor's firm -- manual or printed;

G. **Date** of the audit report (usually the last day of fieldwork).

III. **Unqualified Audit Report** -- Modified, still unqualified.

A. **Opinion based on others:** Opinion based in part on the report of other auditors:

1. When referencing -- affects the introductory, scope, and opinion paragraphs; **does not need an explanatory paragraph;**
2. In the introductory paragraph, indicate the total assets and revenues covered by the other auditors' report(s).

B. **Opinion/Explanatory:** When expressing an unqualified opinion, any explanatory paragraph will follow the opinion paragraph; when issuing a qualified or adverse opinion, the explanatory paragraph will precede the opinion paragraph;

C. Circumstances that may **require an explanatory paragraph** without affecting the unqualified opinion:

1. A **departure** from a promulgated accounting principle -- deemed necessary to keep the financial statements from being misleading (due to unusual circumstances);
2. **Uncertainties** -- when the financial statement treatment is consistent with GAAP, but the uncertainty is sufficiently important that the auditor wants to address it;

3. When there is **substantial doubt about an entity's ability to continue as a going concern** (see AU341) -- when the financial statement treatment is consistent with GAAP, but the uncertainty is sufficiently important that the auditor wants to address it;
4. When a material **change has occurred in the application of accounting principles** -- the auditor should add an explanatory paragraph to describe the nature of the change and refer to the appropriate note in the financials;
5. When **"supplementary information"** required by the FASB or GASB is **omitted;**
6. **Other Information Misleading:** "Other information" presented with the financial statements is misleading (see AU550);
7. **Emphasis of a matter** -- for example:
    a. Major related party transactions;
    b. Entity part of a larger economic entity;
    c. Unusually important subsequent events;
    d. Accounting matter affecting comparability.

IV. Departures from Unqualified Opinions

A. **Qualified opinions** -- taken as a whole, the financial statements are fairly stated, but the auditor expresses reservations...
    1. **Scope limitations** -- insufficiency of evidential matter:
        a. Imposed by circumstances:
            i. Issue a qualified opinion or a disclaimer of opinion;
            ii. Examples include an inability to observe inventory or confirm receivables, or obtain audited financial statements of an investee accounted for using the equity method.
        b. **Imposed by the client** -- ordinarily should disclaim;
        c. Reporting:
            i. Describe the reasons in an explanatory paragraph preceding the opinion paragraph;
            ii. The opinion should refer to "the effects of such adjustments, if any" rather than to the scope limitation itself.
    2. **GAAP departures:**
        a. **Issue a qualified opinion or an adverse opinion;**
        b. Reporting:
            i. Describe the reasons in an explanatory paragraph preceding the opinion paragraph;
            ii. Explain the effects of the matter on the financial statements (or state that such effects are not determinable).
        c. For inadequate disclosure:
            i. Provide the omitted information in the audit report, if practicable;
            ii. Providing the missing statement of cash flows in the audit report, for example, is not necessary
        d. **For accounting changes** -- the auditor should evaluate the method of accounting for the change and management's justification for the change in principle.

B. Adverse Opinions:
    1. Taken as a whole, the financial statements are not fairly stated in conformity with GAAP;
    2. Add an explanatory paragraph preceding the opinion stating the reasons for the adverse opinion and the effects on the financial statements (if reasonably determinable).

C. Disclaimer of Opinion:

1. Add an explanatory paragraph preceding the opinion stating that the scope was insufficient to express an opinion -- do not identify the procedures that were performed (might be misunderstood by users);
2. Disclose any known reservations about the financial statements.

D. **"Piecemeal opinions"** (expressing an adverse opinion or a disclaimer on the statements taken as a whole, but expressing a contrary opinion on certain identified elements within a financial statement) are prohibited.

V. **Reports on Comparative Financial Statements**

A. General Comments:

1. "Taken as a whole" also applies to those financial statements presented for comparative purposes along with the current financial statements;
2. Should be alert for matters that affect the prior financial statements;
3. May issue a different report on the comparative financial statements than for the current financial statements.

B. **Opinion prior changed:** The opinion expressed on the prior financial statements can change from the opinion issued earlier:

1. Should consider any changes in circumstances that affect the prior financial statements and the audit report;
2. If the updated report contains a changed audit opinion -- add a separate paragraph preceding the opinion paragraph and:
   a. Identify the date of the auditor's previous report;
   b. State the type of opinion previously given;
   c. Describe the reasons for the change in the opinion;
   d. State that the opinion differs from the opinion previously expressed.

C. **Predecessor report:** If the report of the predecessor auditor is presented along with the successor's report on the current financial statements:

1. **Reissued:** If the predecessor auditor's report is reissued -- the predecessor should:
   a. Read the current financial statements and compare them with the prior financial statements;
   b. Obtain a letter of representations from the successor (regarding matters that might affect the prior financial statements;)
   c. Make inquiries and perform other appropriate procedures if any matters having possible material effect on the prior financial statements are found;
   d. Use the date of the previous report (unless the financial statements or the audit report are restated -- if so, "dual date" the report).
2. **Not presented:** If the predecessor auditor's report is not presented -- the successor should add appropriate comments to the introductory paragraph:
   a. State that the financial statements of the prior period were audited by other auditors;
   b. Identify the date of the other auditors' report;
   c. Specify the type of opinion issued by the other auditors;
   d. Identify the reasons if their report was other than the standard unqualified report.

AU530 (SAS 1) - Dating of the Report

I. General Comments

A. The auditor's report should not be dated earlier than the date on which the auditor has obtained sufficient appropriate audit evidence to support the opinion. That date should not precede the completion of field work. (The auditor's report may be dated later than the end of field work, depending upon when management has taken responsibility for the financial statements, including footnotes, and when the auditor has reviewed the audit documentation.)

B. The auditor has no responsibility to perform on-going procedures subsequent to the date of the auditor's report.

II. Subsequent Events -- Occurring After Completion of Field Work But Before Issuance of the Auditor's Report (see AU560).

A. For those subsequent events requiring financial statement adjustment:

1. If the financial statements are adjusted without disclosure -- the report should be dated as of the date on which the auditor has obtained sufficient appropriate audit evidence;
2. If the financial statements are adjusted and disclosure is also made (or if no adjustment is made and a qualified opinion is issued as a result) -- the 2 methods of dating described in "B" below are applicable.

B. For those subsequent events requiring only financial statement disclosure -- there are 2 alternatives for dating the audit report when the subsequent event is detected after the original date of the auditor's report but before issuance of the financial statements:

1. **"Dual dating"** -- the overall report is dated as of the original date; however, a reference to the relevant footnote applicable to the subsequent event is added to the date of the audit report, which reference is dated as of the later date;
2. Date the entire report as of the later date -- however, in this case, the auditor would be responsible for all subsequent events up to this later date.

III. Re-Issuance of the Auditor's Report

A. The auditor may reissue an audit report on financial statements (included with an annual report filed with the SEC or in another document submitted to the client or to others) subsequent to the date of the original report.

B. A report may be reissued at the client's request.

C. Dating the reissued report:

1. Using the original report date in a reissued audit report signals that the auditor did not examine or review the records, transactions, or events after that original date;
2. The auditor may decide not to reissue the original audit report if becoming aware that a subsequent event has occurred after the date of the original report that requires financial statement adjustment or disclosure.
    - **a.** When adjustment is required to financial statements previously reported on for a subsequent event in connection with financial statements to be reissued -- **"adjustment with disclosure"** should be made. (Note that the financial statements should not be adjusted unless the matter meets the criteria in the accounting standards for the correction of an error or for prior period adjustments.)
    - **b.** An audit report on the revised financial statements with the added disclosure should be dated either using "dual dating" or a later overall date, as discussed in section "II" above.
3. A subsequent event occurring after the original report date that requires disclosure only - can be disclosed in a separate footnote to the financial statements with a caption to the effect of: "Event (Unaudited) Subsequent to the Date of the Independent Auditor's Report." The reissued report could then use the original date.

AU532 (SAS 87) - Restricting the Use of an Auditor's Report

I. **"General-use" and "Restricted-use" Reports**

A. **General use** - auditors' reports that are not restricted to specified parties.

B. **Restricted use** - auditors' reports that are intended only for specified parties.

C. Reasons for restricting use of auditors' reports:

1. Purpose of the report;
2. Nature of the procedures applied;
3. Assumptions used;
4. Whether procedures used are generally known;
5. Potential for the report to be misunderstood.

D. Reports should be restricted for the following:

1. Subject matter or presentation being reported is based on criteria contained in contracts or regulations that are not GAAP or other comprehensive basis of accounting - should be restricted to the parties to the agreement or to the regulatory agency responsible for the provisions;
2. Report is based on specific procedures to meet the needs of specified parties who take responsibility for the sufficiency - should be restricted to the specified parties responsible for the sufficiency of the procedures for their purposes;
3. Report is issued as a "by-product" of a financial statement audit and is based on procedures performed for purposes of that audit (i.e., procedures not intended to provide assurance on the subject matter of that by-product report).

II. **Reporting as a By-product of a Financial Statement Audit**

A. Examples of "by-product" reports:

1. Reports related to internal control matters noted in an audit;
2. Matters communicated to audit committees;
3. Reports on compliance with contractual provisions or regulations related to a financial statement audit;
4. Reports on one or more specified elements, accounts, or items in accordance with GAAS.

B. Nothing in SAS 87 prevents the auditor from restricting the use of any report.

C. Nature of a "by-product" report - not the primary objective of the engagement, so the procedures performed are usually limited. (This results in potential for misinterpretation or misunderstanding; the report should be restricted.)

D. By-product reports should be restricted to: the audit committee; board of directors; management; others within the organization; specified regulatory agencies; or to the parties to the contract or agreement (when reporting on compliance with aspects of contracts).

E. Limiting the distribution of the reports - the auditor is not responsible for controlling a client's distribution of the restricted-use report (restriction should be clearly identified to alert readers).

III. **Report Language for a Restricted-use Report**

A. Consists of a separate paragraph at the end of the report:

1. State that report is intended solely for the information and use of the specified parties;
2. Identify the specified parties;
3. State that the report is not intended to be and should not be used by anyone other than the specified parties.

B. Example of language - "This report is intended solely for the information and use of (the specified parties) and is not intended to be and should not be used by anyone other than the specified parties."

IV. **Other Matters**

A. Combined reports covering both restricted-use and general-use subject matter or presentations - any such single, combined report should be restricted.

B. Inclusion of a separate restricted-use report in the same document with a general-use report - can include a restricted-use report in a document containing a general-use report without affecting the use of either report.

C. Adding other specified parties - other specified users can be added when reporting on subject matter or a presentation based on criteria contained in contracts or regulations:

1. Obtain other users' understanding (usually in writing) of the nature of the engagement and the criteria used;
2. Ways to add other specified users after the report has been issued:
   a. Report can be reissued - report date should not be changed;
   b. Auditor can provide other written acknowledgment that the parties have been added - this is usually a statement that no procedures have been performed subsequent to report date.

V. **Effective Date** -- for reports issued after 12/31/98 (earlier application is encouraged).

AU534 (SAS 51) - Reports for Other Countries

I. **General Comments**

   A. **Applicability** -- when an auditor practicing in the U.S. is engaged to report on the financial statements of a U.S. client that have been prepared in conformity with the principles of another country for use outside U.S.

   B. Examples:

      1. The financial statements of a U.S. entity are prepared for inclusion in the consolidated financial statements of a non-U.S. parent;

      2. The U.S. entity may have non-U.S. investors or may wish to raise capital outside of the U.S.

   C. The auditor should clearly understand the intended use of such financial statements and obtain appropriate written representations from management;

II. **Audit Procedures**

   A. **Applicability of U.S. GAAS** – the auditor performs the audit procedures necessary in view of the **U.S. general and fieldwork standards;**

   B. **Foreign country principles:** The auditor should understand the accounting principles generally accepted in the foreign country by:

      1. Consulting with persons having the appropriate expertise;

      2. Possibly considering the pronouncements of the International Accounting Standards Committee.

   C. The auditor should also comply with the general and fieldwork standards of the other country (as well as those of the U.S.) when requested to apply the auditing standards of the other country.

III. **Reporting Standards --** When the financial statements are prepared **for use solely outside the U.S.**

   A. **Desired form of report:** The auditor has a choice regarding the desired form of the report:

      1. The audit report may be a modified version of the U.S. report;

      2. The audit report may be that of the foreign country.

   B. When using a modified version of the **U.S. Audit Report** -- the coverage should include the following:

      1. Identify the financial statements covered;

      2. Reference the footnote describing the basis of the presentation (regarding the nationality of the principles used);

      3. State that the audit met U.S. standards (and the other country's standards, as appropriate);

      4. The opinion should state whether the financial statements are fairly stated relative to the basis indicated.

   C. When using the audit **report of a foreign country**, the auditor should:

      1. Understand any applicable legal responsibilities associated with such a report;

      2. Identify the other country in the report when there might be a misunderstanding.

IV. **Other Matters**

   A. If the financial statements are **intended for distribution in the U.S.,** the auditor

      1. Should use the **U.S audit report** (modified as needed for departures from U.S. GAAP);

2. May include a separate paragraph to the report expressing an opinion on whether the financial statements are consistent with the principles accepted in the foreign country.

B. **Cross references:** If the financial statements have been prepared both under U.S. GAAP and the principles accepted in the foreign country with reports issued on each set of the financial statements -- each separate audit report may cross-reference the other report.

AU543 (SAS 1) - Other Independent Auditors

I. **Part of Examination Made by Other Independent Auditors**

II. **Applicability --** when significant parts of the examination have been performed by other independent auditors; it may also apply with respect to material long-term investments accounted for by the equity method when the audit report on the company invested in is a source of primary evidence.

A. An auditor must assess whether participation is sufficient to permit reporting as the "principal auditor."

B. The determination is based on a comparison of the materiality of the respective parts of the financial statements that were audited.

III. **Reporting Requirements**

A. Audit reports do not reference the other auditors:

1. When the principal auditor has knowledge of the standards and competence of the other auditors;
2. When the principal auditor has obtained satisfaction as to the other auditor's examination; or
3. When the other auditors were retained by and worked under the supervision of the principal auditor.

B. Audit reports that do reference the other auditors - represent a modification of the standard report, but not a qualification:

1. Their purpose – is **to clearly indicate the division of responsibility** between the respective auditors (involves both scope and opinion paragraphs);
2. They indicate the respective dollar amounts or percentages examined for total assets, total revenues, or other appropriate criteria; (When 2 or more other auditors are involved, the portion examined by other auditors may be expressed in the aggregate.)
3. They usually do not identify the other auditors by name; may identify the other auditors by name only if their permission is obtained and their report is presented, too.

C. Qualifications in the other auditor's report -- the principal auditors must evaluate the effect of the other auditor's qualification on the overall report:

1. If the other auditor's report is not presented and the effect of the qualification is not material to principal auditor's report, no reference to the other auditor's qualification is required;
2. If the other auditor's report is presented, the principal auditor may want to reference the qualification and its disposition for the overall report.

IV. **Audit Procedures**

A. Reference To Others.

B. Whether or not reference is made to the other auditors:

1. Inquire about their professional reputation -- to the AICPA, other practitioners, bankers, and other appropriate sources (not necessary if the principal auditor already has such knowledge);
2. Obtain a representation from the other auditors as to their independence;
3. Verify with the other auditors their awareness that their work is a component of the principal auditor's audit and that they are familiar with the relevant reporting guidelines (GAAP and GAAS), etc.;
4. If such inquiries indicate that the principal auditor cannot assume responsibility for the part of the engagement performed by the other auditors -- must qualify or disclaim an opinion (due to scope limitation), unless the auditor is able to obtain satisfactory evidence from other procedures.

C. Additional procedures should be considered when reference will not be made to the other auditors. The auditor should:

1. Visit the other auditors and discuss their examination;
2. Review the other auditors' audit programs;
3. Review the other auditors' working papers (especially regarding internal control and major audit areas).

AU544 (SAS 1) - Lack of Conformity with GAAP

I. **Applicability**

   A. When the accounting practices are specified by government regulators (agencies or commissions);

   B. Examples:

      1. Public utilities;

      2. Common carriers;

      3. Insurance companies;

      4. Financial institutions.

   C. Regulatory bodies tend to emphasize the rate-making process, which results in differences relative to GAAP regarding the matching of costs and revenues.

   D. Special Reports (AU623):

   E. AU623, "Special Reports," applies when the financial statements are prepared according to a "comprehensive basis of accounting other than GAAP" (including such "regulatory accounting principles"):

      1. When the financial statements are prepared according to regulatory requirements; and

      2. Distribution is restricted to the regulatory body.

II. **Reporting Requirements --** when the financial statements are prepared according to the regulator's requirements and the auditor is engaged to report on the fairness of the presentation relative to those requirements for purposes other than filings with the regulator. The auditor should:

   A. Use the standard audit report, modified as appropriate for GAAP departures.

   B. Then express an opinion as to whether the financial statements are fairly presented with respect to the prescribed basis.

AU550 (SAS 118) - Other Information in Documents

I. **Introduction**

A. **Scope of this section --** This section addresses the auditor's responsibility in relation to other information in documents containing audited financial statements and the auditor's report (this requires the auditor to read the other information of which he/she is aware).

B. Objective of the auditor is to respond appropriately when the auditor becomes aware that documents containing audited financial statements and the auditor's report include other information that could undermine the credibility of those financial statements and the auditor's report thereon.

C. **Primary definitions**

1. **Other information --** Information other than the financial statements and the auditor's report that is included in a document containing audited financial statements and the auditor's report (can be financial and nonfinancial information, but excludes "required supplementary information").
2. **Inconsistency --** Other information that conflicts with information contained in the audited financial statements (may raise doubt about the auditor's conclusions and the basis for the auditor's opinion).
3. **Misstatement of fact --** Other information that is unrelated to matters appearing in the audited financial statements that is incorrectly presented (may undermine the credibility of the document containing the audited financial statements).

II. **Requirements**

A. **Reading other information --** The auditor should read the other information of which the auditor is aware to identify material inconsistencies with the audited financial statements.

1. Should obtain and read such other information as soon as practicable, preferably prior to the report release date - should communicate the auditor's responsibility for the other information to those charged with governance.
2. If the auditor identifies a material inconsistency -- determine whether the audited financial statements or the other information needs to be revised.

B. Material inconsistencies identified in other information obtained prior to the report release date -- if management refuses to make the revision, the auditor should communicate the matter to those charged with governance and (1) include an explanatory paragraph in the auditor's report to describe the material inconsistency; (2) withhold the auditor's report; or (3) withdraw from the engagement (if that is possible under applicable law or regulation).

C. Material inconsistencies identified in other information obtained subsequent to the report release date:

1. **When management agrees to make the revision --** The auditor may review the steps taken by management to ensure that those receiving previously issued financial statements and other information are informed of the need for revision.
2. **When management refuses to make the revision --** The auditor should notify those charged with governance and take further actions (including seeking advice from the auditor's legal counsel).

D. **Material misstatements of fact --** The auditor should discuss the matter with management; if there is a material misstatement of fact, the auditor should request management to consult with a qualified third party (such as the entity's legal counsel); if management refuses to correct a material misstatement of fact, the auditor should notify those charged with governance of the auditor's concerns.

III. **Application and other explanatory material**

A. **Other information may include --** (1) A report by management or those charged with governance on operations; (2) financial summaries or highlights; (3) employment data; (4) planned capital expenditures; (5) financial ratios; (6) names of officers and directors; and (7) selected quarterly data, for example.

B. **Other information does not encompass --** (1) A press release or cover letter accompanying the document containing audited financial statements; (2) information contained in analyst briefings; or (3) information contained on the entity's Web site, for example.

C. **Reading other information --** Obtaining the other information prior to the report release date enables the auditor to resolve issues with management on a timely basis (may be helpful to obtain an agreement with management as to when other information will be available).

D. When management refuses to revise the other information as deemed appropriate by the auditor:

   1. For material inconsistencies that have been identified in other information (whether obtained prior to or subsequent to the report release date) - the auditor may base action on advice from the auditor's legal counsel.

   2. For material misstatements of fact -- the auditor may obtain advice from the auditor's legal counsel, withhold the auditor's report if it has not been released, or withdraw from the engagement.

E. **Considerations specific to governmental entities**

   1. The term "annual reports of governments" includes comprehensive annual reports or other annual reports containing the entity's financial statements and the auditor's report.

   2. When withdrawal from the engagement or withholding the auditor's report may not be options - the auditor may issue a report to those charged with governance (and the appropriate statutory body, if applicable) detailing the inconsistency.

F. The auditor is not required to reference the other information in the auditor's report, but may choose to include an explanatory paragraph so that readers will not infer an unintended level of assurance -- SAS No. 118 included an exhibit that provided an example of an explanatory paragraph to disclaim an opinion on other information.

Example language when the auditor chooses to disclaim an opinion on other information:

Our audit was conducted for the purpose of forming an opinion on the basic financial statements as a whole. The (identify the other information) is presented for purposes of additional analysis and is not a required part of the basic financial statements. Such information has not been subjected to the auditing procedures applied in the audit of the basic financial statements, and accordingly, we do not express an opinion or provide any assurance on it.

AU551 (SAS 119) - Information Accompanying Documents

I. **Introduction**

A. **Scope of this section --** This section addresses the auditor's responsibility when engaged to report on whether supplementary information is fairly stated, in all material respects, in relation to the financial statements as a whole. (This section may also be applied when engaged to report on whether required supplementary information is fairly stated.)

B. Objective of the auditor when engaged to report on supplementary information in relation to the financial statements as a whole is to evaluate the presentation of the supplementary information and report on whether it is fairly stated, in all material respects, in relation to the financial statements as a whole.

C. **Definition of "supplementary information" --** Information presented outside the basic financial statements. (This excludes required supplementary information that is not considered necessary for the financial statements to be fairly presented in accordance with the applicable financial reporting framework.)

II. **Requirements**

A. Procedures to determine whether supplementary information is fairly stated in relation to the financial statements -- the auditor should determine that:

1. The supplementary information was derived from/related directly to the underlying records used to prepare the financial statements;
2. The supplementary information relates to the same period as the financials;
3. The auditor served as the principal auditor who audited the financial statements;
4. Either an unqualified or qualified opinion was expressed on the financial statements (cannot have issued an adverse opinion or disclaimer of opinion);
5. The supplementary information will accompany the entity's audited financial statements or such audited financial statements will be made "readily available" by the entity.

B. The auditor should obtain an agreement that management takes responsibility for:

1. Preparing the supplementary information in accordance with the applicable criteria;
2. Providing the auditor with required written representations;
3. Including the auditor's report on the supplementary information in any document that contains the supplementary information that refers to the auditor's association with it;
4. Presenting the supplementary information with the audited financial statements (or making the audited financial statements "readily available" to the intended users of the supplementary information).

C. The auditor should perform the following procedures (using the same materiality level as for the audit of the financial statements) -- the auditor's report on supplementary information in relation to the financial statements should not be dated prior to completing these procedures:

1. Inquire of management about the purpose of the supplementary information and the criteria used by management to prepare it;
2. Determine whether the supplementary information complies with applicable criteria;
3. Obtain an understanding about the methods used whether the methods used have changed (and if changed, the reasons for such changes);
4. Compare/reconcile the supplementary information to the financial statements or to underlying records used for the financial statements;
5. Inquire of management about any significant assumptions used;

6. Evaluate the appropriateness and completeness of the supplementary information based on the audit of the entity's financial statements;

7. Obtain written representations from management (a) that management takes responsibility for the presentation of the supplementary information; (b) that management believes the supplementary information is presented in accordance with applicable criteria; (c) that the methods used have not changed relative to the prior period (and if changed, the reason for any changes); (d) about any significant assumptions used; and (e) that management will make the audited financial statements readily available to the users of the supplementary information (when the supplementary information is not presented with the audited financial statements).

D. **Subsequent events --** The auditor has no responsibility for considering subsequent events regarding the supplementary information.

E. **Reporting --** When reporting on supplementary information, the auditor should either (1) add an explanatory paragraph **following the opinion paragraph** of the auditor's report on the financial statements; or (2) issue a separate report on the supplementary information.

1. When reporting on supplementary information in a separate report -- reference the auditor's report on the financial statements, the date of that report, the nature of the opinion expressed, and any report modifications.

2. When the auditor expresses an adverse opinion or a disclaimer of opinion on the financial statements -- the auditor cannot express an opinion on the supplementary information.

3. If the auditor believes that supplementary information is materially misstated in relation to the financial statements:

   a. Discuss the matter with management and propose appropriate revision of the supplementary information;

   b. If management does not revise the supplementary information -- the auditor should either (1) modify the auditor's opinion on the supplementary information and describe the misstatement; or (2) withhold the auditor's separate report on the supplementary information.

III. Application and other explanatory material

A. An auditor has no obligation to apply auditing procedures to supplementary information presented outside the basic financial statements unless reporting on that supplementary information in relation to the audited financial statements. These procedures need not be as extensive as they would be to express an opinion on the information on a stand-alone basis.

B. **Criteria applicable to supplementary information --** May be prepared in accordance with an applicable financial reporting framework, by regulatory or contractual requirements, in accordance with management's criteria, or other requirements.

C. **Meaning of "readily available" --** Information is deemed to be readily available if a third party user can obtain the audited financial statements without any further action by the entity (e.g., financial statements on an entity's Web site are readily available; being available upon request is not readily available).

D. **Understanding of the entity's internal control --** the auditor is not required to obtain a separate understanding of the entity's internal control or to assess fraud risk with respect to supplementary information

E. **Considerations specific to governmental entities --** The auditor's opinion on the supplementary information is in relation to the financial statements as a whole at a level that represents the entire governmental entity (even when the auditor's report on the financial statements includes multiple opinions on reporting units involved).

AU552 (SAS 42) - Selected Financial Data

I. **Applicability**

A. **Reporting on condensed financial statements** -- **for a public client** that is required to file complete audited financial statements with a regulator at least annually.

B. **Reporting on selected financial data** presented in a document including audited financial statements **(for either public or nonpublic clients)**.

II. **Reporting Requirements**

A. **Condensed financial statements** -- **derived from the audited financial statements** (for a public client):

1. State that the auditor has reported on the complete financial statements:

   a. Indicate the date of the audit report on the complete financial statements -- the auditor has no responsibility to investigate or inquire about events that may have occurred between the audit report on the complete financial statements and the report on the condensed financial statement data;

   b. Indicate the type of audit report expressed on the complete financial statements -- describe the nature and reasons if the audit report was other than unqualified (and reference the other auditors if they were referenced in the audit report on the complete financial statements).

2. State an opinion as to whether the condensed financial statement information is fairly stated in view of the complete audited financial statements;

3. The condensed financial statements should be marked **"condensed"** -- since they are not in conformity with GAAP (for example, many required disclosures are omitted);

4. The auditor must report on the condensed financial statements when mentioned in that regard (for a public client) -- unless the condensed financial statements are included in a document containing the complete audited financial statements.

B. **Selected financial data** -- derived from the audited financial statements:

1. State that the auditor has reported on the complete financial statements;

2. Indicate the type of opinion expressed on the complete financial statements;

3. Express an opinion as to whether the selected financial data are fairly stated in view of the complete audited financial statements;

4. The auditor may report separately on the selected financial data or in conjunction with the report on the complete financial statements; if reporting on the selected financial data along with the audit report on the complete financial statements add a separate paragraph to address the selected data.

AU558 (SAS 120) - Required Supplementary Information

I. Introduction

A. Scope of this section -- This section addresses the auditor's responsibility with respect to "required supplementary information" (defined as information that a designated accounting standard setter requires to accompany an entity's basic financial statements for the purpose of placing the basic financial statements in an appropriate operational, economic, or historical context).

B. Objectives of the auditor with respect to required supplementary information are to perform specified procedures to:

1. Describe in the auditor's report whether required supplementary information is presented; and
2. Communicate when (a) some (or all) of the required supplementary information has not been presented in accordance with guidelines established by the designated accounting standard setter; or (b) the auditor has identified material modifications necessary for that information to be in accordance with guidelines established by that standard setter.

C. Primary definitions

1. **Required supplementary information --** Information that a designated accounting standard setter requires to accompany an entity's basic financial statements. (The information is not part of the basic financial statements, but authoritative guidelines for measurement and presentation have been established for the supplementary information.)
2. **Designated accounting standard setter --** A body designated by the AICPA council to establish GAAP pursuant to Rule 202, *Compliance with Standards*.
3. **Basic financial statements --** Financial statements presented in accordance with an applicable financial reporting framework as established by a designated accounting standard setter, excluding required supplementary information.

II. Requirements

A. Procedures -- The auditor should apply the following procedures to required supplementary information:

1. Inquire of management about the methods of preparing the information, including (a) whether it is measured and presented in accordance with prescribed guidelines; (b) whether the methods of measurement or presentation have been changed relative to prior period; and (c) whether any significant assumptions underlie the measurement or presentation of it;
2. Compare the information for consistency with (a) management's responses to the auditor's inquiries; (b) the basic financial statements; and (c) other knowledge obtained during the audit of the basic financial statements;
3. Inform those charged with governance if an inability to complete the above procedures was due to significant difficulties in dealings with management.

B. Reporting -- The auditor should include an explanatory paragraph in the auditor's report (after the opinion paragraph) to refer to the required supplementary information as appropriate.

1. That the required supplementary information is included and the auditor has applied the procedures described above (no material departures);
2. That the required supplementary information is omitted;
3. That some required supplementary information is missing and some is presented in accordance with prescribed guidelines;
4. That the auditor has identified material departures from prescribed guidelines;

5. That the auditor is unable to complete required procedures;
6. That the auditor has unresolved doubts about whether the required supplementary information is presented in accordance with prescribed guidelines.

III. Application and other explanatory material

A. The auditor's report on the financial statements includes a discussion of the responsibility taken with respect to the required supplementary information accompanying the financial statements -- however, the auditor's opinion on the financial statements is not affected by the presentation or omission of such supplementary information.

B. SAS No. 120 included an exhibit that provided examples of explanatory paragraphs for each of the 6 reporting scenarios described above.

Example language when the required supplementary information is included and the auditor has performed the applicable procedures without identifying any material departures from the prescribed guidelines:

(*Identify the applicable financial reporting framework (for example, accounting principles generally accepted in the United States of America)*) require that the (*identify the required supplementary information*) on page XX be presented to supplement the basic financial statements. Such information, although not a part of the basic financial statements is required by (*identify designated accounting standard setter*) who considers it to be an essential part of financial reporting for placing the basic financial statements in an appropriate operational, economic, or historical context. We have applied certain limited procedures to the required supplementary information in accordance with auditing standards generally accepted in the United States of America, which consisted of inquiries of management about the methods of preparing the information and comparing the information for consistency with management's responses to our inquiries, the basic financial statements, and other knowledge we obtained during our audit of the basic financial statements. We do not express an opinion or provide any assurance on the information because the limited procedures do not provide us with sufficient evidence to express an opinion or provide any assurance.

AU560 (SAS 1) - Subsequent Events

I. General Comments

A. Definition--events/transactions that occur after the balance sheet date and before the issuance of the auditor's report which have a material effect on the financial statements and, therefore, require either financial statement adjustment or disclosure.

B. Two types of subsequent events:

   1. Those requiring financial statement adjustment -- events that provide evidence of conditions existing at the balance sheet date (e.g., settlement of litigation for an amount significantly different than that previously recorded);

   2. Those requiring financial statement disclosure only -- events that do not provide evidence of conditions existing at the balance sheet date, but that are sufficiently material that disclosure is required to keep the financial statements from being misleading (e.g., issuance of bonds or capital stock; major uninsured casualty losses; purchase of a business, etc.).

C. The auditor may include an explanatory paragraph to emphasize the matter in the audit report, if desired, for subsequent events requiring only financial statement disclosure.

II. Audit Procedures Related to Subsequent Events

A. "Subsequent period" -- the period after the balance sheet date up to the audit report date. (After the audit report and financial statements are released, it is too late to conveniently make further changes to the financial statements.)

B. Substantive audit procedures related to the "subsequent period" are directed at 3 general purposes (usually performed at or near the completion of field work):

   1. Determining that cutoffs were proper;

   2. Evaluating the valuation of assets and liabilities;

   3. Identifying the occurrence of subsequent events (performed at or near the audit report date):

      a. Review any available interim financial statements;

      b. Make inquiries of management regarding subsequent events (including whether there were any significant changes to long-term debt, working capital, or capital stock; and whether any unusual adjustments were made subsequent to the balance sheet date).

      c. Read minutes of meetings of those charged with governance;

      d. Obtain attorney's letter regarding litigation, claims, and assessments;

      e. Obtain a management representations letter (signed by CEO and CFO, as of the audit report date), which, among other things, addresses subsequent events.

AU561 (SAS 1) - Subsequent Discovery

I. **Applicability --** Applies when the auditor discovers, subsequent to the audit report date, facts existing at the report date, which, if known to the auditor then, would have affected the auditor's opinion.

A. After the report date, the auditor has no obligation to make a continuing investigation of the financial statements reported on.

B. If new information comes to the auditor's attention (information which the auditor would have investigated had it come up during the audit), the auditor must determine the validity of that information and whether the facts existed as of the report date.

C. The auditor should consider whether there are persons currently relying (or likely to rely) on the financial statements and the audit report thereon.

II. **Requirements**

A. The auditor should request that the client make appropriate disclosure to known users:

1. Disclosure consists of issuing revised financial statements with a revised audit report as soon as possible;
2. If the issuance of the subsequent period's financial statements is imminent, then the appropriate disclosure may be made with the new financial statements and report (as long as disclosure will not be delayed);
3. If a prolonged investigation is necessary to ascertain the financial statement consequences, the auditor should request that the client notify all known users that the financial statements and audit report should not be relied on.

B. If the client refuses to make the requested disclosures:

1. Each member of the board of directors should be notified of the refusal to make the disclosure and of the additional steps the auditor will have to take to prevent reliance on the audit report;
2. Notification should be given to the following that the financial statements and the audit report should not be relied on: (Disclose the nature of the effect and the impact on the financial statements and the audit report.)
   a. The client;
   b. Any regulatory agencies having jurisdiction over the client (such as the SEC and stock exchanges);
   c. Each person known to be relying on the erroneous financial statements.
3. The auditor should consult with an attorney regarding notification to the above parties and any legal exposure attributable to the erroneous audit report.

AU623 (SAS 62) - Special Reports

I. **Applicability --** When reporting on one of the following situations, certain GAAS are not applicable, for example, the first standard of reporting (about GAAP).

   A. **Financial statements prepared in conformity with a comprehensive basis other than GAAP.**

   B. **Specified elements, accounts, or items of a financial statement.**

   C. Compliance with contractual agreements or regulatory requirements.

   D. Financial presentations to comply with contractual agreements or regulatory requirements.

   E. Financial information presented in prescribed forms or schedules requiring a prescribed form of the auditor's report.

II. **Financial Statements Prepared in Conformity with a Comprehensive Basis Other Than GAAP**

   A. **Examples** of an "other comprehensive basis" (not GAAP):

      1. Financial statements prepared using requirements of a government regulator;

      2. Reporting under principles used for income tax purposes;

      3. Cash basis;

      4. Any other definite criteria having "substantial support" (e.g. price-level basis of accounting).

   B. The report - usually consists of four paragraphs:

      1. Introduction -- same as a standard audit report;

      2. Scope -- same as a standard audit report;

      3. Explanatory paragraph (preceding the opinion):

         a. Describes the basis used and refers to the appropriate financial statement note;

         b. States that the basis used was an "other comprehensive basis" (not GAAP).

      4. Opinion (similar to the standard audit report, but reference the note to the financial statements describing the basis used) -- any other reservations would be described in an additional explanatory paragraph preceding the opinion.

   C. Other Reporting Considerations:

      1. The auditor should consider whether the financial statements are appropriately titled, since the usual names might imply GAAP;

      2. If the financials are prepared in conformity with the requirements of a government regulator -- restrict the distribution of the report (to the company and the regulatory agency);

      3. To evaluate the adequacy of disclosure, the auditor should include all informative disclosures affecting the usefulness of the financial statements. (The auditor need not quantify the differences between GAAP and the other comprehensive basis used.)

III. **Specified Elements, Accounts, or Items of a Financial Statement**

   A. **Examples** -- rentals, royalties, profit participation, or provision for income taxes, etc.

   B. Applicable Standards:

      1. AU623 (this section) applies when **auditing** the specified elements, accounts, or items;

      2. AU622 applies when using **agreed-upon procedures;**

      3. AT100 applies when **reviewing** the specified elements, accounts, or items.

C. The report -- usually consists of four paragraphs:

1. Introduction;
2. Scope;
3. Explanatory -- describes the basis used for the presentation;
4. Opinion -- discloses any reservations in a separate explanatory paragraph (preceding the opinion).

D. Other Reporting Considerations:

1. If presented to comply with a contract or other agreement (not in conformity with GAAP) -- restrict the distribution of the report;
2. May add another explanatory paragraph to describe additional procedures performed (but should not modify the scope paragraph);
3. If a specified element, account, or item is based upon net income or stockholders' equity -- the CPA must have audited the complete financial statements to express an opinion on the element, account, or item.

IV. Compliance with Contractual Agreements or Regulatory Requirements Related to Audited Financial Statements

A. **Examples** -- payments into sinking funds, maintenance of ratios required by debt covenants, etc.

B. **Negative assurance** may be given relative to such covenants (only if the auditor has audited the financial statements to which the contract or regulatory requirement relate). Such assurance should not be given if the auditor has given an adverse opinion or disclaimer of opinion.

C. Report -- usually consists of **four paragraphs;** (The last 2 paragraphs could be added at the end of the usual audit report.)

1. State that the financial statements were audited; (Indicate the date of the report and any reservations expressed in the report.)
2. Reference the specific covenants and provide negative assurance;
3. Describe the source of any significant interpretations of the agreement made by management;
4. Restrict the distribution to the parties to the contract (or for filing with the regulatory agency).

V. Special-purpose Financial Presentations to Comply with Contractual Agreements or Regulatory Provisions

A. Financial statements prepared on a prescribed basis of accounting (by contract or by regulators) resulting in an incomplete presentation, but which is otherwise in conformity with GAAP or an other comprehensive basis:

1. Example -- a statement of assets sold and liabilities transferred to comply with a contractual agreement;
2. The report -- usually consists of five paragraphs:
    - **a.** Introduction;
    - **b.** Scope;
    - **c.** Explanatory -- refers to the note describing the basis of presentation and states that the presentation is not intended to be a complete presentation;
    - **d.** Opinion; (Any reservations should be disclosed in an additional explanatory paragraph preceding the opinion.)
    - **e.** Restricts the distribution of the report. (Cannot be restricted if the report is filed with a regulator in a document to be distributed to the public.)

B. Financial statements prepared on a basis of accounting prescribed in an agreement that results in a presentation not in conformity with GAAP or other comprehensive basis - when the criteria used do not have "substantial support."

C. Example -- financial statements prepared for the purpose of obtaining a bank loan.

D. The report - usually consists of five paragraphs:

1. Introduction;
2. Scope;
3. Explanatory -- explains the intention of the presentation (refers to the financial statement note describing the basis used) and states that the presentation is not intended to comply with GAAP;
4. Opinion;
5. Restricts the distribution of the report.

E. Circumstances **requiring explanatory language** in an auditor's special report:

1. Lack of consistency in accounting principles -- add an explanatory paragraph (following the opinion) and refer to the applicable financial statement note;
2. Uncertainties and going concern uncertainties;
3. Involvement of other auditors;
4. Comparative financial statements -- when changing the previous opinion expressed;
5. Emphasis of a matter, as deemed appropriate.

VI. **Prescribed Forms or Schedules**

A. When the financial information is presented in **prescribed forms or schedules** -- (for example, when a preprinted report form uses language that the auditor cannot justify) the auditor should **edit the form appropriately or attach a separate report.**

AU625 (SAS 50) - Application of Accounting Principles

I. **Applicability --** This section applies when, in connection with public practice, the "reporting accountant" is asked to comment on the acceptability of accounting principles or the type of opinion the accountant might be able to render given certain circumstances.

A. Applies to the following matters involving a written report:

1. When preparing a written report on the application of accounting principles to "specific transactions" - SAS 97 prohibits issuing a written report on the application of accounting principles to a hypothetical transaction!

2. When asked to provide a written report on the type of opinion that might be issued on a specific entity's financial statements.

B. Applies to the following matters involving verbal advice -- when the reporting accountant believes the advice will be an important factor in the decision making of a principal to the transaction:

1. When advising on the application of accounting principles to "specific transactions;"

2. When providing advice on the type of opinion that might be issued on a specific entity's financial statements.

C. Matters to which this section explicitly does **not** apply:

1. When the **"continuing accountant"** (who has been engaged to report on the financial statements) has also been engaged to:

a. Assist in litigation involving accounting matters;

b. Serve as an expert witness in such litigation;

c. Provide professional advice to another accountant in public practice.

2. This section does not apply to the communication of **"position papers"** for the purpose of expressing views on the application of accounting principles or the type of opinion that may be rendered on an entity's financial statements:

a. Examples of such exclusions include speeches, lectures, and other public presentations, articles, newsletters, letters for the public record, etc.;

b. Note: if the position paper is intended to provide the type of guidance referred to in Applicability Involving Written Reports (above), then this section does apply.

II. **Performance Standards**

A. The general standards apply -- professional competence, due professional care, planning and supervision, sufficient relevant data, and forecasts (see Rule 201 of the rules of conduct).

B. Standards should consider the following:

1. Who the requester of the report is;

2. The circumstances behind the request;

3. The purpose of the request;

4. The requester's intended use of the report.

C. Procedures to be performed:

1. Obtain an understanding of the form and substance of the transaction(s);

2. Review applicable GAAP;

3. If appropriate, consult with other professionals;

4. If appropriate, conduct research regarding the existence of precedents or analogies.

D. When asked to report on accounting principles or the type of opinion that might be rendered on financial statements with respect to specific transactions or a specific entity's financial statements:

   1. **Consult with the continuing accountant to make sure that the reporting accountant has all the relevant facts (regarding "opinion shopping" concerns)**;

   2. Must request the client's permission to contact continuing accountant (due to confidentiality considerations);

   3. Holds the same responsibilities as those defined in AU315, "Communications Between Predecessor and Successor Auditors."

III. **Reporting standards --** A written report should be addressed to the principal to the transaction or to the intermediary acting on the principal's behalf. (The reporting standards apply only to written reports, but may also be useful in providing verbal advice.) The report:

A. Briefly describes the nature of the engagement and references applicable standards of the AICPA.

B. Describes the relevant facts, circumstances, and assumptions (identify any specific principals, unless hypothetical) and states that any differences in these matters may affect the report.

C. Describes the appropriate principles to be used or the type of opinion to be rendered (include reasons for conclusions).

D. States that the proper accounting treatment is the responsibility of the preparers of the financial statements **(who should consult with the continuing accountants).**

AU634 (SAS 86) - Letters for Underwriters

I. "Comfort Letters" -- A letter to underwriters (or other parties) with a statutory due diligence defense under Section 11 of the Securities Act of 1933.

- **A.** Section 11 of the Act provides for liability to underwriters and certain others when there is a material omission or misstatement to a registration statement.
- **B.** A comfort letter may be used to establish that the underwriter or others conducted a "reasonable investigation" under the Act.

II. Applicability -- May provide a comfort letter to underwriters or other parties having a "statutory due diligence defense" under section 11 of the Act.

- **A.** To address a comfort letter to a party other than the named underwriter -- must obtain a letter from an attorney for the requesting party stating that such party has a "statutory due diligence defense" under section 11 of the Act.
- **B.** If such a letter cannot be obtained by such requesting party -- that party must provide the accountant with a "representation letter:" The letter:
  - **1.** Should be addressed to the accountants;
  - **2.** Should include certain boilerplate language stating that requesting party is "knowledgeable with respect to the due diligence review process that would be performed if this placement of securities were being registered pursuant to the Act;"
  - **3.** Should be signed by the requesting party.
- **C.** If a requesting party (without a due diligence defense) does not provide the representation letter, the auditor:
  - **1.** Should not provide a comfort letter but may provide another form of letter;
  - **2.** May report on agreed-upon procedures, but still should not express any negative assurance.
- **D.** "Reasonable investigation" of "unaudited" financial information sufficient to satisfy an underwriter's purposes has not been authoritatively established -- so potential for misunderstanding exists:
  - **1.** Underwriters are concerned with "reasonable investigation" on accounting data **not** "expertized" (i.e., covered by report as experts, based on examination in accordance with GAAS);
  - **2.** To auditors "reasonable investigation" means an audit of the financial information.
- **E.** Comfort letters to underwriters are **not** required under the Act and are not filed with the SEC -- this involves a service tailored to the underwriters or certain other requesting parties:
  - **1.** The scope is specified in the underwriting agreement (between the client and underwriters):
    - **a.** The client and underwriters should give copy of the draft of the agreement to the accountant when available;
    - **b.** The accountant should give them a draft of the report as soon as possible (to resolve any issues that arise);
    - **c.** The accountant should suggest a meeting with the underwriter and the client to discuss procedures to be performed.
  - **2.** The accountant should use care to avoid implying that the procedures were sufficient for the underwriter's (or other parties') purposes.
- **F.** When comfort letters are requested from more than one accountant (e.g., when other accountants' reports are included with the registration statement) -- the principal accountant should read the other accountants' letters and mention that in their own letter.

G. When an underwriter has not been named (e.g., offerings over an extended period by one "shelf" registration statement):

1. Accountant should not agree to furnish a comfort letter (either to the client, legal counsel, or to a nonspecific addressee;)
2. May instead furnish the client or legal counsel with a **draft** comfort letter describing procedures performed and resulting comments.

H. Overview -- a typical comfort letter includes:

1. A statement regarding the independence of the accountants;
2. A positive expression of opinion whether the **audited** financial statements (and schedules incorporated by reference) **comply as to form** with the requirements of the Act;
3. Negative assurance on whether:
   a. The unaudited condensed interim financial information complies as to form with the requirements of the Act;
   b. Any material modifications should be made to the unaudited condensed consolidated financial statements included in the registration statement per GAAP.
4. Negative assurance on whether there has been any change (during a specified period) in capital stock, increase in long-term debt or any decrease in other specified financial statement items.

I. Dating:

1. **Usually dated on or shortly before the effective date -- when registration becomes effective;**
2. The underwriting agreement usually specifies the "cutoff date," the date up to which the procedures were performed. (The letter should note that the procedures did not cover the interval from the cutoff date to the date of the letter.)

J. Addressee -- the letter should not be addressed (or given) to anyone other than the client and named underwriters, broker- dealer, financial intermediary, or buyer or seller.

K. Introductory paragraph -- should identify the financial statements and schedules audited included in the registration statement:

1. When the audit report includes an explanatory paragraph, the nature of that paragraph in the comfort letter is described (not required when dealing with the consistency of accounting principles);
2. The accountant should not repeat his or her opinion if asked by the underwriter to repeat the audit report in the comfort letter;
3. The accountant should not give negative assurance regarding the accountant's report on the audited financial statements;
4. The accountant should not refer to (or attach to the comfort letter) any restricted use report (e.g., agreed-upon procedures).

L. Independence – the letter should include a statement as to the accountant's independence.

M. Compliance with SEC requirements:

1. Give **positive expression of opinion** that **audited** financial statements and schedules **comply as to form** with SEC requirements;
2. Give **negative assurance** that **unaudited** financial statements and schedules **comply as to form** with SEC requirements.

N. Commenting on information other than audited financial statements.

O. Knowledge of internal control -- must have obtained knowledge of I/C related to the preparation of the annual and interim financial statements before commenting on information other than the audited financial statements.

P. Unaudited condensed interim financial information:

1. May provide negative assurance as to the need for modifications to the unaudited condensed interim information and as to whether the information complies as to form with SEC requirements;
2. Identify the unaudited condensed information and issue a disclaimer, since it is unaudited.

Q. Capsule financial information -- consists of unaudited summarized interim information for subsequent periods (in narrative or tabular form):

1. For the most recent interim period and the corresponding period of the prior year;
2. To give negative assurance -- an SAS 71 review of it must have been performed and it must meet disclosure requirements of APB Opinion 28; otherwise, the auditor should limit the report to procedures and findings.

R. Pro forma financial information -- should not comment without having appropriate knowledge of the entity's accounting and financial reporting (i.e., having audited or reviewed the most recent annual or interim financial statements):

1. To give negative assurance -- must have audited the annual financial statements or have performed an SAS 71 review of the relevant interim financial statements (along with having the appropriate knowledge.);
2. If the appropriate knowledge has been obtained, but an audit of the annual financial statements or a review of the interim financial statements has not been performed, the report must be limited to procedures and findings.

S. Financial forecasts -- should not comment without having appropriate knowledge of the entity's accounting and financial reporting:

1. Attach a report on the compilation of a forecast to the comfort letter -- if the applicable compilation procedures have been performed (see AT200);
2. Negative assurance with respect to compliance of the forecast with rule 11-03 of Regulation S-X can be given only if an examination of the forecast has been performed (see AT200);
3. Cannot provide negative assurance on the results of procedures performed.

T. Subsequent changes – include comments that usually relate to any changes in capital stock, increase in long-term debt or decreases in other specified financial statement items:

1. "Change period" -- subsequent to the date and period of the latest financial statements included in the registration statement;
2. Comments are based on limited procedures (i.e., reading the minutes and inquiry of management) which should be indicated;
3. May provide negative assurance as to subsequent changes within **135 days** from the end of the most recent period for which an audit or review was performed;
4. If beyond 135 days from the end of the most recent period for which an audit or review was performed -- comments must be limited to procedures and findings.

U. Tables, statistics, and other financial information:

1. Comments can only be made on information expressed in dollars (or percentages derived from dollars) or on information that has been derived directly from the accounting records and subjected to the entity's controls over financial reporting;
2. Matters that should not be commented on include square footage of facilities, number of employees, backlog information;
3. Negative assurance may be given on the following disclosure requirements of Regulation S-K: Item 301 (Selected Financial Data); Item 302 (Supplementary Financial Information); Item 402 (Executive Compensation); and Item 503(d) (Ratio of Earnings to Fixed Charges);
4. Letter should state that the accountants make no representation involving any matter of legal interpretation.

V. Concluding paragraph -- limits the distribution of the comfort letter to specified parties for the intended purposes.

W. Disclosure of subsequently discovered matters -- regarding matters that may need to be mentioned in the comfort letter that were not mentioned in the draft letter to the underwriter (e.g., changes of items not disclosed in registration statement):

1. Discuss with the client to determine whether disclosure should be made in registration;
2. If disclosure is not made -- inform client that the matter will be disclosed in the comfort letter and that underwriter should be informed promptly;
3. The accountant should ordinarily be present when the client and underwriter discuss the matter.

AU711 (SAS 37) - Federal Security Statutes

I. **Management is Responsible for the Financial Representations Contained in Documents Filed Under the Federal Securities Statutes** -- Similar to financial statements for other purposes.

II. **Independent Accountant's Responsibility** -- (when the accountant's report is included with documents filed under the federal securities statutes) - similar to the responsibility associated with other types of reporting, but the statutes and related SEC rules and regulations specifically address the accountant's responsibility in some detail.

   A. Section 11(a) of the Securities Act of 1933 addresses false or misleading statements in an effective registration statement or for omissions that render statements in such a document misleading on accountants, among others, who prepared or certified any report or valuation associated with the registration statement.

   B. Section 11(b) of the 1933 Act addresses the independent accountant's responsibility as an "expert" when his/her report is included in a registration statement.

   C. Section 11(b) defense [the accountant has the burden of proof] - not liable if he/she had reasonable grounds to believe that the statements in the registration statement were true and that no omission of a material fact was made (based upon "reasonable investigation") or if the registration statement did not fairly represent the accountant's statement as an expert.

   D. The accountant's statutory responsibility under the 1933 Act is determined "in the light of the circumstances" on the effective date of the registration statement.

   E. An independent accountant's "review report" is not a "report" within the meaning of Section 11 of the 1933 Act - when an accountant's review report is presented (or referenced) in a registration statement, the prospectus should clearly state that the review report is not a "report" or "part" of the registration statement within the meaning of sections 7 and 11 of the 1933 Act.

   F. Read the prospectus - the independent accountant should read the prospectus, especially the "experts section," to make sure his/her name is not used in a way that conveys more responsibility than he/she intends.

III. **Subsequent Events Procedures in Filings Under the 1933 Act**

   A. An auditor should extend the procedures related to subsequent events from the date of the audit report up to the effective date of the registration statement (or as close to the effective date as is reasonable in the circumstances).

   B. Following field work - the auditor should arrange with the client to be advised as to the progress of the registration proceedings to facilitate the review of subsequent events: (After the end of field work, the auditor "may rely, for the most part, on inquiries of responsible officials and employees.")

      1. Read the entire prospectus and other relevant portions of the registration statement;

      2. Inquire of officers and other executives responsible for financial and accounting matters and obtain written representations.

   C. An auditor who has audited the financial statements for a prior period included (but not the most recent audited financial statements in the registration statement) - the predecessor auditor has a responsibility to address material subsequent events extending to the effective date of the registration statement:.

      1. The predecessor auditor should read the relevant portions of the prospectus and the registration statement;

      2. Obtain a letter of representation from the successor auditor as to whether any matters were identified that might have a material effect on the financial statements audited by the predecessor;

      3. The predecessor auditor should make inquiries and perform any other procedures considered necessary regarding any adjustment or disclosure affecting the prior audited financial statements.

IV. Response to Subsequent Events and Subsequently Discovered Facts

A. An auditor should follow the guidance in AU560 and AU561 if, subsequent to the date of the report on the financial statements, the auditor discovers subsequent events that require adjustment or disclosure in the financial statements or becomes aware of facts existing at the report date that might have affected the report if the auditor had known of those facts.

B. If the client refuses to make appropriate adjustment or disclosure for a subsequent event or subsequently discovered facts - follow the guidance in AU560 and AU561 and consider withholding consent to use the report on the audited financial statements in the registration statement (with advice of legal counsel).

C. If the auditor concludes that unaudited financial statements or unaudited interim financial information presented (or referenced) in a registration statement are not in conformity with GAAP - insist on appropriate revision and consider withholding consent to the use of the report on the audited financial statements in the registration statement (with advice of legal counsel).

V. Auditing Interpretations Applicable to AU711

A. Question: Under what circumstances does the independent accountant have a responsibility to perform subsequent events procedures after the original effective date of the registration statement?

B. Answer: In general, the accountant should perform the subsequent events procedures (described above) when either (1) a post-effective amendment to the "shelf" registration statement is filed in connection with Regulation S-K; or (2) a filing under the 1934 Act that includes (or amends) audited financial statements is incorporated by reference into the "shelf" registration statement.

1. "Shelf registration" - SEC rules permit companies to register a particular amount of securities for multiple offerings over time (up to 2 years) by filing one "shelf" registration statement without filing a new prospectus and registration statement for each sale of securities.
2. A shelf registration statement can be updated after the original effective date by (a) filing a post-effective amendment; (b) incorporating by reference subsequently filed material; or (c) adding a supplemental prospectus (sometimes referred to as a "sticker").
3. A shelf registration statement is considered to have a new effective date because each post-effective amendment is deemed to be a new registration statement - the accountant should perform subsequent events procedures as close to the new effective date as is practicable.
4. Often a Form 10-Q, 8-K, or other 1934 Act filing can be incorporated by reference into a shelf registration statement without a post-effective amendment - in such cases, the accountant has no responsibility to perform subsequent events procedures (unless the filing includes or amends audited financial statements).

C. Question: Should the auditor consent to being named or referred to as an "expert" in an offering document in connection with offerings other than those registered under the Securities Act of 1933?

D. Answer: No. The term "expert" has statutory meaning under the 1933 Act, but that term (and the corresponding responsibility) is typically undefined outside of the 1933 Act.

1. When a client wants to refer to the auditor's role in an offering document that is not registered under the 1933 Act - the caption "Independent Auditors" should be used to title that section of the document; the term "experts" should not be used in referring to the auditor in the document.
2. If the client refuses to delete such a reference to the auditors as experts - the auditor should not permit use of the auditor's report in the offering document.

AU722 (SAS 100) - Interim Financial Information

AU722 (SAS No. 100) - "Interim Financial Information" - Issued: November, 2002

I. **Introduction --** SAS No. 100 supersedes SAS No. 71 (same name, issued May, 1992)

A. **Purpose** -- to establish standards and provide guidance when conducting a review of "interim financial information" which is defined as "financial information or statements covering a period less than a full year or for a 12-month period ending on a date other than the entity's fiscal year end"

B. The SEC requires a registrant to engage the CPA to review the registrant's interim financial information before filing its Form 10-Q (or Form 10-QSB) -- the SEC requires the review report to be filed if the entity states, in any filing, that the interim financial information has been filed

C. Predecessor-successor communications

1. Such inquiries should be made before accepting an engagement to perform "an initial review" of an entity's interim financial information

a. **Definition of "initial review"** -- when the accountant has not audited the financial statements of the previous year end

b. **Applicability** -- when conducting a review of the interim financial information of an SEC registrant or of a non-SEC registrant that makes a filing with a regulatory agency in preparation for a public offering or listing (if that entity's latest annual financial statements have been or are being audited).

2. **Objective of a review of interim financial information** --

a. **Objective** -- to provide the CPA with a basis for communicating whether material modifications are known that should be made for the interim financial information to comply with GAAP.

b. Procedures consist primarily of (1) analytical procedures and (2) inquiries of management and other personnel responsible for financial and accounting matters

3. **Establishing an understanding with the client about the services to be performed in the engagement** -- the objectives of the engagement, management's responsibilities, the accountant's responsibilities, and the limitations of the engagement (should document the understanding, preferably through a written communication with the client).

a. **Management is responsible for** -- the entity's interim financial information; establishing and maintaining effective internal control over financial reporting; compliance with applicable laws and regulations; making all financial records and related information available; providing a letter stating certain representations made during the review; and adjusting the interim financial information to correct material misstatements.

b. **Accountant is responsible for** -- conducting the review according to AICPA (now PCAOB!) standards

i. Consists primarily of performing analytical procedures and making inquiries of personnel responsible for financial and accounting matters

ii. Obtain sufficient knowledge of the entity's business and internal control applicable to the preparation of annual and interim financial information -- identify the types of material that might occur (and their likelihood).

iii. A review is not designed to provide assurance on internal control or to identify reportable conditions -- when reportable conditions are discovered, the accountant is responsible for communicating them to the audit committee (or others having similar responsibility).

4. **Accountant's knowledge of the business and internal control** --

a. Should have sufficient knowledge of the entity's business and internal control related to the preparation of annual and interim financial information.

i. Identify the types of potential misstatements and their likelihood.

ii. Select the inquiries and analytical procedures that will provide an appropriate basis for communicating any awareness as to whether material modifications should be made.

b. **Planning** -- update the knowledge of the business and internal control to determine the inquiries and analytical procedures (and to identify transactions, events, and assertions to be considered).

i. Read documentation for the prior year's audit and reviews of prior interim periods of the current year (and for the prior year as deemed necessary) -- consider the nature of any corrected material misstatements and uncorrected misstatements, identified risks of material fraud, and other significant financial reporting matters (such as weaknesses in internal control)

ii. Read the most recent annual and prior year financial information

iii. Consider the results of audit procedures applicable to the current year's financial statements

iv. Inquire of management about changes in the entity's business activities

v. Inquire of management about any significant changes in internal control applicable to the interim financial information since the previous audit or review

c. An "initial review" of interim financial information

i. Make appropriate inquiries of the predecessor accountant (if predecessor permits, review that documentation for the prior audit and any interim periods that have been reviewed)

ii. Successor accountant should not refer to the predecessor's report as a basis for the successor's report -- there is no division of responsibility

iii. If the predecessor does not respond to the successor's inquiries (or does not permit access to the predecessor's documentation) -- the successor should use alternate procedures to obtain knowledge about (a) corrected material misstatements; (b) uncorrected misstatements; and (c) identified risks of material fraud; and (d) significant matters affecting financial reporting (including weaknesses in internal control)

iv. Perform procedures to obtain knowledge about internal control applicable to the annual and interim financial information -- internal control over interim financial information may differ from internal control over the preparation of annual financial statements

v. A scope limitation on the review may occur if significant deficiencies in internal control prevent the accountant from effectively performing the necessary review procedures -- in such cases, the review would be "incomplete" (i.e., not an adequate basis for issuing the review report)

5. **Analytical procedures, inquiries and other review procedures** --

a. Review procedures are usually limited to analytical procedures, inquiries, and other procedures applicable to significant accounting and disclosure issues related to interim financial information -- these procedures should be tailored to the engagement to reflect the accountant's knowledge of the entity's business and internal control

b. **Analytical procedures (and related inquiries)** -- analytical procedures provide a basis for identifying unusual items for which further inquiry should be made

i. Compare the quarterly interim information with that of the immediately preceding interim period and compare the quarterly and year-to-date information with the corresponding period(s) of the prior year

ii. Consider plausible relationships among both financial and nonfinancial information, as applicable -- may wish to consider information in a "director's information package" or in a "senior committee's briefing materials"

iii. Compare recorded amounts or ratios to expectations developed by the accountant

iv. Compare disaggregated revenue data (by month and by product line or operating segment) during the current interim period with that of comparable prior periods.

- **v.** Expectations developed for a review of interim financial information are usually less precise than those developed in an audit -- the accountant is not required to corroborate management's responses with other evidence for a review engagement

c. **Inquiries and other review procedures** -- many of these can be performed before or simultaneously with the preparation of the interim information

- **i.** Read the available minutes of stockholder and board meetings (inquire about matters discussed at meetings for which minutes are unavailable)
- **ii.** Obtain reports from other accountants who may have been engaged to review the interim financial information for significant components of the reporting entity
- **iii.** Inquire of management responsible for accounting matters regarding
  1. Whether the interim information is consistent with GAAP
  2. The effect of unusual or complex situations
  3. Significant transactions occurring/recorded in the last few days of the interim period
  4. Status of uncorrected misstatements identified during the previous audit and interim review (i.e., the amounts recorded and period in which such adjustments were made)
  5. Matters for which questions have arisen currently from analytical procedures
  6. Events subsequent to the date of the interim information that could have a material effect on it
  7. Knowledge of any fraud or suspected fraud involving management, employees with significant roles in internal control, or others where the fraud could be material to the financial statements.
  8. Awareness of any allegations of fraud or suspected fraud affecting the entity
  9. Significant journal entries and other adjustments
  10. Communications from regulatory agencies
  11. Significant deficiencies (including material weaknesses in the design or operation of internal control)
- **iv.** Obtain evidence that the interim financial information agrees or reconciles with the accounting records
- **v.** Read the interim financial information for conformity with GAAP
- **vi.** Read any other information that accompanies the interim information in reports to holders of securities or with regulatory agencies

d. Inquiry about litigation, claims and assessments

- **i.** Corroboration of management's responses to inquiries is not usually necessary -- need not send a letter of inquiry to the entity's lawyers(s)
- **ii.** Inquiry of the lawyer is appropriate, however, when the accountant questions whether the interim information concerning litigation, claims and assessments departs from GAAP

e. Inquiry about going concern issues

- **i.** When the accountant has information that indicates the entity's possible inability to continue as a going concern
  1. Inquire about management's plans to overcome those difficulties
  2. Consider the adequacy of the disclosure about such issues
- **ii.** Need not obtain evidence to corroborate "mitigating factors"

f. **Extension of interim review procedures** -- make additional inquiries or perform other appropriate procedures when the accountant becomes aware of information that suggests the interim information may not comply with GAAP.

g. **Coordination with the audit (when also engaged to audit the annual financial statements)** -- some auditing procedures may be performed concurrently with the review of interim information (e.g., reading the minutes or dealing with significant or unusual transactions occurring during the interim period)

6. Written representation from management should be obtained for all interim financial information presented and for all periods covered by the review
   a. Regarding the financial statements
      i. Management's responsibility for the fair presentation of the interim information
      ii. Management's belief that the interim information conforms to GAAP
   b. Internal control
      i. Disclosure of all significant deficiencies in the design or operation of internal control
      ii. Management's responsibility for programs and controls to prevent and detect fraud
      iii. Knowledge of fraud or suspected fraud -- involving management, others with significant roles in internal control, or other where the fraud could have a material effect on the financial statements.
   c. Completeness of information
      i. Availability of all financial records and related data
      ii. Completeness and availability of all minutes for meetings of stockholders, directors, and committees of directors
      iii. Communications with regulatory agencies about deficiencies in financial reporting
      iv. Absence of unrecorded transactions
   d. Recognition, measurement and disclosure
      i. Effects of uncorrected (aggregated) misstatements are immaterial (a summary of such items should be included or attached) -- eliminate this representation if there are no such items
      ii. Plans or intentions that could materially affect valuation or classifications of assets or liabilities
      iii. Information regarding related party transactions and amounts due to or from related parties
      iv. Guarantees (written or oral) for which the entity is contingently liable
      v. Significant estimates and material concentrations required to be disclosed by AICPA Statement of Position 94-6, Disclosure of Certain Significant Risks and Uncertainties
      vi. Violations of laws or regulations that should be considered for adjustment to or disclosure in the interim information
      vii. Unasserted claims or assessments that must be disclosed per SFAS No. 5, Accounting for Contingencies (now FASC Section 450)
      viii. Other liabilities (or gain or loss contingencies) that are required to be accrued or disclosed per SFAS No. 5 (now FASC Section 450).
      ix. Satisfactory title to all owned assets, liens or encumbrances on such assets, and assets pledged as collateral
      x. Compliance with contracts affecting the interim information
   e. Subsequent events
   f. Other matters can add other representations specific to the industry or the entity's business

7. **Evaluating the results of interim review procedures** --

a. When the accountant becomes aware of "likely misstatements", evaluate them individually and in the aggregate to determine whether material modification should be made to the interim information

b. Consider the following matters

   i. Nature, cause (if known), and amount of misstatements

   ii. Whether the misstatements originated in the prior year or interim periods of the current year

   iii. Materiality judgments made in the current or prior year's audit

   iv. The potential effect of the misstatements on future interim or annual periods

c. The review will be "incomplete" when the accountant is unable to perform procedures necessary to achieve the objectives of the review engagement or when management fails to furnish the representations considered necessary

d. If the review cannot be completed must still communicate any known material modifications to the appropriate level of management

8. Communication to management, audit committees, and others

   a. When the accountant believes that material modification should be made to the interim information (or that the entity filed the Form 10-Q or Form 10-QSB prior to the completion of the review), the accountant should communicate the matter(s) to the appropriate level of management

   b. If management is not responsive within a reasonable period of time, the accountant should notify the audit committee (either in writing or orally -- if orally, document the communication)

   c. If the audit committee is not responsive within a reasonable period of time, the accountant should consider whether to resign as the reviewer of the interim information and as the entity's auditor (may wish to consult with an attorney regarding these matters)

   d. If the accountant becomes aware of fraud, notify the audit committee (when the fraud is material or implicates senior management) or the appropriate level of management (when the fraud is not material)

   e. If the accountant becomes aware of possible illegal acts, determine whether the audit committee is adequately informed

   f. If the accountant becomes aware of reportable conditions related to internal control, report such matters to the audit committee

   g. Other matters that should be communicated to the audit committee

      i. The process used by management to develop sensitive estimates

      ii. Any changes in significant accounting policies affecting the interim information

      iii. Adjustments that could be material (individually or in the aggregate)

      iv. Uncorrected misstatements aggregated by the accountant that management viewed as immaterial

   h. Matters to be communicated to the audit committee should be communicated to the audit committee (or at least its chair) and a representative of management

      i. Such information should be made before the entity files its interim information with a regulatory agency

      ii. If the communication cannot be made before such filing, the communication should be made as soon as practicable

9. Accountant's review report on interim financial information

   a. **Form of the accountant's review report** -- each page of the interim information should be clearly marked "unaudited"

      i. Title includes the word "independent"

ii. Identify the interim information that was reviewed

iii. State that the interim information is the responsibility of management

iv. State that the review was conducted according to AICPA (now PCAOB!) standards.

v. Describe the procedures associated with the review

vi. State that a review is substantially less in scope than an audit and include a disclaimer of opinion

vii. State whether the accountant is aware of any material modifications that should be made for the interim information to conform with U.S. GAAP

viii. The report should be signed

ix. **The report should be dated** -- usually the date that the review procedures are completed

b. **Division of responsibility** -- the accountant may use the review report of other accountants and make reference to that report on a significant component of a reporting entity

c. Modification of the accountant's review report

i. **Emphasis of a matter** -- the accountant may add an explanatory paragraph (need not add an explanatory for a lack of consistency in the application of accounting principles, if disclosure is adequate)

ii. **Going concern issues** -- if disclosure is adequate, the review report need not be modified (however, the accountant may choose to add an explanatory paragraph after the concluding paragraph)

iii. **Departure from GAAP** -- add appropriate modification before the concluding paragraph to describe the nature of the modification and (if practicable) the effects on the interim information

iv. **Inadequate disclosure (disclosure for interim information is much less extensive than for annual financial statement purposes)** -- modify the report and (if practicable) provide the necessary disclosure

d. **Subsequent discovery of facts existing at the date of the accountant's report** -- the specific actions to be taken may vary with the circumstances

10. When the client represents in a document filed with a regulatory agency (or issued to stockholders or other outside parties) that the accountant has reviewed the interim financial information included in that document -- the accountant should advise that the review report must be included

a. If the client does not include the review report, request that accountant's name not be associated with the interim information nor referred to in the document

b. If the client does not comply with that request, advise client that the accountant will not consent to use of his/her name or to the reference

c. Advise client to consult with legal counsel about applicable laws/regulations

11. Interim financial information accompanying audited financial statements

a. Each page of the interim information should be clearly marked "unaudited"

b. Auditor's report on the audited financial statements should be modified when

i. **The interim information is not marked "unaudited"** -- should disclaim an opinion on the unaudited interim information in that case

ii. **The interim information does not conform to GAAP** -- the report on the audited financial statements need not be modified, if the accountant refers to the GAAP issue in a separate review report

iii. **The selected quarterly financial data required by Regulation S-K is omitted or has not been reviewed** -- add a paragraph to audit report

12. **Documentation** --

    a. Documentation is the principal record of the review procedures performed and the conclusions reached

    b. **Documentation should include any findings/issues considered to be "significant"** -- e.g., results of review procedures indicating that the interim information could be materially misstated; actions taken to address such findings; and the basis for final conclusions reached

13. **Effective date** -- for interim periods within fiscal years beginning after 12/15/02 (earlier application is permitted)

14. **3 Appendices** --

    a. **Appendix A** -- identified analytical procedures the accountant may consider performing for a review of interim financial information

        i. **Included examples of "key" ratios and indicators** -- current ratio, receivable turnover or days' sales outstanding, inventory turnover, depreciation to average fixed assets, debt to equity, gross profit percentage, net income percentage, and plan operating rates

        ii. **Included examples of disaggregated data** -- comparisons by period (e.g., quarterly, monthly, or weekly amounts), by product line or operating segment, and/or by location (subsidiary, division, or branch)

    b. **Appendix B** -- provided examples of unusual or complex situations for which the accountant would normally make inquiries of management

    c. **Appendix C** -- provided 2 illustrative management representation letters for a review of interim financial information (a "short-form" representation letter and a "long-form" representation letter that is similar to the detail associated with the representation letter used for an audit)

AU722 (SAS 116) - Interim Financial Information

I. Introduction -- Amends SAS No. 100 (having the same name and issued in Nov. 2002).

A. Purpose -- to establish standards and provide guidance when performing reviews of "interim financial information" of **nonissuers**. (This SAS removes the earlier guidance for reviews of interim financial information of issuers, since such guidance is now under the authority of the PCAOB.)

B. Interim financial information -- "financial information or statements covering a period less than a full year or for a 12-month period ending on a date other than the entity's fiscal year end;" may be condensed or in the form of a complete set of financial statements.

C. Need for a written report? -- An accountant is not required to issue a written report on a review of interim financial information, unless the entity states in a written communication containing the interim financial information that it has been reviewed or otherwise references the accountant's association. (In considering whether such a report is warranted, the accountant may consider the risk that a user of the information might otherwise assume too high a level of assurance.)

D. Applicability -- when conducting a review of the interim financial information of an SEC registrant or of a non-SEC registrant that makes a filing with a regulatory agency in preparation for a public offering or listing (if that entity's latest annual financial statements have been or are being audited).

1. The entity's latest annual financial statements have been audited by the accountant or a predecessor;
2. The accountant has been engaged to audit the entity's current year financial statements (or has audited the entity's latest annual financial statements and expects to be engaged to audit the current year's financial statements);
3. The client prepares its interim financial information in accordance with the same reporting framework as used to prepare the annual financial statements; and
4. If the interim financial information is condensed the following conditions are met: (a) the information purports to conform with an appropriate financial reporting framework (including appropriate form and content); (b) the information includes a note that it does not represent complete financial statements and should be read in conjunction with the latest audited financial statements; and (c) the interim financial information accompanies the audited annual financial statements (or the audited financial statements are deemed "readily available" - being available on the entity's Web site is considered readily available, but being available upon request is not).

E. Objective of a review of interim financial information -- to provide the accountant with a basis for communicating an awareness of any material modifications that should be made to the interim financial information for it to conform with the applicable financial reporting framework (based on performing analytical procedures and making inquiries of those responsible for financial and accounting matters).

II. Establishing an Understanding with the Client -- should establish an understanding with the client about services to be performed and document that understanding through a written communication with the client (regarding the objectives of the engagement, the limitations of the engagement, management's responsibilities, and the accountant's responsibilities).

A. Objectives of the engagement

1. The objective of a review is to provide the accountant with a basis for communicating an awareness of any material modifications that should be made to conform with the applicable financial reporting framework;
2. A review includes obtaining sufficient knowledge of the entity's business and its internal control related to the preparation of annual and interim financial information - to identify the types and likelihood of potential misstatements and to select the inquiries and analytical procedures as a basis for the accountant's conclusions.

B. Limitations of a review engagement

1. Does not provide a basis for expressing an "opinion;"
2. Does not provide assurance that the accountant will become aware of all significant matters that would be identified in an audit; and
3. Is not designed to provide assurance on internal control or to identify significant deficiencies (or material weaknesses) in internal control - the accountant is still responsible for communicating any such deficiencies identified in the review engagement.

C. Management's responsibilities -- management is responsible for (a) the entity's interim financial information; (b) establishing and maintaining effective internal control over financial reporting; (c) complying with applicable laws and regulations; (d) making all financial records and related information available to the accountant; (e) providing a management representations letter; and (f) making adjustments for any identified material misstatements.

D. The accountant's responsibilities -- the accountant is responsible for conducting the review in accordance with AICPA standards.

E. Expected form of the communication -- describe the expected form of the accountant's communication at the completion of the engagement (that is, whether a written or oral report).

III. Accountant's Knowledge of the Entity's Business and its Internal Control

A. Should obtain sufficient knowledge of the entity's business and its internal control related to the preparation of financial information (1) to identify the types and likelihood of potential material misstatements and (2) to select the inquiries and analytical procedures as a basis for the accountant's conclusions.

1. If the accountant has audited the financial statements for one or more annual periods - a sufficient knowledge would have been acquired.
2. If the accountant has not audited the most recent annual financial statements - should perform procedures to obtain such knowledge.

B. Planning the review -- the accountant should perform procedures to update the knowledge of the entity's business and its internal control to help determine the inquiries to be made and the analytical procedures to be performed (and to identify the specific events, transactions, or assertions to be addressed).

1. Read documentation for the preceding audit and reviews;
2. Read the most recent annual and comparable prior interim financial information;
3. Consider the results of any audit procedures performed with respect to the current year's financial statements;
4. Inquire of management about changes in the entity's business activities;
5. Inquire of management about any significant changes in internal control related to preparation of financial information since last audit or review.

C. In an initial review of interim financial information -- the accountant obtains this knowledge by making inquiries of the predecessor and reviewing the predecessor's documentation. (If the predecessor does not respond to the successor's inquiries or allow access to the predecessor's documentation, the successor should use alternative procedures to obtain the necessary knowledge of required matters.)

1. The successor accountant should specifically consider the nature of any (a) corrected material misstatements; (b) matters identified in any summary of uncorrected misstatements; (c) identified risks of material misstatement due to fraud; and (d) significant reporting matters that have continuing significance, such as significant deficiencies or material weaknesses in internal control over financial reporting.
2. The successor accountant should not reference the report or work of the predecessor as a partial basis for the successor's own report.

D. Possible scope restriction -- if the entity's internal control appears to contain significant deficiencies such that it would be impracticable for the accountant to effectively perform review procedures that would provide a basis for conclusions.

IV. Analytical procedures, inquiries, and other review procedures -- the specific inquiries and procedures should be tailored to the engagement based on the accountant's knowledge of the entity's business and internal control.

A. Analytical procedures and related inquiries -- should apply analytical procedures to identify and provide a basis for inquiry about matters that appear to be unusual and that may indicate a material misstatement, including the following:

1. Comparing the interim financial information with the preceding interim period (and with the corresponding period in the previous year);
2. Considering plausible relationships among both financial and nonfinancial information, as applicable - may wish to consider information in a director's information package or in a senior committee's briefing materials;
3. Comparing recorded amounts (or ratios developed from recorded amounts) to expectations developed by the accountant;
4. Comparing disaggregated revenue data - e.g., comparing revenue reported by month and by product line or operating segment to comparable prior periods.

B. Expectations developed in a review of interim financial information tend to be less precise than those developed in an audit, and the accountant ordinarily is not required to corroborate management's responses with other evidence - should still consider the reasonableness and consistency of management's responses relative to the results of other review procedures and the accountant's knowledge of the entity's business and its internal controls.

C. Inquiries and other review procedures -- the following inquiries and other review procedures should be performed:

1. Read the available minutes of meetings of stockholders, directors, etc.;
2. Obtain reports from other accountants, if any, who have performed a review of significant components of the reporting entity;
3. Inquire of members of management having responsibility for the following matters: (a) the interim information has been prepared in conformity with the reporting framework; (b) unusual or complex situations may an effect on the interim financial information; (c) significant transactions in the last few days of the interim period; (d) status of any uncorrected misstatements identified during the previous audit and interim review; (e) questions raised by the review procedures; (f) subsequent events; (g) issues related to fraud or suspected fraud; (h) significant journal entries and other adjustments; (i) communications from regulatory agencies; and (j) significant deficiencies, including material weaknesses, in internal control related to the financial information;
4. Obtain evidence that the interim financial information agrees or reconciles with the accounting records;
5. Read the interim financial information to consider whether it conforms with the applicable financial reporting framework;
6. Read any "other information" in documents containing the interim financial information - should exercise judgment if there is a material inconsistency with the interim financial information.

D. Inquiry concerning litigation, claims, and assessments -- ordinarily the accountant does not send a letter of inquiry to an entity's lawyer(s); however, the accountant may choose to do so if information comes to the accountant's attention that calls into question whether the interim information departs from the financial reporting framework.

E. Inquiry concerning an entity's ability to continue as a going concern

1. When becoming aware of conditions indicating possible inability to continue as a going concern - the accountant should inquire of management about plans to address those conditions and should consider the adequacy of the disclosure of such matters.

2. The accountant ordinarily need not obtain evidence to support any mitigating factors involved.

F. **Extension of interim review procedures --** if the accountant becomes aware that the interim information may not be in conformity with the applicable financial reporting framework, additional inquiries should be made or other procedures should be performed to provide an appropriate basis for the review report.

G. **Coordination with the audit --** some audit procedures associated with the annual audit may be performed concurrently with the review of interim financial information (e.g., reading the minutes).

V. **Written Representation from Management --** should be obtained for all interim financial information presented and for all periods covered by the review.

A. **Interim financial information**

1. Management's acknowledgment of responsibility for the fair presentation.
2. Management's belief that the interim information conforms to the applicable financial reporting framework.

B. **Internal control**

1. Management's acknowledgment of responsibility to establish and maintain controls sufficient to provide a reasonable basis for the preparation of reliable interim financial information.
2. Disclosure of all significant deficiencies and material weaknesses related to the preparation of annual and interim financial information.
3. Management's acknowledgment of responsibility for the design and implementation of programs and controls to prevent and detect fraud.
4. Knowledge of fraud or suspected fraud - involving management, others with significant roles in internal control, or others where the effect of the fraud could be material to the interim financial information.
5. Knowledge of any allegations of fraud or suspected fraud - in communications from employees, former employees, analysts, regulators, short sellers, or others.

C. **Completeness of information**

1. Availability of all financial records and related data.
2. Completeness and availability of all minutes for meetings of stockholders, directors, and committees of directors.
3. Communications with regulatory agencies about deficiencies in financial reporting.
4. Absence of unrecorded transactions.

D. **Recognition, measurement and disclosure**

1. Effects of uncorrected (aggregated) misstatements are immaterial - a summary of such items should be included or attached.
2. Plans or intentions that could materially affect valuation or classifications of assets or liabilities.
3. Information regarding related-party transactions and amounts due to or from related parties.
4. Guarantees (written or oral) for which the entity is contingently liable.
5. Significant estimates and material concentrations required to be disclosed by AICPA Statement of Position 94-6, "Disclosure of Certain Significant Risks and Uncertainties."
6. Violations of laws or regulations that should be considered for adjustment to or disclosure in the interim information.
7. Unasserted claims or assessments that must be disclosed per SFAS No. 5, "Accounting for Contingencies."
8. Other liabilities (or gain or loss contingencies) that are required to be accrued or disclosed per SFAS No. 5.

9. Satisfactory title to all owned assets, liens or encumbrances on such assets, and assets pledged as collateral.

10. Compliance with contracts affecting the interim information.

E. **Subsequent events**

F. **Other matters --** can add other representations applicable to the entity's business or industry.

VI. **Evaluating the Results of Interim Review Procedures**

A. **Likely Misstatements --** the accountant's best estimate of the total misstatement in the account balances or classes of transactions that were reviewed.

1. Misstatements (including inadequate disclosure) should be evaluated individually and in the aggregate to determine whether material modification should be made.

2. Considerations - nature, cause (if known), and amount of misstatements; whether the misstatements originated in the prior year or the interim periods of the current year; materiality judgments made in the current or prior year's audit; and the potential effect of the misstatements on future interim or annual periods.

B. **Incomplete Review --** when the accountant is unable to perform the procedures considered necessary to achieve the objectives of the review (or when management fails to provide necessary written representations).

1. An incomplete review is not an adequate basis for issuing a review report.

2. The accountant should appropriately communicate any known material modifications that are necessary even if no review report is issued.

VII. **Communication to Management and Those Charged with Governance**

A. **Communicate with the appropriate level of management --** when the accountant believes that material modification should be made to the interim information (or when the entity issued the interim information before completion of the review).

B. **If management is unresponsive within a reasonable time --** the accountant should inform those charged with governance (either orally or in writing).

C. **If those charged with governance are unresponsive within a reasonable time --** the accountant should consider whether to resign as the reviewer of the interim information and as the entity's auditor (may also wish to consult with an attorney).

D. **If the accountant becomes aware of fraud or possible illegal acts**

1. If fraud is material or involves senior management - inform those charged with governance.

2. If fraud is not material and does not involve senior management - inform the appropriate level of management.

3. Possible illegal acts - the accountant should determine whether those charged with governance are adequately informed.

E. **Internal control matters --** the accountant should communicate any known significant deficiencies or material weaknesses in internal control over financial reporting to management and those charged with governance.

F. **Other matters --** those charged with governance should be informed about:

1. Any changes in significant accounting policies affecting the interim information;

2. Adjustments that could have a significant effect on the entity's financial reporting process, either individually or in the aggregate;

3. Uncorrected misstatements aggregated by the accountant that management regards as immaterial.

G. **Matters to be communicated to those charged with governance --** should be communicated to those charged with governance (or at least the chair of its audit committee) on a timely basis so they can take appropriate action; the communication may be written or oral.

VIII. Accountant's Review Report on Interim Financial Information

A. Form of the accountant's review report -- each page of the interim information should be clearly marked "unaudited."

1. The title includes the word "independent."
2. Identifies the interim information that was reviewed.
3. States that the interim information is the responsibility of management.
4. States that the review was conducted according to AICPA standards.
5. Describes the procedures associated with the review.
6. States that a review is substantially less in scope than an audit and includes a disclaimer of opinion.
7. States whether the accountant is aware of any material modifications that should be made for the interim information to conform with the applicable financial reporting framework.
8. The report should be signed.
9. The report should be dated - usually the date that the review procedures were completed.

B. Modification of the accountant's review report

1. Departure from the applicable financial reporting framework - the modification should describe the nature of the departure(s) and, if practicable, should state the effects on the interim financial information in an explanatory paragraph preceding the concluding paragraph.
2. Inadequate disclosure (Disclosure requirements for interim information is much less extensive than for annual financial statements.) - if information that the accountant believes is necessary for adequate disclosure is omitted, the accountant should modify the report and, if practicable, include the necessary information in an explanatory paragraph preceding the concluding paragraph.
3. Going concern issues - if disclosure is adequate, the accountant is not required to modify the review report; however, the accountant may choose to add an explanatory paragraph for emphasis after the concluding paragraph.

C. Subsequent discover of facts existing at the date of the accountant's report (or completion of the interim review procedures) -- - the specific actions to be taken may vary with the circumstances (should consider the guidance in AU 561).

IX. Client's Representations Concerning a Review of Interim Financial Information

A. If a client represents in a written communication containing the reviewed interim financial information that the accountant has reviewed that information - the accountant should advise the entity that the review report must be included.

B. If the client does not agree to include the review report - the accountant should request that the accountant's name not be associated with the interim financial information, nor referenced in the document.

C. If the client does not comply with that request - communicate the noncompliance with that request to those charged with governance (may also consult with legal counsel and consider what other actions might be appropriate).

X. Interim Financial Information Accompanying Audited Financial Statements

A. Each page of the interim information should be clearly marked "unaudited."

B. The auditor's report on the audited financial statements should be modified if:

1. The interim financial information is not appropriately marked "unaudited" - should then disclaim an opinion on the interim financial information;
2. The interim information does not appear to be presented in conformity with the applicable financial reporting framework - however, need not modify the report on the audited financial statements if those matters are referred to in a separate review report that is presented along with the information.

XI. Documentation -- the quantity, type, and content are matters of professional judgment. Documentation should include:

A. Any findings/issues considered to be "significant" (e.g., indications that the interim information could be materially misstated, actions taken to address such findings, and the basis for the final conclusions reached);

B. Information to enable members of the engagement team having supervisory and review responsibilities to understand the nature, timing, extent, and results of the review procedures performed; the identity of the engagement team members who performed and reviewed the work; and the evidence the accountant obtained in support of the conclusion that the interim financial information agreed or reconciled with the accounting records.

XII. Three appendices -- Appendix A identifies analytical procedures the accountant may consider conducting in a review of interim financial information. Appendix B identifies unusual or complex situation for which the accountant would normally make further inquiries of management. Appendix C provides two illustrative management representation letters for a review of interim financial information (a "short-form" letter and a "long-form" letter).

AU801 (SAS 117) - Compliance Audits

I. Introduction

A. Applicability of this standard -- When an auditor is engaged (or is required by law or regulation) to perform a compliance audit in accordance with (1) generally accepted auditing standards (GAAS); (2) Government Auditing Standards; and (3) a governmental audit requirement requiring an expression of opinion on compliance.

1. This standard applies to the compliance audit, not to the financial statement audit part of such an engagement.
2. This standard is not applicable to an engagement to examine an entity's compliance with specified requirements or to an examination of internal control over compliance - AT 601 (Compliance Attestation) is applicable to those engagements.
3. Some AU sections can be easily adapted/applied to a compliance audit (e.g., by replacing the word "misstatement" with "noncompliance"), whereas other sections are more difficult to adapt/apply - this standard provides more specific guidance on how to adapt/apply certain AU sections to a compliance audit.

B. The objectives of the auditor are to

1. Obtain sufficient appropriate audit evidence to form an opinion and report whether the entity complied in all material respects with applicable compliance requirements (at the level specified in the governmental audit requirement); and
2. Identify audit/reporting requirements specified in the governmental audit requirement that are supplementary to GAAS and Government Auditing Standards and perform procedures to address those requirements.

C. Primary definitions -- Numerous terms are defined, including the following:

1. **Audit risk of noncompliance --** The risk that the auditor expresses an inappropriate audit opinion on the entity's compliance when material noncompliance exists; a function of the risks of material noncompliance and detection risk of noncompliance.
2. **Compliance audit --** A program-specific audit or an organization-wide audit of an entity's compliance with applicable compliance requirements.
3. **Compliance requirements --** Laws, regulations, rules, and provisions of contracts or grant agreements applicable to government programs with which the entity is required to comply.
4. **Governmental audit requirement --** A governmental requirement established by law, regulation, rule, or provision of contracts or grant agreements requiring that an entity undergo an audit of its compliance with applicable compliance requirements related to one or more government programs.
5. **Government Auditing Standards --** Also known as generally accepted government auditing standards (GAGAS) or GAO's "Yellow Book."
6. **Questioned costs --** Costs that are questioned by the auditor because (1) of a violation or possible violation of the applicable compliance requirements, (2) the costs are not supported by adequate documentation, or (3) the incurred costs appear unreasonable and do not reflect the actions that a prudent person would take in the circumstances.
   a. **Known questioned costs --** Questioned costs specifically identified by the auditor (a subset of "likely questioned costs");
   b. **Likely questioned costs --** The auditor's best estimate of total questioned costs, not just the known questioned costs; developed by extrapolating from audit evidence obtained.

D. Management responsibilities -- A compliance audit recognizes that management is responsible for complying with applicable compliance requirements, which includes (1) identifying the entity's government programs and understanding the compliance requirements; (2) establishing/maintaining effective controls over the compliance requirements; (3) monitoring the entity's compliance; and (4) taking corrective action when noncompliance has been identified.

II. Requirements

A. **Adapting and applying the AU sections to a compliance audit --** The auditor should adapt and apply the AU sections to the objectives of a compliance audit. (An appendix to SAS No. 117 specifically excludes certain AU sections from this.)

B. **Establishing materiality levels --** The auditor should establish and apply materiality levels for the compliance audit based on the governmental audit requirement.

C. **Identifying government programs and applicable compliance requirements --** The auditor should determine the "applicable compliance requirements," that is, which government programs and compliance requirements to test.

D. **Performing risk assessment procedures**

1. The auditor should perform risk assessment procedures to obtain a sufficient understanding of the applicable compliance requirements and the entity's internal control over compliance.
2. The auditor should inquire of management about whether there are findings and recommendations resulting from previous audits, attestation engagements, and internal/external monitoring that relate to the objectives of the compliance audit (including management's response to findings and recommendations that could have a material effect on compliance).

E. **Assessing the risks of material noncompliance --** The auditor should assess the risks of material noncompliance whether due to fraud or error for each compliance requirement and consider whether any of those are "pervasive" to compliance.

F. **Performing further audit procedures in response to assessed risks**

1. The auditor should develop an overall response to any risks of material noncompliance that are pervasive to the entity's compliance.
2. The auditor should design and perform further audit procedures, including tests of details, about the entity's compliance with each of the applicable compliance requirements in response to assessed risks of material noncompliance - risk assessment procedures, tests of controls, and analytical procedures alone are insufficient to address those risks.
3. The auditor should perform tests of controls over compliance if (a) the risk assessment includes an expectation of operating effectiveness; (b) substantive procedures alone do not provide sufficient appropriate audit evidence; or (c) such tests of controls over compliance are required by the governmental audit requirement.

G. **Supplementary audit requirements --** The auditor should perform procedures to address any audit requirements that are specified in the governmental audit requirement that are supplementary to GAAS and GAGAS.

H. **Written representations --** The auditor should obtain written representations from management that are tailored to the entity and the governmental audit requirement.

I. **Subsequent events**

1. The auditor should perform audit procedures up to the date of the auditor's report to identify subsequent events related to the entity's compliance - should consider (a) relevant internal auditor's reports; (b) other auditor's reports identifying noncompliance; (c) reports from grantors and pass-through entities regarding noncompliance; and (d) information about the entity's noncompliance obtained through other professional engagements for the entity.
2. The auditor has no obligation to perform any audit procedures related to the entity's compliance during the period subsequent to the period covered by the auditor's report - if the auditor becomes aware of noncompliance in the subsequent period that requires disclosure, the auditor should discuss the matter with management and those charged with governance and include an explanatory paragraph in the audit report describing the matter.

J. **Evaluating the sufficiency and appropriateness of the audit evidence and forming an opinion --** The auditor should form an opinion (at the level specified by the governmental audit requirement) on whether the entity complied in all material respects with the applicable compliance requirements; the auditor should evaluate "likely questioned costs" (not just "known questioned costs") and other noncompliance that may not result in questioned costs.

K. Reporting

1. The auditor may issue: (a) a report on compliance only; (b) a combined report on compliance and on internal control over compliance; or (c) a separate report on internal control over compliance. (AU801 provides specific elements of the auditor's report that are required in each case.)
2. The auditor should modify the opinion on compliance if the auditor identifies noncompliance with the applicable compliance requirements that is material to the entity's compliance, or if the scope of the compliance audit is restricted.
3. The auditor should communicate to those charged with governance the auditor's responsibilities under GAAS, Government Auditing Standards, and the governmental audit requirement, an overview of the planned scope and timing of the compliance audit, and any significant findings.

L. Documentation -- The auditor should document the following:

1. The risk assessment procedures performed, including those related to gaining an understanding of internal control over compliance;
2. Responses to the assessed risks of material noncompliance, the procedures performed to test compliance with the applicable compliance requirements, and the results of those procedures, including any tests of controls over compliance;
3. Materiality levels and the basis on which they were determined; and
4. How the auditor complied with the specific governmental audit requirements that are supplementary to GAAS and GAGAS.

M. Reissuance of the compliance report -- A reissued report should include an explanatory paragraph stating that the report is replacing a previously issued report and describing why the report is being reissued, and any changes from the previously issued report; if additional procedures are performed to obtain audit evidence for all of the government programs being reported on, the auditor's report date should be updated.

III. Application Guidance and Explanatory Material

A. Introduction and applicability -- Example engagements for which SAS No. 117 applies includes an audit under OMB Circular A-133, "Audits of States, Local Governments and Non-Profit Organizations;" also includes a department-specific requirement such as "U.S. Department of Housing and Urban Development Audit Requirements Related to Entities Such as Public Housing Agencies, Nonprofit and For-Profit Housing Projects, and Certain Lenders."

B. Objectives and definitions -- Most (but not all) governmental audit requirements specify that the auditor's opinion on compliance is at the program level; these may also state specific supplementary requirements of the compliance audit.

C. Establishing materiality levels

1. The purpose for establishing materiality levels is to: (a) determine the nature and extent of risk assessment procedures; (b) identify and assess the risks of material noncompliance; (c) determine the nature, timing, and extent of further audit procedures; (d) evaluate whether the entity complied with the applicable compliance requirements; and (e) report findings .
2. Materiality is usually determined relative to the government program taken as a whole - but the governmental audit requirement may specify a different level of materiality for one or more of those purposes .
3. The auditor's determination of materiality is based on consideration of the needs of users as a group, including (but not limited to) grantors.

D. Identifying government programs and applicable compliance requirements

1. Some governmental audit requirements specifically identify the applicable compliance requirements, whereas others provide a framework for the auditor to determine the applicable compliance requirements (e.g., for OMB Circular A-133 audits, the OMB's "Compliance Supplement" provides such a framework).
2. OMB's Compliance Supplement contains the usual compliance requirements and identifies suggested audit procedures applicable to them.

3. The applicable program-specific audit guide issued by the grantor agency may contain the compliance requirements and suggested audit procedures.

4. The auditor may perform other procedures to obtain an understanding of applicable compliance requirements - such as reading the laws, regulations, or grant agreements; making inquiry of management or individuals outside the entity (such as oversight organizations or an attorney); reading the minutes of meetings of the governing board, etc..

E. **Performing risk assessment procedures --** The nature and extent of the risk assessment procedures may vary due to the nature and complexity of the compliance requirements, the auditor's knowledge of internal control over compliance, the level of oversight by the grantor or pass-through entity, and how management addresses findings.

F. **Assessing the risks of material noncompliance**

1. The auditor may consider a variety of factors in assessing the risks of material noncompliance, including the following: (a) the complexity of the compliance requirements; (b) how long the entity has been subject to the applicable compliance requirements; (c) the degree of judgment involved in adhering to the compliance requirements; (d) the entity's compliance with the applicable compliance requirement in prior years, etc.

2. Examples of situations in which there is a "pervasive" risk of material noncompliance: (a) an entity is experiencing financial difficulty and there is an increased risk that grant funds will be used for unauthorized purposes; and (b) an entity's recordkeeping is poor.

G. **Performing further audit procedures in response to assessed risks**

1. The auditor should design procedures to detect both intentional and unintentional material noncompliance.

2. Tests of details (including tests of transactions) may be performed in the following areas: (a) grant disbursements/expenditures; (b) eligibility files; (c) cost allocation plans; and (d) periodic reports filed with grantors.

3. Analytical procedures are usually less effective in a compliance audit than in a financial statement audit, but may be used along with other procedures.

4. **Tests of operating effectiveness --** Some governmental audit requirements (e.g., OMB Circular A-133) require tests of operating effectiveness of controls identified as likely to be effective, even if the auditor believes such testing would be inefficient.

H. **Supplementary audit requirements**

1. Examples of "supplementary audit requirements" are requirements in OMB Circular A-133 for the auditor to (a) perform specified procedures to identify "major" programs; and (b) follow up on prior audit findings to assess the reasonableness of the summary schedule of prior audit findings .

2. When there is conflicting guidance, the auditor may consult with the government agency providing the funding or establishing the audit guidance.

I. **Subsequent events --** An example of noncompliance occurring subsequent to the period being audited (but before the report release date) that may warrant disclosure to prevent report users from being misled is the discovery of noncompliance of such magnitude that it caused the grantor to stop the funding.

J. **Evaluating the audit evidence and forming an opinion --** The auditor may consider the following in evaluating whether the entity has materially complied with applicable compliance requirements: (1) the nature and frequency of the noncompliance; (2) the adequacy of the entity's system for monitoring compliance; and (3) whether the noncompliance resulted in likely questioned costs that are material to the government program.

K. **Reporting**

1. **If the report is a matter of public record --** Removing personally identifiable information regarding noncompliance will reduce the likelihood of disclosing sensitive information.

2. When the auditor communicates significant deficiencies (or material weaknesses) in internal control over compliance to management and those charged with governance - Government Auditing Standards require the auditor to obtain a response from the responsible officials

(preferably in writing) regarding their views on the findings, conclusions, and recommendations (and include a copy of any written response in the auditor's report).

3. If a written response regarding such significant deficiencies is included in a document containing the auditor's written communication to management and those charged with governance about the internal control matters - the auditor may add a paragraph to the written communication to disclaim an opinion on management's written response.

4. If the auditor is submitting a reworded form, schedule, or report (or appropriately worded separate report) - the auditor may include a separate communication to the agency to explain why the form/report was modified.

L. Documentation -- The auditor is not expected to prepare specific documentation as to how the auditor adapted and applied each of the applicable AU sections to the objectives of the compliance audit.

M. Reissuance of the compliance report -- Examples of situations for which the auditor might reissue the compliance report include: (1) a quality control review by a governmental agency indicates that the auditor did not test an applicable compliance requirement; or (2) the discovery subsequent to the date of the compliance report that the entity had another government program that was required to be tested.

AU901 (SAS 1) Public Warehouses

I. **Public Warehouse Operations**

A. The Public Warehouse:

1. A "**warehouse**" involves the business of maintaining custody of goods for others;
2. There are two basic types of warehouses:
    a. "Terminal" -- where the principal economic function is to provide storage;
    b. "Field" -- which is essentially a financing arrangement whereby custody of goods is exchanged for warehouse receipts to be used as collateral for borrowing.

B. Warehouse Receipts:

1. **Warehouse Receipts** are the basic document in warehousing activities;
2. There are two basic types of warehouse receipts:
    a. "Negotiable" -- where the goods may be released only upon surrender of the receipt;
    b. "Non-negotiable" -- where the goods may be released upon valid instructions, even without surrendering the receipt.

C. **Government Regulations** -- a variety of statutes apply to warehousing operations:

1. U.S. Warehouse Act (and related regulations by the U.S. Department of Agriculture);
2. U.S. Commodity Exchange Act;
3. Tariff Act of 1930.

II. **The Warehouseman**

A. Internal controls:

1. Recommend that the auditor obtain an adequate understanding of (and perform appropriate tests) of internal controls related to the warehouseman's **custodial** responsibilities - since significant unrecorded liabilities may result from improperly discharged custodial responsibilities;
2. Proper segregation of duties is the key concept (regarding receiving, storing, and delivering goods);
3. Since warehouse receipts are the basic source documents, controls over these documents must be appropriate.

B. Additional controls for field warehouses:

1. Controls are applied at two points -- the field location and the warehouseman's central office (only non-negotiable warehouse receipts should be issued from field locations);
2. The central office should oversee the field location activities (implies particular control considerations at that level).

C. Procedures of the independent auditor are stated as five recommendations:

1. Study and evaluate internal controls (regarding the accountability for and the custody of all goods stored with the warehouse);
2. Test the records pertaining to accountability for the goods delivered to the warehouse;
3. Compare and reconcile the recorded accountability with the outstanding warehouse receipts;
4. Observe the taking of physical inventory and perform test counts;
5. Confirm accountability, as deemed appropriate, with the holders of warehouse receipts. (The audit concern involves **unrecorded** receipts -- a liability to the warehouseman.)

III. Controls and Auditing Procedures for a Client's Goods Stored in Public Warehouses

A. Internal controls -- include the investigation of the warehouseman prior to delivering goods, as well as an on-going evaluation (review the adequacy of the owner-client's insurance coverage).

B. Audit procedures -- AU331 (specifically paragraph 14) is applicable to inventory held in public warehouses.

SSARS

AR60 - Reporting on Compilation and Review Engagements

I. **Framework for Performing and Reporting on Compilation and Review Engagements --** Issued December, 2009

II. **Introduction --** This section provides a framework and defines and describes the objectives and elements of compilation and review engagements.

  A. **Assurance engagement --** An engagement in which an accountant issues a report designed to enhance the degree of confidence of third parties and management about the outcome of an evaluation or measurement of financial statements (subject matter) against an applicable financial reporting framework (criteria).

  B. **Attest engagement --** An engagement that requires independence, as defined in AICPA Professional Standards.

  C. **Other comprehensive basis of accounting (OCBOA) --** A definite set of criteria, other than U.S. GAAP or IFRS, having substantial support underlying the preparation of financial statements.

  D. **Review evidence --** Information used by the accountant to provide a reasonable basis for obtaining of limited assurance.

  E. **Third party --** All persons, including those charged with governance, except for members of management.

III. **Objectives and Limitations of Compilation and Review Engagements**

  A. **Compilation --** Assists management in presenting financial information in the form of financial statements without providing any assurance; "Although a compilation is not an assurance engagement, it is an attest engagement." (AR 60.05).

  B. **Review --** The objective is to obtain "limited assurance" that there are no material modifications that should be made to the financial statements; "A review engagement is an assurance engagement as well as an attest engagement." (AR 60.07).

IV. **Professional Requirements --** SSARSs contain both professional requirements and explanatory material.

  A. **Requirements --** There are two categories of "requirements."

    1. **"Unconditional requirements" --** The accountant is required to comply with an unconditional requirement when the circumstances exist to which the unconditional requirement applies (an unconditional requirement is indicated by the words "must" or "is required") - No exceptions!

    2. **"Presumptively mandatory requirements"**

      a. The accountant is also required to comply with a "presumptively mandatory requirement" when circumstances exist to which the presumptively mandatory requirement applies - allows for the possibility of exception, however!

      b. In rare circumstances, may depart from a presumptively mandatory requirement - the accountant must document the justification for the departure and how alternative procedures performed in the circumstances were sufficient to achieve the objectives of the presumptively mandatory requirement (a presumptively mandatory requirements is indicated by the word "should").

  B. **Explanatory material --** Defined as the text within a SSARS (excluding any related appendices or interpretations) that may provide further explanation on the professional requirements or describe other procedures or actions possibly applicable to the auditor (practitioner).

1. Such explanatory material is intended to be descriptive and does not impose a professional requirement.
2. Explanatory material is identified by the terms **"may," "might," or "could."**

V. Hierarchy of Compilation and Review Standards and Guidance

A. **SSARSs --** Provide a measure of quality and the objectives to be achieved in both a compilation and review engagement. (Compliance is enforceable by Rule 202 of the AICPA Code of Professional Conduct, *Compliance with Standards*, which requires accountants to adhere to standards promulgated by the ARSC.)

B. **"Interpretive publications"**

1. Consist of compilation and review interpretations (and appendices) of the SSARSs, AICPA Audit & Accounting Guides, and AICPA auditing Statements of Position, to the extent applicable to compilation and review engagements.
2. Accountants should be aware of (and consider) interpretive publications applicable to compilations and reviews - when accountants do not apply such guidance, they should be prepared to explain how they complied with the SSARS provisions related to such interpretive publications

C. **"Other compilation and review publications" --** Other publications have no authoritative status, but they may help the accountant understand and apply the SSARS (for example, articles in the *Journal of Accountancy* and the AICPA's *CPA Letter*, continuing professional education programs, textbooks, etc.).

VI. Ethical Principles and Statements on Quality Control Standards (SQCSs)

A. "When performing a compilation or review engagement, the code (AICPA Code of Professional Conduct) requires an accountant to maintain objectivity and integrity and comply with all other applicable provisions." (AR 60.23)

B. " ...a firm should establish quality control policies and procedures to provide reasonable assurance that personnel comply with SSARSs in compilation and review engagements." (AR 60.24)

C. **Relationship of SSARSs and SQCSs --** "SSARSs relate to the conduct of individual compilation and review engagements; SQCSs relate to the conduct of a firm's accounting practice." (AR 60.25)

VII. There are Five "Elements" that Comprise a Compilation or Review Engagement

A. **Three party relationship --** A compilation or review engagement involves 3 parties: management (or the responsible party), an accountant in the practice of public accounting, and the intended users of the financial statements.

1. **Management (responsible party) --** Management must accept responsibility for the preparation and fair presentation of the financial statements; the accountant may make suggestions about the form or content or even prepare the financial statements based on information that is the representation of management.
2. **Accountant in the practice of public accounting --** If not in public accounting, the issuance of a report under SSARS would not be appropriate.
3. **Intended users --** The accountant has no responsibility to identify the intended users.

B. **An applicable financial reporting framework --** Examples include U.S. GAAP (as promulgated by the FASB, the GASB, or the Federal Accounting Standards Advisory Board); IFRS issued by the International Accounting Standards Board; and OCBOA.

C. **Financial statement or financial information --** The accountant may be engaged to compile or review a complete set of financial statements or an individual financial statement (balance sheet); the financial statements may be for an annual period or for a shorter (or longer) period, depending on management's needs.

D. **Evidence**

1. **Compilation --** The accountant has no responsibility to obtain any evidence .

2. **Review --** Obtain evidence that will provide "a reasonable basis for obtaining limited assurance that there are no material modifications that should be made to the financial statements in order for the statements to be in conformity with the applicable financial reporting framework." (AR 60.44)

E. **Compilation and review reports**

1. **Compilation --** "If the accountant performs a compilation, a report or written communication is required unless the accountant withdraws from the engagement. If the accountant is not independent, he or she may issue a compilation report, provided that the accountant complies with the compilation standards." (AR 60.46)

2. **Review --** "If the accountant performs a review, a written review report is required unless the accountant withdraws from the engagement." (AR 60.47)

AR80 - Compilation of Financial Statements

I. **Establishing an Understanding --** The accountant should establish an understanding with management regarding the services to be performed and document that through a written communication with management.

   A. The understanding should include the objectives of the engagement, management's responsibilities, the accountant's responsibilities, and the limitations of the engagement.

   B. These matters should be communicated in an "engagement letter."

   C. If the compiled financial statements are not expected to be used by a third party (and if the accountant does not expect to issue a compilation report) -- The engagement letter should include an acknowledgment by management that the financial statements will not be used by a third party.

II. **Compilation Performance Requirements**

   A. **Understanding of the industry --** The accountant should possess an understanding of the client's industry, including the accounting principles and practices used in the industry;

   B. **Knowledge of the client --** Should obtain an understanding of the client's business and an understanding of the accounting principles and practices used by the client;

   C. **Reading the financial statements --** The accountant should read the financial statements and consider whether they appear to be appropriate in form and free from obvious material errors, including inadequate disclosure;

   D. **Other compilation procedures --** The accountant is not required to make inquiries or perform any other procedures to verify information supplied by the entity:

   E. If the accountant believes that the financial statements may be materially misstated -- The accountant should obtain additional or revised information;

   F. If the entity refuses to provide the additional or revised information -- The accountant should withdraw from the engagement.

III. **Establishing an Understanding --** The accountant should establish an understanding with management regarding the services to be performed and document that through a written communication with management.

   A. The understanding should include the objectives of the engagement, management's responsibilities, the accountant's responsibilities, and the limitations of the engagement.

   B. These matters should be communicated in an "engagement letter."

   C. If the compiled financial statements are not expected to be used by a third party (and if the accountant does not expect to issue a compilation report) -- The engagement letter should include an acknowledgment by management that the financial statements will not be used by a third party.

IV. **Compilation Performance Requirements**

   A. **Understanding of the industry --** The accountant should possess an understanding of the client's industry, including the accounting principles and practices used in the industry;

   B. **Knowledge of the client --** Should obtain an understanding of the client's business and an understanding of the accounting principles and practices used by the client;

   C. **Reading the financial statements --** The accountant should read the financial statements and consider whether they appear to be appropriate in form and free from obvious material errors, including inadequate disclosure;

   D. **Other compilation procedures --** The accountant is not required to make inquiries or perform any other procedures to verify information supplied by the entity:

E. If the accountant believes that the financial statements may be materially misstated -- The accountant should obtain additional or revised information;

F. If the entity refuses to provide the additional or revised information -- The accountant should withdraw from the engagement.

V. **Documentation in a Compilation Engagement --** The accountant should prepare documentation in sufficient detail to provide a clear understanding of the work performed.

A. **Purpose --** Documentation provides the principal support that the accountant performed the compilation in accordance with SSARSs.

B. **Form, content, and extent of documentation --** Varies with the circumstances and the accountant's judgment, but should include: (1) the engagement letter; (2) any findings or issues that, in the accountant's judgment, are "significant;" and (3) communications (whether oral or written) to the appropriate level of management regarding fraud or illegal acts.

VI. **Reporting on the Financial Statements --** Financial statements that have been compiled should be accompanied by a written report.

A. **Elements of the compilation report**

1. **Title --** "Accountant's Compilation Report" or "Independent Accountant's Compilation Report"
2. Addressee;
3. **Introductory paragraph --** Identifies the financial statements and the nature of the engagement; include a disclaimer of any level of assurance;
4. **Management's responsibility --** For the financial statements and related internal control;
5. **Accountant's responsibility --** To conduct the compilation in accordance with SSARSs issued by the AICPA;
6. Signature of the accountant (either manual or printed);
7. Date of the report (the date of completion of the compilation).

B. **General comments about the compilation report**

1. Each page of the financial statements should reference the accountant's compilation report;
2. The report should not describe other procedures that might have been performed by the accountant;
3. Financial statements prepared under OCBOA are not appropriate unless there is a sufficient description of the OCBOA and the primary differences relative to GAAP (the differences need not be quantified) and the informative disclosures are similar to those required by GAAP.

C. **Reporting on financial statements that omit substantially all disclosures**

1. The accountant may compile such financial statements if the omission of substantially all disclosures is not undertaken with an intention to mislead readers; include a paragraph to the compilation report to comment on the omission of substantially all disclosures.
2. When the entity wishes to include disclosures about a few matters label such disclosures "Selected Information -- Substantially All Disclosures Required by (applicable framework) Are Not Included."

D. **Reporting when the accountant is not independent --** A compilation report may be issued when independence is lacking.

1. Add a statement in a final paragraph of the report: "I am (we are) not independent with respect to XYZ Company."
2. The accountant is permitted (but not required) to disclose the reason(s) for the impairment of independence. If making such a disclosure in the report, the accountant should include all of the reasons involved.

E. **Communications with the client when the compiled financial statements are not expected to be used by a third party --** Not required to issue a compilation report.

1. Each page of the financial statements should be restricted for management;
2. If the accountant discovers that such financial statements have been distributed to third parties, the accountant should discuss this with the client. If client does not comply with the request to recover the financial statements, the accountant should notify known third parties that the financial statements are not intended for the use of third parties (should also consult with legal counsel).

F. **Emphasis of a matter**

1. **Examples --** Uncertainties (going concern issues), related party transactions, subsequent events, etc.
2. Such a paragraph should only be added with respect to a matter that is disclosed in the financial statements -- Should not add an emphasis of a matter paragraph if disclosure is lacking.

G. **Departures from the applicable reporting framework (e.g., GAAP departure)**

1. Consider whether modification of the standard report is an adequate way to disclose the departure. If so, add a separate paragraph to the report. The accountant is not required to determine the effects of the departure if management has not already done so.
2. If modification of the report is not adequate to indicate the deficiencies -- The accountant should withdraw from the engagement (should also consult with legal counsel).

H. **Restricting the use of an accountant's compilation report --** The report should be restricted in certain circumstances (by adding a separate paragraph at the end of the report). The accountant is not responsible for controlling a client's distribution of restricted use reports.

I. **Going concern issues --** If management's conclusions are unreasonable, or if the disclosure of the going concern issues is unreasonable, the accountant should treat the matter as a departure from an applicable financial reporting framework.

J. **Subsequent events --** If the subsequent event is not adequately accounted for (or disclosed), the accountant should treat the matter as a departure from an applicable financial reporting framework.

VII. **Subsequent Discovery of Facts Existing at the Date of the Report --** When, subsequent to the issuance of the compilation report, the accountant becomes aware of facts that may have existed at the report date which might suggest that the information supplied by the entity was incorrect (consider consulting with legal counsel and insurance provider).

A. As soon as practicable, the accountant should try to determine whether the information is reliable, whether the facts existed at the report date, and should obtain additional/revised information.

B. Advise the client to make appropriate disclosure of the newly discovered facts and their impact on the financial statements to known users. (Either issue revised financial statements with the appropriate report; or, when the effect on the financial statements cannot be determined promptly, notify the known users that the financial statements should not be used.)

C. **If the client refuses to make the necessary disclosures --** The accountant should notify the appropriate personnel within the entity (such as the manager, owner, or board of directors) of the refusal. The accountant may also notify applicable regulatory agencies and any known financial statement users that the accountant's report should no longer be used.

D. **The accountant's disclosure --** If the client has not cooperated, the accountant can indicate that information has been obtained which the client has not cooperated in attempting to substantiate and that, if the information is true, the accountant believes the compilation or review report should no longer be used. (The accountant need not detail the specific information and should avoid comments about anyone's motives.)

VIII. **Supplementary Information --** The compilation report should refer to the supplementary information when the accountant has compiled both the basic financial statements and the supplementary information. (Alternatively, the accountant may choose to issue a separate report on the other data.)

IX. **Communicating to Management and Others --** When evidence comes to the accountant's attention that fraud or an illegal act may have occurred (need not report matters regarding illegal acts that are "clearly inconsequential"); should also consider consulting with legal counsel and the accountant's insurance provider.

- **A.** The communication may be oral or written -- If oral, the accountant should document the communication;
- **B.** When the matters regarding fraud or illegal act involve senior management -- Report the matter to an individual or group at a higher level within the entity (e.g., the manager, owner or the board of directors);
- **C.** When the matters regarding fraud or illegal act involve an owner of the business -- The accountant should consider resigning from the engagement;
- **D.** Communicating to parties other than the client's senior management (or the owner or board of directors, as applicable) is ordinarily precluded by ethical requirements regarding confidentiality. However, in some circumstances a duty to disclose to outside parties may exist, although the accountant may wish to consult with legal counsel before discussing such matters with parties outside the client
  - **1.** To comply with applicable legal and regulatory requirements;
  - **2.** To a successor accountant, when inquiring of a predecessor accountant in accordance with SSARS No. 4; or
  - **3.** In response to a subpoena.

X. Change in an Engagement from an Audit or Review to a Compilation -- When the accountant, who has been engaged to audit or review the financial statements of a nonissuer, is requested to change the engagement to a compilation before completion of the engagement.

- **A. Before agreeing to such a change --** The accountant should consider (1) the reason for the client's request (e.g., whether a scope limitation is imposed by the client or by circumstances.); (2) the additional effort required to complete the audit or review; and (3) the estimated additional cost to complete the audit or review .
- **B. Reasonable basis for requesting such a change --** If there is a change in the circumstances that affects the entity's requirement for an audit or review; or if there is a misunderstanding concerning the nature of an audit, review, or compilation. (The report should not reference the original engagement or the reasons for the change.)

AR90 - Review of Financial Statements

I. **Establishing an understanding --** The accountant should establish an understanding with management regarding the services to be performed and document that through a written communication with management.

   A. The understanding should include the objectives of the engagement, management's responsibilities, the accountant's responsibilities, and the limitations of the engagement.

   B. These matters should be communicated in an "engagement letter."

II. **Review performance requirements --** Cannot perform a review engagement if the accountant's independence is impaired for any reason

   A. **Understanding of the industry --** Should possess an understanding of the client's industry, including the accounting principles and practices used in the industry;

   B. **Knowledge of the client --** Should obtain an understanding of the client's business and an understanding of the accounting principles and practices used by the client;

   C. **Designing and performing review procedures --** TV.

      1. **Analytical procedures --** Comparing expectations developed by the accountant to recorded amounts or ratios based on recorded amounts; such procedures may be performed at the financial statement level or at the detailed account level;

      2. **Inquiries and other review procedures --** The accountant should direct inquiries to management about a variety of matters (listed in AR90.19); should also read minutes of board meetings, etc.; should read the financial statements for apparent compliance with the applicable financial reporting framework; and obtain reports from other accountants who have audited or reviewed financial statements of any significant components of the entity;

      3. **Incorrect, incomplete, or otherwise unsatisfactory information --** If the accountant believes that the financial statements may be materially misstated, the accountant should perform additional procedures to obtain limited assurance that there are no material modifications that should be made to the financial statements;

      4. **Management representations --** Written representations are required from management for all financial statements and periods covered by the accountant's review report; (If current management was not present for all such periods, the accountant should still obtain written representations from current management for all such periods.)

      5. **Obtaining an "updating representation letter" --** The accountant should consider obtaining an updating representations letter if there is a significant period of time between the original representations letter and issuance of the review report (or if there is a material subsequent event); "the predecessor accountant should obtain an updating representation letter from the management of the former client."

III. **Documentation in a review engagement --** Should prepare documentation in sufficient detail to provide a clear understanding of the work performed.

   A. **Purpose --** Documentation provides the principal support that the accountant performed the review in accordance with SSARSs.

   B. **Form, content, and extent of documentation --** Varies with the circumstances and the accountant's judgment, but should include: (1) the engagement letter; (2) the analytical procedures performed; (3) additional procedures performed as a follow-up to the analytical procedures; (4) significant matters addressed by inquiries; (5) any findings that are "significant;" (6) any significant "unusual matters" considered and their disposition; (7) communications (whether oral or written) to the appropriate level of management regarding fraud or illegal acts; and (8) the management representation letter.

IV. **Reporting on the financial statements --** Financial statements that have been reviewed should be accompanied by a written report.

   A. **Elements of the review report**

1. **Title --** "Independent Accountant's Review Report"
2. Addressee;
3. **Introductory paragraph --** Identifies the financial statements and the nature of the engagement; state that a review is substantially less in scope than an audit and include a disclaimer of opinion;
4. **Management's responsibility --** For the financial statements and related internal control;
5. **Accountant's responsibility --** To conduct the review in accordance with SSARSs issued by the AICPA;
6. Results of the engagement (expressed as "negative assurance");
7. Signature of the accountant (either manual or printed);
8. Date of the report (not before the date of completion of the review).

B. **General comments about the review report**

1. Each page of the financial statements should reference the independent accountant's review report;
2. **An "incomplete review" --** When the accountant is unable to perform the inquiry and analytical procedures considered necessary (cannot issue a review report under these circumstances);
3. Financial statements prepared under OCBOA are not appropriate unless there is a sufficient description of the OCBOA and the primary differences relative to GAAP (the differences need not be quantified) and the informative disclosures are similar to those required by GAAP

C. **Emphasis of a matter --** The accountant may choose to add a paragraph to the review report to emphasize a matter.

1. **Examples --** Uncertainties (going concern issues), related party transactions, subsequent events, etc.;
2. Such a paragraph should only be added with respect to a matter that is disclosed in the financial statements -- Should not add an emphasis of a matter paragraph if disclosure is lacking

D. **Departures from the applicable reporting framework (e.g., GAAP departure)**

1. Consider whether modification of the standard report is an adequate way to disclose the departure. If so, add a separate paragraph to the report. The accountant is not required to determine the effects of the departure if management has not already done so;
2. If modification of the report is not adequate to indicate the deficiencies -- The accountant should withdraw from the engagement (should also consult with legal counsel).

E. **Restricting the use of an accountant's review report --** The report should be restricted in certain circumstances (by adding a separate paragraph at the end of the report); the accountant is not responsible for controlling a client's distribution of restricted use reports.

F. **Going concern issues --** If management's conclusions are unreasonable or if the disclosure of the going concern issues is unreasonable, the accountant should treat the matter as a departure from an applicable financial reporting framework.

G. **Subsequent events --** If the subsequent event is not adequately accounted for (or disclosed), the accountant should treat the matter as a departure from an applicable financial reporting framework.

V. **Subsequent discovery of facts existing at the date of the report --** When, subsequent to the issuance of the review report, the accountant becomes aware of facts that may have existed at the report date which might suggest that the information supplied by the entity was incorrect (consider consulting with legal counsel and insurance provider).

A. As soon as practicable, the accountant should try to determine whether the information is reliable and whether the facts existed at the report date -- obtain additional/revised information;

- **B.** Advise the client to make appropriate disclosure of the newly discovered facts and their impact on the financial statements to known users; (Either issue revised financial statements with the appropriate report; or, when the effect on the financial statements cannot be determined promptly, notify the known users that the financial statements should not be used.)
- **C.** If the client refuses to make the necessary disclosures -- the accountant should notify the appropriate personnel within the entity (such as the manager, owner, or board of directors) of the refusal; may also notify applicable regulatory agencies and any known financial statement users that the accountant's report should no longer be used;
- **D.** **The accountant's disclosure --** If the client has not cooperated, the accountant can indicate that information has been obtained which the client has not cooperated in attempting to substantiate and that, if the information is true, the accountant believes the review report should no longer be used (need not detail the specific information; should avoid comments about anyone's motives).

VI. **Supplementary information --** The review report should refer to the supplementary information when the accountant has reviewed both the basic financial statements and the supplementary information; disclaim an opinion or any assurance on the supplementary information if it has not be subjected to appropriate review procedures.

VII. **Communicating to management and others --** When evidence comes to the accountant's attention that fraud or an illegal act may have occurred (need not report matters regarding illegal acts that are "clearly inconsequential"); should also consider consulting with legal counsel and the accountant's insurance provider.

VIII. **The communication may be oral or written --** If oral, the accountant should document the communication;

IX. When the matters regarding fraud or illegal act involve senior management -- Report the matter to an individual or group at a higher level within the entity (e.g., the manager, owner or the board of directors);

X. When the matters regarding fraud or illegal act involve an owner of the business -- The accountant should consider resigning from the engagement ;

XI. Communicating to parties other than the client's senior management (or the owner or board of directors, as applicable) is ordinarily precluded by ethical requirements regarding confidentiality. However, in some circumstances, a duty to disclose to outside parties may exist, although the accountant may wish to consult with legal counsel before discussing such matters with parties outside the client.

- **A.** To comply with applicable legal and regulatory requirements;
- **B.** To a successor accountant when inquiring of a predecessor accountant in accordance with SSARS No. 4; or
- **C.** In response to a subpoena.

XII. **Change in an engagement from an audit to a review --** When the accountant who has been engaged to audit the financial statements of a nonissuer is requested to change the engagement to a review before completion of the audit engagement.

- **A.** **Before agreeing to change an audit to a review --** The accountant should consider (1) the reason for the client's request (e.g., whether a scope limitation is imposed by the client or by circumstances); (2) the additional effort required to complete the audit; and (3) the estimated additional cost to complete the audit;
- **B.** **Reasonable basis for requesting such a change --** If there is a change in the circumstances that affects the entity's requirement for an audit; or if there is a misunderstanding concerning the nature of an audit or a review. (The report should not reference the original engagement or the reasons for the change.)

AR110 - Compilation of Specified Elements

I. **This Statement applies --** when an accountant is engaged to compile or issues a compilation report on one or more specified elements, accounts, or items of a financial statement -- examples include schedules of rentals, royalties, profit participation, or provision for income taxes.

II. **Conditions for compiling specified elements, accounts, or items of a financial statement**

   A. An accountant may assist in the preparation of one or more specified elements, accounts, or items of a financial statement without the issuance of a compilation report -- unless engaged to compile such specified elements, accounts, or items of a financial statement (in which case a compilation report is required).

   B. The accountant should consider how the presentation will be used.

   C. Consider issuing a compilation report when associated with the information so that a user will not infer a level of assurance that is unwarranted.

III. **Establish an Understanding with the Entity**

   A. The accountant should establish an understanding with the client as to the services to be performed -- describe the nature and limitations of the services to be performed and the report to be issued.

   B. The understanding should include that the engagement cannot be relied upon to disclose errors, fraud, or illegal acts.

   C. The understanding should include that the accountant will inform the appropriate level of management of any material errors and of any evidence or information that comes to the accountant's attention during the engagement that fraud or an illegal act may have occurred.

IV. **Performance requirements --** The accountant should read such compiled specified elements, accounts, or items of a financial statement and consider whether the information appears to be appropriate in form and free of obvious material errors (i.e., must follow the compilation performance requirements in AR100).

V. **Reporting requirements --** Not required to be independent for such a compilation engagement; if not independent, the report should disclose that lack of independence (without describing the reason for that lack of independence).

VI. **Applicability --** For engagements entered into after 12/15/05 early application is permitted.

AR120 - Compilation of Pro Forma Financial Information

I. **This Statement applies --** when an accountant is engaged to compile or issues a compilation report on pro forma financial information. (Note that presentations of pro forma financial information are not "financial statements" so additional guidance was required.)

   A. Objective of pro forma information -- to show the significant effects on historical financial information associated with a transaction (actual or proposed) had the transaction occurred at an earlier date.

   B. Pro forma information should be labeled in a way that distinguishes it from historical financial information.

II. **Conditions for compiling pro forma financial information**

   A. The accountant may prepare or assist in the preparation of pro forma information without issuing a compilation report -- unless engaged to compile such pro forma information:

      1. Consider how such a presentation will be used;

      2. Consider issuing a compilation report so that a user will not infer an unwarranted level of assurance -- if the accountant may be associated with that information.

   B. To compile the pro forma financial information -- the accountant must have compiled, reviewed, or audited the historical financial statements of the entity on which the pro forma information is based.

   C. The report on the financial statements should be included in the document containing the pro forma financial information (may incorporate by reference).

III. **Understanding with the Entity**

   A. The accountant should establish an understanding (preferably in writing) as to the services to be performed.

   B. That understanding should include a description of the nature (and limitations) of those services and a description of the report:

      1. State that the engagement cannot be relied upon to disclose errors, fraud, or illegal acts; and

      2. State that the accountant will inform the appropriate level of management of any material errors and of any evidence or information obtained that fraud or illegal acts may have occurred -- need not report any matters regarding illegal acts that are "clearly inconsequential" (may agree in advance about communicating such matters).

IV. **Performance requirements --** The accountant should read the compiled pro forma financial information (including the summary of significant assumptions) and consider whether the information appears to be appropriate and is free of obvious material errors.

V. **Reporting requirements**

   A. SSARS No. 14 identifies the basic elements of the compilation report on pro forma financial information (and gives a sample reporting template):

      1. Identify the pro forma financial information;

      2. State that the compilation was performed in accordance with SSARS issued by the American Institute of CPAs;

      3. Reference the financial statements from which the pro forma information is derived (specify whether those financial statements were audited, reviewed, or compiled);

      4. State that the pro forma financial information was compiled;

      5. Describe the basis of the pro forma financial presentation, if not GAAP (when using an "other comprehensive basis of accounting");

6. State that pro forma information is limited to presenting pro forma financial information that is the representation of management;
7. State that the pro forma information has not been audited or reviewed (and disclaim assurance on it);
8. Include a separate paragraph describing the objective of pro forma financial information and its limitations;
9. Sign the report; and
10. Date the report -- using date of completion of the compilation.

B. Other procedures performed by the accountant before or during the compilation engagement -- these should NOT be described in the report.

C. Each page of the compiled pro forma financial information should include a reference such as "See Accountant's Compilation Report."

D. The accountant is not required to be independent to issue a compilation report on pro forma financial information -- if not independent, state that fact, but do not describe the specific reason for the lack of independence

E. Applicability -- for engagements entered into after 12/15/05 early application is permitted.

AR200 - Reporting on Comparative Financial Statements

Issued October, 1979 (Amended Through February, 2008)

I. **General comments --** AR200 provides the standards for reporting on comparative financial statements of a nonissuer when financial statements of one or more periods presented have been compiled or reviewed and reported on.

   A. If client-prepared financial statements of some periods that have not been audited, reviewed, or compiled are presented in a document that also contains financial statements of other periods that have been reported on -- there should be an indication that the accountant assumes no responsibility for the financial statements that have not been audited, reviewed, or compiled. (If the use of the accountant's name or report is inappropriate, consider other actions, such as consultation with an attorney.)

   B. The accountant may modify the report with respect to one or more financial statements for one or more periods while issuing an unmodified report on the other financial statements presented.

   C. When comparative financial statements for one or more, but not all, of the periods presented omit substantially all of the disclosures required by GAAP -- the accountant should not issue a report.

   D. Each page of the comparative financial statements compiled or reviewed by the accountant should include a reference such as "See Accountant's Report."

   E. Distinguishing between an "updated report" and a "reissued report:"

      1. Updated report -- a report issued by a continuing accountant that takes into consideration information obtained during the current engagement (either expressing previous conclusions or expressing different conclusions on the financials statements of a prior period);

      2. Reissued report -- a report issued subsequent to the date of the original report that bears the same date as the original report. (If revised for the effects of specific events, the report should be dual-dated with a separate date that applies to the effects of such events.)

II. **Continuing accountant's standard report**

   A. A continuing accountant is one who performs the same (or a higher level of service) with respect to the current period's financial statements -- should update the report on the financial statements of the prior period presented.

   B. A continuing accountant who performs a lower level of service with respect to the current period's financial statements -- should either (1) include a separate paragraph in the report that describes the responsibility taken for the prior period's financial statements; or (2) reissue the report on the financial statements of the prior period:

      1. For example, for a compilation of the current financial statements and a review of the prior period financial statements -- may issue a compilation report for the current period that includes a description of responsibility for the prior period. (Include the original date of the accountant's report and state that the accountant has not performed any procedures in connection with that review engagement after that date.)

      2. Alternatively, may combine the compilation report for the current period with the reissued review report for the prior period; or may instead present those reports separately.

III. **Continuing accountant's changed reference to a departure from GAAP**

   A. The accountant should be aware that circumstances or events may affect the prior-period financial statement presentation, including the adequacy of disclosure.

   B. When the accountant's report on the prior period's financial statements contains a changed reference to a GAAP departure -- the report should contain an explanatory paragraph identifying (1) the date of the accountant's previous report; (2) the circumstances that caused the reference to be changed; and (3) that the financial statement of the prior period have been changed (when applicable) for a restatement.

IV. Predecessor's compilation or review report -- A predecessor is not required to reissue the compilation or review report on a prior period's financial statements.

- **A.** If the predecessor does not reissue the compilation or review report -- the successor should either reference the predecessor's report or perform a compilation, review, or audit of the prior period's financial statement and report on these appropriately.
- **B.** When the predecessor's report is not reissued and the successor has not compiled or reviewed those financial statements -- the successor's report on the current period's financial statements should include reference to the predecessor's report on the prior period's financial statement. (The explanatory paragraph(s) should include (1) a statement that those financial statements were compiled or reviewed by another accountant; (2) the date of that report; (3) a description of the standard form of disclaimer or limited assurance, as applicable; and (4) a description or quotation of any modifications of the standard report.)
- **C.** The successor accountant should not name the predecessor accountant in the report -- however, the successor accountant may name the predecessor accountant if the predecessor's accounting practice was acquired by (or merged with) that of the successor accountant.
- **D.** When the predecessor's compilation or review report is to be reissued:
  1. Before reissuing a report, the predecessor should consider whether the report is still appropriate; (Considering the current form and manner of presentation of the prior period's financial statement, subsequent events not previously known, and changes in the financial statements that require the addition or deletion of modifications to the standard report.)
  2. The predecessor should perform the following procedures before reissuing the report -- (a) read the financial statements of the current period and the successor's report; (b) compare the prior period's financial statements with those previously issued and with those of the current period; and (c) obtain a letter from the successor accountant that indicates whether there is awareness of any matter that might have a material effect on the financial statements (including disclosures) reported on by the predecessor; (The predecessor should not refer to the letter or report of the successor in the reissued report.)
  3. If the predecessor becomes aware of information that may affect the prior period's financial statements or the report on them -- the predecessor should make inquiries or perform analytical procedures similar to those that would have been performed had the predecessor been aware of such information at the date of the original report, and perform any other procedures considered necessary in the circumstances; (The predecessor may wish to discuss this information with the successor or to review the successor's working papers related to the matters involved.)
  4. When reissuing the report on prior period's financial statements -- the predecessor should use the original date of that report (to avoid the implication that additional procedures were performed after that date); if the predecessor revises the report or if the financial statements are restated, the predecessor should dual-date the report accordingly;
  5. If the predecessor is unable to complete the procedures described above -- the report should not be reissued (and the predecessor may wish to consult with an attorney).
- **E.** Restated prior-period financial statements:
  1. The predecessor may reissue the previously issued report; (See the above section "If the predecessor becomes aware of information that may affect the prior period's financial statements or the report on them.")
  2. If the predecessor does not reissue the report -- the successor accountant may be engaged to report on the prior period's financial statements;
  3. If the predecessor accountant does not reissue the report and the successor accountant is not engaged to report on the prior period's financial statements -- the successor's report should indicate in the introductory paragraph that a predecessor reported on the financial statements before restatement. (The successor may also be engaged to compile or review the restatement adjustment and reference that in the accountant's report.)

V. Reporting when one period is audited and the other period is compiled or reviewed.

- **A.** When the current period financial statements have been audited but those of the prior period were compiled or reviewed, the accountant should follow the applicable Statements on Auditing Standards.

B. When the current-period financial statements have been compiled or reviewed but those of the prior period were audited, the accountant should issue an appropriate compilation or review report for the current period and either: (1) reissue the report on the prior period, or (2) include in the current period's report a separate paragraph that appropriately describe the responsibility taken for the prior period's financial statements.

VI. Reporting on financial statements that previously did not omit substantially all disclosures -- The accountant may report on comparative compiled financial statements that now omit substantially all disclosures if the report includes an additional paragraph that indicates the nature of the previous service rendered with respect to those financial statements and the date of the previous report.

VII. Change of status (issuer/nonissuer) -- The entity's current status determines whether the SASs or SSARSs currently apply for either interim or annual periods; a previously issued report that is not appropriate for the current status of the entity should not be reissued or referred to in the current period's report.

A. If the entity is an "issuer" in the current period and was a "nonissuer" in the prior period -- a compilation or review report previously issued on the prior period's financial statements should not be reissued or referred to in the current report.

B. If the entity is a "nonissuer" in the current period and was an "issuer" in the prior period, the annual financial statements of the prior period may have been audited -- in that case, issue a compilation or review report for the current period and add a separate paragraph to comment on the prior year's audit report.

AR300 - Compilation Reports in Prescribed Forms

I. **Applicability --** When the prescribed form of a nonpublic entity's ("nonissuer's") compiled financial statements is not in conformity with GAAP.

   A. **"Prescribed form"** -- Any standard preprinted form **designed or adopted by a body to which the entity's financial statements are to be submitted** (e.g., trade associations, banks, etc.).

   B. There is a **presumption that the information required by the prescribed form will be sufficient** for the needs of the body that designed or adopted that form -- There is, therefore, no need to inform that body of departures from GAAP by that prescribed form (any other GAAP departures discovered would have to be reported, however).

   C. This section provides an **alternative form of standard compilation report.**

II. **Required Language in this compilation report --** This compilation report consists of 3 paragraphs:

   A. **The first paragraph** -- Identifies the compiled financial statements "included in the accompanying prescribed form" and refers to the Statements on Standards for Accounting and Review Services of the AICPA;

   B. **The second paragraph** -- States that the compilation "was limited to presenting in the form prescribed by (*name of body*) information that is the representation of management" and disclaim an opinion or other assurance;

   C. **The third paragraph** -- States that the financial statements "are presented in accordance with the requirements of (*name of body*), which differ from (GAAP). Accordingly, these financial statements are not designed for those who are not informed about such differences."

AR400 - Predecessor Successor Communications

I. **Applicability --** Applies to communications between the successor and predecessor accountants in conjunction with the acceptance of a compilation or review engagement for a nonpublic client ("nonissuer"); note that the successor is not required to communicate with predecessor, but may choose to do so.

II. **Definitions**

A. **"Successor"** -- The term for the new accountant who has been invited to bid or who has already accepted the engagement.

B. **"Predecessor"** -- Has resigned or been told that services have been terminated (and had been associated with the financial statements in the immediately preceding year); these provisions apparently do not apply when the predecessor is also bidding on the current year's engagement.

III. **Inquiries Regarding Acceptance of an Engagement**

A. Before contacting the predecessor, the successor should seek the client's permission:

1. To allow the successor to initiate the contact; and
2. To allow the predecessor to respond fully to the successor's inquiries.

B. The predecessor should indicate that the **response is limited** if unusual circumstances do not permit a complete response (e.g., litigation).

C. The successor should consider the implications of the **client's refusal** to extend permission or the predecessor's inability to respond fully.

D. Other Inquiries:

1. Other inquiries of the predecessor may be helpful -- Regarding inadequacies known about financial data; areas that have required a disproportionate amount of time, etc.;
2. Usually request permission to review the predecessor's working papers -- Related to matters of continuing financial statement importance (e.g. contingencies);
3. Valid business reasons may cause the predecessor to deny such access to the working papers by the successor (e.g. unpaid fees).

IV. **If the successor concludes that the financial statements reported on by predecessor require revision**

A. The successor should request the client to communicate the information to the predecessor.

B. The successor should consult with legal counsel if the client refuses or if unsatisfied with the predecessor's response.

AR600 - Personal Financial Statements

I. **General Comments**

A. **Applicability --**

1. When **personal financial statements are included** in written personal financial plans prepared by an accountant.

2. Provides an **exemption from AR100** (does not prevent the accountant from complying with AR100 in such matters, however):

   a. When the accountant establishes an understanding with the client (preferably in writing):

      i. That the financial statements will be used solely to assist the client in developing personal financial goals; and

      ii. That the financial statements will not be used to obtain credit or for any other purpose other than developing these goals and objectives.

   b. Nothing comes to the accountant's attention to suggest that the financial statements will be used for any purpose other than developing the client's personal financial goals.

B. The **purpose** of such financial statements is solely to assist in developing the client's personal financial plan -- Therefore, disclosures required by GAAP are frequently omitted.

II. **Reporting requirements --** The report should state the following:

A. That the financial statements are intended solely to help develop the financial plan;

B. That the financial statements may be incomplete or contain other departures from GAAP;

C. That the financial statements have not been audited, reviewed, or compiled.

SSAE

AT20 (SSAE 13) - Defining Professional Requirements

I. Statement on Auditing Standards No. 102; and Statement on Standards for Attestation Engagements No.13 -- "Defining Professional Requirements in Statements on Auditing Standards" and "Defining Professional Requirements in Statements on Standards for Attestation Engagements."

II. Degree of Responsibility

A. The degree of responsibility associated with the terms (1) "must," (2) "is required," and (3) "should" was not previously defined in the SASs and SSAEs -- these 2 standards now define those levels of responsibilities for existing and future SASs and SSAEs:

1. Auditing Standards Board pronouncements apply to "nonissuers" -- a nonissuer refers to any entity not subject to the Sarbanes-Oxley Act or rules of the SEC;

B. The terms discussed in SAS 102 and SSAE 13 are consistent with how the PCAOB uses those terms.

III. Two Categories

A. SAS 102 and SSAE 13 define two categories of professional requirements:

1. "Unconditional requirements" -- the auditor (practitioner) is required to comply with an unconditional requirement when the circumstances exist to which the unconditional requirement applies. (An unconditional requirement is indicated by the words "must" or "is required.") -- No exceptions!

2. "Presumptively mandatory requirements:"

a. The auditor (practitioner) is also required to comply with a "presumptively mandatory requirement" when circumstances exist to which the presumptively mandatory requirement applies -- allows for the possibility of exception, however!

b. In rare circumstances, this may depart from a presumptively mandatory requirement -- the auditor (practitioner) must document the justification for the departure and how alternative procedures performed in the circumstances were sufficient to achieve the objectives of the presumptively mandatory requirement. (A presumptively mandatory requirement is indicated by the word "should.")

IV. Explanatory Material

A. SAS 102 and SSAE 13 also discuss "explanatory material" -- defined as the text within a SAS or SSAE (excluding any related appendices or interpretations) that may provide further explanation on the professional requirements or describe other procedures or actions possibly applicable to the auditor (practitioner).

1. Such explanatory material is intended to be descriptive and does not impose a professional requirement.

2. Explanatory material is identified by the terms "may," "might," or "could."

AT50 (SSAE 14) - SSAE Hierarchy

I. **Attestation Standards**

A. **General Standards**

1. The practitioner must have adequate technical training and proficiency to perform the attestation engagement.
2. The practitioner must have adequate knowledge of the subject matter.
3. The practitioner must have reason to believe that the subject matter is capable of evaluation against criteria that are suitable and available to users.
4. The practitioner must maintain independence in mental attitude in all matters relating to the engagement.
5. The practitioner must exercise due professional care in the planning and performance of the engagement and the preparation of the report.

B. **Standards of Fieldwork**

1. The practitioner must adequately plan the work and must properly supervise any assistants.
2. The practitioner must obtain sufficient evidence to provide a reasonable basis for the conclusion that is expressed in the report.

C. **Standards of Reporting**

1. The practitioner must identify the subject matter or the assertion being reported on and state the character of the engagement in the report.
2. The practitioner must state the practitioner's conclusion about the subject matter or the assertion in relation to the criteria against which the subject matter was evaluated in the report.
3. The practitioner must state all of the practitioner's significant reservations about the engagement, the subject matter, and, if applicable, the assertion related thereto in the report.
4. The practitioner must state in the report that the report is intended solely for the information and use of the specified parties under the following circumstances:
    a. When the criteria used to evaluate the subject matter are determined by the practitioner to be appropriate only for a limited number of parties who either participated in their establishment or can be presumed to have an adequate understanding of the criteria.
    b. When the criteria used to evaluate the subject matter are available only to specified parties.
    c. When reporting on subject matter and a written assertion has not been provided by the responsible party.
    d. When the report is on an attestation engagement to apply agreed-upon procedures to the subject matter.

D. Rule 202 "Compliance with Standards" of the AICPA Code of Professional Conduct requires AICPA members to comply with applicable SSAEs when performing an attestation engagement.

E. If there is a departure from a "presumptively mandatory requirement" - the practitioner must document in the working papers the justification for the departure and how the procedures performed in the circumstances were sufficient to meet the objectives of the presumptively mandatory requirement [see AT 20 (SSAE No. 13) for further discussion of the term "presumptively mandatory requirement"].

II. **Attestation interpretations** -- Recommendations on the application of SSAEs in specific circumstances

A. Meaning of "attestation interpretations" - these consist of Interpretations of the SSAEs, appendices to the SSAEs, attestation guidance included in AICPA Audit and Accounting Guides, and AICPA attestation Statements of Position.

B. If such guidance is not applied - the practitioner should be prepared to explain how he or she complied with the SSAE provisions involved.

III. **Other attestation publications** -- These have no authoritative status

A. These consist of articles in professional journals and newsletters, continuing professional education programs, textbooks, etc.

B. Evaluation of applicability - the practitioner may choose to apply such guidance when it is both relevant and appropriate (perhaps considering the stature of the publication and/or reputation of the author).

AT101 (SSAE 10) - Attestation Standards

I. **Applicability --** SSAE #10 does not apply to engagements already covered by SASs, SSARSs, or SSCSs.

II. **Definitions and underlying concepts**

A. Definition of "attest engagement" -- When a CPA practitioner is engaged to issue (or does issue) an examination, a review, or an agreed-upon procedures report on subject matter, or an assertion about the subject matter that is the responsibility of another party.

B. Definition of "assertion" -- Any declaration about whether the subject matter is in conformity with the criteria selected.

1. Practitioner may report on a written assertion or directly on the subject matter (usually should obtain a written assertion for any examination or review engagement).

2. When a written assertion has not been obtained -- can still report on the subject matter, but restrict the distribution of the report!

C. Definition of "responsible party" -- The person(s) responsible for the subject matter (or a party who has a reasonable basis for making a written assertion about the subject matter).

1. The responsible party must take responsibility for its assertion and the subject matter -- Being able to identify a responsible party is a prerequisite for an attest engagement.

2. Practitioner should obtain written acknowledgment (or other evidence) of the responsible party's responsibility for the subject matter.

D. Definition of "agreed-upon procedure engagement" -- When a practitioner is engaged to issue a report of findings based on specific procedures performed on subject matter (specifically covered in AT 201).

E. Relationship of attestation standards to quality control standards -- The attest practice should be subject to quality control standards. (Note that attestation standards apply to individual attest engagements; quality control standards relate to the firm's attest practice as a whole.)

III. **Attestation standards (amended by SSAE No. 14, issued in 2006)**

A. General standards:

1. Training and proficiency: "The practitioner must have adequate technical training and proficiency to perform the attestation engagement."

2. Knowledge of subject matter: "The practitioner must have adequate knowledge of the subject matter."

3. Criteria: "The practitioner must have reason to believe that the subject matter is capable of evaluation against criteria that are suitable and available to users."

a. Suitability of criteria:

i. Objectivity -- criteria should be free from bias;

ii. Measurability -- criteria should have reasonably consistent measurement of subject matter (qualitative or quantitative);

iii. Completeness -- criteria should not omit relevant factors that could affect the conclusion about the subject matter;

iv. Relevance -- criteria should be relevant to the subject matter.

b. Additional guidance about the suitability of criteria:

i. Criteria established by "due process" procedures are usually considered suitable;

ii. There may be more than 1 set of suitable criteria for a given subject matter (e.g., "customer satisfactions");

iii. When criteria are too subjective or vague, the practitioner should not accept the engagement;

iv. Consideration should be given to the nature of the subject matter (e.g., "soft information," such as forecasts, would have a wider range of reasonable estimates than "hard" data);

v. If criteria are appropriate only for a limited number of users, the report should be restricted to those parties;

vi. This requirement applies equally regardless of the level of assurance conveyed.

c. Availability of criteria -- criteria should be available to users:

i. Available publicly;

ii. Available in the presentation of the subject matter or the assertion;

iii. Available in the practitioner's report;

iv. Well understood by users (although not formally available); or

v. Available to the specified parties.

4. Independence: "The practitioner must maintain independence in mental attitude in all matters relating to the engagement."

a. "... the intellectual honesty and impartiality necessary to reach an unbiased conclusion -- ... a cornerstone of the attest function."

b. "... not the attitude of an advocate or an adversary but an impartiality that recognizes the obligation for fairness."

5. Due care: "The practitioner must exercise due professional care in the planning and performance of the engagement and the preparation of the report." (References Cooley on Torts, a legal treatise, on due care.)

B. Standards of Fieldwork:

1. Planning and supervision: "The practitioner must adequately plan the work and must properly supervise any assistants."

a. This usually considers the following factors:

i. Criteria to be used;

ii. Preliminary judgments about attestation risk and materiality -- note that "attestation risk" consists of (a) inherent risk and control risk (combined) and (b) detection risk;

iii. Nature of the subject matter and items likely to require adjustment;

iv. Conditions that may require modification of attest procedures;

v. Nature of the report expected to be issued.

b. Should establish an "understanding" with the client -- as to objectives of the engagement, management's responsibilities, the practitioner's responsibilities, and limitations of the engagement.

2. Evidence: "The practitioner must obtain sufficient evidence to provide a reasonable basis for the conclusion that is expressed in the report."

a. Required evidence will vary with the engagement -- examination (high level of assurance) versus review (moderate level of assurance).

b. The responsible party usually provides a written assertion:

i. If a written assertion cannot be obtained from the responsible party -- consider effects on the ability to obtain sufficient evidence to form a conclusion;

ii. When the practitioner's client is the responsible party -- a failure to obtain a written assertion should result in a (client-imposed) scope limitation (modify report for an examination; withdraw from a review);

iii. When the practitioner's client is not the responsible party and a written assertion is not obtained -- the practitioner may be able to conclude that there is sufficient evidence to form a conclusion about the subject matter.

c. Representation letter -- In an examination or a review engagement, the practitioner should consider obtaining a representation letter from the responsible party:

i. Even when the client is not the responsible party -- the practitioner should consider obtaining written representations from the client;

ii. The responsible party's (or client's) refusal to furnish written representations, when deemed necessary, constitutes a scope limitation.

C. Standards of reporting:

1. Nature of engagement: "The practitioner must identify the subject matter or the assertion being reported on and state the character of the engagement in the report."

a. The "character of the engagement" has two elements -- (1) a description of the nature and scope of the engagement; and (2) reference to the professional standards governing the engagement ("attestation standards established by the American Institute of CPAs");

b. The terms "examination" and "review" should be used to refer to a high level of assurance and a moderate level of assurance, respectively.

2. Conclusion: "The practitioner must state the practitioner's conclusion about the subject matter or the assertion in relation to the criteria against which the subject matter was evaluated in the report."

a. Examination reports -- state clearly whether the subject matter is based on the criteria in all material respects; or state clearly whether the assertion is fairly presented in all material respects based on the criteria. (Note: if material misstatements exist, usually report directly on the subject matter, not on the assertion!)

b. Review reports -- state whether anything came to the practitioner's attention indicating that the subject matter is not based on the criteria or that the assertion is not fairly presented based on the criteria. (The report should describe any information that caused the subject matter or the assertion to be modified.)

3. Reservations: "The practitioner must state all of the practitioner's significant reservations about the engagement, the subject matter, and, if applicable, the assertion related thereto in the report."

a. Reservation about the engagement -- Any unresolved problem about complying with the attestation standards, interpretive standards, or the specific agreed-upon procedures (includes scope limitations); results in either a qualified opinion, disclaimer, or withdrawal for an examination or a withdrawal for an incomplete review;

b. Reservations about the subject matter -- Any unresolved reservation about the assertion or about the conformity of the subject matter with the criteria; results in either a qualified or adverse opinion for an examination or a modified conclusion for a review.

4. Limited use report: "The practitioner must state in the report that the report is intended solely for the information and use of the specified parties under the following circumstances:

a. When the criteria used to evaluate the subject matter are determined by the practitioner to be appropriate only for a limited number of parties who either participated in their establishment or can be presumed to have an adequate understanding of the criteria;

b. When the criteria used to evaluate the subject matter are available only to specified parties;

c. When reporting on subject matter and a written assertion has not been provided by the responsible party;

d. When the report is on an attestation engagement to apply agreed-upon procedures to the subject matter:"

i. "General use" reports are not restricted to specified parties; (Only examination and review reports can be general use.)

ii. The practitioner should consider informing the client that restricted distribution reports are not intended for unspecified parties; (However, the practitioner is not responsible for controlling the client's distribution of reports.)

iii. To restrict the distribution, add a separate paragraph at the end of the report; (Stating that report is intended solely for specified parties; identify those specified parties; and state that report should not be used by others.)

iv. Other attestation standards may specify additional circumstances that require restricted reports (e.g., a review of "management's discussion and analysis" and certain reports on prospective financial information);

v. Note that the practitioner is not precluded from restricting the use of any report.

IV. Other information in a client-prepared document containing the practitioner's attest report -- Practitioner should read the other information contained in the document to determine whether it is materially inconsistent with the information appearing in the practitioner's report.

A. Consider whether the report might require revision.

B. If the report does not require revision -- request revision of the other information deemed inconsistent. (If the other information is not properly revised, the practitioner might consider adding an explanatory paragraph to the report, withholding the use of the report in the document in question, or withdraw from the engagement.)

C. If there is a material misstatement of fact -- consider notifying the client's management and audit committee in writing; consider consulting with legal counsel for appropriate action.

V. Subsequent events -- The practitioner's responsibility to address subsequent events in an attestation engagement is similar to an audit engagement. (The practitioner is not responsible for detecting subsequent events in an attestation engagement, but should inquire of the responsible party about such matters.)

VI. Attest documentation -- the principal record of attest procedures applied, information obtained, and conclusions/findings reached by the practitioner.

A. Should be sufficient to (1) enable members of the team with supervision responsibilities to understand the procedures performed and results obtained; and (2) indicate the engagement team members who performed and reviewed the work.

B. The practitioner should adopt reasonable procedures to (1) retain the documentation for a reasonable period of time; (2) maintain the confidentiality of client information; and (3) prevent unauthorized access to attest documentation.

VII. Attest services related to consulting service engagements -- issue separate reports on the attest engagement and the consulting service engagement. (If these reports are presented in a common binder, the reports should be clearly identified and separated.)

A. The SSAE applies only to the attest service.

B. Statements on Standards for Consulting Services (SSCS) apply to the rest of the consulting engagement.

AT201 (SSAE 10) - Agreed-Upon Procedures

I. **Introduction and applicability**

A. Additional guidance for certain AUP engagements is provided elsewhere. See AT 301 for financial forecasts and projections; see AT 601 for compliance attestation.

B. This section does not apply to engagements covered by SASs (e.g. AU 324 (Service Organizations); AU 623 (Special Reports); AU 632 (Letters for Underwriters and Certain Other Requesting Parties); AU 801 (Compliance Auditing Considerations in Audits of Governmental Entities and Recipients of Governmental Financial Assistance)), SSARSs, or SSCSs.

II. **Agreed-upon procedures engagements --** where the practitioner is engaged to issue a report of findings based on specific procedures performed on subject matter.

A. Conditions for engagement performance:

1. The practitioner is independent;
2. One of the following circumstances exists;
3. The practitioner and the specified users agree upon the procedures to be performed:
    a. The party seeking to engage the practitioner is responsible for the subject matter;
    b. When a responsible party does not exist - the party seeking to engage the practitioner has a reasonable basis for providing a written assertion about the subject matter;
    c. The party seeking to engage the practitioner is not responsible for the subject matter but is able to provide the practitioner with evidence of a third party's responsibility for the subject matter.
4. Practitioner and specified parties agree upon the procedures (and the specified parties take responsibility for the sufficiency (including the nature, timing, and extent) of the procedures for their purposes);
5. Practitioner and specified parties agree upon criteria to be used;
6. Subject matter can be reasonably consistently measured (evidence providing a reasonable basis for findings is expected);
7. Practitioner and specified parties agree on materiality limits, as applicable (for reporting purposes);
8. Use of the **report is restricted to the specified parties**;
9. for AUP engagements on prospective financial information, a summary of significant assumptions is included.

B. **Sufficiency of Procedures**

C. Agreement on and sufficiency of procedures - the practitioner should not report on an engagement unless the specified users agree upon the procedures and take responsibility for the sufficiency of those procedures:

1. Ordinarily, the practitioner should communicate directly with the specified parties to get their acknowledgment of the sufficiency of the procedures; (The practitioner can do this by meeting with them or by distributing a draft of the anticipated report or a copy of the engagement letter.)
2. if unable to communicate with all of the specified users - the practitioner may satisfy this requirement by: (a) comparing the procedures to the written requirements of the specified parties; (b) discussing the procedures with appropriate representatives of the specified parties; or (c) reviewing relevant contracts or correspondence involving the specified users.

D. **Engagement Letters**

E. Subject matter and related assertions - a "written" assertion is no longer always required in an

AUP engagement. (That is one of the things that is different under SSAE 10 relative to the superseded SSAEs.)

F. **Included in an Engagement Letter**

G. Establish an understanding with the client (regarding services to be performed) - when documented in writing, an "engagement letter" might include the following:

1. Nature of the engagement;
2. Identification of the subject matter (or assertion), the responsible party, and the criteria to be used;
3. Identification of the specified parties;
4. Specified parties' acknowledgment of their responsibility for the sufficiency of the procedures;
5. Practitioner's responsibilities (and reference to AICPA standards) - The practitioner assumes the risk that misapplication of the procedures may result in inappropriate findings being reported;
6. Enumeration of (or other reference to) the agreed-upon procedures;
7. Indication of disclaimers expected to be included in the report;
8. Specification of the limitations on the distribution of the report;
9. Identification of the assistance to be provided to the practitioner;
10. Indication of the role of any specialists expected to be involved;
11. Identification of any agreed-upon materiality limits.

III. **Additional issues related to procedures**

A. **Procedures** to be performed - the procedures may evolve or be modified over the course of an engagement. (In general, there is flexibility as long as the specified parties take responsibility for the sufficiency of such procedures for their purposes.)

B. **Vague terms** (such as general review, limited review, check, or test) should not be used to describe the procedures, unless defined within the agreed-upon procedures.

C. **Examples of inappropriate procedures** that are prohibited - mere reading of work performed by others as a basis for the practitioner's findings; evaluating the competency or objectivity of another party; interpreting documents outside the scope of the practitioner's expertise.

D. **Involvement of a specialist** - " a person (or firm) possessing skill or knowledge in a particular field other than the attest function:"

1. Examples - attorney, medical specialist, environmental engineer, geologist, etc.;
2. The practitioner and specified parties should agree on the involvement of a specialist to assist the practitioner.

E. **Involvement of internal auditors and other personnel**

1. Internal auditors (or others) may prepare schedules and accumulate data or provide other information for the practitioner's use.
2. The practitioner cannot: agree to merely read the internal auditor's report to describe or repeat those findings, take responsibility for procedures performed by the internal auditors as the practitioner's own, or report in any manner that implies shared responsibility for the procedures performed by the internal auditors.

IV. **Reporting**

A. **Findings** - The report should be presented in the form of "procedures" and "findings" ("Materiality" does not apply unless defined in advance.) and should avoid vague language.

B. **Explanatory language** can be added as deemed appropriate (to disclose stipulated facts or assumptions; to describe the condition of records or controls; to explain that the practitioner has no responsibility to update the report, etc.).

C. **Scope limitations** - when circumstances restrict performance of the agreed-upon procedures:

1. Try to obtain agreement from the specified parties for modification of the agreed-upon procedures;
2. If agreement for such a modification cannot be obtained - describe any restrictions on the performance of the procedures in the report or else withdraw from the engagement.

D. **Adding specified parties** ("nonparticipant parties") - The practitioner can agree to add a nonparticipant party as a specified party, based on the identity of that party and the intended use of the report:

1. Obtain acknowledgment (usually in writing) by the nonparticipant party taking responsibility for the sufficiency of the procedures;
2. if added after the practitioner has issued the report - the report may be reissued or the practitioner can provide other written acknowledgment that the party has been added. (Usually state that no procedures have been performed subsequent to the date of the report.)

E. **Dating of the report** - Dated as of completion of the agreed-upon procedures.

F. **Written representations** - The responsible party's refusal to furnish written representations deemed necessary by the practitioner is a limitation on the performance of the engagement. (The practitioner should disclose this fact in the report, withdraw from the engagement, or change the engagement to another form of engagement.)

G. **Knowledge of matters** outside agreed-upon procedures - If the practitioner learns of matters (outside of the agreed-upon procedures, perhaps through an audit or other means) that contradict the subject matter (or assertion) referred to in the practitioner's report, the practitioner should include such matters in the report.

H. **Combined reports** covering both restricted-use and general-use subject matter or presentations - Reports on agreed-upon procedures on specific subject matter can be combined with reports on other services, if the different services are clearly distinguished and applicable standards for each service are followed.

V. **Change to an AUP engagement from another form of engagement**

A. **Scope Limitations -** Before agreeing to change another form of engagement to AUP, the practitioner should consider the following:

1. Certain procedures for another form of engagement may not be appropriate for an AUP engagement;
2. The reason given (especially regarding any related scope limitations);
3. The additional effort required;
4. The reasons for changing from a general-use report to a restricted-use report.

B. **Reasonable basis** for requesting a change - if there is a change in circumstances or a misunderstanding about the nature of the original engagement or the alternatives.

C. **Report Should Not -** if the practitioner concludes that the justification for the change is reasonable - the AUP report should not mention the original engagement or any scope limitation behind the change.

AT301 (SSAE 10) - Financial Forecasts/Projections

I. **Introduction**

A. **Applicability** -- when engaged to issue an **examination, compilation, or agreed-upon procedures** (AUP) report on prospective financial statements that are (or are reasonably expected to be) used by a third party.

B. Does not apply to services involving prospective financial statements used solely in litigation support services. (Since such services are usually subject to thorough analysis by other parties to the legal proceeding.)

C. **Definitions** related to "prospective financial statements."

D. **Prospective financial statement** -- either financial forecasts or financial projections (excludes pro forma financial information and partial presentations).

E. **Financial Forecast** -- represents the expected financial statement outcome (i.e., the predicted results).

F. **Financial Projection** - represents the expected financial statement outcome, given one or more hypothetical assumptions (what if?).

G. **Partial presentation** - a presentation of prospective financial information that excludes one of more items required; not ordinarily intended for general use, so restrict distribution to specified parties.

H. **Responsible party** - the persons responsible for the assumptions underlying the prospective financial statements (usually management).

II. **Uses of prospective financial statements --** May be for "general" or "limited" use.

A. **General use** -- prospective financial statements -- use of the statements by persons with whom the responsible party is not negotiating directly. (Only a financial forecast is appropriate for general use.)

B. **Limited use** prospective financial statements -- use of the statements by the responsible party alone or by the responsible party and third parties with whom the responsible party is negotiating directly:

1. Any type of prospective financial statements is appropriate for limited use - projections must have restricted distribution;

2. A partial presentation must have restricted distribution.

III. **Compilation of prospective financial statements**

A. Not intended to provide assurance on the prospective financial statements or the underlying assumptions:

1. Involves assembling the statements based on the responsible party's assumptions;

2. Must read the statements (with the summaries of significant assumptions and accounting policies) and consider whether presentation is consistent with applicable AICPA guidelines; evaluate whether the information is "obviously inappropriate;"

3. Must issue a compilation report.

B. **Report considerations** -- usually consists of two paragraphs:

1. First paragraph - identifies the prospective financial statements presented; and indicates that these were compiled according to AICPA guidelines;

2. Second paragraph - states that compilation is limited in scope (disclaim opinion); cautions that results may not be achieved; and states that the accountant takes no responsibility for events after report date;
3. If dealing with a projection - add a paragraph describing limitations;
4. If the information is presented as a range - add a paragraph noting that fact;
5. **If not independent** - add a sentence noting that fact (but do not describe the reasons for the lack of independence);
6. May add an explanatory paragraph to emphasize a matter;
7. Any identified deficiencies or omissions should be noted.

C. **Modifications** of the standard compilation report:

1. Add an explanatory paragraph to comment on omitted disclosures - this is permitted if the omission is not intended to deceive (and does not relate to the underlying assumptions);
2. Can add an explanatory paragraph to emphasize a matter, but must be careful not to imply assurance on the compilation;
3. Can compile prospective financial statements when the practitioner is not independent of the entity involved. A sentence can be added to disclose the lack of independence after the last paragraph (but should not comment on the reason for the lack of independence).

IV. **Examination of prospective financial statements**

A. Responsibilities for an examination:

1. Evaluate the preparation of the prospective financial statements;
2. Evaluate the support underlying the assumptions;
3. Evaluate the presentation of the prospective financial statements;
4. Issue an examination report.

B. **Report considerations** - usually consists of three paragraphs:

1. First paragraph - identifies the prospective financial statements presented; identifies management's responsibility and the practitioner's responsibility;
2. Second paragraph - states that the examination complied with AICPA standards and expresses a belief about reasonable basis for opinion;
3. Third paragraph - expresses an opinion (that presentation conforms with AICPA guidelines and that underlying assumptions provide a reasonable basis for the prospective financial statements); cautions that results may not be achieved; and states that practitioner is not responsible for events after the report date;
4. If a projection - a paragraph restricting the report's distribution is added;
5. If presented as a range - a paragraph is added noting that fact;
6. May add an explanatory paragraph to emphasize a matter (or if opinion is based in part on other accountants);
7. Modified opinion:
    a. *Qualified* or *adverse* opinion - when the presentation departs from AICPA guidelines;
    b. *Adverse* opinion - when one or more significant assumptions does not provide a reasonable basis for the forecast or projection (or when one or more significant assumptions is omitted);
    c. *Disclaimer of opinion* - when the scope of the examination is insufficient for expression of an opinion.

V. **Agreed-upon Procedures --** Applying agreed-upon procedures to prospective financial statements.

VI. **Characteristics of engagement to perform agreed-upon procedures**

A. Specified parties are involved in determining the nature and scope of the engagement:

   1. Usually meets with the parties or their representatives;

   2. In the absence of such a meeting - provides the parties with a draft of the report (or copy of the engagement letter) to reduce misunderstandings.

B. Distribution of the report must be restricted to those specified parties.

VII. Reporting on agreed-upon procedures -- (in the form of procedures and findings) - usually consists of four paragraphs:

A. First paragraph - identifies the nature of the engagement and the prospective financial statements;

B. Second paragraph - references AICPA standards; notes that the specified parties are responsible for the sufficiency of the procedures (the practitioner can add separate paragraphs for the procedures and findings or make reference to appendices where those are enumerated);

C. Third paragraph - states that this is not an examination and disclaims an opinion; cautions that results may not be achieved; and states that the accountant is not responsible for events after report date;

D. Fourth paragraph - restrict distribution to the specified parties.

VIII. Practitioner-Submitted Document -- When historical financial statements that the practitioner audited, reviewed, or compiled are included in a **practitioner-submitted** document that includes prospective financial information -- the practitioner should examine, compile, or apply agreed-upon procedures to the prospective information, unless that prospective information is a "budget."

A. Need not issue a report for compilation, examination, or applying agreed-upon procedures if:

   1. The prospective information is labeled "budget;"

   2. It does not extend beyond the end of the fiscal year;

   3. Presented along with interim historical financial statements.

B. Should indicate the level of responsibility taken -- indicate that the budget was not compiled or examined and disclaim an opinion on it.

IX. Client-Prepared Document

A. When the practitioner's report on historical financial statements is included in a **client-prepared** document containing prospective financial information -- The practitioner should not consent to the use of his or her name in the document unless the prospective financial information is covered by an appropriate (examination, compilation, or agreed-upon procedures) report or there is an indication that the accountant takes no responsibility for the prospective financial information.

B. When the practitioner's report on prospective financial information is included in a client-prepared document containing historical financial statements:

   1. The practitioner should not consent to the use of his or her name in the document unless the historical financial statements are covered by an appropriate (examination, compilation, or agreed-upon procedures) report or there is an indication that the practitioner takes no responsibility for the historical financial statements;

   2. If the practitioner believes that a material misstatement of fact exists between the prospective information and the other information appearing in the document with the prospective financial statements - discuss the matter with the responsible party (may consult with other, such as the entity's legal counsel).

X. Minimum presentation guidelines (in Appendix A) -- Prospective information may consist of complete financial statements or may be limited to certain minimum items (below); an omission of one or more of the following items would constitute a "partial presentation" not appropriate for general use:

A. Sales or gross revenues;

B. Gross profit or cost of sales;

C. Unusual or infrequently occurring items;

D. Provision for income taxes;

E. Discontinued operations or extraordinary items;

F. Income from continuing operations;

G. Net income;

H. Basic and diluted earnings per share;

I. Significant changes in financial position;

J. A description of what the responsible party intends the prospective financial statements to represent;

K. Summary of significant assumptions;

L. Summary of significant accounting policies.

AT401 (SSAE 10) - Pro Forma Financial Information

I. **Introduction and applicability**

A. Applies when issuing an examination or review report on pro forma financial information

B. Does not apply when the historical financial statements reflect a transaction after the balance sheet (e.g., revision of EPS due to a stock split or revision of debt maturities). In other words, if a transaction or event after the balance sheet date is required (by GAAP or other applicable accounting framework) to be addressed by adjusting the historical financial statements, then that adjustment is not considered a "pro forma" adjustment.

II. **Presentation of pro forma financial information --** To show the significant effects on historical financial information that might have occurred, had a transaction (actual or proposed) occurred at an earlier date. For example: a business combination, a change in capitalization, the disposition of a significant portion of the business, a change in the form of business or status as an autonomous entity, or the proposed sale of securities and the application of the proceeds.

A. **Adjustments --** Apply the pro forma adjustments to the historical financial information - should be based on management's assumptions and reflect all significant effects attributable to the transaction (event).

B. **Labeling --** Label the pro forma information as such to distinguish it from historical financial information -- the presentation (including a statement that the pro forma information should be read in conjunction with the historical financial information) should include the following:

1. Describe the transaction (event) reflected;
2. Describe the source of the historical financial information involved;
3. Describe the significant assumptions used;
4. Describe any significant uncertainties surrounding those assumptions.

III. **Conditions for reporting** -- the practitioner may agree to conduct an examination or review of pro forma financial information if 3 conditions are met:

A. **Historical Financial Information --** The document containing the pro forma financial information includes or references the complete historical financial information for the most recent year (or the preceding year if those of the most recent year are not yet available); if pro forma information is presented for an interim period, the document also includes or references corresponding historical financial information;

B. **Historical Financial Statements --** The historical financial statements involved have been audited or reviewed - the level of assurance on the pro forma information cannot exceed the level of assurance on the historical financial statements (i.e., if the financial statement information was reviewed, not audited, then only a review is permitted on the pro forma information);

C. **Appropriate Level of Knowledge --** The practitioner should have an appropriate level of knowledge of the accounting and financial reporting practices of the entity involved -auditing or reviewing the historical financial statements would provide the requisite level of knowledge.

IV. **Practitioner's Objective**

A. For an examination of pro forma information - to provide reasonable assurance as to whether:

1. Management's assumptions provide a reasonable basis for presenting the effects of the transaction (event);
2. The pro forma adjustments appropriately reflect those assumptions;
3. The pro forma column properly reflects the application of those adjustments to the historical financial statements.

B. Review -- For a review of pro forma information - to provide negative assurance as to whether anything came to the practitioner's attention to suggest that:

1. Management's assumptions do not provide a reasonable basis for presenting the effects of the transaction (event);
2. The pro forma adjustments do not appropriately reflect those assumptions;
3. The pro forma column does not properly reflect the application of those adjustments to the historical financial statements.

V. Review of Information

A. Procedures for either an examination or review of pro forma financial information:

1. Obtain an understanding of the underlying transaction (event) - read contracts, read minutes, make inquiries;
2. Obtain a level of knowledge of the entity to enable the practitioner to perform the required procedures (communicate with other practitioners?);
3. Discuss assumptions with management;
4. Evaluate whether all significant effects are included;
5. Obtain "sufficient evidence" supporting adjustments (varies with the level of assurance intended);
6. Evaluate whether management's assumptions underlying the pro forma adjustments are presented in a clear and comprehensive manner;
7. Determine that pro forma adjustments are mathematically correct;
8. Obtain written representations from management as to their responsibility for the assumptions used; assertion that the assumptions provide a reasonable basis for the adjustment; and assertion that the significant effects of the transaction (event) are adequately disclosed;
9. Read the pro forma information and evaluate whether (a) the underlying transaction (event), the significant assumption and the uncertainties about those assumptions have been appropriately described; and (b) the source of the related historical financial information has been properly identified.

B. Reporting on pro forma financial information:

1. The report on pro forma information can be added to the practitioner's report on the historical financial information, or presented separately; (If combined and the reports have different dates, the combined report should be dual-dated.)
2. The report on pro forma information should be dated as of the completion of the appropriate procedures;
3. Nothing precludes the practitioner from restricting the use of the report;
4. Restrictions about the scope of the engagement, reservations about the assumptions or the conformity of the presentation with those assumptions, or other reservations may require the practitioner to qualify the opinion, disclaim an opinion, or withdraw from the engagement (must disclose the reasons for the modification of the report;)
5. See the example of an examination report on pro forma information;
6. See the example of a review report on pro forma information.

AT501 (SSAE 15) - Entity Internal Control

I. Internal Control

A. "An Examination of an Entity's Internal Control over Financial Reporting That is Integrated with an Audit of Its Financial Statements" - Issued: October, 2008.

II. Introduction and applicability

Introduction and applicability -- AT 501 applies when engaged to perform an examination of the design and operating effectiveness of an entity's internal control over financial reporting ("examination of internal control") that is integrated with an audit of financial statements ("integrated audit").

A. Timing of an examination of internal control - usually engaged to examine internal control over financial reporting as of the end of the entity's fiscal year. (If engaged to examine internal control for a period of time, the examination should be integrated with an audit of the financial statements covering the same period of time.)

B. This section does not apply to other engagements related to internal control:

1. Engagements to examine the suitability of design of internal control (such engagements may be performed under AT 101);
2. Engagements to examine controls over the effectiveness and efficiency of operations (such engagements may be performed under AT 101);
3. Engagements to examine controls over compliance with laws and regulations (such engagements may be performed under AT 601);
4. Engagements to report on controls at a service organization (see AU 324);
5. Engagements to apply agreed-upon procedures on controls (such engagements may be performed under AT 201);
6. Note: An auditor should **not** accept an engagement to **review** an entity's internal control over financial reporting.

C. Definitions provided include the following, among others:

1. **Control objective --** The aim or purpose of specified controls. Control objectives ordinarily address the risks that the controls are intended to mitigate;
2. **Deficiency --** A deficiency in internal control exists when the design or operation of a control does not allow management or employees, in the normal course of performing their assigned functions, to prevent, or detect and correct misstatements on a timely basis; (A deficiency may pertain to "design" or "operation.")
3. **Internal control over financial reporting --** A process effected by those charged with governance, management, and other personnel, designed to provide reasonable assurance regarding the preparation of reliable financial statements in accordance with the applicable financial reporting framework and includes those policies and procedures that (i) pertain to the maintenance of records that, in reasonable detail, accurately and fairly reflect the transactions and dispositions of the assets of the entity; (ii) provide reasonable assurance that transactions are recorded as necessary to permit preparation of financial statements in accordance with the applicable financial reporting framework, and that receipts and expenditures of the entity are being made only in accordance with authorizations of management and those charged with governance; and (iii) provide reasonable assurance regarding prevention, or timely detection and correction of unauthorized acquisition, use, or disposition of the entity's assets that could have a material effect on the financial statements;
4. **Management's assertion --** Management's conclusion about the effectiveness of the entity's internal control that is included in management's report on internal control;
5. **Material weakness --** A deficiency, or a combination of deficiencies, in internal control such that there is a reasonable possibility that a material misstatement of the entity's financial statements will not be prevented, or detected and corrected on a timely basis;

6. **Relevant assertion --** A financial statement assertion that has a reasonable possibility of containing a misstatement or misstatements that would cause the financial statements to be materially misstated;

7. **Significant deficiency --** A deficiency, or a combination of deficiencies, in internal control that is less severe than a material weakness, yet important enough to merit attention by those charged with governance.

D. Underlying concepts:

1. If one or more material weaknesses exist, then the entity's internal control cannot be considered effective - accordingly, the auditor should plan and perform the examination to obtain sufficient appropriate evidence to obtain reasonable assurance about whether material weaknesses exist as of the date specified;

2. The auditor is not required to search for deficiencies that are less severe than a material weakness;

3. The auditor should use the same suitable and available control criteria to perform the examination of internal control as management uses for its evaluation of the effectiveness of the entity's internal control;

4. An auditor may perform an examination of internal control only if the following 4 conditions are met:

   a. Management accepts responsibility for the effectiveness of the entity's internal control;

   b. Management evaluates the effectiveness of the entity's internal control using suitable and available criteria;

   c. Management supports its assertion about the effectiveness of the entity's internal control with sufficient appropriate evidence; and

   d. Management provides its assertion about the effectiveness of the entity's internal control in a report that accompanies the auditor's report - if management refuses to furnish a written assertion, the auditor should withdraw from the engagement. (If regulation does not allow the auditor to withdraw, then the auditor should disclaim an opinion on internal control.)

III. Integrating the examination with the financial statement audit

A. Basic responsibilities - the auditor should plan and perform the integrated audit to achieve the objectives of both engagements simultaneously; that is, design tests of control (1) to obtain sufficient appropriate evidence to support the auditor's opinion on internal control as of the period end and (2) obtain sufficient appropriate evidence to support the auditor's control risk assessments for purposes of the audit of financial statements.

1. The date specified in management's assertion should correspond to the balance sheet date (or the period ending date of the period covered by the financial statements).

2. The auditor should consider the results of the financial statement procedures in determining the risk assessments and the testing necessary to evaluate the operating effectiveness of a control.

B. Planning the engagement:

1. Role of risk assessment - the same risk assessment process support both the examination of internal control and the audit of the financial statements, and the auditor should focus more attention on the areas of highest risk;

2. Scaling the examination - the size and complexity of the entity, its business processes, and the business units may affect the way in which the entity achieves many of its control objectives; scaling is a natural extension of the risk-based approach and is applicable to examinations of all entities;

3. Addressing the risk of fraud - the auditor should incorporate the results of the fraud risk assessment performed in the financial statement audit:

   a. The auditor should evaluate whether the controls sufficiently address identified risk of material misstatement due to fraud and the risk of management override of other controls;

b. Controls that might address these risks include: (1) controls over significant, unusual transactions, particularly those that result in late or unusual journal entries; (2) controls over journal entries and adjustments made in the period-end financial reporting process; (3) controls over related party transactions; (4) controls related to significant management estimates; and (5) controls that mitigate incentives for, and pressures on, management to falsify or inappropriately manage financial results.

4. Using the work of others - the auditor should evaluate the extent to which the work of others will be used to reduce the work the auditor would otherwise perform:

   a. The auditor may receive the assistance (or use the work) of internal auditors, other entity personnel, and third parties working under the direction of management or those charged with governance that provide evidence about internal control;

   b. The auditor should obtain an understanding of the work of others (to identify those activities relevant to planning the examination of internal control);

   c. The auditor should assess the competence and objectivity of persons whose work the auditor plans to use; (The higher the degree of competence and objectivity, the greater the use the auditor may make of their work.)

   d. In higher risk areas - as the risk associated with a control increases, the need for the auditor to perform the work related to that control increases (using the work of others decreases).

5. Materiality - the auditor should use the same materiality for the examination of internal control as for the audit of the financial statements; significant accounts and disclosures and their relevant assertions are also the same in an integrated audit.

C. Using a top-down approach:

1. A "top-down approach" involves (a) beginning at the financial statement level; (b) using the auditor's understanding of the overall risks to internal control; (c) focusing on entity-level controls; (d) directing attention to accounts, disclosures, and assertions that present a reasonable possibility of material misstatement to the financial statements and related disclosures; (e) verifying the auditor's understanding of the risks in the entity's processes; and (f) selecting controls for testing that sufficiently address the assessed risk of material misstatement to each relevant assertion;

2. Identifying "entity-level" controls - the auditor should test those entity-level controls that are important to the conclusion about whether the entity has effective internal controls (e.g., controls related to the control environment; controls over management override; the entity's risk assessment process; centralized processing and controls; controls to monitor results of operations or to monitor other controls; controls over the period-end financial reporting process; and programs and controls that address significant business control and risk management);

3. Control environment - the auditor should evaluate the control environment and assess whether (a) management's philosophy and operating style promote effective internal control; (b) sound ethical values are developed and understood; and (c) those charged with governance understand and exercise oversight responsibility;

4. Period-end financial reporting process - the auditor should evaluate the period-end financial reporting process and assess (a) the inputs, procedures performed, and outputs of the processes the entity uses to produce its financial statements; (b) the extent of IT involvement in the period-end financial reporting process; (c) who participates from management; (d) the locations involved; (e) the types of adjusting and consolidating entries; and (f) the nature and extent of the oversight of the process by management and those charged with governance;

5. Identifying significant accounts and disclosures and their relevant assertions - the auditor should evaluate the qualitative and quantitative risk factors related to the financial statement items and disclosures to determine the likely sources of potential misstatements (by asking "what could go wrong?");

6. Understanding likely sources of misstatement - the auditor should identify the points within the entity's processes at which a material misstatement could arise (and identify the relevant controls):

   a. Performing walkthroughs - probing questions, along with other walkthrough procedures, provide an understanding of the entity's processes and may identify points at which controls are missing or are ineffective;

b. Selecting controls to test - should test those controls that are important to the auditor's conclusion about whether the entity's controls sufficiently address the risk of material misstatement to each relevant assertion.

D. Testing Controls:

1. Evaluating design effectiveness - procedures include a mix of inquiry, observation of the entity's operations, and inspection of relevant documentation; (A walkthrough that includes such procedures is usually sufficient to evaluate design effectiveness.)

2. Evaluating operating effectiveness - procedures include a mix of inquiry, observation of the entity's operations, inspection of relevant documentation, recalculation, and reperformance of the control;

3. Relationship of risk to the evidence to be obtained - the evidence that should be obtained increases with the risk of the control being tested; (Note that the auditor's objective is to express an opinion on the entity's overall internal control, not on the effectiveness of individual controls.)

4. Nature of tests of controls - procedures performed in increasing order of the resulting evidence: (a) inquiry (inquiry alone does not provide sufficient appropriate evidence about the effectiveness of a control); (b) observation; (c) inspection of relevant documentation; (d) recalculation; and (e) reperformance;

5. Timing and extent of tests of controls - testing controls over a longer period of time (or closer to the date of management's assertion) provides more evidence of effectiveness that testing over a shorter period of time (or testing earlier in the year);

6. Special considerations for subsequent years' examinations - the auditor should incorporate knowledge obtained during past examinations in determining the nature, timing, and extent of testing necessary (might permit reduced testing in subsequent years); note that the auditor should introduce unpredictability into the testing.

E. Evaluating identified deficiencies - the auditor should evaluate the severity of each deficiency to determine whether a material weakness exists:

1. The severity of a deficiency depends on the magnitude of the potential misstatement resulting and the degree of likelihood (whether there is a "reasonable possibility") of a failure; does not depend on whether a misstatement actually occurred;

2. Risk factors affecting whether a misstatement may occur include the following: (a) the nature of the accounts, classes of transactions, disclosures, and assertions involved; (b) the susceptibility of the related asset or liability to loss or fraud; (c) the subjectivity, complexity, or judgment involved; (d) the interaction of the control with other controls; (e) the interaction among the deficiencies; and (f) the possible future consequences of the deficiency;

3. Multiple deficiencies may increase the likelihood of material misstatement and cause a material weakness (or significant deficiency) even though the deficiencies individually may be less severe;

4. Compensating controls - can mitigate the severity of a deficiency, although they do not eliminate the deficiency; (The auditor should test the operating effectiveness of relevant compensating controls.)

5. Indicators of material weaknesses include the following: (a) discovery of any fraud involving senior management; (b) restatement of previously issued financial statements to correct a material error or fraud; (c) identification of any material misstatement during the audit that was not detected by internal control; and (d) ineffective oversight of reporting and controls by those charged with governance.

F. Concluding procedures:

1. Forming an opinion - review reports issued by internal auditors (or others) during the year that address internal control issues;

2. Obtaining written representations from management (a) acknowledging management's responsibility for internal control; (b) stating that management has evaluated the effectiveness of internal control using specified control criteria; (c) stating that management's evaluation was not based on the auditor's procedures; (d) stating management's assertion about internal control as of a specified date; (e) stating that management has disclosed to the auditor all known significant deficiencies or material weaknesses; (f) describing any

material fraud or other fraud involving management or those with internal control responsibilities; (g) stating whether previously communicated significant deficiencies and material weaknesses have been resolved (and point out those which have not); and (h) stating whether any changes affecting internal control occurred subsequent to the date reported - the failure to provide these written representations constitutes a scope limitation;

3. Communicating certain matters identified during the integrated audit - the auditor is not required to perform procedures sufficient to identify all deficiencies, but should communicate identified deficiencies:
    a. Any identified material weaknesses and significant deficiencies should be communicated in writing by the report release date; (For governmental entities, the written communication must take place within 60 days of the report release date.)
    b. Any lesser deficiencies should be communicated in writing to management within 60 days of the report release date (should inform those charged with governance of that communication);
    c. Early communication is not required to be in writing - but all material weaknesses and significant deficiencies must be communicated in writing, even if communicated early (orally) or if the deficiencies were remediated during the examination;
    d. Communicating an absence of deficiencies - the auditor should not issue a report stating that no material weaknesses (or that no deficiencies less severe than a material weakness) were identified in an integrated audit.

IV. Reporting on internal control

A. Separate or combined reports - the auditor may choose separate reports on the financial statements and on internal control or a combined report on both; (If issuing separate reports, the auditor should add a paragraph to each report cross-referencing the other report.)

B. Report date - should be dated when the auditor has obtained sufficient appropriate evidence to support the auditor's opinion; (If issuing separate reports, the reports should have the same date for an integrated audit.)

C. The report on the examination of internal control should have the following elements:
1. A title that includes the word independent;
2. A statement that management is responsible for maintaining effective internal control and for evaluating the effectiveness of internal control;
3. An identification of management's assertion on internal control that accompanies the auditor's report (including a reference to management's report);
4. A statement that the auditor's responsibility is to express an opinion on the entity's internal control (or on management's assertion);
5. A statement that the examination was conducted in accordance with attestation standards established by the AICPA;
6. A statement that such standards require that the auditor plan and perform the examination to obtain reasonable assurance about whether effective internal control was maintained in all material respects;
7. A statement that an examination includes obtaining an understanding of internal control, assessing the risk that a material weakness exists, testing and evaluating the design and operating effectiveness of internal control based on the assessed risk, and performing such other procedures as the auditor considers necessary in the circumstances;
8. A statement that the auditor believes the examination provides a reasonable basis for the opinion;
9. A definition of internal control (the same as used by management in its report);
10. A paragraph describing the inherent limitations of internal control;
11. The auditor's opinion;
12. The signature of the auditor's firm; and
13. The date of the report.

D. Adverse opinions:

1. If there is one or more material weaknesses at the date specified in management's assertion - the auditor should express an adverse opinion (unless there is a scope limitation);
2. When expressing an adverse opinion - the auditor should report directly on the effectiveness of internal control (not on management's assertion);
3. If one or more material weaknesses are omitted from management's report - the auditor should modify the report to state that fact and to describe each such material weakness and its potential effect (should also communicate with those charged with governance);
4. If one or more material weaknesses are included in management's report and the auditor concludes that the disclosure is not fairly presented - the auditor should describe this conclusion and provide information to fairly describe each such material weakness;
5. If an adverse opinion on internal control is expressed - consider the implications to the audit of the financial statements (and disclose whether the opinion on the financial statements was affected).

E. Report modifications - modify the report for the following conditions:

1. If elements of management's report are incomplete/improperly presented, modify the report to include an explanatory paragraph;
2. If there is a scope restriction - the auditor should either withdraw from the engagement or disclaim an opinion (should describe any identified material weaknesses with the disclaimer) and communicate with management and those charged with governance about the matter;
3. For an opinion based partially on the report of another auditor, the auditor should decide whether to reference the examination of internal control performed by the other auditor. (The decision to refer to the other auditor can differ regarding internal control and the financial statements.);
4. If the management's report contains additional information, the auditor should disclaim an opinion on the other information. (For example, corrective action taken for identified deficiencies or management's cost-benefit judgments.)

F. Subsequent events - regarding changes in internal control that occur subsequent to the date as of which internal control is being examined but before the date of the auditor's report:

1. The auditor should inquire of management about any such changes (and obtain written representations about such matters);
2. The auditor should inquire about (a) relevant internal audit reports issued during the subsequent period; (b) other auditor reports of deficiencies; (c) regulatory agency reports on internal control; and (d) information about the effectiveness of the entity's internal control obtained through other engagements.

G. Integration with the financial statement audit:

1. Tests of controls in an examination of internal control - the auditor's opinion relates to the effectiveness of internal control at a point in time (Period tested may be less than the period covered by the financial statements.) and taken as a whole; (This involves testing controls not usually tested in connection with the audit of the financial statements.)
2. Tests of controls in an audit of financial statements - perform test of controls when risk assessment includes an expectation of the operating effectiveness of controls, or when substantive procedures alone do not provide sufficient appropriate audit evidence at the relevant assertion level; auditor is not required to test controls for all relevant assertions;
3. Effect of tests of controls on substantive procedures - the auditor should consider whether any identified deficiency affects the nature, timing, and extent of substantive procedures to be performed; likewise, the auditor should consider whether any substantive procedures affect the auditor's evaluation of the effectiveness of internal control (e.g., misstatements detected).

H. Special topics:

1. Entities with multiple locations - the auditor should assess the risk of material misstatement associated with the location or business unit and correlate the amount of work with the degree of risk (may consider the work performed by others on behalf of management);

2. Use of service organizations - if the service organization's services are part of an entity's "information and communication systems," the auditor should consider the activities of the service organization:

   a. The auditor should obtain an understanding of the controls at the service organization relevant to the entity's internal control (and the controls at the user organization over the activities of the service organization) and obtain evidence that controls relevant to the auditor's opinion are operating effectively;

   b. Evidence that the controls relevant to the auditor's opinion are operating effectively may include (1) obtaining a service auditor's report (including tests of controls); (2) performing tests of the user organization's controls over the service organization's activities; or (3) performing tests of controls at the service organization;

   c. The user auditor should make inquiries concerning the service auditor's reputation, competence, and independence;

   d. As the risk increases, the need for the user auditor to obtain additional evidence increases - e.g., involving the elapsed time between the service auditor's work and the date of management's assertion; the significance of the activities of the service organization, etc.;

   e. The user auditor should not refer to the service auditor's report when expressing an opinion on internal control.

3. Benchmarking of automated controls - the auditor may conclude that automated application controls continue to be effective without repeating prior year's testing (a benchmarking strategy) if general controls over program changes, access to programs, and computer operations are effective and continue to be tested and if the automated application control has not changed; especially effective for entities using purchased software not likely having program changes.

AT601 (SSAE 10) - Compliance Attestation

I. **Applicability**

A. Types of attest engagements -- about an entity's compliance with laws, regulations, contracts, grants, etc.; **or** on the effectiveness of an entity's internal control over such compliance.

B. Conditions for performance -- management accepts the responsibility for compliance; and management evaluates the entity's compliance (and makes an assertion about it).

II. **Scope of Services (cannot accept an engagement to "review" compliance)**

A. Performing **"agreed-upon" procedures:**

1. Procedures:

a. Users should participate in specifying the procedures to be performed and must take the responsibility for the adequacy of such procedures for their purposes;

b. If unable to discuss directly with users -- discuss with an appropriate representative of users and distribute a draft of the anticipated report (or a copy of the proposed engagement letter) to the specified users for their comments;

c. The CPA has no obligation to perform procedures beyond those specifically agreed-upon -- if noncompliance is identified through such other procedures performed, the CPA must include that information in the report.

2. **Reporting** (dated last day of field work):

a. The report should be in form of **procedures and findings** (*do not provide negative assurance!*). The report states the purpose of the procedures; identifies management's assertion; states that the adequacy of the procedures rests with users; and identifies the procedures performed;

b. The auditor should disclaim an opinion and state that the scope is less than an "examination;"

c. The distribution of the report should be restricted to the specified users.

B. Performing an **"examination"** -- requires "reasonable criteria" (must be capable of reasonably consistent estimation or measurement):

1. Consider **"attestation risk"** -- the risk that the practitioner may unknowingly fail to modify appropriately the opinion on management's assertion:

a. Consists of inherent, control, and detection risks;

b. Adjust the nature, timing, and extent of tests for compliance;

c. "Materiality" may differ from a financial statement audit – this may or may not be quantifiable for compliance issues.

2. **Compliance Requirements:** Obtain an understanding of the specified compliance requirements -- consider applicable laws, regulations, contracts, etc.; consider prior engagements and any regulatory reports; consider discussions with appropriate people inside and outside the entity;

3. **Plan the engagement** -- develop an overall strategy; (Consider multiple components, using the work of a specialist, using the internal audit function.)

4. **Consider the internal control over compliance** -- identify the types of potential noncompliance, consider the factors that affect the risk of material noncompliance, and design the appropriate tests for compliance:

a. Understand the design of internal control -- **inquire** of appropriate personnel; **review** applicable documents; **observe** activities;

b. The responsibility to communicate known deficiencies is about the same as for in audit of financial statements (See AU325).

5. **Obtain sufficient evidence** -- the objective is to provide reasonable assurance of detecting material noncompliance (include reading reports of any regulatory examinations);

6. Consider "subsequent events:"

   a. **Those attributable to the period under examination (related to management's compliance and their assertion)** -- consider any internal auditors' reports and regulatory reports issued during the subsequent period;

   b. **Those attributable to the period subsequent to the examination** -- include an explanatory paragraph in the CPA's report if needed to avoid misleading users.

7. **Reporting** for an examination engagement:

   a. The report is analogous to an audit report (with **introduction, scope, and opinion** paragraphs) -- refer to the standards established by the AICPA;

   b. Modifications from the "standard" report:

      i. Material noncompliance => results in a qualified or adverse opinion;

      ii. Material uncertainty;

      iii. Scope limitation;

      iv. Reference to the report of another practitioner;

      v. Explanatory paragraph can be added to emphasize a desired matter;

      vi. Restriction of distribution if criteria by which compliance is evaluated have been "agreed-upon" by management and users.

C. **Management's representations** -- a management representation letter is required for either type of engagement.

III. **Client-Prepared Document** - Other information in a client-prepared document - there is no obligation to perform procedures to corroborate the "other information," but the practitioner should read the other information to consider whether any material inconsistencies exist.

AT701 (SSAE 10) - Management Discussion and Analysis

I. **"Management's Discussion and Analysis" --** (MD&A) Issued January, 2001.

II. **Applicability --** Applies to attestation engagements regarding MD&A using the requirements of the SEC when that MD&A is presented in annual reports or other documents.

A. Two levels of service covered by this standard:

1. Examination of MD&A;

2. Review of MD&A.

B. Applicable to a **public** entity or a **non-public** entity when providing a written assertion that the presentation has been prepared using SEC requirements as criteria.

1. This section does not apply when:

a. Engaged to recommend improvements to MD&A instead of providing assurance;

b. Employing criteria other than SEC requirements;

c. Performing agreed-upon procedures. (Such engagements are governed by ***AT 201***.)

C. SEC requirements are currently stated in Item 303 of Regulation S-K and include:

1. Discussion of financial condition (including liquidity and capital resources);

2. Discussion of changes in financial condition;

3. Discussion of results of operations.

III. **General comments and overview**

A. Conditions for performance of an **examination:**

1. Presentation includes the required elements of the SEC's requirements;

2. Historical financial amounts are accurately derived from the financials;

3. Underlying information, assumptions, etc. provide a reasonable basis for the disclosures within MD&A.

B. To accept engagement - must have audited the financials for the latest period related to the MD&A. (The financials for other periods involved in MD&A must have been audited by the practitioner or a predecessor auditor.)

C. Conditions for performance of a **review** - consists of limited procedures (primarily analytical procedures and inquiries):

1. Purpose - to report whether the practitioner has any reason to believe that:

a. The MD&A does not include all the elements required by the SEC;

b. The historical financial amounts have not been accurately derived from the financial statements;

c. The underlying information, assumptions, etc. do not provide a reasonable basis for the disclosures.

2. To accept engagement for a **public** entity:

a. For an annual period - must have audited the financials for the latest period related to the MD&A; (The financials for other periods involved in MD&A must have been audited by the practitioner or a predecessor auditor.)

b. For an interim period - practitioner issues a review report (or an audit report) on the related interim financials; and the MD&A presentation for the most recent annual period has been examined or reviewed by the practitioner or a predecessor.

3. To accept engagement for a **nonpublic** entity:
    a. For an annual period - must have audited the most recent annual financials (Other financials involved have been audited by the practitioner or predecessor.); and management will provide a written assertion that the MD&A has been prepared using SEC requirements as criteria;
    b. For an interim period - (1) the practitioner has either audited or reviewed the interim financials; (2) the MD&A for the most recent annual period has been (or will be) either examined or reviewed; and (3) management will provide a written assertion that the MD&A has been prepared using SEC requirements as criteria.

D. Responsibilities of management:
1. Management is responsible for the preparation of the MD&A in accordance with SEC requirements;
2. When an entity indicates in a document that MD&A has been examined or reviewed - the following should be included in the document (or, for a public entity, incorporated by reference to documents filed with the SEC):
    a. The MD&A presentation and related practitioner's;
    b. The related financials and the audit (or review) report.

E. The practitioner should obtain an understanding of SEC requirements and management's methodology for preparation of MD&A (the latter by inquiries):
1. Materiality - the relative size of an omission or misstatement determines materiality;
2. Inclusion of pro forma financial information - practitioner should refer to ***AT 401*** in such case (even for information derived from unaudited financials);
3. Inclusion of external information - practitioner should examine or review the external information (e.g., ratings of debt or trade association statistics);
4. Inclusion of forward-looking information - practitioner should examine or review any forward-looking information included in MD&A:
    a. May consider guidance of ***AT 301***;
    b. Considers whether adequate cautionary language has been used;
    c. Determines whether "safe harbor" protections apply to such forward-looking information is a legal matter.
5. Inclusion of voluntary information - entity may voluntarily include other information beyond SEC requirements.

IV. Examination engagement - detailed comments

A. Must limit attestation risk to "an appropriately low level" (a matter of professional judgment).
1. Component risks - **inherent risk** (varies with the nature of the assertion), **control risk, detection risk**;
2. *Assertions* - the representations of management that are embodied in the MD&A presentation:
    a. ***Occurrence*** - whether reported transactions or events have occurred during the period;
    b. ***Consistency*** with the financials - whether historical amounts have been accurately derived from the financials;
    c. ***Completeness*** of the explanation - whether the description of events, trends, uncertainties, etc., comprising the MD&A presentation are complete;
    d. ***Presentation*** and disclosure - whether information in the MD&A is properly classified, described, and disclosed;
    e. These assertions overlap with the assertions associated with the financial statements, but practitioner is **not** expected to test the underlying F/S assertions when examining MD&A.

B. Planning the examination - involves developing an overall strategy:

1. Consideration of audit results - including condition of records, audit adjustments, and likely misstatements;
2. Multiple components - determining the components to which procedures should be applied;
3. Using the work of a specialist - when the MD&A involves specialized skills or knowledge in a field other than accounting;
4. Internal audit function - considering the extent to which internal auditors are involved in testing controls related to the MD&A presentation.

C. Consideration of internal control applicable to the preparation of MD&A:

1. May assess control risk at the maximum - if controls are not perceived as effective (or applicable to an assertion), or if testing of controls is not cost beneficial;
2. After assessing control risk, may seek further reduction of assessed control risk - consider whether tests of controls are cost effective;
3. Must document understanding of internal control components and assessment of control risk;
4. The practitioner has responsibilities to communicate internal control deficiencies in an examination - similar to responsibilities for an audit engagement (see AU325).

D. Obtaining sufficient evidence - usually includes:

1. Reading the MD&A (and non-financial amounts) for consistency with audited financials;
2. Examining other internally and externally generated documents as needed;
3. Obtaining available prospective financial info;
4. Inquiring about plans and expectations;
5. Considering industry and economic trends;
6. Reading minutes of board meetings;
7. Inquiring about communications from SEC;
8. Obtaining press releases and quarterly reports;
9. Considering other public information (news articles, analysts' reports, etc.;)
10. Obtaining written representations from management (as to responsibility for MD&A, completeness of minutes, subsequent events, and other matters deemed appropriate).

E. Consideration of subsequent events - SEC expects MD&A to reflect events at (near) the filing date:

1. If MD&A is included with a 1933 Act document - procedures should extend up to (or near) the filing date;
2. Procedures related to subsequent events:
    - **a.** Read minutes of board meetings;
    - **b.** Read available interim financials and inquire about any significant changes;
    - **c.** Make inquiries of senior management regarding contingencies, etc.;
    - **d.** Consider industry and economic events;
    - **e.** Obtain management representations about subsequent events affecting MD&A.

F. Reporting an opinion on MD&A - the financial statements and the auditor's report should accompany the document containing the MD&A (or be incorporated by reference to documents filed with the regulatory agency):

1. Title - "Independent Accountant's Report;"
2. Standard examination report - four paragraphs:

a. Introductory paragraph - four sentences:
   i. Identifies MD&A presentation;
   ii. States management's responsibility;
   iii. States accountant's responsibility;
   iv. References the audit report on related financial statements.
b. Scope paragraph – three sentences:
   i. References the AICPA standards;
   ii. Describes scope of an examination;
   iii. States that examination provides a reasonable basis for the opinion.
c. Explanatory paragraph – three sentences:
   i. Comments on estimates and assumptions;
   ii. Comments on future expectations;
   iii. Indicates that actual results may differ.
d. Opinion paragraph (one long sentence) whether:
   i. The presentation includes elements required by the SEC;
   ii. Historical amounts are accurately derived from the financials; and
   iii. Underlying information, assumptions, etc. provide a reasonable basis for MD&A.

3. Dating - as of completion of examination procedures (should not precede date of auditor's report on latest financials associated with MD&A);
4. Modifications of the examination report:
   a. Reservations as to presentation (as to a required element excluded from MD&A; historical amounts not accurately derived; or unreasonable basis for MD&A presentation) - may issue a qualified or adverse opinion;
   b. Reservations as to scope - may issue a qualified opinion or a disclaimer;
   c. Reference to another practitioner's report as partial basis for own report;
   d. When engaged to examine MD&A after it has been filed with the SEC;
   e. Emphasis of a matter - presented as a separate paragraph (e.g., information included beyond SEC requirements).

V. Review engagement - detailed comments

A. Obtain understanding of SEC requirements and management's method of preparing MD&A.

B. Plan the engagement - develop overall strategy.

C. Consider relevant portions of internal control affecting MD&A.

D. Apply analytical procedures and make inquiries of management - usually do not obtain corroboration:
   1. Read the MD&A presentation and compare to the audited financials for consistency;
   2. Compare non-financial amounts to the audited (or reviewed) financials or other records;
   3. Should obtain available prospective information (forecasts, budgets, etc.);
   4. Should inquire about communications from the SEC about entity's documents;
   5. If questions arise - practitioner should perform additional procedures necessary to achieve the limited assurance intended.

E. Consider the effects of subsequent events.

F. Obtain written representations from management - regarding responsibility for MD&A, completeness of minutes, subsequent events, and other matters.

G. Form a conclusion - whether practitioner has information suggesting that MD&A does not include all the elements required by SEC, that historical financial amounts are not accurately derived from the financial statements, or that the underlying information, assumptions, etc., do not provide a reasonable basis for the MD&A presentation.

H. Reporting:

1. For a review report on MD&A for an **annual** period - the MD&A must be accompanied by the related financial statements and the auditor's report (or be incorporated by reference);
2. For a review report on MD&A for an **interim** period - the comparative financials for the most recent annual period and the related MD&A should accompany the MD&A on the interim period and the accountant's review report (or be incorporated by reference);
3. Title - "Independent Accountant's Report;"
4. **Standard review report - five paragraphs** (main difference is a restricted use paragraph): Introductory paragraph – three sentences:
    - **i.** Identifies MD&A presentation;
    - **ii.** States management's responsibility;
    - **iii.** References audit report on related financial statements.

    b. Scope paragraph - four sentences:
    - **i.** References AICPA standards;
    - **ii.** Describes a review engagement;
    - **iii.** States that the scope of a review is less than an examination;
    - **iv.** Disclaims an opinion.

    c. Explanatory paragraph – three sentences (same as for an examination report):
    - **i.** Comments on estimates and assumptions;
    - **ii.** Comments on future expectations;
    - **iii.** Indicates that actual results may differ.

    d. Conclusions paragraph (1 long sentence) - limited assurance whether:
    - **i.** Presentation does not include elements required by the SEC;
    - **ii.** Historical amounts are not accurately derived from the financials;
    - **iii.** Underlying information, assumptions, etc. do not provide a reasonable basis for MD&A.

    e. Restricted use paragraph for a **public** entity ***(unless the document is intended to be filed with the SEC, which makes the document publicly available)*** - should be restricted to specified users (also for a non-public entity that is making an offering of securities and it appears that the securities may subsequently be registered with the SEC).
5. Dating - as of completion of the review procedures. (This should not precede date of accountant's report on latest financials covered by MD&A.)
6. Modifications of the standard review report:
    - **a.** Reservations as to presentation (as to a required element excluded from MD&A; historical amounts not accurately derived; or unreasonable basis for MD&A presentation) - modify the report to describe the nature of the misstatement;
    - **b.** Reservations as to scope - the review will be considered incomplete;
    - **c.** Reference to another practitioner's report as partial basis for own report;
    - **d.** When engaged to examine MD&A after it has been filed with the SEC;

e. Emphasis of a matter - presented as a separate paragraph (e.g., information included beyond SEC requirements).

VI. Other technical topics related to MD&A engagements

A. Combined examination and review report on MD&A - may be engaged to examine an MD&A presentation for the most recent fiscal year and to review a separate MD&A presentation for a later interim period.

B. When practitioner is engaged subsequent to the filing of MD&A:

1. Ordinarily a public company would not modify its MD&A once it is filed with the SEC - since significant subsequent events are reported in other ways (e.g., Form 8-K, Form 10-Q, or registration statement);

2. If subsequent events for a public company are adequately disclosed (or if there have been no significant subsequent events) - the practitioner should add a paragraph after the opinion (or conclusion paragraph) stating that the MD&A does not consider such subsequent events;

3. A material subsequent event that has not been adequately disclosed should result in a qualified or adverse opinion for an examination (or modification for a review).

C. When predecessor auditor has audited prior period financial statements related to the MD&A:

1. Practitioner must obtain an understanding of the business and the entity's reporting practices;

2. May consider reviewing predecessor auditor's working papers - will not be a sufficient basis for an opinion on MD&A applicable to such periods;

3. Should inquire of predecessor and management as to any proposed audit adjustments that were not recorded;

4. Communications between the predecessor and successor auditor (governed by AU315) should include specific inquiries by the successor auditor regarding the MD&A if the successor is also engaged to examine or review the MD&A presentation.

D. When another auditor audits a significant part of the financial statements - practitioner may request the other auditors to perform procedures with respect to the MD&A associated with the related component(s):

1. Principal practitioner should not refer to other accountants unless they have issued an examination or review report on the separate MD&A presentation of the component(s);

2. Principal practitioner should perform the procedures considered necessary to take responsibility for the work of the other auditor - reviewing their working papers; discussing their procedures and results; making supplemental tests, etc.

E. Responsibility for other information in documents containing MD&A - practitioner should read the other information for inconsistencies (similar to AU550, regarding documents containing audited financial statements).

F. Communications with the audit committee:

1. When inconsistencies are found and management refuses to make changes - inform the audit committee; (Consider resignation from the MD&A engagement and consider whether to continue as the entity's auditor.)

2. If the practitioner believes that fraud may have occurred - inform an appropriate level of management (similar to fraudulent financials).

G. Obtaining written representations - should obtain written representations from senior management for either an examination or review of MD&A:

1. Specific representations will vary with the circumstances (similar to an audit of financial statements, discussed in AU333);

2. Refusal to provide written representations is a scope limitation:

a. For an examination - sufficient to require a disclaimer of opinion or withdrawal;

b. For a review - sufficient to require withdrawal from the engagement.

AT801 (SSAE 16) - Service Organizations - Issued: April, 2010

I. **Scope of this section --** SSAE No. 16 is applicable to reports by a service auditor regarding controls at service organizations (the focus is controls at service organizations likely to be relevant to user entities' internal controls over financial reporting)

   A. This section complements AU 324 ("Service Organizations").

   B. Management is required to provide the service auditor with a written assertion that is included in (or attached to) management's description of the service organization's system.

   C. The service auditor is required to report directly on the subject matter (that is, the service auditor cannot report on management's assertion about internal control).

II. **Objectives of the service auditor --** to obtain reasonable assurance whether

   A. Management's description of the service organization's system fairly presents the system.

   B. The controls related to the control objectives statement in management's description were suitably designed.

   C. When included in the scope of the engagement, the controls operated effectively.

III. **Selected definitions**

   A. **Complementary user entity controls --** Controls that management of the service organization assumes will be implemented by user entities (should be identified in management's description if necessary to achieve the stated control objectives)

   B. **Control objectives --** The purpose of specified controls at the service organization (control objectives address the risks that controls are intended to mitigate).

   C. **Report on management's description of a service organization's system and the suitability of the design of controls (type 1report) --** A report that consists of (a) management's description of the service organization's system; (b) a written assertion by management of the service organization about whether, in all material respects, and based on suitable criteria, (1) management's description of the service organization's system fairly presents the system that was designed and implemented as of a specified date; and (2) the controls related to the stated control objectives were suitably designed to achieve those control objectives as of the specified date; and (c) a service auditor's report that expresses an opinion on the 2 matters indicated in (b) above.

   D. **Report on management's description of a service organization's system and the suitability of the design and operating effectiveness of controls (type 2 report) --** A report that consists of (a) management's description of the service organization's system; (b) a written assertion by management of the service organization about whether, in all material respects, and based on suitable criteria, (1) management's description of the service organization's system fairly presents the system that was designed and implemented as of a specified date; (2) the controls related to the stated control objectives were suitably designed to achieve those control objectives as of the specified date; and (3) the controls related to the stated control objectives operated effectively throughout the specified period; and (c) a service auditor's report that expresses an opinion on the 3 matters indicated in (b) above.

   E. **Service auditor --** A practitioner who reports on controls at a service organization.

   F. **Service organization --** An organization that provides services to user entities, which are likely to be relevant to those user entities' internal control over financial reporting.

   G. **Subservice organization --** A service organization used by another service organization to perform some of the services provided to user entities that are likely to be relevant to those user entities' internal control over financial reporting.

      1. **Carve-out method --** Management's description of the service organization's system that identifies the nature of the services performed by the subservice organization and excludes

from the description and from the scope of the service auditor's engagement, the subservice organization's relevant control objectives and related controls.

2. **Inclusive method --** Management's description of the service organization's system that includes a description of the nature of the services provided by the subservice organization as well as the subservice organization's relevant control objectives and related controls.

H. **User auditor --** An auditor who audits and reports on the financial statements of a user entity.

I. **User entity --** An entity that uses a service organization.

IV. **Requirements**

A. **Management and those charged with governance --** The service auditor should determine the appropriate person(s) in the service organization with whom to interact (e.g., to obtain representations from or to communicate with).

B. **Acceptance and continuance --** The service auditor should accept or continue an engagement to report on a service organization's controls only if

1. The service auditor has the competence to perform the engagement;
2. The service auditor's preliminary knowledge engagement of the engagement circumstances indicates that (a) the criteria to be used will be "suitable and available" to the intended users and their auditors, (b) the service auditor will have access to sufficient appropriate evidence, and (c) the scope of the engagement will not be so limited to likely affect the usefulness of the engagement (or management's description) to users and their auditors; and
3. Management agrees to the terms of the engagement and accepts its applicable responsibilities (see comments immediately below).

C. **Management's responsibilities are to:**

1. Prepare its description of the service organization's system and its assertion;
2. Have a reasonable basis for its assertion;
3. Select the criteria to be used and state them in the assertion;
4. Specify the control objectives and state them in the description of the service organization's system;
5. Identify the risks that threaten the achievement of the stated control objectives and designing, implementing, and documenting controls that are suitably designed and operating effectively to provide reasonable assurance that the stated control objectives will be achieved;
6. Provide the service auditor with (a) access to all information relevant to management's description of the service organization's system and its assertion; (b) additional information requested by the service auditor; (c) unrestricted access to personnel within the service organization; and (d) written representations at the conclusion of the engagement;
7. Provide a written assertion that will be included in (or attached to) management's description of the service organization's system, and provided to user entities - management's refusal to provide a written presentation constitutes a scope limitation and the auditor should withdraw from the engagement (if law or regulation prohibits withdrawal, the service auditor should disclaim an opinion).

D. **Assessing the suitability of the criteria --** The service auditor should assess whether management has used suitable criteria in preparing its description and in evaluating whether controls were suitably designed (and, for a type 2 report, in evaluating the operating effectiveness throughout the specified period).

1. In assessing the suitability of the criteria used in management's description - the criteria should include:

   a. Whether management's description presents how the service organization's system was designed and implemented (including types of services provided; procedures used; related accounting records involved; the process used to prepare reports for user entities; the specified control objectives and controls designed to achieve those objectives; and other matters, such as risk assessment, etc.).

   b. For a type 2 report - whether management's description includes relevant changes during the period covered by the description.

   c. Whether management's description omits or distorts relevant information, while acknowledging that specific matters of interest to some individual users (and their auditors) may not be addressed.

2. In assessing the suitability of the criteria to evaluate whether the controls are suitably designed - the service auditor should determine if the criteria include (a) the risks that threaten achievement of the stated control objectives and (b) the controls that, if the controls are operating as described, would provide reasonable assurance of mitigating those risks.

3. In assessing the suitability of the criteria to evaluate whether controls operated effectively - the service auditor should determine whether the controls were consistently applied as designed throughout the period.

E. **Obtaining an understanding of the service organization's system --** The service auditor should obtain an understanding of the service organization's system (defined as: "the policies and procedures designed, implemented, and documented, by management of the service organization to provide user entities with the services covered by the service auditor's report").

F. **Obtaining evidence regarding management's description --** The service auditor should read management's description of the service organization's system, determine whether the service organization's system has been implemented, and evaluate whether the items comprising the description are fairly presented.

1. Whether stated control objectives are reasonable;
2. Whether controls identified were implemented;
3. Whether any complementary user entity controls are adequately described;
4. Whether services performed by any subservice organization are adequately described (and whether the inclusive or carve-out method has been used).

G. **Obtaining evidence regarding the design of controls --** The service auditor should assess whether controls were suitably designed to achieve the control objectives by (1) identifying risks that threaten achievement of the control objectives and (2) evaluating the linkage of the controls with those risks.

H. **Obtaining evidence regarding the operating effectiveness of controls --** (for a type 2 engagement)

1. Evidence obtained in prior engagements about the operating effectiveness of controls does not provide a basis for reduction in testing in the current period;

2. The service auditor should inquire about changes in the service organization's controls during the period covered by the report and should determine whether any changes considered significant by users (and their auditors) are included in management's description; if not included, the service auditor should describe those changes and consider the effect on the report;

3. When designing/performing tests of control - the service auditor should

   a. Perform procedures in addition to inquiry to determine how the control was applied, whether the control was applied consistently, and by whom or by what means the control was applied;

   b. Determine whether the controls to be tested depend on other controls (and whether it is necessary to obtain evidence supporting the operating effectiveness of those other controls);

   c. Determine an effective method for selecting items to be tested.

I. **Using the work of the internal audit function --** The service auditor should determine whether the internal audit function is likely to be relevant.

1. When the service auditor contemplates using the work of the internal audit function - the service auditor should evaluate (a) the objectivity and competence of the internal auditors; (b) whether their work is likely to be conducted with due professional care; and (c) whether effective communication between the internal audit function and the service auditor is likely;

2. When the service auditor determines that the work of the internal audit function is likely to be adequate for the engagement - the service auditor should evaluate (a) the nature and scope of the specific work to be performed by the internal audit function; (b) the significance of that work to the service auditor's conclusions; and (c) the degree of subjectivity involved;

3. Reporting implications - the service auditor should not reference the internal audit function's work in the service auditor's opinion (there is no such division of responsibility); however, for a type 2 report, the service auditor's description of tests of controls performed should include a description of the internal auditor's work in that area and the service auditor's procedures with respect to that work.

J. Written representations

1. The service auditor should request certain written representations from management;

2. The service auditor should obtain certain written representation from management of the subservice organization when the service organization's management uses the inclusive method;

3. The representations letter should have the same date as the service auditor's report;

4. If management does not provide one or more of the requested written representations - the service auditor should discuss the matter with management, evaluate the effect of such refusal on the assessment of management integrity, and take appropriate action (such as disclaiming an opinion or withdrawing from the engagement).

K. Other information

1. The service auditor should read any other information included in a document containing management's description of the service organization's system and the service auditor's report to identify inconsistencies with that description.

2. Any material inconsistencies or misstatements of facts in the other information should be discussed with management.

L. Documentation

1. The service auditor should prepare sufficient documentation so that an experienced service auditor who is not associated with the engagement, could understand (a) the nature, timing, and extent of procedures performed to comply with applicable requirements; (b) the results of the procedures performed and the evidence obtained; and (c) the significant findings or issues, the conclusions reached, and significant professional judgments.

2. In documenting the nature, timing, and extent of procedures performed - the service auditor should record (a) the identifying characteristics of the specific items tested; (b) who performed the work and the date completed; and (c) who reviewed the work and the date and extent of the review.

3. The service auditor should document discussions of significant findings or issues with management and others (including the nature of such issues, when the discussions occurred, and with whom).

4. The service auditor should document how any inconsistent information identified relative to the final conclusion regarding a significant finding or issue was addressed.

5. The service auditor should assemble the engagement documentation in an engagement file and complete the assembly of the final engagement file on a timely basis (no later than 60 days following the report release date).

M. Reports -- An appendix provides sample reports (both type 1 and type 2 reports)

1. The type 1 report ("Independent Service Auditor's Report on a Description of a Service Organization's System and the Suitability of the Design of Controls") - should be addressed to "XYZ Service Organization" and normally consists of the following sections

   a. Scope - identifies the nature of the engagement and date involved;

   b. Service organization's responsibilities;

   c. Service auditor's responsibilities - reference attestation standards established by the AICPA and describe an examination; disclaim an opinion on operating effectiveness;

   d. Inherent limitations;

e. Opinion - (1) that the description fairly presents the system that was designed and implemented as of the specific date; and (2) that the controls related to the stated control objectives were suitably designed to provide reasonable assurance that the control objectives would be achieved if the controls operated effectively as of the specific date;

f. Restricted use - notifies that distribution should be restricted to the service organization, user entities, and the user entities' independent auditors.

2. The type 2 report ("Independent Service Auditor's Report on a Description of a Service Organization's System and the Suitability of the Design and Operating Effectiveness of Controls") - should be addressed to "XYZ Service Organization" and normally consists of the following sections

   a. Scope - identifies the nature of the engagement and period involved;

   b. Service organization's responsibilities;

   c. Service auditor's responsibilities - reference attestation standards established by the AICPA and describe an examination;

   d. Inherent limitations;

   e. Opinion - (1) that the description fairly presents the system that was designed and implemented throughout the period; (2) that the controls related to the stated control objectives were suitably designed to provide reasonable assurance that the control objectives would be achieved if the controls operated effectively throughout the period; and (3) that the controls tested operated effectively throughout the period;

   f. Description of tests of controls - reference the pages of the service auditor's report identifying the specific controls tested and the nature, timing, and results of those tests;

   g. Restricted use - notifies that distribution should be restricted to the service organization, user entities, and the user entities' independent auditors.

3. **Modified opinion --** The service auditor's opinion should be modified and the report should clearly describe all the reasons for the modification

   a. Management's description of the service organization's system is not fairly presented;

   b. The controls are not suitably designed to provide reasonable assurance that the stated control objectives would be achieved if the controls operated as described;

   c. For a type 2 report - the controls did not operate effectively throughout the specified period;

   d. The service auditor is unable to obtain sufficient appropriate evidence.

N. Other communication responsibilities

1. If there are incidents (excluding those that are "clearly trivial") of noncompliance with laws and regulations, fraud, or uncorrected errors attributable to the service organization - the service auditor should determine the effect of such incidents on management's description of the service organization's system, the achievement of control objectives, and the service auditor's report.

   The service auditor should also determine whether this information has been communicated appropriately to affected user entities - and, if not and if management is unwilling to do so, the auditor should take appropriate action (e.g., obtain legal advice, communicate with those charged with governance, modify the service auditor's report, or withdraw from the engagement).

SQCS

QC10 - A Firm's System of Quality Control

I. **Introduction --** Supersedes SQCS #2-6 (SQCS #1 was previously superseded by SQCS #2); SQCS #7 is effective as of January 1, 2009.

   A. Statements on Quality Control Standards (SQCS) are issued by the Auditing Standards Board. (The AICPA's QC Standards do not purport to include any specific modifications that might be required by PCAOB requirements.)

   B. This section requires a CPA firm to design and implement a system of quality control applicable to its "accounting and auditing practice" - for audit, attestation, compilation, review and any other services covered by Rules 201 or 202 of the AICPA's Code of Professional Conduct.

II. **System of quality control --** Regarding (1) performing engagements in accordance with professional standards and regulatory and legal requirements; and (2) issuing reports that are appropriate in the circumstances.

   A. **Basic requirement** - "The firm must establish a system of quality control designed to provide the firm with reasonable assurance that the firm and its personnel comply with professional standards and applicable regulatory and legal requirements. A system of quality control consists of policies designed to achieve these objectives and the procedures necessary to implement and monitor compliance with those policies:"

      1. **Reasonable assurance** - "a high, but not absolute, level of assurance;"

      2. The specific policies and procedures that comprise the system of quality control may vary among firms - e.g., depending upon the size and operating characteristics of the particular firm.

   B. **Professional requirements** - SQCSs have two categories of professional requirements that determine the specific degree of responsibility imposed:

      1. **Unconditional requirements** (no exceptions) - the firm is required to comply in all cases in which the circumstances exist (indicated by "must" or "is required");

      2. **Presumptively mandatory requirements** (some exceptions) - required to comply in cases in which such circumstances exist, except that (in rare circumstances) the firm may depart from a presumptively mandatory requirement; must document the justification for the departure and how the procedures performed in the circumstances were sufficient to achieve the objectives of the requirement (indicated by "should");

   C. **Explanatory material** - the professional requirements are to be applied in the context of the explanatory material that provides application guidance (indicated by the words "may"; "might"; and "could"):

      1. Defined as the text within the SQCS that provides further explanation and guidance on the professional requirements, or that identify and describe other procedures or actions relating to the firm (excludes any interpretations that may exist);

      2. Explanatory material is intended to be descriptive rather than imperative - it explains the objective of the professional requirements or explains why the firm might consider particular procedures (provides additional information for the firm to consider in exercising judgment about quality. Control).

III. **Documentation and communication of quality control policies and procedures**

   A. **Documentation** - the firm should document its quality control policies and procedures. (The extent of the documentation may vary depending upon the size, structure, and nature of the practice of the firm.)

   B. **Communication** - the firm should communicate its quality control policies and procedures to its personnel: (The communication is not required to be in writing, although that may enhance the communication.)

      1. Describe the quality control policies and procedures and their objectives;

2. Emphasize that each individual has a personal responsibility for quality and is expected to know and comply with the policies/procedures;

3. Request feedback on the system of quality control from personnel.

IV. Elements of a system of quality control

A. The system of quality control consists of six elements:

1. Leadership responsibilities for quality within the firm ("tone at the top");
2. Relevant ethical requirements;
3. Acceptance and continuance of client relationships and specific engagements;
4. Human resources;
5. Engagement performance;
6. Monitoring.

B. Leadership responsibilities for quality within the firm ("tone at the top"):

1. The firm should promote an internal culture that emphasizes quality - the firm's leadership should assume ultimate responsibility for the firm's system of quality control;

2. That internal culture depends upon consistent messages from all levels of the firm's management that emphasize the firm's quality control policies and procedures - the firm should recognize and reward quality work;

3. The firm's business strategy is subject to the overarching requirements of quality control - the firm should establish policies to (a) assign management responsibilities so that commercial considerations do not override quality considerations; (b) address performance evaluation and reward systems to be consistent with the objectives of quality control; and (c) devote sufficient resources to quality control matters;

4. Anyone assigned operational responsibility for quality control should have adequate experience and ability, including the necessary authority.

C. **Relevant ethical requirements** - The firm should establish policies and procedures to provide reasonable assurance that independence is maintained as required:

1. Basic responsibility - communicate the independence requirements to appropriate personnel; and identify/evaluate threats to independence and take appropriate action to mitigate those threats by applying safeguards or withdrawing from the engagement;

2. The firm's policies and procedures should require (a) the engagement partner to consider relevant information (e.g., scope of service issues) to evaluate the overall effect on independence requirements; (b) personnel to promptly notify the engagement partner and firm of all threats to independence (or breaches of independence requirements); (c) communication of timely information to appropriate personnel so that independence requirements can be met and so that identified threats to independence may be appropriately addressed;

3. The firm should obtain written confirmation of compliance with independence requirements from all necessary personnel at least annually (either in paper or electronic form);

4. The firm's policies and procedures should address applicable regulatory requirements that require periodic rotation of personnel.

D. Acceptance and continuance of client relationships and specific engagements:

1. The firm should have policies and procedures to provide reasonable assurance that it will accept/continue an engagement only where the firm (a) has considered the integrity of the client and the risks associated with the engagement; (b) is competent to perform the engagement; and (c) can comply with applicable legal and ethical requirements;

2. Policies and procedures should provide for obtaining an understanding with the client about services to be performed - professional standards may provide guidance about whether the understanding should be written or may be oral;

3. When issues have been identified and the firm has decided to accept or continue the engagement, it should document how the issues were resolved;

4. Matters to be considered in accepting or continuing an engagement include whether: (a) firm personnel have adequate knowledge of relevant industries or subject matters; (b) firm personnel have experience with relevant regulatory or reporting requirements; (c) the firm is able to complete the engagement within the reporting.

E. **Human resources** - the firm should establish policies and procedures to provide reasonable assurance that it has sufficient personnel with the capabilities, competence, and commitment to ethical principles required:

1. Such policies and procedures address (a) recruitment and hiring; (b) determining capabilities and competencies; (c) assigning personnel to engagements; (d) professional development; and (e) performance evaluation, compensation, and advancement;

2. Recruitment and hiring – involve selecting people who have the characteristics to enable them to perform competently (e.g., meeting minimum academic requirements, maturity, integrity, and leadership traits);

3. Determining capabilities and competencies – describes the knowledge, skills, and abilities that qualify personnel to perform an engagement: (Assessing overall competency is essentially a qualitative judgment.)

   a. Capabilities and competence are developed through professional education, continuing professional education, work experience, and mentoring;

   b. Competencies of the engagement partner - should have policies and procedures to provide reasonable assurance that the engagement partner has the competencies to fulfill the engagement responsibilities, including (1) understanding of the role of a system of quality control and the Code of Professional Conduct; (2) understanding the service to be performed; (3) technical proficiency; (4) familiarity with the industry; (5) professional judgment (such as the kind of report that is appropriate in the circumstances); and (5) understanding the organization's information technology systems (and whether an IT professional is needed);

   c. Interrelationship of competencies and other elements of a firm's system of quality control - the competencies (identified above) are interrelated;

   d. Relationship of the competency requirement of the Uniform Accountancy Act (UAA) to the human resource element of quality control - compliance with this Standard (QC10) is deemed to meet the competency requirement referred to in the UAA;

   e. Assignment of engagement teams - the firm should assign responsibility for each engagement to an appropriate engagement partner and should assign appropriate staff with the necessary capabilities, competence, and time to meet engagement requirements; (Generally, the need for direct supervision decreases as the ability and experience levels of assigned staff increases.)

   f. Professional development - all levels of firm personnel should participate in general and industry-specific continuing professional education to fulfill the responsibilities assigned and to meet CPE requirements of the AICPA and regulatory agencies;

   g. Performance evaluation, compensation, and advancement - personnel selected for advancement should have the necessary qualifications to fulfill their responsibilities (should give due recognition and reward for competence and commitment to ethics); the structure of the performance evaluation process may vary by the firm's size and circumstances. (Smaller firms may be less formal.)

F. **Engagement performance** - the firm should establish policies and procedures to provide reasonable assurance that engagements are consistently performed in accordance with professional standards and regulatory and legal requirements, and that the appropriate reports are issued in the circumstances:

1. Required policies and procedures should address (a) engagement performance; (b) supervision responsibilities; and (c) review responsibilities;

2. Confidentiality, safe custody, integrity, accessibility, and retrieval of engagement documentation - the firm should establish policies and procedures to address each of these considerations as appropriate for documentation purposes (includes password usage and appropriate back-up routines for electronic documentation, and restricted access and proper distribution and storage of confidential documentation);

3. Retention of documentation - the firm should establish procedures for the retention of engagement documentation for a period sufficient to meet the needs of the firm, professional standards, and applicable laws/regulations;
4. Consultation - the firm should establish policies and procedures to provide reasonable assurance that consultation takes place as appropriate regarding significant technical, ethical and other contentious issues (includes discussion at the appropriate level within or outside the firm);
5. Differences of opinion - the firm should establish policies and procedures for dealing with and resolving differences of opinion within the engagement team, with those consulted, and between the engagement partner and the engagement quality control reviewer (including that the conclusions reached are documented and implemented and that the report is not released until the matter is resolved);
6. Engagement quality control review - the firm should establish criteria to determine whether an engagement quality review should be performed before the report is issued: (The criteria may include the nature of the engagement, the identification of unusual risks, or regulatory issues.) The firm should include:
    a. Objective evaluation of the significant judgments made by the engagement team and the conclusions reached (e.g., significant risks identified and responses; judgments made with respect to materiality; significance of corrected and uncorrected misstatements; matters communicated to management and those charged with governance);
    b. Reading the financial statements (or other subject matter) and the report to consider the appropriateness of the report;
    c. A review of selected engagement documentation related to the significant judgments made and conclusions reached (should include a discussion with the engagement partner regarding significant findings and issues);
    d. Timeliness - the quality review should be done on a timely basis (may be conducted at appropriate stages during the engagement);
    e. Independence - although not a member of the engagement team, the quality reviewer should meet the independence requirements;
    f. Allowance for small firms to use other firms for quality reviews if insufficient personnel are available to serve in such a capacity;
    g. Documentation - the firm should establish policies and procedures that provide for appropriate documentation, including that (1) required review procedures have been performed; (2) the quality review has been completed before the report is released; and (3) the reviewer is not aware of any unresolved matters regarding significant judgments and conclusions of the engagement team.

G. **Monitoring** - the firm should establish policies and procedures to provide the firm with reasonable assurance that the policies and procedures of the system of quality control are relevant, adequate, operating effectively, and in compliance:

1. Purpose of monitoring compliance - to evaluate (a) adherence to professional standards and legal and regulatory requirements; (b) the design and implementation of quality control policies and procedures; and (c) whether the policies and procedures have been operating effectively;
2. Inspection procedures involves selection of individual engagements; (This may be performed on a cyclical basis, e.g., to include at least one engagement for each engagement partner over a cycle spanning three years.)
3. Deficiencies identified during the monitoring process do not necessarily indicate that the firm's system of quality control is insufficient - deficiencies should result in one or more of the following: (a) taking corrective action applicable to the engagement or personnel; (b) communication of the findings to those responsible for training; (c) changes to the quality control policies and procedures; or (d) disciplinary action against those who fail to comply, especially if done so repeatedly;
4. If the report issued may be inappropriate - determine what further action is appropriate to comply with professional standards, etc. (consider obtaining legal advice);

5. The firm should establish policies and procedures to appropriately document monitoring and to communicate the result of monitoring its quality control systems (at least annually) to appropriate members of the firm, including the firm's leadership - should include a description of the monitoring procedures performed, the conclusions drawn from those procedures, and a description of systemic, repetitive, or other significant deficiencies and actions take to address those deficiencies;
6. Relationship of peer review to monitoring - a peer review under AICPA standards may substitute for the inspection of engagement working papers, reports, and clients' financial statements for the period of the peer review;
7. Complaints and allegations - the firm should establish policies and procedures to provide reasonable assurance that it deals appropriately with complaints and allegations of substandard work or noncompliance with the system of quality control:
    a. Should have clearly defined channels for personnel to raise any such concerns without fear of reprisal;
    b. Investigations of complaints and allegations should be supervised by someone having appropriate experience without other involvement in the engagement in question;
    c. Should appropriately document any complaints and allegations, including the responses to them.

H. Documentation of the operation of quality control policies and procedures - the firm should establish policies and procedures requiring appropriate documentation of the operation of each element of the system of quality control:

1. Form and content - a matter of judgment and varies with the circumstances (e.g., the size of the firm, number of offices, nature and complexity of the firm's practice);
2. Retention - the firm should establish policies and procedures to require retention of documentation for a period sufficient to permit evaluation of the firm's compliance with its system of quality control (or for a longer period as required by law or regulation).

I. **Effective date** - applicable to a CPA firm's system of quality control for its accounting and auditing practice as of January 1, 2009.

PCAOB

AS8 - Audit Risk

I. **Released by the PCAOB on August 5, 2010 - Approved by the SEC on 12/23/10**

II. **Objective --** The objective is to conduct the audit of financial statements in a manner that reduces audit risk to an appropriately low level.

III. **Audit Risk --** The audit risk is "the risk that the auditor expresses an inappropriate audit opinion when the financial statements are materially misstated, i.e., the financial statements are not presented fairly in conformity with the applicable financial reporting framework."

- A. Basic auditor responsibility - the auditor must plan and perform the audit to obtain reasonable assurance about whether the financial statements are free of material misstatement due to error or fraud.
- B. "Reasonable assurance" is obtained by reducing audit risk to an appropriately low level (by exercising due professional care and obtaining sufficient appropriate audit evidence).
- C. Audit risk is a function of the risk of material misstatement and detection risk.

IV. **Risk of Material Misstatement --** The auditor should assess the risks of material misstatement at two levels: (1) at the financial statement level; and (2) at the assertion level.

- A. At the financial statement level - the risk of material misstatement relates pervasively to the financial statements as a whole and potentially affects many assertions.
- B. At the assertion level - the risk of material misstatement consists of two component risks: (1) inherent risk; and (2) control risk (which is a function of the effectiveness of the design and operation of internal control).
    1. The auditor assesses inherent risk using information obtained from performing risk assessment procedures and considering the characteristics of the accounts and disclosures in the financial statements.
    2. The auditor assesses control risk using tests of controls (if the auditor plans to rely on those controls) and from other sources.

V. **Detection Risk --** This risk is affected by (1) the effectiveness of the auditor's substantive procedures and (2) their application by the auditor (whether due professional care was exercised).

- A. "The higher the risk of material misstatement, the lower the level of detection risk needs to be in order to reduce audit risk to an appropriately low level."
- B. The level of detection risk is determined by the nature, timing, and extent of the auditor's substantive procedures.
- C. When the auditor is performing an "integrated audit of financial statements and internal control over financial reporting" - the risks of material misstatement of the financial statements are the same for both the audit of financial statements and the audit of internal control over financial reporting.

AS9 - Audit Planning

I. **Released by the PCAOB on August 5, 2010 - Approved by the SEC on 12/23/10**

II. **Objective --** The objective is to plan the audit so that the audit is conducted effectively.

III. **Responsibility of the Engagement Partner --** "The engagement partner is responsible for the engagement and its performance. Accordingly, the engagement partner is responsible for planning the audit and may seek assistance from appropriate engagement team members in fulfilling this responsibility."

IV. **Planning an Audit --** "Planning the audit includes establishing the overall audit strategy for the engagement and developing an audit plan, which includes, in particular, planned risk assessment procedures and planned responses to the risks of material misstatement. Planning is not a discrete phase of an audit but, rather, a continual and iterative process that might begin shortly after (or in connection with) the completion of the previous audit and continues until the completion of the current audit."

A. **Preliminary Engagement Activities --** The auditor should perform the following activities at the beginning of the audit: (1) perform procedures regarding the continuance of the client relationship and the specific audit engagement; (2) determine compliance with independence and ethics requirements; and (3) establish an understanding with the client regarding the services to be performed.

B. **Planning Activities --** The nature and extent of planning activities depend on the size and complexity of the company, the auditor's previous experience with the company, and changes in circumstances that occur during the audit; the auditor should ordinarily consider whether the following matters will affect the audit.

1. Knowledge of the company's internal control over financial reporting.
2. Matters affecting the industry in which the company operates (e.g., financial reporting practices, economic conditions, regulations, etc.).
3. Matters related to the company's business (e.g., operating characteristics, capital structure, etc.).
4. Recent changes affecting the company, including internal control over financial reporting, its operations, etc.).
5. The auditor's preliminary judgments about materiality and risk and about the effectiveness of internal control over financial reporting.
6. Control deficiencies previously communicated to the audit committee.
7. Legal or regulatory matters known to the company.
8. Available evidence regarding to the effectiveness of the company's internal control over financial reporting.
9. Knowledge about risks related to the company evaluated in connection with the auditor's client acceptance and retention decision.
10. The relative complexity of the company's operations.

C. **Audit Strategy --** The auditor should establish an overall audit strategy that sets the scope, timing, and direction of the audit and guides the development of the audit plan; the overall audit strategy should take into consideration the following:

1. The reporting objectives of the engagement and the nature of the communications required by PCAOB standards;
2. The factors that are significant in directing the activities of the engagement team;
3. The results of preliminary engagement activities and the auditor's evaluation of important planning activities considered by the auditor;

4. The nature, timing, and extent of resources necessary to perform the audit.

D. **Audit Plan --** The auditor should develop and document an audit plan that includes: (1) the planned nature, timing, and extent of the risk assessment procedures; (2) the planned nature, timing, and extent of tests of controls and substantive procedures; and (3) any other planned audit procedures required to comply with PCAOB standards.

E. **Multi-location Engagements --** The auditor should determine the locations or business units at which audit procedures should be performed (including the nature, timing, and extent of procedures to be performed at the various locations); the auditor should "... correlate the amount of audit attention devoted to the location or business unit with the degree of risk of material misstatement associated with that location or business unit." Relevant factors include:

1. Nature and amount of assets, liabilities and transactions executed at the location or business unit (including significant transactions that are outside the normal course of business for the company or that appear unusual).
2. The materiality of the location or business unit.
3. The specific risks associated with the location or business unit that present a "reasonable possibility of material misstatement" to the company's consolidated financial statements.
4. The degree of centralization of records or information processing.
5. The effectiveness of the control environment and management's ability to effectively supervise activities at the location or business unit.
6. The frequency, timing, and scope of monitoring activities at the location or business unit. (The auditor may also consider relevant activities performed by internal audit.)

F. **Changes During the Audit --** The auditor should modify the audit strategy and the audit plan as necessary for significantly changed circumstances encountered (including revisions of the risks of material misstatement or the discovery of a previously unidentified risk of material misstatement).

G. **Persons with Specialized Skill or Knowledge (Specialists) --** The auditor should have sufficient knowledge of the subject matter involved to enable the auditor to (1) communicate the objectives of that person's work; (2) determine whether that person's procedures meet the auditor's objectives; and (3) evaluate the results of that person's procedures with respect to effects on the auditor's report.

H. **Additional Considerations in Initial Audits**

1. The auditor should do the following before starting an initial audit: (a) perform procedures regarding acceptance of the client relationship and the specific engagement; and (b) communicate with the predecessor auditor when there is a change in auditors.
2. The auditor should determine the additional planning activities necessary to establish an appropriate audit strategy and audit plan, including determining the audit procedures required to obtain sufficient appropriate audit evidence regarding the company's beginning balances. (Note that the auditor has responsibilities regarding the consistency of the company's financial statements.)

AS10 - Supervision

I. **Released by the PCAOB on August 5, 2010 - Approved by the SEC on 12/23/10**

II. **Objective --** The objective is to supervise the audit engagement so that the work is performed as directed and supports the conclusions reached.

III. **Responsibility of the Engagement Partner --** "The engagement partner is responsible for the engagement and its performance. Accordingly, the engagement partner is responsible for proper supervision of the work of engagement team members and for compliance with PCAOB standards, including standards regarding using the work of specialists, other auditors, internal auditors, and others who are involved in testing controls."

IV. **Supervision of Engagement Team Members**

A. Inform engagement team members of their responsibilities regarding (1) the objectives of the procedures that they are to perform; (2) the nature, timing, and extent of procedures they are to perform; and (3) matters that could affect the procedures to be performed or the evaluation of the results of those procedures.

B. Direct engagement team members to bring significant accounting and auditing issues to the attention of the engagement partner (or other applicable supervisors) for evaluation.

C. Review the work of the engagement team members to evaluate whether (1) the work was performed and documented; (2) the objectives of the procedures were achieved; and (3) the results of the work support the conclusions reached.

V. **The Extent of Supervision Required Varies with the Circumstances**

A. The nature of the company, including its size and complexity;

B. The nature of the work assigned to engagement personnel.

C. The risks of material misstatement - the extent of supervision should be commensurate with the risks of material misstatement.

D. The knowledge, skill, and ability of each engagement team member.

AS11 - Materiality in Planning/Performing an Audit

I. **Released by the PCAOB on August 5, 2010 - Approved by the SEC on 12/23/10**

II. **Materiality in the Context of an Audit --** The auditor should plan and perform the audit to detect misstatements that, individually or in the aggregate, would result in material misstatement of the financial statements.

   A. This includes misstatements that could be material due to quantitative or qualitative factors.

   B. Ordinarily it is not practical to design audit procedures to detect misstatements that are material due solely to qualitative factors.

   C. The auditor should use the same materiality considerations for planning the audit of internal control over financial reporting as for the audit of the financial statements.

III. **Establishing Materiality for the Financial Statements as a Whole**

   A. The auditor should establish a materiality level for the financial statements that is appropriate in light of the particular circumstances.

   B. To determine the nature, timing, and extent of audit procedures, the materiality level for the financial statements needs to be expressed as a specified amount.

   C. If the financial statements for the audit period are unavailable, the auditor may establish the initial materiality level based on estimated or preliminary financial statement amounts.

IV. **Establishing Materiality for Particular Accounts or Disclosures --** When there is a substantial likelihood that misstatements of lesser amounts than the materiality level established for the financial statements would influence the judgment of a reasonable investor, the auditor should establish separate materiality levels for those accounts or disclosures and design the nature, timing, and extent of the audit procedures accordingly.

V. **Determining Tolerable Misstatement**

   A. The auditor should determine tolerable misstatement for purposes of assessing risks of material misstatement and planning and performing audit procedures at the account or disclosure levels. Tolerable misstatement should be less than the materiality level for the financial statements as a whole (and, if applicable, the materiality level or levels for particular accounts or disclosures).

   B. Prior periods - the auditor should take into account the nature, cause, and amount of misstatements that were identified in audits of prior periods.

   C. Considerations for multi-location engagements - the auditor should determine tolerable misstatement for the individual locations or business units (so that there is an appropriately low level probability that the total of uncorrected and undetected misstatements would result in material misstatement of the consolidated financial statements).

VI. **Considerations as the Audit Progresses --** The auditor should reevaluate the established materiality level(s) in light of changes in circumstances or additional information that comes to the auditor's attention.

   A. When the initial materiality level(s) and tolerable misstatement were based on estimated or preliminary amounts that differ significantly from actual amounts.

   B. When events or changed conditions occurring after the materiality level(s) and tolerable misstatements were initially established are likely to affect investors' perceptions about the company's financial statements (e.g., significant new contractual arrangements involving a particular aspect of a company's business that is separately disclosed in the financial statements).

AS12 - Identifying/Assessing Risks of Material Misstatement

I. **Released by the PCAOB on August 5, 2010 - Approved by the SEC on 12/23/10**

II. **Objective --** The objective is to identify and appropriately assess the risks of material misstatement, thereby providing a basis for designing and implementing responses to the risks of material misstatement.

III. **Performing Risk Assessment Procedures --** The auditor should perform risk assessment procedures that are sufficient to provide a reasonable basis for identifying and assessing the risks of material misstatement (whether due to error or fraud) and designing further audit procedures.

A. Risks of material misstatement arise from external factors (e.g., industry conditions) and company-specific factors (e.g., internal control issues). Audit procedures for identifying and appropriately assessing the risks of material misstatement should include consideration of these external factors and company-specific factors.

B. This standard focuses on the following risk assessment procedures:

1. Obtaining an understanding of the company and its environment;
2. Obtaining an understanding of internal control over financial reporting;
3. Considering information from the client acceptance and retention evaluation, planning activities, prior audits, and other engagements performed for the company;
4. Performing analytical procedures;
5. Conducting a discussion among engagement team members regarding the risks of material misstatement;
6. Inquiring of the audit committee, management, and others within the company about the risks of material misstatement.

C. **Top-down Approach --** The auditor should begin by identifying and assessing the risks of material misstatement at the financial statement level (with the auditor's overall understanding of the company and its environment) and then work down to the significant accounts and disclosures and their relevant assertions.

D. **For an Integrated Audit --** The auditor's risk assessment procedures apply to both the audit of internal control over financial reporting and the audit of the financial statements. (That is, the risks of material misstatement are the same for both audits.)

IV. **Obtaining an Understanding of the Company and Its Environment**

A. Obtaining an understanding of the company includes understanding the following:

1. Relevant industry, regulatory, and other external factors;
2. The nature of the company;
3. The company's selection and application of accounting principles;
4. The company's objectives and strategies and the business risks that might reasonably be expected to result in risks of material misstatement;
5. The company's measurement and analysis of its financial performance.

B. The auditor should also evaluate whether significant changes in the company from prior periods affect the risks of material misstatement.

C. Industry, regulatory, and other external factors - include the competitive environment and technological developments, the applicable financial reporting framework, the legal and political environment, and general economic conditions.

D. Nature of the company

1. Obtaining an understanding includes understanding the following matters:
   a. The company's organizational structure and management personnel;
   b. The sources of funding of the company's operations and investment activities (including the capital structure and debt funding);
   c. The company's significant investments (including equity method investments, joint ventures, and variable interest entities);
   d. The company's operating characteristics (including its size and complexity);
   e. The sources of the company's earnings (including the relative profitability of key products and services);
   f. Key supplier and customer relationships.
2. The auditor should also consider the following:
   a. Reading public information about the company relevant to the auditor's evaluation of the risks of material misstatement;
   b. Observing or reading transcripts of earnings calls and (if publicly available) other meetings with investors or rating agencies;
   c. Obtaining an understanding of compensation arrangements with senior management (including incentives, special bonuses, etc.);
   d. Obtaining information about trading activity (and holdings) in the company's securities by significant holders to identify potentially significant unusual developments.

E. Selection and application of accounting principles, including related disclosures.

1. The auditor should evaluate whether the company's selection and application of accounting principles are appropriate.
2. The auditor should develop expectations about the disclosures necessary for the financial statements to be presented fairly.
3. The auditor should consider the following matters relevant to understanding the company's accounting principles, including disclosures:
   a. Significant changes in the company's accounting principles or disclosures (and the reasons for such changes);
   b. The competence of personnel involved in selecting and applying significant accounting principles;
   c. The accounts or disclosures involving judgment (estimates and assumptions) in the application of significant accounting principles;
   d. Significant accounting principles in controversial or emerging areas for which there is a lack of guidance or consensus;
   e. Methods used to account for significant and unusual transactions;
   f. Financial reporting standards and laws/regulations that are new to the company (and how and when the company will adopt them).

F. Company objectives, strategies, and related business risks.

1. The purpose of obtaining this understanding is to identify business risks that might result in material misstatement of the financial statements.
2. Examples of business risks that might result in material misstatements:
   a. Industry developments/changes;
   b. New products and services;
   c. Use of information technology;
   d. New accounting requirements;
   e. Expansion of the business;

f. Current and prospective financing requirements;

g. Regulatory requirements.

G. Company performance measures.

1. The purpose of obtaining this understanding is to identify performance measures that affect the risks of material misstatement.

2. Examples of performance measures that might affect the risks of material misstatement:

a. Measures that form the basis for contractual commitments or incentive compensation arrangements;

b. Measures used by external parties (e.g., analysts, rating agencies, etc.) to review the company's performance;

c. Measures used to monitor the company's operations to identify unexpected results or trends.

V. **Obtaining an Understanding of Internal Control over Financial Reporting --** The auditor should obtain a sufficient understanding of each component of internal control to (a) identify the types of potential misstatements, (b) assess the factors affecting the risks of material misstatements, and (c) design further audit procedures.

A. Obtaining an understanding of internal control includes evaluating the design of controls relevant to the audit and determining whether controls have been implemented.

1. Procedures to obtain evidence about design effectiveness - inquiry of appropriate personnel, observation of the company's operations, and inspection of relevant documentation. (Walkthroughs, ordinarily, are sufficient to evaluate design effectiveness.)

2. Procedures to determine whether a control has been implemented - inquiry of appropriate personnel, in combination with observation of the application of controls or inspection of documentation. (Walkthroughs, ordinarily, are sufficient to determine whether a control has been implemented.)

B. Internal control over financial reporting consists of five components. The auditor should use the same control framework that management uses for its annual evaluation of internal control over financial reporting:

1. Control environment;

2. Risk assessment process - includes obtaining an understanding of the risk of material misstatement identified and assessed by management;

3. Information and communication;

4. Control activities.

5. Monitoring.

C. Performing walkthroughs.

1. The auditor may perform walkthroughs to understand the flow of transactions, to evaluate the design of controls relevant to the audit, and to determine whether those controls have been implemented.

2. Walkthrough procedures include a combination of inquiry, observation, inspection of relevant documentation, and reperformance of controls.

D. Relationship of "understanding of internal control" to "tests of controls" - the procedures performed to obtain an understanding of internal control might provide evidence that is relevant to the auditor's evaluation of entity-level controls.

VI. **Considering Information --** Considering information from the client acceptance and retention evaluation, audit planning activities, past audits, and other engagements.

A. Client acceptance/retention and audit planning activities - the auditor should evaluate whether information obtained is relevant to identifying risks of material misstatement;

B. Past audits - the auditor should use knowledge obtained in past audits to identify risks of material misstatement (especially regarding changes in the company or its environment);

C. If relying on past audits to limit the auditor's risk assessment procedures - the auditor should evaluate the relevance and reliability of the prior years' information

D. Review engagements - the auditor should evaluate whether information obtained in the review is relevant to identifying risks of material misstatement in the audit.

VII. Performing Analytical Procedures

A. The auditor should perform analytical procedures designed to (1) enhance the auditor's understanding of the client's business and significant transactions/events since the prior year; and (2) identify specific risks to the audit (e.g., unusual transactions and events that warrant investigation).

B. Regarding revenue - the auditor should perform analytical procedures to identify unusual or unexpected relationships involving revenue accounts.

C. Analytical procedures performed as risk assessment procedures often use data that is aggregated at a high level (and, as a result, do not have the level of precision needed for substantive purposes).

VIII. Conducting a Discussion Among Engagement Team Members About Risks of Material Misstatement

A. Key members of the team should discuss (1) the company's selection and application of accounting principles and (2) the risk of material misstatement to the financial statements due to error or fraud.

B. The engagement partner (or other key team members) should communicate the important matters discussed to team members not involved in the discussion.

C. Discussion of the potential for material misstatement due to fraud - the discussion among key members of the team should include the following:

1. "Brainstorming" about the company's susceptibility to fraud;
2. Consideration of known external and internal factors that might (a) create incentives/pressures to commit fraud; (b) provide the opportunity to commit fraud; and (c) indicate a culture or environment that enables management to rationalize committing fraud;
3. Consideration of the risk of management override;
4. Consideration of the potential audit responses to the fraud risks.

IX. Inquiries Regarding Fraud Risks -- The auditor should make a variety of specific inquiries of management, of the audit committee, of the internal audit function, and of others; the auditor should obtain evidence to address inconsistencies in responses to the inquiries.

X. Identifying and Assessing the Risks of Material Misstatement -- The auditor should identify and assess the risks of material misstatement both at the financial statement level and at the assertion level.

A. Auditor responsibilities - the auditor should:

1. Identify risks of material misstatement (from risk assessment procedures);
2. Evaluate whether the risks pervasively affect the financial statements (that is, potentially affect many assertions);
3. Evaluate the types of potential misstatements that could occur - asking "What could go wrong?"
4. Assess the likelihood and magnitude of the potential misstatement;
5. Identify significant accounts and disclosures (and relevant assertions);
6. Determine whether any of the identified risks are "significant risks."

B. Identifying significant accounts and disclosures and their relevant assertions

1. The auditor should evaluate the qualitative and quantitative risk factors, including:
   a. Size and composition of the account;
   b. Susceptibility to misstatement due to error or fraud;

c. Volume of activity and complexity of transactions involved;

d. Nature of the account or disclosure (and changes in characteristics relative to the prior period);

e. Accounting and reporting complexities associated with the account;

f. Exposure to losses in the account;

g. Possibility of significant contingent liabilities arising;

h. Existence of related party transactions.

2. For an integrated audit - the significant accounts and disclosures are the same for the audit of the financial statements and the audit of internal control over financial reporting.

3. When there are multiple locations or business units - the auditor should identify significant accounts and disclosures and their relevant assertions based on the consolidated financial statements.

C. Factors relevant to identifying fraud risks - the auditor should presume that there is a fraud risk involving improper revenue recognition; the auditor should also consider the risk of management override of controls.

D. Factors relevant to identifying "significant risks" - the determination of whether a risk of material misstatement is a "significant risk" is based on inherent risk (without regard to the effect of controls); note that a fraud risk is a significant risk.

E. Further consideration of controls - when the auditor identifies a "significant risk" the auditor should evaluate the design of the company's controls (and whether those controls have been implemented) intended to address those risks.

XI. **Revision of Risk Assessment --** The assessment of the risks of material misstatement should continue throughout the audit; the auditor should revise the risk assessment and modify planned audit procedures as needed in response to the revised risk assessments.

AS13 - Responses to Risks of Material Misstatement

I. **Released by the PCAOB on August 5, 2010 - Approved by the SEC on 12/23/10**

II. **Objective --** The objective is to address the risks of material misstatement through appropriate overall audit responses and audit procedures.

III. **Responding to the Risk of Material Misstatement --** Discusses two types of audit responses:

  A. Responses that have an overall effect on how the audit is conducted;

  B. Responses involving the nature, timing, and extent of the audit procedures to be performed.

IV. **Overall Responses**

  A. Making appropriate assignments of significant engagement responsibilities based on the knowledge, skill, and ability of team members;

  B. Providing the extent of supervision that is appropriate for the circumstances;

  C. Incorporating elements of unpredictability in auditing procedures to be performed;

  D. Evaluating the company's selection and application of significant accounting principles - especially subjective measurements and those subject to bias;

  E. Determining whether it is necessary to make pervasive changes to the nature, timing, and extent of audit procedures - e.g., increase the substantive testing of valuation in view of deteriorating market conditions; obtain more persuasive audit evidence from substantive procedures when there are pervasive weaknesses in the company's control environment.

V. **Responses Involving the Nature, Timing, and Extent of Audit Procedures --** The auditor should address the assessed risks of material misstatement for each relevant assertion of each significant account and disclosure.

  A. Audit procedures performed in response to the assessed risks of material misstatement can be classified into two categories: (1) tests of controls; and (2) substantive procedures.

  B. Responses to "significant risks" - the auditor should perform substantive procedures, including tests of details, that are responsive to the assessed risks.

  C. Responses to fraud risks - the auditor should perform substantive procedures, including tests of details, that are responsive to the assessed fraud risks.

    1. Fraud risks may cause planned audit procedures to be modified in terms of nature (obtaining more reliable evidence), timing (moving procedures closer to year-end), and extent (increasing sample sizes).

    2. The auditor should perform audit procedures to address the risk of management override of controls - examining journal entries, reviewing accounting estimates for biases, and evaluating the business rationale for significant unusual transactions.

VI. **Testing Controls**

  A. **Testing Controls in a Financial Statement Audit**

    1. Controls to be tested - If the auditor plans to assess control risk at less than the maximum level (relying on controls), the auditor must perform tests of controls during the entire period of reliance.

    2. The auditor is not required to assess control risk at less than the maximum for all relevant assertions - the auditor may choose not to do so for a variety of reasons

    3. Tests of control must be performed for each relevant assertion for which substantive procedures alone cannot provide sufficient appropriate evidence.

    4. The persuasiveness of evidence required from tests of control increases as the degree of reliance placed on a control increases.

  B. **Testing Design Effectiveness --** Procedures include a mix of inquiry, observation, and inspection of documentation; walkthroughs including these procedures are usually sufficient to evaluate design effectiveness.

C. Testing Operating Effectiveness

1. Meaning that the control is operating as designed and that the person performing the control possesses the authority and competence to perform the control effectively.
2. Procedures include a mix of inquiry, observation, inspection of documentation, and re-performance of the control (presented in order from least to most persuasive).

D. Nature of Tests of Controls -- Inquiry alone does not provide sufficient evidence to support a conclusion about the effectiveness of a control.

E. Extent of Tests of Controls -- Matters that could affect the extent of testing in relation to the degree of reliance include the following:

1. The frequency of the performance of the control by the company;
2. The length of time during the audit period that the auditor is relying on the control;
3. The expected rate of deviation from a control;
4. The relevance and reliability of evidence to be obtained about the control;
5. The nature of the control (whether manual or automated); and for an automated control, the effectiveness of relevant IT general controls.

F. Timing of Tests of Controls -- The auditor must obtain evidence about the operating effectiveness during the entire period of reliance. (When tests of control are performed at an interim date, the auditor should update the results of testing through the remaining period of reliance.)

G. Assessing Control Risk

1. Control risk should be assessed at the maximum level when (a) the controls are ineffective; or (b) the auditor has not obtained sufficient appropriate evidence to support a control risk assessment below the maximum level .
2. When deficiencies affecting the controls on which the auditor intends to rely are detected, the auditor should evaluate the severity of the deficiencies and the effect on the auditor's risk assessment.

VII. Substantive procedures -- The auditor should perform substantive procedures for each relevant assertion of each significant account and disclosure (regardless of control risk).

A. As the assessed risk of material misstatement increases, the evidence from substantive procedures should also increase; also, more evidence is needed from substantive procedures for relevant assertions that have a higher susceptibility to management override or breakdowns resulting from human failures.

B. Nature of substantive procedures

1. Inquiry alone does not provide sufficient appropriate evidence to support a conclusion about relevant assertions.
2. Substantive procedures related to the period-end financial reporting process - the auditor's substantive procedures related to the period-end financial reporting process must include the following: (a) reconciling the financial statements with the underlying accounting records; and (b) examining material adjustments made.

C. Extent of Substantive Procedures -- The necessary extent of a substantive audit procedure depends on the materiality of the account or disclosure, the assessed risk of material misstatement, and the necessary degree of assurance from the procedure

D. Timing of Substantive Procedures -- When substantive procedures are performed at an interim date, the auditor should obtain a reasonable basis for extending the audit conclusions to the end of the period (by performing substantive procedures or substantive procedures combined with tests of controls).

Dual-purpose Tests -- The auditor should design the dual-purpose test to achieve the objectives of both the test of the control and the substantive test.

AS14 - Evaluating Audit Results

I. **Released by the PCAOB on August 5, 2010 - Approved by the SEC on 12/23/10**

II. **Objective --** The objective is to evaluate the results of the audit to determine whether the audit evidence obtained is sufficient and appropriate to support the opinion.

III. **Evaluating the Results of the Audit of Financial Statements --** The auditor should consider all relevant audit evidence, whether is corroborates or contradicts the financial statements.

A. The auditor should evaluate the following:

1. The results of analytical procedures performed as the overall review;
2. Misstatements accumulated during the audit (especially uncorrected ones);
3. The qualitative aspects of the company's accounting practices;
4. Conditions identified during the audit related to fraud risk;
5. The presentation of the financial statements, including disclosures;
6. The sufficiency and appropriateness of the audit evidence obtained.

B. Performing analytical procedures in the overall review.

1. The auditor should read the financial statements and disclosures and perform analytical procedures to (a) evaluate the auditor's conclusions regarding significant accounts and disclosures and (b) assist in forming an opinion on the financial statements as a whole.
2. The auditor should perform analytical procedures relating to revenue through the end of the period.
3. The auditor should obtain corroboration for management's explanations regarding significant unusual or unexpected transactions, events, amounts, or relationships.

C. Accumulating and evaluating identified misstatements.

1. Accumulating identified misstatements - the auditor should accumulated misstatements identified during the audit, other than those that are "clearly trivial."
2. The accumulation of misstatements should include the auditor's best estimate of the total misstatements in the accounts and disclosures tested, not limited to misstatements specifically identified.
3. Misstatements involving accounting estimates - the auditor should treat the difference between the company's estimate and a "reasonable" estimate as a misstatement.
4. Considerations as the audit progresses - the auditor should determine whether the audit strategy and audit plan need to be modified. (If the accumulated misstatements could be material or approach the materiality level(s) used in planning.)
5. Communications - the auditor should communicate accumulated misstatements to management on a timely basis to give management an opportunity to correct them.
6. Evaluation of uncorrected misstatements - the auditor should determine whether uncorrected misstatements are material, individually or in the aggregate; the auditor should evaluate the misstatements in relation to the specific accounts and disclosures and to the financial statements as a whole (considering relevant quantitative and qualitative factors).
7. Effect of prior year's misstatements - the auditor should evaluate the effects of uncorrected misstatements associated with prior years.
8. Intentional misstatements - when the auditor believes that a misstatement may be intentional, the auditor should obtain additional evidence to determine whether fraud occurred and the effect on the financial statements; the auditor should also evaluate the implications to the integrity of management or employees and the effect on the audit.

D. Evaluating the qualitative aspects of the company's accounting practices - the auditor should evaluate the qualitative aspects of the company's accounting practices, including potential bias in management's judgments

1. Examples of management bias include: (a) the selective correction of misstatements; (b) the identification by management of additional adjusting entries that offset misstatements accumulated by the auditor; (c) bias in the selection and application of accounting principles; and (d) bias in accounting estimates.
2. The auditor should evaluate whether the auditor's risk assessments (especially the assessment of fraud risks) and the related audit responses remain appropriate .
3. Evaluating bias in accounting estimates - the auditor should evaluate whether the differences between the recorded amounts and that supported by the audit evidence indicate a possible bias by management .

E. Evaluating conditions relating to the assessment of fraud risks - the auditor should evaluate whether the accumulated results of the audit procedures affect the assessment of fraud risks and whether the audit procedures should be modified; the engagement partner should determine whether there has been appropriate communication among audit team members throughout the audit about fraud risks.

F. Evaluating the presentation of the financial statements - the auditor should evaluate whether the financial statements contain the information essential for fair presentation in conformity with the applicable financial reporting framework.

G. Evaluating the sufficiency and appropriateness of audit evidence - the auditor must reach a conclusion as to whether sufficient appropriate audit evidence has been obtained to support the opinion on the financial statements.

AS15 - Audit Evidence

I. **Released by the PCAOB on August 5, 2010 - Approved by the SEC on 12/23/10**

II. **Objective --** The objective is to plan and perform the audit to obtain appropriate audit evidence that is sufficient to support the opinion expressed in the auditor's report.

III. **Sufficient Appropriate Audit Evidence**

- **A.** Sufficiency is a measure of the quantity of evidence and is affected by:
  - **1.** The risk of material misstatement (or the "risk associated with the control" for the audit of internal control over financial reporting) - as that risk increases, the amount of evidence required also increases;
  - **2.** Quality of the evidence obtained - as the quality of evidence increases, the amount of evidence required decreases.
- **B.** Appropriateness is the measure of the quality of evidence, and involves:
  - **1.** Relevance - the relationship between the evidence and the assertion (or to the objective of the control) being tested.
  - **2.** Reliability - ranking of the reliability of audit evidence:
    - **a.** Evidence obtained directly by the auditor is more reliable than evidence obtained indirectly;
    - **b.** Evidence obtained from a knowledgeable source that is independent of the company is more reliable than evidence obtained only from internal company sources;
    - **c.** The reliability of information generated internally by the company is increased when the company's controls are effective;
    - **d.** Evidence provided by original documents is more reliable than evidence provided by photocopies or facsimiles or documents that have been converted into electronic form.
  - **3.** Using information produced by the company - the auditor should evaluate whether the information is sufficient and appropriate for audit purposes:
    - **a.** Test the accuracy and completeness of the information (or test the controls over the accuracy and completeness of the information);
    - **b.** Evaluate whether the information is sufficiently precise and detailed for audit purposes.

IV. **Financial Statement Assertions that are Implicitly or Explicitly Made by Management**

- **A.** The PCAOB identifies five traditional financial statement assertions:
  - **1.** Existence - that the assets or liabilities exist at a given date or that the recorded transactions have occurred during a given period;
  - **2.** Completeness - that all transactions and accounts that should be presented are included;
  - **3.** Valuation or allocation - elements are included in the financial statements at appropriate amounts;
  - **4.** Rights and obligations - the company has the rights to the assets and the liabilities are the obligations of the company at a given date;
  - **5.** Presentation and disclosure - the elements of the financial statements are properly classified, described, and disclosed.
- **B.** The PCAOB states, "The auditor may base his or her work on financial statement assertions that differ from those in this standard if the assertions are sufficient for the auditor to identify the potential misstatements... " (presumably referring to AICPA or IFAC standards that present such assertions differently).

V. Audit Procedures for Obtaining Audit Evidence -- Procedures can be classified into the following categories: (a) "risk assessment procedures;" and (b) "further audit procedures" (consisting of tests of controls and substantive procedures, including tests of details and substantive analytical procedures).

- **A.** Inspection - involves examining records/documents (whether internal or external, whether paper or electronic) or physically examining an asset;
- **B.** Observation - consists of looking at a process or procedure being performed by others;
- **C.** Inquiry - consists of seeking information from knowledgeable persons within or outside of the company; (Note that inquiry of company personnel, by itself, does not provide sufficient evidence to reduce audit risk to an appropriately low level or to support a conclusion about the effectiveness of a control.)
- **D.** Confirmation - consists of obtaining evidence from a third party;
- **E.** Recalculation - consists of checking the mathematical accuracy of records or documents;
- **F.** Reperformance - involves independently performing the procedures or controls that were originally performed by company personnel;
- **G.** Analytical procedures - evaluations of financial information made by a study of plausible relationships among both financial and nonfinancial data.

VI. Selecting items for testing to obtain audit evidence -- The alternatives are (a) selecting all items (100% testing); (b) selecting specific items; and (c) audit sampling.

Inconsistency in (or doubts about the reliability of) audit evidence -- The auditor should perform the procedures necessary to resolve the matter and determine any effect on other aspects of the audit.

Alphabetical Index

CPAexcel
CPA Review

Auditing and Attestation

Donald E. Tidrick, Ph.D., CPA, CMA, CIA
Robert A. Prentice, J.D.

EFFICIENT LEARNING SYSTEMS™

PO Box 4223 Sedona, AZ 86340-4223
888.884.5669 N.America 928.204.1066 International

www.cpaexcel.com

Made in the USA
Monee, IL
08 November 2026

68055346R00142